Object-Oriented
Programming in

java™

A Graphical Approach

Object-Oriented Programming in

java™

A Graphical Approach

Kathryn E. Sanders

RHODE ISLAND COLLEGE

Andries van Dam

BROWN UNIVERSITY

PEARSON

Addison
Wesley

Boston San Francisco New York
London Toronto Sydney Tokyo Singapore Madrid
Mexico City Munich Paris Cape Town Hong Kong Montreal

Publisher	Greg Tobin
Senior Acquisitions Editor	Michael Hirsch
Editorial Assistant	Lindsey Triebel
Production Supervisor	Marilyn Lloyd
Cover Designer	Joyce Wells
Electronic Publishing Specialist	Laura Wiegleb
Media Producer	Bethany Tidd
Marketing Manager	Michelle Brown
Marketing Assistant	Dana Lopreato
Senior Prepress Supervisor	Caroline Fell
Text Design	Gillian Hall/The Aardvark Group
Illustrations	Dartmouth Publishing, Inc.
Cover Image	© 2005 David Tipling/Digital Vision

Many of the designations used by manufacturers and sellers to distinguish their products are claimed as trademarks. Where those designations appear in this book, and Addison-Wesley was aware of a trademark claim, the designations have been printed in initial caps or all caps.

Library of Congress Cataloging-in-Publication Data

Sanders, Kathryn E.
   Object-oriented programming in Java : a graphical approach / Kathryn E. Sanders, Andries van Dam.-- Preliminary ed.
      p. cm.
   ISBN 0-321-24574-1
   1. Object-oriented programming (Computer science) 2. Java (Computer program language) I. van Dam, Andries, 1938- II. Title.
   QA76.64.S26 2005
   005.13'3--dc22

                                                    2005018441

3 4 5 6 7 8 9 10—CRS—09

Dedication

To Robert, Xantha, Jason, and Joan

— ks

To John Gannon, the archetype of the superb Brown
CS undergraduate — In memoriam

— avd

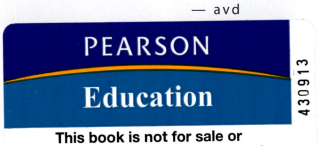

Preface

Who should read this book and why

This book is an introduction to object-oriented modeling, problem solving and design using Java™. It is aimed at students who are learning to program for the first time. Experienced programmers who want to learn Java may also find the approach enjoyable, although they will want to skim through some of the introductory material.

Many other introductory programming books on the market feature Java. Before writing another text, we looked at dozens of them, but found that none was quite what we wanted. This book has five key goals that we didn't find altogether satisfactorily attained in other texts:

1. Cover object-oriented programming first, not just objects first
2. Make it fun
3. Make it real
4. Prepare students for a rapidly changing field by covering transferable concepts and ideas, not just Java
5. Manage the detail

Object-oriented programming first

The most distinctive feature of this book is that it covers all of object-oriented programming first. Object-oriented languages have three defining characteristics: encapsulation, inheritance, and polymorphism. True object-oriented programming requires the programmer to use all three.

Many Java books now do "objects early." That is, they teach students how to define classes and instantiate objects early, but postpone inheritance and polymorphism until late in the semester: objects are early, but object-oriented programming is late.

It could be argued that students who learn "objects early" are simply learning good, structured, procedural programming. "Objects early," after all, is not so different from the old idea of abstract data types that we taught to students programming in Pascal. While this approach can be easier to teach, its downside is that late in the course, or perhaps in the second semester, when the instructor introduces the ideas of inheritance and polymorphism, the students must unlearn their procedural mindset.

Another tempting approach is to teach objects and inheritance early, but postpone polymorphism. We tried this but found that without polymorphism, good object design is impossible. We were forced either to create artificial examples that didn't require polymorphism, or to use examples that forced the students to code by hand (using conditional branching) what the compiler should do for them. We were sacrificing design in order to teach polymorphism late.

Because object-oriented design is so important to our approach, we decided to try teaching polymorphism early, immediately after objects and inheritance. We had two concerns. Would the concept of polymorphism be too difficult? And would introducing polymorphism early require us to go into detail about topics we'd rather postpone till later in the semester?

In nearly a decade of experience with our approach, we saw that students find the concept of polymorphism manageable and that teaching it early did not force us to introduce too much additional detail. Moreover, introducing polymorphism early had all the benefits we'd hoped for. Students have more practice using polymorphism. They don't have to break the habit of using conditionals instead. And we can begin talking about object-oriented design early in the semester.

Making it fun—the graphical approach

We believe that programming is fun. When we learned to program, just making the computer say "Hello world!" was fun, and text-based and arithmetic-based programs were sufficient motivation to start us down the road towards being computer scientists.

Today's students come to programming from a different background. Most of them are already familiar with computers. Nearly all of them have used the Web, email, and computer games. They are familiar with graphical interfaces (GUIs), but few of them have seen a command-line interface to a computer. Arithmetic and text-based programs don't give them the same sense of excitement and mastery over the computer that they gave students years ago.

In order to give our students the same feeling of excitement about programming that we had, we use graphics for all the examples and assignments in the first part of the book. Students write simple animations, GUIs, and games. Numeric and text-based computing are covered later in the book.

Making it real

Even though the examples are fun, students are learning to program in Java, one of the most widely used programming languages today. By the end of the course, the class libraries we work with are the standard libraries used by professional programmers.

Writing graphical programs is not just fun. It is also a marketable skill, since nearly every software package now on the market has a graphical interface. Indeed, given that most programs our students will write will be interactive programs with graphical interfaces, learning to use simple graphical objects should be part of their introduction to programming. And there is a very natural mapping from the notion of graphical shapes and UI widgets to objects in an object-oriented language like Java.

Preparing students for a rapidly changing field

One of the greatest challenges for computer-science instructors is preparing students for the rapid changes in the field. Even if we could teach our students every detail of today's hundred most popular tools and software packages, it would not be enough. Five years from now the list of "essential" software will have changed, and the students would have to start over. Even more than instructors in other fields, we must teach our students how to learn and give them a basic framework within which to fit the new things they will learn.

As a result, this book covers not just Java but also object-oriented modeling and design as implemented in Java. We stress that programs are models and that object-oriented programs model a set of cooperating objects (each of which is typically decomposable as a subsystem of cooperating objects). We provide a process for designing object-oriented models, numerous examples in the text, and challenging assignments.

This text is well suited for the first course in a two-course objects-first sequence or the first two courses in a three-course sequence as described in *Computing Curricula 2001*. The book contains chapters on data structures and recursion and brief introductions to searching and sorting algorithms and analysis of algorithms, plus a separate chapter on design patterns. The instructor wishing to follow *Computing Curricula 2001* exactly can supplement our text with some material on the history of computing and the risks involved in computing.

Managing the detail

One of the greatest challenges for anyone teaching Java is to give students the amount of detail they need when they need it, and no more. Java is a large and complex language. An instructor must avoid showing students so many trees that they never see the forest—or, in this case, so much syntax that they never understand the concepts. This is especially difficult if you want students to be able to write fun programs right from the start and very nearly impossible if you want the students to write graphical programs.

In order to focus students' attention on key concepts without burying them in syntax, we provide a custom graphics library called Wheels (as in "training wheels"). Wheels is a very simple wrapper around Java's own graphics libraries, AWT and Swing. It allows the instructor to introduce graphics without having to explain all the complexities of AWT and Swing.

Wheels is very easy to learn. It contains only six interfaces and fourteen classes. Students need to know only six of the classes: `Frame`, `Ellipse`, `Line`, `Rectangle`, `RoundedRectangle`, and `ConversationBubble`. With these classes, they can create a window and pictures (made up of two-dimensional shapes) in the window. In addition, the `ConversationBubble` class lets them create cartoons. If desired, the shapes can be made clickable, but this is hidden initially for simplicity. All of the code for Wheels is provided on the CD that accompanies this text.

Because we want the students to use "real" Java before the end of the semester, Wheels is used only with chapters 1-6 of the text. Immediately following those chapters (which cover the basics of object-oriented programming, arithmetic, and conditionals), there are two chapters on graphics programming in Java. In these two chapters we give the students a good working subset of AWT and Swing and briefly describe event-handling. Thereafter students use the AWT and Swing libraries directly.

Order of the chapters

At Brown we cover Chapters 0-16, almost the entire book, in one 14-week semester. At RIC, we cover Chapters 0-11 and 13 (object-oriented programming, graphics and GUI, arithmetic, conditionals, loops, and arrays) in the same amount of time. Other variations are possible. It is important to cover all of Chapters 0-5 (object-oriented programming through polymorphism) first. Chapters 7 (graphics) and 8 (GUI) depend on the material in those chapters, plus Chapter 6 (arithmetic and conditionals). After Chapter 8, the chapters can be read in any order. Those who prefer to cover Chapters 7 and 8 after later chapters (or omit them entirely) can do so, but they will need to substitute their own programs for the "Working Out With" sections in the later chapters.

Features of the book

Organization: To distinguish between material that is language-independent and material that is specific to Java, we have organized each chapter consistently. Sections called

Concepts primarily cover information that is useful for more than one language; sections called Mechanics deal primarily with Java-specific details.

Key concepts: Throughout the margins of this book are icons pointing you to some of the most important concepts of each chapter. Students should pay close attention when reading the sections surrounding the Key Concepts. The Key Concept list also should serve as a tool to help students review before exams.

"Working Out With" sections: The best way to understand Java programming is to work through the development of programs. Every chapter ends with a "Working Out With" section that applies the concepts and mechanics of each chapter to a runnable program, suitable for exploration in an in-class lab. Source code for these programs is provided on the CD accompanying this book.

Exercises and projects: At the end of the chapters are several types of exercises. The Self-Check questions are simple factual questions about the material covered in the chapter. The Applying the Facts questions and Debugging Code questions are pencil-and-paper exercises that require a little more thought. The Modifying Programs questions involve adapting a given program (generally the program from the "Working Out With" section in the same chapter), If you have your students work through the "Working Out With" program in a closed lab, you may want to use some of the Modifying Programs exercises in connection with that lab. Finally, the Writing Programs questions, as their name suggests, involve writing a program from scratch.

Supplementary materials

If purchased new, this book is accompanied by a CD that includes:

- Complete source code files from the "Working Out With" sections of the book
- The Wheels library
- Sun's J2SE 5.0

These supplements are also available via download from www.aw.com/cssupport

The following supplements are available to qualified instructors only. Visit Addison-Wesley's Instructor's Resource Center at www.aw.com/irc, or contact your local Addison-Wesley representative for information about how to access them.

- PowerPoint slides
- Solutions
- Test Bank

Acknowledgements

This book would not have been possible without the help of our students, our colleagues, and our families. In particular, we would like to thank Brook Conner for the idea of a radical objects-first approach; Brook Conner and Robert Duvall for early drafts of the object oriented programming chapters; the many generations of undergraduate teaching assistants who worked on versions of Wheels (especially Matt Chotin and John Goodwin); the students in CS015 at Brown, CS201 at RIC, and CSE133 at UConn who patiently used many rough drafts of the chapters; and our students and former students at Brown and RIC who read critically, commented on drafts, and participated in lengthy discussions, both on- and off-line, especially Michael Black, Matt Chotin, David Eustis, David Goldberg, John Goodwin, Bernie Gordon, Erik Holder, Katherine (Casey) Jones, Christopher Maloney, Aaron Myers, Shirin Oskooi, Leah Pearlman, Devon Penney, Janete Perez, James Piechota, Jason Sobel, Christopher (Zeke) Swepson, Dana Tenneson, Susan Warren, Stacy Wong, and A. J. Young.

Special thanks to Teresa McRann for writing most of the debugging exercises; Zeke Swepson for the Blobs; Charles Berube for the original `FoodServiceProfessional` example; Marc René for discussions of software testing at the introductory level; Anna Eckerdal of the University of Uppsala for hospitality and encouragement during the final editing phase; Robert McCartney and Ruth Simons of the University of Connecticut and Ann Moskol of Rhode Island College for alpha-testing multiple versions of the chapters in their own classes and providing invaluable feedback; Tom Doeppner of Brown University for reading and commenting on Chapter 18; and Shriram Krishnamurthi and Steve Reiss, of Brown University and Laurent Michel of the University of Connecticut for helpful discussions of programming language and design questions. Helen Salzberg, chair of the Mathematics and Computer Science Department at Rhode Island College, and Richard Weiner, Dean of the Faculty of Arts and Sciences at Rhode Island College, deserve particular thanks for their encouragement and support.

Thanks to the external reviewers for their helpful comments, including Carl Alphonce, SUNY Buffalo; Elizabeth Boese, Colorado State University; Fazli Can, Miami University of Ohio; Jacques Cohen, Brandeis University; Sherif Elfayoumy, University of North Florida; Henry Etlinger, Rochester Institute of Technology; Stan Kwasny of Washington University; Michael Lipton of Northeastern University; Mark Llewellyn, University of Central Florida; Mauricio Manengoni of Marist College; John McGregor, Clemson University; Shyamal Mitra, University of Texas at Austin; Sridhar Narayan, University of North Carolina at Wilmington; Richard Povinelli, Marquette University; Roger Priebe, University of Texas at Austin; Stuart Regis of the University of Washington; Jerry Ross, Lane Community College; Ben Schafer, University of Northern Iowa; Dave Small, University of Florida; Esther Steiner, New Mexico State University; Gary Thai of

Montgomery College; Kent Vidrine, George Washington University; and Karl Wurst, Worcester State College.

Thanks to Trina Avery for superb copy-editing, Rosemary Simpson for her vision of the ideal index and her implementation of the one we had to settle for given space constraints, Lauren Clarke for serencly keeping us organized, and the entire Addison–Weslcy team who worked on the book, particularly Michael Hirsch, Susan Hartman, Patty Mahtani, Joyce Wells, and Marilyn Lloyd.

Thanks to the National Science Foundation for their support of the development and adaptation of materials related to the approach taken in this book under grant DUE-0410546. Any opinions, findings, and conclusions or recommendations expressed in this material are those of the authors and do not neccessarily reflect the views of the National Science Foundation.

And finally, thanks to Robert and Debbie. We owe you.

Contents

Preface   vii

Chapter 0   Background   1

0.1   Introduction   1
0.2   Computer hardware   1
0.3   Computer software   3
0.4   Programming languages and Java   4
0.5   Executing a program   6
0.6   Software tools for programming   6
0.7   How compilation works in Java   8
0.8   The process of writing programs   9
0.9   What if your program doesn't work?   12
     Summary   13
     Self-Check Questions   14
     Exercises   14

Chapter 1   Introduction to Objects   17

1.1   Introduction   17
1.2   Concepts   18
     1.2.1   What is a model?   18
     1.2.2   How are models built?   19
     1.2.3   How to have different objects of the same type: classes and instances   21
     1.2.4   Managing complexity   22
     1.2.5   What makes a good software model?   23
1.3   Mechanics   25
     1.3.1   The rubber stamp: declaring and defining a class   25
     1.3.2   Modeling properties: instance variables   28
     1.3.3   Modeling capabilities I: constructors   31
     1.3.4   Giving properties their values: assignment statements   32
     1.3.5   Modeling capabilities II: more about methods   34
     1.3.6   UML diagrams   37
1.4   Working Out with Objects—getting started with Java   39
     1.4.1   Getting started   39
     1.4.2   Background: the Wheels library of graphical shapes   40
     1.4.3   Analysis   42
     1.4.4   Design   42

1.4.5	Implementation	43
1.4.6	Steps of execution	44
1.4.7	Testing	45
1.4.8	Followup	45
	Summary	45
	Self-Check Questions	46
	Exercises	48
	Programming Projects	52
	New Style Conventions	52

Chapter 2	**Methods with Parameters**	**55**
2.1	Introduction	55
2.2	Concepts	56
2.2.1	Parameters	56
2.2.2	Return values	58
2.3	Mechanics	59
2.3.1	Parameters	59
2.3.2	Constructors with parameters	61
2.3.3	Debugging tips for method calls	63
2.3.4	Parameters, local variables, and instance variables	64
2.3.5	Return types	67
2.3.6	Method signatures and overloading	68
2.4	Working Out with Objects—the talking sun	69
2.4.1	Background: more about Wheels	70
2.4.2	Analysis	70
2.4.3	Design	72
2.4.4	Implementation: version 1	73
2.4.5	Imports, packages, and libraries	73
2.4.6	Version 2: adding the constructor body	75
2.4.7	Java's built-in colors	75
2.4.8	Testing version 2	75
2.4.9	Putting shapes in different locations in the `Frame`	76
2.4.10	Implementation: version 3	77
2.4.11	Testing version 3	79
2.5	Working Out with Composite Objects—the snowman	79
2.5.1	Analysis	79
2.5.2	Design	80
2.5.3	Implementation: reusing the `SunCartoon`	80
2.5.4	Testing: the first piece of the program	81
2.5.5	Implementation: the `Hat`	81
2.5.6	Testing the Hat: part 1	81
2.5.7	Setting the location of a composite object: the `Hat`	82
2.5.8	Testing the `Hat` (continued)	86

	2.5.9	Pulling it all together: implementing the `Snowman`	87
	2.5.10	Testing the `Snowman`: part 1	88
	2.5.11	Implementing the `Snowman` (continued)	88
	2.5.12	Testing the `Snowman` (continued)	89
Summary			90
Self-Check Questions			90
Exercises			91
Programming Projects			93

Chapter 3 Inheritance **99**

3.1	Introduction		99
3.2	Concepts		100
3.3	Mechanics		102
	3.3.1	Simple inheritance	102
	3.3.2	Overriding inherited methods	104
	3.3.3	Implementing abstract methods	107
	3.3.4	Inheriting properties: pseudo-inheritance	108
	3.3.5	Method resolution	111
3.4	Working Out with Inheritance—the Blobs		113
	3.4.1	Background: mouse methods in Wheels	113
	3.4.2	Analysis	114
	3.4.3	Design	115
	3.4.4	Implementation: `BlobApp` with one `Blob`	116
	3.4.5	Testing (part 1)	117
	3.4.6	Implementation: a `BlobApp` with a `WinkingBlob`	117
	3.4.7	Testing (part 2)	119
	3.4.8	Implementation: a `BlobApp` with a `WinkingBlob` and a `Talkative Blob`	120
	3.4.9	Final Testing	120
Summary			121
Self-Check Questions			121
Exercises			122
Programming Projects			125

Chapter 4 Interfaces **127**

4.1	Introduction		127
4.2	Concepts		128
4.3	Mechanics		129
	4.3.1	Defining and implementing interfaces	129
	4.3.2	Classes that implement multiple interfaces	130
	4.3.3	Extending interfaces	133
	4.3.4	Design choices: interfaces vs. `abstract` classes	134
	4.3.5	Design choices: how many interfaces to use	135
	4.3.6	Design choices: which capabilities to put in which interface	135

4.4		Working Out with Interfaces—a movable sun	136
	4.4.1	Writing an interface	136
	4.4.2	Writing a class that implements an interface	138
	4.4.3	Implementing the mouseDragged method	138
	4.4.4	Implementing the Frame: MovableSunApp	140
4.5		Working Out with Interfaces and Composite Shapes—a movable hat	141
	4.5.1	Getting started: the interface and the movableHatApp	142
	4.5.2	Creating a part that knows about its container: the HatPart class	143
	4.5.3	Creating a composite object that moves as a unit: the Hat class	144
4.6		Recipes	146
	4.6.1	Defining classes	147
	4.6.2	Initializing instance variables	147
	4.6.3	Instance variables with default values	148
	4.6.4	Accessors and mutators	149
	4.6.5	Parts that know about their containers	151
		Summary	153
		Self-Check Questions	153
		Exercises	154
		Programming Projects	155

Chapter 5   Polymorphism   157

5.1		Introduction	157
5.2		Concepts	158
5.3		Mechanics	161
	5.3.1	Inheritance polymorphism	161
	5.3.2	Interface polymorphism	163
	5.3.3	Determining which method is invoked	164
5.4		Working Out with Polymorphism—the sketch pad	166
	5.4.1	Analysis	166
	5.4.2	Design	167
	5.4.3	Implementation	168
	5.4.4	Testing	171
		Summary	173
		Self-Check Questions	174
		Exercises	175
		Programming Projects	180

Chapter 6   Introduction to Arithmetic and Conditional Statements   183

6.1		Introduction	183
6.2		Concepts	184
	6.2.1	Representing numbers	184
	6.2.2	Arithmetic operators	184
	6.2.3	Conditional statements and Boolean logic	185
	6.2.4	Relational operators	188

6.2.5   Object equality   188

6.2.6   Choosing when you have one yes-no alternative   189

6.2.7   Choosing from two different alternatives   189

6.2.8   Choosing from many alternatives   190

6.2.9   When to use conditional statements   191

6.3   Mechanics   192

6.3.1   Numbers in Java   192

6.3.2   Arithmetic operators   194

6.3.3   Increment and decrement   195

6.3.4   Boolean operators   196

6.3.5   Relational operators   197

6.3.6   Single decisions   198

6.4   Working Out with Arithmetic and Conditionals—Daisy,
       Daisy, give me your answer do   200

Summary   206

Self-Check Questions   206

Exercises   207

Programming Projects   210

Chapter 7   Two-Dimensional Graphical Shapes   **211**

7.1   Introduction   211

7.2   Concepts   212

7.3   Working Out with Windows and Shapes—`FirstApp` revisited   213

7.3.1   `JFrames`   213

7.3.2   `JPanels`   215

7.3.3   Layout   217

7.3.4   Putting an ellipse in a `JPanel`   218

7.3.5   Creating a "smart" ellipse   218

7.3.6   Drawing shapes and the `Graphics` object   221

7.4   Working Out with Events and Animation—the bouncing ball   225

7.4.1   The Java event model   225

7.4.2   Using events: making the ballApp bounce   230

7.4.3   Rotating shapes   234

7.5   Working Out with Events and Composite Shapes—the fish tank   236

7.6   Working Out with Design—building our own Wheels   246

7.6.1   Java's built-n shape classes   246

7.6.2   Our new `ColorShape` classes   247

Summary   252

Self-Check Questions   253

Exercises   253

Programming Projects   255

Chapter 8   Graphical User Interfaces and Event-Handling   **259**

8.1   Introduction   259

8.2	Concepts	261
	8.2.1 Design principles	261
	8.2.2 Design tools	264
8.3	Mechanics	266
	8.3.1 Arranging components on the screen: layouts	266
	8.3.2 Components	270
	8.3.3 Making the program respond to input: event handling and `SmartComponents`	276
8.4	Working Out with GUI—a user-controlled bouncing ball	282
	8.4.1 Part 1: layout	283
	8.4.2 The `ControlPanel`	285
	8.4.3 The `QuitButton`	286
	8.4.4 Adding the `BallPanel` with the `BouncingBall`, adding the color buttons, and making them work	287
	8.4.5 Adding sliders	289
Summary		295
Self-Check Questions		295
Exercises		297
Programming Projects		299

Chapter 9   Design Patterns   **301**

9.1	Introduction	301
9.2	Concepts	302
9.3	Mechanics	303
9.4	Working Out with the Holder Pattern—part of a drawing program	303
	9.4.1 Modeling the current color: the Holder Pattern	305
	9.4.2 `ColorHolderApp`	306
	9.4.3 The `ControlPanel` class and the button classes	307
	9.4.4 `ColorShapePanel`	308
9.5	Working Out with the Proxy Pattern—race cars	311
9.6	Working Out with the Composite Pattern—the space alien	327
Summary		332
Self-Check Questions		333
Exercises		333
Programming Projects		333

Chapter 10   Advanced Arithmetic and Conditional Statements   **335**

10.1	Introduction	335
10.2	Concepts	336
	10.2.1 Modeling real numbers	336
	10.2.2 Operations on floating-point numbers	336
	10.2.3 Casting and coercion	336
	10.2.4 Modeling choices within choices	337
10.3	Mechanics	339

10.3.1	Floating-point numbers in Java	339
10.3.2	Arithmetic operations on floating-point numbers, casting, and coercions	340
10.3.3	Java's `Math` class: static variables and methods	342
10.3.4	Random numbers	343
10.3.5	Constants: how, where, and when to define them	344
10.3.6	Modeling choices within choices: nested conditionals	347
10.3.7	Short-circuiting	349
10.3.8	Switch statement	350
10.4	Working Out with floating point numbers, nested conditionals, and random numbers—`ColorBounceApp`	353
	Summary	359
	Self-Check Questions	359
	Exercises	360
	Programming Projects	362

Chapter 11 Loops   **365**

11.1	Introduction	365
11.2	Concepts	366
11.3	Mechanics	366
11.3.1	`Vectors`	366
11.3.2	Indefinite loops: `while` loops	370
11.3.3	Iterators	373
11.3.4	Indefinite loops: `do-while`	374
11.3.5	Definite loops: the `for` loop	374
11.3.6	`Break` and `continue` in loops	377
11.3.7	Choosing between loops	378
11.3.8	Recipes for writing loops	379
11.3.9	Debugging loops	381
11.3.10	Flow of control	384
11.4	Working Out with Loops—`ButterflyApp`	386
	Summary	392
	Self-Check Questions	393
	Exercises	393
	Programming Projects	395

Chapter 12 Recursion   **397**

12.1	Introduction	397
12.2	Concepts	398
12.3	Mechanics	399
12.3.1	An example with one recursive call: factorial	399
12.3.2	An example with more than one recursive call: Towers of Hanoi	401
12.3.3	Debugging tips	404

		12.3.4	Choosing between iteration and recursion	404
	12.4	Working Out with Recursion—`SpiralApp`		407
	12.5	Working Out with Recursion—`TreeApp`		413
	Summary			418
	Self-Check Questions			418
	Exercises			418
	Programming Projects			419

Chapter 13   Arrays, Vectors, and ArrayLists   421

	13.1	Introduction		421
	13.2	Concepts		421
	13.3	Mechanics		422
		13.3.1	Declaring and initializing arrays, `ArrayLists`, and `Vectors`	422
		13.3.2	Accessing and using elements	424
		13.3.3	Passing as parameters	425
		13.3.4	Multidimensional structures	425
		13.3.5	Debugging tips: common array errors	427
		13.3.6	Comparing and contrasting arrays, `Vectors`, and `ArrayLists`	429
		13.3.7	The mainline revealed	429
	13.4	Working Out with Arrays—`ClickApp`		431
	Summary			436
	Self-Check Questions			436
	Exercises			436
	Programming Projects			438

Chapter 14   Introduction to Data Structures   441

	14.1	Introduction		441
	14.2	Concepts		442
		14.2.1	Stacks	443
		14.2.2	Queues	444
		14.2.3	Lists	444
		14.2.4	Dictionaries	446
		14.2.5	Implementing ADTs with linked lists	446
		14.2.6	Instance diagrams	447
	14.3	Mechanics		448
		14.3.1	The `Node` class	449
		14.3.2	A `StackADT` interface	451
		14.3.3	The `Stack` class	451
		14.3.4	A `QueueADT` interface	454
		14.3.5	The `Queue` class	454
		14.3.6	A `ListADT` interface	457
		14.3.7	Implementing `List` and the Iterator design pattern	457
		14.3.8	A `DictionaryADT` interface	458
		14.3.9	The `Dictionary` class	462

14.4 Working Out with Data Structures—Driver programs   471

Summary   473

Self-Check Questions   474

Exercises   475

Programming Projects   477

Chapter 15   Trees   479

15.1 Introduction   479

15.2 Concepts   480

    15.2.1 Modeling with trees   480

    15.2.2 Implementing dictionary operations efficiently with trees   483

    15.3.3 In-order, pre-order, post-order   486

15.3 Mechanics: Binary Search Trees   490

    15.3.1 Declaring the `BinarySearchTree` class   491

15.4 Working Out with Trees—Driver Program   500

Summary   502

Self-Check Questions   502

Exercises   502

Chapter 16   Sorting and Searching   505

16.1 Introduction   505

16.2 Concepts   506

    16.2.1 Sorting: overview   508

    16.2.2 Bubble sort   509

    16.2.3 Insertion sort   513

    16.2.4 Selection sort   516

    16.2.5 Merge sort   517

    16.2.6 Recurrence relations   518

    16.2.7 Searching: overview   522

    16.2.8 Searching: arrays   523

    16.2.9 Searching: linked lists   524

    16.2.10 Searching: binary trees   524

    16.2.11 Searching: n-ary and hybrid trees   525

    16.2.12 Searching: hash tables   527

Summary   530

Self-Check Questions   530

Exercises   531

Programming Projects   532

Chapter 17   Strings and Text I/O   533

17.1 Introduction   533

17.2 Concepts   533

17.3 Mechanics: `Strings`   534

    17.3.1 Combining `Strings`   535

17.3.2   Extracting parts of `Strings`   536

17.3.3   Comparing `Strings`   536

17.3.4   Reversing `Strings`   537

17.3.5   Summarizing the `String` class   539

17.4   Working Out with Strings—GUI Text I/O   540

17.4.1   A boilerplate GUI for simple text I/O programs   540

17.4.2   A simple program: `EchoApp`   545

17.4.3   A second application: `StringMethodsApp`   546

17.4.4   A third application: `EqualTestApp`   546

Summary   551

Self-Check Questions   551

Exercises   551

Programming Projects   552

Chapter 18   Console I/O, File I/O, and Exceptions   555

18.1   Introduction   555

18.2   Concepts   556

18.2.1   Console I/O   556

18.2.2   File I/O   557

18.2.3   Saving objects to files and reading them back in   559

18.2.4   Exceptions   559

18.3   Mechanics   562

18.3.1   Console I/O   562

18.3.2   Exceptions   569

18.3.3   File I/O   576

18.4   Working Out with File I/O—Saving and restoring objects   579

Summary   583

Self-Check Questions   583

Exercises   584

Programming Projects   584

Index   585

Listings

Chapter 1	Introduction to Objects	**17**
Listing 1.1	The properties and capabilities of the iguana object	21
Listing 1.2	`FirstApp.java`	43
Chapter 2	**Methods with Parameters**	**55**
Listing 2.1	Actual and formal parameters: aliases for the same thing	61
Listing 2.2	Examples of variables and their scope (indicated by the lines on the left)	66
Listing 2.3	`SunCartoon` (version 1)	74
Listing 2.4	`SunCartoon` (version 2)	76
Listing 2.5	`SunCartoon` (version 3)	78
Listing 2.6	`SnowCartoon` (version 1)	82
Listing 2.7	`Hat` (version 1)	83
Listing 2.8	`SnowCartoon` (version 2)	83–84
Listing 2.9	Version 2 of `Hat` class	84
Listing 2.10	Final version of `Hat` class	86
Listing 2.11	`Snowman` class (version 1)	87
Listing 2.12	Final version of `Snowman` class	88–89
Chapter 3	**Inheritance**	**99**
Listing 3.1	Mouse methods for the shapes in Wheels	114
Listing 3.2	`BlobApp.java`	117
Listing 3.3	`Blob.java`	118
Listing 3.4	`WinkingBlob.java`	119
Listing 3.5	`TalkativeBlob.java`	120
Chapter 4	**Interfaces**	**127**
Listing 4.1	`Box`, a class that implements two interfaces	132
Listing 4.2	The `Draggable` interface	137
Listing 4.3	The `Sun` class	139
Listing 4.4	The `MovableSunApp` class	141
Listing 4.5	The `MovableHatApp` class	143
Listing 4.6	The `HatPart` class	144
Listing 4.7	The `Hat` class	145–146
Listing 4.8	The class-definition recipe	148
Listing 4.9	The default-value recipe	149
Listing 4.11	The basic mutator recipe	150
Listing 4.12	Recipe for objects that know their container	151–152

Chapter 5	**Polymorphism**	**157**
Listing 5.1	The SketchApp class	169
Listing 5.2	The superclass DrawButton	170
Listing 5.3	The UpButton class	172
Listing 5.4	The Cursor class	173
Chapter 6	**Introduction to Arithmetic and Conditional Statements**	**183**
Listing 6.1	The DaisyApp class	202
Listing 6.2	The Daisy class	203–204
Listing 6.3	The Petal class	205
Chapter 7	**Two-Dimensional Graphical Shapes**	**211**
Listing 7.1	The BallApp class	215
Listing 7.2	The BallPanel class	217
Listing 7.3	The BallPanel class (version 2)	219
Listing 7.4	The SmartEllipse class	219–220
Listing 7.5	BallPanel's paintComponent method	223
Listing 7.6	SmartEllipse's fill method	223
Listing 7.7	SmartEllipse's draw method	224
Listing 7.8	MoveTimer	227
Listing 7.9	MoveListener class	228
Listing 7.10	The Mover interface	229
Listing 7.11	The MoveTimer class modified	230
Listing 7.12	The BallPanel class modified	231
Listing 7.13	The BouncingBall class	233
Listing 7.14	BouncingBall's move method	234
Listing 7.15	BouncingBall's getMinBound methods	235
Listing 7.16	BouncingBall's getMaxBound methods	235
Listing 7.17	The FishApp class	238
Listing 7.18	The FishPanel class	238–239
Listing 7.19	The Fish class	240
Listing 7.20	The Fish's move method	241
Listing 7.21	Fish's getMinBound and getMaxBound methods	242
Listing 7.22	Fish's setLocation method	242
Listing 7.23	Accessor methods for the Fish's location	242
Listing 7.24	The Fish's methods related to rotation	243
Listing 7.25	The Fish's fill and draw methods	244
Listing 7.26	The SmartArc class	245
Listing 7.27	The ColorShape class	248
Listing 7.28	ColorRectangle, an alternative to SmartRectangles	251
Chapter 8	**Graphical User Interfaces and Event-Handling**	**259**
Listing 8.1	The ColorButton class	278–279
Listing 8.2	The LocationSlider (with references to steps in Figure 8.9)	280

Listing 8.3	`ColorShapePanel`	281–282
Listing 8.4	The `GUIBounceApp` class	284
Listing 8.5	Stubs for `BallPanel` and `ControlPanel`	285
Listing 8.6	`ControlPanel` (version 2), with `GridLayout`	285
Listing 8.7	`ControlPanel` (version 3), with `QuitButton`	286
Listing 8.8	The `QuitButton` class	287
Listing 8.9	The `ControlPanel` class (version 4), with `ColorButtons`	288
Listing 8.10	The `Colorable` interface	289
Listing 8.11	The `BallPanel` class's new `getBall` method	290
Listing 8.12	The `BouncingBall` class	291
Listing 8.13	The `ControlPanel` class (version 5), with sliders	292–293
Listing 8.14	The `SpeedSlider` class	293–294
Listing 8.15	The `Accelerator` interface	294

Chapter 9   Design Patterns   301

Listing 9.1	The `ColorHolder` class	306
Listing 9.2	The `ColorHolderApp` class	308
Listing 9.3	`ControlPanel` for `ColorHolderApp`	309
Listing 9.4	The `ColorShapePanel` class	310–311
Listing 9.5	The `CarProxy` class	316–317
Listing 9.6	The `CarProxyApp` class	318
Listing 9.7	The `CarProxyPanel` class)	318–319
Listing 9.8	`CarProxyPanel`'s move method	319
Listing 9.9	`CarProxyPanel`'s paintComponent method	320
Listing 9.10	`CarProxyPanel`'s `MyMouseListener` class	320
Listing 9.11	The `ControlPanel` class	321
Listing 9.12	The `SpeedButton` class	322
Listing 9.13	The `Image` class	323
Listing 9.14	`Image`'s setSelected and paint methods	325
Listing 9.15	The `Car` class	325
Listing 9.16	`Car`'s move method	326
Listing 9.17	The `SpaceAlien` class	330–331

Chapter 10   Advanced Arithmetic and Conditional Statements   335

Listing 10.1	The `Utilities` class	344
Listing 10.2	The `ColorBounceApp` class	354
Listing 10.3	The `BouncePanel` class	355
Listing 10.4	The `BouncingBall` class	356–358
Listing 10.5	The `BounceConstants` class	358

Chapter 11   Loops   365

Listing 11.1	The `ButterflyApp` class	387
Listing 11.2	The `ButterflyPanel` class	388
Listing 11.3	The `Butterfly` class	389–390

Chapter 12	Recursion		397
	Listing 12.1	The `SpiralApp` class	408
	Listing 12.2	The `SpiralPanel` class	409
	Listing 12.3	The `Spiral` class	410–411
	Listing 12.4	The `TreeApp` class	414
	Listing 12.5	The `TreePanel` class	415
	Listing 12.6	The `Tree` class	415–417
Chapter 13	**Arrays, Vectors, and ArrayLists**		**421**
	Listing 13.1	The `ClickApp` class	432
	Listing 13.2	The `ClickPanel` class	433
	Listing 13.3	The `ClickPanel`'s constructor	433
	Listing 13.4	The `ClickPanel`'s `paintComponent` method	434
	Listing 13.5	The `ClickPanel`'s inner class `MyMouseListener`	434
	Listing 13.6	The `ClickSquare` class	435
Chapter 14	**Introduction to Data Structures**		**441**
	Listing 14.1	The Node class	450
	Listing 14.2	The `StackADT` interface	451
	Listing 14.3	The `Stack` class	452
	Listing 14.4	The `QueueADT` interface	454
	Listing 14.5	The `Queue` class	455–456
	Listing 14.6	The `ListADT` interface	457
	Listing 14.7	The `DictionaryADT` interface (version 1 of 5)	459
	Listing 14.8	The `DictionaryADT` interface (version 2 of 5)	459
	Listing 14.9	The `KeyProvider` interface	460
	Listing 14.10	The `DictionaryADT` interface (version 3 of 5)	461
	Listing 14.11	`DictionaryADT` interface (version 4 of 5)	461
	Listing 14.12	`DictionaryADT` interface (version 5 of 5)	463
	Listing 14.13	The `Dictionary` class	464
	Listing 14.14	The `Dictionary` class's `search` method	464
	Listing 14.15	The `Dictionary` class's `searchAux` method	465
	Listing 14.16	The `Dictionary`'s `delete` method	466
	Listing 14.17	The `Dictionary`'s `deleteAux` method	467
	Listing 14.18	The `Dictionary`'s `insert` method	467
	Listing 14.19	The `Dictionary`'s `insertAux` method	469
Chapter 15	**Trees**		**479**
	Listing 15.1	The `BinarySearchTree` class	492–493
	Listing 15.2	The `BinarySearchTree`'s `Node` class	494
	Listing 15.3	The `BinarySearchTree`'s `insert` method	496
	Listing 15.4	The `BinarySearchTree`'s `insertAux` method	496
	Listing 15.5	The `BinarySearchTree`'s `search` method	497
	Listing 15.6	The `BinarySearchTree`'s `searchAux` method	498

Listing 15.7	The `BinarySearchTree`'s delete method	498
Listing 15.8	The `BinarySearchTree`'s deleteAux method	499

Chapter 17   Strings and Text I/O   533

Listing 17.1	The `StringGUI` class	541–542
Listing 17.2	The `LabeledTextBox` class	544
Listing 17.3	The `EchoApp` class	545
Listing 17.4	The `StringMethodsApp` class	547–548
Listing 17.5	`TwoInputStringGUI`	548
Listing 17.6	The `EqualTestApp` class	549–550

Chapter 18   Console I/O, File I/O, and Exceptions   555

Listing 18.1	The `ConsoleOutput` class	564
Listing 18.2	The `ConsoleOutput` class with concatenation	565
Listing 18.3	The `ScannerApp` class	566
Listing 18.4	The `Echo` class	567
Listing 18.5	The `EchoInteger` class	568
Listing 18.6	The `EchoInteger2` class	572
Listing 18.7	The `EchoInteger3` class	574
Listing 18.8	The `FileToConsole` program	577
Listing 18.9	The `ConsoleToFile` class	578
Listing 18.10	The `Character` class	579
Listing 18.11	The `CharApp` class	581–582

chapter **0**

Background

OBJECTIVES

After reading this chapter, you should be able to:

☑ Define hardware, software, and algorithm

☑ List the basic hardware and software tools needed for writing programs

☑ Compare and contrast the waterfall process, the spiral process, and the extreme-programming process for designing and implementing software

☑ Explain the difference between syntax errors and semantic errors in a program

☑ Briefly explain what debugging is and discuss the process of debugging a program

■ 0.1 ■ Introduction

This chapter is a very brief introduction to the process of writing programs and the hardware and software tools that you will use. If you have already done some programming in another language, you may want to skim this chapter or even skip it entirely. In Chapter 1, we begin talking specifically about object-oriented programming and Java and present the first Java programs.

■ 0.2 ■ Computer hardware

Computers are machines for manipulating information. That information could be poetry. It could be equations or mathematical surfaces or pictures or music. It could be space aliens in a video game. To manipulate all these kinds of information, the computer must have ways to get the information, store it, process it, and respond to the user.

The first thing you notice about a computer is its hardware. **Hardware** is the part of the computer you can touch: the screen (also called the monitor), the keyboard, the mouse (or equivalent input devices), and maybe a separate box housing various kinds of electronics and the hard drive, CD player, etc. (illustrated in Figure 0.1). The keyboard and the mouse are both **input devices**: that is, they let you send information to the computer (or "input" it) by typing or clicking respectively. The monitor, the speakers, and the printer are **output devices**: they let the computer send information back to you (or "output" it).

Between reading your information in and outputting a response, the computer processes the information. This processing is controlled by the brains of the computer, a **central processing unit**, or **CPU**. If your computer has a separate box, the CPU is located in that box.

Finally, the computer needs a way to remember things, both information and instructions about how to process the information. Computers remember things in two ways, short-term and long-term (much like humans). If you read advertisements for computers, you see references to the amount of memory they have and the size of their hard drive or disk. **Memory** (shorthand for systems memory, primary memory, or random-access memory (RAM)) is short-term and fast: it is located close to the CPU where it can be accessed quickly, but generally anything stored in this memory goes away when your computer is turned off.

The **disk** is an example of long-term storage, also called secondary memory. The hard disk is located in the same box as the CPU and memory, but it takes longer to access than primary memory. On the other hand, it generally holds much more (as you can see from the advertisements), and it continues to remember things even when the computer is turned off. Other examples of long-term storage include floppy disks, CDs, and memory sticks. There is a separate memory for the graphics card that controls the display, called video memory. All of these forms of storage are measured in bytes. A **byte** is one

keyconcept

Hardware is the part of the computer you can touch.

keyconcept

Input devices let you send information to the computer.

keyconcept

Output devices let the computer send information to you.

keyconcept

The central processing unit, or CPU, is the part of the computer that controls the processing of information.

keyconcept

Random access memory (RAM) is short-term and fast. Secondary memory is slower but larger and longer lasting.

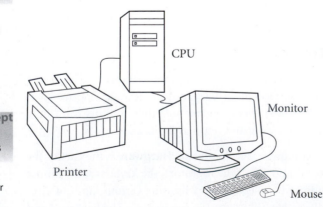

CPU

Monitor

Printer

Mouse

Figure 0.1 ■ The parts of a computer.

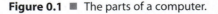

unit of computer storage, consisting of eight bits (**bi**nary digi**t**s, 0 and 1). A **megabyte** (MB) is approximately a million bytes, and a **gigabyte** (GB) is approximately a billion bytes. And generally speaking, more is better.

To understand the difference between short-term and long-term computer storage, think of the difference between remembering someone's phone number in your head and writing it in an address book. If you know the number by heart, it's much quicker—until you forget it! If you write it down in an address book, it takes longer to look it up, but you have it forever (or at least until someone spills a cup of coffee on your address book). Table 0.1 summarizes the different kinds of storage on a computer.

Computers store your input in their own language. The computer's language represents everything in a binary code of sequences of bits, 1s and 0s. The letter A, for example, is represented as the byte 01000001, and K is 01001011. There are standard ways of representing letters, numbers, and even pictures and sound, but each type of computer has its own built-in vocabulary of commands for processing data, known as its **machine language**.

keyconcept
Each computer has its own built-in language called machine language.

Table 0.1 ■ Different ways of storing information in a computer.

	Short-term	Long-term
Name(s)	RAM, primary memory, systems memory	Secondary memory
Location	Near the CPU	In the box (hard drive) or on CD, floppy disk, or memory stick
Accessibility	Fast	Slow
Longevity	Short	Long
Compare to	Phone number in your head	Phone number in an address book

■ 0.3 ■ **Computer software**

Computers need both hardware and software to operate. The ways in which computers get input, process it, and generate output are all controlled by computer software (programs). You might infer from the definition of hardware above that software is the part of the computer you *can't* touch, and that's right as far as it goes.

An **algorithm** is an unambiguous, executable list of instructions for performing some task or exhibiting some behavior. Cookbook recipes are algorithms, for example, as are the instructions for downloading music onto an IPod™. "Buy low, sell high" is not an algorithm, because it's too ambiguous. "To fly, just open your umbrella and hold it over

keyconcept
An algorithm is an unambiguous, executable list of instructions for performing some task or exhibiting some behavior.

your head" is not an algorithm, because people can't execute it (most people, anyway).

keyconcept
A computer program is an algorithm (or collection of algorithms) that can be executed by a computer.

A **computer program** is an algorithm (or collection of algorithms) that can be executed by a computer: a list of instructions for the CPU.

■ 0.4 ■ Programming languages and Java

Do we have to write our programs in binary machine language? Fortunately not. In the late 1940s, early computer programmers did use the computer's own language, but as you can imagine, writing programs in long sequences of 1s and 0s was slow and prone to error.

On the other hand, we can't use English either. If we used English to describe software to a computer, the computer wouldn't be able to understand it, because most English sentences, like sentences in all human languages (also called **natural languages**), contain ambiguities and incomplete thoughts. Humans rely on one another to fill in the gaps using the prior knowledge and context each person possesses, but computers can't fill in the gaps because they don't have such context, as Table 0.2 suggests. (One of the goals of artificial intelligence is to give a computer context and common-sense reasoning so it can understand and translate natural languages.) When giving instructions to a computer, we need to use a **programming language**: a language for writing programs that has precise structure and meaning and avoids ambiguities completely.

Table 0.2 ■ If computers spoke English...

Phrase	How a human might respond	How a computer might respond
What's up?	Not much.	A noun, referring to the direction of the sky.
I'm sleeping in tomorrow.	Good—you need it.	In what?
Do you have the time?	It's 4 o'clock.	Yes.
Hang 10.	Like, totally!	Loading ...1...2...3

Since computers don't understand human language, and humans have a hard time with machine language, we need something in between. The first solution was assembly language. An **assembly language** is the same as a computer's machine language, except that words are substituted for some of the numeric codes. Instead of a sequence of 0s and 1s like 1101 0110 0111 1100, we might see ADD #9, D3. Assembly language is much easier to use than machine language, but it still has disadvantages. It's not as readable as it could be, and worse, because it's the same as machine language, there's a different type of assembly language for each type of computer. That means we'd have to write one program for a Dell, and one for a Macintosh, and one for a Compaq—and so on. We want something even closer to human language, and we want it to stay the same regardless of what computer we run it on.

In the 1950s, computer scientists began to design high-level programming languages for this purpose. A **high-level programming language** is a language that is more readable than machine language, more precise and unambiguous than human language, and includes some mathematical notation to express arithmetic. It is far enough from machine language that programs written in a high-level language, unlike assembly language programs, need not be rewritten for every type of machine on which they are run. Programs written in high-level languages can't be understood by the computer, but because the high-level languages are so precise, they can be automatically translated into machine language by other programs called **compilers**. (See Figure 0.2.)

The particular high-level language we use in this book is called Java. Java, like other languages (both programming and natural), uses a **grammar**—a set of rules that you must follow in order to be understood. The difference is that, in a natural language, if you hear someone use incorrect grammar, you usually can determine what the person meant anyway. ("Less calories, with the same great taste!") In a programming language, however, if your sentence is not grammatically correct, the computer has no idea what you meant. Again, this is because computers have no imagination; they cannot make educated guesses.

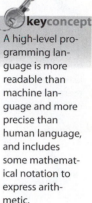

keyconcept

A high-level programming language is more readable than machine language and more precise than human language, and includes some mathematical notation to express arithmetic.

keyconcept

Compilers are programs that translate other programs from high-level programming languages into a computer's machine language.

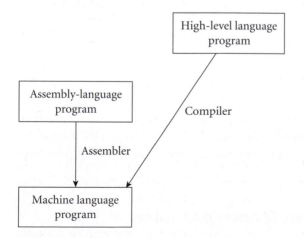

Figure 0.2 ■ Levels of programming languages.

keyconcept

Errors in a program are called **bugs**, and the process of finding these errors is called **debugging**.

Java's grammar rules describe the formal structure, or **syntax**, of the language. Grammatical mistakes in a program are called **syntax errors**. Just one syntax error, even a missing punctuation mark, keeps an entire program from being translated by the compiler. This can be very frustrating—it's as if you built an entire mansion and it fell down because you left off one doorknob. But as in a good poem, every word and every punctuation mark in a program has a purpose.

keyconcept

Grammatical errors are called **syntax errors**; a program that is grammatically correct but does the wrong thing is said to have **semantic errors**.

Since you are learning a new language, we will spend a good deal of time at first studying its syntax. However, you must not be so focused on the syntax that you forget the **semantics** of the language, the meaning behind the syntax. A program that is syntactically correct may still not do what you want. Such a program is said to have semantic errors.

Just as there are many natural languages, there are many programming languages, for example, VisualBasic®, Perl, Python, Lisp, C, C#, and C++. Each programming language has its own syntax. Just as you can say the same thing in languages as different as French and Chinese, you can write programs in different programming languages that do the same thing (that is, they have the same semantics).

Many programming languages can be, and have been, used as introductory programming languages. The basic concepts examined in these chapters can be found in many different languages. We are using Java as an introductory language for a number of reasons. First, it is a relatively simple language. Second, Java is widespread, especially on the World Wide Web, and it is used by students and professional programmers throughout the world for developing applications. It is a modern, object-oriented language. Finally, Java is powerful enough to develop any application, from databases to animated web content.

■ 0.5 ■ Executing a program

Writing a program is like writing a to-do list: nothing happens until you actually start doing the tasks on the list. Once you've successfully compiled your program, you have a to-do list for the computer, but nothing will happen until you tell the computer to do the tasks on the list. Telling the computer to do the tasks on its list is also known as **running the program**, or **executing the program**. Exactly how you enter the commands to tell the computer to run your Java program varies; your instructor will explain how this works.

■ 0.6 ■ Software tools for programming

You will need tools that are themselves software in order to build more software, which is a little like using tools to build more tools. The tool you will probably use most often is the text editor, which lets you enter and edit your programs in the Java language. A **text editor** is a program like a word processor. Most text editors for programming have additional features beyond what more general-purpose word processors provide, in order to make programming easier. For example, they may automatically highlight **reserved words** (also called **key words**, words that have specific meaning in Java) and automatically format your program with indentation, both techniques that make your program easier to read (and easier for you to write).

You will also use a compiler. Recall that a compiler is a program that translates a program in a higher-level language into the machine language that the computer can understand. After you have designed and written a program in a higher-level language, and before you can run it, you must **compile** it, that is, give it to the compiler to be translated. The compiler analyzes your program using the grammar of some programming language and then translates it into a machine-language version; this process is called **compilation**. The original program is also called **source code**; the machine-language translation is known as **binary code**, or a **binary**, or **object code**.

If a program is not grammatically correct, it won't compile. Instead of translating your program, the compiler gives you messages describing the syntax errors it found. It's like giving a book to a proofreader and getting it back with all the grammatical mistakes pointed out. Sometimes you have misspellings, sometimes you've got the punctuation wrong, sometimes your meaning isn't clear—the proofreader is nice enough to point all these out so your book doesn't get published with mistakes that make it unreadable.

The editor, compiler, and other tools are often combined into an **integrated development environment (IDE)**. Examples of IDEs include JBuilder®, CodeWarrior®, BlueJ®, Visual J++®, Eclipse®, and the Java Development Environment for Emacs (JDEE), among others. We will not be teaching you how to use a specific IDE in this book, since so many IDEs are available. We will simply refer to "the editor" and "the compiler."

There are five essential features of any IDE:

1. how to start it;
2. how to stop it;
3. how to edit a program;
4. how to compile a program; and
5. how to run (or execute) a compiled program.

Most IDEs have additional features, but if you learn these five, you will know enough to work through the examples and run the programs in this text.

You will also use a web browser to learn more about Java. There's a lot of helpful information about Java on the Web, particularly at the Sun website (http://java.sun.com/api/ index.html). In addition, your instructor may provide **support code**, files written in Java that you can use to help in the execution of your programs. For example, suppose you're trying to write a program that simulates a rock concert. Your instructor may give you the code that builds a headliner, an opening act, a few thousand crazy fans, and speakers that hurt your ears just thinking about them, and your job will be to put these parts together in a way that makes sense. Or you might be writing Solitaire for the computer: your instructor gives you the code for the cards themselves, and your job is to write the code that says what happens when a card is moved from one pile to another.

■ *0.7 ■ **How compilation works in Java**

Note: A star in front of a section indicates optional material.

We simplified the explanation of how compilation works in Java quite a bit, and in case you want to know how it really works, here's a more thorough explanation. Compiling a program in Java is a little different from the way it is done in most other languages. Instead of translating your program into machine language all at once, the Java compiler first translates it part way, into an intermediate language called **Java byte code**. At first, it seems that going part way wouldn't be as good, but in fact, this method of translation has been a big reason for Java's success. Remember that we said that every type of computer has its own machine language? Naturally, that means that every type of computer must have its own compiler in order to translate each programming language properly. In addition, compilers are large and difficult programs to write, requiring teams of programmers over many years. But because all Java programs are compiled into Java byte code, the Java compiler only had to be written once.

But wait, you're thinking. The program is still only in Java byte code instead of machine language, so the computer still can't understand it, right? You're absolutely correct. We still need a program to interpret and execute the Java byte code, and this program, known as the **Java virtual machine** (or JVM), must be written for each type of computer. A program like the JVM that executes code is called an **interpreter**. Because Java byte code is much simpler than Java, however, these programs are relatively easy to write, and essentially all computers now have a Java virtual machine. Thus the job of writing a Java compiler for a new machine is reduced to writing a much simpler byte-code interpreter, a big advantage over writing the entire compiler from scratch. For those of you with some programming background, the difference between a compiler and an interpreter is that the former translates the entire program for subsequent execution, while an interpreter translates and immediately executes each instruction in turn. See Figure 0.3.

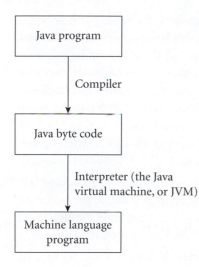

Figure 0.3 ■ How compilation works in Java.

■ 0.8 ■ **The process of writing programs**

People rarely build things correctly the first time. What's more, if they build something that is successful, it will nonetheless need to be changed and improved as time goes by. Today's airplanes are very different from the ones the Wright brothers flew. Telephones have been modified many times since they were first invented.

The larger the program, the longer it is used, and the more people who work on it, the more important it is to have a well-defined approach to building it. If you're working on a small class project that will never be used again, you may do well without taking any kind of systematic approach. If it's a large project, or if you're ever going to use it again, or if you're working as part of a team, or if someone else is going to work on it afterward, it's important to be more systematic.

The traditional model of the software development process compares it to a waterfall, as shown in Figure 0.4. In this process, each step is like a basin where the water pools for a while before continuing downward. Programs are written step by step, just as the water flows step by step down the waterfalls. In their typical order, the steps in the **waterfall model** are:

- ■ *Analysis*. First, describe the problem to be solved in a human language, such as English. ("Design a bicycle.") Next, analyze the problem definition in detail and work with the potential users to develop a thorough understanding of the problem. This precise description is also known as a **specification**. ("Design a bicycle for city use by one person.")

keyconcept

The steps of the waterfall model are analysis, specification, design, implementation, testing, and maintenance.

■ *Design.* Now you've figured out what you're going to do, figure out how you're going to do it, using both components you design from scratch and others you adapt and reuse. ("The handlebars, the frame, and the gears will be standard; the seat will be customized to make it more comfortable, and there will be a specially designed basket for carrying books or groceries.") Your finished design should include an overview and a detailed description of all the components of the system. In addition to a verbal description, your design may include UML diagrams (discussed in Chapter 1) and sketches or mock-ups of what the user might see on the screen when the program is run.

■ *Implementation.* Next, build the program using a computer programming language (Java in our case). If your design is good enough, most of the hard work should already be done before this phase. (At this point, we build the bicycle out of the parts we selected from our shelves or built from scratch.)

■ *Testing.* Even if you know you built it right, test it thoroughly to make sure. Computer programs almost never work right the first time, even when (or maybe especially when) you expect them to. (Now we actually take the bicycle out for a test ride.)

■ *Maintenance.* Finally, keep the program working and current. Once people start using the program, they will find things that need to be fixed and/or features they want added. In a successful piece of software, maintenance is often said to be 80% of the effort. (The bicycles skip gears too often, so we need to find a new supplier. People want to ride the bicycle at night, so we need to add extra reflectors and lights.)

The waterfall model has been popular for many years, but it's not perfect. For example, it doesn't capture the fact that we often go back and forth, repeating earlier steps, or even

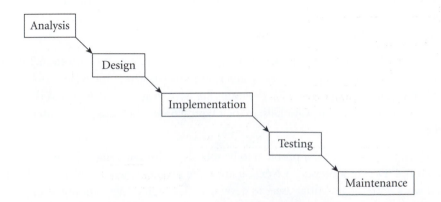

Figure 0.4 ■ The waterfall process for building, testing, and maintaining software.

jump around. For example, when developing a detailed design, you may realize that your analysis was incomplete, or even that the specification was unclear. (Was this bicycle for regular commuting in heavy traffic, or just for recreation?) You can jump from design to testing and test your design by thinking it through, working it through on paper, or even prototyping pieces of it, before you implement it. Your actual process may be more like the one shown in Figure 0.5. In short, these steps are guidelines to help give structure to the software development process, not an immutable linear sequence of activities.

This process is probably one with which you are already quite familiar. It is useful for many things, from applying to college, to planning a party, to building a bridge. Indeed, an outline for a history or English paper can be thought of as the detailed specifications for the paper.

Another, more recent software development model is the **spiral model**. Here, the basic idea is to design, implement, and test a small version of the system, and then repeat these steps for larger and larger versions of the system. The spiral model has many advantages. First, implementers and users can see a small version of the program running early on. It's always easier to evaluate a program you can see rather than having to visualize a full-bore one from a detailed specification. Second, the program is thoroughly tested at each stage, instead of waiting until after all the features have been added. If we manage the changes carefully, we're adding to the program at each stage, rather than completely reinventing it. Since we have a working program at each stage, we can be more confident that our final program is error-free. (In terms of the example above, start by building a very basic bicycle, test it, then add the custom seat, then test it again, then add the basket, then test it again....)

Finally, a third model that is growing in popularity is **extreme programming**. This approach is used by experienced programmers working in teams. Developed in response to older

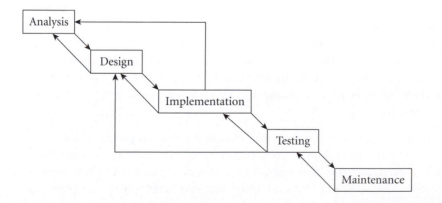

Figure 0.5 ■ A more realistic view of the waterfall process, with backtracking.

models of program development, it is motivated by three main considerations. First, many believe that older methods are too rigid and bureaucratic, particularly for smaller programs. Second, the older methods were based on methods for building things like bridges and dams. Software is much easier to modify during the development process than a bridge or a dam. Third, specifications change as projects develop. As a result of all these factors, the advocates of extreme programming argue that it is not necessary, or even desirable, to do all the design early. Instead, they de-emphasize detailed upfront design. Programmers start implementing immediately and test the program right from the beginning. The whole process is driven by testing, rather than design. (First, decide that the bicycle must be suitable for regular commuting in city traffic and must go for 1000 miles without a flat tire. Then order parts, fasten them together, and start riding the bicycle.)

The extreme-programming process can work well for small teams of experienced programmers who already have strong design skills. If inexperienced programmers start programming without designing their programs carefully, they can easily write a program that's so complicated it can't be modified without starting all over again. In this text, we emphasize design, so that you can develop the skills to let you adopt the extreme programming approach later, if you choose to.

These models of software development are quite different, but they all have one thing in common: they all attempt to manage the complex process of building a large piece of software by providing a structure for that process.

■ 0.9 ■ What if your program doesn't work?

Once you have removed all the syntax errors, you can get your program to run. But does it do everything it was supposed to? And does it do it all correctly?

You need to go back to the specifications and develop ways to test your program. Suppose you have written a calendar program. You might consider the following tests: does it work for months with 30 and with 31 days? Does it handle February correctly? Does it handle leap years correctly? There are too many possible sequences of calendar entries to test them all, so you have to choose the tests that are most likely to uncover any errors. Designing good tests is an art in itself, and if you become interested, you may decide to specialize in this area.

As you go through your testing, you may notice **bugs** or errors in the program. **Debugging** is the process of removing those bugs. Some bugs are obvious; others are very subtle and only appear in particular cases. For example, you may have heard of the Y2K bug that caused great anxiety in the late 1990s just before the year 2000. Back in the 1960s and 1970s, a lot of software used only two digits for the date: "72," for example, instead of

"1972." The good news was that this software was so successful that people were still using it in 1999, contrary to its designers' expectations. The bad news was that all the software had to be revised because the dates were now ambiguous. "72" could refer to 1972 or 2072. This revision of thousands of programs in common use cost many billions of dollars.

Finding bugs in a program can frustrate even the best programmers, and even the best programmers write imperfect code. The Y2K bug was unusual in that it was a conscious choice that made sense at the time: computer storage was expensive, saving two digits out of four on every date was worthwhile, and no one anticipated that the software would still be in use at the turn of the century. What seemed a smart design choice under the circumstances became an unanticipated bug much later. Most bugs, however, are simply mistakes. So it shouldn't alarm you if the program you have entered doesn't perform exactly as you intended; a certain amount of trial and error is common.

Because bugs are so common, it is essential to test your program carefully. To minimize frustration, take the time to find the bug before you enter a change in your program—even if that means walking away from your computer for a while. Haphazard changes in your program can introduce more bugs than they remove—like adding salt to a dish that actually needed garlic, or dyeing your hair the wrong color because you didn't like your haircut.

■ Summary ■

In this chapter, we give a brief introduction to computer hardware and software and the process of writing programs. The part of the computer you can touch is called hardware: it includes input devices (keyboard, mouse, etc.), a central processing unit, or CPU, memory, and output devices (monitors, printers, etc.). Software controls what the computer does. An algorithm is an unambiguous, executable list of instructions for performing some task or exhibiting some behavior. A computer program is an algorithm (or collection of algorithms) that can be executed by a computer: it is a list of instructions for the CPU. Software is another term for a collection of programs.

Several models have been developed to describe the process of writing software. We discuss three in this chapter: the waterfall model, the spiral model, and the extreme programming model. Program design, implementation, testing, and maintenance are all important phases of the process, although they have different emphases in different models.

■ Self-Check Questions ■

(The answers to these questions can be found on the book's website, www.aw.com/sanders)

1. What is hardware?
2. What is an algorithm?
3. What is software?
4. What is machine language?
5. What is an input device? Give three examples.
6. What is an output device? Give two examples.
7. Compare and contrast RAM and a hard disk as ways of storing information.
8. What is a high-level programming language?
9. What is a compiler?
10. What is the difference between syntax and semantics?
11. How is a text editor for programs different from a general-purpose word processor?
12. What is an integrated development environment (IDE)? What are the five essential parts of an IDE?
13. What is the waterfall process for writing programs? What are its stages? What is its major flaw?
14. What is the spiral process for writing programs, and what are its stages?
15. What is the extreme-programming process for writing programs?
16. What does it mean to execute a program?
17. What does it mean to debug a program?

■ Exercises ■

Applying the Facts

1. Give an algorithm for making a peanut-butter-and-jelly sandwich.
2. Explain how you might plan a party using each of the following processes. Which do you prefer? Why?
    a. The waterfall model
    b. The spiral model
    c. The extreme programming model
3. Explain how you might write a paper using each of the following processes. Which do you prefer? Why?

    a. The waterfall model

    b. The spiral model

    c. The extreme programming model

4. Explain how you might cook dinner using each of the following processes. Which do you prefer? Why?

    a. The waterfall model

    b. The spiral model

    c. The extreme programming model

5. Suppose you want to write a word processor. It should model the process of writing documents with a pen and paper. In addition, it should allow the user to copy text from one place to another; cut and paste text; and choose between right-justified and ragged-right text. It should be possible to put text in bold or italics as well as regular (Roman) type. Explain how you might write the word processor using each of the following processes. Which do you prefer? Why?

    a. The waterfall model

    b. The spiral model

    c. The extreme programming model

6. Find an IDE for Java, start it, find the editor, the compiler, and the mechanism for running programs, and then stop it. Give a written explanation of how it works as if you were describing it to another student in the class who'd never tried it.

1

Introduction to Objects

OBJECTIVES

After reading this chapter, you should be able to:

☑ Define object-oriented program

☑ Give seven criteria for evaluating software models

☑ Explain the importance of managing software complexity

☑ Explain three techniques for handling software complexity

☑ Define properties, capabilities, class, and instance

☑ Identify objects, properties, and capabilities in a written problem description

☑ Explain how an object's properties and capabilities are modeled in Java

☑ Declare and define a class

☑ Declare and initialize instance variables

☑ Write simple methods, including a mainline and a constructor

☑ Draw a simple class diagram in UML

■ 1.1 ■ **Introduction**

Imagine how the people felt who created Tetris™ and then saw it played all over the world. Imagine writing the programs for burglar alarms or breathalyzers that save people's lives, designing new features for instant messaging, or being one of the people who start the next Microsoft or the next Google. Imagine the satisfaction of simply writing a program to help your fellow students register for class more easily.

Writing computer programs like these is an activity that many people enjoy. It can be intellectually challenging, like solving puzzles. It can be creative. It provides tangible results—when you're done, you've got something you, and others, can use.

To write a program, you need to give the computer a detailed and precise description that it can understand and execute. For example, to write a game like Tetris, you need to describe the size and shape of the game board, the size and shape of the pieces, and exactly what moves the player can make. If you're writing a program to help your fellow students register, you need to describe courses, classrooms, instructors, and students.

Although detailed, the description must be simplified. For example, the registrar's software doesn't include every fact about every student! We have to choose which details to include and which to leave out. Every model has a purpose. We focus on the details that are most relevant to that purpose. Thus, your graduation year and course schedule are included; your favorite band and your great-grandmother's maiden name are not.

A simplified representation of something else is called a **model**. You're probably familiar with model airplanes and model cars. You may have built model buildings out of LEGO® bricks, or played with dolls (which are models of people), or built model castles out of sand at the beach.

At a low level, a computer program is a list of machine-language instructions for the CPU, but at a high level, a **program** is a model written in a programming language. An **object-oriented program**, the type of program we focus on in this book, is made up of a collection of parts (called objects) cooperating to perform some task or exhibit some behavior. Objects can model tangible things, like a roller coaster and all its parts, LEGO pieces, or plants that are part of a garden. Objects can model concepts, like the date or a meeting between two people. Objects can also model processes, like writing a paper or playing a computer game. Objects cooperate by sending each other messages that request actions to be performed—objects are programmed to respond to such messages in order to carry out the requested actions.

Object-oriented programming is the process of writing a model in an object-oriented programming language by defining the objects it contains and the relationships among them. In this chapter, we introduce the structure of object-oriented programs, a technique for identifying the set of cooperating objects needed to build a model, and the syntax for creating those objects in Java. We introduce four key ideas: properties, capabilities, classes, and instances.

■ 1.2 ■ Concepts

1.2.1 What is a model?

Consider the definition of "model": a simplified representation of something else. Starting from the last word, "else," we already see what a model is not. A model is not the same as the "else," the thing being modeled. LEGO bricks are easier to work with than real bricks and mortar. Weather models let us predict where hurricanes will be hours in the future. The registrar's software makes it possible to find your transcript in seconds, twenty-four hours a day. Models allow us to do things that would be much harder—or impossible—with the original.

Working backwards, the next word is "something," referring to the thing being modeled. This may seem a little obvious, but it can be surprisingly easy to lose track of the thing being modeled. If you ever started to look up information about a college on the Web, followed links to read about the city or town it's in, the restaurants and clubs located there, the coming attractions at those clubs, a particularly interesting band and its latest album ... only to remember that you still needed to find out how to download the application form, you understand this problem. It's important to keep focused on the facts that are most relevant to your purpose, or the purpose of the model you are building.

The next important word in the definition of a model is "representation": a model is nothing without some way to represent it. Models can be made out of all kinds of things. Model airplanes are made out of wood. Barbie® dolls are made out of plastic. Mathematical models of the weather are made out of mathematical equations and statistical information. Models of current events can be documentaries, the evening news, or *People* magazine. The process of cooking a meal can be modeled in words (as a set of recipes) or on film (as a TV cooking show). Our models here will be built using a programming language, which has some of the precision of mathematics and some of the expressiveness of ordinary prose.

Focusing on the "representation" means focusing on the *solution domain*. Programming techniques are critically important, and indeed we spend much of the rest of this book discussing them; as you learn these new techniques, however, remember that programs are *about* something. The stereotype of a computer programmer is someone who spends all his or her time programming. In fact, such seclusion can be a real disadvantage. The more you know about other fields—business, art, medicine, police work, sports, cooking, whatever—the better you will be able to model them. Some of the most effective (and most valuable) programmers are also experts in some other field.

1.2.2 How are models built?

Everything we want the computer to know, we have to tell it explicitly. Suppose we're trying to model something simple, say a pet iguana. When building a software model, we often start with a verbal description:

> The iguana is green. It lives in a cage, eats lettuce from a food dish, and moves around the cage.

Whatever the purpose of our model, we need much more detail. For example, if we're designing the model for a vet, we need to include lots of detail about iguana biology and possible diseases. If we're designing it as a character in an online game, we want it to look, move, and perhaps behave like an iguana. But for now, let's keep it simple.

How can we get started? A grammatical analysis of the verbal description can help us identify the objects we need. Objects often correspond to nouns, so our list of possible objects would include "iguana," "cage," "lettuce," and "food dish."

After identifying the objects in our model, we need to describe each of them. There are two kinds of information we need to include. The things an object can do (i.e., the messages it responds to) are called its **capabilities**. These often correspond to verbs. For example, iguanas have the capabilities "live," "eat," and "move."

The things an object knows are called its **properties**. There are three kinds of properties: components (or parts), attributes, and associations with peer objects. Parts are easy to identify: the iguana's head, tail, and legs, for example, are all parts of the iguana. The iguana's location and size are examples of **attributes**: characteristics of an object that don't make any sense apart from the object itself. And the cage, the food dish, and the lettuce are examples of **peer objects**: independently existing objects that are associated with the object we're describing, not components or attributes.

Properties have values. Most properties have values that are objects themselves: for example, the iguana's "cage" property could have a value that is also an object, the cage itself, which in turn may have its own parts among its properties.

The problem definition gives us clues about the different kinds of object properties and some of their possible values:

- An object generally "has," is "composed of," or "contains" its components (iguanas "have" a tail).
- Attributes of an object are often suggested by adjectives ("green," "long").
- Objects often can be said to know about their peer objects (for example, iguanas know about their cage and their food dish).

The properties and capabilities of the iguana object are summarized in Listing 1.1. (The // notation signifies an explanatory comment.)

This grammatical analysis of the problem definition is a simple and widely used method for identifying objects, properties, and capabilities. As you can see, it's just a start. The description didn't include any information about the iguana's legs, for example, and we're going to need those in order to give it a "move" capability. Identifying the objects we need isn't a mechanical process, and there is typically more than one possible design. The main thing is to understand your options and be able to defend your choices. Making these judgment calls is both the challenge and the fun of programming.

```
1    Iguana
2       Properties
3          color // an attribute
4          leftBackLeg, rightBackLeg // components
5          cage, food dish // peer objects
6       Capabilities:
7          live
8          eat
9          move
```

Listing 1.1 ■ The properties and capabilities of the iguana object

1.2.3 **How to have different objects of the same type: classes and instances**

What if we want several iguanas, not just one? Software objects that have the same capabilities and the same type of properties are grouped together into a **class**. What we really want, then, is an Iguana *class*. The class of an object is also known as its **type**.

A particular object that belongs to a class is called an **instance**. All instances have the same capabilities, for example, the ability to eat and move, but at any given moment, they may be doing different things. One may be eating, while another is walking in its cage. Similarly, instances of a given class all have the same properties, but they may have different *values* for their properties. For example, two iguanas may have the same length, but they may have different colors and weights, certainly have different locations, and each has its own legs.

A property can change values during the execution of a program. It is likely, for example, that the location of an iguana will change. We call the collection of all the values of an instance's properties at a given time the instance's **state** at that time; change the value of any property, and the state of the instance changes as well.

We can think of a class as a rubber stamp (Figure 1.1). A rubber stamp knows how to make a particular kind of picture. Each picture can have its own specific color and location, however. The rubber stamp supplies the basic pattern, but each individual image has its own property values.

From now on, we use the terms "class" and "instance." We continue to use the word "object" informally, either for a class or for a particular instance, when the context makes it clear which one is meant.

keyconcept

A class corresponds to a group of software objects with the same capabilities and the same type of properties. A particular object that belongs to a class is called an instance.

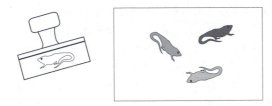

Figure 1.1 ■ A class and three instances that have different values for instance variables "color" and "position."

1.2.4 **Managing complexity**

keyconcept

Software models of interesting situations can be very complex. Techniques for managing this complexity include parts hierarchies, encapsulation, and inheritance.

What if, even after we have eliminated all the detail we can from our model, it is still very large and complex? Object-oriented programming offers us several techniques for managing that complexity. In this section, we introduce three such techniques:

1. encapsulation
2. parts hierarchies (or containment hierarchies)
3. inheritance

Encapsulation lets us hide the details that another object doesn't need to know, like medicine hidden inside a capsule. We don't need to know what's inside a medicine capsule in order to benefit from taking the medicine. Similarly, the electrical system in your house is generally hidden, except for light switches and outlets. When we define the objects in our model, an object-oriented language lets us choose which of their properties and capabilities will be hidden and which will be publicized to the other objects in the model so they can use them.

keyconcept

Encapsulation is information hiding: hiding details about an object that other objects don't need to see.

Another technique is to describe an object by identifying its parts, defining objects corresponding to those parts, then defining objects corresponding to *their* parts, and so forth. At each level, the parts become smaller, and by focusing on one part at a time, we can reduce a large problem to a group of smaller, more manageable ones. For example, we could model an amusement park as a collection of rides. Then we could model, say, the merry-go-round as a platform, an organ, a collection of painted horses, and a ring. The horses could be modeled as a painted wooden body, a saddle, and a pole, and so on. The collection of an object, its parts, subparts, sub-subparts, and so forth is called a **parts hierarchy** or **component hierarchy**.

keyconcept

The collection of an object, its parts, subparts, sub-subparts, and so forth is called a parts hierarchy.

Note: Dividing a problem into parts so as to focus on one part at a time is a strategy known as **divide and conquer**, which has been an effective means of controlling complexity since ancient times. It is the classic problem-solving technique.

Finally, **inheritance** lets us look at the objects in our model and factor out the properties and capabilities they have in common. For example, palaces and beach houses are kinds of houses. Because both are kinds of houses, they have things in common: they both contain rooms where people can sleep and eat, for example. If we list all the properties and capabilities of palaces, and then all the properties and capabilities of beach houses, we'll have to list a lot of the same things twice.

Instead of listing the same properties and capabilities over and over, inheritance lets us put them in one place. In this example, we could define a "house" class that includes the properties and capabilities all houses have in common. Then we could define a "palace" class that contains the properties and capabilities that are specific to palaces (moats, thrones, etc.) and a "beach house" class that contains those properties and capabilities that are specific to beach houses (near the ocean, has outdoor showers, etc.). If we're also modeling office buildings, we can go further and define a "building" class that includes the properties and capabilities all buildings have in common (number of stories, location, etc.), along with more specific "house" and "office building" classes.

Inheritance, like subdividing an object into parts, is a kind of divide-and-conquer strategy: it enables us to focus on the general properties that buildings all have in common, then on the properties that are special about houses, and then on the properties that make beach houses different from other houses. An object, its subcategories, sub-subcategories, and so forth are collectively called an **inheritance hierarchy**. Of course, our choice of objects to include in an inheritance hierarchy depends on the purpose of the model. If we're creating a model for a small-town developer who builds only houses, for example, we probably won't need either palaces or office buildings; instead, we'll include much more detail about the types of houses he or she builds. Chapter 3 discusses the mechanism and application of inheritance.

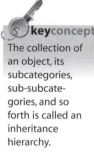

keyconcept
The collection of an object, its subcategories, sub-subcategories, and so forth is called an inheritance hierarchy.

1.2.5 **What makes a good software model?**

How can we decide if our software model is good? Or if we're considering buying software, how can we choose between one product and another? Some key factors are:

keyconcept
Seven criteria for evaluating models are: how well they fulfill their purpose, appearance, reliability, efficiency, usability, flexibility, and maintainability.

1. What does it do?
2. Is it reliable?
3. Is it easy to learn and to use?
4. What is its look and feel?
5. Is it efficient?
6. Can it easily be adapted to new uses?
7. How hard is it to maintain?

The first thing we look at in evaluating a model is what it does: its **functionality**. When buying a car, we ask, "Does it run?" We might then ask, "How many people does it hold?" or "How much can it carry?" In the same way, when buying a piece of software off the shelf, we look at the features it has—will it entertain us? Let us type our papers more easily? Help us do our taxes?

The next thing to consider is **reliability**: how often does the model break? If you've ever had a car that broke down all the time, or if you've ever used a piece of software when it "shut down unexpectedly," you understand why people tend to be loyal to reliable products. Making software as bug-free as possible is a huge challenge. Computer scientists also refer to a reliable piece of software as **robust**.

How frustrating is it when you buy a new product, take it home, and discover that it's hard to learn, or hard to use when you have learned it? **Usability** is the quality of being easy to use (both at first, when you're learning, and then afterward). Some car radios have so many buttons, for example, that you could have an accident finding the one you want. Usability experiments suggest concrete ways to improve the layout of graphics on a computer screen to best convey information and make a program more usable. Nevertheless, combining functionality and usability continues to be a challenge.

Another important factor is the software's **look and feel**. When you're using the software, what does each screen look like? If there are menus and buttons, where are they located? What colors are used? How easy is it to figure out the sequence of instructions required to perform a particular function? Once learned, how natural are those interactions? How easy are they to remember? A user's response to these questions might seem completely subjective. But, like usability (to which it is closely related), look and feel can be tested experimentally.

People are impatient with products that take too long to work. For example, think about the last really long web search you did. Similarly, we'd like our cars to use less fuel, and our mobile phones to be smaller and easier to carry around. The quality of using as few resources as possible is called **efficiency**.

The more people use a model, the more they want it to do. If your car is too small, it may work for driving to school, but you won't be able to give all your friends a ride to the beach or attach a trailer to move all your furniture to your new apartment. A model that can adapt over time has **flexibility**. Unfortunately, flexibility does not come for free—it must be planned from the beginning.

Finally, if a software model is going to last, someone must be able to make the changes that keep it current or make it more reliable. The more easily these changes can be made, the more **maintainable** the software model is. If the software model is so complicated that it cannot be understood by others, then it cannot be maintained.

Figure 1.2 ■ Rube Goldberg cartoon showing component parts of a system. Rube Goldberg is the ® and © of Rube Goldberg, Inc.

Consider Figure 1.2, one of cartoonist Rube Goldberg's machines that models a rather simple action with a variety of extremely incongruous parts. While his model may solve the problem, it is a very fragile system. Each part must be precisely triggered by the previous component. This model may work well (to those who cannot see how it is actually implemented), but it certainly does not look good to the person who must maintain it. What happens when we need to replace the monkey?

■ 1.3 ■ **Mechanics**

Now that we have introduced the concepts of classes, instances, capabilities, and properties, let's take a look at how to express these concepts in Java. (Most chapters in this book have a Mechanics section like this one to introduce the Java syntax for that chapter. In general, the Concepts section includes principles and ideas that you can use in other languages, not just in Java; the Mechanics section may include a few principles, but primarily includes implementation details that are relevant only to Java.)

1.3.1 **The rubber stamp: declaring and defining a class**

Each entry in a dictionary has a word, followed by one or more definitions. Similarly, in Java, we first name a new class (i.e., **declare** it) and then **define** it. The class definition is the basis of all Java programs. In fact, a Java program is just a collection of class definitions, much as a dictionary is just a collection of word definitions. Every Java statement that can be executed occurs inside some class definition.

We can declare an Iguana class like this:

```
public class Iguana
```

Some of the words in this declaration are predefined in Java (that is, they are **reserved words**, or **keywords**), and others are words chosen by the programmer to name objects and their properties and capabilities. Here, `public` and `class` are keywords; `Iguana`, the class's name, is chosen by the programmer.

The keyword `public` means that this class is available to the public. In other words, any other class in the program can know about it. We will discuss the issue of who can know about what information (also called **visibility**) in more detail in later chapters; for right now, though, simply take it as a rule that all classes should be public and their definitions preceded by the Java keyword `public`.

Having declared the class, we are now ready to define it. A **class definition** tells the compiler what the properties and capabilities of the class are. We follow the class declaration with a "{", a left curly brace to begin the definition. We end the definition with a "}", a right curly brace. Within these braces, we later put the Java code that defines the properties and capabilities of the class. The part of a definition between the first and last curly brackets is called the **body** of the definition.

Here, then, is the simplest class that can be defined:

```
public class Iguana {
}
```

The curly braces are simply **body delimiters** (they indicate the beginning and end—the limits—of the body). So far, the body is just empty. This class can be compiled, but it does not do anything. In other words, it is syntactically (grammatically) correct but has no semantics (meaning).

The names (called **identifiers**) that you choose for your classes (and for their properties and capabilities) are very important. Names start with a letter or an underscore(_); after that, you can put as many letters, numbers, or underscores as you want. Spaces are *not* allowed. We couldn't name our class `char`, because that happens to be a reserved word in Java. But this rule gives us a wide variety of choices, even more than the number of words in English and all other languages combined. For example, we could have called our class `iguANA`, or `_iGUana73`, or `xq234`, or simply `x`.

Not all the legal names are good choices, however. There are two important rules in choosing names:

- make them meaningful
- follow a good set of style conventions

A **convention** is a rule that isn't required by the syntax of the language, but is generally accepted as good practice. Our simple class definition illustrates two style conventions:

- Class names start with a capital letter (like `Iguana`).
- The opening bracket of the class body is placed on the same line as the class name, and the closing bracket is on a line by itself, aligned with the "p" in the keyword "`public`."

Another important naming conventions is:

- If a class name is made up of two words, each word should start with a capital letter.

Thus, if we wanted to declare a class just for pet iguanas, we could call it `PetIguana`. Some conventions are widespread among Java programmers (like these); others are specific to a particular workplace or project (or to this book). Like the layout of your programs, naming conventions are part of the programming style you adopt when you program. A good consistent style makes your programs much easier to read and fix later on.

Comments also make your program easier to read. **Comments** are statements included in a program to explain something to the reader; they are ignored by the compiler. Java has three kinds of comments:

1. A **documentation comment** starts with /** and ends with */.
2. An **inline comment** starts with // and ends at the end of the line.
3. A **standard comment** starts with /* and ends with the next */.

We can rewrite our basic Java class definition with comments like this:

```
/**
 * Chapter 1: Iguana.java
 * Our first Java class definition.
 * This class is a very simple model of an iguana.
 */
public class Iguana {
    // here model the properties and capabilities
}
```

This documentation comment explains what the class does. If we run the built-in program `javadoc` on a file of Java code that contains documentation comments, it automatically produces documentation. As you write these comments, therefore, it's a good idea to imagine that someone is reading them separately from the code itself.

Inline comments are used to explain something local: the purpose of a single line of code for example, or, as here, the intended contents of an empty definition.

Finally, standard comments can be used for any multi-line comments. They are most useful, however, for something called "commenting out" a block of code. **Commenting out code** is the technique of making part of your code into a comment. Occasionally when you're writing a program, you want the compiler to ignore part of what you've written, but you don't want to delete it entirely. Maybe you're not quite done with that part of the program yet, but you want to try out the rest of it. Maybe you think that part of the program has a syntax error, and you want to see if the program will compile without it. The easiest way to do this in Java is by using a standard comment: all you have to do is put `/*` at the beginning of the code you want to comment out, and `*/` at the end. When you want the compiler to stop ignoring that piece of code, just delete the comment symbols.

Even more important than following a good set of naming conventions is using meaningful names. A name like `Iguana` or `Camel` tells us (and any teammates or instructors who may be reading our code) what the class is intended to model. Names like `C` or `X` or `XQ22` provide no information and are bad choices.

Be careful, however: naming something doesn't make it true! If we write

```
public class Camel {
    ...
}
```

and then say that the `Camel` is a small purple fruit that can be made into wine, then `Camel` is not an accurate name (at least, not in English). This is one example of a more general point. It's easy to convince ourselves that, because our classes have the right names, our model does what it is supposed to do. But just because we call a class `Camel` or `Iguana` doesn't mean the class is an accurate model of a camel or an iguana. All it means is that the class is *supposed* to model a camel or an iguana. We must still test our programs carefully to make sure that they do what they're supposed to do.

1.3.2 Modeling properties: instance variables

An object's properties are modeled in Java by instance variables. An **instance variable** is a variable that is associated with each instance of a class. Computer variables, like mathematical variables, stand for a value that can change. Each instance variable models a single property and holds a current value for that property. With very few exceptions, which we will learn about later, properties have values that are themselves objects. Instance variables don't hold these objects directly. Instead, an instance variable stores the address of an object. The address of an object is its location in the computer's memory; it is also called a **reference** or a **pointer** to the value. (See Figure 1.3). Java takes care of all the bookkeeping required to store and retrieve objects in memory—all we care about is having the right values in the right variables to suit our model.

Just like classes, instance variables have to be **declared**: that is, we have to tell the compiler their names and their types. The declarations, like all the class's other capabilities and properties, go inside the body of the class definition, like this:

```
public class Iguana {
    // first, model the properties
    // starting with the attributes
    private Color _color;
}
```

Note: In code that is a modified version of a previous example, the changes are printed in boldface type.

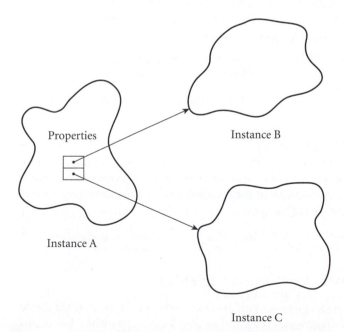

Instance B

Properties

Instance A

Instance C

Figure 1.3 ■ Instance variables that reference other objects.

A declaration introduces a property to the compiler. There are four parts to this introduction. First, we state the visibility of the instance variable (`private`). The keyword `private` means that only instances of this class and no other objects in the program can send messages to this variable. For now, just as all classes are `public`, assume that all instance variables are `private`.

Second, we give the type of the instance variable (i.e., the kind of object it is). This type must be defined somewhere. It can be any other Java class, built-in or defined by the programmer, or a primitive type such as a number. Here, for example, **Color** is a pre-defined class. In Java properties are most often objects themselves, so the compiler must know what class to use to stamp out an instance and must be able to find the definition of that class.

Third, we give the name of the instance variable. Note that we start all instance variables with an underscore, followed by a lower-case letter. Starting variable names with an underscore is a convention of this book, not a general Java convention, but it's very helpful. If you follow this convention, you will easily be able to identify the instance variables in your code. You will quickly spot the difference between class `Color` and instance variable `_color`. You can read this statement as "class `Iguana` contains a private instance variable of type `Color` called `_color`."

The name you use for an instance variable need not be related to its type, but it does make it easy for you to remember the type of an instance variable if they are close. Not only does the compiler retrieve information about the instance variable based on its type, but knowing the type of an instance variable helps the compiler verify the correctness of your program. When your code later on refers to the `Iguana`'s `_color`, the compiler will make sure that it's referring to an instance of the `Color` class.

Finally, the semicolon is like a period in English—it indicates the end of a statement.

The general form for declaring all instance variables is the same:

```
private <type> <identifier>;
```

Except for Java generics (discussed in Chapter 14), in our code examples pointed brackets (<>) indicate a place where you must fill in the specified kind of value; anything outside pointed brackets is a required part of the syntax.

Generally, our objects have several properties. We can simply list their declarations one after another, like this:

```
public class Iguana {
    // first, model the properties
    // starting with attributes
    private Color _color;
    // then components
```

```
    private Leg _leftBackLeg;
    private Leg _rightBackLeg;
    // then peer objects
    private Bowl _foodDish;
    private Cage _cage;
}
```

We have to define the `Leg`, `Bowl`, and `Cage` classes—every class we refer to must be defined, unless it's built into Java.

For convenience, if we are declaring more than one instance variable of the same type, Java lets us put them on the same line. So we could shorten the above definition by saying

```
    private Leg _leftBackLeg, _rightBackLeg;
```

Thus, we have a second possible form for variable declarations:

```
    private <type> <identifier>, ..., <identifier>;
```

The list of identifiers can contain as many items as we want; we just have to put a comma between each pair of items and a semicolon after the last one.

1.3.3 Modeling capabilities I: constructors

Other classes can send our class a message to tell it to activate any of its capabilities. Therefore it is our responsibility to say what an instance of the class being defined will do in response to such a message. In object-oriented programming, the definition of what an instance will do in response to a message is called a **method**, short for "the method of responding to the message."

Whenever an instance is created (i.e., an object is **instantiated**), Java sets aside space in memory for its properties and does the bookkeeping necessary to make sure the instance actually exists. Java then sends a message to the new instance to activate its constructor. A **constructor** is a particular kind of method, the method that is called when an instance of a class is first created.

> **keyconcept**
> A constructor is a special method that is called whenever an instance of a class is created. Its job is to initialize the object's instance variables.

If Java has already taken care of the bookkeeping, what is left for the constructor to do? The purpose of a constructor is to prepare the new instance so that another object can send it messages. All instances are born with the same capabilities; what they don't yet have is initial values for their properties. Giving a property its initial value is called **initializing** the property; giving each of the object's properties an initial value is called initializing the instance, and this is the job of the constructor.

The constructor, like all the `Iguana`'s other capabilities and properties, goes inside the body of the class definition. By convention, we put instance variables first and method definitions second:

```
public class Iguana {
    // first, model the properties
    // starting with attributes
    private Color _color;
    // then components
    private Leg _leftBackLeg, _rightBackLeg;
    // then peer objects
    private Bowl _foodDish;
    private Cage _cage;

    // put the constructor second
    public Iguana() {
    }
}
```

Like a class definition, a constructor begins with a visibility modifier, public. Next comes the name of the constructor, always the same as the class, followed by a set of parentheses, "( )," whose purpose we will learn in Chapter 2. We complete the definition by adding open and closed curly brackets, an empty body for the moment, just as we did for the class.

There are several things to note here. First, the constructor's definition looks very similar to the basic framework of the class itself. Can you spot the differences? (The constructor has parentheses; the class has the keyword class.)

Second, the constructor's definition is contained within its class's definition. And third, if you do not define a constructor for a class, one is typically defined for you. This constructor, the default constructor, simply initializes the object's properties with default values. However, this is rarely what we want, so it is always a good idea to define a constructor explicitly.

The general form for defining a class and its constructor is:

```
public class <ClassName> {
    // instance variable declarations
    public <ClassName> ()  {
    }
}
```

1.3.4 Giving properties their values: assignment statements

Thus far, we have simply declared instance variables, without giving them useful values. So, since we did not specify values, Java has automatically given them default values of null. The Java value null just means "nothing"—it is not a legal reference to some other instance.

Thus, every instance of our `Iguana` class has properties that represent nothing. If we send one of these instances, say `_tail`, a message while our program is running, we get an error called a `NullPointerException` that halts the program.

We give a value to a variable using an **assignment statement**, like this:

```
_color = GREEN;
```

On the left is the name of the variable whose value is being changed; in the middle is an equals sign, the **assignment operator**; and on the right is the new value, followed by a semicolon. Here we are assigning a constant value, not an instance, to the `_color` attribute. In order not to confuse the assignment operator with the equals sign in mathematics, it helps to pronounce this statement, "`_color` gets `GREEN`." In other words, the `Iguana` is now green.

Suppose we want to create a new instance and make that the value of a property. We can do that using a variant on an assignment statement, like this:

```
_leftBackLeg = new Leg();
```

As above, this assignment statement begins with the name of an instance variable, followed by the assignment operator. But now, instead of a constant value, we have the Java keyword `new`. The `new` keyword is a signal that we're going to invoke a constructor to create a new instance of (i.e., instantiate) an object. The name of the class whose instance we are creating follows the word `new`, and a pair of parentheses and a semicolon concludes the statement. These assignment statements in a programming language are like sentences in a human language: each is a complete thought.

How can you tell the difference between a class name and a call to the constructor for a class? Both the class and the constructor have the same name, but the constructor's name is followed by two parentheses. (`Leg` vs. `Leg()`.) There also is context, of course— the class declaration is at the top of a class definition, and the constructor is the first method in its body.

We can now fill in the body of the `Iguana` constructor like this:

```
public class Iguana {
    // first, model the properties
    // starting with attributes
    private Color _color;
    // then components
    private Leg _leftBackLeg, _rightBackLeg;
    // then peer objects
    private Bowl _foodDish;
    private Cage _cage;
```

```
        // put the constructor second
        public Iguana() {
           _color = GREEN;
           _leftBackLeg = new Leg();
           _rightBackLeg = new Leg();
           // foodDish and _cage not initialized for now
        }
    }
```

We have not assigned any value at all to the peer objects. Objects don't create their own peer objects. Peer objects exist independently. Objects *do* initialize their peer objects in the constructor, but we can't explain exactly how until Chapter 2, after we discuss parameters.

Finally, there are some more style conventions to observe in this code:

■ Instance variable declarations are indented three spaces inside the class body

■ The constructor definition is also indented three spaces inside the class body

■ The statements inside the constructor body are indented three additional spaces

1.3.5 Modeling capabilities II: more about methods

So far, we've seen how to define what an object does when it is first instantiated, but we haven't seen how to define what it does later. Constructors, as we said earlier, are a special case of methods. Now we see how to define a more typical method. We want our `Iguana` to be able to move.

A Java method has several parts, including what its name is, what it does, and what (if anything) it sends back in return to the object that sent the message. We discuss methods that return something in Chapter 2. First, let's look at the syntax for declaring a method that returns nothing at all:

```
public void move
```

So far, our method definition looks similar to both a class declaration and an instance variable declaration. It starts with the keyword `public`, which we have seen before. For now, assume that just as classes are `public` and instance variables are `private`, methods are `public`. The next part of the method definition is the keyword `void`, indicating that the method doesn't return anything, followed by the name of the method. It is a general Java convention to start method names with a lower-case letter.

Next, we need to add some syntax that says what the method will do. We start by adding parentheses after the name and curly braces for the body, as with the constructor.

Here's the empty method definition within the context of the `Iguana` class. Like our very first class definition, this method definition is syntactically correct—it can be compiled—but so far, it has no semantics.

```
public class Iguana {
    // first, model the properties
    // starting with attributes
    private Color _color;
    // then components
    private Leg _leftBackLeg, _rightBackLeg;
    // then peer objects
    private Bowl _foodDish;
    private Cage _cage;

    // put the constructor second
    public Iguana() {
        _color = GREEN;
        _leftBackLeg = new Leg();
        _rightBackLeg = new Leg();
        // foodDish and _cage not initialized for now
    }

    // then any other methods
    public void move() {
    }
}
```

Now we need to say what the method will do. We do this by enclosing a list of statements in the method body (between the curly brackets). We can use any kind of statement, such as assignment statements or messages to other objects.

Here's an extremely simple model of the way an iguana moves:

```
public class Iguana {
    // first, model the properties
    // starting with attributes
    private Color _color;
    // then components
    private Leg _leftBackLeg, _rightBackLeg;
    // then peer objects
    private Bowl _foodDish;
    private Cage _cage;

    // put the constructor second
```

```
public Iguana() {
    _color = GREEN;
    _leftBackLeg = new Leg();
    _rightBackLeg = new Leg();
    // foodDish and _cage not initialized for now
}

// then any other methods
public void move() {
    _leftBackLeg.move();
    _rightBackLeg.move();
}
}
```

We've defined our method by simply giving the work to some other objects. This may seem too easy to be true—but in fact, it's a very common recipe. Obviously, there's a lot of work left to be done on our model. We haven't yet discussed how the individual legs move, or how their movement is coordinated. Nevertheless, as far as it goes, this method is quite typical. Just as Donald Trump delegates work to his subordinates, the Iguana delegates work to its components. This method is another example of divide-and-conquer: the problem of making an individual leg move is smaller and easier than the problem of making the whole iguana move.

Sending a message to another object is also known as **invoking a method**. The general form of a method invocation is:

```
<instance variable name>.<method name>();
```

First, we specify the name of the instance to which we want to send the message, followed by a period, followed by the name of the message we want to send, followed by parentheses. Finally, we end each of the statements in the method body with a semicolon. We say "call move on _leftBackLeg" as a shorthand for "send the move message to instance variable _leftBackLeg."

The public parts of a class are collectively known as a class's **interface**. In general, it is good for a class to know *what* another class is able to do, but bad to know *how*. For this reason, we generally make all methods public and all instance variables private.

Even though the method is public, the body of the method (between the curly braces) is still completely hidden. Other objects in the program know that they can send a move message to instances of class Iguana, but they don't know exactly how the object will respond. Hiding the instance variables and hiding the details of how a method does its job are both examples of encapsulation.

1.3.6 **UML diagrams**

It often helps to summarize information about a class in a diagram. We use the standard way to write diagrams for object-oriented programs, known as the Unified Modeling Language (UML). It's a very extensive language, so we just give a small subset of it, enough for our purposes here.

Note: The earliest prototype of UML was introduced in 1995 and adopted as a standard by the Object Management Group in 1997. A good source for further information is Martin Fowler, *UML Distilled: a brief guide to the standard object modeling language.* 4th ed., Addison-Wesley 2004 (with Kendall Scott).

In UML, classes are represented by class boxes, as shown in Figure 1.4. The box shows the class name in boldface at the top. Next the diagram shows the property types that each instance of the class has (and optionally the identifiers we use to refer to each property). Finally the diagram shows the important capabilities that instances of the class can perform, indicating only what an object can do, not how it does it. A plus symbol indicates that a property or capability is `public`; a minus symbol, that it is `private`.

Sometimes, though, we want to see more information on how a class relates to the other classes in the system. For this we use a class diagram, as shown in Figure 1.5. A class diagram is composed of multiple class boxes, connected by different types of arrows that indicate the relationships between the classes. Figure 1.5 shows a small part of the class diagram for our model of an iguana.

In addition to the important properties and capabilities of a class, a class diagram shows the type of relationships among classes. For example, there are three different ways to express the relationship between a class and the three types of properties it can have. First, a simple arrow, like the one connecting `Iguana` with `Bowl`, indicates that there is an *association* relationship between two peer objects. Note that the arrow goes from the property of an object to its value (the peer object). In other words, each instance of

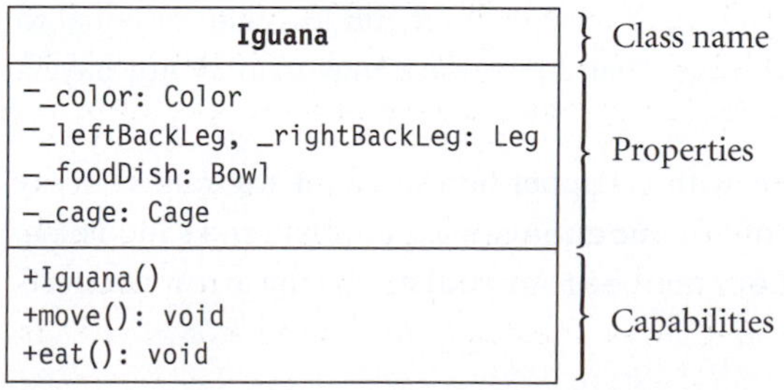

Figure 1.4 ■ Class box for our `Iguana` class.

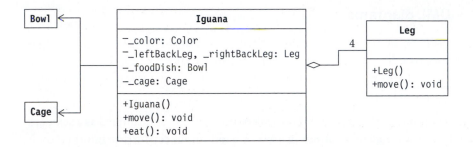

Figure 1.5 ■ Class diagram for `Iguana` and related classes.

`Iguana` has a property that is an instance of `Bowl`, but `Bowl`s do not have properties that are `Iguana`s.

Second, an arrow with a diamond arrowhead, like the one connecting `Iguana` and `Leg`, means that one class is a component of the other. The arrowhead goes next to the container object, not the component.

Attributes are a special case. Sometimes they are primitive types, not objects. In that case, we couldn't draw a class box for them. But even if they are objects (as here), we don't draw a box for them. Perhaps they don't rate a box of their own because it doesn't make sense to talk about, say, an object's color on its own, apart from the object. In any event, an object's attributes are just indicated by a line in the class box.

Finally, as shown, we can annotate the arrows with information about the number of objects involved. The annotations go on the arrow next to the component or the peer object. For annotations, we can use either an exact number or a range. The annotations are written as follows:

- A number by itself means "exactly this number." (For example, the "4" in Figure 1.5 next to the `Leg` class box means that each instance of the `Iguana` class must have exactly four `Leg`s.)

- *x* .. *y* means some number greater than or equal to *x* and less than or equal to *y*. (For example, if we wanted to say that an `Iguana` may or may not have a `Tail`, we would write `"0..1".`)

- A * by itself means "0 or more, with no upper bound." So if we wanted to say that there can be any number of `LettuceLeaves` in the `Iguana`'s food dish, we could add a class box for `LettuceLeaf` and put a * on the arrow connecting `Bowl` to `LettuceLeaf`.

- A `*` can also be the upper bound of a range. In that case, it means that there is no upper limit. For example, if we wanted to say that everyone should have at least one pet `Iguana` and maybe more, we'd add a box for `Human` and annotate the arrow connecting `Human` to `Iguana` with "`1..*`"

These annotations are optional. If no annotation is present, the number of objects involved in the relationship is unspecified. This is not necessarily a bad thing: if the diagram becomes too cluttered, it will not be useful.

■ 1.4 ■ Working Out with Objects—getting started with Java

Objectives:
- ☑ Edit, compile, and run a Java program
- ☑ Get used to your Java environment
- ☑ Use the Java syntax to define a class
- ☑ Use the Wheels library

We encourage you to get the program described in this section from the book's website (www.aw.com/sanders) or the book's CD and try it out. There will be a "Working Out with ..." section in most of the chapters from here on, and you should treat all of them the same way: compile the programs, run them, modify them, compile and run them again—until you're comfortable that you understand exactly how they work.

You will find, in fact, that it is difficult to read the Working Out with ... sections without trying out the code. This is intentional. Just like driving a car, programming can't be learned without doing it—and you wouldn't want to. So log in, start up your Java environment, and have fun!

1.4.1 **Getting started**

In this section we give you the code for a very simple Java program that creates a window displaying a red circle on a white background. The red circle could model the Japanese flag, a sunrise, or a checker on a checkerboard. A screenshot of this program is given in Figure 1.6.

Step 1: Start up your Java environment. If it has windows, menus, and icons, take a few minutes to explore them. In particular, find the commands to edit, compile, and run a program.

Step 2: Quit. Not learning to program! Quit the Java environment (just so you know you can) and start it up again.

Figure 1.6 ■ Screenshot of our first Java program.

1.4.2 **Background: the Wheels library of graphical shapes**

Generally, a program that is ready to be used is called an **application**. These range from small games to large word-processing programs. We're going to create a graphical application—that is, a program that creates a model of a visual image.

To understand the graphical part of this, let's take a brief look at **computer graphics**, the area of computer science that deals with modeling still and animated images. Typical computer displays are organized as a grid of individual lighted points, called **pixels** (short for picture elements). In fact, when you look at a computer screen you are looking at over a million tiny colored points of light. Software controls the color of each point, and how the points are colored determines what you see on the screen.

Computer graphics includes techniques for drawing all kinds of primitive shapes, including common two-dimensional ones like lines, ovals, and rectangles, as collections of pixels. These basic shapes are needed very often, and it would be silly for programmers to recreate them from individual pixels every time. Therefore, programmers have written **libraries**: collections of objects that can be used again and again. Libraries are an important part of programming. You can think of a library as a parts catalog. Instead of defining the same classes from scratch each time, we can use pre-defined classes from a library and focus on the unique parts of a program.

Java provides some libraries that make up the core of its language. In the first few chapters of this book, we use a very simple graphics library called Wheels (so called because it's like a set of training wheels to get you started). Later we introduce you to Java's built-in graphics libraries, known as AWT and `Swing`, and you'll take off the training wheels and zoom.

Just as you can go through a catalog deciding what parts to order to assemble into a car or a bicycle, you can go through a class library deciding what classes to use to build bigger and more useful classes. This type of code reuse is one of the major benefits of object-oriented programming. We call it being **appropriately lazy**, and the need to be lazy—in the right way, of course—is one of the themes of this book.

It is easy to choose the objects in a graphical program because they correspond almost one-to-one to graphical images on the computer screen. This is one of the primary reasons we have chosen a graphical approach to teaching object-oriented programming.

Wheels is very easy to learn. It provides only seven objects: four shapes (modeling an ellipse, a line, a rectangle, and a rounded rectangle), an image class that lets you include picture files in your model, a conversation bubble like the ones in cartoons, and a `Frame` class that lets you create a window on your computer screen to display your pictures in. These seven classes are enough to let us write a surprising variety of interesting programs. For instructions on how to use Wheels with various computing environments, see the book's website, www.aw.com/sanders.

The shape classes and the conversation bubble are summarized in Figure 1.7. We will see how to display all of these shapes in a window with different sizes and colors. By default, however, if we don't say otherwise, all the Wheels shapes are bright red and located in the middle of the window.

The `Frame` class creates a very generic rectangular window with a white background. A blank white window is never what we want; we'll always want to put something in it. But there's no way Wheels could know about every possible application for which you would want to use a `Frame`.

When we write programs using `Frame`s, we will write a specific type of `Frame` that knows how to do everything the generic `Frame` does and more. To do this, we will extend the generic `Frame` class to add specific capabilities and properties for our model. Extending classes is another word for inheritance—a means of organizing classes that is so central to object-oriented programming that we spend an entire chapter on it (Chapter 3). For now, all that you need to know is that by extending a generic `Frame`, we can define specific properties and capabilities that your computer can run and display.

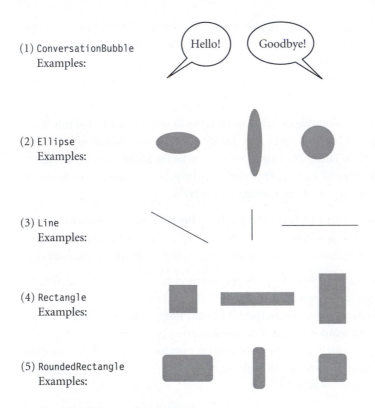

(1) `ConversationBubble`
Examples:

(2) `Ellipse`
Examples:

(3) `Line`
Examples:

(4) `Rectangle`
Examples:

(5) `RoundedRectangle`
Examples:

Figure 1.7 ■ The shapes Wheels lets us create.

1.4.3 **Analysis**

Recall that our program is supposed to display a red circle on a rectangular white background. There are two nouns in the problem description: circle and background. These are possible objects.

What are the adjectives? Red, rectangular, and white. "Red" is an attribute of the circle, and "rectangular" and "white" are attributes of the background.

1.4.4 **Design**

Since we have already done a good analysis, creating the design is fairly easy. We know that we have to start with the `Frame`, and we've been told that it does a good job of modeling a displayable rectangular area. Better still, it already has a white background. The only other component is the red circle. All graphical objects must be properties of the `Frame` (or properties of properties of the `Frame`, etc.). Thus, since we have only two classes and one must be an instance variable of the other, the relationship is clear. The `Ellipse` will be a property—specifically, a component—of the `Frame`.

Wheels makes sure that all objects know how to display themselves in a window once they are created. By default, the `Ellipse` is a red circle located in the center of the window. Therefore, we don't even need to send any messages to the `Ellipse` once it has been created. We'll see how to define our own, more interesting behaviors for various kinds of shapes later.

1.4.5 Implementation

When we actually get down to writing our program, it is extremely simple. The code is given in Listing 1.2. After the keywords `public` and `class` is the name of our `Frame`, `FirstApp` (short for "first application program"). The `Frame` is the basic window through which the user interacts with our program, the place where our graphical shapes are displayed and users will eventually provide input. Accordingly, we think of the `Frame` as the application, even though it is really only a part.

After the name `FirstApp` is a keyword `extends` that we have not seen before. This keyword is the mechanism that Java provides for us to add on to another pre-existing class,

```
1   /**
2    * Chapter 1: FirstApp.java
3    * Our first runnable Java program.
4    * It displays a red circle on a white background.
5    */
6   public class FirstApp extends wheels.users.Frame {
7       private wheels.users.Ellipse _ellipse;
8
9       public FirstApp () {
10          _ellipse = new wheels.users.Ellipse();
11      }
12
13      //magic to let FirstApp execute
14      public static void main(String[] args) {
15          FirstApp app = new FirstApp();
16      }
17  }
```

Listing 1.2 ■ `FirstApp.java`

and we explore it in great detail in Chapter 3. Next, there is the name of the pre-existing class, `wheels.users.Frame`. The dot notation indicates that the class in question, `Frame`, is contained in the `users` package (so named because it contains all the classes you're most likely to use) in the Wheels library.

Next, we declare an instance variable of type `Ellipse`. (The dot notation here is the same as for the `Frame`.) We then define a constructor for `FirstApp` and initialize the instance variable inside the constructor, using syntax familiar from Section 1.3. `FirstApp` contains a component, the `Ellipse`, but has no attributes or associated peer objects. We see examples of both of these shortly, in Chapter 2.

The other new syntax is the line that says

```
public static void main(String[] args).
```

Notice that this looks similar to a method declaration. Indeed, `main` is a special kind of method known as the **mainline** (or main **method**). Recall from Chapter 0 that the Java Virtual Machine (JVM) is a program that runs the Java byte code version of your program. It always starts a program by calling the mainline.

As you can see, the `main` method then uses the `new` operator to create an instance of `FirstApp`. The mainline is almost like a method that doesn't belong to any class. It may be a little mystifying, especially with the `static`, `void`, and `String[] args` terms that we have not explained. For now, just accept that this magic mainline is required for your program to work; we will gradually reveal the significance of each of these terms in future chapters.

1.4.6 **Steps of execution**

When this program is executed, first, we use whatever command our programming environment provides for running a program. This command tells the system to invoke the Java VM and run the mainline of the class `FirstApp`. The `main` method invokes the constructor of `FirstApp`.

The only thing the `FirstApp` constructor does is to instantiate the `Ellipse` (by invoking its constructor in turn). With the `Ellipse` on the screen, the last step of the `FirstApp` constructor (and of the program) has been executed.

The last step of the program has been executed, but the window will not disappear. Any program that uses a Wheels `Frame` continues to run until the user quits the program. Most environments provide several options for quitting: clicking on the Quit button, selecting Quit from the menu, and clicking on the X icon at the corner of the window.

Going through the steps a program should execute one by one like this, on paper, is called a **walk-through** or a **trace**. Tracing code is an invaluable technique, both for understanding and for debugging.

1.4.7 Testing

Because this program is extremely short, there is not much to test after verifying that it is syntactically correct. However, you should still run the program to make sure that it meets the specifications laid out in the beginning of this section. This two-phase testing plan allows you to switch roles; you first implement and test your code as a programmer, then pretend to be a user to test it again, assuming no knowledge of the code.

1.4.8 Followup

A surprising amount of programming involves adapting programs written in the past, rather than creating new programs from scratch. It's not too soon to begin collecting the programs you have written and learning to adapt them. To help develop this skill, most of the chapters in this book have a section in the end-of-chapter exercises called Modifying Programs. Now would be a good time to look at those questions and write some new programs based on `FirstApp`.

■ Summary ■

People use computers to model things—abstract like the concept of an animal, concrete like a roller coaster, real like a deck of cards and imaginary like the perfect pet—by writing programs. A program, like any model, is a simplified representation of something else, different from the thing being modeled.

Object-oriented programming creates software models by defining computer "objects" that correspond to objects or processes in the real world (or imaginary ones), the relationships among those objects, and the messages they send to one another. Object-oriented models are collections of communicating, collaborating objects, and the individual objects are defined in terms of their properties and capabilities. Properties are things the object knows, and capabilities are things the object can do. Object properties make it possible for an object to communicate with other objects: an object can only communicate directly with the objects it knows about (that is, the objects that are its properties). By communicating, objects work together to create models.

A class is a group of objects that share the same capabilities and the same type of properties. An instance of a class is a specific object that belongs to a class. Instantiating a class is another way of saying "creating an instance of a class." Each instance is a unique instantiation of a class.

Computer models can be extremely complex. We talked about techniques for managing this complexity: encapsulation, parts hierarchies, and inheritance hierarchies. Parts hierarchies express the relationship among an object and its parts; inheritance hierarchies express the relationship between a category (such as "Animal") and subcategories (such as "Mammal" or "Reptile") and allow us to factor out what classes have in common so we can concentrate on how they differ.

The first test of whether a model is good is whether it fits its purpose. Other criteria, which may be even more important, include its appearance, how easy it is to use, how reliable it is, its efficiency, how easily it can be adapted to new uses (flexibility), and how easy it is to maintain.

When designing code, it is often useful to express the design as a diagram. The standard diagrams for object-oriented designs are written in UML (Unified Modeling Language). UML provides a way to diagram individual classes, using a class box, and the relationships among classes, using a class diagram.

■ Self-Check Questions ■

(The answers to these questions can be found on the book's website, www.aw.com/sanders)

1. Define each of the following and give an example of each:
   a. software model
   b. object-oriented programming
   c. program
   d. encapsulation
   e. parts hierarchy
   f. inheritance
   g. object property
   h. object capability
   i. object state
   j. (object) class
   k. (object) instance
   l. attributes
   m. components
   n. associations
   o. object type
   p. class
   q. instance
   r. instantiation

s.   instance variables
t.   constructor
u.   method
v.   class declaration
w.   class definition
x.   identifier
y.   UML
z.   class diagram
aa.   class box

2. Give the seven criteria for a good model, with examples of models that satisfy (and fail to satisfy) each.

3. Which things in a problem description correspond to:

    a. objects
    b. capabilities
    c. object attributes
    d. object components

4. Which characters can appear in a Java identifier?

5. What goes inside the curly brackets in a class definition?

6. What is the purpose of the `new` keyword in Java?

7. What does the name of a constructor have to be?

8. What does the modifier of a constructor have to be?

9. What happens if you do not define a constructor for a class?

10. What is the significance of an underscore at the beginning of a variable name?

11. What does the Java keyword `private` mean?

12. What is the assignment operator, and what does it do?

13. If the naming conventions are followed, how can you tell if an identifier refers to a class, a method, a constructor, or an instance variable?

14. What does it mean to invoke a method?

15. Why should methods be `public` and instance variables `private`?

16. Give a simple UML diagram and explain its parts.

■ **Exercises** ■

Applying the Facts

1. Consider your driver's license. It contains a very simplified (and probably not ideal) model of you, created for the purpose of identifying drivers. The model includes a photograph and a very brief written description with such information as your height, weight, eye color, hair color, and birth date. Evaluate this model in terms of the seven criteria for software models.

2. Consider the word processor you use for typing papers. Originally word processors modeled the process of typing on a typewriter, but they have added many features that were not available on a typewriter. Suppose the purpose of the word processor now is not to model a typewriter, but to model an ideal word processor. Explain how that ideal word processor works, describe the features of the program you actually use, and compare them based on the seven criteria for software models.

3. Consider the email program you use. How well does it model the process of sending and receiving letters? Describe its features and evaluate it with respect to the seven criteria for models.

4. Consider the web search engine you use. It models the work of a reference librarian, who listens to what you want to know and finds information for you. Describe the search engine you use and evaluate it using our seven criteria for software models.

5. Suppose we're building a software model of each of the following objects. List three properties and three capabilities that we might include for each.

   a. a cell phone
   b. Barney the Dinosaur
   c. a glass of wine
   d. a political campaign
   e. a parachute
   f. a newspaper
   g. a three-legged dog

6. Suppose we're building a software model of a deck of cards to be used as part of several different online card games. You need at least two classes: a deck class and a card class. List three properties and three capabilities for each class.

7. Suppose we're building a software model of a chess game to be the basis for an online version of the game. It should have different levels of play, depending on the skill level of the player. List six classes that you might need for an online chess game, along with three relevant properties and three

relevant capabilities for each. Explain your choices. (For reference, the rules of chess can be found at many different sites, including http://www.conservativebookstore.com/chess/.)

8. Suppose we're building a software model of a soccer game. This model is part of a tutoring system, to be used in teaching beginners to play soccer. List four classes we might need, along with three relevant properties and three relevant capabilities for each.

9. Explain how you might use a divide-and-conquer strategy to plan a party.

10. Most people use their VCR without opening it up and looking inside. This illustrates one of the techniques for managing complexity discussed in this chapter. What is the name of that technique? Explain, and give another illustration of the same technique.

11. Describe a parts hierarchy for this book. List the objects involved in the hierarchy with a brief description of each, and explain their relationships.

12. Describe an inheritance hierarchy in which the top-level category is "student." List the objects involved in the hierarchy with a brief (one-sentence) description of each, and explain their relationship.

13. Describe an inheritance hierarchy where the top-level category is "vehicle." List the objects involved in the hierarchy with a brief description of each, and explain their relationship.

14. Suppose you are creating a software model of your classroom.

    a. Suppose the purpose of your model is to create an animated movie of a class. List at least five objects that are relevant to that purpose.

    b. Suppose the purpose of your model is to generate seating charts for classes in a given classroom. What objects are relevant to this problem? How would you change the list you gave in part (a)?

    c. Suppose the purpose of your model is to support classroom maintenance, by providing your school's maintenance department with the ability to determine from a central location whether all the equipment in the room is working correctly. What objects are relevant to this problem? How is your list different from the list you gave in (a) or (b)?

15. Suppose you are trying to model the game of Monopoly®.

    a. Briefly describe the game (if you are not familiar with it, you may ask one of your fellow students or find a description on the Web).

    b. Identify at least five objects that are important in the game. List the objects and some properties and capabilities for each.

    c. Now compare your answer to this question with a fellow student's. Imagine you're working together as a team to write this program.

c1. Identify any duplication in your lists.

c2. Identify any conflicts between your lists.

c3. Combine your two lists into a single list, eliminating any duplication and resolving any conflicts you have found.

16. Which of the following are legal Java class names? Explain each of your answers.

a. R2D2

b. Chameleon

c. public

d. 23skidoo

e. _hello

17. Which of the following are both legal and satisfy the conventions for Java class names? Explain each of your answers.

a. R2D2

b. Chameleon

c. public

d. 23skidoo

e. _hello

18. Write class definitions with empty bodies for each of the following classes:

a. Skyscraper

b. Greyhound

c. Elephant

d. Sportscar

e. Ski

19. Add constructors with empty bodies to each of the classes you defined for Question 18.

20. Modify your answer to question 18(c) so that the Elephant class has one instance variable of type Tail and four instance variables of type Leg.

21. Modify your answer to question 18(d) so that the Sportscar has instance variables of type Color and EngineType.

22. Consider the following problem description.

We want to model a game of tic-tac-toe. Tic-tac-toe has two players and a gameboard made up of three rows of three squares each. The players take turns to choose an empty square and mark it. The first player marks a square with an X and the second player uses an O. As soon as all the squares in any row, column, or diagonal are marked with the same symbol, the player corresponding to that symbol wins the game. If all squares have been filled without either player winning the game, the result is a draw.

Using grammatical analysis, identify the objects, attributes, components, peer objects, and capabilities in the problem description.

Debugging Programs

Identify the error(s) in each of the following incomplete code fragments:

1. ```java
public class Animal;
```

2. ```java
public class Animal {
    private Animal() {
    }
}
```

3. ```java
public class Animal {
    public Tail _tail;
    public Animal() {
        _tail = new Tail();
    }
}
```

4. ```java
public class Animal {
    private Tail _tail;
    public Animal() {
        _tail = new Tail();
    }
    void wagTail() {
        _tail.wag();
    }
}
```

5. ```java
public class Octopus {
    private Leg _one _two _three _four _five _six _seven;
    private Leg _eight;
    public Octopus {
    ... // code for constructor
    }
}
```
```

■ **Programming Projects** ■

Modifying Programs

For each of the following questions:
   a. Identify on paper the lines of code in the original program that need to be changed (you may find it helpful to print out the code and make notes on the printout).
   b. Explain the changes that are necessary.
   c. Edit, compile, and run the revised program.

   1. Modify the `FirstApp` program so that it displays a red rectangle on a white background, instead of a circle.

   2. Modify the `FirstApp` program so that it displays a rounded red rectangle on a white background, instead of a circle.

   3. Modify the `FirstApp` program so that it displays a red line on a white background, instead of a circle.

   4. Modify the `FirstApp` program so that it creates both an `Ellipse` and a `Rectangle`. What happens? Why do you think it happens?

   5. Shapes in Wheels know how to display themselves on the screen in response to a `show` message; they also know how to hide themselves in response to a `hide` message. Modify your code from Exercise 4 to add the following line at the end of the constructor: `_rectangle.hide();` Now what happens when you run the program? Why?

■ **New Style Conventions** ■

(These are general Java conventions unless otherwise noted.)

Names

   ■ Class names start with a capital letter.
   ■ If a class name is made up of two words, each word should start with a capital letter.
   ■ Instance-variable names start with an underscore, followed by a lower-case letter. (This is a convention specific to this book.)
   ■ Method names start with a lower-case letter.

Indentation and Spacing

- The opening bracket of the class body is placed on the same line as the class name, and the closing bracket is on a line by itself, aligned with the `p` in the keyword `public`.
- Instance variable declarations are indented inside the class body.
- The constructor definition is also indented inside the class body.
- The statements inside the constructor body are indented further.

Ordering

- Inside a class definition, declare all the instance variables first (if any), then the constructor, then any other method definitions. (Specific to this book.)

2

Methods with Parameters

OBJECTIVES

After reading this chapter, you should be able to:

☑ Explain how parameters make methods more general

☑ Compare and contrast parameters, local variables, and instance variables

☑ Identify the scope and lifetime of parameters, local variables, and instance variables

☑ Write and invoke methods with parameters

☑ Write methods that return a value

☑ Use the Wheels library to write programs that display simple cartoons

■ 2.1 ■ Introduction

Consider the `Ellipse` class in Chapter 1. The `Ellipse` knew how to draw itself, but only in the center of the window. The other Wheels shapes—the `Rectangle`, `RoundedRectangle`, and `Line`—all drew themselves at the same location: right in the middle of the window. They were all bright red, and there was no way to change their size.

If we're going to use these shapes to create a picture, we need to be able to tell them to change their locations. Suppose the window is 400 wide by 600 tall and we want the `Ellipse` to be able to draw itself at a particular *x* and *y* location in the window. We could model this capability with a set of methods: `setXLocation0`, `setYLocation0`, `setXLocation1`, `setYLocation1`, and so forth. But we'd have to write a thousand methods, one for each possible *x* location and one for each possible *y* location on the screen. Worse, we would be writing almost the same code for each method, over and over.

In order to control this unacceptable complexity, we use the powerful tool of abstraction. Instead of many different `setLocation` methods, we write a single general one. But to do that, somehow we need to tell the `Ellipse` what its new location should be: we need to model the fact that the *x* and *y* locations are details associated with that message.

To model the details associated with a message, we use parameters. A **parameter** is a piece of information that is sent along with a message. The `setLocation` method could have *x* and *y* parameters. Concerts can be held at different times, at different places, or with different performers, so the `schedule` method in a `Concert` class might have a `time` parameter, a `venue` parameter, and an `act` parameter. The `prepare` method in a `Pizza` class might have a `topping` parameter. Parameters model the fine details that are different about otherwise similar messages—they allow the method to be more general than it would be if it were restricted to specific values.

In addition to customizing messages with parameters, in this chapter we also show how to model getting an answer back from a message. Before you buy concert tickets, you probably want to know what the act is, and where and when the concert is being held. Before you order pizza, you may want to ask what kind of toppings it has—if the pizza returns anchovies, you know not to eat it. If we only talked to other people and never listened to the answers, cooperation would be impossible. Similarly, it would be hard to design a system of objects that could cooperate to solve a problem without some way for them to get answers to their messages.

■ 2.2 ■ Concepts

2.2.1 Parameters

Imagine living in the world of the future. You have just bought a new household robot. You want to give it a plan for making breakfast. You could say

> Make orange juice, coffee, and an omelet with toast for breakfast. (or cold pizza, or whatever your favorite breakfast happens to be).

We already know the syntax for this kind of message in Java; it could look like this:

```
_robot.makeOrangeJuiceCoffeeOmeletToast();
```

But you don't want the same meal every day. Weekends you might like orange soda, black coffee, and cold pizza. If you have company you might want cappuccino and croissants. So you give it a more general plan, like this:

> Make _____, _____, and _____ for breakfast.

This is certainly general. But if you don't fill in the blanks the next morning, the robot might give you toothpaste, soap, and a pile of clean socks for breakfast. Your robot needs a little more guidance.

You decide on a general plan for breakfast:

Make _____, _____, and _____ for breakfast.
    fruit juice   Caffeinated Beverage   breakfast entrée

In other words, this plan says, "Make me some kind of fruit juice, some kind of caffeinated beverage, and some breakfast entrée." You have specified the type of item to fill in each blank. This way, the robot is much more likely to make a breakfast you will like.

You also want to tell it that in general, Tuesday's breakfast should be different from Monday's. You try this:

Make _____ on Monday and make _____ on Tuesday.
        breakfast entrée   breakfast entrée

_____ must be different from _____.
breakfast entrée   breakfast entrée

but that doesn't quite work. Your robot decides that you mean:

Make <u>oatmeal</u> on Monday and make <u>oatmeal</u> on Tuesday. <u>Scrambled eggs</u> must be different from <u>waffles</u>.

Oatmeal is fine, but not two days in a row. So you think about it for a few days, and the next week you try again. You can't put in the actual values, because you want a general plan. Instead, you fill in some working names for each item, in addition to their types:

Make <u><Monday's entrée></u> on Monday and make <u><Tuesday's entrée></u> on Tuesday.
        breakfast entrée   breakfast entrée

<u><Monday's entrée></u> must be different from <u><Tuesday's entrée></u>.
<u>breakfast entrée</u>   <u>breakfast entrée</u>

Finally, success. Now in addition to filling in the blanks with values that match the type, the robot has to fill in the same value wherever it sees the same working name. Whatever it chooses to give you on Monday must be a breakfast entrée and must be different from the breakfast entrée it gives you on Tuesday. On Monday, you wake up to the smell of home-cooked waffles, and on Tuesday there are pancakes with maple syrup. Life is good.

When we write a method with parameters, Java requires the same information as your successful breakfast plan: the types of the parameters you want and a working name for each. The working names are called **formal parameters**. The details that are filled in, like "waffles" or "pancakes with maple syrup," are called **actual parameters** (because these are the values you fill in when you actually use the method).

keyconcept
Formal parameters are the working names for details that will be filled in later. Actual parameters are the values you fill in when you actually use the method.

For another example, think about geometry. What good would a line segment be if it always went from the origin to the Cartesian point (100, 100)? What if all circles had a radius of twenty-five? Or what if only equilateral triangles existed? When we define a line segment that can vary its end points, for example, L = (x1, y1, x2, y2), we are creating a very general kind of line segment: one that can represent an infinite number of particular lines.

In the case of our general line L, the end points, x1, y1, x2, y2, are formal parameters because they represent any pair of Cartesian (x, y) coordinates. If we were to construct a specific line segment, say L1 = (0, 0, 100, 100), then these particular coordinates are the actual parameters that determine the length and orientation of the line segment.

The identifiers used for the formal parameters (the placeholders x1, y1, etc.) are arbitrary. We could have named them anything: for example, L = (startX, startY, endX, endY). The formal parameter names should make some sense—for example, L = (george, john, ringo, paul) might be confusing to anyone reading your code—but what really matters is the actual parameters.

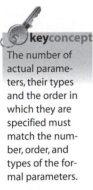

keyconcept

The number of actual parameters, their types and the order in which they are specified must match the number, order, and types of the formal parameters.

Note that we need such a distinction between actual and formal parameters because when the method is defined, it can't be known what the parameters being passed in will be, either in name or in value; only their types are specified. The function definition with formal parameters is similar to a function definition in mathematics, such as $f(x) = x^3 + 3x + 5$. Here x is the formal parameter and could just as well be called p, t, or alice. If we then write $f(2)$, 2 is the actual parameter that we plug in to compute the value of the function.

Because the types of the formal parameters are specified in the method definition, the compiler can (and does) check the requirement that the types of the actual parameters match the types of the formal parameters. Sending a message with an actual parameter of the wrong type or too few or too many actual parameters is an error: *there must be a one-to-one correspondence between actual and formal parameters*. The number of actual parameters, their types, and the order in which they are specified must match the number, types, and order of the formal parameters.

keyconcept

The return value is something an object gives back to whatever object invoked one of its methods. The type of the return value is the method's return type.

2.2.2 Return values

When asked to do something, an object may give something back to whatever asked it to perform the action: the results of the action, the answer to an inquiry, or perhaps only an acknowledgment. (See Figure 2.1). The value that is sent back is called the **return value** of a method, and the type of the return value (the class to which it belongs) is the method's **return type**. In the field of programming languages, a method that returns a value is also known as a **function**; a method that does not return a value is also known as a **procedure**.

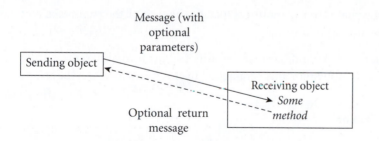

Figure 2.1 ■ Objects exchanging information through parameters and return values.

■ 2.3 ■ **Mechanics**

2.3.1 **Parameters**

The Java syntax for defining a method with a parameter is very simple. We can give our `Robot` a move method like this:

```
public class Robot {
    ...
    public void move (Room aRoom) {
        ...
    }
}
```

The syntax for this method definition is the same as the definitions we saw in Chapter 1, except that now we see the real use of the parentheses. They're not just flags to tell the compiler that this is a method; they also contain the type of the formal parameter followed by its name. Here, the formal parameter must be of type `Room`, and we give it the working name `aRoom`. A method definition may have zero, one, or more parameters; if there are two or more, they are separated by commas, much like a list in real life.

Here's how we use this method to send a message to the `Robot` telling it to go to the kitchen:

```
_robot.move(myKitchen);
```

Let's go through the parts of this syntax in order. The message begins the same way as any other message: we specify the receiver of the message (`_robot`), followed by a period and the name of the message we're sending. After the method name, instead of the type and formal parameter, we now see an actual parameter. In this case, the actual parameter is a variable name, `myKitchen`. It could be the name of any instance of the class `Room`. Both formal and actual parameters are listed between parentheses; the easiest way to tell the difference is that formal parameters include the type of the parameter, and actual parameters do not.

During the execution of a method, Java temporarily assigns formal parameters the same values as their corresponding actual parameters. In effect, Java inserts at the beginning of the method

```
aRoom = myKitchen;
```

In other words, for now `aRoom` and `myKitchen` are different names for the same instance, which exists somewhere else in the computer's memory (see Listing 2.1).

Suppose that while the robot is moving, it automatically picks up the clutter in whatever room it is in. When the method is done executing, `myKitchen` will be clutter-free. Later on, we can call the same method with another parameter, for example,

```
_robot.move(myLivingRoom);
```

Now `aRoom` refers to `myLivingRoom` instead of `myKitchen`. The robot will go to `myLivingRoom` and straighten it up, instead of `myKitchen`.

When we call a method, the actual parameters must have the same type as the formal parameters. Since the `move` method has a formal parameter of type `Room`, the actual parameter also has to be of type `Room`. (We discuss some exceptions to this rule in Chapter 5, but for now, assume that it is always true.) Thus, this is an indoor `Robot`; unless it has some other method we don't know about yet, we can send it to any room we like, but we can't say

```
_robot.move(CENTRAL_PARK);
```

There can be zero or more actual parameters, and if there are two or more, they are separated by commas, like the formal parameters. Indeed, when we invoke a method, we must give it exactly the same number and type of actual parameters as it has formal parameters.

You may have noticed a naming convention we often use: the formal parameter is the parameter's type prefixed with "a" (or "an") to indicate a generic instance of that type, while the actual parameter prefixes the type with "the" (or "my") to indicate the specific instance.

To summarize what we have seen so far, the Java syntax for a method definition for a method that receives parameters is

```
<modifier> void <name> (<type1> <name1>, ...) {
    ...
}
```

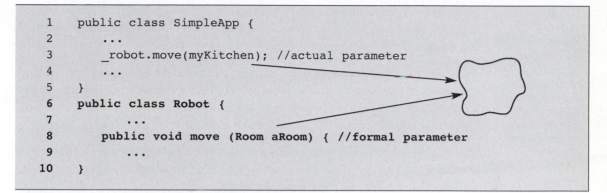

```
 1    public class SimpleApp {
 2        ...
 3        _robot.move(myKitchen); //actual parameter
 4        ...
 5    }
 6    public class Robot {
 7        ...
 8        public void move (Room aRoom) { //formal parameter
 9            ...
10    }
```

Listing 2.1 ■ Actual and formal parameters: aliases for the same thing

The syntax for sending a message with actual parameters is:

```
<receiver-name>.<method-name>(<actual1>, <actual2>, ...)
```

2.3.2 **Constructors with parameters**

Let's try another example. Suppose our `Robot` knows its battery life. With this knowledge, it can automatically recharge its batteries before they run down. We can model this knowledge by giving the `Robot` an instance variable:

```
public class Robot {
    private int _batteryMinutes;
    ...
}
```

To give the `Robot` the ability to change its battery life, we could say:

```
public class Robot {
    private int _batteryMinutes;
    ...
    public void setBatteryMinutes (int minutes) {
        _batteryMinutes = minutes;
    }
}
```

The syntax of this method fits the general pattern for methods with parameters, shown above. The result of the method is that the value of the actual parameter is saved in the instance variable. If we send the message:

```
_robot.setBatteryMinutes(120);
```

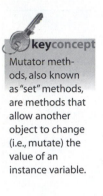

the `Robot` will know that its battery will run down in two hours. This is a very common type of method, so common that it has a name: a mutator. A **mutator** is a method that changes the value of one of the class's instance variables.

Note the type of the instance variable `_batteryMinutes`. We want this to be some kind of number. In Java, numbers are modeled by a kind of "primitive type." **Primitive types** are types that are not objects, but are predefined parts of Java. Their names are keywords. They include, among other things, `int`, which is one of Java's models of an integer.

Now suppose robots' initial battery life is always set in the factory, when the battery is first installed. As we've seen, we can model that by initializing the `Robot`'s `_batteryMinutes` variable inside the `Robot`'s constructor, like this:

```
public class Robot {
    private int _batteryMinutes;
    public Robot () {
       _batteryMinutes = 600;
    }
    ...
}
```

But what if some of our robots have batteries that last longer than others? The robot industry would thrive if it could charge more for robots with longer battery life. The robot manufacturers are definitely going to build their robots with this value flexible.

So just as with other methods, we'd like a more general constructor, and the solution is just the same: use parameters. Then we could say:

```
_robot = new Robot(1440);
```

for a `Robot` that needs to be recharged once a day, or

```
_robot = new Robot(120);
```

for the cheaper version that needs to be recharged every two hours (just enough time to cook breakfast, serve it, clear the table, and do the dishes afterward). As we've seen before, a message to a constructor starts with the Java keyword `new`, followed by the name of the class the constructor belongs to. The rules for calling constructors with parameters are the same as those for other constructors.

How about defining a constructor with parameters? You can probably already guess, since it's just like a constructor definition plus a parameter list. Here's how the `Robot`'s constructor would look with a parameter:

```
public class Robot {
    private int _batteryMinutes;
```

```
    public Robot (int minutes) {
        _batteryMinutes = minutes;
    }
    ...
}
```

When a constructor has parameters, they are typically used to initialize the object's instance variables.

To summarize, in Java, the general form for invoking a constructor with parameters is:

new <class-name> (<actual1>,<actual2>, ...))

And the general form for *defining* a constructor with parameters is:

```
<modifier> <class-name> (<type1> <name1>,
                         <type2> <name2>...) {
    ...
}
```

2.3.3 Debugging tips for method calls

The most important thing to remember about method calls in Java is that the number, order, and types of the actual parameters must match the number, order, and types of the formal parameters; there must be an exact correspondence.

The compiler can find many errors of this sort for you. Suppose we have the method call

```
_robot.makeBreakfast(myJuice, myCoffee, myOmelet);
```

where `myJuice` is a variable of type `FruitJuice`, `myCoffee` is a variable of type `CaffeinatedBeverage`, and `myOmelet` is a variable of type `BreakfastEntree`. For this code to work, the `makeBreakfast` method must expect a `FruitJuice` first, a `CaffeinatedBeverage` second, and a `BreakfastEntree` third. The method call

```
_robot.makeBreakfast();
```

is wrong, because it has too few parameters. You'll go hungry if you try it. The method call

```
_robot.makeBreakfast(myJuice, myOmelet, myCoffee);
```

is wrong, because the parameters are in the wrong order. Java won't let you get your omelet in a mug and your coffee on a plate—you'll just get an error message for breakfast. In other words, the object receiving the message needs exactly the right information in the right order.

What happens when you write a method call with too few, or too many, parameters? The compiler assumes that what you wrote is what you meant and looks for a method with that number of parameters. Similarly, if you write a method call with the wrong type of parameters, the compiler looks for a method with that type of parameters. If it can't find a method definition that matches the method call, the compiler gives you a message like "Cannot resolve symbol." The exact text of the message depends on your compiler, but if the compiler says it can't find something, consider the possibility that your parameter list is wrong.

There are some parameter errors that the compiler can't help you with. For example, suppose you ask the `Robot` to bake you a cake and the method call is:

```
_robot.bakeCake(myChocolate, myVanilla);
```

If you accidentally put the parameters in the wrong order, you might end up with a vanilla cake with chocolate frosting when you wanted a chocolate cake with vanilla frosting (or vice versa). Either way, the compiler would have no way to tell, if both are `Flavor` parameters. Which one you want is a question of the meaning—in computer terms, the semantics—of the statement and of any statements in the body of the method that refer to these parameters. The compiler can't tell whether you said what you meant. It can only tell whether you obeyed the rules of the Java language.

2.3.4 **Parameters, local variables, and instance variables**

keyconcept

Local variables are declared inside a method. They model objects that are needed temporarily by that method to do a job.

There are three kinds of variable a method can use in Java: instance variables, parameters, and local variables. All three variable types are declared inside a class and all three are names for values stored somewhere in memory. The differences lie in how long they exist and which statements can access them. We have seen instance variables, which are declared outside of any method definition. They are easily recognized in the code in this book, because their names start with an underscore (_): `_robot`, `_redCircle`, `_moose`, and so forth. We have also seen formal parameters, whose names start with a lower-case letter, often (in this book) the letter "a" (as in `aKitchen`, `aSpoon`).

Local variables are declared inside a method. They model objects that are needed temporarily by that method to do a job. For example, suppose our `Robot` is baking a cake. It might have a local variable to model the spoon, or the mixing bowl, or the batter. Local variable names also start with a lower-case letter (as in `spoon`). Imagine sitting down to watch TV without a remote control—if you were an object in Java you could just create a local variable, `remoteControl`, use it while you watch TV; when you're done watching, the remote just disappears instead of cluttering your living room.

The name of an instance is separate from its identity. Each instance of an object has its own identity, but it may have any number of distinct names that others use to refer to it. Similarly, in real life, people can go by different names in different situations. After all, your friends call you by one name, while your mother might very well use another (perhaps one you would rather your friends didn't know).

Conversely, during its lifetime, a single variable name can refer to several different instances. Similarly, in real life, the same name may refer to several different people. If you and your friend both talk about "Chris," for example, you may without knowing it be talking about two entirely different people.

Unlike people, the compiler must always know exactly which instance a particular name refers to at any given moment. Consider the following four examples from the code in Listing 2.2.

1. Suppose one method wants to use a variable that's declared inside another method. For example, suppose the `Robot` wanted to use the `spoon` from the `bakeCake` method when it was weeding the garden.

2. The `Robot`'s `setLocation` and `put` methods both have `x` and `y` parameters.

3. Two different methods in the `Robot` class refer to the variable `_gripper`, which is not defined inside either method.

4. The `Robot` and `Spoon` classes both have private instance variables called `_x` and `_y`.

The **scope** of a variable is the part of the program where it can be used. The scope of any variable starts where it is declared: you can never use a variable before you declare it. The scope of a local variable ends at the end of the block that contains it (i.e., at the next closing curly bracket). Thus, the scope of the variable `spoon` in Listing 2.2 starts where it is declared and ends at the end of the `bakeCake` method; it can't be used by the `weedGarden` method, because it is defined only inside `bakeCake`.

The scope of `_gripper` in Listing 2.2, like all instance variables, ends at the curly bracket that ends the class in which it is declared. Thus, it is defined throughout both the `bakeCake` and `weedGarden` methods (and all of the class's other methods) and can be used anywhere it's defined. The `Robot`'s `private _x` and `_y` instance variables can also be used anywhere from the point where they are declared to the end of the `Robot` class. They *cannot* be used outside the class in which they are declared, however, so the `Spoon` can have instance variables called `_x` and `_y` without causing any problems for the compiler.

The scope of a formal parameter name starts where it is declared in the parameter list in a method declaration and goes to the end of the method definition. Thus, the scope of the variable name `x` in the parameter list of the `Robot`'s `setLocation` method starts where it is declared and ends with the curly bracket that ends that method. We can

```
1    public class Robot {
2        private int _x, _y;
3        private Gripper _gripper;
4        ...
5        public void bakeCake(Flavor myFrosting, Flavor myCake){
6            Spoon spoon = new Spoon();
7            _gripper.grab(spoon);
8            ...
9        }
10
11       public void put (Object object, int x, int y) { ... }
12
13       public void setLocation (int x, int y) { ... }
14
15       public void weedGarden () {
16           Weed weed = new Weed();
17           _gripper.grab(weed);
18           _gripper.pull();
19           ...
20       }
21   }
22
23       public class Spoon {
24           private int _x, _y;
25               ...
26           public void stir(){ ... }
27   }
```

Listing 2.2 ■ Examples of variables and their scope (indicated by the lines on the left)

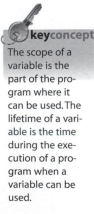

reuse the parameter name **x** without ambiguity, because each parameter is limited to the method in which it is declared.

Which type of variable we choose is related to its scope. Local variables are the right choice when a variable will only be used inside a single block of code such as a method. Parameters are the right choice when a method needs to get information from outside in order to do its job. And instance variables are the right choice when a variable will be used by at least two methods within a class.

Another way to look at the distinction between a local variable and an instance variable is to consider the variable's lifetime. The **lifetime** of a variable is the period of time during the execution of a program when you can use that variable. The lifetime of an instance variable is the same as the lifetime of the instance that contains it. As long as _robot exists, it will have some _gripper that it knows about (although the identity of the gripper may change from time to time).

The lifetime of a local variable or a parameter is only the length of time during which the method that contains them is executing in response to a particular message. As noted above, creating a local variable is like creating a remote control each time you watch TV and having it disappear conveniently when you're done.

How do we know when to use which kind of variable? The answer depends on whether and how the object is used outside of the current method. If we want to model information that a method needs but can get only from outside, we need a parameter. If we want to model something that a method uses only temporarily to accomplish a task, we need a local variable. And if we want to model something that is used by more than one method in a class, we need an instance variable. Table 2.1 compares parameters, local variables, and instance variables in Java.

2.3.5 Return types

Recall that we wrote a method to change a Robot's battery life. Suppose instead that we just want to ask it what its battery life is. We could write a method like the code in boldface type:

```
public class Robot {
    private int _batteryMinutes;
        ...
    public int getBatteryMinutes () {
```

Table 2.1 ■ Scope and lifetime of different types of variables.

	Scope ends	Lifetime	When used	Names
Instance variables	At end of class in which declared	While instance of class exists	To model something used to accomplish more than one task	Start with an underscore (_)
Local variables	At end of block in which declared (i.e., next close curly bracket)	During response to particular message	To model something used temporarily to accomplish a particular task	Start with a lower-case letter
Parameters	At end of method in which declared	During response to particular message	To model information, obtained from outside a method, that is used to accomplish a particular task	Formal parameter names start with a lower-case letter, often "a"

```
                            return _batteryMinutes;
                    }
            }
```

This method is called an **accessor**, because it gives access to one of the class's instance variables.

The method starts, like all the methods we've seen, with `public`. But then there's something new. The second word in a method definition is usually its return type. Until now, the word in this position has been the Java keyword `void`, because all the methods we have seen returned nothing at all. This method, instead, returns an `int`.

Inside the method, we see the Java keyword `return`. `Return` indicates the beginning of a `return` statement. **Return statements** say what the method will use as its return value, and they are required in any method that returns a value, except for constructors. (Constructors always return a new instance of their class.)

A return statement always begins with `return` and continues with a value of a primitive type, an identifier that refers to a value of a primitive type or an object, or the result of another message. Here it is the name `_batteryMinutes`.

A `return` statement always ends with a semicolon. The `return` statement is the last statement executed in a method. For now, that just means it must be the last statement in a method. Note that the type of `_batteryMinutes` matches the return type of `getBatteryMinutes`. These types are required to match or the code will not compile.

This method illustrates the simplest type of return value computation: all it does is look up the value of one of the object's properties. Methods are limited to returning a single value, but a method can perform an arbitrary amount of computation, including calls to other methods, in order to compute the value to be returned. For example, suppose someone asked you your age: you'd just remember the fact and spit it out. If someone asks you how many hairs you have on your head, though, you might have to do some work before you give them an answer. You may sometimes want to return more than one value. If so, you can either write a method for each of them and make two method calls, or you can return a composite data structure. We discuss various data structures in Chapters 13–15 of this book.

2.3.6 **Method signatures and overloading**

The combination of a method's name, the types of its parameters, and the order of its parameters is its **signature**. For example, the signature of the `Robot`'s `makeBreakfast` method is

```
makeBreakfast(FruitJuice, CaffeinatedBeverage,
    BreakfastEntree)
```

The signature is not a Java statement. It is not a method definition or a method call. It is just a way of identifying a method. Like a person's signature, a method's signature must be unique, and defining two methods in the same class with the same signature is an error (even if they have different return types).

It is possible in Java to define two methods with the same name but different signatures in the same class. Specifically, two methods can have the same name but different parameter lists. Defining two methods with the same name but different signatures is called **method overloading**.

keyconcept

Defining two different methods with the same name and different signatures is called method overloading.

There's no new syntax for overloaded methods; we define them in the same way as any other method. For example, suppose we want two kinds of breakfast, one for ordinary days and one for holidays. We could have a method with the signature

```
makeBreakfast(CaffeinatedBeverage)
```

for the days when we're in a hurry, and another with the signature

```
makeBreakfast(FruitJuice, CaffeinatedBeverage,
        BreakfastEntree)
```

for the days when we want to relax.

Method overloading can be very useful. For example, one of the constructors for the Wheels `Ellipse` class takes no parameters and automatically places a red `Ellipse` in the center of the `Frame`; another allows us to specify the initial location of the `Ellipse`, and a third allows us to specify the initial color.

■ 2.4 ■ Working Out with **Objects**—the talking sun

Objectives:
- ☑ Write a program with parameters
- ☑ Learn more about Wheels
- ☑ Have fun

In the last chapter, we built a simple program using the `Ellipse` object from the Wheels library. The `Ellipse` could only draw itself as a red circle, and it could only draw itself in the center of the window. If you tried adding more than one shape, you probably noticed that they all ended up on top of each other.

Now we can take advantage of the magic of parameters to make the circle move, change its color, size, and dimensions, and add more shapes to the `frame`. In this section, we give you a warmup program, so you can get comfortable with parameters; in the next (optional) section, we show you how to design more elaborate cartoons.

Our step-by-step development of these programs also illustrates an important technique, **incremental development**. If you write your programs this way, a little bit at a time, testing them after each step, any bugs that creep in are much easier to identify and fix.

2.4.1 Background: more about Wheels

In Chapter 1, we introduced the Wheels classes that you will use. You saw how to use their default constructors, the ones with no parameters. Each of these objects has additional methods with parameters, including constructors, that we can now begin to use. These methods are summarized in Table 2.2.

As you can see, each of the shapes has its own constructors, allowing us to specify such things as the shape's initial color, location, or degree of rotation. The additional methods are all accessors and mutators (recall that by convention, these start with `get` and `set`). All shapes have accessors and mutators that let us change their color, location, or rotation. `Ellipses` (ovals and circles), `Rectangles` (including squares), `RoundedRectangles`, and `ConversationBubbles` also have methods that let us change the thickness of their outline, or change the color of the shape's outline and the color of the inside of the shape. In these method names, "fill" refers to the inside of the shape and "frame" refers to its outline.

The `ConversationBubble` has two additional `set` methods, `setText` and `setTailDirection`, that let us change what the conversation bubble says, or which part of the cartoon its tail is pointing to. The `Line` has a `set` method that let us change its thickness (if only humans had such a method!). All the shapes have methods for changing their color, their location, their size, and for making them disappear from the window (`hide()`). In addition, `Rectangles`, `RoundedRectangles`, `Ellipses`, and `ConversationBubbles` have methods that allow us to give the outline and the middle of the shape different colors, and to change the thickness of the outline. We're halfway to creating a Picasso!

2.4.2 Analysis

Here's the problem description for our first program with parameters:

> Write a program that displays the sun on a white background, with a conversation bubble that says, "Here comes the sun!"

Table 2.2 ■ Some useful methods from Wheels.

Type of shape	Methods

`Lines`, `Ellipses`, `Rectangles`, `RoundedRectangles`, `ConversationBubbles`	`java.awt.Color getColor ()`
	`int getRotation ()`
	`void setRotation (int degrees)`
	`void setColor (java.awt.Color aColor)`
	`    //makes whole shape one solid color`
	`void hide ()`

All of the above, except for `Lines`	`java.awt.Color getFrameColor ()`
	`java.awt.Color getFillColor ()`
	`int getFrameThickness ()`
	`int getXLocation ()`
	`int getYLocation ()`
	`int getWidth ()`
	`int getHeight ()`
	`void setFrameColor(java.awt.Color aColor)`
	`    // sets color of shape's outline`
	`void setFillColor (java.awt.Color aColor)`
	`    //sets color of inside of a shape`
	`void setFrameThickness (int thickness)`
	`void setLocation (int x, int y)`
	`void setSize (int width, int height)`

`ConversationBubble`	`ConversationBubble (String text)`
	`//draws bubble with "text" inside`
	`ConversationBubble(String text,int tailDir)`
	`// same bubble, but allows us to change the`
	`    // direction of its "tail": 0 for left and`
	`    // 1 for right.`
	`void setText (String text)`
	`void setTailDirection (int direction)`

`Ellipse`	`Ellipse ()`
	`Ellipse (java.awt.Color aColor)`
	`Ellipse (int x, int y)`
	`Ellipse (int degrees)`

`Line`	`Line()`
	`Line(int x1, int y1, int x2, int y2)`
	`void setThickness(int thickness)`
	`void setPoints(int x1,int y1,int x2,int y2)`

`Rectangle`	`Rectangle ()`
	`Rectangle (java.awt.Color aColor)`
	`Rectangle (int x, int y)`
	`Rectangle (int degrees)//sets shape's rotation`

`RoundedRectangle`	`RoundedRectangle ()`
	`RoundedRectangle (java.awt.Color aColor)`
	`RoundedRectangle (int x, int y)`
	`RoundedRectangle (int degrees)`

Let's start with a grammatical analysis of the problem description. The nouns in this description are "program," "sun," "background," and "conversation bubble," so these are candidates for objects in our system. The only adjective is "white." There's no mention of "has" or "part of" or "composed of," so there are no explicit component relationships. Finally, the only verbs are "display" and "say."

The information provided by this grammatical analysis is pretty limited, and after all, we're talking about a visual image, so as a next step, let's sketch a picture of what the output might look like (see Figure 2.2).

2.4.3 Design

We know from the previous chapter that Wheels has an object called `Frame` that we can use to model a displayable rectangular area. It also has an `Ellipse` that we can use to model the sun.

Without parameters, the `Ellipse` won't quite work, however. In the last chapter, when we instantiated an `Ellipse` like this:

```
new Ellipse();
```

it was always solid red and always located in the center of the screen. According to our picture, we want a circle that's yellow and located off to the side.

Fortunately, Wheels has overloaded the constructors for these classes. As you can see from Table 2.2, there's another constructor in which the sender object uses a parameter to specify the color of the ellipse, and a third that lets us use parameters to specify the `Ellipse`'s location. We can choose either one of these; if we specify the color in the

Figure 2.2 ■ Sketch of desired output of `SunCartoon`.

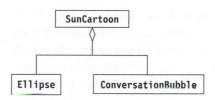

Figure 2.3 ■ A UML class diagram for our first program with parameters.

constructor, we can set the location later using `setLocation`, and if we specify the location, we can set the color later using `setColor`.

Finally, Wheels provides a `ConversationBubble` class that takes the bubble's text as a parameter. The `ConversationBubble` resizes itself to fit whatever text you put into it. There's no method that gives both the text and the location of the bubble to the constructor, but there's a `setLocation` method that lets us position the conversation bubble where we want it after it's created.

In summary, we will define a kind of `Frame` called a `SunCartoon`. This is the top-level class, and it will contain the method called `main`. The `SunCartoon` also has two components, an `Ellipse` to model the sun and a `ConversationBubble` to model what the sun says. A UML diagram for this design is given in Figure 2.3.

2.4.4 **Implementation: version 1**

Let's start with the basic framework for our program, shown in Listing 2.3. Read it first, and we'll explain the new terms afterward.

2.4.5 **Imports, packages, and libraries**

We start by importing the Users package in the Wheels library. **Package** is a Java keyword for a group of related classes. In Java, a **library**, like Wheels is a larger package, often containing subpackages, provided for use in programs. Wheels has two subpackages, Users and Etc. The `Frame` and the shape objects are all in the Users subpackage, so that is the only one we need to import. The `*` in the program above is a wild card; think of it as a fill-in-the-blank. It indicates that we want to import any class whose name starts with "wheels.users" from the Users package. If we wanted to, we could specify one particular class to import, like `wheels.users.Line`, but this way, we get them all.

What does it mean to import something? In Java, an import statement, which starts with the keyword `import` (tricky, right?), lets us use short names in our code. The full name of an object includes the packages that it's in. For example, the full name of our `Ellipse` object is `wheels.users.Ellipse`. The full name of the `Frame` is `wheels.users.Frame`.

keyconcept
Package is a Java keyword for a group of related classes. A library is a larger package, often containing subpackages, provided for use in programs.

keyconcept
An import statement lets us use short names for objects, instead of their full name.

The rightmost part of a name is the name of an object. Before that is the name of the package, and so forth. It's similar to the way we name ourselves; our last names show the group we come from and our first names specify us as individuals, but we need them both together to describe who we are. Except for Madonna and Prince—but there are no exceptions like these in Java. To separate the names of the packages, subpackages, and objects, Java uses a dot. (Note that the official names of these packages are all in lower case; these are the names we must use in our programs. To distinguish the name of the package from ordinary English words, however, we use an initial capital letter when *writing* about the packages.)

Importing a package has two advantages. First, it is convenient not to have to type the long names all the time. Second, if for some reason a class is moved from one package to another or the name of a package is changed, we need to modify only the import statement. Otherwise, we would have to look through the code and change every reference to that package.

It is important to remember the real name of each object, however. If we import two packages and both contain, say, a `Rectangle` (as would be true if we imported both Wheels

```
1    /**
2     * Chapter 2: SunCartoon, Version 1 of 3
3     * Displays a sun (yellow circle) on a white background,
4     * with a comment in a conversation bubble.
5     * Uses parameters to customize the location of its contents.
6     */
7    import wheels.users.*;
8
9    public class SunCartoon extends Frame {
10       private Ellipse _sun; // components
11       private ConversationBubble _bubble;
12
13       public SunCartoon() {
14           // we will fill this in soon
15       }
16
17       public static void main ( String[] args ) {
18           SunCartoon cartoon = new SunCartoon();
19       }
20   }
```

Listing 2.3 ■ SunCartoon (version 1)

and Java's graphics library), we would still need to distinguish between the two objects by using their full names. Such full names are officially called **fully qualified names**.

The rest of the code above follows our standard pattern for defining classes. We define a class that extends `Frame` and name it `SunCartoon`. Then we declare the instance variables we need: the sun and the conversation bubble, which are modeled by built-in Wheels classes. After declaring the instance variables we define a constructor, which has an empty body for now. Finally, there's the code for the mainline, which just creates an instance of the class it's contained in, `SunCartoon`.

2.4.6 **Version 2: adding the constructor body**

In the constructor, the first thing to do is to initialize the instance variables. In the next version of `SunCartoon`, shown in Listing 2.4, we've initialized all the instance variables by calling the appropriate constructor. (We do this inside the constructor, because the `Ellipse` and the `ConversationBubble` are components of `SunCartoon`.)

Note: A Java statement can be continued on the next line, as in lines 15 and 16 of Listing 2.4. The end of the statement is indicated by the semicolon.

2.4.7 **Java's built-in colors**

You may be wondering about the parameter to the `Ellipse` constructor. Basically, Java provides some built-in colors we can use: red, green, blue, yellow, pink, orange, cyan, magenta, black, white, gray, dark gray, and light gray. If you're a big heliotrope fan, you'll have to do something tricky. We'll explain it later, but if you're ready to zoom ahead, you can find the answer in the online Java documentation.

Because these colors are defined in the `Color` class of the `java.awt` library, we refer to them by their full name. These colors are constants—meaning that their values do not change—and the convention for constant names in Java is that they are in upper-case letters, with an underscore between words. Thus, the names look like `java.awt.Color.GREEN` and `java.awt.Color.DARK_GRAY`. In general, the fully qualified names of these colors have the form:

```
java.awt.Color.<COLOR_NAME>
```

2.4.8 **Testing version 2**

Enter, compile, and run version 2 of the program. You will notice that it's not completely satisfactory: the `CartoonBubble` is in the top left-hand corner of the `Frame`, with its tail pointing the wrong way, away from the `Sun`. But before we try to fix that semantic error, change the color of the `Sun` a few times. (Why not? How many times in your life do you have the chance to change the color of the sun?) Try out the built-in colors to see how they look on your computer. Then change the message in the `ConversationBubble`. You can make your sun say just about anything—have fun with it.

2.4.9 Putting shapes in different locations in the `Frame`

Now we'll see how to put the sun and the `ConversationBubble` in the right place. As shown in Figure 2.4, all Java's shapes have a `setLocation` method. In general, the form of a call to the `setLocation` method is:

```
<shape-name>.setLocation(<x-position>, <y-position>);
```

What do those numbers mean? First you have to understand that graphical shapes in Wheels (and in Java) are considered to be surrounded by invisible rectangles called "bounding boxes," as in Figure 2.4. Giving the location of a shape just involves giving the location of the upper left-hand corner of its bounding box.

```
1    /**
2     * Chapter 2: SunCartoon Version 2 of 3
3     * Displays a sun (yellow circle) on a white background,
4     * with a comment in a conversation bubble.
5     * Uses parameters to customize the location of its contents.
6     */
7    import wheels.users.*;
8
9    public class SunCartoon extends Frame {
10       private Ellipse _sun; // components
11       private ConversationBubble _bubble;
12
13       public SunCartoon() {
14          _sun = new Ellipse(java.awt.Color.YELLOW);
15          _bubble = new
16             ConversationBubble("Here comes the sun!");
17       }
18
19       public static void main ( String[] args ) {
20          SunCartoon cartoon = new SunCartoon();
21       }
22    }
```

Listing 2.4 ■ SunCartoon (version 2)

But what is location (300, 40)? Locations are measured in pixels (short for picture element). By convention, measurement starts at the top left-hand corner of the `Frame`. Unlike the normal Cartesian plane, a `Frame` has (0, 0) as its upper-left corner. The first (x) value goes up as you go to the right; the second (y) value goes up as you go down, as in Figure 2.5. One way to remember this is that it is numbered the same way we read English, left to right, top to bottom. Specifying the position of an object with pixels this way is known as **absolute positioning** (even though, of course, it's relative to the corner of the `Frame`). It gives us precise control over positioning, but it's not a perfect system. Figuring out what numbers you want is tricky: the best way is to draw your picture on graph paper. And even then, the results may look different on different computers. In Chapter 8, we see ways of arranging the contents of a frame in a Java window that give us less precise control but are easier to use.

keyconcept

Calculating where an object should appear relative to the top left-hand corner of the window is called absolute positioning. Calculating where an object should appear relative to another object is called relative positioning.

2.4.10 **Implementation: version 3**

Now let's modify our class definition to specify the locations of the sun and the conversation bubble. The next version of the code, with these changes, is shown in Listing 2.5.

Figure 2.4 ■ Bounding boxes for graphical shapes.

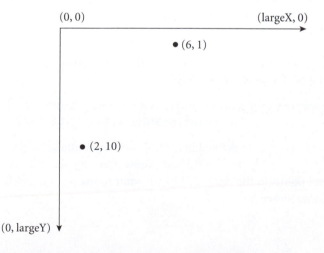

Figure 2.5 ■ x and y locations in a Java window.

```
1    /**
2     * Chapter 2: SunCartoon
3     * Version 3 of 3
4     * Displays a sun (yellow circle) on a white background,
5     * with a comment in a conversation bubble.
6     * Uses parameters to customize the location of its contents
7     */
8    import wheels.users.*;
9
10   public class SunCartoon extends Frame {
11       private Ellipse _sun; //components
12       private ConversationBubble _bubble;
13
14       public SunCartoon () {
15           _sun = new Ellipse(java.awt.Color.yellow);
16           _sun.setLocation (300, 40);
17           _bubble = new
18               ConversationBubble("Here comes the sun!",
19                                 ConversationBubble.TAIL_DIR_LEFT);
20           _bubble.setLocation(110, 110);
21       }
22
23       public static void main ( String[] args ) {
24           SunCartoon cartoon = new SunCartoon();
25       }
26   }
```

Listing 2.5 ■ SunCartoon (version 3)

We fix the tail of the conversation bubble so it points the other way by specifying the direction we want in the bubble's constructor, like this:

```
_bubble = new ConversationBubble("Here comes the sun!",
                                ConversationBubble.TAIL_DIR_LEFT);
```

TAIL_DIR_LEFT is a constant of type int defined in the ConversationBubble class. We explain constants in Chapter 10. For now, just know that by default, the ConversationBubble's tail points to the right, and if you want to make it point left, use the constructor in the form shown here.

2.4.11 **Testing version 3**

Enter, compile, and run version 3 of our program. You will probably not be satisfied with these locations—modify the parameters to the `setLocation` methods until you have something that matches our specifications. Remember: increasing the *x* value moves something to the right, and decreasing it moves something to the left; increasing the *y* value moves something down, and decreasing it moves something up.

Now you have a cartoon! Try adding more shapes of different sizes, in different locations, to make a picture of your own.

■ 2.5 ■ Working Out with **Composite Objects**—the snowman

Objectives:
- ☑ Create composite objects
- ☑ Use relative positioning
- ☑ Create an object with a peer relationship to another object
- ☑ Create interesting, fun cartoons

2.5.1 **Analysis**

Here's the problem description for our next program:

> Draw a snowman inside a rectangle. Put a sun in the top right-hand corner of the rectangle.

Again, we start with a grammatical analysis of the problem description. The nouns in this description are "snowman," "rectangle," "corner," and "sun," so these are candidates for objects in our system. The only adjectives are "top" and "right-hand." There's no mention of "has" or "part of" or "composed of," so there are no explicit component relationships. Finally, the only verbs are "draw" and "put."

Figure 2.6 contains a picture of what the output might look like. For fun, we have added a conversation bubble and a hat for the snowman.

Suppose we check with the users (that is, whoever we're writing the program for) and they approve our sketch. Now we have substantially more information. The snowman has several parts: a hat, a head, two eyes, and a body. The head, the eyes, and the body are circles. The eyes are solid black circles. The head and body are black outlines around a white circle; the sun is a solid yellow circle. The hat has two parts: two rectangles,

Figure 2.6 ■ A sketch of the desired output of `SnowCartoon`.

both black, but different shapes. The snowman is on the left, the conversation bubble is in the middle, and the sun is on the right.

2.5.2 **Design**

This cartoon is similar to the one in the last section. Just as before, we can use the `Frame` to model a displayable rectangular area, the `Ellipse` to model the sun, and the `ConversationBubble` to display the snowman's message.

Unlike the cartoon in the last section, this one contains two objects with components: the snowman and the hat. We can use the `Ellipse` to model the eyes, the head, and the bottom of the snowman. And we can use a `Rectangle` to model the two parts of the hat. We will see how to make the pieces fit together.

In summary, we define three new classes. First, just as in the `SunCartoon`, we have an extension of a `Frame` (here called `SnowCartoon`). This is the top-level class, and it will contain the `main` method. We also write `Hat` and `Snowman` classes. The `SnowCartoon` contains an `Ellipse` (the sun), the `Hat`, the `Snowman` and a `ConversationBubble`. The `Snowman` is made up of `Ellipses`, and the `Hat` is made up of `Rectangles`. This design is summarized in the UML diagram in Figure 2.7.

2.5.3 **Implementation: reusing the `SunCartoon`**

Now we have an opportunity to be appropriately lazy. We've only written two programs, and we already have some code we can reuse. We can write the first part of the

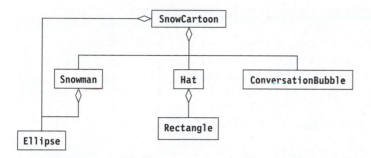

Figure 2.7 ■ UML diagram for the `SnowCartoon` program.

`SnowCartoon`—the sun and the conversation bubble—by modifying the program in the last section, as shown in Listing 2.6.

With minor changes—adding in the two new instance variables, changing the class's name, and changing the message in the conversation bubble—we have written most of our first class.

2.5.4 **Testing: the first piece of the program**

Note that we've put comment symbols before and after the lines with `Hat` and `Snowman` in them. This is called **commenting something out**: that is, telling the compiler to ignore one or more lines of code for now, because they're not ready. Because those lines of code are commented out, even though we haven't defined the `Hat` or the `Snowman` classes, we can compile and test our program. So take the opportunity now to do that, and modify the parameters until the sun and the conversation bubble are in the right place for our new cartoon.

2.5.5 **Implementation: the `Hat`**

The hat is the next simplest part of our program, since it only has two parts. Both of them are black rectangles. Our first pass at code for a `Hat` class is shown in Listing 2.7. The `Hat` has two parts, both black `Rectangles`. So far, so good. Now, to test what we have so far, uncomment the lines creating and initializing the `Hat` in `SnowCartoon`, as shown in Listing 2.8.

2.5.6 **Testing the `Hat`: part 1**

Before you test this program, can you guess what the bug will be? What about the location of the `Hat`? If you compile and test the program now, you will find a predictable bug: the two parts of the hat are the same size, and they both show up on top of each other in the middle of the `Frame`.

```
1     /**
2      * Chapter 2: SnowCartoon
3      * Version 1 of 2
4      * Displays a picture of a snowman.
5      * Similar to SunCartoon, but with composite objects.
6      */
7     import wheels.users.*;
8
9     public class SnowCartoon extends Frame {
10        /* private Snowman _snowman;
11        private Hat _hat; */
12        private Ellipse _sun;
13        private ConversationBubble _bubble;
14
15        public SnowCartoon () {
16            /*_snowman = new Snowman();
17            _hat = new Hat();
18            _hat.setLocation(20, 180); */
19            _sun = new Ellipse(java.awt.Color.YELLOW);
20            _sun.setLocation (300, 40);
21            _bubble = new
22                ConversationBubble("Happy snow day!",
23                    ConversationBubble.TAIL_DIR_LEFT);
24            _bubble.setLocation(110, 110);
25        }
26
27        public static void main ( String[] args ) {
28            SnowCartoon snowCartoon = new SnowCartoon();
29        }
30    }
```

Listing 2.6 ■ SnowCartoon (version 1)

2.5.7 Setting the location of a composite object: the Hat

ConversationBubbles and Ellipses already have accessor and mutator methods for their location (called, as usual, getLocation and setLocation). What about Hat? We're writing the Hat class ourselves, so if we want it to know how to set its location, we have to tell it.

The revised Hat class is shown in Listing 2.9.

```
1   /**
2    * Chapter 2: Hat.java
3    * Models a top hat.
4    * Version 1 of 3.
5    */
6   import wheels.users.*;
7
8   public class Hat {
9       private Rectangle _hatBrim, _hatUpper;
10      public Hat() {
11          _hatBrim = new Rectangle(java.awt.Color.BLACK);
12          _hatUpper = new Rectangle(java.awt.Color.BLACK);
13      }
14  }
```

Listing 2.7 ■ Hat (version 1)

```
1   /**
2    * Chapter 2: SnowCartoon
3    * Version 2 of 2
4    * Displays a picture of a snowman.
5    * Similar to SunCartoon, but with composite objects.
6    */
7   import wheels.users.*;
8   public class SnowCartoon extends Frame {
9       /* private Snowman _snowman; */
10      private Hat _hat;
11      private Ellipse _sun;
12      private ConversationBubble _bubble;
13
14      public SnowCartoon () {
15          /* _snowman = new Snowman(); */
16          _hat = new Hat();
17          /* _hat.setLocation (20, 180); */
18          _sun = new Ellipse(java.awt.Color.YELLOW);
19          _sun.setLocation (300, 40);
20          _bubble = new
21              ConversationBubble("Happy snow day!",
22                  ConversationBubble.TAIL_DIR_LEFT);
23          _bubble.setLocation(110, 110);
```

Listing 2.8 ■ SnowCartoon (version 2) (*continued on next page*)

```
24          }
25
26          public static void main ( String[] args ) {
27              SnowCartoon snowCartoon = new SnowCartoon();
28          }
29      }
```

Listing 2.8 ■ SnowCartoon (version 2)

Consider the Hat's setLocation method. It simply delegates the job to _hatBrim and _hatUpper, the Hat's two parts, by sending them messages to set their locations. This delegation works because _hatBrim and _hatUpper are both Rectangles, which, like Ellipses, have a setLocation method.

Let's look a little more closely at the body of the method. What's happening with the actual parameters in a method call like this?

```
_hatBrim.setLocation(x, y + 50);
```

```
 1   /**
 2    * Chapter 2: Hat.java
 3    * Models a top hat.
 4    * Version 2 of 3.
 5    */
 6   import wheels.users.*;
 7
 8   public class Hat {
 9       private Rectangle _hatBrim, _hatUpper;
10
11       public Hat() {
12           _hatBrim = new Rectangle(java.awt.Color.BLACK);
13           _hatUpper = new Rectangle(java.awt.Color.BLACK);
14       }
15
16       public void setLocation(int x, int y) {
17           _hatBrim.setLocation(x, y + 50);
18           _hatUpper.setLocation(x + 10, y);
19       }
20   }
```

Listing 2.9 ■ Version 2 of Hat class

This is the first time we've seen arithmetic in Java. We'll talk about it in detail in Chapters 6 and 10, but for now, you can assume that these operations work pretty much the same way they would in mathematics or on your calculator.

So basically, what we're saying here is, whatever the first actual parameter was when the Hat's setLocation method was called, let that be the *x* location of the brim of the Hat. (If you look back at SnowCartoon, you will find this was a 20.) Then we're saying, whatever the second actual parameter was when the setLocation method was called, the *y* value for the brim should be that number plus 50. (In this case, it would be 180 + 50, or 230.)

Note that we are using the result of an arithmetic calculation as one of the actual parameters. Recall that we said earlier that we could use the return value from a method call as a parameter, like this:

```
_robot.bringDrink(theBeer, myKitchen.getRefrigerator(),
        myLivingRoom);
```

Why do we need this computation? Because the parameters model the location of the Hat, not the brim or the upper part of the Hat. If you draw the Hat on graph paper, the *x* and *y* values are the location of the top left-hand corner of the box surrounding the whole Hat, as in Figure 2.8.

We have the location of the Hat; we need to figure out where the brim and the upper part of the hat should go in relation to the Hat as a whole. In this case, we're saying that if the Hat is at position (20, 180), the _hatBrim should be at position (20, 230) and the _hatUpper should be at position (30, 180). If the Hat were at position (0, 0), the _hatBrim would be at position (0, 50) and the _hatUpper would be at position (10, 0). Calculating where an object should appear relative to another object is called **relative positioning**, and it is a useful technique whenever you are trying to position an object that is made up of more than one shape. We will see relative positioning again in the setLocation method for the Snowman.

If you enter, compile, and run the program now, you will see that the Hat is not the right shape. We want to fix the size of the Hat. The problem is that both parts of the Hat have

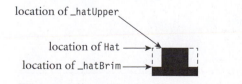

location of _hatUpper

location of Hat ⟶

location of _hatBrim ⟶

Figure 2.8 ■ Locations of the parts of the Hat, relative to the Hat.

the default size for a `Rectangle` in Wheels: 50 by 50 pixels. Wheels shapes have a `setSize` method that we can use to solve this problem. The basic form of a call to the `setSize` method is:

```
<shape-name>.setSize(<width>, <height>);
```

The width and height of a shape are both measured in pixels, like its location. (And if you have trouble remembering which comes first, width or height, it may help to remember that in `setLocation`, the *x* position comes first and then the *y* position; and both the *x* value and width are measured horizontally, while the *y* value and height are vertical.) The code for the `Hat` with the sizes is given in Listing 2.10.

2.5.8 Testing the `Hat` (continued)

Now that we have the `Hat` class's `setLocation` method, uncomment the line

```
_hat.setLocation(20, 180);
```

```
1   /**
2    * Chapter 2: Hat.java
3    * Models a top hat.
4    * Version 3 of 3.
5    */
6   import wheels.users.*;
7
8   public class Hat {
9       private Rectangle _hatBrim, _hatUpper; // components
10
11      public Hat() {
12          _hatBrim = new Rectangle(java.awt.Color.BLACK);
13          _hatBrim.setSize(80, 20);
14          _hatUpper = new Rectangle(java.awt.Color.BLACK);
15          _hatUpper.setSize(60, 60);
16      }
17
18      public void setLocation(int x, int y) {
19          _hatBrim.setLocation(x, y + 50);
20          _hatUpper.setLocation(x + 10, y);
21      }
22  }
```

Listing 2.10 ■ Final version of `Hat` class

to the `SnowCartoon`. Recompile both classes and test the program again. How does it look? Try some different locations. Change the message to one the `Hat` might say. Now you have a cartoon with a composite object—congratulations! This is a significant step up from the `SunCartoon`.

2.5.9 **Pulling it all together: implementing the `Snowman`**

Looking back at our original picture, we see that the `Snowman` needs a head, a body, and two eyes. We can model all these parts with `Ellipses`. We know how to make them different sizes, how to position them in the right location, and how to make the head and body white and the eyes black. A first pass at the code for the `Snowman` class is shown in Listing 2.11.

```
1   /**
2    * Chapter 2: Snowman.java
3    * Models a simple snowman.
4    * Version 1 of 2.
5    */
6   import wheels.users.*;
7
8   public class Snowman {
9       private Ellipse _head, _body, _leftEye, _rightEye;
10
11      public Snowman() {
12          _head = new Ellipse(java.awt.Color.WHITE);
13          _head.setSize(80, 80);
14          _head.setLocation(20, 240);
15          _body = new Ellipse(java.awt.Color.WHITE);
16          _body.setSize(100, 100);
17          _body.setLocation(10, 300);
18          _leftEye = new Ellipse(java.awt.Color.BLACK);
19          _leftEye.setSize(15, 15);
20          _leftEye.setLocation(35, 265);
21          _rightEye = new Ellipse(java.awt.Color.BLACK);
22          _rightEye.setSize(15, 15);
23          _rightEye.setLocation(75, 265);
24      }
25  }
```

Listing 2.11 ■ Snowman class (version 1)

2.5.10 **Testing the Snowman: part 1**

Revise SnowCartoon so the reference to Snowman is no longer commented out, initialize the _snowman variable, and compile and test the program. You should now see the Snowman's eyes just below the Hat, but no Snowman! What happened?

You may already have spotted this problem in the code: the body and head of the snowman are modeled as white ellipses, which is the same color as the background. We need one more thing: a way to make the outline of a shape a different color from the inside.

2.5.11 **Implementing the Snowman (continued)**

In Wheels, we can draw the outline of a shape using the setFrameColor method. The basic form of a call to setFrameColor is:

```
<shape-name>.setFrameColor(java.awt.Color.<color>);
```

And just for fun, we can also set the thickness of the outline using a setFrameThickness method, like this:

```
<shape-name>.setFrameThickness(<number-of-pixels>);
```

Instead of putting everything in the constructor (which would make it quite long), let's write a method for the Snowman that sets the thickness of the Snowman's body and its head at the same time. The revised version of the Snowman is shown in Listing 2.12.

```
1    /**
2     * Chapter 2: Snowman.java
3     * Models a simple snowman.
4     * Version 2 of 2.
5     */
6    import wheels.users.*;
7
8    public class Snowman {
9        private Ellipse _head, _body, _leftEye, _rightEye;
10
11       public Snowman() {
12           _head = new Ellipse(java.awt.Color.WHITE);
13           _head.setSize(80, 80);
14           _body = new Ellipse(java.awt.Color.WHITE);
15           _body.setSize(100, 100);
16           _leftEye = new Ellipse(java.awt.Color.DARK_GRAY);
```

Listing 2.12 ■ Final version of Snowman class (*continued on next page*)

```
17              _leftEye.setSize(15, 15);
18              _rightEye = new Ellipse(java.awt.Color.DARK_GRAY);
19              _rightEye.setSize(15, 15);
20
21              _body.setLocation(10, 300);
22              _head.setLocation(20, 240);
23              _leftEye.setLocation(35, 265);
24              _rightEye.setLocation(75, 265);
25              this.setOutline(java.awt.Color.BLACK, 2);
26          }
27
28          public void setOutline (java.awt.Color color, int thickness) {
29              _body.setFrameColor(color);
30              _body.setFrameThickness(thickness);
31              _head.setFrameColor(color);
32              _head.setFrameThickness(thickness);
33          }
34      }
```

Listing 2.12 ■ Final version of Snowman class

2.5.12 **Testing the Snowman (continued)**

Compile and test this version of the program. Testing should be a simple process, since the cartoon doesn't do much—just run the program and make sure the cartoon's appearance matches our original specifications.

■ Summary ■

This chapter has given you some very powerful tools. You can now write general methods that take detailed information in the form of parameters. If we had to write methods to cover every possible situation, our programs would be impossibly complex. But by using parameters, we can write methods that are both general and customizable to fit particular situations. Thus, using parameters is yet another example of the use of abstraction to control complexity, a continuing theme of this book.

Methods use instances to do their job. Sometimes these instances are provided from outside, like parameters; sometimes they are created and used temporarily within a method, like local variables; and sometimes they are accessible to all the methods in a particular class, like instance variables. These different kinds of variables are distinguished by their scope (the part of the program in which they can be used) and lifetime (the time during the execution of the program during which they are defined).

Methods can also return information to the object that called them. Methods that return a value are also known as functions; methods that do not return a value are known as procedures. The syntax for returning a value is very simple, but the concept is an extremely powerful one. If objects cannot only send messages (by invoking methods), but also get an answer back, it becomes possible for them to cooperate.

Finally, using the Wheels library, you have seen how to create a program with classes that cooperate to display a simple cartoon, using a variety of shapes and colors. The program positioned shapes in a displayable rectangular area using absolute positioning (giving the location of the shape within the displayed area).

Now that you have seen how to write classes and methods, Chapter 3 discusses inheritance. Inheritance is a way of organizing groups of classes and one of the most powerful concepts in object-oriented programming.

■ Self-Check Questions ■

(The answers to these questions can be found on the book's website, www.aw.com/sanders)

1. What kind of parameter errors can the compiler find for you? Explain and give examples.
2. What kind of parameter errors *can't* the compiler find for you? Why not? Give examples.
3. What is a formal parameter?
4. What is an actual parameter?
5. What is a method's signature?

6. What is method overloading?

7. What is a local variable?

8. Define the term "scope," and compare and contrast the scopes of instance variables, formal parameter names, and local variables.

9. What is the lifetime of a variable? Compare and contrast the lifetimes of instance variables, formal parameter names, and local variables.

10. How can you decide whether to use a local variable, instance variable, or parameter?

11. What conventions do we use for naming instance variables, local variables, and parameters?

12. What is a return value?

13. What is a return type?

14. What does the Java keyword `void` mean?

15. What is incremental development?

16. What is a package?

17. What is a library?

18. What is an import statement?

19. What is the difference between absolute and relative positioning of graphical objects?

■ Exercises ■

Applying the Facts

1. Why is it unnecessary to declare local variables and parameters `private`?

2. Find the source code for Wheels on the book's website (or on the CD that accompanies this text) and look through it. (*Note:* Don't worry if you don't understand it all yet—if you do, you're probably in the wrong class! The point is just to get used to the structure of method definitions.)

    a. Circle five method definitions in Wheels.
    b. List five parameter types that you find in Wheels.
    c. List five return types that you find in Wheels.
    d. List the names of three accessor methods that you find in Wheels.
    e. List the names of three mutator methods that you find in Wheels.

3. Based on the definition of the `Hat` class in the `Snowman` program, if we send the message `_hat.setLocation(100, 100)`, what will the location of `_hatBrim` and `_hatUpper` be?

4. Based on the definition of the Hat class in the Snowman program, if we send the message _hat.setLocation(210, 160), what will the location of _hatBrim and _hatUpper be?

5. Based on the definition of the Hat class in the Snowman program, suppose you have placed the Hat at position (20, 80) and it seems to be about 20 pixels too far to the left. Fill in the numbers for _hat.setLocation(___, ___) that will cause _hat to appear 20 pixels to the right of (20, 80).

6. Based on the definition of the Hat class in the Snowman program, suppose you have placed the Hat at position (20, 80), and it seems to be about 50 pixels too high. Fill in the numbers for _hat.setLocation(___, ___) that will cause _hat to appear 50 pixels lower than (20, 80).

Debugging Programs

Identify the error(s) in each of the following code fragments:

1.
```java
public void eatFood(_apple) { ... }
```

2.
```java
public class Student
      private Pencil _pencil;
      public Student() {
             ...
            _pencil = new Pencil();
      }
      public void takeNotes() {
          this.write(Pencil pencil);
      }
   ...
}
```

3.
```java
public class TeachingAssistant {
   ...
   public void gradePaper(Paper paper, Pen pen) { ... }
   ...
}
//new class
public class Professor {
   private TeachingAssistant _ta;
   private Pen _pen;
     ...
   public void giveTAWork(Paper paper) {
          _ta.gradePaper(_pen, paper);
   }
      ...
}
```

```
4. public class LunchMaker {
      ...
      public Sandwich makeSandwich() {...}
      public Salad makeSalad() {...}
      public Lunch makeLunch() {
          Lunch lunch = new Lunch();
          Salad salad = new Salad();
          return salad;
      }
   }
5. public class PainterPalette {
      private Brush _brush;

      public PaintColor getCurrentColor() {
          PaintColor pColor = _brush.getColor();
          return pColor;
      }
      public void changeCurrentColor(PaintColor newColor) {
          pColor = newColor;
      }
   }
```

■ Programming Projects ■

Modifying Programs

1. Modify the SnowCartoon program so that there is a different message in the conversation bubble. Compile, test, and run your revised program.

2. Modify the SnowCartoon program to change the sun from yellow to one of the other built-in colors. Compile, test, and run your revised program.

3. Modify the SnowCartoon program so that the Snowman class can be re-used. Suppose we want a Snowman in a different position on the screen at some point. Accomplish this by giving the Snowman its own setLocation method that, as with Hat, delegates setLocation to its components. Be sure to modify the Snowman's constructor as well so that we can specify the Snowman's location when we call its constructor.

4. Modify the SnowCartoon program so that wherever the Snowman is, the Hat is on its head. Accomplish this by giving the Hat the Snowman as a peer object and giving the Snowman instance variables for its *x* and *y* position and accessors and mutators for both.

5. Modify the `SnowCartoon` program so that wherever the sun is located, the `Hat` is located ten pixels directly below it. Compile, test, and run your revised program.

6. Modify the `SnowCartoon` program so that there are two instances of `Snowman` in the program at two different locations, each with a separate cartoon bubble. One of them should say, "Oh-oh, feels like the temperature is rising," and the other should answer, "Ahh! A talking snowman!" Compile, test, and run your revised program.

Writing Programs

1. Write a program that displays a picture, made up of `Ellipses` from Wheels, of a poached egg (if you're vegan, make a plate with a spot of mustard instead). Compile, test, and run your program. Hand in a UML diagram for the classes in your program, a printout of the Java code for the program, and a printout of the cartoon that appears when your program is run.

2. Write a program that displays a picture, made up of `Ellipses` from Wheels, of the Olympic symbol: five interlocked rings, colored (from left to right) blue, yellow, black, green, and red. Compile, test, and run your program. Hand in a UML diagram for the classes in your program, a printout of the Java code for the program, and a printout of the cartoon that appears when your program is run.

3. Write a program that displays a picture, made up of shapes from Wheels, of a target (see Figure 2.9). Compile, test, and run your program. Hand in a UML diagram for the classes in your program, a printout of the Java code for the program, and a printout of the picture that appears when your program is run. (If you want to get mean, you could put that target on one of your snowmen.)

Figure 2.9 ■ A target.

4. Write a program that displays a picture, made up of shapes from Wheels, of a stereotypical alien (see Figure 2.10). Compile, test, and run your program. Hand in a UML diagram for the classes in your program, a printout of the

Java code for the program, and a printout of the cartoon that appears when your program is run.

Figure 2.10 ■ A space alien.

5. Write a program that displays a picture, made up of shapes from Wheels, of a car. Compile, test, and run your program. Hand in a UML diagram for the classes in your program, a printout of the Java code for the program, and a printout of the picture that appears when your program is run.

6. Write a program that uses Wheels's `Line` class to display your initials in red and blue on a white background. Compile, test, and run your program. Hand in a UML diagram for the classes in your program, a printout of the Java code for the program, and a printout of the picture that appears when your program is run.

7. Write a program that displays a picture, made up of shapes from Wheels, of a stick figure (see Figure 2.11). Compile, test, and run your program. Hand in a UML diagram for the classes in your program, a printout of the Java code for the program, and a printout of the picture that appears when your program is run.

Figure 2.11 ■ A stick figure.

8. Write a program that displays a picture of a flag made up of shapes from Wheels. There are many flags that can be made using rectangles and ellipses, for example the flags of France, Sierra Leone, Botswana, and Bangladesh, or you can design your own. Compile, test, and run your program. Hand in a UML diagram for the classes in your program, a printout of the Java code for the program, and a printout of the picture that appears when your program is run.

9. Write a program that displays a (highly stylized) picture of a dog. Compile, test, and run your program. Hand in a UML diagram for the classes in your program, a printout of the Java code for the program, and a printout of the picture that appears when your program is run.

10. Write a program that displays a picture of a house. Compile, test, and run your program. Hand in a UML diagram for the classes in your program, a printout of the Java code for the program, and a printout of the cartoon that appears when your program is run.

11. The painter Mondrian is known for paintings that are made up of rectangles of different colors arranged together in patterns like this one (see Figure 2.12). Write a program that displays a Mondrian-like picture in a window. There must be at least nine rectangles, and they must be aligned so that they fill the window without any gaps. There must be at least two different colors, or at least two different sizes of rectangles, or both. Compile, test, and run your program. Hand in a UML diagram for the classes in your program, a printout of the Java code for the program, and a printout of the picture that appears when your program is run.

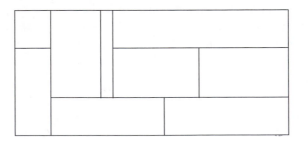

Figure 2.12 ■ Sample layout for Mondrian-like picture.

12. Write a program that displays a simple cartoon. You might include, for example, spaceships, faces, houses, and/or robots. Your cartoon must display at least two characters, at least one of which must be composed of four or more smaller shapes, plus a cartoon bubble for each character. Hand in a UML diagram for the classes in your program, a printout of the Java code for the program, and a printout of the cartoon that appears when your program is run.

■ **New Style Conventions** ■

Names

- Parameter names start with a lower-case letter. Formal parameters often start with "a" (as in `aKitchen`, `aSpoon`.) Specific to this book.
- Local variable names also start with a lower-case letter.
- The names of accessor methods start with "get."
- The names of mutator methods start with "set."
- Package names often start with a lower-case letter. When *writing* about packages, however, we use an initial upper-case letter.

3

Inheritance

After reading this chapter, you should be able to:

- ☑ Define inheritance
- ☑ Define superclass and subclass
- ☑ Explain why inheritance is important
- ☑ Identify the use of inheritance in Java code
- ☑ Create a Java inheritance hierarchy
- ☑ Explain method resolution
- ☑ When a method is called in Java, identify the method definition that the invocation refers to

■ 3.1 ■ Introduction

In the previous chapter, we implemented a program with three classes, substantially more complex than anything we had discussed before. Imagine, then, the complexity of a program with hundreds or even thousands of classes. Suppose we are modeling the items in a supermarket, for example, and we need a class for every item it sells: every brand of spaghetti sauce, every type of produce, and every gossip magazine. Not only will there be hundreds of classes, but many of them will have the same properties (for example, weight and price) and the same capabilities (being shelved, being added to the shopping cart, being checked out).

Stores help us to deal with this complexity by organizing their products into categories: meat, vegetables, sodas, prepared foods, and so forth. Organizing things into categories is a common strategy for dealing with complexity. We group poodles and greyhounds together as dogs, and chairs and tables together as furniture. We may even use a hierarchy of categories: fresh fruit and vegetables may be grouped together as produce; meat, produce, and baked goods grouped together as perishable food; and so on.

In object-oriented programming, inheritance lets us model the way people organize things into categories. **Inheritance** is a relationship between two classes in which one class (the **subclass**) inherits all of the properties and capabilities of another (the **superclass**). Superclasses themselves can have superclasses. For example, we could define a class `Okra`, with a superclass `Vegetable`, which has a superclass `PerishableFood`, which has a superclass `Food`, which has a superclass `SupermarketItem`.

In addition to being a powerful modeling tool, inheritance can save us a tremendous amount of work. Suppose every one of the classes in our supermarket model needs a `getPrice` method. Instead of writing it over and over in every class, we can write it once in the `SupermarketItem` class—another example of appropriate laziness. Every one of the subclasses—all the other classes in our model—can use that method. Subclasses define only the properties and capabilities that make them different from their superclass.

Inheritance is usually seen as one of the three most powerful aspects of object-oriented programming, along with encapsulation (which we have already seen) and polymorphism (which we will see in Chapter 5). Because inheritance adds so much to our ability to model and provides so much in terms of code reuse and the ability to make incremental improvements in a system, most computer scientists feel that without inheritance, there is no object-oriented programming.

■ 3.2 ■ **Concepts**

Among the easiest inheritance hierarchies to understand are hierarchies of animals. Consider the hierarchy in Figure 3.1. This diagram illustrates a new part of the Unified Modeling Language introduced in Chapter 1. It expresses in a compact form the idea that reptiles, mammals, and birds are all animals, iguanas are reptiles, monkeys are mammals, and penguins, swans, and crows are all birds.

In UML, the inheritance relationship is represented by an arrow connecting the subclass and the superclass, with an arrowhead shaped like an open triangle pointing toward the superclass. These diagrams are also called "tree diagrams." (As you will see in Chapter 15, computer scientists frequently draw trees upside-down—maybe we don't get out enough.)

There's a lot more English terminology for subclasses, superclasses, and the process of defining the relationship between them than there is Java syntax. For example, we can say that `Monkey` subclasses `Mammal`, or extends it, or specializes it. Sometimes, more colloquially, we say that `Monkey` is-a `Mammal`, and we say that the inheritance hierarchy implements is-a relationships. You will sometimes hear superclasses referred to as the parent class, base class, or ancestor class, and subclasses referred to as the child class, derived class or descendant class.

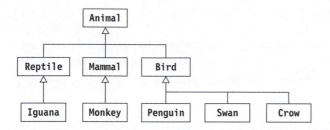

Figure 3.1 ■ Inheritance hierarchy for some animals.

Be careful not to confuse subclasses with instances of a class: a subclass is itself a class, and can be used to generate its own instances. `Monkey` is a subclass of `Mammal`, but Curious George is a particular instance of `Monkey`.

Classes can't throw any of their inheritance away. And they inherit a lot: a class inherits all of the properties and capabilities of its superclass, which inherits all the properties and capabilities of *its* superclass, and so on. For example, all Java classes have the built-in class `Object` as an ancestor, and all Java classes can respond to the `equals` message defined in `Object`. For this reason, we can guarantee that an instance of one class can do everything an instance of one of its ancestor classes can do, so that the subclass truly is-a kind of ancestor class, as a `Monkey` is-a `Mammal`.

Perhaps fortunately, because they inherit so much from one superclass, Java classes cannot have more than one superclass. Some object-oriented programming languages do allow a class to have more than one superclass; this language feature is called **multiple inheritance**. Languages like Java that allow one superclass at most are said to have **single inheritance**.

Since Java classes inherit all of their ancestors' capabilities, they must be able to respond to all the `public` messages any of their ancestors could handle—but they don't have to respond in the *same way*. A class can do something in an entirely different way by **overriding** an ancestor's method. For example, most birds fly, but penguins do not. Instead of flying through the air, penguins have a way of swimming that is almost like flying, except underwater. Alternatively, a class can **partially override** an inherited method, if it doesn't want to reject its ancestors' way of doing things completely. For example, most birds flap their wings while they fly, but waterfowl such as swans both run and flap their wings as they take off, so that they appear to run along the water.

Inheritance and overriding used together give us the advantages of both reuse and flexibility. Just as methods with parameters let us factor out the parts of a method that we would otherwise have to write again and again, inheritance lets us factor out the common elements in entire classes. Just as we can customize methods by varying parameters, we can customize classes by adding instance variables and overriding or adding methods.

keyconcept

Every class in Java has exactly one superclass; a class can have any number of subclasses.

keyconcept

A class must inherit all the methods from its superclasses, but it can override (or partially override) one or more of the inherited methods.

■ 3.3 ■ **Mechanics**

Making effective use of inheritance is much more a matter of learning good design and good modeling techniques than a matter of learning Java syntax. In fact, Java requires very little syntax to provide all the concepts we have been discussing, and we have seen most of it in the previous two chapters.

3.3.1 **Simple inheritance**

For purposes of illustration, let's model part of the Animal hierarchy in Java. We know how to define any of the classes we might want. For example, we could write:

```
public class Swan {
    private Heart _heart;
    ...
    public void sleep() {...}
    public void breathe() {...}
    ...
}
```

and

```
public class Penguin {
    private Heart _heart;
    ...
    public void sleep() {...}
    public void breathe() {...}
    ...
}
```

and

```
public class Crow {
    private Heart _heart;
    ...
    public void sleep() {...}
    public void breathe() {...}
    ...
}
```

and the same for Iguana, Monkey, and whatever other classes we want to add to our model.

But as you can see, we'd be repeating a lot of the same code over and over again. All these classes have a lot of properties and capabilities in common: they all breathe, sleep, and so forth. This is a perfect time to be appropriately lazy. We can just factor out that commonality, put it in a superclass, `Animal`, and create an inheritance hierarchy.

This is one of the two contexts in which we encounter inheritance. On the one hand, you may notice, as we did here, that two or more of your classes are starting to overlap a lot. In that case, inheritance lets you factor out the code they have in common, define a superclass, and put the common code in the superclass. This process is known as **bottom-up design**, since it starts with something specific and moves to something more general. Alternatively, you may start with a class, either your own or someone else's, and realize that you need one or more subclasses of that class. This process is an example of **top-down design** (so called because you are starting with something general and making it more specific). We have already seen this several times: for example, when we extended the Wheels `Frame` class to create `FirstApp`, `SunCartoon`, and `SnowCartoon`.

The syntax for creating an inheritance relationship in Java is very simple. To say that `Crow` is a subclass of `Bird`, for example, we simply write:

```
public class Crow extends Bird {
    ...
}
```

This definition starts the same as all the other class definitions we've seen, with the Java keyword `public` followed by the keyword `class` and the name of the class. Next, the Java keyword **extends** indicates that the class being defined is a subclass of another class, and then follows the name of the superclass.

You should recognize this: it's the same syntax we used when we declared the `FirstApp` class in Chapter 1 and the `SunCartoon` and `SnowCartoon` classes in Chapter 2:

```
public name <classname> extends Frame {
    ...
}
```

In all three cases, the new class had all the properties and capabilities of a Wheels `Frame`, and more. The `FirstApp` class defined in Chapter 1 had the ability to display itself on the screen and all the other properties and abilities of a `Frame`, and it also knew how to display a red circle in the middle of the `Frame`. The `SunCartoon` class had the abilities and properties of a basic `Frame`, plus the ability to display a picture of the sun and a cartoon bubble. The `SnowCartoon` was a basic `Frame` that could also display a picture of a snowman.

We don't have to write the inherited methods in the subclass; we get them for free. To add more properties or methods to a subclass, we simply list them in the class definition as we would for any class.

What about classes that don't have the keyword `extends` in the class definition, such as the `Snowman` class in Chapter 2? They don't appear to have a superclass, but in fact they do. All Java classes except for one have exactly one superclass. If the class definition doesn't explicitly give the name of the superclass, Java provides a default, the class `Object`. So all Java classes have as a superclass either a class that is named in the class definition, or the class `Object`. The only exception is the `Object` class itself, which has no superclass.

Thus, all Java classes, both the built-in ones and the ones we define ourselves, are part of a single, large inheritance hierarchy. Figure 3.2 shows that part of the hierarchy containing the classes defined for `FirstApp`, `SunCartoon`, and `SnowCartoon`. (The classes between the Wheels `Frame` class and the `Object` class have been omitted here. These built-in Java classes are discussed further in Chapter 7.)

3.3.2 Overriding inherited methods

A more detailed class diagram for part of the `Animal` hierarchy is shown in Figure 3.3. The diagram includes the information we need for these examples, but for brevity omits many classes and many details about each class.

Let's examine Figure 3.3 closely, as it includes a lot of information in a very compact form. Recall that each class box is divided into three parts, the top one for the class name, the middle one for the instance variables, if any, and the bottom one for the methods defined in that class. For brevity, methods are listed only in classes where they are defined, not in subclasses where they are inherited. You may notice that some of the class and method names are in italics; we explain that notation in Section 3.3.3. The names of variables are given first, followed by a colon, followed by their type; similarly, the names of methods are given first, followed by a parameter list. For methods that have a return type (unlike these), the parameter list is followed by a colon and the return type.

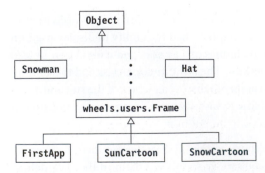

Figure 3.2 ■ Inheritance hierarchy containing classes defined for `FirstApp`, `SunCartoon`, and `SnowCartoon`.

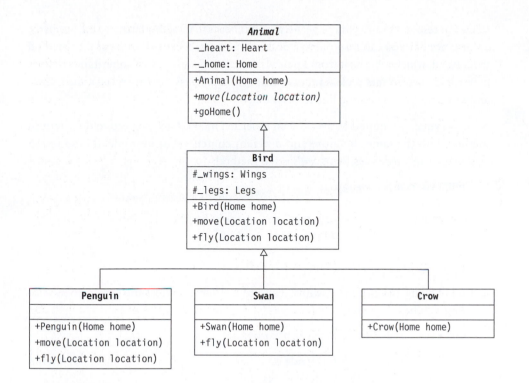

Figure 3.3 ■ An expanded class diagram for part of the `Animal` hierarchy.

One other new feature of this diagram is the use of "+," "−," and "#" before variable or method names. These symbols indicate which other classes can see these properties and capabilities (i.e., their visibility). "+" indicates that a variable or method is pub-lic, "−" indicates that it is `private`, and "#" indicates that it is `protected`. Expect to see `private` instance variables and `public` methods (and in certain circumstances, `protected` instance variables). We discuss these different types of visibility further in Section 3.3.4.

For now, let's look at the methods defined in the various classes. Each of the classes defines its own constructor; this is consistent with our practice that a class definition should always include a constructor, even if it is empty. In addition, `Animal` has two methods: `move` and `goHome`. `Bird` inherits all of these and adds a new method, `fly`. `Bird` also repeats `move`. `Crow` inherits all the methods shown in `Bird`; `Swan` repeats `fly`; and `Penguin` repeats both `move` and `fly`.

If a class inherits a method, it can respond to a message even though the correspond-ing method is not included explicitly in its class definition. For example, an instance of

`Crow` can respond to a `fly` message, because it inherits that method from `Bird`. Similarly, an instance of `Crow` can respond to a `goHome` message, because it inherits that method from `Bird`, which inherits it from `Animal`. Subclasses pass on their inheritance to their own subclasses, so that a class inherits from its superclass, its superclass's superclass, and so on all the way up the line to `Object`.

No new syntax is required to override an inherited method: all we need to do is write a method with the same signature and different contents. For example, the `Penguin` class completely redefines the `Bird`'s `move` method:

```
public class Penguin {
    ...
    public void move(Location location) {
        this.swim(location);
    }
}
```

Instead of flying, the `Penguin` swims. It also completely overrides the `fly` method, substituting a stub:

```
public void fly (Location location) { }
```

It is also possible to partially override an inherited method. For example, our `Swans` fly, but to do so, they both flap their wings and run:

```
public class Swan extends Bird {
    ...
    public void fly (location) {
        _legs.run(location);
        super.fly(location);
    }
}
```

keyconcept
The Java keyword super is a convenient way to refer to any superclass.

Java uses the keyword **super** as a convenient way of referring to the superclass of the class we're in, so a class doesn't need to worry about the names of its ancestors. Here, when a `Swan` is sent a message to `fly`, it starts by running and then invokes the `fly` method from its superclass, `Bird`. Because the `Swan`'s `fly` method adds to the superclass's method, it is an example of partial overriding. (And yes, we know that a real swan runs and flaps its wings at the same time and this code is sequential and therefore isn't a very good model of the actual behavior, but since this isn't executable code, we'll ignore this bit of stretching.)

The method being overridden doesn't have to be a method that's defined in the class's immediate superclass; classes inherit, and can override, methods from all of their ancestor classes. But one typically overrides methods in immediate ancestors only.

3.3.3 **Implementing abstract methods**

We can define a standard `goHome` method that's the same for all `Animals`:

```
public void goHome() {
    Location location = _home.getLocation();
    this.move(location());
}
```

In other words, go home by finding out where home is and then moving to that location. Similarly, we can define a `fly` method for all `Birds`:

```
public void fly (Location location) {
    _wings.flap();
       . . .
}
```

Some subclasses of `Bird`, such as `Swan` and `Penguin`, override this method, but most can use the default definition.

But what if there isn't a default? For example, consider the `move` method: all `Animals` move, but `Iguanas`, `Monkeys`, `Swans`, and `Penguins` move in very different ways. When you want all the subclasses of a given class to define the same method, but there's no standard implementation, the solution is to define an `abstract` method. In Java, an **abstract method** is preceded by the keyword `abstract` and does not have a body, not even empty braces. Instead of a method body, an `abstract` method has only a semicolon.

To declare an `abstract` `move` method for `Animal`, we can write:

```
public abstract void move(Location location);
```

This statement means that no definition is provided for `move`, but it must be defined in all subclasses, which is exactly what we want. More precisely, it means that this class (the class containing the `abstract` method) cannot be instantiated, and the method must be defined in all subclasses that are ever going to be instantiated.

In Java, a class that contains an `abstract` method must itself be declared as an **abstract class**, like this:

```
public abstract class Animal {
       . . .
}
```

The definition of an `abstract` class includes the keyword `abstract`, just as the definition of an `abstract` method does. If you forget to use the keyword `abstract` and your

keyconcept

If a class contains an abstract method, that method must be defined in all subclasses that will ever be instantiated.

class contains an `abstract` method, the compiler will print an error message. In UML, the name of an abstract class or method is italicized. Alternatively, the work "<>" may be added after the name.

Compare the strategy of declaring an `abstract` method to declaring a **stub** (i.e., a method with no method body), like this:

```
public void move (Location location) {}
```

A stub is useful during incremental development. With a stub, we could instantiate and test `Animal`, and then add in a method body for `move` when the rest of the class is working. Stubs are also useful when we want to model a subclass that doesn't have one of its superclass's capabilities. For example, while `Penguins` can't fly, since they are a bird we might still want to send them the `fly` message but have them essentially ignore it. We do this by giving a stub for the definition:

```
public class Penguin {
    ...
    public void fly(Location location) { }
}
```

In summary, an `abstract` method is appropriate when (1) we don't want to define the method in a particular class but (2) we do want all concrete subclasses to define the method. In Chapter 5, we show why being able to count on all the subclasses having certain capabilities is useful.

`Abstract` classes are useful because they set policies for their subclasses. By declaring an `abstract` method, an `abstract` class declares a capability that subclasses must have. For example, because `Animal` contains the `abstract` method `move`, we can count on all of its subclasses also being able to `move`. `Abstract` methods don't provide any reuse: we still have to write the code for their method bodies. Nevertheless, an `abstract` method must be implemented by any concrete subclass, no matter how far down in the class hierarchy. In this way, `abstract` methods give the superclass designer some control over what the subclasses can do.

Because they can't be instantiated, `abstract` classes are also useful for modeling abstract categories (like Animal, or Shape, or SupermarketItem). Chances are good that we don't ever want these classes to be instantiated because, frankly, they are too general. By declaring a class `abstract`, we can ensure that it is never instantiated, even if all the methods it contains are concrete.

3.3.4 Inheriting properties: pseudo-inheritance

Java classes don't just inherit all of the capabilities of their ancestors, they also inherit all of their properties. `Animals` have an instance variable `_heart` of type `Heart`, for example, so `Birds, Reptiles, Mammals,` and their subclasses all have `_heart` instance variables as well. The superclass methods that the subclass inherits most likely involve accessing instance variables defined in the superclass, so those inherited methods must have access to the instance variables, hence the need to have the superclass inherit the properties along with the methods that use them.

We call this **pseudo-inheritance**, because in Java, classes inherit properties without "knowing" it. In other words, any instance variable that is declared `private` in the superclass cannot be directly accessed by a subclass. The subclass is treated the same as any other class—if it wants to change the value of a `private` instance variable inherited from a superclass, it must use whatever methods that superclass has provided for that purpose. This is another (admittedly sometimes extreme) form of encapsulation.

keyconcept

In Java, any instance variable that is declared `private` in the superclass cannot be directly accessed by a subclass, although it is inherited by the subclass.

How are these superclass properties initialized, then, if they can't be accessed directly in a subclass? When an object is instantiated, the first thing its constructor does is to call the superclass's constructor. Recall that the `Swan` used the Java keyword `super` to refer to its superclass when defining a `fly` method above. We can use the same keyword on its own, followed by parentheses, to invoke the superclass's constructor. When we defined our `SunApp` class, for example, we could have written:

```
public class SunApp extends wheels.users.Frame {
    ...
    public SunApp() {
        super();
        ...
    }
    ...
}
```

keyconcept

The first thing a Java constructor does is to call the constructor of its superclass to initialize the superclass's instance variables.

In other words, the first thing the `SunApp` constructor does is to create a `Frame`.

We can also call the superclass's constructor with parameters, if appropriate. For example, we could define a `Sun` class that is a subclass of `Ellipse` as follows:

```
public class Sun extends wheels.users.Ellipse {
    ...
    public Sun() {
        super(Color.YELLOW);
        ...
    }
    ...
}
```

Here, the first thing the constructor does is to create a yellow `Ellipse`.

If we do not explicitly invoke the superclass's constructor, Java does so for us. Since Java can't guess what parameters we might want, it invokes the simplest form of the constructor:

```
super();
```

Up until now, since we hadn't covered inheritance, we relied on this default version of the superclass's constructor. But now that we can, we will often invoke a superclass's constructor with parameters. And even if the default version of the constructor is what we want, it is a good idea to write it explicitly, just as a reminder that it is being called.

The superclass's constructor is responsible for initializing the superclass's instance variables. When we create a new `Crow`, first its constructor calls the `Bird`'s constructor. Then, before doing anything else, the `Bird`'s constructor calls the `Animal`'s constructor, which calls Java's `Object` class's constructor. (Recall that unless we say otherwise, all Java classes `extend` the `Object` class.) The `Object` constructor creates a very basic `Object` and initializes any instance variables that `Object` may have. Then the `Bird`'s constructor takes the `Object`, adds the instance variables and methods of a `Bird`, and initializes the `Bird`'s instance variables. Finally, we're back to the `Crow`'s own constructor, which adds the instance variables and methods and initializes any instance variables that are unique to a `Crow`.

What good is inherited data that a class can't access directly? Well, consider a `Bird`'s `Heart`, for example. The `Bird` needs its heart to keep beating, but it doesn't need (or want) to control it consciously, at least not in our simplistic model. Alternatively, to look at this question from Java's point of view, the `Bird` subclass doesn't need to know about its `Heart`; only the methods it inherits need to know. If `Animal` defines a `maintainCirculation` method, for example, any of its subclasses can use this method, even though they don't explicitly know that they have a `Heart`.

Sometimes both a subclass and a superclass need to know about the same property. Consider the `Bird`'s `_wings`, for example. The `Bird` needs to know about these in order to define its `fly` method. The `Penguin` needs to know about its `_wings` in order to define the method that will propel it through the water.

When a superclass and a subclass both need to access the same instance variable, define the variable in the superclass, along with any related methods that should be available to all subclasses. Then you have two choices:

1. If you want all other classes in the program to be able to access the variable, make the variable `private` and provide an appropriate method for accessing it. (We'll learn about a standard way of providing such access, through so-called accessor and mutator methods, in the next chapter.)

🔑 keyconcept

When a superclass and a subclass both need to access the same instance variable and unrelated classes do not, define the variable in the superclass and declare it `protected`.

2. If only the subclasses need access to the variable, make it `protected`, like this:

```
protected Wings _wings;
```

The Java keyword **`protected`** corresponds to the UML symbol "#" shown in Figure 3.3. Declaring a variable `protected` is like keeping it in the family: it's accessible, but only to the class, its subclasses, and other classes in the same package as the class.

It's important to be careful about making variables `protected`. Making `private` variables available only in a class, and hidden even from its subclasses, has its advantages. It means that the only methods that can change the variable are the ones defined in the same class as the variable. In effect, it's another example of encapsulation for safety's sake—after all, the designer of a class has no idea what the designer of a subclass might do, advertently or inadvertently, and yet the class and all its methods must work as advertised. If the `Bird` class modifies the `Heart` property, the `maintainCirculation` method might fail (which would not be good for the `Bird`). If you want the ultimate protection, keep variables `private` and provide methods that make instance variables accessible to any other object, but only on the class's own terms.

To summarize, a class can directly access:

- its own variables
- its own methods
- `protected` or `public` instance variables of its superclasses
- `protected` or `public` methods belonging to its superclasses
- `public` methods of other classes it knows about

3.3.5 **Method resolution**

Given that classes can inherit methods and even instance variables, and that sometimes their ancestors may define things in different ways, how does Java know which variable or method is being referred to? If Java sees a call to a `move` method in the `Penguin` class, for example, where does it look to find out more about that method? If someone sends a `Swan` a `fly` message, how does the `Swan` know what to do? Any given variable or method could be defined in the class itself and/or any number of superclasses.

The answer is method resolution. **Method resolution** is a technique for determining which method a name refers to. When Java determines that you are calling a method on an instance of a class, it checks to see if that method is explicitly defined in that class. If not, Java assumes it must be an inherited method and checks the immediate superclass. If it is defined there, Java is done. If not, it continues to check successive superclasses until it either finds the method or hits the highest-level superclass, `Object`. By

keyconcept

Method resolution is a technique for determining which method a name refers to.

using this technique, illustrated in Figure 3.4, Java properly finds an overridden definition in a subclass rather than the original definition in its superclass. If Java never finds a definition of the method, it generates an error.

For example, suppose someone sends a `Penguin` a `fly` message. Java looks first in the `Penguin` class definition and finds the definition right there. The fact that the method is also defined in `Bird` does not matter, since it never gets to check `Bird`. Alternatively, suppose someone sends a `Crow` a `fly` method. The compiler starts by looking in the `Crow` class definition. This time, however, it won't find the definition. So it continues to `Crow`'s superclass, `Bird`. It finds a definition there, so it stops.

Finally, suppose someone sends the `Crow` a `goHome` message. Java looks first in the class definition of `Crow`. It won't find the definition there, so it looks next in the definition for `Crow`'s superclass, `Bird`. Once again, it fails to find a definition, so it continues to the definition of `Bird`'s superclass, `Animal`. Here at last it finds a definition for the method, so it stops.

In theory, Java follows the same procedure for finding instance variables as for method definitions: look in the current class. If Java finds the desired variable there, it stops; otherwise, it checks the superclass, and keeps going until it either finds it or reaches the class

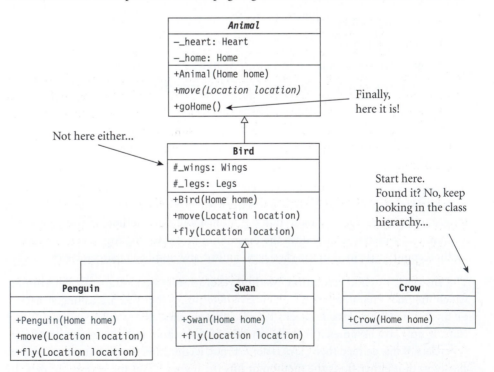

Figure 3.4 ■ Method resolution: Java finds the `goHome` method for `Crow`.

`Object` and can go no further. In practice, there is a big difference: instance variables that have been declared `private` in a superclass don't count. The variable Java's looking for must either be in the current class or be in some ancestor class and not be declared `private`—which rules out most of the instance variables in ancestor classes.

One last point about declaring a variable `public`: you should never declare a `public` variable in the code you write connected with this book, as it is a violation of encapsulation, but you should be able to recognize the Java syntax for using a `public` variable when you see it. Just as methods are invoked by using the name of an instance variable belonging to the right class, followed by a dot, followed by the name of the method (plus its parameters), public instance variables are referred to by using the name of an instance variable belonging to the right class, followed by a dot, followed by the name of the instance variable within that class.

■ 3.4 ■ Working Out with **Inheritance**—the Blobs

O b j e c t i v e s :
- ☑ Practice using inheritance
- ☑ Write an interactive program
- ☑ Write a program that accepts mouse input

In the last chapter, we built a cartoon using shapes from the Wheels library. Now instead of a `Sun`, we're going to have characters called `Blobs`. Instead of just sitting on the screen, the `Blobs` will react when we click on them. They will turn blue when we press the mouse and red when we let go. And instead of one `Sun`, we're going to create two kinds of `Blobs`—a talkative `Blob` and a `Blob` that winks—and organize them into an inheritance hierarchy.

3.4.1 Background: mouse methods in Wheels

We need one more piece of information to write this program: how to make graphical shapes react when we click on them. We'll see how to do this from scratch in Chapters 7 and 8, but for now, Wheels has done a lot of the work for us. All of the shapes in Wheels inherit the four stubs shown in Listing 3.1. These methods are called automatically when the mouse is pressed, released, or clicked, respectively, on one of the shapes in Wheels, or when one of the shapes is dragged with the mouse. (Note that a mouse click is the same as a mouse press plus a mouse release; a mouse drag includes a press, some movement, and then a release. We will not use a mouse click in this program, because we don't want to change the `Blobs` permanently; we just want to make something happen temporarily

```
1   public void mousePressed (java.awt.event.MouseEvent e) {}
2   public void mouseReleased (java.awt.event.MouseEvent e) {}
3   public void mouseClicked (java.awt.event.MouseEvent e) {}
4   public void mouseDragged (java.awt.event.MouseEvent e) {}
```

Listing 3.1 ■ Mouse methods for the shapes in Wheels

while we're holding the mouse down.) Up to now, there has been no sign that our shapes responded to mouse input. Because the methods have empty bodies, if we clicked on the sun in the `SunCartoon` nothing happened, so there was no way to tell that the method was actually being called.

These methods make things easy for us because they do the work of detecting the mouse input. All we need to do is to override one or more of them by filling in its method body to make something actually happen. Whatever statements we put in the method body will be executed when the corresponding event happens.

3.4.2 Analysis

Here's our problem description:

> The program should display two `Blobs`. `Blobs` have a round, red face and two round black eyes. They respond to a mouse press by turning blue, and turn back to red when we let go. There are two types of `Blobs`. In addition to turning blue, one displays a cartoon bubble with a message; the other winks. When we let go, the `Blobs` return to their original non-winking, non-talking state. The program should display one instance of each type of `Blob`.

Let's start with a grammatical analysis of the problem description. The nouns in this description are "program," "`Blobs`," "face," "eyes," "types," "cartoon bubble," "message," and "instance." `Blob` is the name of an object. "Two types" suggests that there are two subclasses of `Blob`. The verb "have" indicates that the eyes and the face are parts of the `Blobs`. We need a cartoon bubble, which naturally will contain a message of some kind.

The adjectives are "two," "round," "red," "blue," "black," and "one." Round shapes are circles—`Ellipses` whose height and width are equal. The face and eyes of the `Blobs` will all be circles. `Ellipses` have a built-in color attribute, so all we need to do is to set the color attribute's value to black for the eyes and red for the face. To display our `Blobs`, as usual, we write a subclass of `Frame`. The `Frame` contains two objects, one of each type of `Blob`.

Finally, the verbs, other than "have," are "display," "turn," "are," "click," "release," and "wink." The `Blobs` must all have the capability of responding to a mouse press and mouse release. One type of `Blob` must have the capability of making a conversation bubble appear and disappear; the other must have the capability of winking its eye.

A screenshot of the program we're going to write, just after the user has pressed the mouse on the `TalkativeBlob`, is shown in Figure 3.5.

3.4.3 **Design**

As usual, we use a `Frame` to model a displayable rectangular area. This time we call it `BlobApp`. We define a class `Blob`, which is an `Ellipse`, with two more `Ellipses` for its eyes. `Blob` has two subclasses, `TalkativeBlob` and `WinkingBlob`, and the `Frame` contains one of each of those. Finally, we use a `ConversationBubble` to model the conversation bubble that one of the `Blobs` needs to display.

A UML diagram for our design is shown in Figure 3.6. The eyes (which are `Ellipses`) and `ConversationBubble` are not shown, because they are both classes from Wheels, rather than classes we need to define for this program. The top-level class is `BlobApp`, and this is the class that will contain our `main` method. It contains the `TalkativeBlob` and `WinkingBlob` classes, which are both subclasses of `Blob`.

Figure 3.5 ■ The `BlobApp` program, just after the user presses the mouse on `TalkativeBlob`.

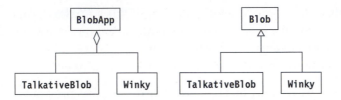

Figure 3.6 ■ UML diagram for the `BlobApp` program. (For readability, we break the diagram into two parts, one showing containment and the other showing inheritance.)

`TalkativeBlob` and `WinkingBlob` are not parts of the `BlobApp` in the same way that the `Blob`'s eyes are part of the `Blob`. It seems more accurate to say that they're contained in the window. We will often see this kind of graphical containment relationship between two objects.

Both the containment relationship and the component relationship are represented using the same diamond-headed arrow. And both share key characteristics: an instance of `TalkativeBlob` is initialized in the same way as a component—the constructor creates a new object—and the `TalkativeBlob` lasts no longer than the `BlobApp` that contains it. Nevertheless, the two relationships model different things, and for clarity we distinguish between them by using "contains" and "containment" for one relationship and "component" and "is composed of" for the other.

3.4.4 **Implementation: `BlobApp` with one `Blob`**

Let's go through the classes we need one by one, starting with the top-level class `BlobApp`, shown in Listing 3.2. This is very similar to the two subclasses of `Frame` we have defined already. The main method calls the constructor, and the constructor in turn creates instances of the `Frame`'s two peer objects, one `WinkingBlob` located at (300, 300) and one `TalkativeBlob`, located at (400, 200).

Now consider the `Blob` class shown in Listing 3.3. Our `Blob` is an `Ellipse` with two eyes. Note that the eyes are declared `protected`. We can infer that one or more of the `Blob`'s subclasses need to access the eyes. The `Blob`'s constructor takes two `int`s as parameters, so we use absolute positioning to place the `Blob` in the `Frame`; we then use relative positioning to place the eyes relative to the `Blob`. The eyes' color is set to black. We don't need to set the color of the `Blob` itself, because its default color is red.

Finally, consider the `mousePressed` and `mouseReleased` methods. See how easy it is to make the `Blob` respond? With only one line of code, we make the `Blob` respond to a mouse press by turning blue, and with another line of code, we make the `Blob` turn red again when the mouse is released. Between our mouse press (the stimulus) and the `Blob`'s response, Java and Wheels do a lot of work behind the scenes. We don't need to know about any of that now. (We'll show how it works later, in Chapters 7 and 8.) The parameter `MouseEvent` includes useful information such as exactly where the mouse was pressed. We ignore it for now, because we do not need any of its information here.

3.4.5 **Testing (part 1)**

Create a `BlobApp` now with just a `Blob` in it, instead of the `WinkingBlob` and `TalkativeBlob`, to make sure that the program is working so far.

3.4.6 **Implementation: a `BlobApp` with a `WinkingBlob`**

Next, let's create a `Blob` that can wink. The code for the `WinkingBlob` class is given in Listing 3.4. `WinkingBlob`'s constructor calls its superclass's constructor and passes on

```
1    /**
2     * Chapter 3: BlobApp.java
3     * Our first interactive program.
4     * Displays two "Blobs" that respond to mouse clicks.
5     */
6    import wheels.users.*;
7
8    public class BlobApp extends Frame {
9        private WinkingBlob _winkingBlob;
10       private TalkativeBlob _talkativeBlob;
11
12       public BlobApp() {
13           super();
14           _winkingBlob = new WinkingBlob(300, 300);
15           _talkativeBlob = new
16               TalkativeBlob(400, 200, "I'm so Happy!");
17       }
18
19       public static void main (String[] args) {
20           BlobApp app = new BlobApp();
21       }
22   }
```

Listing 3.2 ■ `BlobApp.java`

the location for the `Blob`. `WinkingBlob`'s properties are the same as the `Blob`'s, but it overrides two of the `Blob`'s capabilities. When the mouse is pressed on an instance of `WinkingBlob`, `WinkingBlob` winks by changing the shape of its left eye. When the mouse is released, `WinkingBlob` restores its eye to its original shape.

Does an instance of `WinkingBlob` still turn blue when the mouse is pressed? According to the specifications, it should. Can you tell from the code what happens?

In fact, `WinkingBlob` does still turn blue, in addition to winking. We can tell because of the statement

```
super.mousePressed(e);
```

```
1    /**
2     * Chapter 3: Blob.java
3     * Models a creature with two eyes.
4     */
5    import wheels.users.*;
6
7    public class Blob extends Ellipse {
8        protected Ellipse _leftEye, _rightEye;
9
10       public Blob(int x, int y) {
11           super(x, y);
12           _leftEye = new Ellipse(java.awt.Color.BLACK);
13           _rightEye = new Ellipse(java.awt.Color.BLACK);
14           this.setSize(100, 100);
15           _leftEye.setSize(30, 30);
16           _rightEye.setSize(30, 30);
17           _leftEye.setLocation(this.getLocation().x+22,
18                                  this.getLocation().y+10);
19           _rightEye.setLocation(this.getLocation().x+47,
20                                  this.getLocation().y+10);
21       }
22       public void mousePressed(java.awt.event.MouseEvent e){
23               this.setFillColor(java.awt.Color.BLUE);
24       }
25       public void mouseReleased(java.awt.event.MouseEvent e){
26           this.setFillColor(java.awt.Color.RED);
27       }
28   }
```

Listing 3.3 ■ `Blob.java`

```
1    /**
2     * Chapter 3: WinkingBlob.java
3     * Extends the Blob class to add the
4     * ability to wink when clicked on.
5     */
6    import wheels.users.*;
7
8    public class WinkingBlob extends Blob {
9        public WinkingBlob (int x, int y) {
10           super(x, y);
11       }
12
13       public void mousePressed(java.awt.event.MouseEvent e){
14           super.mousePressed(e);
15           _leftEye.setSize(30, 5);
16           _leftEye.setLocation(_leftEye.getLocation().x,
17                                _leftEye.getLocation().y+15);
18       }
19
20       public void mouseReleased(java.awt.event.MouseEvent e){
21           super.mouseReleased(e);
22           _leftEye.setSize(30, 30);
23           _leftEye.setLocation(_leftEye.getLocation().x,
24                                _leftEye.getLocation().y-15);
25       }
26   }
```

Listing 3.4 ■ `WinkingBlob.java`

This statement says, "Look in my superclasses until you find a version of this method, and invoke it." Similarly, we can tell that `WinkingBlob` turns back to red when the mouse is released because of the line

```
super.mouseReleased(e);
```

in `WinkingBlob`'s `mouseReleased` method. These are two more examples of partial overriding, a very useful technique.

3.4.7 Testing (part 2)

Create a `BlobApp` now with just a `WinkingBlob` in it, instead of the `Blob` you had earlier, to make sure that the program is working so far. Compile and run your program.

3.4.8 **Implementation: a `BlobApp` with a `WinkingBlob` and a `TalkativeBlob`**

Finally, consider the definition of the fourth class, `TalkativeBlob`, shown in Listing 3.5. This class has a `ConversationBubble` as its peer object. After creating a basic `Blob`, the constructor initializes the `ConversationBubble` with whatever text was given as a parameter and uses relative positioning to place the bubble relative to the `TalkativeBlob`. Then we see a useful method, `hide`, which causes the `ConversationBubble` to disappear from sight. When the mouse is pressed, the `show` method causes it to appear again briefly, until the mouse is released and `hide` is invoked again.

3.4.9 **Final Testing**

First, modify the program so that it has a `TalkativeBlob` instead of a `WinkingBlob`. Enter, compile, and run this program. When you're sure that the `TalkativeBlob` works

```
1    /**
2     * Chapter 3: TalkativeBlob.java
3     * Extends the Blob class to add
4     * the capability of displaying a message when clicked on.
5     */
6    import wheels.users.*;
7
8    public class TalkativeBlob extends Blob {
9        private ConversationBubble _bubble;
10
11       public TalkativeBlob(int x, int y, String speech) {
12           super(x, y);
13           _bubble = new ConversationBubble(speech);
14           _bubble.setLocation(x-100, y-100);
15           _bubble.hide();
16       }
17       public void mousePressed(java.awt.event.MouseEvent e){
18           _bubble.show();
19       }
20       public void mouseReleased(java.awt.event.MouseEvent e){
21           _bubble.hide();
22       }
23   }
```

Listing 3.5 ■ `TalkativeBlob.java`

just as it is supposed to, modify the program so you have both a `TalkativeBlob` and a `WinkingBlob` in your `BlobApp`, as shown in Figure 3.5. Compile, run, and test this final version. Voilà! You have written an interactive program!

■ Summary ■

The use of abstraction as a tool to control complexity is a theme of this book. We have seen more than one example already. When designing our models, for instance, we include only the classes, properties, and capabilities that we need, abstracting from the real world. In our picture of a sun in the last chapter, for example, we didn't model the temperature, or the distance of the sun from the earth: the only aspects of the sun we modeled were its shape and color. Methods with parameters are another example: rather than giving our classes hundreds of specific methods, we write a few general methods and use parameters to model the details associated with the message. `Ellipses` have a single `setSize` method, rather than `setWidthTo0`, `setWidthTo1`, `setWidthTo2`, `setWidthTo3`, `setHeightTo0`, and so on for every possible width and height. Inheritance is yet another example of abstraction: it lets us organize classes into groups of similar classes, modeling the way that people organize the things they encounter in the world.

Inheritance also illustrates a second key theme: appropriate laziness and reuse. If several classes share methods and/or instance variables, it would not be appropriately lazy to write the same code for these methods and variables over and over. Instead, inheritance lets us factor them out and define them just once, in a superclass. Subclasses inherit all of the properties and capabilities of their superclasses and can simply reuse them.

Inheritance is a powerful modeling mechanism for describing both what is similar about objects (abstracted in the superclass) and what is different (encoded in added properties and methods, overridden methods, and definitions for `abstract` methods). In addition, it has tremendous potential for saving us work by allowing us to reuse methods written and tested for one class in any number of subclasses.

■ Self-Check Questions ■

(The answers to these questions can be found on the book's website, www.aw.com/sanders)

1. What is inheritance in Java? Explain and give an example from real life.
2. Why is inheritance an important concept in object-oriented programming?
3. What is an is-a relationship?
4. What is a superclass?

5. What is a subclass?

6. What does it mean to override an inherited method? How is it different from method overloading, which we discussed in Chapter 2?

7. What is the syntax for overriding an inherited method?

8. What is the function of the Java keyword `super`?

9. What is an `abstract` class?

10. When do you absolutely have to make a class `abstract`?

11. In general, when should you make a class `abstract`?

12. What properties and capabilities do subclasses inherit from their superclasses in Java?

13. What is the role of the built-in Java class `Object`?

14. Explain the `protected` keyword in Java.

15. What are the pros and cons of declaring something `protected` in Java?

16. What is method resolution?

17. What is Java's technique for method resolution?

18. How many superclasses can a Java class have?

19. What is a stub?

■ Exercises ■

Applying the Facts

1. Write the code (with an empty body) for a new `abstract` class, `Student`.

2. Write the code (with an empty body) for a new `abstract` class, `CartoonCharacter`.

3. Write the code (with an empty body) for two classes, `HighSchoolStudent` and `CollegeStudent`, that are subclasses of the `abstract` class `Student`.

4. Write the code (with an empty body) for three classes, `PrairieDog`, `BlueJay`, and `Walrus`, that are subclasses of the `abstract` class `Animal`.

5. Use UML notation to diagram two classes, `CollegeStudent` and `HighSchoolStudent`, and show that they are subclasses of the `abstract` class `Student`.

6. Use UML notation to diagram three classes, `PrairieDog`, `BlueJay`, and `Walrus`, and show that they are all subclasses of a fourth class, `Animal`.

7. If Java allowed a class to inherit from more than one superclass (as C++ does), what problems might that cause for method resolution?

8. Suppose we want to declare a variable _gpa in the Student class, but the CollegeStudent and HighSchoolStudent classes also need explicit access to that variable. What should we do? Give a Java statement that would solve this problem and explain where in your program you would put that statement.

9. Suppose we've designed three classes, MusicalInstrument, Drums, and Guitar, and we find that we're repeating a lot of the same code in the three classes. What should we do?

10. Write a stub for the Perch class called swim. It should take two ints as parameters, an *x*-distance and a *y*-distance, so that it knows how far to swim, and return nothing.

11. Suppose the Perch class has instance variables for three parts, _body, _tail and _fin, and each of those parts has a setLocation method. Fill in the body of the swim method from question 10.

Answer questions 12–20 with reference to Figure 3.7.

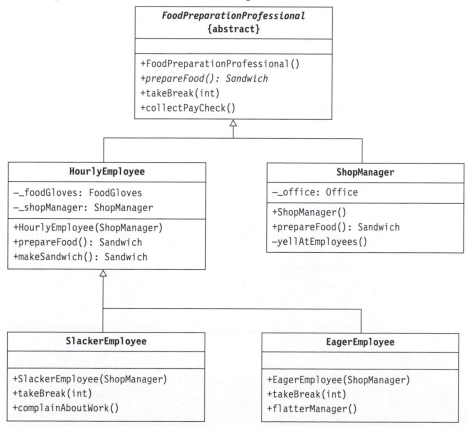

Figure 3.7 ■ Diagram for questions 12–20.

12. If another object sends a `makeSandwich` method to an instance of `EagerEmployee`, which method definition is executed (if any)? Why?

13. If another object sends a `takeBreak` message to an instance of `SlackerEmployee`, which method definition is executed (if any)? Why?

14. If another object sends a `takeBreak` message to an instance of `ShopManager`, which method definition is executed (if any)? Why?

15. If someone sends a `takeBreak` message to a `FoodPreparationProfessional`, which method definition is executed (if any)? Why?

16. If someone sends a `yellAtEmployees` method to a `ShopManager`, which method definition is executed (if any)? Why?

17. If another object sends a `complainAboutWork` message to a `SlackerEmployee`, which method definition is executed (if any)? Why?

18. If another object sends a `complainAboutWork` message to an `HourlyEmployee`, which method definition is executed (if any)? Why?

19. If another object sends a `complainAboutWork` message to an `EagerEmployee`, which method definition is executed (if any)? Why?

20. If another object sends a `prepareFood` message to an `EagerEmployee`, which method definition is executed (if any)? Why?

Debugging Programs

Identify the error(s) in each of the following code fragments:

1.
```java
public abstract class Guitar {...}
public class BassGuitar extends Guitar {...}
public class Drums {...}
public class Drums {
        private Drums _drums;
        private Guitar _guitar;

        public Band() {
            _drums = new Drums();
            _guitar = new Guitar();
        }
    }
```

2.
```java
public abstract class Student {
        ...
        public abstract goToClass() { ...}
    }
```

```
3.  public abstract class Student {
            ...
            public abstract goToClass();
            public abstract takeNotes();
            public abstract study();
    }
    public class CompSciStudent extends Student {
    ...
    public CompSciStudent() {...}
    public void takeNotes {...}
    public void study {...}
    }
```

■ Programming Projects ■

Modifying Programs

1. Modify the BlobApp program so that there is a HappyBlob that is a subclass of TalkativeBlob that always says "I'm so happy!" and a SadBlob, also a subclass of TalkativeBlob, that always says "I'm sad!"

2. Modify the BlobApp program so that WinkingBlob blinks its right eye instead of its left.

3. Modify the BlobApp program to add a GreedyBlob that gets larger and larger when you click on it.

4. Modify the BlobApp program to add a ShyBlob that moves away when you click on it.

5. Modify the BlobApp program to add a MeltingBlob that gets smaller and smaller when you click on it.

Writing Programs

1. Write a program that models a simple game. It should display three rectangles of the same color (they can be any color but yellow); exactly one of these rectangles, when clicked on, should turn yellow. The user must guess which rectangle is hiding the "gold." Your program should include a rock class that is clicked on and does nothing, and a subclass of that class that turns yellow when clicked on.

2. Design an inheritance hierarchy with a superclass Robot and two subclasses that are different types of Robots. Like the Blobs, each type of Robot should behave slightly differently. Write a program that displays an instance of each type of Robot.

3. Write a program that displays two `Blobs` on the screen, `LeaderBlob` and `FollowerBlob`. When the mouse is pressed on the `FollowerBlob`, nothing happens; when the mouse is pressed on the `LeaderBlob`, they both turn green. When the mouse is released, they both turn back to red.

4. Using techniques from both Chapter 2 and this chapter, write a program that displays a snowman. When you click on it, the snowman should melt (i.e., get smaller and smaller) and gradually disappear. Its hat should stay on its head as it melts and eventually be left sitting on the ground. This `MeltingSnowman` should be a subclass of the `Snowman` from Chapter 2.

chapter **4**

Interfaces

OBJECTIVES

After reading this chapter, you should be able to:

- ☑ Define interface
- ☑ Explain how interfaces are used in Java
- ☑ Compare and contrast Java interfaces with concrete and abstract classes
- ☑ Write a Java interface
- ☑ Learn some simple recipes for writing programs
- ☑ Use Java interfaces to set a policy for class methods

■ 4.1 ■ Introduction

Classes let us group similar objects together, and inheritance lets us group similar classes together. Sometimes, however, we'd like to group together objects that are related only because they all play a particular role. For example, we might like to group together classes that model humans, birds, ants, space aliens, and robots, because they all can walk. These classes may not have anything else in common. It wouldn't be appropriate to give them a single superclass, because there isn't a useful category that contains them all, but they do share a particular ability. In this chapter, we discuss the mechanism provided by Java for modeling such a situation, called an interface.

In addition, we give you some simple recipes for writing programs. After you see enough class and method definitions, you observe certain patterns: ways of writing code that are repeated over and over even though they are not required by the syntax of the language. Recognizing and using these patterns, or recipes, will help you to write code more quickly and easily.

127

■ 4.2 ■ **Concepts**

Java's **interface**s specify a set of responsibilities, or in other words, a role. A class doesn't have to implement any interfaces at all, but if it does, the interface describes the capabilities it needs to have. In effect, it's like a job description for classes.

Similarly, implementing an interface is like accepting a job. Any concrete class that implements an interface is promising that it can and will do the job defined by the interface. An `abstract` class that implements an interface makes the same promise on behalf of its concrete subclasses: any concrete subclass will have the capabilities needed to do this job.

The interface defines a job that an object is willing to do for other objects, but it provides absolutely no code reuse. An interface is even more abstract than an `abstract` class: it never includes any instance variables or method bodies. The body of an interface contains only a list of method signatures. The method bodies must be written over and over in each class that implements the interface.

Nevertheless, because each class that implements an interface must use the same method names and signatures, interfaces help us to write cleaner, more consistent, more readable, and more maintainable code. If we need a `walk` method in six different classes, we could define it in those classes, with or without using an interface. But without an interface, we might have a `walk` method that takes one parameter in one class and a `walk` method that takes two parameters in another class, both performing the same task. Or we might have `walk`, `amble`, `stroll`, `toddle`, and `stride`, all performing similar tasks, in different classes. If we enforce some consistency in the signatures of these methods, it is much easier to design and write the other objects that call them.

Interfaces allow us to highlight the different roles played by each class in our model. A single class can implement many interfaces. One class might implement the interfaces `Walker`, `Runner`, `Pilot`, `Friend`, `Musician`, and more. Looking at this from another angle, interfaces let us model the fact that a given class has capabilities in common with different groups of other classes: the group of `Walker`s, the group of `Musician`s, and so forth.

If we look at an object in terms of just one of its interfaces, however, we are getting a limited view. An interface typically models only part of an object's capabilities. If we look at a class just as a `Musician`, we may miss the fact that it also has the ability to run a marathon. Thus there's a tradeoff: if we think of an object in very general, abstract terms, we can't take advantage of its distinctive characteristics.

■ 4.3 ■ Mechanics

Like inheritance, interfaces in Java require very little syntax. Making effective use of interfaces is, once again, more a matter of learning good design and modeling skills than learning the syntax. We introduce the syntax you need in this section, along with some examples.

4.3.1 Defining and implementing interfaces

Suppose we want to capture the fact that a number of things in our model—including dogs, planets, and bicycles—can all move. We can model that similarity by creating an interface `Mover`, like this:

```java
public interface Mover {
    public void move(int x, int y);
    public Location getLocation();
}
```

As you can see, interface definitions look a lot like class definitions. They start with the word `public`, followed by the Java keyword `interface` instead of `class`, followed by the name of the interface. Interface names often end in -er: `Mover`, `Walker`, and so forth. Another common type of interface name ends in "able": we might want to group objects according to whether they are `Movable`, for example. (There isn't really a good way to choose the -er versus the -able suffix; just pick the name that best describes what you are trying to model.) Finally, after the name of the interface, its body is enclosed in curly brackets.

keyconcept

Interface names often end in -er or -able.

The syntax for an interface definition is almost the same as for a class definition, but not quite. First, interfaces do not use the keyword `abstract`. Because all interface methods are `abstract`, there's no need to say so; it would be redundant to say `public abstract interface Mover`. Second, interfaces never include instance variables or method bodies. And finally, interface definitions never include a constructor, because interfaces can never be instantiated.

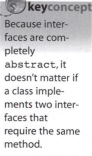

keyconcept

Because interfaces are completely abstract, it doesn't matter if a class implements two interfaces that require the same method.

Once we have defined an interface, we define a class that implements that interface. For example, if we have a class `Dog` and we want that class to take on the responsibilities of the `Mover` interface, we use the Java keyword `implements` in the class definition, like this:

```java
public class Dog implements Mover {
    ...
}
```

We define a class that both implements an interface and extends a superclass like this:

```
public class Dog extends Animal implements Mover {
    ...
}
```

A class can both implement an interface and extend a superclass at the same time, because interfaces and superclasses represent different forms of modeling.

If a class implements an interface, it must define every method declared in that interface or be declared `abstract`. Its subclasses must also define (or inherit a definition for) every method declared in the interface, or they too must be declared `abstract`. To satisfy an interface, the class's method definition must exactly match the signature given in the interface: return the same type, have the same name, and accept the same parameters in the same order.

Once we have defined an interface, we can use the interface name almost anywhere we could have used a class name. The only exception is in an initialization statement after the keyword `new`. Even this makes sense, however, since we can't use an abstract class there either.

> **keyconcept**
>
> You can use an interface name anywhere you could have used a class name, except in an initialization statement after the keyword `new`.

Figure 4.1 gives part of a class diagram showing that three classes, `Dog`, `Bicycle`, and `Planet`, all implement the interface `Mover`. In a UML class diagram, the arrows connecting a class to its interface are like inheritance arrows, with a triangle for an arrowhead pointing toward the interface, but they are drawn with dotted lines. Interfaces are indicated by a box containing their name, just like classes, but with the word "interface" inside double angle brackets, as shown.

4.3.2 Classes that implement multiple interfaces

What happens when a class implements more than one interface? Let's consider the class definition for a box, something that can both hold things and be held—something that implements both `Holder` and `Holdable`.

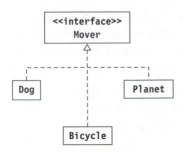

Figure 4.1 ■ Class diagram illustrating UML for interfaces.

First we need to define the `Holder` interface. We want to model things that can hold other things. Of course, this is a very general specification: it could apply to almost anything, from grocery sacks to hotels to cargo vehicles. In fact, just about the only obvious property or capability these objects have in common is that they can hold things. Since holding things is a behavior, and it does not correspond to an obvious class, we model the ability to hold things with an interface.

For our purposes, all that objects implementing `Holder` need to be concerned about is holding onto and releasing other objects that implement `Holdable` (which we will define in a moment). Here's our definition:

```
public interface Holder {
    void add(Holdable toBeHeld);
    Holdable release();
}
```

Next, we need to define `Holdable`. `Holders` do not necessarily hold the same things: grocery sacks hold food, hotels hold people (and luggage), and cargo vehicles hold packages (which in turn hold other things). We must find some commonality among those objects that are being held.

What are the responsibilities of the `Holdable` role? Or, from another perspective, what characteristics are important to an object that must hold another? For our purposes, all that the containing object cares about is the object's size and weight. We can represent our simple `Holdable` objects with the following interface:

```
public interface Holdable {
    Weight getWeight();
    Dimensions getDimensions();
}
```

If we extend this model, we might add other characteristics to the interface, such as the object's value and whether it's alive or fragile.

Now we've defined the interfaces, here's the class definition for a `Box`. (See Listing 4.1.) (Our `Box` keeps track of its `Holdable` contents by adding them to or releasing them from an imaginary `HoldableBag` that implements `Holder` and can contain an arbitrary number of `Holdables`. We take this somewhat awkward approach, because we do not yet have the syntax to test whether the `Box` is full before adding another `Holdable`.)

Aside from the `implements` clause, the remainder of the syntax for this definition is the same as other class definitions. The `Box` class contains three instance variables, which model its weight, its dimensions, and the `HoldableBag` for its contents.

```
 1   /**
 2    * Chapter 4: Box.java
 3    * A class that implements two interfaces.
 4    */
 5   public class Box implements Holder, Holdable {
 6       private Weight _weight; // attributes
 7       private Dimensions _size;
 8       private HoldableBag _bag; // component
 9
10       public Box(Weight emptyWeight, Dimensions size) {
11           super();
12           _weight = emptyWeight;
13           _size = size;
14           _bag = new HoldableBag();
15       }
16       //implement Holder methods
17       public void add(Holdable toBeHeld) {
18           _bag.add(toBeHeld);
19           _weight.increaseBy(toBeHeld.getWeight());
20       }
21       public Holdable release() {
22           Holdable holdable = _bag.release();
23           _weight.decreaseBy(holdable.getWeight());
24           return holdable;
25       }
26
27       //implement Holdable methods
28       public Weight getWeight() {
29           return _weight;
30       }
31       public Dimension getDimensions() {
32           return _size;
33       }
34   }
```

Listing 4.1 ■ Box, a class that implements two interfaces

The constructor accepts the box's empty weight and dimensions as parameters. This makes sense, because we may want to have different types of boxes in our model, like cardboard, plastic, or steel, and we want to be able to model boxes of different sizes. We use classes to represent these data because we do not know (or care) what units are used to represent these values, we just want them to match. Treating units in a general way is very important in Java programs because they may be used internationally. Thus, `Weight` may be represented in pounds or grams; `Dimensions` may be in feet or meters. The class will keep track of the units and deal with converting between all the different measures so that you do not need to worry about it.

Next, the class includes a method definition for each method named in each interface it implements—necessary, if the class is to be concrete. The method bodies may vary from class to class; the interface just requires that there be some definition. Typically, the class would also implement some additional methods specific to that class, not just the methods specified by the interface.

What happens if a class implements two interfaces that each require the same method? Because the interfaces only say what has to be done and not how, there's no conflict between them. You should consider revising the interfaces to eliminate the overlap, but if one or both of them is contained in a package written by someone else, that may not be possible. In any event, if two methods really are the same—that is, if their signatures are the same—the class can satisfy both at the same time by defining one method with that signature.

4.3.3 **Extending interfaces**

Just as classes can extend other classes, interfaces can extend other interfaces. Consider the problem of transporting `Holdable` objects from one place to another. Many real-world things solve this problem: taxis transport people, freight elevators transport packages up and down, and pack elephants transport luggage. Let's look at the interface for something that transports things from place to place:

```
public interface Transporter extends Holder, Mover {
    Currency chargeFee();
}
```

This sort of an object acts as `Mover` and a `Holder` because it knows how to move itself and it must be able to hold things while it is doing so. Additionally, these objects generally charge a fee for their efforts.

keyconcept

Just as classes can extend other classes, interfaces can extend other interfaces. Sub-interfaces inherit all the methods declared in their super-interfaces.

Like classes, interfaces use the keyword `extends` to indicate that an interface adds to an existing interface or interfaces. To extend multiple interfaces, we simply list the names of all the interfaces, separated by commas. Any new methods are then declared in the interface as usual.

As expected, any concrete class that implements this interface must provide definitions for the `chargeFee` message as well as the messages declared in the super-interfaces `move`, `getLocation`, `add`, and `release`.

4.3.4 **Design choices: interfaces vs. `abstract` classes**

If we want to capture the fact that a group of objects all have the ability to move, we could write either an abstract class or an interface. Not only do the interface and the `abstract` class have very similar syntax, but they have the same effect: they both require classes to implement methods with particular signatures. So how can we choose?

The main thing to take into account is that classes should model a thing or a category; interfaces should model a role or a behavior. If you want to model the relationship between a Labrador Retriever and the more general category of Dog, for example, you could define a concrete `Labrador` class and an abstract `Dog` class and use inheritance to model the relationship between the two. On the other hand, if you want to model the fact that dogs, trucks, and spaceships all move, you could define a `Dog` class, a `Truck` class, a `Spaceship` class, and a `Mover` interface and have all three classes, whether abstract or concrete, implement the same interface.

A second important factor is that classes must have exactly one superclass, but may implement any number of interfaces, or none at all. Suppose we want to model the facts that Labradors are a kind of dog, that they move, and that they chew shoes and telephone cords (and other valuable things). Only one of these facts can be modeled as a superclass, but the others can be interfaces. Moving and chewing valuable things are behaviors, so they should be interfaces; Dog is a category, so it should be modeled by a class.

Let's look at this from another angle. Suppose we have a task that requires something to make noise at the right time. The only important thing about this "something" is that it make noise at a specified volume for a specified duration. In truth, almost anything can provide these capabilities, but we do not care what other capabilities it has. Having recognized the precise capabilities needed to fulfill a specific role, we can then take advantage of any object that has accepted the responsibilities implied by the role.

We could model this situation by creating a (very) abstract superclass that captures the relevant features of a noisemaker. Many objects in our system would inherit from this common class because a wide variety of objects can make noise. We are in essence saying that each of these objects "is-a" noisemaker.

But if we want to model both noisemakers and containers as superclasses, we run into trouble. Cars, trucks, trains, and airplanes are all both noisemakers and containers, so which superclass should they extend? This model would almost certainly be wrong. Instead, we should define interfaces for each of these roles, making noise and containing things, and ask each class in our model to implement the appropriate interface (if any). Table 4.1 summarizes the differences between an interface and an abstract class.

Table 4.1 ■ Comparison of interface and abstract class.

Interface	Abstract class
Models a *role*; defines a set of responsibilities	Models an *object* with properties and capabilities
Factors out common capabilities of potentially *dissimilar* objects	Factors out common properties and capabilities of *similar* objects
Declares, but does not define, methods	Declares methods and may define some or all of them
A class can implement *multiple* interfaces	A class can extend *only one* superclass

4.3.5 **Design choices: how many interfaces to use**

Since each object can have any number of interfaces, how should we choose? Like many tools in Java (or any programming language, for that matter), interfaces can be overused, leading to an overly complex model. Compare balancing eight roles with juggling eight balls and you get an idea of how hard it is to make a good design from so many simultaneous roles. Balancing two or three roles is much easier, like juggling two or three balls. Your system design is much simpler, and you have a much better chance of success.

> **keyconcept**
> Interfaces factor out the commonality between *dissimilar* objects in a model, while classes factor out commonality between *similar* objects.

A model with several interfaces can be unwieldy, but if it is an accurate model and effectively factors out the common capabilities of many classes, it may in fact be perfectly understandable. Wheels's shapes, for example, implement the interfaces `Colorable`, `Locatable`, `Rotatable`, and `Sizable`.

To make a good decision, consider the following questions:

1. *Do the roles represented by the interface overlap in any way?* Overlapping roles may suggest that some roles are very similar, or even the same.

2. *Are these roles so disparate that no one class should be implementing all of them?* Remember that a class should have a clear purpose, even if it takes on many roles.

3. *Will the interface be implemented by more than one unrelated class?* It is not necessary that every capability be part of an interface. Interfaces are primarily useful if several implementations of the interface exist.

4.3.6 **Design choices: which capabilities to put in which interface**

Like classes, interfaces should be coherent. All the methods they list should be related to a particular role. And if you can identify a subset of the methods that you would like to use separately, they should probably be made into a separate interface.

This may all seem vague right now, but we will see an example in the next section.

■ 4.4 ■ Working Out with
Interfaces—a movable sun

O b j e c t i v e s :
☑   Write an interface and a class that implements it
☑   Create a simple shape that can be dragged using the mouse
☑   Design the interface in such a way that it can be reused for composite objects

Here's the problem description for our next program:

Write a program that contains a picture of the sun on a white background. It should be possible for the user to position the sun in the window using a mouse.

We will need two classes, a Sun and an extension of `Frame` that we call `MovableSunApp`. We'll specify the methods the `Sun` has to implement in an interface called `Draggable`.

Figure 4.2 is a UML diagram showing our design for this program. It shows our two classes, `MovableSunApp` and `Sun`, and the `Draggable` interface.

The diagram also captures two important relationships. First, the `Sun` class is contained in `MovableSunApp`. Second, the `Sun` class implements the `Draggable` interface. As noted above, the line connecting a class to an interface that it implements has the same arrowhead as the arrow for an inheritance relationship, but is made with a dotted line.

4.4.1 **Writing an interface**

We can easily put a yellow circle on a white background; we've written programs like this several times now. The challenge here is to let the user use the mouse to position the sun in a window.

Let's consider exactly what we want to happen. When the user moves the mouse over the sun and presses the mouse, we want the sun to change color, in order to give the user

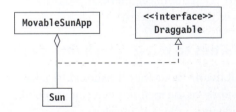

Figure 4.2 ■ UML class diagram for the `MovableSunApp` program.

feedback indicating that it has been clicked on. We want it to change back to its original color when the mouse is released. We want it to respond to being dragged by changing location. In sum, we want our sun object to have the following five capabilities:

1. setting its color

2. setting its location

3. responding to a mouse press

4. responding to being dragged with the mouse

5. responding to a mouse release

Now we have to face a design question: which of these capabilities should go into the `Draggable` interface? `Locatable` and `Colorable` are very useful interfaces; in fact, they're built into Wheels. Should we leave setting the color and setting the location out of the interface, since we know that Wheels shapes already implement `Colorable` and `Locatable`? No, because in the next section, when we create a composite object, we want to be able to reuse the same interface, and composite objects don't have these methods built in. Should we just make the composite object implement `Colorable` and `Locatable`, since those interfaces already exist? We could do that, but if we do, we'll have to write accessor methods that we don't need, because `Colorable` and `Rotatable` both require them.

To make sure that draggable objects, whether simple or composite, have the capabilities we want, and to avoid writing the unnecessary accessor methods, we put all five of the capabilities we want into an interface called `Draggable`. The code for that interface is shown in Listing 4.2. These are all familiar methods. Recall that the Wheels shapes all have `setColor` and `setLocation` methods, and they inherit the mouse methods, only

```
 1    /**
 2     * Chapter 4: Draggable.java
 3     * An interface for objects that can be dragged with a mouse.
 4     */
 5    public interface Draggable {
 6        public void setColor(java.awt.Color aColor);
 8        public void setLocation(int x, int y);
 9        public void mousePressed(java.awt.event.MouseEvent e);
10        public void mouseDragged(java.awt.event.MouseEvent e);
11        public void mouseReleased(java.awt.event.MouseEvent e);
12    }
```

Listing 4.2 ■ The `Draggable` interface

with empty bodies. All we will need to do is to override the mouse methods with methods that achieve the desired results.

4.4.2 **Writing a class that implements an interface**

Writing a class that implements an interface is very simple. For our interface, all we need to do is to say that the class "implements Draggable" and then make sure that it defines all the methods required by the interface.

Here's the skeleton of the code we need:

```
import wheels.users.*;
public class Sun extends Ellipse implements Draggable {
        ...
    public void mousePressed(java.awt.event.MouseEvent e){}
    public void mouseDragged(java.awt.event.MouseEvent e){}
    public void mouseReleased(java.awt.event.MouseEvent e){}
}
```

We don't need to include the setColor and setLocation methods, because our new class extends the Ellipse class, and so it will inherit those methods.

4.4.3 **Implementing the mouseDragged method**

The full code for the Sun class is shown in Listing 4.3.

The Sun has an instance variable called _lastMousePosition that is initialized to a Point. Point is a built-in Java class that models a mathematical point with an x and y value. Notice the syntax for getting the x and y values of the two instances of Point, currentPoint and _lastMousePosition:

```
<instance-name>.<variable-name>
```

This is the syntax for referring to a public instance variable. As remarked earlier, it is extremely risky to make instance variables public. Java's designers decided that, because the x and y values of Point are accessed so frequently and speed is important in computer graphics, the risk was justified in this case. Since we don't specify the initial x and y values for the Sun's _lastMousePosition, they are arbitrarily set to (0.0). The Sun is always yellow, and its initial location is supplied by the x and y parameters to the constructor.

The mousePressed and mouseReleased methods are both straightforward. The parameter e refers to the mouse press, and e.getPoint() returns the location of the point where the mouse was pressed. The method first uses the _lastMousePosition instance variable to save this location, and then changes the Sun's color to blue, to give the user some visual feedback that the mouse press was received. The `mouseReleased` method simply changes the `Sun`'s color back to yellow.

The `mouseDragged` method is more interesting. Here again there's a parameter e, but this time `e.getPoint(` represents the current location of the mouse as it is being dragged. Thus the line:

```
int diffX = currentPoint.x - _lastMousePosition.x;
```

```
1    /**
2     * Chapter 4: Sun.java
3     * A class that implements the Draggable interface.
4     */
5    import wheels.users.*;
6
7    public class Sun extends Ellipse implements Draggable {
8        private java.awt.Point _lastMousePosition; // attribute
9
10       public Sun(int x, int y) {
11           super(java.awt.Color.YELLOW);
12           _lastMousePosition = new java.awt.Point();
13           this.setLocation(x, y);
14       }
15
16       public void mousePressed(java.awt.event.MouseEvent e) {
17           _lastMousePosition = e.getPoint();
18           this.setColor(java.awt.Color.BLUE);
19       }
20       public void mouseDragged(java.awt.event.MouseEvent e) {
21           java.awt.Point currentPoint = e.getPoint();
22           int diffX = currentPoint.x - _lastMousePosition.x;
23           int diffY = currentPoint.y - _lastMousePosition.y;
24           this.setLocation(this.getLocation().x + diffX,
25                             this.getLocation().y + diffY);
26           _lastMousePosition = currentPoint;
27       }
28       public void mouseReleased(java.awt.event.MouseEvent e) {
29           this.setColor(java.awt.Color.YELLOW);
30       }
31   }
```

Listing 4.3 ■ The Sun class

computes how far the mouse has been dragged in the *x* direction from the place where it was first pressed (`_lastMousePosition`) to the current location. Similarly,

```
int diffY = currentPoint.y - _lastMousePosition.y;
```

computes how far the mouse has been dragged in the *y* direction.

Thus, `diffX` and `diffY` indicate how much we should change the location of the `Sun` to respond to the mouse drag. These lines of code get the old location of the `Sun` and move it the distance we have computed:

```
this.setLocation(this.getLocation().x + diffX,
                 this.getLocation().y + diffY);
```

Finally, we save the current point as the new value of `_lastMousePosition`, so that we can use it the next time the `Sun` is moved with the mouse:

```
_lastMousePosition = currentPoint;
```

After reading this method, you might be asking, "Why make things so complicated?" Why can't we just set the new location of the `Sun` to be the same location as the current point, like this:

```
public void mouseDragged(java.awt.event.MouseEvent e) {
    java.awt.Point currentPoint = e.getPoint();
    this.setLocation(currentPoint.x, currentPoint.y);
}
```

This code is much simpler, but unfortunately (as you will see if you try it out) it doesn't work. Why not? Well, the mouse is being pressed somewhere in the *middle* of the `Sun`. Recall that the "location" of the `Sun`, like all Wheels shapes, is the top left-hand corner of an imaginary box drawn around it. Suppose we press the mouse right in the center of the `Sun` and drag it a tiny amount to the right, say just one pixel. The `Sun`'s location would now be just to the right of where its center was a moment ago, causing it to move with a sudden jerk. This is why we have to compute `diffX` and `diffY` and add them to the `Sun`'s location; even though this computation increases the complexity of the code, it's necessary to make the `Sun` move the way we want it to move.

4.4.4 **Implementing the `Frame`: `MovableSunApp`**

Finally, as usual, we need a class that extends `Frame`, to create a window and display the new draggable `Sun`. The code for this class is given in Listing 4.4. This code is very straightforward, similar to the `Frame` subclasses we have already seen.

Now compile this program and try it out. Drag the `Sun` around the window, change the `Sun`'s color and starting location, and test it again until you are convinced that it works.

```
1    /**
2     * Chapter 4: MovableSunApp.java
3     * Displays a yellow circle (the sun)
4     * that can be repositioned using the mouse.
5     */
6    import wheels.users.*;
7
8    public class MovableSunApp extends Frame {
9        private Sun _sun; // component
10
11       public MovableSunApp() {
12           super();
13           _sun = new Sun(300, 40);
14           _sun.setSize(60, 60);
15       }
16
17       public static void main ( String[] args ) {
18           MovableSunApp app = new MovableSunApp();
19       }
20   }
```

Listing 4.4 ■ The MovableSunApp class

■ 4.5 ■ Working Out with
Interfaces and Composite Shapes—a movable hat

Objectives:
☑ Write an interface and two classes that implement it
☑ Create simple and composite shapes that both implement the same interface
☑ Create a composite shape that can be dragged as a unit using the mouse
☑ Create parts that know about their container
☑ Implement methods using delegation

Here's the problem description for our next program:

Write a program that contains a picture of a black hat made up of two rectangles, similar to the one in Chapter 2, on a white background. The user should be able to position the hat in the window using a mouse.

What's the difference between this and the `MovableSunApp`? In fact, they are very similar, and we can reuse much of the code from the last section. There is one key difference, however: the `Hat` is a composite object, that is, it is made up of more than one shape. This has two consequences:

1. We want the whole `Hat` to move at once, so when the `Hat` moves, it must send a message to both of its parts to move.

2. In Wheels, it's the individual shapes that know they have received some mouse input. So when we press, drag, or release the mouse over one of the parts of the hat, it must send a message to the `Hat` that contains it.

We need three classes: an extension of `Frame`, which we call `MovableHatApp`, a `Hat`, and a `HatPart` class to model the individual parts of the `Hat` that know enough to pass on a message about mouse input to the `Hat` that contains them.

Figure 4.3 is a UML diagram showing the classes in our program and their relationships. This diagram captures a lot of information, so let's examine it carefully. The `MovableHatApp` contains the `Hat`, which contains the `HatPart` (actually, two instances of `HatPart`). Both the `HatPart` and the `Hat` must implement the `Draggable` interface.

Finally, the diagram captures the relationship between the `Hat` and `HatPart` classes. The `HatPart` is not only contained by the `Hat`, it also knows about its container. In effect, it has its container as a peer object. The relationship between one object and another peer object is shown by an arrow with a simple arrowhead.

4.5.1 Getting started: the interface and the `MovableHatApp`

The `Draggable` interface is just the same as the one in the previous section, so we can just use it again without any changes. `MovableHatApp` is very simple, and similar to

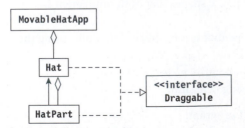

Figure 4.3 ■ UML class diagram for the `MovableHatApp` program.

extensions of the `Frame` class that we have used, both in the previous section and in earlier programs. The new code is shown in Listing 4.5.

We create a new `Hat`, give it an initial location and a size, and we're done.

4.5.2 **Creating a part that knows about its container: the `HatPart` class**

This next class includes something new, a part that knows about its container, but it is still fairly simple (see Listing 4.6). The `HatPart` is a `Rectangle`. We give it an initial color of white, so it will blend into the background until it is given its initial location. Then we initialize the _hat instance variable using a parameter, like any other peer object.

The `HatPart` implements `Draggable`, so it must be able to respond to the `setColor`, `setLocation`, `mousePressed`, `mouseReleased`, and `mouseDragged` methods. The `HatPart` is a `Rectangle`, so, like the `Sun` in the previous section, it inherits `setLocation` and `setColor` from its superclass. We must define the three mouse methods here, but that's easy: they just call the corresponding method in the `Hat`. Whenever we click on

```
1    /**
2     * Chapter 4: MovableHatApp.java
3     * Displays a composite object (a hat)that can be
4     * repositioned using a mouse.
5     */
6    import wheels.users.*;
7
8    public class MovableHatApp extends Frame {
9        private Hat _hat; // component
10
11       public MovableHatApp() {
12           super();
13           _hat = new Hat(java.awt.Color.BLACK);
14           _hat.setLocation (300, 40);
15           _hat.setSize(80, 70);
16       }
17
18       public static void main ( String[] args ) {
19           MovableHatApp app = new MovableHatApp();
20       }
21   }
```

Listing 4.5 ■ The `MovableHatApp` class

```
1    /**
2     * Chapter 4: HatPart.java
3     * Models part of a top hat.
4     * Knows about the Hat that contains it.
5     */
6    import wheels.users.*;
7
8    public class HatPart extends Rectangle implements Draggable {
9        private Hat _hat; // a peer object
10       public HatPart(Hat aHat) {
11           super(java.awt.Color.WHITE);
12           _hat = aHat;
13       }
14       public void mousePressed(java.awt.event.MouseEvent e){
15           _hat.mousePressed(e);
16       }
17       public void mouseDragged(java.awt.event.MouseEvent e){
18           _hat.mouseDragged(e);
19       }
20       public void mouseReleased(java.awt.event.MouseEvent e){
21           _hat.mouseReleased(e);
22       }
23   }
```

Listing 4.6 ■ The `HatPart` class

one of the `Hat`'s parts, the `Hat` will behave as if we had clicked on the whole `Hat`, which is just what we want.

4.5.3 Creating a composite object that moves as a unit: the `Hat` class

The last class in our program is the longest, because we have to write methods like `setColor`, `setSize`, and `setLocation` that the Wheels shapes simply inherit. In addition, this class includes code for the three mouse methods. The three mutator methods are simple, however, and the mouse methods are almost identical to those we just saw in the previous section.

The code for the `Hat` class is given in Listing 4.7. The three mutator methods, `setColor`, `setLocation`, and `setSize`, are all very similar: each one hands off its task to the `Hat`'s two parts. The only difference is that before handing off its task, `setLocation` saves the `Hat`'s current location.

```
1    /**
2     * Chapter 4: Hat.java
3     * Models a top hat. Similar to the top hat in Chapter 2,
4     * but can be repositioned using a mouse.
5     */
6    import wheels.users.*;
7
8    public class Hat implements Draggable {
9        private int _x, _y; // attributes
10       private java.awt.Point _lastMousePosition;
11       private HatPart _hatUpper, _hatBrim; // components
12
13       public Hat(java.awt.Color aColor) {
14           super();
15           _x = 80;
16           _y = 100;
17           _lastMousePosition = new java.awt.Point();
18           _hatUpper = new HatPart(this);
19           _hatBrim = new HatPart(this);
20           this.setColor(java.awt.Color.BLACK);
21           this.setLocation(80, 100);
22       }
23       public void setColor(java.awt.Color aColor) {
24           _hatBrim.setColor(aColor);
25           _hatUpper.setColor(aColor);
26       }
27       public void setLocation(int x, int y) {
28           _x = x;
29           _y = y;
30           _hatBrim.setLocation(x, y + 50);
31           _hatUpper.setLocation(x + 10, y);
32       }
33       public void setSize (int width, int height) {
34           _hatBrim.setSize(80, 20);
35           _hatUpper.setSize(60, 60);
36       }
37       public void mousePressed(java.awt.event.MouseEvent e) {
38           _lastMousePosition = e.getPoint();
39           this.setColor(java.awt.Color.BLUE);
40       }
41       public void mouseDragged(java.awt.event.MouseEvent e) {
```

Listing 4.7 ■ The Hat class (continued on next page)

```
42          java.awt.Point currentPoint = e.getPoint();
43          int diffX = currentPoint.x - _lastMousePosition.x;
44          int diffY = currentPoint.y - _lastMousePosition.y;
45          this.setLocation(_x + diffX, _y + diffY);
46          _lastMousePosition = currentPoint;
47      }
48      public void mouseReleased(java.awt.event.MouseEvent e){
48          this.setColor(java.awt.Color.black);
50      }
51  }
```

Listing 4.7 ■ The Hat class

The code for the three mouse methods is almost identical to the code we saw for the Sun. The mousePressed method is, in fact, identical. The mouseReleased method is identical except that it sets the Hat's color to black, while the Sun's normal color was, naturally, yellow. And the mouseDragged method is the same, except that in the Sun's code, we needed to use accessors to get its x and y position, and here the x and y position of the Hat are stored in instance variables.

In this code, you have examples of several important points. First, you have the design of a composite object passing commands to its parts. We have seen this before, with the Hat class in Chapter 2. Second, we have the parts passing information back to the object that contains them and, in order to make this work, we have parts that take their container as a peer object. And finally, we have the computation necessary to make a mouse-move operation work. (From a common-sense point of view, it may not seem as if the "peers" of an object A could include the object that contains A or the object that A is a part of. Recall from Chapter 1, though, that any instance variable that is neither an attribute nor a component is a peer.)

■ 4.6 ■ Recipes

One of the themes of this book is "appropriate laziness": when programming, never do any more work than you have to! This applies in a concrete way to code: reuse code whenever you legitimately can, and write your code so that it can be reused in the future.

Another kind of reuse is more abstract. Experienced programmers recognize that certain ways of writing methods, objects, and combinations of related objects occur again and again. If you can identify a useful pattern and know when to follow it, you can save yourself a lot of work. In real life, for example, if you were designing a supermarket, you might use the pattern "put the milk in the far back corner" instead of inventing an original layout. (As you may have noticed, many supermarkets are laid out this way. It is an effective arrangement, because the many customers who stop just for milk are more likely to buy other things if they have to walk all through the store to find it.)

Design patterns, patterns of related objects that help to design a solution to a problem, are so important that we spend all of Chapter 9 discussing them. Here, we point out a number of simpler patterns that we call "recipes." These recipes are related to the way in which classes, or methods, or parts of methods are written. By now you have seen several programs and you may have begun to recognize these patterns already. Giving them names makes them easier to recognize and use in the future.

4.6.1 Defining classes

The first recipe we look at is the **class-definition recipe**, the set of general rules for writing class definitions shown in Listing 4.8. We have seen examples of this recipe already and will see more throughout the book. This is a recipe you should follow in nearly every class you write. A class definition starts with the instance-variable declarations, followed by the constructor or constructors, then the method definitions, and finally, the `main` method (if any).

4.6.2 Initializing instance variables

Now let's look at one part of the class-definition recipe more closely: the initialization of instance variables inside the constructor. According to the class-definition recipe, attributes should be declared first, then components, then peer objects. All instance variables should be initialized in the constructor, and they should be initialized in the order in which they were declared.

Components and contained objects are always initialized like this:

```
_<component name> = new <component type>(<optional
                                         parameters>);
```

In other words, if we're constructing an object, we construct each part of the object at the same time. This part of the class-definition recipe has been illustrated several times, starting with the `Ellipse` that is created in `FirstApp`'s constructor in Chapter 1.

Instance variables that hold a reference to a peer object are initialized in a different way. Here, the problem is to model the fact that the object being defined is associated with another object that exists independently. The object can't create its peer object in its constructor, because it already exists. So how can an object find out about its peer object? Someone has to tell it. And the way we model telling an object something when

keyconcept
Certain ways of writing methods, objects, and combinations of related objects occur again and again. If you can identify a useful pattern and know when to follow it, you can save yourself a lot of work.

```
 1    public class <classname> {
 2        /* (1) declare the instance variables */
 3        //first any attributes
 4        // then any components
 5        // then any associated peer objects
 6
 7        /* (2) the constructor */
 8        public<classname> (<parameterList>) {
 9            // invoke the superclass's constructor
10            super(<optional parameters>) ;
11
12            // initialize the attributes
13            // then the components
14            // then the peer objects
15
16            /* (3) method definitions (not main) */
17            /* (4) finally, the main method (optional) */
18        }
19    }
```

Listing 4.8 ■ The class-definition recipe

it's first constructed is by giving a parameter to the object's constructor, which then assigns it to an instance variable to "remember" it, like this:

```
_<peer object name> = <some formal parameter name>;
```

For example, when we defined the `HatPart` class in Listing 4.6, we gave it the `Hat` as a peer object.

Finally, attributes may be initialized with parameter values, with base types, or with newly created objects. Attributes can't be distinguished from components or peer objects by the syntax used to initialize them; they are distinguished by what they model.

4.6.3 Instance variables with default values

Next is the **default-value recipe**. Recall that the shapes in Wheels are colored red by default. It's useful to have some default, but we often want to create a shape with a different color. The solution is to provide two constructors. Here's how that code might be written (we have simplified it for clarity, but this is the basic idea).

```
public class Ellipse extends RectangularShape {
    public Ellipse () {
        this(java.awt.Color.RED);
    }

    public Ellipse (java.awt.Color c) {
        super(..., c);
    }
    ...
}
```

The second constructor allows the user to specify a color. The first constructor takes no parameters, supplies the default value (`java.awt.Color.RED`), and uses Java's `this` keyword to call the constructor that takes a `Color` parameter. (Java uses the keyword `this` followed by parentheses when an object calls its own constructor.) Note that the first constructor (the one with no parameters) calls the second constructor for us.

The default-value recipe is another example of appropriate laziness. Most of the code that needs to be in the constructor is written only once, in the constructor with parameters. The basic form for this recipe is shown in Listing 4.9.

4.6.4 **Accessors and mutators**

The problem this recipe solves is how to make an object's properties generally available, at least to some degree, without making them `public`. An object whose instance variables are `public` has no control—or even knowledge—of how and when they are

```
 1    public class <classname> {
 2        private <Type1> _<instance variable1>;
 3
 4        public <classname> (<Type1> <aType1>) { // general
 5            _<instance variable1> = <aType1> ; // constructor
 6
 7        }
 8        public <classname> ()   { // default constructor
 9            this(<some default value of Type1>) ;
10        }
11
12    }
```

Listing 4.9 ■ The default-value recipe

changed. On the other hand, making them completely inaccessible means that other objects that need those values can't get them. An alternative solution is to make the variables `protected`, but that solution applies only to the special case of providing access to subclasses.

The solution is to write accessor and mutator methods. **Accessor** methods are methods written specifically for the purpose of providing limited information about the values of an object's instance variables. **Mutator methods** allow the sender to change the value of a particular property in a safe way. Typically accessors and mutators come in pairs for each variable that needs access, but it may also be useful to have just an accessor method. Accessors and mutators are also commonly known as get and set methods, because, by convention, accessors start with "get" and mutators with "set." We first used Wheels's accessor and mutator methods in Chapter 2, and we have written accessor and mutator methods, including those for the `MovableHatApp`. The basic recipe for accessor and mutator methods is given in Listings 4.10 and 4.11.

At this point, you might be wondering: what's the difference between this simple mutator recipe and a `public` instance variable? Whoever calls this method can change the property's value any way they want. There is a critical difference, however. If an object has `public` instance variables, other objects (possibly written by other programmers whom we don't even know about) may include code that references those variables. If we find that other objects are assigning illegal values to the object's properties, the only way to fix it is to track down all of that other code and change it. Finding and changing all these references will be difficult, perhaps even impossible, if some of them are contained in other people's code.

On the other hand, if we have used even a minimal mutator method like the one in the above recipe, the only thing we need to change is the method body in this class. We can

```
1    public <property-type> get<property-type> () {
2        return <property-instance-variable>;
3    }
```

Listing 4.10 ■ The basic accessor recipe

```
1    public void set<property-type> (<property-type> <name>) {
2        <property-instance-variable> = <name>;
3    }
```

Listing 4.11 ■ The basic mutator recipe

check to make sure that the new property passed as a parameter is within an acceptable range for the class and reject any unacceptable values (for example, no negative numbers for the location of the `Snowman`). And we can change the body of the method *without modifying the code of any other class that might call it.* This type of encapsulation is a huge advantage in a program with many interacting objects. The fewer objects that are affected by each change, the better.

Another advantage of using accessors and mutators is that they can include any arbitrary computation. For example, we might have the mutator convert dates into a standard internal form, such as the number of days since January 1, 1900, and have the accessor convert them back into a more readable form. And again, we can change the method body to make any computation that it performs more efficient, without modifying the code of any of the other classes that call this method.

4.6.5 **Parts that know about their containers**

The final recipe in this chapter is the recipe for creating an object that knows about its container. We saw this for the first time in the `MovableHatApp`, earlier in this chapter, where each part of the `Hat` knew if it had been clicked on and had to send a message to the `Hat` so that the `Hat` could move all its parts together.

This very simple recipe is shown in Listing 4.12. We just initialize the component by creating a new object in the constructor, as usual. The only difference is that we use the keyword `this` as a parameter to the component's constructor. `This` is the keyword a Java object uses to refer to itself, so the object is giving its component a reference to itself. All the component needs to do is to save that value in an instance variable for future reference, as shown in Listing 4.12.

```
1   public class <ContainerClass> {
2       ...
3     private <PartClass> _<part>;
4
5     public <ContainerClass>(...) {
6         ...
7       _<part> = new <PartClass>(this);
8         ...
9     }
10      ...
11  }
```

Listing 4.12 ■ Recipe for objects that know their container (*continued on next page*)

```
12
13   public class <PartClass> {
14       private <ContainerClass> _<container>:
15
16       public <PartClass> (<ContainerClass> <aContainer>) {
17           ...
18           _<container> = <aContainer>;
19           ...
20       }
21           ...
22   }
```

Listing 4.12 ■ Recipe for objects that know their container

■ Summary ■

In this chapter, we have discussed a mechanism provided by Java called an interface. A Java interface lists one or more capabilities that define some coherent role; any object that implements the interface agrees to provide those capabilities declared by the interface. In this way, an interface allows us to model the relationship between a group of objects that share a common role. In addition, because each class that implements an interface must use the same method names and signatures, interfaces help us to write cleaner, more consistent, more readable, and more maintainable code. Classes can implement any number of interfaces but extend only one class.

In addition, we presented some simple "recipes" for writing programs. These included a class-definition recipe, a recipe for initializing the three types of instance variables, a default-value recipe, recipes for defining accessors and mutators, and a recipe for defining objects that know about their containers. Recognizing these recipes will help you to write code more quickly and easily.

■ Self-Check Questions ■

(The answers to these questions can be found on the book's website, www.aw.com/sanders)

1. What does a Java interface model?
2. What does a Java interface contain?
3. What does a class need to provide in order to implement an interface?
4. Syntactically, where can the name of an interface be used in a program?
5. What do interface names end in?
6. What is the smallest number of interfaces a class can implement? The largest?
7. What happens if a class implements two interfaces that require the same method?
8. Can interfaces inherit from classes? Why or why not?
9. Can interfaces extend other interfaces?
10. How many classes can implement a given interface?
11. What are recipes?
12. What is the class-definition recipe?
13. What is the default-property-value recipe? What problem does it solve?
14. What is an accessor? What problem does it solve?
15. What is a mutator? What problem does it solve?
16. What is the recipe for components that know about their container?

■ Exercises ■

Applying the Facts

1. Compare and contrast the syntax for class definitions and interface definitions.

2. What are the two big advantages of using interfaces? Explain with an example of each.

3. Why don't we need to use the term `abstract` in an interface definition?

4. Suppose we have classes for three shapes, `Rectangle`, `Ellipse`, and `Triangle`. Draw a UML diagram showing that they all implement the interface `Colorable`.

5. Compare and contrast interfaces and `abstract` classes.

6. Suppose you have three classes, `Cod`, `Trout`, and `Goldfish`, and you want to model the fact that they are all fish. Would you use an interface or a class? Explain.

7. Suppose you have three classes, `Trout`, `Otter`, and `Submarine`, and you want to model the fact that they all know how to swim (or at least propel themselves through the water). Would you use an interface or a class? Explain.

8. Compare and contrast Java's design, which lets a class inherit from one class and extend multiple interfaces, with a language design that allows multiple inheritance.

Debugging Exercises

Find the bugs (if any) in the following code. Explain your answers.

1.
```java
public interface Paintable {
    Surface getSurfaceToPaint();
    Color getColor();

    public Paintable() { ...}
}
```

2. For purposes of this question, assume we have a `Paintable` interface similar to the one above, with any errors corrected.

```java
public class Canvas implements Paintable {
        ... // instance variable declarations
    public Canvas () {...}
    public getSurfaceToPaint() { ... }
}
```

■ **Programming Projects** ■

Modifying Programs

1. Modify `MovableSunApp` so that the program displays a draggable green rectangle.

2. Modify `MovableSunApp` so that the program displays a draggable black line.

3. Modify `MovableSunApp` so that the program displays a draggable magenta rounded rectangle.

4. Modify `MovableSunApp` so that the program displays a draggable conversation bubble.

5. Modify `MovableSunApp` so that the program displays several shapes, all of which can be dragged separately. You must include at least four different shapes, some duplicates, and a conversation bubble with an appropriate message.

6. Modify `MovableHatApp` so that the two classes also implement the `Locatable` interface from Wheels. (Look at the Wheels documentation to find the methods required by this interface.)

7. Modify `MovableHatApp` so that the two classes also implement the `Colorable` interface from Wheels. (Look at the Wheels documentation to find the methods required by this interface.)

8. Modify `MovableHatApp` so that the two classes also implement the `Sizeable` interface from Wheels. (Look at the Wheels documentation to find the methods required by this interface.)

9. Modify `MovableHatApp` so that the two classes also implement the `AdvancedColorable` interface from Wheels. (Look at the Wheels documentation to find the methods required by this interface.)

10. Modify `MovableHatApp` so that the program displays a draggable `Sun` and a draggable `ConversationBubble` as well as the `Hat`.

Writing Programs

1. Write a program that displays a `Snowman` like the one from Chapter 2, a `Sun`, and a `ConversationBubble`. All three should implement the `Draggable` interface.

2. Write a program that displays `Blob`s like the ones from Chapter 3. Each of the `Blob` classes should be `Draggable`.

3. Write a program that displays three ellipses. Two of them should be draggable individually. When the third one is dragged, however, the other two should follow along. Define a new class `Leader` for the ellipses that carry the others along with them.

5

Polymorphism

OBJECTIVES

After reading this chapter, you should be able to:

☑ Define polymorphism

☑ Explain how polymorphism relates to inheritance and interfaces

☑ Identify polymorphism when used in a Java program

☑ Use polymorphism in a Java program

☑ Explain the pros and cons of polymorphism

■ 5.1 ■ Introduction

Polymorphism is one of the most important parts of object-oriented programming. In general, it means "having many shapes"; in programming languages, it refers to the ability of a variable to have more than one type.

Let's introduce it with an example. Suppose the villain has tied you to the train tracks, like the heroine of an old silent movie, and the train is near. You have only moments to live, when you see a blur on the horizon—someone approaching fast. You know by the cape that it's some kind of superhero, but you don't have time to find out if it's an X-Man®, or a native of the planet Krypton, or some other kind of superhero you haven't even heard of. You do know, though, that all superheroes have a `saveMe` method, because saving people is what superheroes do. So you shout "Superhero, save me!"—and you're saved.

One reason polymorphism is so powerful is that it allows different (but related) objects the flexibility to respond differently to the same message. Note that these superheroes each implement `saveMe` in his or her own way. They may command the lightning to cut the ropes that are binding you, or use their claws to undo them, or simply teleport you, leaving the ropes behind.

The other reason polymorphism is so powerful is that it allows objects to treat other objects in a general way. You don't have time to find out how the superhero will respond

to the "save me" message—and you don't need to know. All you need to know is that whoever you're sending your message to belongs to the superhero class and therefore will be able to respond to the message.

Similarly, if a college's library software sends a "check out" message to something you're trying to borrow, the object in question may be a video, a book, or a reserve book. Each of these types of object has its own way of being checked out: some for 24 hours, some for two weeks, some for use only within the library, and so forth. The circulation desk's software has the convenience of being able to send a single "check out" message, and the flexibility to implement that type of message differently for each type of object (i.e., class).

The disadvantage of polymorphism is that, when you use it, you *must* treat different objects in a general way. You can't take advantage of specific capabilities that a particular type of object might have. For example, if the library software sends a message to a "circulating item," it can ask the object to check itself out or in, but it can't ask it to rewind itself. The only specific type of circulating item that can be rewound is the video subtype.

Polymorphism is generally considered one of the three most important features of object-oriented programming, along with encapsulation (introduced in Chapter 1) and inheritance (discussed in Chapter 3). There is no new syntax involved in polymorphism. Nevertheless, as you will see, using it takes practice. Accordingly, in this chapter we consider some examples to help you get a feel for how and when to use polymorphism.

■ 5.2 ■ Concepts

Polymorphism lets us code generically. Like parameters, it lets us write code that is both general and tailored to a particular situation. In terms of the example above, we have the convenience of yelling "save me," while the superhero has the flexibility to decide how best to get us off the train tracks. Thus, polymorphism is yet another example of how abstraction helps to control complexity.

To understand how this actually works, we need to return to the topic of assignment. Recall that in an assignment statement, the type of the variable (on the left-hand side) and the type of the value being assigned to it (on the right-hand side) must be the same. If we see

```
SuperHero _hero = _wonderWoman;
```

we know that _wonderWoman must be of type SuperHero.

Similarly, when a method is called, the values of the actual parameters are assigned to the formal parameter variable names. So when a method is called, the type of the actual parameters must be the same as the type of the formal parameters. If we see:

```
    _hero.leap(obstacle);
```

and the `SuperHero`'s `leap` method has the signature

```
    leap (TallBuilding aBuilding)
```

then we know `obstacle` must be a tall building.

Now for some terminology. Suppose we have a variable of type `SuperHero`. We have declared the variable like this:

```
    SuperHero _hero;
```

Not surprisingly, `SuperHero` is called the **declared type** of `_hero`, because it is the type the variable is given when it is declared. Now suppose we assign a value to the variable `_hero`:

```
    _hero = someHero;
```

keyconcept

The type we give a variable when we declare it is its declared type.

The type of the value that is assigned to the variable (`someHero`) is the **actual type**. Similarly, if we have a method, we refer to the type of the formal parameter as the declared type, and the type of the actual parameter as the actual type. With that terminology we can rephrase our type-matching rule for parameter passing or assignment: the actual type of a parameter or variable's value must be the same as the declared type of the parameter or variable.

keyconcept

The type of the value assigned to a variable is the variable's actual type.

Polymorphism lets us relax that rule in two ways: one based on inheritance, and one based on interfaces. Inheritance polymorphism says that the actual type of a parameter or variable's value must be the same as the declared type *or any subclass of the declared type* (**subtype** for short). Thus, for example, if `SuperHero` is a subclass of `Person`, we could say:

```
    Person person = new SuperHero();
```

Similarly, if `Skyscraper` is a subclass of `TallBuilding`, we can say,

```
    SuperHero hero;
    Skyscraper skyscraper;
        ...
    hero.leap(skyscraper);
```

This means that if we declare a variable (or define a method with a parameter) of a very general type, say the Wheels `Shape`, the actual type of the variable or parameter's value can be an `Ellipse`, or a `Line`, or a `Rectangle`, or any other `Shape` class in the inheritance hierarchy.

Interface polymorphism lets us be even more general: we can declare a variable (or define a method with a parameter) whose type is an interface, say `Colorable`, and then the actual type of the variable or parameter's value can be any class that implements the interface. Thus, for example, if we have an interface `Mover` that is implemented by classes `Meteor`, `Whale`, and `Bicycle`, we can write:

```
Mover mover = new Meteor();
```

or

```
Mover mover = new Whale();
```

or

```
Mover mover = new Bicycle();
```

We can go even further and combine inheritance and interface polymorphism. Suppose the class `Person` also implements `Mover`, and `SuperHero` (as before) is a subclass of `Person`. We can say

```
Mover mover = new SuperHero();
```

Then when we send the message

```
mover.move();
```

the variable will move according to its actual type: flash across the night sky, swim, roll, or swing on a spiderweb. The `mover` variable can take many forms: a meteor, a hawk, a bicycle, or a superhero. Hence the name polymorphism.

Since this is true, you might be wondering, why don't we just declare all variables of type `Object`? We could, but there's a big catch. We can only send an object messages that its declared type knows about. Since it's so general, `Object` has very few messages that would be helpful in any particular application. Similarly, if an object's declared type is `Mover`, the *only* thing we can ask it to do is to move. We can't tell the `Hawk` to catch a mouse, or the `Bicycle` to carry a rider, or the `SuperHero` to save someone. If we think of an object in very general terms, we can't take advantage of its specific characteristics.

In sum: the actual type of a parameter or variable's value must be the same as the declared type of the parameter or variable, or any subclass of the declared type (if the declared type is a class), or any class that implements the declared type (if the declared type is an interface), or any subclass of any class that implements the declared type (again, if the declared type is an interface). We can only send an object messages that its declared type knows about, however. And when the object responds to a message, it will respond according to the specific type of its value, using method resolution.

Given the pros and cons of polymorphism, how can we recognize when to use it? Here's the key: are we modeling a situation where several different classes of object can do the same thing? There are many such situations. Just for a start, here are a few examples:

- Different employee classes, all of which have a `computePay` method
- Different shape classes, all of which have a `draw` method or a `computeArea` method
- Different athlete classes, all of which have a `printStatistics` method
- Different library item classes, all of which have a `checkout` method
- Different store-inventory classes, all of which have a `checkout` method
- Different chess-piece classes, all of which have a `computeNextMove` method
- Different musical instrument classes, all of which have a `playSound` method
- Different classes that can be displayed in a computer window and all have a `draw` method

Once you've recognized this type of situation, ask yourself: are the classes in question naturally related by inheritance, or by the fact that they all share a role? The answer to that question will tell you whether to use inheritance polymorphism, interface polymorphism, or (possibly) a combination of the two.

■ 5.3 ■ Mechanics

Suppose we have a class `Gardener` and a hierarchy of `Plants` that the `Gardener` knows how to plant. Some of the plants in the hierarchy are given in Figure 5.1.

5.3.1 Inheritance polymorphism

First, consider the definition of the `Gardener`'s grow method:

```
public class Gardener {
    ...
    public void grow (...) {
        ...
    }
}
```

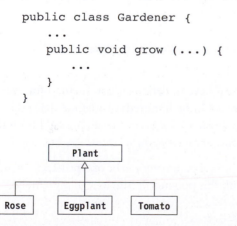

Figure 5.1 ■ Some of the plants that instances of the `Gardener` class can grow.

Suppose that we have the tools of parameters and inheritance that we learned about in earlier chapters, but no polymorphism. In other words, we must use strict type matching for parameter passing. Suppose also that we have defined a large inheritance hierarchy of plants (part of which is given in Figure 5.1), with the `abstract` class `Plant` at its root.

What should the formal parameter of `grow` be? Everything we want the `Gardener` to grow is a `Plant`, so suppose we write the method header like this:

```
public void grow (Plant plant)
```

But wait—if there's no polymorphism, we must use strict type matching. The formal parameter is a `Plant`, so the actual parameter must always be an instance of `Plant`, not any of its subclasses. And because `Plant` is an `abstract` class, there can't be any instances of `Plant`. So this solution won't work.

What if we overload the `grow` method? Then we can give the `Gardener` the capabilities it should have by defining a method for each subclass of `Plant`, like this:

```
public class Gardener {
    ...
    public void grow (Rose rose) {...}
    public void grow (Eggplant eggplant) {...}
    public void grow (Tomato tomato) {...}
    public void grow (Blueberries blueberries) {...}
    public void grow (Okra okra) {...}
    ...
}
```

Then, whenever the `Gardener` wants to grow a `Plant`, it can just call its `grow` method:

```
this.grow(_plant);
```

and Java will pick the method definition whose formal parameter type matches the actual type of `_plant`.

This solution works, but it's really ugly. We'd have to define a `grow` method for every single kind of `Plant` in our model—there could be hundreds of method definitions. Worse still, every time we add a new subclass to the `Plant` hierarchy, we'll have to revise the `Gardener` class and give it yet another new `grow` method.

Relaxing the type-matching rule so that the actual parameter can be of type `Plant` *or any of its subtypes* solves all these problems. With this polymorphism, we can say simply:

```
public class Gardener {
    ...
```

```
      public void grow (Plant plant) {
         ...
      }
   }
```

This single `grow` method works for instances of every class that is now in the `Plant` hierarchy. Thus we can call `_marthaStewart.grow(tomato)` or `marthaStewart.grow(okra)` and Java will execute the same `grow` code, dealing with method calls inside `grow` such as `digHoleFor(plant)` by calling `digHoleFor` on whatever type of `Plant` was actually passed to `grow`. Not only that, if we later add another subclass to the `Plant` hierarchy, we won't have to change the `Gardener` class definition at all. The `grow` method will still work for any instance of any class that we may add to the `Gardener` hierarchy in the future. (For more details of exactly how this works, see Section 5.3.3.)

5.3.2 Interface polymorphism

Now suppose we have a subclass of `Gardener` called `AmbitiousGardener`. This class assumes that anything that holds things can be turned into a planter. We can define a method that takes `Holder` as a parameter:

```
public void createPlanter (Holder holder) {
    _holder.add(new Dirt());
    _holder.add(new Seeds());
    _holder.add(new Water());
}
```

Suppose also that we have a class `Truck` that `implements` the `Mover` and `Holder` interfaces from Chapter 4 and `extends` `Vehicle`. We can create an instance variable whose declared type is `Holder` and use it to hold a value of type `Truck`:

```
Holder _holder;
    _holder = new Truck();
```

and similarly with `Mover`:

```
Mover _mover;
    _mover = new Truck();
```

Now even a truck, if you add enough dirt, seeds, and water, could become a garden:

```
_ambitiousGardener.createPlanter(new Truck());
```

This is allowed because your code does not care what the actual object implementing the `Holder` role is, only that the role's capabilities are concretely defined.

As usual with polymorphism, however, the cost of creating such general, flexible code is that we can't take advantage of the specific capabilities of a class. The only capabilities of the parameter that `createPlanter` can use are the ones that all `Holders` have: `add` and `release`. If an object is referenced through an interface, it is a compiler error to send any messages to the object that are not declared within that interface. For example, since the `AmbitiousGardener` thinks of the `Truck` as just a `Holder`, it can't send the `Truck` a message to `move` or `getLocation`, even though instances of `Truck` have both of those capabilities as well.

5.3.3 Determining which method is invoked

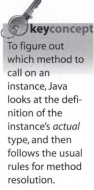

keyconcept
To figure out which method to call on an instance, Java looks at the definition of the instance's *actual* type, and then follows the usual rules for method resolution.

With a complex set of classes and superclasses, determining how a particular instance will respond to a message may seem difficult. We can always figure it out, though, by looking at the instance's *actual type* and following the rules for method resolution described in Chapter 3.

Consider another hierarchy from the plant kingdom, given in Figure 5.2. Suppose we have the following code:

```
private Tree _tree;
    ...
_tree = new Oak();
    ...
_tree.prepareForWinter();
```

The declared type of `_tree` is `Tree`, so the first thing Java does is to check to see if `prepareForWinter` is a method that all `Trees` have. It is, so `prepareForWinter()` is a legitimate message to send to the `_tree` variable. (Our simplified model does not include trees from regions such as the tropical rain forest that have no winter.)

Next, to find out which particular definition of `prepareForWinter` will be used, Java starts by looking at the actual type of `_tree`'s value—`Oak`. Java finds a definition of `_prepareForWinter` right away in the class definition for `Oak`, so it's done. This tree is an oak, so it will prepare for winter by losing its leaves.

Suppose instead that `_tree` is a `Pine`. In other words, we have the code:

```
private Tree _tree;
    ...
_tree = new Pine();
    ...
_tree.prepareForWinter();
```

In this case, the `Tree`'s actual type is `Pine`. Java starts method resolution by looking in the definition of actual type `Pine`. The `Pine` class definition contains its own definition of the `prepareForWinter` method, so we use that one. This tree is a pine, so it prepares for winter by doing nothing—pines are already very well adapted for winter.

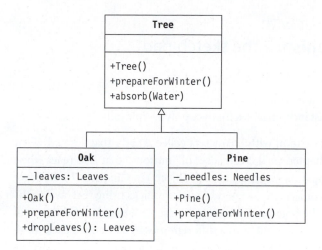

Figure 5.2 ■ A `Tree` hierarchy.

Finally, suppose that it rains, and the `Tree` receives a message to `absorb(water)`. There's a definition of an `absorb(Water water)` method in the `Tree` class, so `absorb(water)` is a legitimate message to send to the `_tree` variable. To find out which definition of the method is used, again, Java starts with the class definition for the actual type (`Pine`). There is no definition of `absorb(Water)` in the `Pine` class, so Java looks in its superclass, `Tree`, and uses the definition it finds there. As you can see, there's nothing new here: we're just using method resolution, as we did in Chapter 3.

Thinking in terms of method resolution can also help us to understand the downside of coding polymorphically. Suppose we have a variable of type `Plant`:

    Plant _plant;

If we want to send it a message to `growBlueberries`, we can't. Our variable is declared a `Plant`, understands only `Plant` messages, and only the `Blueberries` subclass has a `growBlueberries` method.

Java always:

1. checks first to see if the method is one that *every* subclass has (because it is defined in the superclass), and

2. if it is, uses method resolution to determine which version of the method is executed.

■ 5.4 ■ Working Out with **Polymorphism**—the sketch pad

O b j e c t i v e s :
- ☑ Define a class with a peer object
- ☑ Define instance variables that act polymorphically

In the last chapter, we built a cartoon with characters called `Blobs` that reacted when we clicked on them. In this chapter, we'll create a set of "buttons" that also react when we click on them—by sending a message to another object. (In Chapters 7 and 8, we see how to define buttons and objects that respond to mouse clicks using real Java, without Wheels.) The buttons will be organized into an inheritance hierarchy, and they will behave polymorphically: each button will send a different message when we click on it.

5.4.1 **Analysis**

Here's our problem description:

> The program should display a drawing board and four buttons. When the program is run, an invisible cursor is located somewhere in the middle of the drawing board. By clicking on the buttons, the user makes the cursor go up, down, left, or right. (There is one button for each direction). The cursor never becomes visible, but as it moves, it draws a line along its path. (Those of you who know the toy Etch-a-Sketch™ will already be familiar with this basic idea.)

As usual, we start with a grammatical analysis of the problem description. "Program" will likely correspond to a subclass of `Frame`, as in our previous Wheels programs. The `Frame` will "display," or contain, five things: one drawing board and four buttons. We can put objects on `Frames`, so we'll let the `Frame` be our "drawing board." "Button" is another object for our program. There are up buttons, down buttons, left buttons, and right buttons: possible subclasses of our button class. "Cursor," "line," and "path" are other nouns that may indicate classes. The adjective "invisible" describes a property of the cursor.

The verbs, besides "display," are "run," "locate," "click," "make go," "move," and "draw." The program should be runnable—that is, it should have a `main` method. The cursor should have a `setLocation` method. The buttons should respond to mouse clicks, possibly with a `mouseClicked` method, possibly with `mousePressed` or `mouseReleased` methods. The cursor must be able to move and the user must make it go by pressing buttons, so the buttons should send a message to the cursor. The cursor also needs a method for drawing lines. Figure 5.3 shows what the output of our program might look like, after we have drawn a simple picture.

Figure 5.3 ■ What our `SketchApp` should look like.

5.4.2 **Design**

As usual, we use a `Frame` to model a displayable rectangular area. This time let's call it `SketchApp`. We define a superclass `DrawButton`, which is an `Ellipse`, and four subclasses of `DrawButton`: `LeftButton`, `RightButton`, `UpButton`, and `DownButton`. Finally, we'll need something to represent the cursor. The cursor is invisible, according to our problem description. All it has is a location, the location that tells us where we should start drawing the next line. All the different buttons need to be able to access that location and then update it after each new line is drawn. We'll create a class `Cursor` to keep track of the location for us.

UML diagrams for our design are shown in Figure 5.4. The two diagrams could be combined; we have separated them for clarity. The diagram on top shows a containment hierarchy. The top-level class in the containment hierarchy is `SketchApp`, and this is the class that will include our `main` method. `SketchApp` contains four buttons, all of which inherit from the superclass `DrawButton` (as shown in the lower diagram). `SketchApp` also contains a `Cursor`, which is (as shown in the lower diagram) a peer object of the buttons.

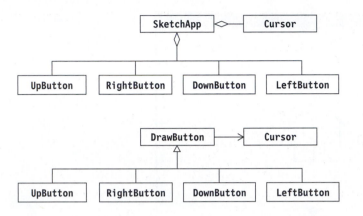

Figure 5.4 ■ Two UML diagrams for the `SketchApp` program: a containment hierarchy (above) and an inheritance hierarchy (below).

5.4.3 **Implementation**

Let's go through the classes we need one by one, starting with the top-level class `SketchApp` shown in Listing 5.1. The `SketchApp` class is very simple; we could almost write it straight from the UML diagram. It contains a `Cursor` and four buttons. The declared type of each button is `DrawButton`, but they each have a different actual type. As usual, there's a `main` method that calls the constructor of the object that contains it. The buttons' parameters are their locations (x and y values) and the `Cursor`. Note that the `UpButton` is drawn at the highest location, the `LeftButton` is on the left, the `RightButton` on the right, and the `DownButton` on the bottom. Thus, although we don't give the buttons labels, the user should easily be able to remember which is which.

Next, let's look at the button hierarchy. The buttons have a lot of code in common, which we factor out and put in the superclass, `DrawButton`, as shown in Listing 5.2. As a result, although the class is not complicated, it is the longest class in our program. Let's consider it carefully.

The `DrawButton` class extends `Ellipse`. Our buttons will be round, like elevator buttons. (If you prefer rectangular buttons, how would you revise this code?)

All the button classes have a peer object that is a `Cursor`; it is an instance variable in this superclass, and its value is one of the parameters to the class's constructor. Recall that this is the usual pattern for peer objects. Whatever object calls the constructor will supply the location of the button, but they are all the same size, 20 pixels in diameter. They are all red at first, since that is the default color for `Ellipses` in Wheels.

```
1    /**
2     * Chapter 5: SketchApp.java
3     * Displays four buttons and a drawing
4     * board and lets the user draw simple pictures.
5     */
6    import wheels.users.*;
7
8    public class SketchApp extends Frame {
9        private Cursor _cursor; // components
10       private DrawButton _upButton, _downButton;
11       private DrawButton _leftButton, _rightButton;
12
13       public SketchApp() {
14           super();
15           _cursor = new Cursor();
16           _upButton = new UpButton(350, 400, _cursor);
17           _downButton = new DownButton(350, 440, _cursor);
18           _leftButton = new LeftButton(330, 420, _cursor);
19           _rightButton = new RightButton(370, 420, _cursor);
20       }
21
22       public static void main (String[] args) {
23           SketchApp app = new SketchApp();
24       }
25   }
```

Listing 5.1 ■ The SketchApp class

The DrawButton class has a mousePressed method that turns the button blue when you click on it—this is useful feedback to the user that something is happening. The real work is done in the mouseReleased method, however. First it gets the current location of the cursor. Then, based on that point, it computes where the next point is going to be and draws a line from the last point to that next point (whatever that is). We make the line black and two pixels thick; you can vary the color or thickness if you like. Then we save the new location of the cursor, and finally, turn the button back to red.

Finally, DrawButton contains one abstract method, computeNextPoint. This is the method that determines where the cursor is going. Each of the buttons will implement it in its own way. It returns a java.awt.Point, and takes one as a parameter. This is a built-in Java class that models a mathematical point. It has two instance variables, x and y, which hold the x and y values of the point.

```
1    /**
2     * Chapter 5: DrawButton.java
3     * The abstract superclass for a hierarchy of buttons that move
4     * the cursor.
5     */
6    import wheels.users.*;
7
8    public abstract class DrawButton extends Ellipse {
9        private Cursor _cursor; // peer object
10
11       public DrawButton (int x, int y, Cursor cursor) {
12           super(x, y);
13           _cursor = cursor; // store reference to peer cursor
14           this.setSize(20, 20);
15       }
16
17       public void mousePressed(java.awt.event.MouseEvent e){
18           this.setFillColor(java.awt.Color.BLUE);
19       }
20
21       public void mouseReleased(java.awt.event.MouseEvent e){
22           java.awt.Point lastPoint = _cursor.getLocation();
23           java.awt.Point nextPoint = computeNextPoint(lastPoint);
24           Line line = new Line(lastPoint, nextPoint);
25           line.setColor(java.awt.Color.BLACK);
26           line.setThickness(2);
27           _cursor.setLocation(nextPoint);
28           this.setFillColor(java.awt.Color.RED);
29       }
30
31       public abstract java.awt.Point computeNextPoint
32           (java.awt.Point lastPoint);
33   }
```

Listing 5.2 ■ The superclass `DrawButton`

`DrawButton` and its subclasses are an example of the use of polymorphism. Each subclass of `DrawButton` implements `computeNextPoint` differently, because each type of button moves the cursor in a different direction. Thus, we can click on each of the buttons—giving each of them the same input—and get different results from each button.

Now consider one of `DrawButton`'s subclasses (shown in Listing 5.3). Because we did most of the work in the superclass, the `UpButton` class is very simple. It has a constructor, which simply calls `DrawButton`'s constructor. And, as required, it implements the `computeNextPoint` method. This method gets the *x* and *y* values of the cursor's current location (`lastPoint`) and creates a new point with the same *x* value and a *y* value that is five pixels higher. To define the `DownButton`, we simply *add* 5 to the *y* value, like this:

```
return new java.awt.Point(lastPoint.x, lastPoint.y+5);
```

Similarly, to define the `LeftButton` and `RightButton` classes, we create new points with the same *y* value as `lastPoint`. Instead of changing the *y* value, we add 5 to (or subtract 5 from) the *x* value. Because the `DownButton`, `LeftButton`, and `RightButton` are so similar to the code given here, we leave them for you to write.

Now let's look at the last of the classes for this program, the `Cursor`, shown in Listing 5.4. The whole purpose of this class is to hold one value—the location of the cursor—make it available to any other object that asks for it, and allow any other object to modify it. The constructor creates the initial point, located at (350, 250) (which happens to be the center of the `Frame`). The two other methods are the most basic accessor and mutator.

5.4.4 Testing

For the first time we have a program that has many different possible inputs. With the `Snowman` program, for example, once it was complete, all we could do was run it; either the picture was displayed correctly or it wasn't. With the `Blobs`, we ran the program to see if they were displayed, and then clicked on each one to see if the right thing happened. In each case, we could do what is called **exhaustive testing**, that is, we could try every possible input and see if the program responded correctly.

Here we have four different buttons that can be pressed in many different combinations. In fact, they can be pressed in so many different combinations that we can't test them exhaustively. We have to choose.

Choosing an appropriate set of test cases is a challenging and interesting problem. As so often in programming, there are no easy, mechanical answers. We can give you a few guidelines, though. First, try boundary cases. These are cases at the limits of the possible inputs. For example, for this program, one boundary case might include running the program without clicking on any buttons at all. So give that a try. Does the `Frame` appear? Are the buttons in the right place?

Another boundary case might be running the program and clicking on only one button. So if the `Frame` appears and everything looks right, try clicking on the `UpButton`,

keyconcept

When your program has many possible inputs, you must choose which ones to use in testing. Boundary cases are a good start.

```
1    /**
2     * Chapter 5: UpButton.java
3     * Subclass of DrawButton that moves the cursor up.
4     */
5    import wheels.users.*;
6
7    public class UpButton extends DrawButton {
8        public UpButton (int x, int y, Cursor cursor) {
9            super(x, y, cursor);
10       }
11
12       public java.awt.Point computeNextPoint
13                         (java.awt.Point lastPoint) {
14           return new java.awt.Point(lastPoint.x,
15                               lastPoint.y-5);
16       }
17   }
```

Listing 5.3 ■ The `UpButton` class

say. Does the button change to blue when you press it, and then change back to red when you release it? Does clicking the `UpButton` move the cursor upward? Does the line start in the middle of the `Frame` as it's supposed to? Does the line go upward? If you keep clicking on the `UpButton`, does the line keep going upward?

Once the `UpButton` is working perfectly, quit the application and start over. Now try one of the other buttons, say, the `RightButton`. This way we can make sure that it works from the starting point, without any possible interference from the `UpButton`. Repeat all the tests that you tried for the `UpButton` until the `RightButton` is working perfectly, and then go through the same process for the remaining two buttons.

Now you have four buttons that work separately, it's time to try combining them. Start up the program and draw a simple picture or two. Even better, if you can, find a friend to try it out for you. Often testers who are unfamiliar with the code are better at finding bugs.

```
1    /**
2     * Chapter 5: Cursor.java
3     * A class that holds the current
4     * location of the cursor.
5     */
6    import wheels.users.*;
7
8    public class Cursor {
9        private java.awt.Point _location; // component
10
11       public Cursor () {
12           super();
13           _location = new java.awt.Point(350, 250);
14       }
15
16       public void setLocation(java.awt.Point point) {
17           _location = point;
18       }
19
20       public java.awt.Point getLocation () {
21           return _location;
22       }
23   }
```

Listing 5.4 ■ The Cursor class

■ Summary ■

Now we have finished covering the object-oriented features of Java: encapsulation, inheritance, and polymorphism. Polymorphism builds on the power of inheritance and interfaces. It allows us to relax the rule that a variable's value must be the same type as the variable itself.

Four key facts that make polymorphism work are:

1. The actual type of a parameter or variable's value can be any concrete class that is

   a. the same as the declared type, or any subclass of the declared type (if the declared type is a class), or

   b. any class that implements the declared type (if the declared type is an
       interface), or

   c. any subclass of any class that implements the declared type (if the
       declared type is an interface).

2. The messages that can be sent to an object depend on its *declared* type.

3. The way the object responds depends on its *actual* type.

4. Java has dynamic binding: that is, given a number of methods with the same
    name, it doesn't decide until runtime which one will be executed.

When a method is called on a polymorphic variable, Java checks to see if the method is
defined in the class definition of the variable's declared type. If so, the method invocation is legitimate. When deciding at runtime which definition of a method will be executed, Java looks first in the class definition of the actual type of the variable to which
the message is sent, then follows the usual rules for method resolution.

It makes sense to use polymorphism in building a model if the situation we're modeling involves several different classes of object that can do the same thing. If the classes
in question are all related by inheritance, then consider inheritance polymorphism; if
they are not naturally part of an inheritance hierarchy, but they share a role, then interface polymorphism is a better choice.

■ Self-Check Questions ■

(The answers to these questions can be found on the book's website, www.aw.com/sanders)

1. What is polymorphism?

2. What are the two reasons why polymorphism is powerful?

3. What are the characteristics of a situation that suggest you should model it
    using polymorphism? Explain and give an example.

4. What is a variable's declared type?

5. What is a variable's actual type?

6. What is a method binding?

7. In programming languages, what does it mean for something to be static?

8. In programming languages, what does it mean for something to be dynamic?

9. What does it mean for a method name to be dynamically bound?

10. Why is dynamic binding important for polymorphism?

11. What types can the actual parameter to a method have?

12. What types can the value of a variable have?

13. What messages can be sent to an object?

14. How does Java find the method that is being called on a polymorphic instance?

15. What does a `java.awt.Point` model? What are its properties, and why is it useful?

16. Explain the syntax `lastPoint.x` in the program in Section 5.3.

■ Exercises ■

Applying the Facts

1. Consider three classes: `Dog`, `Poodle`, and `StandardPoodle`. `StandardPoodle` is a subclass of `Poodle`, and `Poodle` is a subclass of `Dog`. None of them is an `abstract` class.

    a. Draw a UML class diagram of these classes showing their inheritance relationships.

    b. If we have a method with a formal parameter of type `Poodle`, what are the possible declared types of the actual parameter and why?

    c. If we have a method with a formal parameter of type `Poodle`, what are the possible actual types of the actual parameter and why?

    d. If we have a method with a formal parameter of type `StandardPoodle`, what are the possible declared types of the actual parameter and why?

    e. If we have a method with a formal parameter of type `StandardPoodle`, what are the possible actual types of the actual parameter and why?

    f. If we have a method with a formal parameter of type `Dog`, what are the possible declared types of the actual parameter and why?

    g. If we have a method with a formal parameter of type `Dog`, what are the possible actual types of the actual parameter and why?

2. Revise the UML diagram in question 1 to add the following methods: the `Dog` class has a `bark` method, the `Poodle` class has a `lookElegant` method, and the `ToyPoodle` class has a `wearRaincoat` method.

    a. If a variable's declared type is `Dog` and its actual type is `Dog`, which methods can be called on that variable?

    b. If a variable's declared type is `Dog` and its actual type is `Poodle`, which methods can be called on that variable?

    c. If a variable's declared type is `Dog` and its actual type is `ToyPoodle`, which methods can be called on that variable?

    d. If a variable's declared type is `Poodle` and its actual type is `Poodle`, which methods can be called on that variable?

    e. If a variable's declared type is `Poodle` and its actual type is `ToyPoodle`, which methods can be called on that variable?

    f. If a variable's declared type is `ToyPoodle` and its actual type is `ToyPoodle`, which methods can be called on that variable?

3. Consider the following classes: `Tree`, `DeciduousTree`, `Conifer`, `Maple`, `Oak`, and `Pine`. `Tree` is an abstract class. `Conifer` and `DeciduousTree` are subclasses of `Tree`. `Maple` and `Oak` are subclasses of `DeciduousTree`, and `Pine` is a subclass of `Conifer`.

    a. Draw a UML class diagram of these classes showing their inheritance relationships.

    b. If we have a method with a formal parameter of type `Maple`, what are the possible actual type(s) of the actual parameter and why?

    c. If we have a method with a formal parameter of type `Maple`, what are the possible declared type(s) of the actual parameter and why?

    d. If we have a method with a formal parameter of type `Conifer`, what are the possible actual type(s) of the actual parameter and why?

    e. If we have a method with a formal parameter of type `Conifer`, what are the possible declared type(s) of the actual parameter and why?

    f. If we have a method with a formal parameter of type `Tree`, what are the possible actual type(s) of the actual parameter and why?

    g. If we have a method with a formal parameter of type `Tree`, what are the possible declared type(s) of the actual parameter and why?

4. Revise the UML diagram in question 3 to add the following methods: the `Tree` class has a `grow` method, the `DeciduousTree` class has a `changeLeafColor` method, the `Conifer` class has a `dropNeedles` method, and the `Oak` class has a `dropAcorns` method. The `DeciduousTree` class has a `dropLeaves` method, and the `Maple` and `Oak` classes each contain their own `dropLeaves` methods, all three with the same signature.

    a. If a variable's declared type is `Tree` and its actual type is `DeciduousTree`, which methods can be called on that variable?

    b. If a variable's declared type is `Tree` and its actual type is `Conifer`, which methods can be called on that variable?

    c. If a variable's declared type is `Tree` and its actual type is `Oak`, which methods can be called on that variable?

    d. If a variable's declared type is `DeciduousTree` and its actual type is `Oak`, which methods can be called on that variable?

    e. If a variable's declared type is `Oak` and its actual type is `Oak`, which methods can be called on that variable?

5. Consider the following classes: Shape, Ellipse, RoundedRectangle, and ConversationBubble. In this hierarchy (which is similar to but simpler than the hierarchy in Wheels), Shape is an abstract class, Ellipse and RoundedRectangle are subclasses of Shape, and ConversationBubble is a subclass of RoundedRectangle.

    a. Draw a UML class diagram of these classes, showing their inheritance relationships.

    b. If we have a method with a formal parameter of type Shape, what are the possible actual type(s) of the actual parameter and why?

    c. If we have a method with a formal parameter of type Shape, what are the possible declared type(s) of the actual parameter and why?

    d. If we have a method with a formal parameter of type Ellipse, what are the possible actual type(s) of the actual parameter and why?

    e. If we have a method with a formal parameter of type Ellipse, what are the possible declared type(s) of the actual parameter and why?

    f. If we have a method with a formal parameter of type ConversationBubble, what are the possible actual type(s) of the actual parameter and why?

    g. If we have a method with a formal parameter of type ConversationBubble, what are the possible declared type(s) of the actual parameter and why?

6. Revise the UML diagram in question 5 to add the following methods: the Shape class has a setColor method, the RoundedRectangle class has a setSize method, and the ConversationBubble class has setSize, setColor, and setTailDirection methods. (Assume for purposes of this question that these are the only methods and that if methods have the same name, they also have the same signature.)

    a. If a variable's declared type is Shape and its actual type is RoundedRectangle, which methods can be called on that variable?

    b. If a variable's declared type is Shape and its actual type is ConversationBubble, which methods can be called on that variable?

    c. If a variable's declared type is RoundedRectangle and its actual type is RoundedRectangle, which methods can be called on that variable?

    d. If a variable's declared type is RoundedRectangle and its actual type is ConversationBubble, which methods can be called on that variable?

    e. If a variable's declared type is ConversationBubble and its actual type is ConversationBubble, which methods can be called on that variable?

Consider the following two questions in relation to Figure 5.2.

7. Suppose we have the following code:

```
Tree tree = new Pine();
tree.prepareForWinter();
```

What definition of `prepareforWinter()` will be used?

8. Suppose we have the following code:

```
Tree tree = new Oak();
tree.prepareForWinter();
```

What definition of `prepareforWinter()` will be used?

9. Suppose we want to model a circus parade.
   a. Identify at least four classes that might appear in this model.
   b. Identify some properties and capabilities for each class.
   c. Give a detailed UML diagram for your inheritance hierarchy, including properties and capabilities for each class.

   Make sure your example illustrates inheritance relationships, abstract classes, and polymorphism.

10. Suppose we want to model a public beach on a summer's day.
    a. Identify at least four classes that might appear in this model.
    b. Identify some properties and capabilities for each class.
    c. Give a detailed UML diagram for your inheritance hierarchy, including properties and capabilities for each class.

    Make sure your example illustrates inheritance relationships, abstract classes, and polymorphism.

Modifying Programs

1. Modify `SketchApp` so that the buttons are rectangular rather than round. Compile, test, and run your new program.

2. Modify `SketchApp` so that the line is a different color. Compile, test, and run your new program.

3. Modify `SketchApp` so that the line is a different thickness. Compile, test, and run your new program.

4. Modify `SketchApp` so that instead of four buttons, there are eight, arranged like this:

The corner buttons should each make the line go diagonally (i.e., five pixels in the *x* direction and five pixels in the *y* direction). The rest of the buttons should continue to work as they do now. Compile, test, and run your new program.

5. Modify `SketchApp` to add buttons that let the user change the color of the line to red, blue, or yellow at any point during the program's execution. Compile, test, and run your program.

6. Modify `SketchApp` to add buttons that let the user change the thickness of the line at any point during the program's execution. Compile, test, and run your new program.

7. Modify `SketchApp` so that the user can click in the drawing area at any point to change the location of the cursor. The user should now be able to draw separate, disconnected things, for example a house, a tree, and a sun, in the same picture. (Hint: you should add a `Rectangle` to the `Frame` before you add the buttons; the `Frame` is not clickable in Wheels.)

Debugging Programs

Consider the following class definitions:

```
public abstract class ShoppingBag {
    private Handle _handleOne, _handleTwo;
    private int _maxWeightCapacity;
    private int _maxVolumeCapacity;
        ...
}


public class PlasticBag extends ShoppingBag {...}

public class PaperBag extends ShoppingBag {...}
```

Find the bugs (if any) in the following code. Explain your answers.

```
1. public class Supermarket {
        public PaperBag _paperBag;
            ...

        public Supermarket () {
            _paperBag = new ShoppingBag();
                ...
        }
    }
```

```
2. public class Supermarket {
       public PlasticBag _plasticBag;
           ...

       public Supermarket () {
           _plasticBag = new PaperBag();
               ...
       }
   }
3. public class Supermarket {
       public ShoppingBag _shoppingBag;
           ...

       public Supermarket () {
           _shoppingBag = new PaperBag();
               ...
       }
   }
```

■ Programming Projects ■

Writing Programs

1. Write a program that contains an ellipse and three buttons. The ellipse should start out red and the buttons, when clicked on, should change the ellipse's color to blue, yellow, or green.

   a. Write, compile, and run your program until you are convinced that it works.
   b. Explain what inputs you chose to test your program and why.

2. Write a program that contains two ellipses and three color buttons. The user must click on an ellipse to select it, and then click on a button to change the color of that ellipse. (Hint: you should create an object to keep track of the current ellipse, just as we created an object to hold the current cursor position in SketchApp.)

   a. Write, compile, and run your program until you are convinced that it works.
   b. Explain what inputs you chose to test your program and why.

3. Write a program that contains a simple picture of a car and lets the user select part of the car and then click on a button to change the color of that part of the car. (Hint: you should create an object to keep track of the current car part, just as we created an object to hold the current cursor position in SketchApp.)

    a. Write, compile, and test your program until you are convinced that it works.

    b. Explain what inputs you chose to test your program and why.

4. Write a program that simulates a string of lights that turns on when you plug in the plug connected to the endmost light (that is, click on a rectangle). There should be two types of lights:

- middle lights, which turn on (i.e., change color) when they receive a message to turn on and then send a message to the next light to turn on as well, and

- end lights, which turn on but don't have a "next light" to send a message to.

When you click on the plug, all the lights should turn on; when you release it, they should turn off again.

    a. Write, compile, and run your program until you are convinced that it works.

    b. Explain what inputs you chose to test your program and why.

chapter **6**

Introduction to Arithmetic and Conditional Statements

OBJECTIVES

After reading this chapter, you should be able to:

☑ Define primitive types

☑ Give truth tables for the boolean operators and, or, and not

☑ Compare and contrast identity equality, property equality, and deep property equality

☑ List and explain the four types used to model integers in Java

☑ Read and write in Java

  ✓ arithmetic expressions
  ✓ expressions containing increment and decrement operators
  ✓ expressions containing boolean operators
  ✓ expressions containing relational operators
  ✓ if statements and if-else statements

■ 6.1 ■ Introduction

So far, we've shown how powerful object-oriented programming is, and how natural it is to model complex systems using this methodology. In this chapter, we introduce two topics that object-oriented programming shares with all other types of programming: arithmetic and conditional statements. We discuss simple arithmetic using integers and simple conditional statements here. More advanced arithmetic and conditional statements are covered in Chapter 10.

■ 6.2 ■ **Concepts**

Computers' ability to do arithmetic, along with other more complex mathematical calculations, is the main reason they were first built. Although many computer applications still primarily do "number crunching," numbers and numerical expressions are also used in building models. For example, a banking model uses numbers to model money and numerical expressions to record transactions and to calculate interest on the accounts. A census model uses numbers to keep track of population statistics. And a model of the solar system uses numerical expressions to express the way the motion of the planets obeys the laws of physics.

keyconcept

Because computers have limited memory, there's a limit to the size of the numbers that a computer can model.

Conditional statements model decisions. Many models include decisions, alternatives, or forks in the road. For example, we might want to model a car that slows down if the speed limit changes, or changes direction when it reaches a turn.

6.2.1 **Representing numbers**

We begin with arithmetic. Numbers on a computer are not quite the same as the numbers you learned about in grade school. Numbers in Java (and in any programming language) are a model of these abstract numbers—a very good model, but not perfect. Perhaps the biggest influence on this model is that no computer has unlimited memory. The larger an integer is, or the more decimal places a fraction has, the more memory its model takes up. As a result, there's a limit to the size of the numbers that a computer can model.

keyconcept

Java models numbers using primitive types. Primitive types are basic to the Java language and have their own syntactic rules different from those of objects. They are immutable and have no constructors.

Numbers are used so frequently that it is generally easier for object-oriented programming languages not to represent numbers as objects. Thus, numbers in Java are called **primitive types**, because they are basic to the Java language, and they have their own syntactic rules that differ from those of objects. Because numbers are not objects, they have no constructors or any other methods; instead, we use arithmetic operators to combine them. In order to initialize a number, we must assign it a value using an initialization statement.

6.2.2 **Arithmetic operators**

We might find it difficult to work with numbers if we had to send messages to them like objects. For example, if we wrote the expression $x + y * (z - 2)$ as a series of message sends, it might look something like this:

```
x.plus(y.times(z.minus(2)))
```

This expression represents "Call z's `minus` method, passing it 2, in effect computing $(z - 2)$, then take the result of that computation and give it to y's `times` method as a parameter, computing $y * (z - 2)$, and finally, take the result of *that* computation and give it to x's plus method as a parameter, computing $x + y * (z - 2)$. This sequence doesn't correspond at all to the way we normally read equations. Moreover, we could not use our standard mathematical symbols (like + and –) because message names must start with an alphabetic character.

Instead, programming languages, like calculators, generally define arithmetic operators using familiar symbols such as +, –, *, and /, and let us use them to create arithmetic expressions. An **expression**, in general, is an arbitrary combination of variables, constants, operators, and parentheses that has a value. An **arithmetic expression**, in particular, is a combination of numeric variables, numeric constants, arithmetic operators, and parentheses that has a numeric value, such as $2 + 2 - 17 * - (x + y)$. Arithmetic expressions can be used anywhere a numeric constant could be used.

Even with familiar operators, we can still run into problems. To choose a simple example, suppose we write $2 * 3 + 4$. Is this $2 * (3 + 4)$ or $(2 * 3) + 4$? The value of the first expression is 14 and that of the second is 10. Because of this ambiguity, mathematicians have introduced the notion of precedence. If one operator in an expression has higher **precedence** than another, it is executed first. The operators in a programming language also have precedence. For arithmetic operators, the precedence in programming languages is generally the same as in mathematics: unary minus first (e.g., -3), then multiplication and division, then addition and subtraction. Thus, $2 * -3 + 4$ is equivalent to $(2 * (-3)) + 4$. As in mathematics, if we have two operators of the same precedence, the one on the left goes first. And finally, if there's any doubt, add parentheses: just as in mathematics, the expression in parentheses is evaluated first.

6.2.3 **Conditional statements and boolean logic**

Up to now, when we had a sequence of statements in a method, each one was executed, one after another. Now we want to write **conditional statements**: statements that perform a test and, based on the result of the test, choose which statements to execute or whether to execute any at all. Our running example in this chapter is a cookie factory. We want to say things like, "If cookie sales are up, give everyone a raise," and "If demand for chocolate-chip cookies is up, bake more chocolate-chip cookies, otherwise bake more oatmeal cookies."

In order to write a conditional statement, we need to express the test. To model English-language statements that are true or false, programming languages use **boolean logic**, a simple model of reasoning named after its inventor, the mathematician George Boole (1815–1864). Java gives us the **boolean constants** "true" and "false" and **boolean variables**, variables that have only those two possible values. Using booleans, we can define a variable such as `_cookieSalesUp` to model the test in a conditional statement. If the variable has the value true, then everyone gets a raise; if its value is false, they won't. Booleans, like numbers, are a primitive type in Java, and they can be used anywhere other variables can be used: as instance variables, local variables, and parameters.

There are three main boolean operators: "and," "or," and "not." Just as arithmetic operators can be used to build arithmetic expressions, boolean operators can be used to build boolean expressions. A **boolean expression** is an expression that has a boolean value. It can be created by combining boolean constants and boolean variables using boolean operators and parentheses. It can also be created, using relational operators.

The first boolean operator, "and," combines two boolean expressions to create a larger one. For example, we can say, "Our factory makes chocolate-chip cookies AND our factory makes peanut-butter cookies." Just as you would guess, the combined expression is true *only if* both parts are true. If the factory does not make any chocolate-chip cookies or does not make any peanut-butter cookies, then the whole combined expression is false.

"Or" also combines two expressions, but with a different result. Suppose we combine our two expressions by saying, "Our factory makes chocolate-chip cookies OR our factory makes peanut-butter cookies." In normal spoken English we tend to assume that this is an **exclusive or**: that is, that one or the other of the English-language sentences is true, but not both. Boolean logic is different. The Boolean "or" means "either-or." Thus, in Boolean logic, the above combined expression is true if the cookie factory really makes chocolate-chip cookies, or if the factory makes peanut-butter cookies, or both.

The third important boolean operator is "not." "Not" is a unary operator (i.e., it takes one argument), and it means just what you would expect: if an expression is true, the "not" of that expression is false, and vice versa. Thus, if "The factory makes chocolate-chip cookies" is true, then "NOT (the factory makes chocolate-chip cookies)" is false.

We summarize the effect of these operators in Tables 6.1–6.3. This type of table, called a **truth table**, is used often in logic. A **truth table** lists all possible combinations of input values and the value of some expression built up out of those values. For example, the first line of Table 6.1 tells us that if two logical expressions, expression1 and expression2, are both false, then the combined expression, expression1 AND expression2, is also false. The next line of the table tells us what happens if the first expression is false and the second one is true, the third one tells us what happens if the first expression is false and the second one is true, and so on. Similarly, Tables 6.2 and 6.3 give the truth tables for OR and NOT.

To summarize, the two **boolean constants** are "true" and "false." **Boolean expressions** are expressions that have a boolean value. Just as the arithmetic operators can be used

keyconcept

A boolean expression is an expression that has a boolean value, i.e., true or false. Boolean expressions model the conditions in conditional statements.

keyconcept

A truth table lists all possible combinations of input values and the value of some expression built up out of those values.

Table 6.1 ■ Truth table for AND.

<expression1>	<expression2>	<expression1> AND <expression2>
False	False	False
False	True	False
True	False	False
True	True	True

Table 6.2 ■ Truth table for OR.

<expression1>	<expression2>	<expression1> OR <expression2>
False	False	False
False	True	True
True	False	True
True	True	True

Table 6.3 ■ Truth table for NOT.

<expression>	NOT <expression>
False	True
True	False

to put together arithmetic expressions, boolean operators can be used to build boolean expressions. For example, if we have boolean variables we can say

    p AND q OR NOT s AND NOT r.

And just like arithmetic expressions, the boolean expressions can be ambiguous, so mathematicians have introduced rules of precedence. In the same way that multiplication takes precedence over addition, boolean operators have different precedences: NOT is the highest, followed by AND and then OR. Just as in arithmetic, we can use parentheses to group boolean expressions to change the precedence of these operators. Thus, the above expression is equivalent to:

    (p AND q) OR ((NOT s) AND (NOT r)).

We can also write **Boolean methods**. These are analogous to arithmetic methods—given some inputs, they give back a boolean value. For example, we could write a method

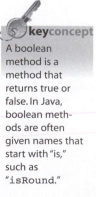

keyconcept
A boolean method is a method that returns true or false. In Java, boolean methods are often given names that start with "is," such as "isRound."

`highProduction` that would test the number of cookies produced today and return true if that number is particularly high. We use boolean methods to help us make decisions in our programs.

6.2.4 **Relational operators**

Relational operators are operators that compare one thing with another, and they also can be used to create boolean expressions. For example, the statement "the number of cookies made today is *greater than* 1000" is either true (the factory produced more than 1000 cookies) or false (the factory produced 1000 cookies or fewer). Of course, we can only make these comparisons between things that have some sense of order.

Since these relational expressions have a boolean value, we can combine them with boolean operators. For example, we can say:

> The number of cookies produced by the factory is greater than 1000 AND the number of peanut-butter cookies is less than 200.

Relational operators such as "greater than" have a higher precedence than the boolean operators. Thus, the above statement is equivalent to

> (The number of cookies produced by the factory is greater than 1000) AND (the number of peanut-butter cookies is less than 200).

6.2.5 **Object equality**

Determining when two objects are equal is harder than it might first appear. Before making such a decision, we need to decide what we mean by "equal." Equality seems as if it should be a simple concept—after all, if two objects are the same, then they are equal. In fact, for primitive types, this is all that is required. For example, if two distinct boolean variables are both true, they are equal. Similarly, if two integer variables both have the value 2, they are also regarded as equal.

The problem is that equality for objects is not that simple. We can create two distinct instances of an object with the same properties. Should they be equal or not? At first glance, we might say no. Two distinct instances of the class `Cookie` should not be the same. The cookie I have in my hand is not the same as the one you're holding; my copy of the textbook is not the same as yours.

But consider the `java.awt.Point` class. Are two instances of `Point` necessarily different? Suppose the two instances have the same coordinate values. A `Point` models a position, and the same coordinate values indicate the same position. In this case, we may want to say that two different instances are in fact the same.

If the only way two instances can be the same is by being the same instance, we call this **identity equality**. If two instances can be the same by simply having the same properties, we call this **property equality**. And if we have to consider the properties of the properties, or the properties of the properties of the properties, or even more, to determine if two instances are equal, then we call it **deep property equality**.

Choosing what kind of equality we mean when designing a model is a fundamental design decision, and what we choose ultimately depends on the purpose of our model. Consider books, for example. For purposes of the bookstore, one copy of a textbook is the same as another, as long as they have the same author and title, they're the same edition, they're both new, etc. In other words, we want *property equality*. For purposes of the library, on the other hand, each copy is different. Two copies of a book might be checked out to two different people, or one might be checked out and one might be checked in. For the library software, we want *identity equality* for the books. Similarly for `Points`: suppose one `Point` is one of the corners of a rectangle and another is one of the corners of a triangle. We might want to consider them as distinct points, even if they have the same *x* and *y* values. For each type of object in the domain that you want to model, ask, "When should two of these objects be considered the same *for purposes of this model?*"

6.2.6 **Choosing when you have one yes-no alternative**

There are several kinds of conditional statement. We can say, for example, "If the cookie factory produced over 70,000 cookies today, give everyone a raise." This is the simplest kind of conditional statement, also called an **if-statement**. If the result of the test is true, the action is executed; if not, it isn't. The if-statement gives us two paths through a method: the path where the result of the test is true and one or more statements are executed, and the path where the result of the test is false and the statements that go with it are not executed. Figure 6.1 shows these two paths. The type of diagram shown in Figure 6.1 is also called a **flow chart**, because it shows the flow of execution in a method from one statement to the next.

6.2.7 **Choosing from two different alternatives**

Instead of having the computer do nothing when the condition is false, we can give it two different alternatives: either do statement A or do statement B. This type of conditional statement is a simple form of **if-else statement**. For example, if the factory sells more chocolate-chip cookies than peanut-butter cookies, increase production of chocolate-chip; otherwise increase production of peanut-butter cookies. Figure 6.2 shows the flow chart for a simple if-else statement with two options.

keyconcept

Identity equality is a very strict definition of equality for objects: two objects are only considered equal if they are the same instance.

keyconcept

Property equality is a definition of equality that allows two instances to be equal if their properties are equal, even if they are not the same instance.

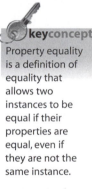

keyconcept

Deep property equality looks at the properties of the properties of the properties... to determine if two instances are equal.

keyconcept

A flow chart shows the flow of execution in a method from one statement to the next.

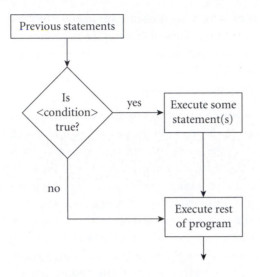

Figure 6.1 ■ Flow chart for a very simple choice.

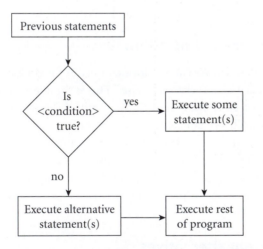

Figure 6.2 ■ Flow chart for two-alternative choice.

keyconcept

Conditional statements model decisions. They can model simple yes-no choices, a choice between two alternatives A and B, or a choice among several alternatives.

6.2.8 **Choosing from many alternatives**

A third kind of choice that is treated separately in many programming languages is a choice with more than two alternatives. For example, we might want to implement the rule "If customers prefer chocolate-chip cookies, make more chocolate-chip cookies; otherwise, if customers prefer peanut-butter cookies, make more peanut-butter cookies; otherwise, if they prefer oatmeal cookies, make more oatmeal cookies." This type of conditional statement is a more complicated version of an if-else statement. The flow chart for an if-else statement with more than two options is shown in Figure 6.3.

6.2.9 **When to use conditional statements**

It can be tricky deciding when to use conditionals and when to use polymorphism, especially if you're used to procedural programming. Here's a rule of thumb:

■ To model a *single* type of object whose behavior changes during the execution of a program in response to an external input, such as a car responding appropriately to the state of a traffic signal, use conditionals: if light is red, stop, else if...

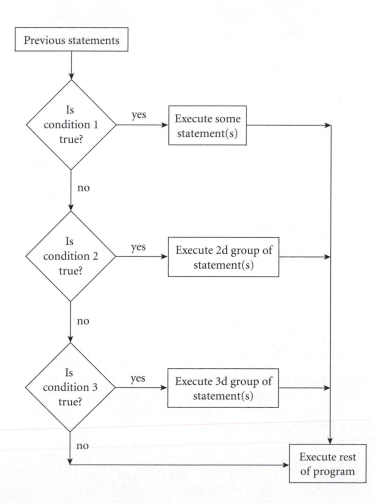

keyconcept
To model a single type of object whose behavior changes during a program, use conditionals. To model different types that make different choices, use polymorphism.

Figure 6.3 ■ Flow chart for choice with four alternatives.

■ To model *different* types of objects that each make different choices depending on their nature, define a class corresponding to each type, send instances of these classes a message, and let them respond polymorphically. For example, to model types of cars that accelerate at different speeds, send all the cars the same message to start and let each car respond in its own way.

As you read through the rest of the book, you will see more examples of both conditionals and polymorphism that illustrate when to make each choice.

■ 6.3 ■ **Mechanics**

In this section, we show how to implement arithmetic and conditional statements in Java. We continue with our hypothetical cookie factory as a running example. First we define a cookie factory class, and then show how to accomplish tasks such as keeping track of how many cookies are sold in a day.

6.3.1 **Numbers in Java**

keyconcept
The four types used to model integers in Java are byte, short, int, and long.

Earlier we said that computers have different ways of storing numbers with different precision. In the realm of integers, we have four different levels of precision we can use, called, in order of increasing precision, byte, short, int, and long. An 8-bit **byte** can hold any number between −128 and 127, inclusive. A **short** can hold many more values, between −32,768 and 32,767, again inclusive. An **int** can hold much more, ranging from −2,147,483,648 to 2,147,483,647. Finally, a **long** has the greatest precision of all, ranging from −9,223,372,036,854,775,808 all the way to 9,223,372,036,854,775,807.

To begin with, we want to declare variables to hold the total number of cookies produced and the number of hours the factory is running during a particular day. We'll make the number of cookies an int, since we hope to produce more than 32,767 cookies in a day. The total numbers of hours in a day is only 24, so we'll use a byte variable for that quantity.

Here's a definition for our CookieFactory class:

```
public class CookieFactory {
    private int _totalCookies; //notice we declare
          // numbers just like any other object
    private byte _numHoursWorked;

    public CookieFactory() {
       _totalCookies = 0; // always initialize, for
       _numHoursWorked = 0; // safety
```

```
        }
    }
```

We assign a value to a numeric variable using the assignment operator:

```
    _totalCookies = 0;
```

This looks the same as when we use the assignment operator to assign a value to a variable whose type is an object:

```
    _ellipse = new Ellipse();
```

In fact, however, assignment works quite differently for primitive-type variables. In both cases, assignment changes the value in the memory location referred to directly by the variable (e.g., 42, in Figure 6.4.). But recall that a variable whose type is an object holds a reference to the object, not the object itself. In other words, it holds the object's address in memory. On the other hand, if a variable belongs to a primitive type, the variable holds the value itself, *not* a reference to the value.

Because assignment works differently for primitive-type variables, passing parameters also works differently. When the actual parameter to a method is an object-type variable, the variable contains a reference to the object, not the object itself. When this value is assigned to the formal parameter, the formal parameter will also contain a reference to the same object. As a result, the method can go to the address of the object and change it. It can't change the contents of the formal parameter—the address of the object—but it can change the object itself. And any changes it makes will affect the actual parameter, since the actual parameter refers to the same address (see Figure 6.5).

But when the actual parameter to a method is a primitive-type variable, the variable contains its value (say, 12 dozen). When this value is assigned to the formal parameter, the

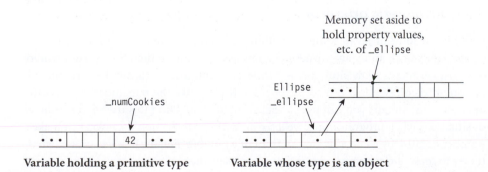

Figure 6.4 ■ Comparison of primitive-type variables and variables whose type is an object.

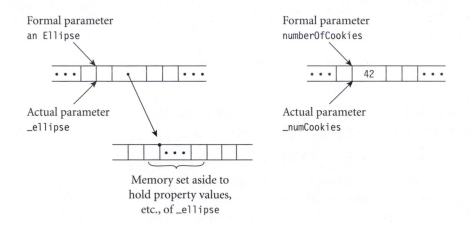

Figure 6.5 ■ Comparison of primitive-type parameters and parameters whose type is an object.

formal parameter also contains the value 12 dozen. The method can't change the contents of the variable, and it has no address to go to, so it can't change the parameter at all (see Figure 6.5). For this reason, primitive types are said to be **immutable**; in other words, they can't be changed.

Because methods can't change them, primitive types are also referred to as **safe**. Suppose one of your fellow students wants to borrow some money. There's a difference between lending him the money and giving him your keys so he can find it in your apartment. Giving a method a primitive type is like lending a friend some money. Giving a method the reference to an object is like giving a friend your house keys. It requires considerably more trust.

6.3.2 **Arithmetic operators**

Let's look at some of Java's common arithmetic operators. We can add numbers using + and subtract them using –. Multiplication uses * (because there is no cross symbol on most keyboards). Division, too, is a little different, using / (again, because there is no long-division symbol on most keyboards). If you'd like the remainder of a division operation on integers, you can use % (called "mod." You'll find this useful in a number of situations when programming; we'll see an example in Section 6.4). You can make a number negative by using a single – in front of a number. Finally, Java lets us use parentheses to make it clear which expression we actually mean.

Any arithmetic operator can be used in an assignment statement by following it with an equals sign, like this:

```
x *= 2;
y += 7;
```

Any statement in this form, a `<op>= b`, is a shorthand for `a = a <op> b`. So the above statements are equivalent to:

```
x = x*2;
y = y+7;
```

Both versions are syntactically correct; which one you use is a matter of personal preference, but it's necessary to recognize both, since you will see them in other people's code.

Here's another example: if people eat some of the cookies before they are supposed to, we would have to subtract the amount they ate from the total produced by the `CookieFactory`:

```
public void loseInventory(Employee hungryEmployee) {
    // returns number of cookies eaten
    int numEaten = hungryEmployee.eatCookies();
    // subtract the number eaten from our total
    _totalCookies -= numEaten;
}
```

You must be careful when using non-commutative operators like subtraction. Just as $5 - 3$ is not the same as $3 - 5$, `_totalCookies - numEaten` does not produce the same result as `numEaten - _totalCookies`. This means that you must be careful when using the `-=` operator (or the `/=` operator for that matter): use it only when the variable would appear immediately to the right of the assignment operator.

6.3.3 Increment and decrement operators

If we want a method to increase the number of hours that the factory has been operating, it is fairly simple. We simply need to increment the number by one each time that method is called. One way that we might do this is using our friend the `+=` operator. That line might look like

```
_numHoursWorked += 1;
```

This operation is used so often that yet another shortcut has been created by Java—the `++` operator. `++` is equivalent to `+=1` (and `–` is equivalent to `-=1`). Thus we can rewrite the above statement as simply

```
_numHoursWorked++;
```

Attaching the ++ to the right-hand side of the variable is called the **postfix operator**. What is actually happening above is the variable is being accessed for its old value, then being incremented by one. So if we had _numHoursWorked = 10 and we said

```
int oldNumHours = _numHoursWorked++;
```

after this statement had been executed, the value of oldNumHours would be 10 and the value of _numHoursWorked would be 11.

Sometimes, however, we want to use the ++ (or --) operator on the other side of the variable to receive a slightly different result. If we put the ++ before the variable (as a prefix), thus saying

```
int newNumHours = ++_numHoursWorked;
```

the incrementing takes place before the actual assignment. As a result, after this statement is executed, the value of newNumHours is 11 and the value of _numHoursWorked is 11 (see Table 6.4).

Table 6.4 ■ Comparison of assignment statements involving pre- and post-increment operators.

a is 0 and b is 10	
a=b++;	a=++b;
Step 1. assignment: a is 10, b is 10	Step 1. increment b: a still 0, b is 11
Step 2. increment b: a is 10, b is 11	Step 2. assignment: a is 11, b is 11

6.3.4 **Boolean operators**

Next, we want to determine whether the cookie factory is producing enough cookies to satisfy its customers. To do this, we use boolean expressions and conditional statements. Java models true and false logical variables using the primitive type boolean. Declaring boolean variables is analogous to declaring a variable of type int or float. Boolean variables are much more restrictive, however, than the other types of variables we have seen; their only possible values are true and false.

Java provides three boolean operators: *and*, *or* and *not*. *And* is represented by a double ampersand (&&). *Or* is represented by a double vertical bar, or pipes (||). The last operator, *not*, is a unary operator represented by an exclamation mark, or bang (!): !true is false, and !false is true.

We can define methods corresponding to other operators in terms of the three basic operators. For example, consider exclusive or, which is true only if one side is true and the other is false (remember that normal or is true in this situation but is also true if both sides are true). We can model this with the following method:

```
public boolean exclusiveOr (boolean left, boolean right) {
    return (left || right) && (!(left && right));
}
```

Notice that this returns `true` only if exactly one of `left` and `right` is `true`. If both are `true` or both are `false`, `exclusiveOr` returns `false`.

6.3.5 Relational operators

Java also provides relational operators, listed in Table 6.5. These operators take numbers as arguments and return a `boolean`. They let us check the numerical values of situations. For example, we can see if the factory's `_cookiesPerHour` is greater than or equal to the minimum number of cookies specified by the factory. If it is not, the manager needs to increase productivity somehow.

Table 6.5 ■ Java's relational operators.

Operator	Meaning
!=	not equal to
>	greater than
<	less than
<=	less than or equal to
>=	greater than or equal to
==	equal to

The simplest relational operator is equality, represented by two equals signs (= =) (remember that a single equals sign (=) is the assignment operator). This operator works for any Java primitive type or object, testing identity equality. The opposite of == is != (not equal) and can also be used for both objects and numbers.

The other relational operators work only on numbers (and on `Strings`, as discussed in Chapter 17). They are less than (<), greater than (>), less than or equal (<=) and greater than or equal (>=). They take numbers and return `booleans`.

We call methods that return `true` or `false` **predicates** and often give them names starting with "is": for example, `isChocolateChipCookie`. We can use a predicate to write a method for our manager to check to see if the factory is producing enough:

```
public boolean isSellingEnoughCookies() {
    _cookiesPerMonth = this.computeCookiesSoldPerMonth();
```

```
        return _cookiesPerMonth >= MINIMUM_COOKIES_PER_MONTH;
    }
```

Table 6.6 summarizes the operators we've seen so far and their precedence levels.

Table 6.6 ■ Summary of operators seen so far and their precedence levels.

Precedence level	Operators	Description
Highest	++	Increment
	--	Decrement
	–	Unary minus
	!	Logical not
	*	Multiplication
	/	Division
	%	Mod
	+	Addition
	–	Subtraction
	<	Less than
	<=	Less than or equal
	>	Greater than
	>=	Greater than or equal
	==	Identity equality
	!=	Not equal
	&&	Logical and
	||	Logical or
Lowest	=, +=, –=, *=, etc.	The assignment operators

6.3.6 **Single decisions**

We can now use a conditional statement to make our factory as productive as possible. If the factory is not producing enough cookies, the manager will do something to increase production. To do this, we'll use an `if`-statement (see Figure 6.1). To write a very simple `if`-statement in Java, we use the keyword `if`, a `boolean` expression inside parentheses, and a single additional statement. If the expression in parentheses is true, then the additional statement will be executed. Otherwise, nothing will happen. So for our factory, we can write:

```
// if we are not selling enough cookies, add new flavor
```

```
if (!this.isSellingEnoughCookies())
    this.addOatmealCookies();
```

If we want more than one statement after our `if`, we can group several statements between curly brackets to create a compound statement:

```
if (!this.isSellingEnoughCookies()) {
        this.addOatmealCookies();
        this.addPeanutButterCookies();
}
```

Caution: if you want to group statements together inside a conditional statement, but you forget the curly brackets, like this:

```
if (!this.isSellingEnoughCookies())
        this.addOatmealCookies();
        this.addPeanutButterCookies();
```

then *only* the first statement is part of the conditional. Here, the factory will add peanut-butter cookies regardless.

To write a conditional statement with two alternatives in Java, we use an `if-else` statement. An **if-else statement** is similar to an `if`-statement, but adds a second statement after the keyword `else` (see Figure 6.2). If the condition is `true`, the first statement is executed. If the condition is `false`, the second statement is executed. As before, we can group multiple statements together using curly brackets.

```
if (!this.isSellingEnoughCookies())
        this.addOatmealCookies();
else
        this.giveEmployeeBonus();
```

Finally, to write a conditional statement with three or more alternatives in Java, we can use an `if-else-if` statement (see Figure 6.3). For example, we could do this to respond to consumer demand in the cookie market:

```
if (_consumerCookiePreference == "oatmeal")
        this.addOatmealCookies();
else if (consumerCookiePreference == "peanutButter")
        this.addPeanutButterCookies();
else
    this.addChocolateChipCookies();
```

■ 6.4 ■ Working Out with Arithmetic and Conditionals—Daisy, Daisy, give me your answer, do

Objectives:
- ☑ Use arithmetic
- ☑ Use a boolean expression
- ☑ Use a conditional statement

We design and implement a program in this section that displays a daisy on the screen and allows the user to get answers from it by "plucking" its petals one by one. It makes some basic use of arithmetic and conditionals; we will see much more of both of these in future chapters. Figure 6.6 shows a screenshot of this program.

We use three classes: a `DaisyApp` class for the whole application, a `Daisy` class to model the flower, and a `Petal` class to model the individual petals. As the user clicks on petals, they should disappear and the message in the `ConversationBubble` should change. Figure 6.7 shows a UML class diagram for this program.

The `DaisyApp` class is very simple. (See Listing 6.1.) It just needs to create the `ConversationBubble`, tell it what to say initially, and create the `Daisy`. The

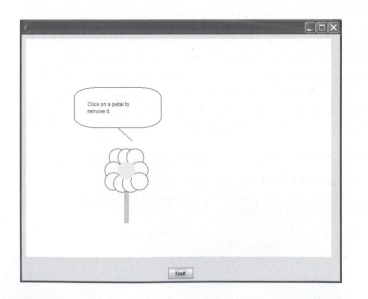

Figure 6.6 ■ Screenshot of `DaisyApp`.

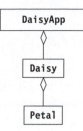

Figure 6.7 ■ UML class diagram for `DaisyApp` program.

`ConversationBubble` will contain the instructions to the user: "click on a petal to remove it."

The Daisy class creates the Daisy with a stem, a center, and petals, sizes the various parts and locates them in the window. It also contains a method, `petalPlucked`, that is called when the user clicks on one of the Daisy's petals. Examine the code for the Daisy class (given in Listing 6.2). The constructor is mainly concerned with displaying the flower properly on the screen. The *x* and *y* parameters to the Daisy's constructor are the location of the flower's center. The stem and the petals are all located in relation to the center of the flower. The center is created last, so it is superimposed on the stem and petals. In addition to displaying the flower, the constructor also records the initial number of petals in the variable `_numPetalsPlucked`. Because the `Daisy` doesn't have more than 127 petals, this variable can be a `byte`.

The `Daisy` class also has a method `petalPlucked`. When the first petal is plucked, we want the `ConversationBubble` to say "Loves me"; when the second petal is plucked, it should say "Loves me not," then "loves me," "loves me not," and so forth until all the petals have been removed. In other words, it should say "Loves me," for petals 1, 3, 5, ... (the odd-numbered petals), and "Loves me not," for petals 2, 4, 6, 8, ... (the even-numbered petals). Thus, we want our conditional statement to say

If the number of petals that have been plucked is an even number

Send the conversation bubble a message to say "Loves me not."

Otherwise (that is, if the number is odd)

Send the conversation bubble a message to say "Loves me."

This is a conditional statement with two alternatives, so the Java syntax we need is

```
if (...) {
    _conversationBubble.setText("Loves me not.");
```

```
    }
    else {
        _conversationBubble.setText("Loves me.");
    }
```

The only part left to fill in is the condition itself. How do we say that something is an even number? There's a cliché for this in programming languages. Mathematically, an even number is a number that is divisible by 2. In other words, when we divide by 2, the remainder is 0. Remember the % operator in Java, the one that gives the remainder if we divide one number by another? The condition uses that operator. In effect, it says, "if we take the number stored in _numPetalsPlucked and divide it by two and the remainder is 0, the number must be even."

Finally, we define a class `Petal` (shown in Listing 6.3). The `Petal` should be an `Ellipse` that, given a location, knows how to give itself the right size and color and position

```
1    /**
2     * Chapter 6: DaisyApp.java
3     * Displays a picture of a daisy
4     * whose petals can be removed by
5     * clicking on them, plus a conversation bubble.
6     */
7    import wheels.users.*;
8
9    public class DaisyApp extends Frame {
10       private ConversationBubble _bubble; // components
11       private Daisy _daisy;
12
13       public DaisyApp() {
14           super();
15           _bubble = new ConversationBubble(
16               "Click on a petal to remove it.");
17           _daisy = new Daisy(210, 280, _bubble);
18           _bubble.setLocation(110, 110);
19       }
20
21       public static void main ( String[] args ) {
22           DaisyApp app = new DaisyApp();
23       }
24   }
```

Listing 6.1 ■ The `DaisyApp` class

```
 1    /**
 2     * Chapter 6: Daisy.java
 3     * Models a daisy with a center, nine petals, and a stem.
 4     */
 5    import wheels.users.*;
 6
 7    public class Daisy {
 8        private byte _numPetalsPlucked; // attribute
 9        private Rectangle _stem; // components
10        private Petal _petal1, _petal2, _petal3, _petal4;
11        private Petal _petal5, _petal6, _petal7, _petal8;
12        private Petal _petal9;
13        private Ellipse _center;
14        private ConversationBubble _bubble; // peer object
15
16        public Daisy(int x, int y, ConversationBubble aBubble){
17            // first call superclass constructor
18            super();
19            // then initialize instance variables, in order
20            _numPetalsPlucked = 0;
21            _stem = new Rectangle(java.awt.Color.GREEN);
22            _petal1 = new Petal(x-20, y-30, this);
23            _petal2 = new Petal(x, y-30, this);
24            _petal3 = new Petal(x+20, y-30, this);
25            _petal4 = new Petal(x-30, y, this);
26            _petal5 = new Petal(x+30, y, this);
27            _petal6 = new Petal(x-30, y+25, this);
28            _petal7 = new Petal(x-10, y+30, this);
29            _petal8 = new Petal(x+10, y+30, this);
30            _petal9 = new Petal(x+30, y+25, this);
31            _center = new Ellipse(java.awt.Color.YELLOW);
32            _bubble = aBubble;
33            // then set size and location of stem, center
34            _stem.setSize(10, 100);
35            _stem.setLocation(x+15, y+40);
36            _center.setSize(40, 40);
37            _center.setLocation(x, y);
38        }
39
40        public void petalPlucked () {
41            _numPetalsPlucked++;
```

Listing 6.2 ■ The Daisy class (*continued on next page*)

```
42              if (_numPetalsPlucked % 2 == 0)
43                  _bubble.setText("Loves me not.");
44              else
45                  _bubble.setText("Loves me.");
46          }
47      }
```

Listing 6.2 ■ The Daisy class

itself on the screen. It should also know how to "disappear" when it is plucked. It should notify the Daisy that it has lost a Petal. Finally, it should only respond the first time the user clicks on it; if the user clicks in the same general area a second time, nothing should happen.

A petal is "plucked" when the user clicks on it. Since the Petal is an Ellipse, it inherits a mouseClicked method. By default, the body of this method is empty, so nothing happens when the user clicks; but if we want something to happen, all we need to do is to override that method, just as we have done with the other mouse methods in earlier programs.

The constructor creates the petal and displays it in the location specified by its x and y parameters. All petals are the same size, and each is white with a black outline, but they can be at different locations.

The mouseClicked method first checks to see if the Petal has already been plucked once. Because we need to know this, a boolean variable _plucked has already been declared and initialized to false. The first time the user clicks on a particular Petal, then, the value of this variable is still false and the conditional statements are executed. First, we remove the petal from the window. Then we notify the Daisy that a Petal has been plucked, calling its petalPlucked method. And finally, we set the value of the _plucked variable to true, so that if the user clicks on the Petal again, nothing will happen.

Now enter, test, and run this program.

```
 1   /**
 2    * Chapter 6: Petal.java
 3    * Models the petal of a daisy.
 4    * Another example of an object that has its container as a peer.
 5    */
 6   import java.awt.event.*;
 7   import wheels.users.*;
 8
 9   public class Petal extends Ellipse {
10       private boolean _plucked; // attribute
11       private Daisy _daisy; // peer object
12
13       public Petal(int x, int y, Daisy daisy) {
14           super();
15           _plucked = false;
16           _daisy = daisy;
17           this.setColor(java.awt.Color.WHITE);
18           this.setSize(40, 40);
19           this.setLocation(x, y);
20           this.setFrameColor(java.awt.Color.BLACK);
21       }
22
23       public void mouseClicked (MouseEvent e){
24           if (!_plucked) {
25               this.hide(); // remove petal from screen
26               _daisy.petalPlucked();
27               _plucked = true;
28           }
29       }
30   }
```

Listing 6.3 ■ The Petal class

■ Summary ■

In this chapter, we have covered Java's arithmetic operators and the four basic types used by Java to model integers, `int`, `byte`, `short`, and `long`. The basic arithmetic operators are the ones we're familiar with from calculators—+, −, *, and /—plus a fifth operator, %, for remainders. Java uses the same rules of precedence for the arithmetic operators as we're used to from mathematics.

We have also covered conditional statements, statements that are executed only if some condition is true. Java uses a model of Boolean logic to model true and false statements and to express conditions. It has a `boolean` primitive type for variables whose only possible values are `true` and `false`, and the logical operators `&&`, `||`, and `!` to combine those variables into larger expressions. Relational operators such as < and > can also be used to create boolean expressions. Truth tables show the value of compound boolean expressions.

We saw three forms of conditional statements. The simplest form is where a statement is either executed or not. The next simplest form is where there are two options, and we want the program to execute either option A or option B. The third form of conditional statements covered in this chapter is the form where there are three or more options.

Conditionals should be used when you have a single type of object that may need to behave differently at different points in the program. If you have more than one object and they behave differently because they are different types of object, use polymorphism to model their behavior rather than conditionals.

Chapter 7 introduces Swing, Java's own graphics library, and provides more opportunities to apply what you have learned about arithmetic and conditional statements.

■ Self-Check Questions ■

(The answers to these questions can be found on the book's website, www.aw.com/sanders)

1. What is one major difference between integers in mathematics and computer models of those integers? Why is that difference part of all computer implementations of integers?

2. Define "primitive types."

3. What does it mean to say that numbers in Java are immutable?

4. List the four types used to model integers in Java and give the values that each type can hold.

5. Give Java's arithmetic operators for addition, subtraction, multiplication, division, and mod.

6. Give the precedence rules for Java's arithmetic operators.

7. List and explain five different assignment operators in Java.

8. List and explain four increment and decrement operators in Java.

9. Explain why the order of operations is important and give an example.

10. Explain when to use conditional statements and when to use polymorphism, and give an example.

11. Define "truth table."

12. Give truth tables for the logical operators.

13. Explain the difference between the logical operator or and the logical operator xor.

14. Give the two values of a boolean variable in Java.

15. Give the precedence rules for logical operators in Java.

16. List Java's relational operators.

17. Which of Java's relational operators work on both numbers and objects, and which work only on numbers?

18. What is the relative precedence of relational and logical operators?

19. Define and give an example of identity equality.

20. Define and give an example of property equality.

21. Define and give an example of deep property equality.

22. Give the syntax for an if-statement in Java.

23. Give a flowchart for an if-statement in Java.

24. Give the syntax for an if-else statement with two alternatives in Java.

25. Give a flowchart for an if-else statement with more than two alternatives in Java.

■ Exercises ■

Applying the Facts

1. In each of the following arithmetic expressions, explain what order the operations are executed in and why, and give the result. Before each expression is evaluated, assume the value of x is 3 and the value of y is 10.

    a. `x * y++`

    b. `x * y + 1`

    c. `x * y / 2`

    d. `x * y - 3`

      e. x * -y + 6

      f. x * y % 2

      g. x + y % 2

      h. x = y+7

      i. x *= 2 * y

      j. x *= x + 3

      k. x = ++x

2. In each of the following boolean expressions, explain what order the operations are executed in and why, and give the result. Before each expression is evaluated, assume the value of x is 3 and the value of y is 10.

      a. x < y

      b. x > y

      c. x <= y

      d. y <= x

      e. x < y && x < 7

      f. x < y && x > 7

      g. x < y || x > 7

      h. x < y + 6 * 7 − 16 % 5 || y++ > 12

3. Suppose we have a pizza with N pieces to divide among 10 people. Write an arithmetic expression to determine how many whole pieces each person can have.

4. Suppose we have a pizza with N pieces to divide among 10 people. Write an arithmetic expression to determine how many pieces will be left over, if we divide the pieces evenly among the guests and everyone eats only whole pieces.

5. Define a Year class and a method isLeapYear that returns true if it is a leap year, otherwise false.

Answer questions 6–9 with respect to MyEllipse, an extension of the Ellipse class.

6. Write a method isCircle that returns true if the Ellipse is a circle, otherwise false.

7. Write a method isWiderThan that takes an Ellipse and returns true if the instance of MyEllipse is wider than the parameter, otherwise false.

8. Write a method isTallerThan that takes an Ellipse and returns true if the instance of MyEllipse is taller than the parameter, otherwise false.

9. Write a method isLargerThan that takes an Ellipse and returns true if the instance of MyEllipse is large enough to contain the parameter, otherwise false.

Answer questions 10–14 with respect to `MyRectangle`, an extension of the Wheels `Rectangle` class.

10. Write a method `isSquare` that returns `true` if the instance of `Rectangle` is square, otherwise `false`.

11. Write a method `isWiderThan` that takes a `Rectangle` and returns `true` if the instance of `MyRectangle` is wider than the parameter, otherwise `false`.

12. Write a method `isTallerThan` that takes a `Rectangle` and returns `true` if the instance of `MyRectangle` is taller than the parameter, otherwise `false`.

13. Write a method `isLargerThan` that takes a `Rectangle` and returns `true` if the instance of `MyRectangle` is large enough to contain the parameter, otherwise `false`.

14. Write a method `intersects` that takes a `Rectangle` and returns `true` if the instance of `MyRectangle` has any points in common with the parameter, otherwise `false`.

15. Suppose we're writing a program with a `Frame` and we want to place an `Ellipse` in the center of the `Frame`. Write an arithmetic expression to compute the correct location for the `Ellipse`.

16. Suppose we want to place eight squares next to each other. Each square is a `Rectangle`, ten pixels by ten pixels. Suppose the location of the leftmost square is position (x, y). Write an arithmetic expression that computes the location for square s, where s indicates how far the square is from the left (i.e., the 0th square, the first square, the second, etc.)

17. Suppose we have a tic-tac-toe gameboard and `byte` variables referring to each square: `_upperLeft, _upperCenter, _upperRight, _midLeft, _midCenter, _midRight, _downLeft, _downCenter,` and `_downRight`. Each square has the value 0 (if it is empty), −1 (if it is an X) or 1 (if it is O). Write the conditional statements necessary to test whether the game is over and if so, to determine who has won.

Debugging Programs

Find the errors, if any, in the following code fragments. Explain your answers.

1. `2 + 2 * 3`
2. `NumCookies > 100 && < 1000`

3.
```
public void makeSandwich() {
        Bread bread = this.getBread();
        PeanutButter pb = this.getPeanutButter();
        this.makeSandwiches(bread, pb);
        _totalSandwiches+;
    }
```

4.
```
if (_numSandwiches = 6) {
        this.eatSandwich();
    }
    else {
        this.makeSandwich();
    }
```

5.
```
public void buyItem(Item anItem) {
        int cost = anItem.getCost();
        _moneyInWallet =- cost;
    }
```

■ Programming Projects ■

Modifying Programs

1. Modify `DaisyApp` to change the color of the `Daisy` and the number of petals it has.

2. Modify `DaisyApp` so that there are three messages: "Loves me," "Possibly loves me," and "Loves me not."

3. Examine the Wheels documentation on `Ellipses` and find out how to rotate them. Then modify the `DaisyApp` so that the petals are oval and angled in different directions from the center of the flower.

Writing Programs

1. Write a program that displays a window containing an `Ellipse` that the user can move around using the mouse. This program should be similar to the code in Chapter 4, except that when the `Ellipse` touches the side of the `Frame` it should stop and not let the user drag it any farther in that direction.

Two-Dimensional Graphical Shapes

OBJECTIVES

After reading this chapter, you should be able to:

- ☑ Give an overview of AWT and Swing
- ☑ Define shape classes
  - ✓ based on Java2D classes such as `Ellipse2D.Double` and `Rectangle`
  - ✓ that know their own color and rotation
  - ✓ that can display themselves in a window
  - ✓ that can be rotated
  - ✓ that can be animated
- ☑ Write and explain simple graphical programs using
  - ✓ the Java Swing class `JFrame`
  - ✓ the Java Swing class `JPanel`
  - ✓ the shape classes you have defined
- ☑ Explain the Java event model

■ 7.1 ■ Introduction

We now start a two-chapter sequence, the first teaching you how to draw and animate basic two-dimensional shapes, the second teaching you how to use basic user-interface components such as buttons and sliders. Up to now, we have been using Wheels, a library designed to make it easy for beginning programmers to write graphical programs in Java. Now that you've learned the basics of object-oriented programming, you're ready to try Java's own graphics libraries, AWT and Swing, on top of which Wheels was built.

We begin by showing you how to use the real Java libraries to write code that does most of the things Wheels provided for us. Like Wheels, AWT and Swing let us display lines, ellipses, and rectangles in various colors. We show how to create a window for the output of a program to be displayed in; how to create points, ellipses, lines, and rectangles;

how to position them and display them in the window. Then we add something new that we couldn't do in Wheels: animating the shapes we create.

Then we develop two simple programs: one that displays a ball bouncing around a window, and one that displays an aquarium with fish swimming around in it. These examples give you a powerful set of tools and a basic framework that you can reuse for many graphical programs. Later chapters cover additional elements of Swing as you learn the concepts necessary to use them effectively. The AWT and Swing libraries are extensive, however, and we can give you only a small subset of them in this text. If you want to learn more, there is excellent documentation online at the Sun website (http://java.sun.com/api/index.html).

Although we spend much of our time in this chapter and the next on the details of Java's AWT and Swing libraries, the programs we write continue to illustrate the object-oriented techniques introduced in Chapters 1–5. These programs provide more extensive examples of encapsulation, inheritance, polymorphism, and delegation.

■ 7.2 ■ **Concepts**

Before we start working with real Java graphics, it helps to know a little history. AWT, which stands for "Abstract Windowing Toolkit," has been part of Java from its beginning. It is a library of classes related to graphics that can be used either in applets or in application programs.

Swing and Java2D are extensions to AWT that fix some of its limitations and provide many additional capabilities. You can think of AWT as the bottom layer, and Swing and Java2D

AWT and Swing: Some Background

Java 1.0 was the original minimal version of the language; AWT was added in Java 1.1. Java 1.2 was a major revision of the language. Java 1.2's additions to the graphics facilities of Java included both Swing (for windows, menus, buttons, etc.) and the Java2D classes (for 2D graphical shapes). Most of

Swing is contained in the javax.swing package. Most of the Java2D classes are contained in the java.awt.geom package, but some classes, such as java.awt.Graphics2D, were added to the older java.awt package. Java 1.3 and 1.4 made minor changes to these libraries. Java 1.5 (the current version as of this writing) made major changes to other aspects of Java, but AWT and Swing were relatively unchanged.

as each adding part of a second layer on top of AWT. Swing and Java2D are the current technology for Java application programs. Since AWT is part of Swing, we discuss some AWT classes in this chapter, including the `java.awt.Color` and `java.awt.Point` classes you have already seen, but we focus primarily on Swing and Java2D.

AWT, Java2D, and Swing are toolboxes for you to use, but they are also themselves illustrations of object-oriented design. As you learn the tools, don't forget to notice how the designers of AWT and Swing make use of classes, inheritance, polymorphism, and interfaces.

■ 7.3 ■ Working Out with
Windows and Shapes—`FirstApp` revisited

Objectives:
- ☑ Use `JFrames` and `JPanels`
- ☑ Use Java's shape classes
- ☑ Rewrite `FirstApp` from Chapter 1 in real Java

In this section, we show you how to create a window in Java and place a shape in the window. In the process, we build a very simple application, `BallApp`, that displays a red ball in a window with a white background. This application has the same output as `FirstApp`, the first program we wrote in Chapter 1 when we began to use Wheels.

7.3.1 `JFrames`

Like Wheels, Swing calls its basic window a frame, or specifically a `JFrame` (see Figure 7.1.) The fully qualified name of the `JFrame` class is `javax.swing.JFrame`. (Many classes in the Swing library begin with J, for Java.) `JFrames` provide the outside frame of the window, and the programmer specifies what goes inside. In general, they are used for the main window of an application.

`JFrame` is an extension of the AWT `Frame` class. Both can be used to provide the main window for an application, but `JFrames` can be easily configured either to mimic the look and feel of whatever windowing system the program is running on, or to have their own independent look and feel. Notice that the Java designers didn't have to throw out all the AWT classes and start over in order to make this change. They just extended the old `Frame` class. This is an example of how Java itself makes use of object-oriented programming.

The code for `BallApp`, a simple extension of `JFrame`, is given in Listing 7.1. `BallApp` is the top-level class for our simple program and also illustrates a recipe for building

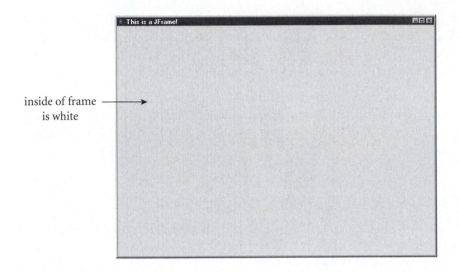

inside of frame is white

Figure 7.1 ■ A basic `JFrame` with nothing in it.

graphical programs. The boilerplate is *not* underlined; you can copy this code and use it again and again by filling in the "blanks" (i.e., substituting for the code that has been underlined).

Let's step through this code. First, look at the mainline, where Java would start executing the code. Other than the title for the top of the window, this mainline is exactly the same as the one we would write using Wheels.

Next, consider the constructor. All this code is new—Wheels took care of all of this for us before. The first line of the constructor calls `JFrame`'s constructor and passes on the title to be placed on top of the window. The second line gives the size for the window—here, 600 pixels wide and 450 tall. This is a reasonable choice, but you can change it if you like.

The next line probably seems somewhat obscure at first. It turns out that `JFrames`, although they have the usual close icons you would expect, do not automatically know how to respond when the user closes them. This makes sense: an application might have several windows, and closing a window shouldn't necessarily cause the entire program to quit. When the user closes the main window of the application, however, you do want Java to halt the program, and that's what this line of code causes to happen. `JFrame.EXIT_ON_CLOSE` is a constant defined in the `JFrame` class that, as you might imagine, causes Java to exit your program when the window is closed.

```
1    /**
2     * Chapter 7: BallApp.java
3     * Displays a window with a red circle on a white background.
4     * Similar to FirstApp.java (ch.1), but written without Wheels.
5     * Used (with adaptations) in all programs from here on.
6     */
7    public class BallApp extends javax.swing.JFrame {
8        public BallApp (String title) {
9            super (title);
10           this.setSize(600, 450);
11           this.setDefaultCloseOperation(
12               javax.swing.JFrame.EXIT_ON_CLOSE);
13           // add code for panels here — in next section
14           this.setVisible(true);
15       }
16
17       public static void main (String[ ] args) {
18           BallApp app =
19               new BallApp ("This is a JFrame!");
20       }
21   }
```

Listing 7.1 ■ The `BallApp` class

Finally, the last line of the constructor, as you might guess from its name, makes the application visible on the screen. Without this line, the program would compile and run but we wouldn't see anything. Making the code invisible until we explicitly set it visible is very useful: it allows us to set things up before displaying them on the screen.

Almost all this code will be the same in every graphical program you write. The only variables are the name of the program itself, the size of the `JFrame`, the title to be placed on top of the window, and of course, the code for whatever you want to appear in the `JFrame` (more about this in the next section).

Now compile and test this code exactly as is (without the extra code from the next section). You will see an empty window appear—your first program with a real Java window!

7.3.2 `JPanels`

`JFrames` by themselves are not very interesting. If we're going to have a `JFrame`, we want to put something inside it. We want to add buttons, menus, cartoons, etc.

Before we add anything else, however, we need to add a JPanel to the JFrame. JFrame and JPanel both derive from Java's java.awt.Container class, a class modeling graphical objects that can contain other graphical objects. JPanels are Containers that sit invisibly inside another Container (such as a JFrame). You can think of the JPanel as the canvas inside the frame on which your graphics will be painted. The fully qualified name for a JPanel is javax.swing.JPanel. Figure 7.2 shows how the JPanel and JFrame classes fit into Java's inheritance hierarchy.

In order to use a JPanel, first we need to modify the BallApp class to add a new instance of a BallPanel defined below. Substitute the line

```
this.add(new BallPanel()); // code to add Panel to BallApp
```

for the placeholder comment in the previous section:

```
// add code for panels here -- in next section
```

The code for the BallPanel itself is given in Listing 7.2. Like BallApp, this class illustrates a recipe. The code you need to modify when using the recipe is underlined.

BallPanel is a subclass of JPanel that will contain and display a bouncing ball. For now, the constructor simply calls the JPanel's constructor. To show the difference between the plain BallApp and the BallApp with the BallPanel added, we set the color of the BallPanel to blue.

Finally, the paintComponent method is called automatically by the system whenever the panel is resized, reopened after being minimized, etc. We explain the details of this method below, when we show how to add shapes to the panel.

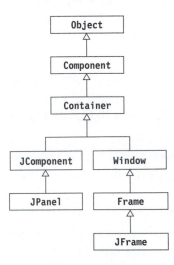

Figure 7.2 ■ JPanel's place in the Java inheritance hierarchy.

```
 1    /**
 2     * Chapter 7: BallPanel.java
 3     * Creates the panel to be placed inside the BallApp window.
 4     * Used (with adaptations) in all programs later in this book.
 5     * Version 1 of 3
 6     */
 7    public class BallPanel extends javax.swing.JPanel {
 8        // add instance variables for contents of panel, if needed
 9
10        public BallPanel () {
11            super ();
12            this.setBackground(java.awt.Color.BLUE);
13            // insert code to define contents of panel
14        }
15
16        public void paintComponent (java.awt.Graphics aBrush) {
17            super.paintComponent (aBrush);
18            // insert code to paint contents of panel
19        }
20    }
```

Listing 7.2 ■ The BallPanel class

Meanwhile, compile and test the revised version of BallApp along with the BallPanel class. You should now see the same window as before, only filled with blue. The blue BallPanel fills the entire inside of the BallApp frame.

7.3.3 Layout

The next step is to put the bouncing ball in the BallPanel. Whenever we put a shape in a panel, we want to control where it's placed. There are a variety of ways to do this using Java objects called LayoutManagers, which are discussed in more detail in Chapter 8.

For now, we'll be giving the pixel locations for graphical shapes using what is known as absolute positioning, just as we did in Wheels. As in Wheels, we use x values that give the number of pixels from the left-hand edge of the JPanel, and y values that give the number of pixels down from the top (see Figure 7.3). And as before, we'll use trial and error to determine the locations that make our pictures look right.

keyconcept
To position shapes, we can use absolute positioning, as in Wheels.

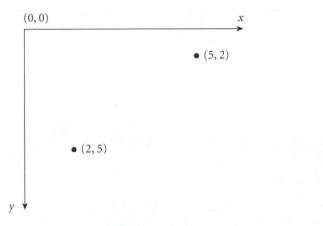

Figure 7.3 ■ Absolute positioning.

7.3.4 **Putting an ellipse in a `JPanel`**

In order to add an ellipse to the `BallPanel`, we need to modify the `BallPanel` class definition, as shown in Listing 7.3 (new code appears in boldface).

The code for declaring and initializing the instance variables is very similar to what we would have written using Wheels (except that it's in a `JPanel` class). `INIT_X`, `INIT_Y`, and `DIAMETER` are names given to the numbers 75, 75, and 60 to make the code more readable. The Java keyword `final` means their values cannot be changed. An instance variable whose value cannot be changed is also called a **constant**. We change the background from blue to white, as in `FirstApp`.

7.3.5 **Creating a "smart" ellipse**

AWT provides a library of shapes for us in the `java.awt.geom` package, but they're very primitive. They don't know what color they are, whether they've been rotated, how to respond to mouse clicks, or even how to draw themselves.

For our programs, we will always want something more sophisticated. At the very least, we want our shapes to be smart enough to have a color and know how to draw themselves. Before we go any further, then, we define a `SmartEllipse` class (shown in Listing 7.4).

This class extends Java's `Ellipse2D.Double` class (pronounced "ellipse 2D dot double"). It gives the ellipse two colors, one for its outline (`_borderColor`) and one to fill in the outline (`_fillColor`), plus a mutator for each color. The ellipse also has a rotation and a constant, `STROKE_WIDTH`, to indicate the thickness of the outline.

```
1    /**
2     * Chapter 7: BallPanel.java
3     * Version 2 of 3
4     */
5    public class BallPanel extends javax.swing.JPanel{
6        private final int INIT_X = 75; // attributes
7        private final int INIT_Y = 75;
8        private final int DIAMETER = 60;
9        private SmartEllipse _ball; // component
10
11       public BallPanel () {
12           super();
13           _ball = new SmartEllipse(java.awt.Color.RED);
14           this.setBackground(java.awt.Color.WHITE);
15           _ball.setLocation(INIT_X, INIT_Y);
16           _ball.setSize(DIAMETER, DIAMETER);
17       }
18
19       public void paintComponent (java.awt.Graphics aBrush) {
20           super.paintComponent(aBrush);
21           // insert code to paint contents of panel
22       }
23   }
```

Listing 7.3 ■ The `BallPanel` class (version 2)

```
1    /**
2     * Chapter 7: SmartEllipse.java
3     * Extends Java's Ellipse2D.Double class, adding the capabilities to
4     * set color, rotation, location, and size, to move to a specified
5     * location, and to display itself on a panel.
6     */
7    public class SmartEllipse extends java.awt.geom.Ellipse2D.Double {
8        private java.awt.Color _borderColor, _fillColor; // attributes
9        private int _rotation;
10       private final int STROKE_WIDTH = 2;
11
12       public SmartEllipse(java.awt.Color aColor){
13           super();
14           _borderColor = aColor;
```

Listing 7.4 ■ The `SmartEllipse` class (*continued on next page*)

```
15              _fillColor = aColor; // solid color to start
16              _rotation = 0; // no rotation for now
17          }
18          // methods not provided by Java
19          public void setBorderColor (java.awt.Color aColor) {
20              _borderColor = aColor;
21          }
22          public void setFillColor (java.awt.Color aColor) {
23              _fillColor = aColor;
24          }
25          public void setColor (java.awt.Color aColor) {
26              _fillColor = aColor;
27              _borderColor = aColor;
28          }
29          public void setRotation (int aRotation) {
30              _rotation = aRotation;
31          }
32          // more readable versions of methods provided by Java
33          public void setLocation (double x, double y) {
34              this.setFrame (x, y, this.getWidth(), this.getHeight());
35          }
36          public void setSize (int aWidth, int aHeight) {
37              this.setFrame(this.getX(), this.getY(), aWidth, aHeight);
38          }
39          public void move (int aChangeInX, int aChangeInY) {
40              this.setFrame((int)this.getX()+aChangeInX,
41                              (int)this.getY()+aChangeInY,
42                              this.getWidth(), this.getHeight());
43          }
44          // insert code to display ellipse
45      }
```

Listing 7.4 ■ The SmartEllipse class

Note: As explained in Chapter 1, Java class names start with a capital letter and package names with a lower-case letter. So the fully qualified name javax.swing.JFrame refers to the JFrame class in the swing package, which is inside the javax package. Knowing this, you may be wondering why the class java.awt.geom.Ellipse2D.Double has two parts with capital letters. That's because both Ellipse2D and Double are classes. Double is an **inner class,** a class defined inside another class (in this case, inside

`Ellipse2D`). Classes defined as inner classes have certain advantages in terms of encapsulation and efficiency. We discuss how to write inner classes in Section 7.5.

In addition, the class definition includes three methods that aren't strictly necessary but make our code easier to read: `setSize`, `setLocation`, and `move`. For some reason, the designers of Java's shape classes assumed we would always want to set the size and location of a shape at the same time, so they provided a `setFrame` method that does both tasks at once. Its interface is:

```
public void setFrame(double x, double y, double w, double h);
```

This approach is fine in the constructor, when we usually do want to set both size and location. Later on, however, we almost never change both at the same time. Accordingly, we define separate `setSize` and `setLocation` methods, similar to the ones in Wheels.

The `move` method is similar to `setLocation`, except that it doesn't specify a particular destination. Instead, it causes the ellipse to change its location by the given amount. In computer graphics we call `setLocation` an absolute translation and `move` a relative one.

Finally, there must be methods that define how the ellipse will paint itself. They are explained in the next section.

7.3.6 Drawing shapes and the `Graphics` object

After we create a graphical shape, we want it to show up in a panel. Wheels took care of displaying shapes for us, but in Swing, we have to write the code ourselves.

There are three things you need to know about in order to cause shapes to appear in a panel:

- the `repaint` method,
- the `paintComponent` method, and
- the `Graphics` object.

repaint. Repaint is the method we call if our code has changed something on a `JPanel`. All `JPanel`s come with a `repaint` method. The method `repaint()`, with no parameters, causes the whole `JPanel` to be redrawn.

paintComponent. When we call `repaint()`, the request is put on a schedule, along with whatever other painting requests Java is dealing with at the moment. When it's our `JPanel`'s turn, the system calls `paintComponent`. `PaintComponent` is another method that all `JPanel`s have. In addition to calling `paintComponent` in response to our `repaint` message, the system calls it when a `JPanel` is opened or resized, when another window that was in front of a `JPanel` is closed, and in general, whenever the `JPanel`'s appearance is altered and its contents need to be refreshed.

keyconcept
Java's `repaint` method causes a `JPanel` to be redrawn. It is called automatically when the window containing the `JPanel` is opened, maximized, etc., and can also be called by the programmer.

keyconcept

When the repaint method is called, it in turn calls the JPanel's paint-Component method, which we must override to say what should be drawn.

Here's the minimal `paintComponent` method, the one we used for the first version of `BallPanel`, above:

```
public void paintComponent (java.awt.Graphics aBrush) {
    super.paintComponent(aBrush);
    // insert code to paint contents of panel
}
```

All this simple method says thus far is: call the superclass's `paintComponent` method (i.e., `JPanel`'s method), using the paintbrush supplied by the system, to paint the `JPanel` itself. Debugging tip: it's a common error to forget this call to the superclass's method, and your program will not behave properly if you do.

As we saw earlier, this method works fine if we just want to paint the panel. If we want to put some shapes in the panel, we'll need to add something more.

The Graphics object. The `Graphics` object is the parameter to the `paintComponent` method, an instance of `java.awt.Graphics`. Despite its name, the `Graphics` object is a collection of attributes, not a shape. You may want to think of it as a very sophisticated paintbrush. Its properties include the current color.

keyconcept

The paint-Component method takes a Graphics object as a parameter, but by casting, we can take advantage of the more useful Graphics2D class.

Taking advantage of polymorphism, we can also use `java.awt.Graphics`'s newer and more powerful subclass, `java.awt.Graphics2D` (added as part of Java2D in Java 1.2). The `Graphics2D` object, unlike the `Graphics` object, can draw the shapes in the `java.awt.geom` package (and also our `SmartEllipse`). In addition, it can draw lines of various widths and draw at an angle.

Now we can write the final methods we need for our program. First, consider the `BallPanel`'s complete `paintComponent` method (shown in Listing 7.5). It overrides the built-in `paintComponent` method and adds the ball to the panel.

keyconcept

Graphics and Graphics2D are like paint-brushes used to draw the JPanel, but only the Graphics2D object knows how to draw the Java2D shapes.

The `paintComponent` method is older than the `Graphics2D` class, so it takes a `Graphics` object as its formal parameter, rather than `Graphics2D`. The actual parameter is a `Graphics2D` object, fortunately, so it is able to paint our ellipse, as long as we force the actual parameter to be considered as a `Graphics2D` object. Java allows us to force an instance of a class to be treated as an instance of one of its subclasses. Explicitly stating that a variable of one type should be considered as belonging to another type, as here, is known as **explicit coercion** or **casting**.

Finally, here are the `SmartEllipse`'s methods for displaying itself in a window. We define two methods: `draw` to paint the outline of the shape, and `fill` to paint a solid shape. The `SmartEllipse`'s `fill` method is shown in Listing 7.6.

```
1    public void paintComponent (java.awt.Graphics aBrush) {
2        super.paintComponent(aBrush);
3        java.awt.Graphics2D betterBrush =
4            (java.awt.Graphics2D) aBrush;
5        _ball.fill(betterBrush);
6    }
```

Listing 7.5 ■ BallPanel's paintComponent method

The paintbrush already has a color (and a number of other attributes). The system uses the same paintbrush over and over, so one of the first things the SmartEllipse needs to do is to set the color of the paintbrush to the SmartEllipse's own color. Note that we save the old color of the paintbrush and restore it again at the end of the method. This is not strictly necessary, but it's a good idea: the next method that wants to draw may be relying on the previous color, and cleaning up now can save us some painful debugging later.

The paintbrush, as a Graphics2D object, has two methods for painting shapes: a fill method for coloring inside the outline and a draw method for drawing just the outline, or drawing the outline in a separate color. Here we only need the fill method, because we want a solid shape.

Finally, we give the SmartEllipse a method for drawing its border (see Listing 7.7). This method is useful if we just want to draw the outline of an ellipse, or if we want to have an ellipse whose border color is different from the color inside the border.

Again, we save the old border color and give aBrush the ellipse's border color to use. We also use a new feature of the Graphics2D object: its ability to draw lines of differing widths. The default border is thin (only one pixel), so we give aBrush a wider line (STROKE_WIDTH, which, as you recall, is equal to 2). We save and restore the stroke width just as we do the border color.

```
1    public void fill (java.awt.Graphics2D aBetterBrush){
2        java.awt.Color savedColor = aBetterBrush.getColor();
3        aBetterBrush.setColor(_fillColor);
4        aBetterBrush.fill(this);
5        aBetterBrush.setColor(savedColor);
6    }
```

Listing 7.6 ■ SmartEllipse's fill method

```
1    public void draw (java.awt.Graphics2D aBrush) {
2        java.awt.Color savedColor = aBrush.getColor();
3        aBrush.setColor(_borderColor);
4        java.awt.Stroke savedStroke = aBrush.getStroke();
5        aBrush.setStroke(new java.awt.BasicStroke(STROKE_WIDTH));
6        aBrush.draw(this);
7        aBrush.setStroke(savedStroke);
8        aBrush.setColor(savedColor);
9    }
```

Listing 7.7 ■ `SmartEllipse`'s draw method

Now we have all the code we need to run the `BallApp` program. Modify `BallApp` to change the title of the window, compile and run the program, and you should see a window that looks like Figure 7.4.

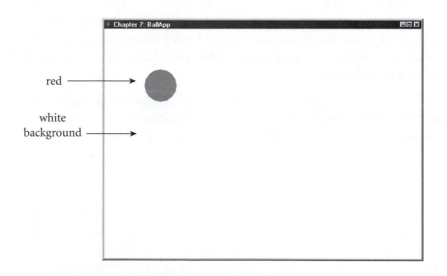

Figure 7.4 ■ Screenshot for `BallApp` program.

■ 7.4 ■ Working Out with
Events and Animation—the bouncing ball

Objectives:
- ☑ Understand the Java event model
- ☑ Learn a basic design for event-based programs in Java
- ☑ Write an event-based program
- ☑ Use a `javax.swing.Timer`
- ☑ Write a program with animated shapes

The basic idea behind animation is very simple: you just draw a graphical image over and over with slight changes from one time to the next, so that it looks as if it's moving, changing size, angle, color, etc. To make this work, Java provides something called a `Timer`. The fully qualified name of the `Timer` we use here is `javax.swing.Timer`.

keyconcept
We can create animations by writing code that makes our graphical shapes respond to Java's `javax.swing. Timer`.

A `javax.swing.Timer` doesn't work like a kitchen timer. With a kitchen timer, we give it an amount of time—say four minutes—and after that amount of time it goes off, to remind us of some task we wanted to perform, like taking the popcorn out of the microwave. After it goes off, it's done until the next time you set it. Instead, a `Javax.swing.Timer` works more like a metronome. Once we start it, it keeps on going until we stop it. While going, it provides a steady, regular "ticking" that only the program can hear, and on each tick, certain actions, which we can specify, are performed. To understand how this works, you need to understand what is known as the Java Event Model.

Note: Java has two other classes called `Timer`, `java.util.Timer`, and `javax.management.timer.Timer`, which work slightly differently and have different uses. When working with Swing, make sure to use the Swing `Timer`. As long as we use its fully qualified name `javax.swing.Timer`, there is no ambiguity.

7.4.1 The Java event model

The term "Java event model" sounds complicated but is actually very simple. The idea is this. When a timer ticks, or when the user presses a button, selects a menu item, opens or closes a window, or clicks the mouse, that's an **event**. Any object that's interested in hearing about a particular event can register with the source of the event (the timer, the button, the window, etc.) as a listener. When the event happens, Java notifies the listeners automatically, and they must respond. Each listener decides for itself how it will respond.

keyconcept
An event is something happening outside our program that we want the program to respond to, such as a mouse click, keystroke, or timer.

We have written event-handling code before, using Wheels. The `BlobApp` in Chapter 3 and the `SketchApp` in Chapter 5, for example, both involved classes that reacted to mouse input. Wheels hid the details of how this code is written in Java, however.

There are many ways to design event-handling code in Java. Here, we give you a simple, workable design to get you started; once you are comfortable with this design, you can experiment and try alternatives of your own. Our design has three parts:

1. a source (some object that generates an event, like a `Timer` or a subclass of `Timer`)

2. a middleman object called a listener that registers with the source

3. one or more responders, the objects that will ultimately respond to the event

Whenever there's an event, the source object automatically notifies the listener, and the listener then passes on the information to the responders, as in Figure 7.5.

For example, suppose we want a `Timer` that will make shapes move. First, define a subclass of `Timer` called `MoveTimer` (shown in Listing 7.8).

When the `MoveTimer` is created, likely by a subclass of `JPanel`, it is given two parameters:

1. a `Mover`

2. the time interval between the ticks (that is, how fast the `MoveTimer` should tick)

The `Mover` is the object that responds (or coordinates the response) to the `MoveTimer`. Any instance of a class that implements the `Mover` interface can play this role.

The first thing any constructor has to do is call the superclass's constructor. Here, the superclass (`Timer`)'s constructor requires two parameters: the interval, which we have, and a middleman object, a listener. Since we haven't instantiated a `MoveListener` yet,

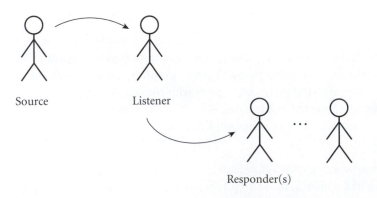

Source   Listener

Responder(s)

Figure 7.5 ■ Simple design for event-handling code.

```
1    /**
2     * Chapter 7: MoveTimer.java
3     * A subclass of javax.swing.Timer
4     * that can be used for animation.
5     * It also serves as an example of the code
6     * for an "event source" object.
7     * Version 1 of 2
8     */
9    public class MoveTimer extends javax.swing.Timer {
10       private Mover _mover; // peer object
11
12       public MoveTimer (int anInterval, Mover aMover) {
13          super(anInterval, null);
14          _mover = aMover;
15          this.addActionListener(new MoveListener(_mover));
16       }
17
18       // more code to be added later
19   }
```

Listing 7.8 ■ `MoveTimer`

we let the second parameter be `null`. Then we create a new `MoveListener`, pass the `Mover` parameter on to it, and register it as an `ActionListener` with the `MoveTimer`.

We've made it part of the way. We have a source object, we've initialized a middleman listener object and registered it with the source, and the source object knows about the responder.

Next, we need to define the listener class. A first draft of a class called `MoveListener` is shown in Listing 7.9.

`MoveListener` implements `ActionListener`, and the only thing the `ActionListener` interface requires is an `actionPerformed` method. `actionPerformed` is the method that is executed on each beat of the `MoveTimer` by the middleman listener object. All it does here is to forward a message to the responder:

The `actionPerformed` method doesn't even look at its `ActionEvent` parameter. The parameter is required by the `ActionListener` interface, but it contains details of the event that are not needed for this simple example. `ActionEvent` is part of Java's hierarchy of `AWTEvent` classes. These classes model various kinds of events. They all include information about the type and source of the event, plus additional information depending on the

```
1    /**
2     * Chapter 7: MoveListener.java
3     * Public class that could be (but isn't)
4     * used as a listener in our event-handling design.
5     * Instead, we use an inner class defined inside the
6     * MoveTimer, as shown in Listing 7.11.
7     */
8
9    public class MoveListener implements java.awt.event.ActionListener{
10       private Mover _mover; // peer object
11
12       public MoveListener (Mover aMover) {
13           super();
14           _mover = aMover;
15       }
16
17       public void actionPerformed(java.awt.event.ActionEvent e){
18           _mover.move();
19       }
20   }
```

Listing 7.9 ■ MoveListener class

event's type. The KeyEvent class, for example, has a method that returns the key that was pressed to cause the event. Similarly, the MouseEvent class has a getPoint method that returns the point on the screen where the mouse was clicked.

We don't have to use the information contained in these event objects, however. In Chapter 3's BlobApp program, we didn't use the MouseEvent parameter to the mouseClicked method. Here again, we don't use the parameter. In Chapter 4's MovableSunApp, on the other hand, we did use the MouseEvent's getPoint method, and in Chapter 8 (when we show how to handle mouse clicks) we will see examples where the event objects are used again.

Finally, we need a responder, the object that ultimately responds to the MoveTimer's message. This object must be something that knows how to move, that is, some object with a move method. It could be a bouncing ball, a swimming fish, or any other simple or composite shape that we want to animate. Since all we care about is the object's behavior, we define an interface, Mover (shown in Listing 7.10).

```
1    /**
2     * Chapter 7: Mover.java
3     * Interface for objects that can move.
4     * Responders to a MoveTimer must implement this.
5     */
6    public interface Mover {
7        public void move();
8    }
```

Listing 7.10 ■ The Mover interface

There's still one problem with this code. It doesn't seem quite right for the MoveListener to be an independent class, given that the MoveTimer is the only object that will send it messages. In fact, we'd like to prevent other objects from sending the MoveListener an actionPerformed message. How can we hide the MoveListener from the rest of the program?

Here's the solution: define an inner class, a class inside another class. An **inner class** is useful in situations like this, where one class is closely related to another and does not interact with the rest of the program.

To define an inner class, all we need to do is to write one class definition inside another, like this:

```
public class <name> {
    ...

    private class <inner-class-name> {
        // body of inner class
    }
    ...
}
```

By making the inner class private, we can hide it from the rest of the program.

Our final version of the MoveTimer is shown in Listing 7.11. This is the design we will use for all our event-handling code.

As you can see, the MoveListener is shorter now that it's an inner class. One additional advantage of using inner classes is that inner classes, like methods, have access to the instance variables of the outer class. This often makes it possible to shorten the inner

keyconcept

Inner classes are classes defined inside another class. They can be more efficient and provide greater encapsulation than a separate class.

class. Because the inner class has access to the outer class's instance variables (_mover in this case), it doesn't need to have them passed as parameters to the constructor.

The steps for handling other types of events are the same as for ActionEvents; only some of the names are different. For example, there are MouseListeners, WindowListeners, MouseEvents, and WindowEvents. We discuss techniques for handling additional kinds of events in Chapter 8.

7.4.2 Using events: making the ball bounce

Just for fun, let's modify the BallApp program so that the red circle moves in a diagonal line from one edge of the window to another. This is about the simplest animated program we could write.

```
 1    /**
 2     * Chapter 7: MoveTimer.java
 3     * A subclass of javax.swing.Timer
 4     * that can be used for animation.
 5     * Also serves as an example of the
 6     * code for an "event source" object.
 7     * Version 2 of 2
 8     */
 9    public class MoveTimer extends javax.swing.Timer {
10        private Mover _mover; // peer object
11
12        public MoveTimer (int anInterval, Mover aMover) {
13            super(anInterval, null);
14            _mover = aMover;
15            this.addActionListener(new MoveListener());
16        }
17
18        // our first inner class
19        private class MoveListener implements java.awt.event.ActionListener{
20            public void actionPerformed(java.awt.event.ActionEvent e){
21                _mover.move();
22            }
23        }
24    }
```

Listing 7.11 ■ The MoveTimer class modified

BallApp and BallPanel. The `BallApp` class does not need any changes. The `BallPanel` class must be modified slightly, as shown in Listing 7.12 (new code is given in boldface).

```
1   /**
2    * Chapter 7: BallPanel.java
3    * BallPanel from Listing 7.3, modified to add animation.
4    * BallPanel version 3 of 3
5    */
6   public class BallPanel extends javax.swing.JPanel implements Mover {
7       private final int INIT_X = 75; // attributes
8       private final int INIT_Y = 75;
9       private final int DIAMETER = 60;
10      private final int INTERVAL = 100;
11      private BouncingBall _ball; // components
12      private MoveTimer _timer;
13
14      public BallPanel () {
15          super();
16          this.setBackground(java.awt.Color.WHITE);
17          _ball = new BouncingBall (java.awt.Color.RED, this);
18          _timer = new MoveTimer (INTERVAL, this);
19          _ball.setLocation(INIT_X, INIT_Y);
20          _ball.setSize(DIAMETER, DIAMETER);
21          _timer.start();
22      }
23
24      public void move() {
25          _ball.move();
26          this.repaint();
27      }
28
29      public void paintComponent (java.awt.Graphics aBrush) {
30          super.paintComponent(aBrush);
31          java.awt.Graphics2D betterBrush =
32              (java.awt.Graphics2D) aBrush;
33          _ball.fill(betterBrush);
34      }
35  }
```

Listing 7.12 ■ The `BallPanel` class modified

The `BallPanel` class now contains a `MoveTimer`. The shape in the `BallPanel` is no longer a `SmartEllipse`; instead, it's a `BouncingBall`, a subclass of `SmartEllipse` that knows how to move and change direction when it reaches the edge of the panel containing it.

When instantiating `MoveTimer`, we need to make two decisions: how often it will tick, and what object (if any) should be the first to register with the `MoveTimer`. This `MoveTimer` ticks every 100 milliseconds. This is a reasonable interval, but you can vary it if you like.

The second parameter to the `MoveTimer`'s constructor is the object that's going to respond to the `MoveTimer` (the responder). What should that be? There are two possibilities, depending on the situation.

1. Our panel contains only one object that is being animated by the `MoveTimer`. In that case, that object is the responder.

2. Our panel contains, or may contain in the future, more than one animated object. In that case, the panel is the responder; it will coordinate the response of the other objects.

We have one `BouncingBall` here, but we might want to add more, so we make the `BallPanel` the responder. To make this possible, the `BallPanel` also has to implement `Mover`.

BouncingBall. An overview of the last piece of our program, the `BouncingBall` class itself, is given in Listing 7.13. This code is entirely new.

The constructor initializes the instance variables. Because `MOVE_LEN` is positive, the `BouncingBall` moves in a positive direction at first.

Next we need the methods that define how the `BouncingBall` moves. It's easy to get the current location and add the necessary amount (`_changeX` or `_changeY`). The trick is to detect when the new location is at the edge of the window and make the `BouncingBall` change direction.

Start by assuming that we have some methods—`getMinBoundX`, `getMinBoundY`, `getMaxBoundX`, and `getMaxBoundY`—that give us the minimum and maximum locations for the `BouncingBall`. If we have those, all we need to do is to compute the new location, check to see if it's out of bounds, and if so, change direction (see Listing 7.14).

Note the use of a conditional in this method. This is a good example of where a conditional statement is appropriate: where an object needs to respond to conditions that change during the execution of a program (such as its location), conditions that are not determined by the type of the object.

```
1    /**
2     * Chapter 7: BouncingBall.java
3     * Extends SmartEllipse, adding the ability to
4     * "bounce."
5     */
6    public class BouncingBall extends SmartEllipse implements Mover {
7        private int _changeX, _changeY; // attributes
8        private final int MOVE_LEN = 5;
9        private javax.swing.JPanel _panel; // peer object (and container)
10
11       public BouncingBall (java.awt.Color aColor,
12                            javax.swing.JPanel aPanel){
13           super(aColor);
14           _changeX = MOVE_LEN;
15           _changeY = MOVE_LEN;
16           _panel = aPanel;
17       }
18
19           // methods so the BouncingBall knows how to move
20   }
```

Listing 7.13 ■ The `BouncingBall` class

We assumed we had methods to tell us the boundaries of the panel, so now we have to write them. Fortunately, they're pretty easy. The minimum *x* and *y* values are the same as the `BallPanel`'s, as shown in Listing 7.15.

To get the maximum *x* value for the `BouncingBall`, we take the minimum value for the `BallPanel` and add the width of the `BallPanel` and similarly for the maximum *y* value, as shown in Listing 7.16.

Now you have an animated program, completely written in Java! Compile and test it, and then vary it. For example, try varying the number of pixels by which the `BouncingBall` changes at each step; the trick is to make it fast enough to be interesting, and slow enough that the motion doesn't appear jerky. Five pixels each way is a reasonable start, but you may find something you like better, or something that works better for your particular computer. Also, try making `_changeX` or `_changeY` negative at first, varying the size and color of the bouncing ball, and so forth. Keep making changes until you are sure you understand how the program works.

```
1    public void move() {
2        int nextX = (int)this.getX() + _changeX;
3        int nextY = (int)this.getY() + _changeY;
4        if (nextX <= this.getMinBoundX()) {
5            _changeX *= -1;
6            nextX = this.getMinBoundX();
7        }
8        else if (nextX >= this.getMaxBoundX()) {
9            _changeX *= -1;
10           nextX = this.getMaxBoundX();
11       }
12       if (nextY <= this.getMinBoundY()) {
13           _changeY *= -1;
14           nextY = this.getMinBoundY();
15       }
16       else if (nextY > this.getMaxBoundY()){
17           _changeY *= -1;
18           nextY = this.getMaxBoundY();
19       }
20       this.setLocation(nextX, nextY);
21   }
```

Listing 7.14 ■ `BouncingBall`'s move method

7.4.3 **Rotating shapes**

In the next section, we write code for an animated fish tank. We did not need rotation in the bouncing ball program—no matter how much you rotate a circle, it looks the same. But to make it look as if the fish are swimming back and forth, we'd like to be able to draw the same fish at different angles.

`Java`'s `Graphics2D` paintbrush has a `rotate` method that will help us to solve this problem. The first argument to the `rotate` method is the angle: how far we want it to rotate. Unlike the `Arc2D`'s angles, these angles are measured in radians. Suppose we're drawing a rectangle. Basically, an angle of 0 means the rectangle isn't rotated at all; an angle of π means it has been turned 180 degrees; 2π means it's back to where it started; and so forth. Fortunately, Java has a math library with PI as a built-in constant, so we can just refer to it by name as `Math.PI`. We don't even need to import the math library, since it's a core part of Java.

```
1    public int getMinBoundX() {
2        return (int) _panel.getX();
3    }
4    public int getMinBoundY() {
5        return (int) _panel.getY();
6    }
```

Listing 7.15 ■ BouncingBall's getMinBound methods

```
1    public int getMaxBoundX() {
2        return (int) (_panel.getX() + _panel.getWidth()
3                        - this.getWidth());
4    }
5
6    public int getMaxBoundY() {
7        return (int) (_panel.getY() + _panel.getHeight()
8                        - this.getHeight());
9    }
```

Listing 7.16 ■ BouncingBall's getMaxBound methods

The second and third arguments are the *x* and *y* values of the point around which to rotate. If we had to draw a shape at an angle on a piece of paper, we would mentally rotate the shape and then draw it. Java, on the other hand, models this situation by rotating the paper in the opposite direction and then drawing the shape. It's as if we put a pen down on a piece of paper, pushed down, turned the paper around that point, and then drew the shape.

Two things follow from this: first, we need to be careful what point we put our pen down on; and second, we have to make sure to turn the paper back again when we're done. Generally, we want to put the pen down on the center of the shape, and that's what we do here. Finally, we undo the rotation of the paper when we're done by rotating the same distance in the opposite direction (−_rotation). In Java, the Graphics2D object knows the amount by which the drawing surface has been rotated. Our SmartEllipses know their own rotation, however, and they have a setRotation mutator method for changing it (see Section 7.3.5).

▪ 7.5 ▪ Working Out with
Events and Composite Shapes—the fish tank

Objectives:
- ☑ Gain practice with Java2D, Swing, and AWT
- ☑ Write a second event-driven program
- ☑ Use a `Timer` to animate a composite shape
- ☑ Demonstrate how `Mover`, the interface implemented above by a simple shape, can also be implemented by a composite shape

In this section, we give a program that displays a fish tank with a simple fish swimming back and forth. Figure 7.6 contains a screenshot of the program. There's only one fish so far, and it's small—so there's lots of room for you to add more if you want.

A UML containment diagram for this program is given in Figure 7.7. The program includes five new classes: `FishApp` (an extension of `JFrame`), `FishPanel` (an extension of `JPanel`), `Fish`, `SmartRectangle`, and `SmartArc`. In addition, it uses the same `Mover`, `MoveTimer`, and `SmartEllipse` as the `BallApp`.

The `FishPanel` contains a `SmartRectangle` (which models the fish tank) and `Fish`. The `FishPanel` implements `Mover`, as the `BallPanel` class did earlier in this chapter, since both coordinate the response to the `MoveTimer`. The `Fish` is composed of a `SmartEllipse` (which models its body) and a `SmartArc` (which models its tail). The

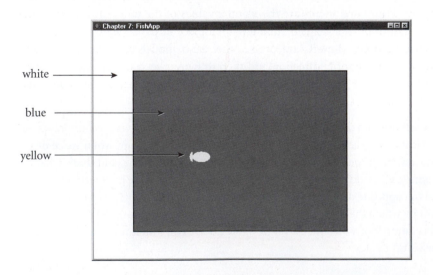

Figure 7.6 ▪ A screenshot of the `FishApp` program.

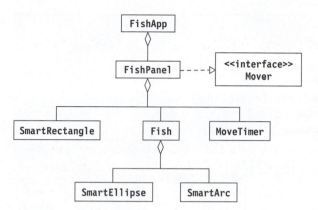

Figure 7.7 ■ Containment diagram for `FishApp`.

`SmartRectangle` and `SmartArc` are shape classes, very similar to the `SmartEllipse`, that build on the primitive shapes provided by Java.

The code for the `FishApp` class is given in Listing 7.17. It follows our recipe for building graphical programs. As usual, the new code is in boldface. Since this class definition follows the recipe, there is nothing new to explain; only the class names and the title of the window have changed.

The code for the `FishPanel` class is shown in Listing 7.18. This class is very similar to `BallPanel`, the corresponding class in the `BallApp` program. Again we create a subclass of `JPanel` that implements `Mover`, with an instance variable (here, `_yellowFish`) for the object to be animated. There are the same three methods: a constructor, `move`, and `paintComponent`. The `move` method is exactly the same, except for the name of the instance variable (`_yellowFish` instead of `_ball`). The `paintComponent` method is exactly the same, except that the `betterBrush` has to draw the fishtank and a fish instead of a bouncing ball.

The `SmartRectangle` is exactly like the `SmartEllipse`: a shape based on one of the Java shapes, with the added capabilities of setting its color, rotating itself, and displaying itself in a window. All you need to do to is to copy the `SmartEllipse` code and replace `ellipse` with `rectangle` everywhere it appears.

Next, consider the `Fish` class. Because it is a composite shape—a shape made up of smaller shapes—we need to explicitly define methods such as `setLocation` that the `Ball` could simply inherit. As a result, this class definition is longer.

The first part of the code for the `Fish` class is given in Listing 7.19. Again, we have a class that implements `Mover`. It has `_changeX` and `_changeY` variables, like the `BouncingBall`,

```
1    /**
2     * Chapter 7: FishApp
3     * A second animated object. A composite
4     * object (the fish) is animated.
5     * Follows the same recipes as BallApp
6     * for displaying and animating 2D
7     * graphical shapes and for event handling.
8     */
9    public class FishApp extends javax.swing.JFrame {
10       public FishApp (String title) {
11          super(title);
12          this.setSize(600, 450);
13          this.setDefaultCloseOperation(
14             javax.swing.JFrame.EXIT_ON_CLOSE);
15          this.add(new FishPanel());
16          this.setVisible(true);
17       }
18
19       public static void main (String [ ] args) {
20          FishApp app = new FishApp ("Chapter 7: FishApp");
21       }
22    }
```

Listing 7.17 ■ The FishApp class

```
1    /**
2     * Chapter 7: FishPanel.java
3     * The JPanel in which the fish tank and
4     * fish are displayed.
5     * Similar to BallPanel.
6     */
7    public class FishPanel extends javax.swing.JPanel implements Mover {
8       private final int TANK_X = 75; //attributes
9       private final int TANK_Y = 75;
10      private final int TANK_WIDTH = 400;
11      private final int TANK_HEIGHT = 300;
12      private final int INTERVAL = 100;
13      private SmartRectangle _tank; //components
14      private Fish _yellowfish;
```

Listing 7.18 ■ The FishPanel class (*continued on next page*)

```
15          private MoveTimer _timer;
16
17          public FishPanel () {
18              super();
19              _tank = new SmartRectangle(java.awt.Color.BLUE);
20              _yellowfish = new Fish(java.awt.Color.YELLOW, _tank);
21              _timer = new MoveTimer(INTERVAL, this);
22              this.setBackground(java.awt.Color.WHITE);
23              _tank.setBorderColor(java.awt.Color.BLACK);
24              _tank.setLocation(TANK_X, TANK_Y);
25              _tank.setSize(TANK_WIDTH, TANK_HEIGHT);
26              _yellowfish.setLocation(TANK_X,
27                                      TANK_Y + TANK_HEIGHT/2);
28              _timer.start();
29          }
30
31          public void move() {
32              _yellowfish.move();
33              this.repaint();
34          }
35
36          public void paintComponent(java.awt.Graphics aBrush){
37              super.paintComponent(aBrush);
38              java.awt.Graphics2D betterBrush =
39                  (java.awt.Graphics2D) aBrush;
40              _tank.fill(betterBrush);
41              _tank.draw(betterBrush);
42              _yellowfish.fill(betterBrush);
43          }
44      }
```

Listing 7.18 ■ The FishPanel class

but _changeY is 0: the fish just swim straight back and forth, not up or down. Fish do have an instance variable _rotation that stores the angle they're facing, since they turn around when they reach the edge of the tank. The parts of the fish are modeled by a SmartEllipse and a SmartArc. Just as the Ball had a reference to the BallPanel that contained it in order to determine when it had reached the edge of the panel, the Fish has a reference to the SmartRectangle in which it is swimming. Finally, there are constants to hold the width and height of the fish and its parts.

```
 1    /**
 2     * Chapter 7: Fish.java
 3     * Models a fish in a fish tank.
 4     */
 5    public class Fish implements Mover {
 6        private final int BODY_WIDTH = 34; // attributes
 7        private final int TAIL_WIDTH = 12;
 8        private final int FISH_WIDTH = 44;
 9        private final int FISH_HEIGHT = 20;
10        private final int MOVE_LEN = 5;
11        private int _changeX, _changeY;
12        private double _rotation;
13        private SmartEllipse _body; // components
14        private SmartArc _tail;
15        private SmartRectangle _tank; // peer
16
17        public Fish(java.awt.Color aColor, SmartRectangle aRectangle){
18            super();
19            _changeX = MOVE_LEN;
20            _changeY = 0; // fish swims horizontally
21            _rotation = 0;
22            _body = new SmartEllipse(aColor);
23            _tail = new SmartArc(90, 180,
24                                java.awt.geom.Arc2D.PIE, aColor);
25            _tank = aRectangle;
26            _body.setSize(BODY_WIDTH, FISH_HEIGHT);
27            _tail.setSize(TAIL_WIDTH, FISH_HEIGHT);
28        }
29        // code that implements move, etc. goes here
30    }
```

Listing 7.19 ■ The Fish class

The constructor initializes all the instance variables, gives the parts of the Fish their sizes, and positions them in the fish tank.

The move method for the Fish is almost identical to the move method for the bouncing ball. The only difference is that in addition to computing the next location of the Fish, we also need to compute its rotation. The Fish's move method is shown is Listing 7.20.

```
1   public void move() {
2       int nextX = (int)this.getX() + _changeX;
3       int nextY = (int)this.getY() + _changeY;
4       if (nextX <= this.getMinBoundX()) {
5           _changeX *= -1;
6           nextX = this.getMinBoundX();
7       }
8       else if (nextX >= this.getMaxBoundX()) {
9           _changeX *= -1;
10          nextX = this.getMaxBoundX();
11      }
12      if (nextY <= this.getMinBoundY()) {
13          _changeY *= -1;
14          nextY = this.getMinBoundY();
15      }
16      else if (nextY > this.getMaxBoundY()){
17          _changeY *= -1;
18          nextY = this.getMaxBoundY();
19      }
20      if (_changeX < 0)
21          this.setRotation(Math.PI);
22      else
23          this.setRotation(0);
24      this.setLocation(nextX, nextY);
25  }
```

Listing 7.20 ■ The `Fish`'s move method

The `getBound` methods for the fish are also very similar to the `getBound` methods for the bouncing ball (see Listing 7.21). The only difference is that instead of comparing the location of the `BouncingBall` to the edge of the `BallPanel`, now we're comparing the location of the `Fish` to the edge of the fish tank.

In the `setLocation` method, the `Fish` delegates work to its parts. (See Listing 7.22). Because the `Fish` and its parts have `setLocation` methods with the same signatures, client code using the `Fish` doesn't need to know whether it's sending a message to a simple shape or a composite one. This is an example of a design pattern called the Composite Pattern, which we discuss in more detail in Chapter 9.

The `Fish` also needs to define `getX` and `getY` methods, two methods that the `SmartEllipse` just inherits. It defines them by delegating to the tail (a `SmartArc`), as

```
1    public int getMinBoundX() {
2        return (int) _tank.getX();
3    }
4    public int getMaxBoundX() {
5        return (int) (_tank.getX() + _tank.getWidth()
6                      - FISH_WIDTH);
7    }
8    public int getMinBoundY() {
9        return (int) _tank.getY();
10   }
11   public int getMaxBoundY() {
12       return (int) (_tank.getY() + _tank.getHeight()
13                     - FISH_HEIGHT);
14   }
```

Listing 7.21 ■ Fish's getMinBound and getMaxBound methods

```
1    public void setLocation (int x, int y) {
2        _body.setLocation(x+5, y);
3        _tail.setLocation(x, y);
4    }
```

Listing 7.22 ■ Fish's setLocation method

```
1    public int getX () {
2        return (int) _tail.getX();
3    }
4    public int getY() {
5        return (int) _tail.getY();
6    }
```

Listing 7.23 ■ Accessor methods for the Fish's location

shown in Listing 7.23. Why the tail rather than the body of the Fish? Because, as you can see in Figure 7.8, the top left-hand corner of the tail is the same as the top left-hand corner of the Fish.

location of tail
and fish

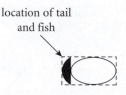

Figure 7.8 ■ Bounding boxes for the `Fish`.

```
1    public void setRotation (double aNumberDegrees) {
2        _rotation = aNumberDegrees;
3    }
4    public double getCenterX () {
5        return this.getX() + FISH_WIDTH/2;
6    }
7    public double getCenterY () {
8        return this.getY() + FISH_HEIGHT/2;
9    }
```

Listing 7.24 ■ The `Fish`'s methods related to rotation

The `Fish` has three methods related to rotations: first, a mutator to set the amount of the rotation, and then two methods for computing the center point of the `Fish` around which it rotates (see Listing 7.24).

Finally, the `Fish` defines its own `fill` and `draw` methods. After rotating `aBrush`, the `Fish` calls the corresponding methods on its parts, another example of the Composite Pattern (see Listing 7.25).

There are two things to notice about the way in which the `Fish` is drawn. First, the drawing is rotated around the center of the `Fish`; if the tail and body were rotated individually, it wouldn't look right. Second, when the `Fish` swims from right to left, it is upside down. It's swimming on its back—not generally a good sign in fish! As long as the `Fish` are symmetric top-to-bottom, this makes no difference (the picture in the window looks exactly the same). If you change the `Fish`, for example by adding fins, you will need to deal with some added complexity to rotate it properly, which we do not cover here.

We need one last class to write this program, the `SmartArc`. The `SmartArc` is the same as the `SmartEllipse` and the `SmartRectangle` except for its constructor. The class definition is shown in Listing 7.26.

```
1    public void fill (java.awt.Graphics2D aBrush){
2        aBrush.rotate(_rotation,
3                        this.getCenterX(),this.getCenterY());
4        _body.fill(aBrush);
5        _tail.fill(aBrush);
6        aBrush.rotate(-_rotation,
7                        this.getCenterX(),this.getCenterY());
8    }
9    public void draw (java.awt.Graphics2D aBrush){
10       aBrush.rotate(_rotation,
11                        this.getCenterX(),this.getCenterY());
12       _body.draw(aBrush);
13       _tail.draw(aBrush);
14       aBrush.rotate(-_rotation,
15                        this.getCenterX(),this.getCenterY());
16   }
```

Listing 7.25 ■ The Fish's fill and draw methods

The Arc2D.Double is a Java2D shape that models a curve. It is basically a piece of an ellipse, as if the paintbrush stopped after painting only part of the ellipse. (Figure 7.9 top). We can use this class to model not only open curves, but also filled-in shapes (Figure 7.9 middle), and pie slices, where lines are drawn from each of the endpoints to the center of the ellipse (Figure 7.9 bottom).

Clearly, we need to provide more information in order to draw arcs than rectangles or ellipses. Since the arcs are based on ellipses, we start by giving the location of the top

Figure 7.9 ■ Kinds of shapes that can be drawn with Java's Arc2D.

```
1    /**
2     * Chapter 7: SmartArc.java
3     * Extends Java's Arc2D.Double
4     * class, adding the same
5     * capabilities the
6     * SmartEllipse has.
7     */
8    public class SmartArc extends java.awt.geom.Arc2D.Double {
9        private java.awt.Color _borderColor, _fillColor; // attributes
10       private int _rotation;
11       private final int STROKE_WIDTH = 2;
12
13       public SmartArc (double aStart, double anExtent,
14                        int aType, java.awt.Color aColor) {
15           super (0, 0, 0, 0, aStart, anExtent, aType);
16           _borderColor = aColor;
17           _fillColor = aColor;
18           _rotation = 0;
19       }
20
21       // copy methods from SmartEllipse in here
22   }
```

Listing 7.26 ■ The SmartArc class

left-hand corner of the ellipse, its width, and its height, just as if we were drawing the whole thing. These *x*, *y*, width, and height values are the first four parameters to the Arc2D's constructor. The next parameter is aStart, the starting point. The starting point is given in degrees, starting at 3 o'clock and going counter-clockwise around the ellipse. Three o'clock is represented by 0, noon is 90, 9 o'clock is 180, and so forth. (The angles in between may seem a little wrong if your ellipse isn't a perfect circle, because the angle from the center of the ellipse to the corner of its bounding box is always considered to be 45 degrees from the horizontal. Just play with the numbers until the shape looks right to you.)

Next we need to say how much of the ellipse to draw (anExtent). We give the number of degrees, so if we want to draw the top half of the ellipse starting from 3 o'clock, we say 180. If we want to draw the bottom half of the ellipse, that's also 180 degrees, but we say −180, because we're going clockwise. Finally, we need to choose whether we want a curve (Arc2D.OPEN), a filled-in curve (Arc2D.CHORD), or a pie slice (Arc2D.PIE).

With fairly small modifications, reusing most of the code from the previous example, we now have a program that is significantly more complex. Compile the code for the `FishApp` and try it out for yourself, varying it until you are comfortable that you understand the material.

■ 7.6* ■ Working Out with Design—building our own Wheels

In this section we show you an alternative design for a simple replacement to Wheels. When we extended the shape classes provided by Java, we needed to repeat a lot of code. `SmartEllipse` and `SmartRectangle` are each 47 lines long, and only two of those lines are at all different. It's easy to write that code using cut-and-paste, but all things being equal, it would be a better design if we could somehow avoid all that repetition.

Here we define a `ColorShape` superclass and factor out all the common methods from our `SmartShapes` into that superclass. A class diagram for our new shapes hierarchy is given in Figure 7.10.

7.6.1 **Java's built-in shape classes**

The design we're about to show you avoids the repeated code of the earlier design, but at a cost. With this design, it's more difficult to add lines or polygons, if we wish to do so. To understand why, we need to look more closely at Java's built-in shape classes.

AWT modeled points with integer x and y values, as we have seen, using the `java.awt.Point` class. It also contained a model of a polygon, `java.awt.Polygon`, and a rectangle, `java.awt.Rectangle`. Java2D added several new shape classes, including the `Ellipse2D.Double`, `Arc2D.Double`, and `Rectangle2D.Double` that we have already used. A portion of the inheritance hierarchy for these classes is given in Figure 7.11.

The classes modeling primitive rectangles, ellipses, and arcs are all closely related—they all extend the `RectangularShape` superclass. They are all described in terms of a rectangular bounding box, and they share many useful methods. The classes modeling lines and

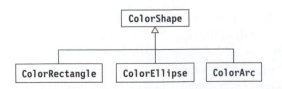

Figure 7.10 ■ A class diagram showing the `ColorShapes`.

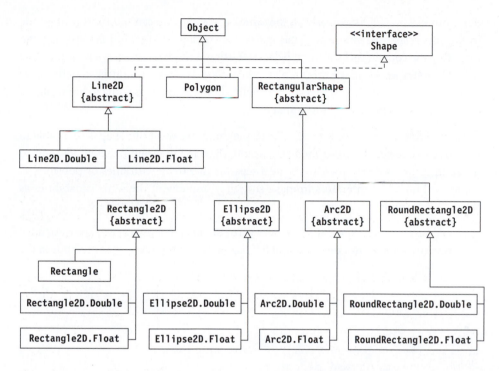

Figure 7.11 ■ Portion of inheritance hierarchy for Java2D shapes.

polygons, however, share relatively little with the `RectangularShapes`: only the methods required by the `Shape` interface. (Recall that the dotted line indicates that a class implements an interface.) If we simply extend each of the shape classes we're interested in to create a new `SmartShape`, as in the earlier part of the chapter, we can easily add lines and polygons. The design we're about to show you is successful in factoring out code because it focuses on `RectangularShapes`, which have a lot of methods in common; but for the same reason, it does not easily lend itself to modeling lines or polygons.

7.6.2 **Our new `ColorShape` classes**

As with `SmartEllipse` and `SmartRectangle`, we want our smart shape classes to be able to do several things:

- color themselves
- rotate themselves
- size themselves
- position themselves in a window
- display themselves in a window

Since our classes will have nearly all the same capabilities, we can put most of the code in the superclass `ColorShape`. That makes the superclass long, but it saves us from repeating the code in each of the subclasses. Listing 7.27 gives an overview of the code for `ColorShape`. We make this an `abstract` class, because it models something we don't want to instantiate; any object we actually put in a window is going to be an ellipse, or an arc, or a rectangle, not just a shape.

We also define an interface for each one of the things we want our shapes to be able to do: `Colorable` for the color methods, `Rotatable` for the rotation methods, and so forth. In future, we may want to create a separate hierarchy with lines or polygons. If so, we will use these interfaces to make sure they implement the same capabilities as the classes we're defining here.

We could have `ColorShape` extend `RectangularShape`, just as `SmartEllipse` extended `Ellipse2D.Double`. But then we wouldn't have access to the specialized methods of the

```
 1   /**
 2    * Chapter 7.6*: ColorShape.java
 3    * An alternative implementation of smart shapes
 4    * based on containment and delegation.
 5    */
 6   public abstract class ColorShape {
 7       private java.awt.Color _borderColor, _fillColor; // attributes
 8       private double _rotation;
 9       private final int STROKE_WIDTH = 2;
10       private java.awt.geom.RectangularShape _shape; // component
11
12       public ColorShape (java.awt.geom.RectangularShape s) {
13           _borderColor = java.awt.Color.WHITE;
14           _fillColor = java.awt.Color.WHITE;
15           _rotation = 0;
16           _shape = s;
17       }
18       // code implementing color methods
19       // code implementing rotation methods
20       // code implementing location methods
21       // code implementing size methods
22       // code implementing draw and fill methods
23   }
```

Listing 7.27 ■ The `ColorShape` class

individual shape classes, such as `Ellipse2D.Double`. We want to model specific shapes, not just `RectangularShapes`. So instead, we make the `RectangularShape` a component of `ColorShape`. This contained `_shape` object is used to store the `ColorShape`'s height, width, and location. All the other attributes (the border color, the fill color, and the amount of rotation) are stored in instance variables, just as in the earlier design. The accessors and mutators for the color and rotation variables are also the same as in our previous design. The default color of the `ColorShape` is white (both the outline and the fill), and the default rotation is 0.

The `ColorShape`'s color methods are the same as for the `SmartShapes`:

```java
public void setBorderColor (java.awt.Color aColor) {
    _borderColor = aColor;
}

public void setFillColor (java.awt.Color aColor) {
    _fillColor = aColor;
}
```

To be able to rotate, a `ColorShape` must be able to compute its center (because it rotates around its center). The `SmartShapes` in our earlier design simply inherited these methods, which are provided by Java's built-in `RectangularShape` classes. Here we must define them explicitly:

```java
public double getCenterX () {
    return _shape.getCenterX();
}

public double getCenterY () {
    return _shape.getCenterY();
}
```

We delegate the work to `_shape`, because it is a `RectangularShape`.

Similarly, we can write methods for getting the boundaries of the shape by delegating work to the `_shape` variable. These are additional methods we did not have to write in our earlier design, because the shapes inherited them:

```java
public double getMaxX () {
    return _shape.getMaxX();
}

public double getMaxY () {
    return _shape.getMaxY();
}
```

```
                    super(new java.awt.geom.Ellipse2D.Double());
                    super.setBorderColor(aBorderColor);
                    super.setFillColor(aFillColor);
                }
        }
```

The only difference is that here we're drawing an ellipse, instead of a rectangle.

The `ColorArc`'s class definition is almost as short as the others:

```
    /**
     * Chapter 7.6*: ColorArc
     * An alternative to SmartArc
     */
    public class ColorArc extends ColorShape {
        public ColorArc(double aStart, double anExtent,
                        int aType,java.awt.Color aColor){
            super(new java.awt.geom.Arc2D.Double
                  (0, 0, 0, 0, aStart, anExtent, aType));
            this.setFillColor(aColor);
            this.setBorderColor(aColor);
        }
    }
```

In sum, both designs have their pros and cons. The clean, short subclasses are the best part of the design presented here, and this design also avoids the repeated code of the inheritance-based design. On the other hand, the `ColorShape` class here is very long, and it must define several methods that simply delegate tasks to `_shape`, methods that don't have to be defined at all in the inheritance-based design. Moreover, the inheritance-based design can easily be extended to include lines or polygons; this design can't, because Java's line and polygon classes don't inherit from `RectangularShape`. We leave it to you to decide which one you prefer.

■ Summary ■

You have now been given a powerful set of tools. You have learned about Swing's built-in `JFrame` and `JPanel` classes, about creating shapes, positioning them on the screen, giving them color, rotating, and animating them, and you have been introduced to Java's event model. These are only a subset of the tools available in Swing, but they are sufficient to enable you to create simple animated pictures. In addition, you have seen a significant example of object-oriented design, in AWT and Swing.

In the next chapter, we will discuss graphical user interfaces and introduce you to another part of Java's AWT and Swing libraries.

■ Self-Check Questions ■

(The answers to these questions can be found on the book's website, www.aw.com/sanders)

1. What is a JFrame used for?

2. What is a JPanel used for?

3. When do you call the repaint method?

4. What are the properties and capabilities of the Graphics object?

5. What built-in method takes the Graphics object as a parameter?

6. What is the difference between a Graphics object and an instance of its subclass, Graphics2D?

7. List five built-in shape classes provided by Java2D.

8. What is the main difference between graphical shapes in AWT and graphical shapes in Java2D?

9. What is an inner class?

10. Explain how a javax.swing.Timer works.

11. Briefly explain the Java event model.

12. What interface is necessary for objects that listen to Timers?

13. Summarize the steps necessary in order to use a Timer.

14. Give the basic framework for graphical programs in the rest of this text (i.e., the boilerplate from the definitions of BallApp and BallPanel).

15. What does it mean to cast an object?

■ Exercises ■

Applying the Facts

1. Suppose we wanted to write a program with squares moving around a window, instead of a bouncing ball. Why would it be more difficult to write this program? Explain.

2. (Examine the online Java documentation at http://java.sun.com/j2se/1.5.0/docs/api/allclasses-noframe.html for the answer to the following question.) What is the difference between Java's RectangularShape's setFrame method and the Polygon's translate method? Discuss how the use of an interface might have helped in the design of this portion of the Java2D library.

3. Compare and contrast the two designs given in the chapter for defining shape classes. Which do you prefer and why? Justify your answer.

4. Explain the purpose of the line `super(title)` in `BallApp`'s constructor.

5. Explain the purpose of the line

   `this.setDefaultCloseOperation(JFrame.EXIT_ON_CLOSE)` in `BallApp`.

6. Inside `paintComponent`, why is it sometimes useful to cast the `Graphics` object as a `Graphics2D` object?

7. Inside `paintComponent`, why should the first line be `super.paintComponent()`?

Debugging Programs

Identify the error(s) in each of the following code fragments, if any. Explain your answers.

1.
```java
public class MyApp extends JFrame
    public MyApp (String title) {
        super(title);
        this.setSize(600, 450); // the size may vary
        this.setDefaultCloseOperation(
            JFrame.EXIT_ON_CLOSE);
        // specific code for your application goes here
    }

    public static void main (String [] args) {
        new MyApp ("This text will go on the frame.");
    }
}
```

2.
```java
// Assume setColor methods are defined in "Shape" class
Shape shape1 = new Shape();
shape1.setColor(java.awt.Color.PURPLE);
Shape shape2 = new Shape()'
shape2.setColor(new java.awt.Color(-10, 0, 300));
```

3.
```java
// code to make some Rectangles
    import java.awt.*;
    import java.awt.geom.*;
    ...
    RectangularShape rect1 = new Rectangle(25, 25, 100,
    100);
    RectangularShape rect2 = new Rectangle2D(40, 40, 50,
    50);
    RectangularShape rect3 = new Rectangle2D.Double(100,
    10, 30, 60);
```

```
4.  import java.awt.event.*
    import javax.swing.Timer;
    public class DancingShape extends MyShape {
        ...
        public DancingShape(Timer aTimer) {
        ...
        aTimer.addActionListener(this);
        }
        public void actionPerformed (ActionEvent e) { ...}
    }
```

■ Programming Projects ■

Modifying Programs

1. Modify the `BallApp` program to change the height and width of the `JFrame`.

2. Modify the `BallApp` program to change the color of the ball and the background. (Choose any two different colors).

3. Modify the `BallApp` program so that the `Ball` only moves horizontally, back and forth.

4. Modify the `BallApp` program so that the `Ball` only moves vertically, up and down.

5. Modify the `BallApp` program to speed up and slow down the `Ball`. Which speed do you like best? Why?

6. Modify the `BallApp` program to change the direction in which the `Ball` bounces when it hits the wall so that it always makes a right angle.

7. Modify the `BallApp` program to add a second bouncing ball of a different color to the picture.

8. Modify the `BallApp` program to create a `SquareApp` program with a square bouncing around a window.

9. Modify the `ColorShape` hierarchy to add a `ColorRoundedRectangle`. Write a program that displays a blue `ColorRoundedRectangle` on a white background (without animating it).

10. Modify the `FishTankApp` program to add two new fish, one blue and one yellow.

11. Modify the `FishTankApp` program to create a new color for the fish tank. Create a custom blue-green color that you find more attractive than the built-in cyan color.

12. Modify the `FishTankApp` program so that the fish is painted before the fish tank.

    a. Before you run the program, predict the result of this change.
    b. Compile, test, and run the modified program. What happens? Does it match your prediction? How do you explain the result?

13. Modify the `FishTankApp` program until the fish is about two inches long on your screen.

14. Modify the `FishTankApp` program so that the fish starts on the right-hand side of the tank, facing left.

15. Modify the `FishTankApp` program to add a new subclass of `Fish`, `MotleyFish`, that has a body and tail of different colors. Add an instance of `MotleyFish` to the fish tank.

16. Modify the `FishTankApp` program so that one of the fish swims vertically. It should move up until it reaches the top of the tank, then move down to the bottom, then back up to the top, and so on. For now, let it continue to face right.

17. Modify the `FishTankApp` program so that one of the fish swims vertically. It should move up until it reaches the top of the tank, then move down to the bottom, then back up to the top, and so on. Make sure it faces in the direction it is moving.

18. Modify the `FishTankApp` program so that one of the fish swims on a diagonal. It should move continuously, changing direction each time it reaches the edge of the tank. For now, let it continue to face right.

19. Modify the `FishTankApp` program so that one of the fish swims on a diagonal. It should move continuously, changing direction each time it reaches the edge of the tank. Make sure it faces in the direction it is moving.

20. Modify the `FishTankApp` program so that one large fish gets smaller and smaller as it moves to the right, until it disappears completely.

21. To redraw just part of a `JPanel` we can call `repaint(x, y, width, height)`, giving the location, width, and height of the rectangle we want repainted. For example, if we just want to repaint a single shape, we can give the location, width, and height of its bounding box, like this:

    ```
    _somePanel.repaint(this.getBounds());
    ```

    Modify `BallApp` so that it only repaints (1) the area the ball is leaving and (2) the area it will be located in. Some argue that this version of the code is slower than calling `repaint` on the entire panel—do you find a difference? What if you add more instances of `BouncingBall`—then do you find a difference? Measure the times as precisely as you can and give data to support your conclusion.

Writing Programs

1. Write a program to display the shapes from Tetris® in a window. The shapes are each made up of four squares, as shown in Figure 7.12.

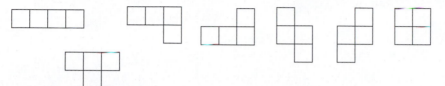

Figure 7.12 ■ Tetris shapes.

2. Write a program to create the Tetris shapes (in question 1) one after another at the top of the screen and move them to the bottom. Each shape should stop as soon as it either reaches the bottom of the window or touches another shape below it. The program should halt when one of the shapes touches the top edge of the window.

3. Write a program that displays a cartoon figure performing jumping jacks.

4. Write a program that displays a simple picture of a house with clouds moving across the sky above it. Each cloud should be composed of at least two ellipses.

5. Write a program in Java, without using Wheels, that displays the Snowman picture from Chapter 2.

chapter **8**

Graphical User Interfaces and Event-Handling

OBJECTIVES

After reading this chapter, you should be able to:

☑ Define user-centered design, describe the process of creating a user interface, and give some guidelines for determining whether an interface is user-centered

☑ Discuss the pros and cons of a given interface with respect to the guidelines

☑ Use Java's built-in Swing and AWT classes to implement an interface with windows, pushbuttons, and radio buttons

☑ Use Java's `FlowLayout`, `GridLayout`, and `BorderLayout` classes to arrange the components of a user interface in a window

☑ Implement Smart Components: buttons, radio buttons, or sliders that have the ability to handle the events they generate

☑ Explain our recipe for handling mouse input

☑ Implement simple programs that handle mouse input

■ 8.1 ■ Introduction

An interface can be defined as "the point at which independent systems or diverse groups interact." (The American Heritage Dictionary of the American Language, 3d edition. Boston: Houghton Mifflin (1992).) So a Java `interface` is a kind of interface, because it defines the way in which one object interacts with another. The seashore is the interface between the ocean and the land. The steering wheel, brake, gas pedal, and dashboard are parts of the user interface to a car. User interfaces, the subject of this chapter, are the point at which a product interacts with the user—that is, us.

The interface is the part of the product we see and manipulate. In our technological society, we encounter user interfaces every day. When we set a clock radio, turn the television on or off, program a VCR, cook something in the microwave, call a friend on a cell phone, or play music on the CD player, we are using an interface.

In the 2000 United States presidential election, a bad interface design may have changed history. Florida was the state whose votes determined the result, and Palm Beach County was a key location in Florida. The Palm Beach ballot is shown in Figure 8.1. Ballot designs are determined locally and vary from place to place in the United States. Examine this ballot carefully. To cast a vote, you must punch one of the holes in the center column. Gore's name is third if you consider the left- and right-hand columns together, but second in the left-hand column. To cast a vote for Gore, the voter needed to punch the third hole, but it seems that some voters—perhaps enough to change the result of the election—mistakenly punched the second hole, casting a vote for Buchanan when they intended to vote for Gore.

The interface defines a product for its users. Because the user interface is the only part of a piece of software that the users see, user-interface design is key to the success of a software project. Designing good user interfaces is also a challenging and interesting field. User-interface designers may or may not be programmers, but they must understand how software is designed and implemented. In addition, they must understand people: their physical and cognitive limitations, what they find easy to learn, easy to use, and appealing.

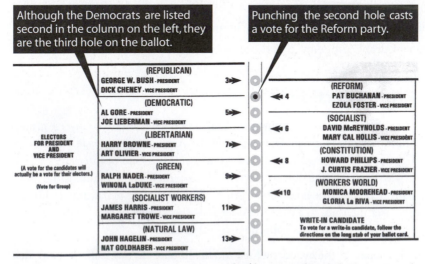

Confusion at Palm Beach County polls

Some Al Gore supporters may have mistakenly voted for Pat Buchanan because of the ballot's design.

Graphic courtesy of South Florida Sun-Sentinel

Figure 8.1 ■ How user interface designers can change history.

In this chapter, we give a brief overview of user interface design, including some general design principles, and a basic toolkit for creating graphical user interfaces in Java. For the rest of the book, you will build user interfaces of your own for your programs.

■ 8.2 ■ Concepts

8.2.1 Design principles

The main principle of user interface design is that the interface should work for the user. We should provide usable, functional, safe, efficient systems for the people who use them. This approach is known as *user-centered design*.

How do we create a user-centered interface? The process is similar to any software project: analysis, design, implementation, testing, and maintenance. In the analysis phase, the first step is to get as much information as possible about the potential users. Creating an interface that will work for someone else requires an effort of imagination. The more relevant information we have about the users, the better, starting with general background information about human capabilities and preferences. For example, humans are not good at remembering random five-digit numbers while concentrating on another task. An interface that requires users to memorize a five-digit code and remember it while searching through several screens for the place to enter it is badly designed.

We must also gather as much information as possible about the users of this software. Who are they? How experienced are they with computers and their application programs? What software have they used? What are their ages, educational levels, cultural characteristics, disabilities, general attitudes toward computers, and typing abilities? How long will they have to learn the new system? How many will be occasional users likely to forget how to use various features, and how many everyday "power users" for whom efficiency is more important than ease of learning and remembering? Will they be using it at home, at work, or on the road?

One particularly good question to ask is how users are currently solving the problem your software is designed to solve. The more you know about what they like and dislike about their current solution, the more appealing you can make your software, and the easier you can make the transition from the old solution to the new one. In one case, for example, the shipping department of a large corporation ordered a custom piece of software. The software's job was to determine the routes the company's trucks should use to deliver its products to a given set of locations most efficiently. This is a well known, much studied problem in computer science, and the software engineers wrote a program that computed very efficient routes.

keyconcept

The main principle of user-interface design is that the interface should work for the user. This approach is also known as *user-centered design*.

keyconcept

Interface design is software design. The process is the same: analysis, design, implementation, testing, and maintenance, and we use the same technique of incremental development and debugging.

Despite its excellent performance, however, the program was not being used. In order to find out why, the designers observed the users. Instead of using the software, the users kept solving the problem the old way: they put pins in a large map to mark the delivery locations and worked from there. The software designers modified their user interface to display a map on which users could mark locations with a "pin" by clicking on them. The revised software was much more popular than the first version—even though the actual routes it computed were exactly the same. Ideally, we find out this kind of information about how users solve their problems early in the analysis phase.

In the design phase, we need to identify the key concepts in the application, as we would for any program: what are the objects? What are their properties? What actions can they perform? What are the relations between objects? How can we model those objects and their relationships in Java?

Then we need to define the content of the information the user gives to the program, and the information the program presents to the user. What order can/must the user provide information in? When does the computer tell the user something, and what?

Next we need to design the form of the information exchanged between the user and the computer:

1. How will the user provide input to the program (e.g., mouse selections from menus, mouse clicks on icons, keyboard shortcuts, typed commands, or voice commands)?

2. What kind of feedback should the system provide? (Feedback might include highlighting the object the mouse is hovering over to show that it is selectable, or changing the color of an item to show that it has been selected at least once.)

3. If the program gets input from the user, which object(s) provide feedback? Which objects provide other forms of response?

4. How can we cause the user input to go to the object(s) that need it?

5. What should the object that receives the input do in response? (We distinguish between temporary feedback during a user interaction and response to the user's input.)

6. How can we model that response in Java?

7. How will the user's options, the program's feedback, and the program's output be arranged on the screen?

8. How can we create the desired spatial arrangement, using Java's built-in abilities to lay out graphical components and/or doing absolute positioning ourselves?

At this design stage, we should also begin to predict specific user inputs, in order to identify potential problems.

Once we have a draft, how can we tell if we have a good user-centered design? Here are some guidelines:

- Let the user be in control
- Make the interface
  - □ physically comfortable and easy to use
  - □ as quick as possible to use (in computer-science terms, efficient)
  - □ easy to learn
  - □ easy to remember
  - □ fun to use
  - □ unobtrusive
- Make it harder, not easier, to make mistakes
- Follow the "law of least astonishment"

Computer scientists call an unobtrusive interface **transparent**: a good interface, like a clean window, lets the user look through it and focus on the task being performed. A bad interface, like a dirty window, draws attention to itself.

keyconcept
A transparent interface lets users focus on the task.

The **law of least astonishment** means "don't surprise the users." If users have expectations about interfaces, take advantage of them. For example, if your users, from experience with other applications, expect "quit" or "exit" to be on the bottom of the left-hand menu, put it there (unless you can make a compelling argument that it is better *for the user* another way). If the users are comfortable with a map, make your interface look like a map. If the users know that a triangle pointing to the right means "play," use that symbol when designing an interface for an online music player. If users are accustomed to using a browser's back button to return to a previous page, let them.

keyconcept
The law of least astonishment means "Don't surprise the users."

Sometimes these rules reinforce each other and sometimes they conflict. An interface that obeys the law of least astonishment is likely to be easier to learn. On the other hand, an interface that takes more initial effort to learn may be much faster to use once mastered. That is certainly true for keyboard shortcuts designed to avoid menu selections. As designers, we must determine how to make the tradeoffs in each case or provide the user with options.

The implementation and testing phases are similar to any other part of a software project, except that it's even more important to involve the users—real users, both novice and expert—early and often. We can make our best guess as to whether our interfaces satisfy the principles given above, but the real test is whether they work for the users.

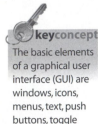

8.2.2 **Design tools**

The basic components of a graphical user interface (GUI) include, among other things, windows, icons, menus, text, push buttons, toggle buttons, radio buttons, combo boxes, and sliders. The kind of GUI using such graphical components (also called "widgets") is often referred to as a WIMP GUI, shorthand for Windows, Icons, Menus and Pointer (typically the mouse).

Icons are graphical shapes that usually correspond to a file, a folder, or a device such as a CD-ROM drive, a hard disk, or a printer. **Menus** are a list of predefined choices. When you select one, it's like pushing a button. **Text** basically means words. It can also include sentences, paragraphs, or mathematical expressions—in short, anything that can be typed on a keyboard. Some text objects can be modified by the user, and some cannot. **Push buttons** work like the button on a doorbell: when you push them, something happens. Other buttons let the user choose between a set of values. **Toggle buttons** go back and forth between two states, like light switches. They let the user choose whether or not something is true. For example, should the background color be white or blue? **Radio buttons** let the user choose one of a set of separate, mutually exclusive values. Just like the buttons on your car radio, radio buttons let you select only one option at a time, so that the user can choose black, white, blue, or green for the background. **Sliders** let the user choose one of a range of possible (discrete) values. With a slider, the user can choose integers between a minimum and a maximum, or one of a range of possible colors.

We need a way to arrange the GUI components and the objects they control in a window. Up to now, we have used absolute positioning of shapes. In this chapter, we see three of the alternative automatic layout methods Java provides, called `BorderLayout`, `FlowLayout`, and `GridLayout`.

Finally, we need a way for the program to respond to the user's input. Menus, text, buttons, sliders, mouse clicks, and mouse drags all allow users to give information to the program. In Java, when users give information to a program in any of these ways, the users' action generates an event. Just as the `Fish` in Chapter 7 responded to the events generated by the `Timer`, objects can be programmed to respond to (or handle) events generated by the user.

WIMP GUIs: Some Background

WIMP GUIs are the standard interface for all personal computers and are more than three decades old. The WIMP GUI was invented at Xerox Palo Alto Research Center in the early seventies, as part of the Smalltalk programming environment. Smalltalk was the first full-featured object-oriented programming language, a precursor to Java.

Table 8.1 ■ An overview of the main Swing containers and components.

Top-Level Containers	
`JApplet`	for small programs that run inside another program (usually a web browser)
`JOptionPane`	for dialog boxes
`JFrame`	for the main window(s) of an application
Mid-Level Containers	
`JPanel`	the basic mid-level container. Contained inside a top-level container (or another mid-level container), `JPanels` in turn contain other containers or components
`JScrollPane`	provides a container with scrollbars, a scrollable way of looking at another component
`JSplitPane`	a container divided into two parts, each showing a different component
`JTabbedPane`	a set of one or more rectangular components where the "top" component only is visible, each component looks like an index card with a tab, and the user brings a component to the front by clicking on its tab
`JToolBar`	contains a row of buttons; usually placed along the top of another container
Components: getting user input	
`JButton`	a push button
`JComboBox`	a drop-down list
`JList`	a list from which the user can select one or more items. May be large
`JMenu`	a software menu
`JRadioButtons`	allow the user to push one of a set of mutually exclusive buttons
`JSlider`	lets the user select a value by sliding a button from side to side (or up and down)
`JSpinner`	like a drop-down list except that it takes up less space (the user cycles through the values by pressing an arrow)
`JTextField`	allows the user to enter a single line of text
`JPasswordField`	allows the user to enter a single line of text; indicates that something was entered without displaying it
`JFormattedTextField`	allows the user to enter a single line of text that matches a specified set of characters

(continued on next page)

Components: getting user input (continued)	
JTextArea	allows the user to enter multiple lines of text
JColorChooser	displays possible colors and allows the user to choose
JFileChooser	displays a list of files and allows the user to select one (e.g., to open)

Components: output only	
JLabel	displays a small amount of text or a picture or both
JProgressBar	shows how much of a task has been completed
JToolTip	information that appears when the user hovers the mouse over a component

■ 8.3 ■ Mechanics

The three main things we need to know to define a GUI are:

1. how to create the components of the GUI, such as buttons

2. how to arrange the components in a window

3. how to make them respond to user input

keyconcept

In Java, the basic elements of a GUI interface, called components, each correspond to a class. These classes are contained in the AWT and Swing libraries.

In Java, the basic components of a GUI each correspond to a class. These classes are contained in the AWT and Swing libraries and, as you can see from the overview in Table 8.1, there are quite a few of them.

Fortunately, however, you don't need to learn all of Java's component classes—at least not right away. In this chapter, we describe a few representative components. The main emphasis, however, is on the layout and event-handling mechanisms of Java, which underlie all components and are the real subject of this chapter. When you master this material, you will be able to learn from the online documentation how to use additional components as you need them. There is a particularly helpful visual index of components at http://java.sun.com/docs/books/tutorial/uiswing/components/components.html, with links to the documentation for each component.

8.3.1 Arranging components on the screen: layouts

In Chapter 7, we used absolute positioning to locate graphical shapes in a JPanel. The problem with this solution is that—as you've probably already noticed—it's hard to figure out what the positions should be. It's hard to remember how we figured it out, too, so that modifying the program is difficult. In addition, the program might look different on different types of computer screens, making it less portable.

As an alternative to absolute positioning, Java provides several built-in solutions for arranging graphical shapes and components. In true object-oriented fashion, Java models these solutions with classes, each of which implements the `LayoutManager` interface. (`LayoutManager` is an interface rather than an abstract superclass because `LayoutManager` is a role, a set of behaviors that we want the classes to have.). By being appropriately lazy and using a `LayoutManager`, we sacrifice fine control over placement of components to get reasonable, if not optimal defaults for their placement.

Each of the classes that implements the `LayoutManager` interface corresponds to a particular way of arranging components. We discuss three of the most popular in this chapter: `BorderLayout`, `FlowLayout`, and `GridLayout`.

BorderLayouts. **`BorderLayout`** is the default layout for the contents of a `JFrame`. This built-in layout arranges components into five regions, called "North," "South," "East," "West," and "Center." As you might expect, these regions are at the top, bottom, left, right, and middle, respectively, of the `JFrame` or `JPanel`. Each of the regions of a `BorderLayout` can contain at most one component. The size of the regions depends on the size of their contents, and regions expand to fill the area left over by other regions. Figure 8.2 shows some of the possible configurations of a `BorderLayout`. For clarity, we outline the `BorderLayout`'s regions in color; the boundaries of these regions are normally invisible. The code for drawing the outlines is given later in the chapter.

In fact, although you may not realize it, we have seen `BorderLayout` before. When we added the `FishPanel` to the `FishApp` in Chapter 7, like this:

```
this.add(new FishPanel());
```

we were actually adding to the center region of a `BorderLayout`. So this line of code is equivalent to:

```
this.add(new FishPanel(), java.awt.BorderLayout.CENTER);
```

If we want to add another component to the bottom of the `JFrame`, we can add it explicitly to the south region of the `BorderLayout`:

```
this.add(_someComponent, java.awt.BorderLayout.SOUTH);
```

Similarly, if we want a component on the left-hand side, we add it to `BorderLayout.WEST`, and if we want a component on the right, we add it to `BorderLayout.EAST`. Order matters: if we add two components to the same region of a `BorderLayout`, only the second one is displayed.

Nested panels and `FlowLayouts`. What if we want to add more than one component to a particular region of a `BorderLayout`? With a `BorderLayout`, we can only have

keyconcept
Three built-in ways of arranging the contents of a `JPanel` are `BorderLayout`, `FlowLayout`, and `GridLayout`. `BorderLayout`, `FlowLayout`, and `GridLayout` are all objects themselves and are associated with a container whose components they arrange.

keyconcept
`BorderLayout` holds one component per region; to add more than one, we add a subpanel to the region and then add components to the subpanel.

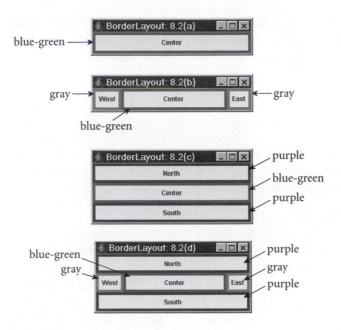

Figure 8.2 ■ Some `BorderLayout`s.

one component per region. If we add two components, one after another, the `BorderLayout` puts them on top of one another, and we see only the second one.

Here's a solution: use a subpanel. Start by creating a new `JPanel`. Then add the components to the `JPanel` and put the `JPanel` in the `JFrame`, instead of putting the components directly into the `JFrame`. Here's the code we need, as a reusable recipe:

```
// use this code inside a JFrame subclass
_panel = new JPanel();
_panel.add(<_component1>);
_panel.add(<_component2>);
    ... // add more components if desired
this.add(_panel, BorderLayout.<someRegion>);
```

The components are now displayed correctly, because the default layout for a `JPanel` is a different kind of layout, called `FlowLayout`. **FlowLayout** arranges components from left to right, top to bottom, like the words on this page.

An example of a `FlowLayout` is shown in Figure 8.3. First, five panels (numbered 1–5) were added to another panel (outlined in purple). Then the panel containing the numbered panels was added to the south region of the `JFrame`.

Unlike `BorderLayout`, `FlowLayout` does not expand objects to fill the space available. For that reason, `FlowLayouts` are a good choice for components such as buttons that don't look right when they're expanded arbitrarily.

Nested panels and `GridLayouts`. Suppose we want to arrange components in rows and columns, like the keys on a calculator or the buttons on a telephone. The Java layout called `GridLayout` solves this problem. When we add components to a `GridLayout`, they expand to fit the space. In an $n \times m$ grid, they are all 1/nth of the width of the panel and 1/mth of the height of the panel, so this layout is best suited for components that should be uniform in size.

`GridLayout` arranges its contents into rows and columns. The number of rows is given first and then the columns, for example:

```
new GridLayout(5, 10)
```

Be sure to remember the order of the parameters here. It's the opposite of `setLocation`, where x is first and y second, and `setSize`, where the horizontal dimension (width) is first and the vertical (height) second.

As long as we add exactly the right number of components to a `GridLayout` (here, 50), this syntax creates a layout with five rows and ten columns. Otherwise, it creates five rows and divides the components among them, ignoring the number of columns. If the number of columns is important but we don't know what the number of rows is going to be, set the row number to zero:

```
new GridLayout(0, 10)
```

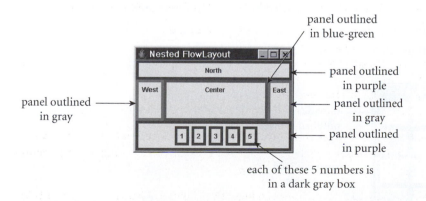

Figure 8.3 ■ A `FlowLayout`, nested inside a `BorderLayout`.

This code creates a layout with ten columns. The first ten components are added to the top row, from left to right, then components 11–20 are added to the second row, and so forth, until all the components have been added.

Similarly,

```
new GridLayout(1, 0)
```

creates a single row with any number of columns, depending on the number of items you add.

We can add a GridLayout to the JFrame in the same way we added a FlowLayout: create a new JPanel, add the components to the JPanel, and add the JPanel to the JFrame using the following recipe:

```
JPanel _panel;
_panel = new JPanel(new GridLayout(<rows>, <columns>));
_panel.add(_component1);
_panel.add(_component2);
   ...
this.add(_panel, BorderLayout.<region>);
```

An example of a GridLayout is shown in Figure 8.4.

8.3.2 **Components**

Now we have some techniques for arranging components in a window, let's look at how to create the components themselves. In this section, we discuss how to create four representative components: push buttons, radio buttons, sliders, and labels.

Push buttons.   Push buttons are modeled in Java using JButtons. We can create a button with a label like this:

```
new JButton("Move right >>");
```

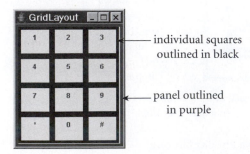

individual squares
outlined in black

panel outlined
in purple

Figure 8.4 ■ A GridLayout with 0 rows and 3 columns, nested inside the Center region of a BorderLayout.

or like this:

```
new JButton("Quit");
```

If desired, we can change the color of a button, like this:

```
someButton.setBackground(java.awt.Color.BLUE);
```

Figure 8.5 shows some JButtons.

To arrange the buttons, we put them inside a JPanel (outlined here in purple), and then add the JPanel to the JFrame, like this:

```
_panel.add(new JButton("<< Move left"));
_panel.add(new JButton("Quit"));
_panel.add(new JButton("Move right >>"));
this.add(_panel, java.awt.BorderLayout.SOUTH);
```

(We put buttons at the bottom of the window (in the SOUTH), but you can vary this if you like.)

Why don't we just add the buttons directly to the desired region of the JFrame? Experiment and try this for yourself. If you do, you will see that (as noted earlier), when we add more than one component to the same region of a BorderLayout, only the last one added is visible. If instead we nest the components inside a JPanel, because the default layout for JPanels is FlowLayout, we get what we want: the components are all shown in the order in which they were added.

Radio buttons. To model a situation where the user picks one of a set of mutually exclusive choices, Java provides a component called a JRadioButton. Suppose we want to let the user choose the color of a shape. First we need to declare instance variables of class JRadioButton for each of the possible choices:

```
private JRadioButton _greenButton;
private JRadioButton _blueButton;
```

We can add as many buttons as we want, but for purposes of illustration we'll just use two. Next add code instantiating the buttons:

```
_greenButton = new JRadioButton("green");
_blueButton = new JRadioButton("blue");
```

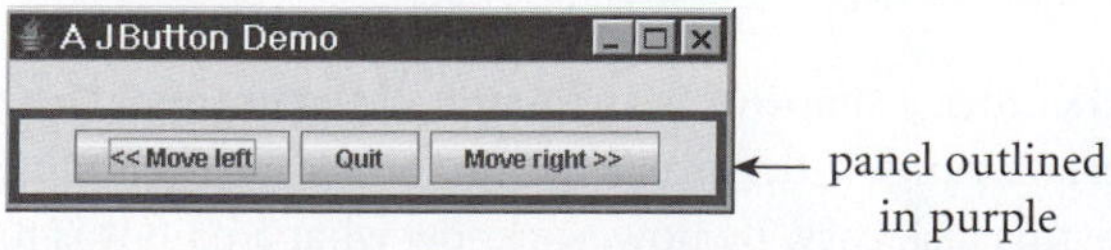

Figure 8.5 ■ Some JButtons inside a JPanel inside a JFrame.

This syntax is entirely similar to the syntax for JButtons. On the screen, however, you will see that the names of JRadioButtons appear next to them, instead of on the button.

We can also indicate which button should be selected at the start of the program, by using the setSelected method. If we add this line of code after creating the JRadioButtons, the green button is selected at first:

```
_greenButton.setSelected(true);
```

Alternatively, we can set true as a second parameter in a constructor:

```
_greenButton = new JRadioButton("green", true);
```

Finally, we group the buttons together, so that only one can be selected at a time.

```
ButtonGroup group = new ButtonGroup();
group.add(_greenButton);
group.add(_blueButton);
```

(Wonder what happens if you forget to group the buttons? Try it and see!)

Figure 8.6(a) shows a screenshot of these radio buttons. Once again, the buttons are nested inside a JPanel (here, outlined in purple) that is added to one of the regions of a JFrame.

If we color the buttons instead of giving them labels, users who can perceive the colors will have an easier time associating the buttons with what they do. In addition, buttons with colors instead of labels are language-independent, and the interface is elegantly minimal.

We can create the buttons without a label and give them associated colors like this:

```
_blueButton = new JRadioButton();
_blueButton.setBackground(java.awt.Color.BLUE);
```

Figure 8.6(b) shows the interface with colors instead of labels on the buttons.

Since some users will have difficulty seeing the colors, however, the best interface uses what is called "dual coding," combining colors and labels. We can do this easily:

```
_blueButton = new JRadioButton("blue");
_blueButton.setBackground(java.awt.Color.BLUE);
```

The combined version is shown in Figure 8.6(c).

Sliders. Suppose we want to let users move a shape or vary its size. We want them to be able to enter a number within a certain range—the size, location, or speed of a shape, for example—and we want to make this task easy. By now, we know what a pain it is to

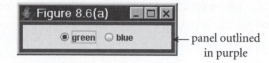

Figure 8.6(a) ■ Java's `JRadioButtons` inside a `JPanel`, nested inside the South region of a `JFrame`.

Figure 8.6(b) ■ `JRadioButtons` with colors instead of labels, nested inside a `JPanel`, inside the South region of a `JFrame`.

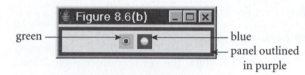

Figure 8.6(c) ■ The preferred solution: `JRadioButtons` with both colors and labels.

figure out the right pixel numbers for the size or location of a shape. We don't want the user to have to type in number after number.

The solution to this problem is a slider: a widget that lets the user enter a number by dragging a knob back and forth. We can create a horizontal slider like this:

```
_xSlider = new JSlider();
```

and a vertical slider like this:

```
_ySlider = new JSlider(JSlider.VERTICAL);
```

By default, the numbers on horizontal sliders run from left to right and the numbers on vertical sliders run from the bottom to the top. Since y values run from the top to the bottom, if we're using the slider to control the y location of an object, we want to reverse the orientation on our vertical slider, like this:

```
ySlider.setInverted(true);
```

By default, the minimum and maximum values of a slider are 0. Java provides mutators to change those values:

```
_xSlider.setMaximum(400);
_xSlider.setMinimum(0);
```

One additional useful method is the one to set the initial value of the slider:

```
_ySlider.setValue(200);
```

Alternatively, we can set the orientation, the minimum and maximum values, and the initial value all at once in the constructor. For example, we could write:

```
_xSlider = new JSlider(JSlider.HORIZONTAL, 0, 100, 20);
```

A GUI with two sliders is shown in Figure 8.7. Here, the vertical slider is contained inside a JPanel (outlined in purple), which has been added to the EAST region of a JFrame. The horizontal slider, similarly, has been nested inside another JPanel, which has been added to the SOUTH region. And finally, a JPanel (outlined in blue) has been added to the CENTER region. Later, this JPanel could hold whatever items the sliders are manipulating. We can improve this GUI by adding labels to the sliders, so the user knows which values he or she can choose from (see Figure 8.8). To add labels to a JSlider called _xSlider, we need the following code:

```
_xSlider.setPaintTicks(true);
_xSlider.setPaintLabels(true);
_xSlider.setMajorTickSpacing(10);
_xSlider.setMinorTickSpacing(1);
```

The first line of code specifies that we want the tick marks (the vertical lines). The sec-

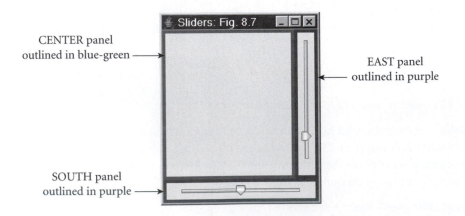

Figure 8.7 ■ A GUI with two JSliders and a central JPanel.

ond line of code gives us the numeric labels. Note that the tick marks are of two different sizes. The third line of code specifies how often we want the major tick marks (the larger ones, with the labels); the second line of code specifies how often we want the minor tick marks.

JLabels. Labels were helpful with sliders—how about adding them to other parts of our GUI? Suppose we want to say "Welcome!" or "Error!" or "The current *x* position of the ellipse is 257"? We can do this with a `javax.swing.JLabel`, like this:

```
_label = new JLabel("Welcome!");
```

For example, Figure 8.6 used `JLabel`s to label the regions of a `BorderLayout`. Here's the code to create one of these labels and put it in a panel:

```
javax.swing.JPanel subPanel = new javax.swing.JPanel();
javax.swing.JLabel label =
          new javax.swing.JLabel(<message>);
subPanel.add(label);
subPanel.setBorder(new
    javax.swing.border.LineBorder(<color>, <thickness>));
```

If we want to include the value of a numeric variable in a label, we can do it like this:

```
int xPos;
   ...
_label = new JLabel("X position: " + xPos);
```

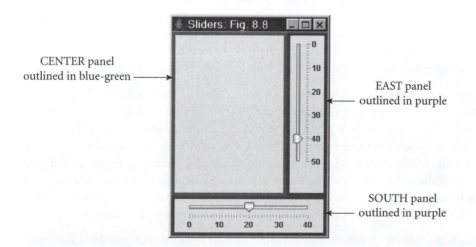

Figure 8.8 ■ `JSliders` with labels.

The plus symbol is overloaded in Java. When we're combining two numeric values, it means addition. When we're combining two `Strings` or, as here, a `String` and a number, it creates a longer `String` by attaching (or "concatenating") the second string onto the end of the first. Note that Java converts (or casts) the integer `xPos` to a string so it can concatenate the two strings and assign the result to the `JLabel`.

8.3.3 Making the program respond to input: event handling and `SmartComponents`

`JButtons`, `JRadioButtons`, and `JSliders` cause events, just as the `Timers` discussed in Chapter 7 do. Just like the ticks of a `Timer`, the user's click on a `JButton`, `JRadioButton`, or any other part of a `JFrame` generates an event. But if you run the program as we have written it up to this point and click on any of the buttons, you get feedback—it's clear that you clicked on the button—but nothing happens! Similarly, mouse clicks cause events, but if you click on the `BouncingBall` in Chapter 7, nothing happens. That's because the program doesn't do anything with these events; to use the technical term, it doesn't **handle** the events. An **event handler** is a piece of code that defines how the program responds to a particular event. The event handler is responsible for knowing which object(s) are to respond, and how, when a particular component is activated by the user.

In this section, we make our components into Smart Components by enabling them to handle the events they generate. We give each component a built-in event handler. In addition, we show how to make our shapes respond when the user clicks on them.

Smart JButtons and JRadioButtons. Like `Timers`, `JButtons` and `JRadioButtons` both generate `ActionEvents`, so to make a listener object respond to a button press, we follow the same recipe we used for `MoveTimers` (shown in Figure 8.9). The listener's `actionPerformed` method is called every time the user presses the `JButton` or selects the `JRadioButton` and will forward a message to the responder object(s).

For example, Listing 8.1 shows how to define a `ColorButton`, a `JRadioButton` that sends a message to an associated responder object (any kind of `Colorable`) to change its color. When the button is pushed, it sends a message to its internal `ColorListener`, which then sends a message to the particular `Colorable` that is associated with this button. This definition follows most of the steps of our event-handling recipe, as indicated in the comments. The only one omitted is Step 1, define an interface; the interface (`Colorable`) must be defined separately. The `getColorName` method gives us the label we need for the button, so we can include both names and colors, as recommended above.

Smart JSliders. Unlike `Timers`, `JButtons`, or `JRadioButtons`, `JSliders` generate `javax.swing.event.ChangeEvents`. `ChangeEvents` are very similar to

keyconcept

Push buttons are modeled in Java using `JButtons`, which generate `ActionEvents`.

keyconcept

To model a situation where the user picks one of a set of mutually exclusive choices, Java uses `JRadioButtons`. `JRadioButtons` generate `ActionEvents`.

keyconcept

Sliders are modeled using `JSliders`. `JSliders` generate `ChangeEvents`.

1.   Define an interface for objects that respond to the component (the "responder interface, e.g., `Mover`, `Colorable`, etc.) (except for mouse events)

2.   Define a subclass of the component class (or, for mouse events,) of `JPanel`

3.   Give that new subclass one or more peer objects that implement the responder interface or, in the case of mouse events, component objects that can be graphically contained in a `JPanel` (the "responder objects")

4.   Define a `private` inner class inside the new subclass that implements the appropriate listener interface (here, `java.awt.event.ActionListener`) or, in the case of mouse events, extends the `MouseInputAdapter` class

5.   Register an instance of the new `private` class with the class that contains it

6.   Define a method in the `private` class that is called when the event occurs and sends a message to the responder object(s)

Figure 8.9 ■ Event-handling recipe.

`ActionEvents`. To handle `ChangeEvents`, we need a `javax.swing.event.ChangeListener`. The `ChangeListener`'s `stateChanged` method is called every time the user moves the `JSlider`. Otherwise, we follow the same recipe.

For example, Listing 8.2 shows the code for `LocationSlider`, a smart `JSlider` that changes the location of an object. Like `ColorButton` (Listing 8.1), `LocationSlider` follows the event-handler recipe shown in Figure 8.9.

The only significant difference between this class definition and `ColorButton`'s is that here, the `private` listener class has an instance variable and a constructor. Why is that, when the `LocationListener` has access to the `LocationSlider`'s instance variables? Because the `LocationListener` needs to refer to the one thing it can't access: the `LocationSlider` itself. It needs to get the `LocationSlider`'s current value in order to pass it on to the `Mover`. To make this possible, the `LocationSlider` gives the `LocationListener` a reference to itself, which is stored in the `LocationListener`'s `_slider` instance variable.

Handling mouse input. Mouse input—clicks, drags, and so forth—generates two new types of event, `MouseEvents` and `MouseMotionEvents`. The basic recipe for handling these events is the same as for `ActionEvents` and `ChangeEvents`. The source of all mouse input is considered to be the `JPanel`, so we create a subclass of `JPanel` (as we do for most of our programs anyway) and give it an inner class that acts as a listener.

Consider the code in Listing 8.3 for a `ColorShapePanel`. The `ColorShapePanel` contains two shapes, an `Ellipse` and a `Rectangle`. When the user clicks on the

```
 1   /**
 2    * Chapter 8: ColorButton.java
 3    * Controls the color of some Colorable object.
 4    * Illustrates the event-handler recipe.
 5    */
 6
 7   // Step 2
 8   public class ColorButton extends javax.swing.JRadioButton {
 9       private java.awt.Color _color; // attributes
10       private String _colorName;
11       private Colorable _colorable; // peer object (Step 3)
12       public ColorButton (java.awt.Color aColor,
13       String aColorName;
14                           Colorable aColorable,
15                           javax.swing.ButtonGroup aGroup,
16                           boolean isSelected) {
17           super(aColorName, isSelected);
18           _color = aColor;
19           _colorable = aColorable;
20           this.setBackground(aColor); // make button display its color
21           this.addActionListener(new ColorListener()); // Step 5
22           aGroup.add(this);
23       }
24
25       // Step 4
26       private class ColorListener
27               implements java.awt.event.ActionListener {
28           // Step 6
```

Listing 8.1 ■ The `ColorButton` class (*continued on next page*)

```
29              public void actionPerformed (java.awt.event.ActionEvent e) {
30                  _colorable.setColor(_color);
31              }
32          }
33
34          public String getColorName() {
35              return _colorname;
36          }
37      }
```

Listing 8.1 ■ The ColorButton class

ColorShapePanel, the ColorShapePanel checks to see if the mouse click is contained in one of the shapes and, if so, sends it a message to change its color.

The listener is notified any time the user clicks anywhere on the JPanel, not just inside a shape. Since we want to respond only if one of the shapes has been clicked, we need to determine whether the mouse click is contained in one of the shapes. We find out where the mouse was clicked by using the Event parameter to mouseClicked. These parameters hold a variety of information about the event in question. When the mouse is clicked, for example, the MouseEvent includes the point at which the mouse was clicked. Once we know where the mouse was clicked, we use the shapes' contains method, which they inherit from the built-in Java2D classes, to determine whether the point is inside one of the shapes.

There is one way in which this class does not satisfy the event-handling recipe: the responder objects (the SmartEllipse and the SmartRectangle) are instances of a class, not an interface. They are components of the ColorShapePanel and need to do a variety of things not just respond to mouse clicks. To take advantage of the components' full capabilities, we make them class instances.

Why do we only define one method inside the listener? MouseListener, unlike the ActionListener and ChangeListener interfaces, requires five different methods, and MouseMotionListener requires another two. How do we avoid defining all seven of these methods?

Here's the trick: instead of implementing MouseListener and/or MouseMotion-Listener, the inner class extends MouseInputAdapter. MouseInputAdapter is a clever solution to our problem. It's a class provided by Java that implements both MouseListener and MouseMotionListener and defines all seven required methods with empty method bodies. If we extend this class, we inherit empty definitions for

```
1   /**
2    * Chapter 8: LocationSlider.java
3    * A slider that controls the location of a Mover object.
4    * Illustrates the event-handler recipe.
5    */
6   public class LocationSlider extends javax.swing.JSlider { // Step 2
7       private Mover _mover; // peer object (Step 3)
8
9       public LocationSlider (int anOrientation, Mover aMover,
10                             int aMinLocation, int aMaxLocation,
11                             int aCurrentLocation) {
12          super(anOrientation, aMinLocation, aMaxLocation,
13              aCurrentLocation);
14          _mover = aMover;
15          // set labels, etc. for slider
16          // ...
17          this.addChangeListener(new LocationListener(this)); // Step 5
18      }
19
20      // Step 4
21      private class LocationListener
22              implements javax.swing.event.ChangeListener{
23          private LocationSlider _slider; // peer object
24
25          public LocationListener (LocationSlider aSlider) {
26              _slider = aSlider;
27          }
28          // Step 6
29          public void stateChanged(javax.swing.event.ChangeEvent e){
30              _mover.setXLocation (_slider.getValue());
31          }
32      }
33  }
```

Listing 8.2 ■ The LocationSlider (with references to steps in Figure 8.9)

all of the required methods. To get the behavior we want, we just override the methods corresponding to the events we want to handle. Here, because we want the object to respond to mouse clicks, we override `mouseClicked`.

Compare `ColorShapePanel` carefully with `MoveTimer`, `ColorButton`, and `Location-Slider`, until you understand our basic recipe for writing event handlers.

```
1    /**
2     * Chapter 8: ColorShapePanel.java
3     * A subclass of RadioButton that controls the color of a
4     * particular object.
5     * This class illustrates the event-handler recipe from page
6     * 177 by extending a Component (JRadioButton), giving it a peer
7     * object that implements an interface (Colorable), defining a
8     * private inner class (ColorListener) that implements the
9     * listener interface that the listener to a JRadioButton needs,
10    * and registering an instance of ColorListener with itself.
11    */
12   public class ColorShapePanel extends javax.swing.JPanel{ // Step 2
13       private SmartEllipse _ellipse; // components // Step 3
14       private SmartRectangle _rectangle;
15
16       public ColorShapePanel (ColorHolder aHolder) {
17           super();
18           _ellipse = new SmartEllipse(java.awt.Color.BLUE);
19           _rectangle = new SmartRectangle(java.awt.Color.RED);
20           _ellipse.setSize(60, 60);
21           _ellipse.setLocation(200, 200);
22           _rectangle.setSize(20, 100);
23           _rectangle.setLocation(100, 130);
24           this.setBackground(java.awt.Color.WHITE);
25           this.addMouseListener(new MyMouseListener()); // Step 5
26       }
27
28       public void paintComponent(java.awt.Graphics aBrush){
29           super.paintComponent(aBrush);
30           java.awt.Graphics2D betterBrush =
31               (java.awt.Graphics2D) aBrush;
32           _ellipse.fill(betterBrush);
33           _ellipse.draw(betterBrush);
34           _rectangle.fill(betterBrush);
```

Listing 8.3 ■ `ColorShapePanel` *(continued on next page)*

```
35                 _rectangle.draw(betterBrush);
36         }
37
38         // Step 4
39         private class MyMouseListener
40                 extends javax.swing.event.MouseInputAdapter {
41             public void mouseClicked (java.awt.MouseEvent e){ // Step 6
42                 if (_ellipse.contains(e.getPoint()))
40                     _ellipse.setColor(color);
41                 else if (_rectangle.contains(e.getPoint()))
42                     _rectangle.setColor(color);
43             }
44         }
45     }
```

Listing 8.3 ■ `ColorShapePanel`

■ 8.4 ■ Working Out with
GUI—a user-controlled bouncing ball

O b j e c t i v e s :

☑ Gain practice with Swing and AWT
☑ Gain practice with `BorderLayout`, `FlowLayout`, and `GridLayout`
☑ Use `JButtons`, `JRadioButtons`, and `JSliders`
☑ Create a `QuitButton` that can be reused in future programs
☑ Create `ColorButtons` that can be reused in future programs
☑ Create a `SpeedSlider` that can be reused in future programs
☑ Define and use inner classes
☑ Gain practice with event-handling

In this section, we create a program that displays a bouncing ball and allows the user to control the color and speed of the ball. This program is a simple example of user-controlled animation; it provides you with an example that you can modify to create animations of your own.

Figure 8.10 is a screenshot showing the interface of this program, `GUIBounceApp`. The panel that contains the ball is basically the same as the one in the `BallApp` program in Chapter 7. In addition, here, the user can control the speed of the ball by moving the slider and can change the color of the ball, even in mid-bounce, by clicking on a color button. The user exits the program by clicking on the Quit button. The slider is set to zero, so the ball is stationary until the user chooses a different speed. The ball is red, and the red color button is selected.

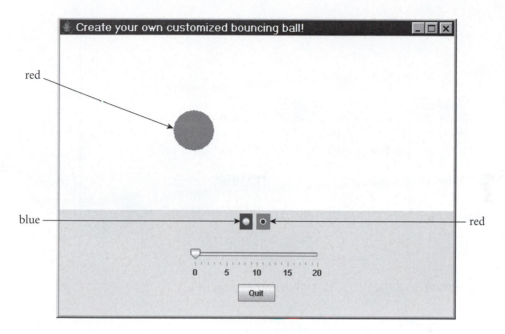

Figure 8.10 ■ Screenshot for `GUIBounceApp`.

8.4.1 **Part 1: layout**

Now that we see how the user interface should look, how can we use Java's layout managers (and/or absolute positioning) to get the look we want? All the layouts we've seen are based on some idea about rows and columns. What rows and columns can we see in the screenshot? There is a column of four elements: the area with the bouncing ball, the color buttons, the slider, and the quit button. The color buttons, in turn, are lined up in a row. Thus, we need to implement a column of four elements, one of which is a row.

As usual, we're starting with a `JFrame`, though, and the `JFrame`'s `BorderLayout` lets us have a column of three elements at most, in the North, Center, and South regions. How can we reduce the number of elements in the column? The four rows we can see in the screenshot can be divided into two groups: the area with the bouncing ball, where things happen, and the control panel with buttons and sliders. Accordingly, we define a `JFrame` that contains a column made up of two `JPanels`—a `BallPanel` in the Center region and a `ControlPanel` below it, in the South region—and add all the buttons and sliders to panels nested inside the `ControlPanel`, as in Figure 8.11.

Listing 8.4 gives the code for the `GUIBounceApp`. So far, the only code that's different from previous chapters is the explicit use of the `BorderLayout`. If you create two new empty class definitions, or **stubs**, for `BallPanel` and `ControlPanel`, as shown in Listing 8.5, you can compile and test the program so far.

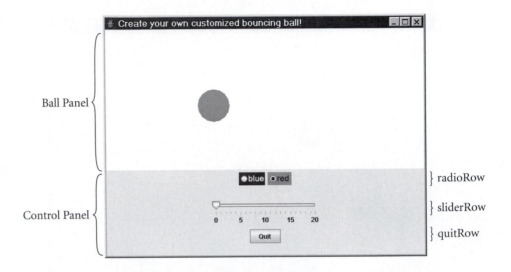

Ball Panel

Control Panel

} radioRow

} sliderRow

} quitRow

Figure 8.11 ■ Layout of the GUIBounceApp program.

```
1    /**
2     * Chapter 8: GUIBounceApp.java
3     * Window that contains two panels,
4     * one that displays a bouncing ball
5     * and one that holds control buttons.
6     */
7    public class GUIBounceApp extends javax.swing.JFrame {
8        public GUIBounceApp (String title) {
9            super(title);
10           this.setSize(600, 450);
11           BallPanel ballPanel = new BallPanel();
12           ControlPanel controlPanel = new ControlPanel(ballPanel);
13           this.add(ballPanel, java.awt.BorderLayout.CENTER);
14           this.add(controlPanel, java.awt.BorderLayout.SOUTH);
15           this.setDefaultCloseOperation(javax.swing.JFrame.EXIT_ON_CLOSE);
16           this.setVisible(true);
17       }
18       public static void main (String [ ] args) {
19           GUIBounceApp app = new GUIBounceApp(
20               "Create your own customized bouncing ball!");
21       }
22   }
```

Listing 8.4 ■ The GUIBounceApp class

```
1   /**
2    * Chapter 8: BallPanel.java
3    * Contains a bouncing ball.
4    */
5   public class BallPanel extends javax.swing.JPanel {
6   }
7   /**
8    * Chapter 8: ControlPanel.java (version 1 of 5)
9    * Contains buttons that
10   * control the bouncing ball's color and speed.
11   */
12  public class ControlPanel extends javax.swing.JPanel {
13      public ControlPanel (BallPanel aPanel) {
14      }
15  }
```

Listing 8.5 ■ Stubs for `BallPanel` and `ControlPanel`

8.4.2 The `ControlPanel`

The `ControlPanel` is a column of three elements: the color buttons, the slider, and the quit button. Since we want a column, we give it a `GridLayout`, as shown in Listing 8.6.

```
1   /**
2    * Chapter 8: ControlPanel.java (version 2 of 5)
3    * Contains buttons that
4    * control the bouncing ball's color and speed.
5    */
6   public class ControlPanel extends javax.swing.JPanel {
7       public ControlPanel (BallPanel aPanel) {
8           super(new java.awt.GridLayout(0, 1));
9           // create radio buttons
10          // create slider
11          // create quit button
12          // put it all together
13      }
14  }
```

Listing 8.6 ■ `ControlPanel` (version 2), with `GridLayout`

Recall that `GridLayouts` arrange their contents in rows and columns, and the parameters (0, 1) used here indicate that there will be one column with an arbitrary number of rows. We'll start with one row (the `QuitButton`) and add the others one by one.

8.4.3 The `QuitButton`

To add a `QuitButton` to our GUI, first revise the `ControlPanel` (see Listing 8.7). We create a `JPanel`, put the button in the `JPanel`, and then add the `JPanel` to the `ControlPanel`. Why? Experiment for yourself. Put the `QuitButton` directly into the `ControlPanel` and you will see. `GridLayout` expands the button to fill its cell in the grid. If we nest the button inside another `JPanel` and take advantage of the `JPanel`'s `FlowLayout`, the button is the right size.

The code for the `QuitButton` itself is shown in Listing 8.8. This is a `JButton` that we can use over and over, in any program where we want to give the user the option of clicking a button to exit from the program. This class follows our event-handling recipe: it's a subclass of a component (a `JButton`) that contains its own listener as a `private` class. The only difference is that there is no responder object. In this case, the listener calls the method, `System.exit`, that causes the program to halt.

```
1    /**
2     * Chapter 8: ControlPanel.java
3     * Contains buttons that
4     * control the bouncing ball's color and speed.
5     * Version 3 of 5
6     */
7    public class ControlPanel extends javax.swing.JPanel {
8        public ControlPanel (BallPanel aPanel) {
9            super(new java.awt.GridLayout(0, 1));
10           // create radio buttons
11           // create slider
12           // create quit button
13           javax.swing.JPanel quitRow = new javax.swing.JPanel();
14           quitRow.add(new QuitButton());
15
16           // put it all together
17           this.add(quitRow);
18       }
19   }
```

Listing 8.7 ■ `ControlPanel` (version 3), with `QuitButton`

```
1    /**
2     * Chapter 8: QuitButton.java
3     * Lets the user quit a program.
4     * A very simple illustration of the
5     * event-handler recipe, with no user-defined
6     * responder objects.
7     */
8    public class QuitButton extends javax.swing.JButton {// Step 2
9        public QuitButton() {
10           super("Quit");
11           this.addActionListener(new QuitListener()); // Step 5
12       }
13
14       // Step 4
15       private class QuitListener
16               implements java.awt.event.ActionListener {
17           // Step 6
18           public void actionPerformed(java.awt.event.ActionEvent e) {
19               System.exit(0);
20           }
21       }
22   }
```

Listing 8.8 ■ The `QuitButton` class

Compile, test, and run this program. Try the quit button to make sure it works. Congratulations! You've now created your first GUI program in real Java!

8.4.4 Adding the `BallPanel` with the `BouncingBall`, adding the color buttons, and making them work

In this section, we add the central panel, the bouncing ball, and the radio buttons to our program, and add the code necessary to make the radio buttons control the ball's color.

Code for adding the color buttons to the `ControlPanel` is shown in Listing 8.9. First create a group for the buttons to belong to and get the object (the `BouncingBall`) that they're supposed to control. Then create the color buttons, giving them their group and the bouncing ball as parameters. Finally, add the buttons to a `JPanel` and add the `JPanel` to the `ControlPanel`. The object these buttons control can be any object that satisfies the `Colorable` interface (shown in Listing 8.10).

`setColor` is a new method we will define soon (in Listing 8.12) that sets both the border color and the fill color of an object to the same color. Thus, we can use these `ColorButtons` with any object whose color can be set.

```
1    /**
2     * Chapter 8: ControlPanel.java (version 4 of 5)
3     * Contains buttons that
4     * control the bouncing ball's color and speed.
5     */
6    public class ControlPanel extends javax.swing.JPanel {
7        public ControlPanel (BallPanel aPanel) {
8            super(new java.awt.GridLayout(0, 1));
9
10           // radio buttons
11           javax.swing.ButtonGroup group = new
12               javax.swing.ButtonGroup();
13           Colorable colorable = aPanel.getBall();
14           ColorButton redButton = new
15               ColorButton(java.awt.Color.RED, colorable,
16                           group, true);
17           ColorButton blueButton = new
18               ColorButton(java.awt.Color.BLUE, colorable,
19                           group, false);
20           javax.swing.JPanel radioRow =
21               new javax.swing.JPanel();
22           radioRow.add(blueButton);
23           radioRow.add(redButton);
24
25           // slider
26           // quit button
27           javax.swing.JPanel quitRow =
28               new javax.swing.JPanel();
29           quitRow.add(new QuitButton());
30
31           // put it all together
32           this.add(radioRow);
33           this.add(quitRow);
34       }
35   }
```

Listing 8.9 ■ The `ControlPanel` class (version 4), with `ColorButtons`

```
1    /**
2     * Chapter 8: Colorable.java
3     * Interface that must be implemented by any object
4     * that responds to a ColorButton.
5     */
6    public interface Colorable {
7        public void setColor (java.awt.Color aColor);
8    }
```

Listing 8.10 ■ The Colorable interface

Also note that we're adding the `ColorButtons` to two objects: the `ButtonGroup` and `radioRow`. Adding the buttons to the `ButtonGroup` is necessary in order to make them mutually exclusive. Adding them to `radioRow` is optional—they will still work if we don't—but is necessary to make them look the way we want them to look. The `ButtonGroup` is conceptual and the `radioRow` is visual. Both are necessary, but for different reasons.

Next, we replace the stub of the `BallPanel` class (see Listing 8.11.) The actual class is almost identical to the `BallPanel` in Chapter 7. The only new code is the accessor for the `BouncingBall`, necessary because the color buttons and the slider send messages directly to the `BouncingBall`.

The `BouncingBall` class is also very similar to the corresponding class in Chapter 7 (see Listing 8.12). Like the `BouncingBall` in Chapter 7, this one is a `Mover`. In addition, it's `Colorable`, since it needs to respond to `ColorButtons`. To implement `Colorable`, it has a `setColor` method.

We reuse the `ColorButton` from Listing 8.1 and the `Mover`, `MoveTimer`, and `SmartEllipse` from Chapter 7 without any change. With those additions, we have all we need for this part of our program. Compile, test, and run the program and try adding some more colors, until you are comfortable with the `ColorButtons`.

8.4.5 **Adding sliders**

To add sliders, first we modify the `ControlPanel` as shown in Listing 8.13. The code we need is very similar to the code we used to add the color buttons. First, get the object that the component needs to control; then instantiate the new component, giving it the object it controls as a parameter. Then nest the component (the slider) in a `JPanel` and add the `JPanel` to the `ControlPanel`.

```
1    /**
2     * Chapter 8: BallPanel.java (version 2 of 2)
3     * Contains a bouncing ball.
4     */
5    public class BallPanel extends javax.swing.JPanel
6              implements Mover {
7        private final int INIT_X = 75; // attributes
8        private final int INIT_Y = 75;
9        private final int DIAMETER = 60;
10       private final int INTERVAL = 100;
11       private BouncingBall _ball; // components
12       private MoveTimer _timer;
13
14       public BallPanel () {
15           super();
16           _ball = new BouncingBall (java.awt.Color.RED, this);
17           _timer = new MoveTimer(INTERVAL, this);
18           _ball.setLocation(INIT_X, INIT_Y);
19           _ball.setSize(DIAMETER, DIAMETER);
20           this.setBackground(java.awt.Color.WHITE);
21           _timer.start();
22       }
23       public void move() {
24           _ball.move();
25           this.repaint();
26       }
27
28       public BouncingBall getBall() {
29           return _ball;
30       }
31
32       public void paintComponent(java.awt.Graphics aBrush) {
33           super.paintComponent(aBrush);
34           java.awt.Graphics2D betterBrush =
35               (java.awt.Graphics2D) aBrush;
36           _ball.fill(betterBrush);
37       }
38   }
```

Listing 8.11 ■ The `BallPanel` class's new `getBall` method

```
1    /**
2     * Chapter 8: BouncingBall.java
3     * A SmartEllipse that can change color or speed
4     * on command.
5     */
6    public class BouncingBall extends SmartEllipse
7            implements Mover, Colorable, Accelerator {
8       private int _changeX, _changeY; // attributes
9       private javax.swing.JPanel _panel; // peer object (and container)
10
11      public BouncingBall (java.awt.Color aColor,
12                              javax.swing.JPanel aPanel){
13          super(aColor);
14          _changeX = 0;
15          _changeY = 0;
16          _panel = aPanel;
17      }
18
19          // same move method as in Chapter 7
20          // same getMinBoundX, etc. as in Chapter 7
21
22      public void setSpeed (int xSpeed, int ySpeed) {
23          _changeX = xSpeed;
24          _changeY = ySpeed;
25      }
26
27      public void setColor (java.awt.Color aColor) {
28          this.setFillColor(aColor);
29          this.setBorderColor(aColor);
30      }
31   }
```

Listing 8.12 ■ The BouncingBall class

Note that the same object—the BouncingBall—is referred to at one point as a Colorable, at another point as a Mover, and at yet another point as an Accelerator. The only aspect of the BouncingBall that the ColorButtons need is the fact that it can set its color; the only aspect the MoveTimer needs is that it can move; the only aspect that the SpeedSlider needs is that it can change its speed. Interfaces let all three components work with the same object in very different ways.

```
 1   /**
 2    * Chapter 8: ControlPanel.java (version 5)
 3    * Contains buttons that
 4    * control the bouncing ball's color and speed.
 5    */
 6   public class ControlPanel extends javax.swing.JPanel {
 7      private final int MAX_SPEED = 20; // attribute
 8
 9      public ControlPanel (BallPanel aPanel) {
10         super(new java.awt.GridLayout(0, 1));
11
12         // radio buttons
13         javax.swing.ButtonGroup group = new
14            javax.swing.ButtonGroup();
15         Colorable colorable = aPanel.getBall();
16         ColorButton redButton = new
17            ColorButton(java.awt.Color.RED, colorable,
18                        group, true);
19         ColorButton blueButton = new
20            ColorButton(java.awt.Color.BLUE, colorable,
21                        group, false);
22         javax.swing.JPanel radioRow =
23            new javax.swing.JPanel();
24         radioRow.add(blueButton);
25         radioRow.add(redButton);
26
27         // slider
28         Accelerator accelerator = aPanel.getBall();
29         javax.swing.JPanel sliderRow =
30            new javax.swing.JPanel();
31         sliderRow.add(new
32            SpeedSlider(javax.swing.JSlider.HORIZONTAL,
33                        accelerator, 0, MAX_SPEED, 0));
34
35         // quit button
36         javax.swing.JPanel quitRow =
37            new javax.swing.JPanel();
38         quitRow.add(new QuitButton());
39
40         // put it all together
41         this.add(radioRow);
```

Listing 8.13 ■ The `ControlPanel` class (version 5), with sliders (*continued on next page*)

```
42            this.add(sliderRow);
43            this.add(quitRow);
44        }
45    }
```

Listing 8.13 ■ The `ControlPanel` class (version 5), with sliders

We need one last class to complete our program, the `SpeedSlider`. Its code is shown in Listing 8.14. This class follows the same recipe for handling events as the `MoveTimer`, the `ColorButton`, and the `ColorShapePanel` and is almost identical to the `LocationSlider` discussed earlier. See if you can identify the lines of code that correspond to the steps of the event-handler recipe given in Figure 8.9.

```
1    /**
2     * Chapter 8: SpeedSlider.java
3     * Controls the speed of some Accelerator object.
4     * Illustrates the event-handler recipe.
5     */
6    public class SpeedSlider extends javax.swing.JSlider {
7        private Accelerator _accelerator; // peer object
8
9        public SpeedSlider (int anOrientation,
10                            Accelerator anAccelerator,
11                            int aMinSpeed, int aMaxSpeed,
12                            int aCurrentSpeed) {
13            super(anOrientation, aMinSpeed,
14                  aMaxSpeed, aCurrentSpeed);
15            _accelerator = anAccelerator;
16            this.setValue(0);
17            this.setMinimum(0);
18            this.setMaximum(aMaxSpeed);
19            this.setMajorTickSpacing(5);
20            this.setMinorTickSpacing(1);
21            this.setPaintTicks(true);
22            this.setPaintLabels(true);
23            this.addChangeListener(new SpeedListener(this));
24        }
25
26        private class SpeedListener implements
```

Listing 8.14 ■ The `SpeedSlider` class (*continued on next page*)

```
27                          javax.swing.event.ChangeListener {
28              private SpeedSlider _slider; // peer object
29
30              public SpeedListener (SpeedSlider aSlider) {
31                  _slider = aSlider;
32              }
33              public void stateChanged
34                      (javax.swing.event.ChangeEvent e) {
35                  _accelerator.setSpeed(_slider.getValue(),
36                                        _slider.getValue());
37              }
38          }
39      }
```

Listing 8.14 ■ The `SpeedSlider` class

`SpeedSliders` control the speed of `Accelerator` objects. Recall that this in one of the interfaces implemented by the `BouncingBall`. Its definition is given in Listing 8.15. And with that, we're done with the third part of the program. Compile, test, and vary it until you are comfortable using the sliders.

```
1   /**
2    * Chapter 8: Accelerator.java
3    * Interface for objects that can change their speed.
4    * Must be implemented by objects that respond to
5    * SpeedSliders.
6    */
7   public interface Accelerator {
8       public void setSpeed(int xSpeed, int ySpeed);
9   }
```

Listing 8.15 ■ The `Accelerator` interface

■ **Ex**

Applyi

1.

2.

■ **Summary** ■

The main principle of user-interface design is "Put the user first." Such user-centered design requires an effort of imagination to understand the user's point of view; it also requires getting (and listening to) as much user feedback as possible, at all stages of development. To deal with this feedback effectively, you need to be able to keep your own ego out of the way, even though getting and accepting criticism is hard.

Java gives us many tools for developing user interfaces. In this chapter, we showed how to design interfaces with buttons, radio buttons, sliders, and labels using Java's event model. Like the `Timers` we saw in Chapter 7, Java's `JButtons` and `JRadioButtons` generate `ActionEvents`. We must create a listener object to respond to each component's `ActionEvents`. This listener object must implement the `ActionListener` interface and register itself with the button generating the event. To be a listener the object must contain a definition of the method `actionPerformed`.

Java also gives us `JSliders`, widgets that allow the user to select from a range of discrete numerical values by sliding a control back and forth. `JSliders` generate `ChangeEvents`. Like the button classes, `JSliders` require us to create a listener object to respond to the `ChangeEvents`. The process is very similar to the way we handle `ActionEvents`: the listener object for `JSliders` must implement an interface (`ChangeListener`) and define a specified method (`stateChanged`).

Since all of these components require listeners, we face a design decision: where to put the code for the listeners? We present a design for Smart Components, each of which has the ability to respond to the events it generates. For each task we want a component to perform—for example, a quit button or a slider to change the location of an object— we define a subclass of the appropriate component. This subclass contains a `private` inner class that provides the necessary event-handling code.

3.

4.

5.

■ **Self-Check Questions** ■

(The answers to these questions can be found on the book's website, www.aw.com/sanders)

1. What is user-interface design and why is it important?

2. What is the main principle of user-interface design?

3. List ten pieces of information that should be gathered during the analysis phase of developing a user interface.

4. Give four guidelines for user-interface design.

5. What does it mean to say an interface is transparent?

6.

7.

```
1    /**
2     * Chapter 9: ColorHolder.java
3     * Illustrates the Holder Pattern
4     */
5    public class ColorHolder implements Colorable {
6        private java.awt.Color _color; // component
7
8        public ColorHolder () {
9            super();
10           _color = java.awt.Color.RED; // default
11       }
12
13       public void setColor (java.awt.Color color ) {
14           _color = color;
15       }
16       public java.awt.Color getColor () {
17           return _color;
18       }
19   }
```

Listing 9.1 ■ The `ColorHolder` class

accessor and mutator methods for `SomeObject`. Any number of clients can then access `SomeObject` by using the holder's get and set methods. A holder object is thus no more than a simple encapsulation of an instance variable and its accessor/mutator method(s).

A class diagram for our program is given in Figure 9.3. Consider the Holder Pattern in context. In general, the Holder object in the Holder Pattern has association relationships with two or more client objects, and the Holder object and its clients are all created by the same container object. As you can see, this program follows the general rule. The `ColorHolder` is a peer object for both the `ControlPanel` and the `ColorShapePanel`, and all three classes are created by the `ColorHolderApp`.

The immediate clients of the Holder object don't necessarily use its data themselves; they may simply pass it on. The `ControlPanel`, for example, needs to know about the `ColorHolder` so that it can pass the information along to the `ColorButtons`.

9.4.2 `ColorHolderApp`

Let's construct the rest of the program top-down, starting with the top of the containment hierarchy. As usual, the first thing we need is a subclass of `JFrame`. This subclass is called

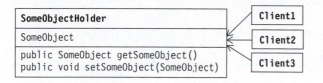

Figure 9.2 ■ Class diagram for Holder pattern.

ColorHolderApp. Like the GUIBounceApp class in Chapter 8, ColorHolderApp graphically contains two subclasses of JPanel, one for shapes and the second for buttons.

To implement the Holder Pattern, ColorHolderApp creates a ColorHolder and passes it to both panels as a parameter (see Listing 9.2). The panel layout is the same as the layout used for GUIBounceApp in Chapter 8.

9.4.3 The ControlPanel class and the button classes

There are some small differences between the ControlPanel class we use here (shown in Listing 9.3) and the one we saw in Chapter 8. There's no slider, and there are three color buttons instead of two.

More important, however, is the code that remains the same: the code for creating the buttons in the ControlPanel, and the code for the button classes themselves. The QuitButton is very generic and takes no parameters, so it's not surprising that we can re-use it. The ColorButton needs the right kind of parameter, however. In Chapter 8, the ColorButtons took the bouncing ball itself as its actual parameter; here, they take the ColorHolder. Both the BouncingBall and the ColorHolder implement the Colorable interface, however, and that's all the ColorButton requires. As a result, we can re-use the ColorButton class without changing it at all. This is another example of the value of interface polymorphism.

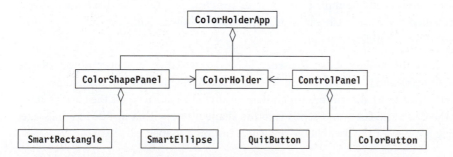

Figure 9.3 ■ Class diagram for ColorHolderApp.

```
1    /**
2     * Chapter 9: ColorHolderApp.java
3     * Creates a window that contains a
4     * very small drawing program.
5     */
6    public class ColorHolderApp extends javax.swing.JFrame {
7
8        public ColorHolderApp (String title) {
9            super(title);
10           this.setSize(600, 450);
11           ColorHolder holder = new ColorHolder();
12           ColorShapePanel shapePanel = new ColorShapePanel(holder);
13           ControlPanel controlPanel = new ControlPanel(holder);
14
15           this.add(shapePanel, java.awt.BorderLayout.CENTER);
16           this.add(controlPanel, java.awt.BorderLayout.SOUTH);
17           this.setDefaultCloseOperation
18               (javax.swing.JFrame.EXIT_ON_CLOSE);
19           this.setVisible(true);
20       }
21       public static void main (String [ ] args) {
22           ColorHolderApp app =
23               new ColorHolderApp("Design Patterns I: Holder");
24       }
25   }
```

Listing 9.2 ■ The `ColorHolderApp` class

9.4.4 **ColorShapePanel**

The last class we need to complete the `ColorHolderApp` program is `ColorShapePanel`. We presented this class in Chapter 8 as an example of how to handle mouse clicks; now examine it from a different angle.

Notice how the holder object is used. The `ColorHolder` is a peer object of the `ColorShapePanel`. When the mouse is clicked inside one of the shapes, the `ColorShapePanel` determines which shape was clicked; it then gets the current color from the `ColorHolder` and sends it to the shape along with a `setColor` message. Nothing happens if the user clicked anywhere but on a shape.

Now that we have all the classes we need, compile, test, and run this program. Try all the different combinations of colors. Then modify the program: add more color buttons and then more shapes. Compile and test your new program. Continue until you are comfortable with the program and the Holder Pattern.

```
1   /**
2    * Chapter 9: ControlPanel.java
3    * Contains the buttons that control the ColorHolderApp's shapes.
4    */
5   public class ControlPanel extends javax.swing.JPanel {
6
7       public ControlPanel (Colorable aColorable) {
8           super(new java.awt.GridLayout(0, 1));
9
10          // radio buttons
11          javax.swing.ButtonGroup group = new javax.swing.ButtonGroup();
12          ColorButton blueButton = new
13              ColorButton(java.awt.Color.BLUE, aColorable, group, true);
14          aColorable.setColor(java.awt.Color.BLUE);
15          ColorButton greenButton = new
16              ColorButton(java.awt.Color.GREEN,aColorable,group, false);
17          ColorButton redButton = new
18              ColorButton(java.awt.Color.RED,aColorable,group, false);
19          javax.swing.JPanel radioRow = new javax.swing.JPanel();
20          radioRow.add(greenButton);
21          radioRow.add(blueButton);
22          radioRow.add(redButton);
23
24          // quit button
25          javax.swing.JPanel quitRow = new javax.swing.JPanel();
26          quitRow.add(new QuitButton());
27
28          // put colorbutton row above quitbutton row
29          this.add(radioRow);
30          this.add(quitRow);
31      }
32  }
```

Listing 9.3 ■ ControlPanel for ColorHolderApp

```
1   /**
2    * Chapter 9: ColorShapePanel.java
3    * The panel that contains shapes for ColorHolderApp.
4    */
5   public class ColorShapePanel extends javax.swing.JPanel {
6       private SmartEllipse _ellipse; // components
7       private SmartRectangle _rectangle;
8       private ColorHolder _holder; // peer object
9
10      public ColorShapePanel (ColorHolder aHolder) {
11          super();
12          _ellipse = new SmartEllipse(java.awt.Color.BLUE);
13          _rectangle = new SmartRectangle(java.awt.Color.RED);
14          _holder = aHolder;
15          _ellipse.setSize(60, 60);
16          _ellipse.setLocation(200, 200);
17          _rectangle.setSize(20, 100);
18          _rectangle.setLocation(100, 130);
19          this.setBackground(java.awt.Color.WHITE);
20          this.addMouseListener(new MyMouseListener(this));
21      }
22
23      // paintComponent method omitted-see ColorShapePanel Chapter 8
24
25      private class MyMouseListener
26              extends javax.swing.event.MouseInputAdapter {
27          private ColorShapePanel _panel; // peer object
28
29          public MyMouseListener (ColorShapePanel aPanel) {
30              _panel = aPanel;
31          }
32          public void mouseClicked (java.awt.event.MouseEvent e){
33              if (_ellipse.contains(e.getPoint())) {
34                  _ellipse.setColor(_holder.getColor());
35                  _panel.repaint();
36              }
37              else if (_rectangle.contains(e.getPoint())) {
38                  _rectangle.setColor(_holder.getColor());
39                  _panel.repaint();
40              }
41          } // end of mouseClicked
```

Listing 9.4 ■ The ColorShapePanel class (*continued on next page*)

```
42        } // end of MyMouseListener
43     } // end of ColorShapePanel
```

Listing 9.4 ■ The `ColorShapePanel` class

The Holder Pattern: recap. Here's a summary of our first design pattern:

Name: Holder Pattern

Problem solved: an object (A) needs to be accessed or replaced by two or more other classes (the clients).

Structure: Create a second object, the Holder, whose sole purpose is to contain the current object A and provide accessor and mutator methods to be used by the client objects.

Pros and cons: On the down side, we have to create an extra object. None of the client objects can now access object A directly. On the up side, the holder object is simple, coherent, and easy to write and read (and encapsulated). By putting the management of object A in the holder class, we simplify the code for the client classes.

■ 9.5 ■ Working Out with the Proxy Pattern—race cars

O b j e c t i v e s :
- ☑ Practive writing programs with GUI interfaces
- ☑ Use the Proxy Pattern

Here are the specifications for our next program:

Design a frame that contains two regions. One region should contain two pictures of cars. The other region should contain three buttons. Clicking on a car selects it (that is, makes it the current car). Once selected, a car remains selected until the user clicks on another car (selecting it instead) or clicks elsewhere in the region. Clicking a button makes the current car (if any) move to the right, move to the left, or stop. If no car is selected, clicking a button should have no effect. Once started, a car keeps moving until either (1) it reaches the edge of the region containing it or (2) the user selects it and clicks the stop button.

keyconcept

Use the Proxy Pattern to store a changing value that needs to be sent messages to perform some action.

As usual, start by underlining the nouns.

> Design a <u>frame</u> that contains two <u>regions</u>. <u>One region</u> should contain two <u>pictures</u> <u>of cars</u>. The <u>other region</u> should contain <u>three buttons</u>. Clicking on a <u>car</u> selects it (that is, makes it the <u>current</u> <u>car</u>). Once selected, a <u>car</u> remains selected until the user clicks on another <u>car</u> (selecting it instead) or clicks elsewhere in <u>the region</u>. Clicking a <u>button</u> makes the <u>current car</u> (if any) move to the right, move to the left, or stop. If no <u>car</u> is selected, clicking a <u>button</u> should have no effect. Once started, a <u>car</u> keeps moving until either (1) it reaches the <u>edge of the region containing it</u> or (2) the user selects it and clicks the <u>stop button</u>.

Based on this grammatical analysis, our candidate classes include a frame, two regions of a frame (which we model, as usual, with panels), a car, and buttons that make the current car move. In addition, we somehow need to model the idea of "current car." We don't need a class to model "edge of a region"; instead, we treat that as an attribute of the region.

When we run the program, the output should look something like Figure 9.4. Can you tell which is the current car by looking at the screenshot? A good interface should provide visual feedback for the user when he or she performs an action such as selecting an object or clicking on a button. In the Holder example, the radio buttons indicated which was the current color. Here, the current car is outlined. When the user selects one of the cars, its outline appears and the other car's outline disappears. When the user clicks somewhere else in the panel, not on one of the cars, both outlines should disappear.

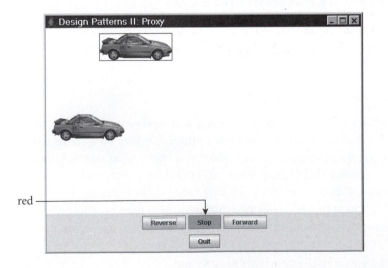

Figure 9.4 ■ Screenshot of `CarProxyApp`, a program illustrating the Proxy Pattern.

How can we model the "current car"? Suppose for argument's sake that the program has several buttons and sliders, not just three buttons, and they all need to access the car. We could give each of them a reference to the current car. Call this Design 1. Figure 9.5 shows a class diagram for Design 1.

This design would work, but it has problems. We know that the current car is likely to change often, and every time that happens, any object that has a reference to it will have to be updated. In fact, even if the user clicks on the car that is already current, the sliders and buttons all need to do some work, if only to check to see if the current car has changed.

In object-oriented design, the amount of connection between classes is called **coupling**. Visually, the amount of coupling corresponds to the number of lines connecting class boxes in a complete class diagram. Syntactically, two classes are coupled if one is mentioned in the class definition of the other. Thus, classes are coupled to their attributes (like `java.awt.Color`), their components, their peer objects, and any other objects that are used as parameters or local variables.

Some coupling is necessary to make object-oriented programs work—without any coupling, objects couldn't cooperate at all. But in general, given two designs that accomplish the same task, the one with less coupling is better.

We can improve this design. Suppose instead, we use a `CarHolder`. The idea of a "current car" sounds a lot like "current color" from Section 9.4. We could have each car put itself in a holder when it's clicked on, and components could get the current car from the holder when they need it. Call this "Design 2"; Figure 9.6 shows its class diagram.

Design 2 is definitely an improvement over Design 1. As we can see from the diagram, the client objects depend on the `CarHolder`, not the `Car`. Since the `CarHolder` doesn't change, we don't have to update all the client objects' references to it each time the user clicks on

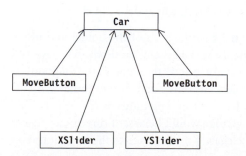

Figure 9.5 ■ Class diagram for Design 1 for `CarProxyApp`.

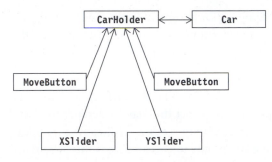

Figure 9.6 ■ Class diagram for Design 2 for `CarProxyApp`.

a car. Instead, we just change the contents of the holder. By separating the frequently changing `Car` from the GUI components, we have a much more loosely coupled design.

The drawback of Design 2 is that the code for the client objects is still more complicated than we'd really like. The client objects first have to get the car from the holder and then send the car a message (to move right, move left, or stop):

```
Car car = _holder.getCurrentCar();
car.move();
```

Compare this with the color holder example, where the client object simply gets the object from the holder and passes it along:

```
_ellipse.setColor(_holder.getColor());
```

We'd like the code in the client objects here to be even simpler, if possible.

The Proxy Pattern solves this design problem. Like a holder object, a proxy object always has a reference to the current car. But while a holder object simply acts as a centralized container through which client objects can reference the current object, a proxy stands in for the object and can do everything the object can do. All the client objects (here, GUI components) have a reference to the proxy object, which does not change.

The difference between Design 2 and Design 3 lies in details of the holder and proxy classes. If we don't consider the classes' instance variables and methods, the class diagram (Figure 9.7) for this design (Design 3) looks exactly the same as the diagram for Design 2. The difference is that a Holder object has only accessor and mutator methods, while a Proxy object, unlike a Holder, has the same methods as the objects it's a Proxy for. The clients send the same message they would have sent directly to the car itself, and the Proxy simply forwards (i.e., delegates) the message to the current `Car`.

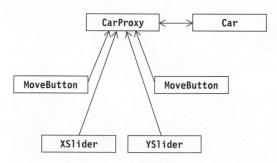

Figure 9.7 ■ Class diagram for Design 3 for `CarProxyApp`.

The code for the `CarProxy` is shown in Listing 9.5. Proxy objects are generally very easy to write, and this one is no exception: we just take each of the `Car`'s methods and write a simple method with the same signature that delegates the task to the current `Car`. Here, for example, we have `move`, `setSpeed`, `setSelected`, and a group of methods for determining the *x* and *y* values within which the `Car` can move. The only complication is that in this program, the proxy sometimes is unemployed: if no car is selected, the car has no one to forward its messages to. We solve this problem for the `void` methods by simply doing nothing when `_car` is `null`. For the methods that return the boundaries within which the car can move, we have them all return 0; since the minimum and maximum locations are all 0, the car does not move. The only additional code required is a simple mutator method, used to change the current `Car`.

To make sure the `CarProxy` and the `Car` both implement the methods we need with the same signatures, we specify the required methods in an interface called `Mover`. To modify the `CarProxy` to work with other images or graphical shapes, all we'd need to do is have the new shapes implement the `Mover` interface. Moreover, as we see below, we write the buttons to work with any `Mover`, not just the `CarProxy`.

Figure 9.8 shows a containment diagram for our new program. Like the `ColorHolder`, the `CarProxy` has a peer relationship with some client objects, and the `CarProxy` and its client objects are all created by a third container object, the `CarProxyApp`. In addition, we include a `MoveTimer` to control the cars' motion. Following the event-handling recipe defined in Chapter 8, the `MoveTimer` sends ticks to the `CarProxyPanel`, which in turn forwards them to the cars.

For the first time, we are using a photographic image instead of graphical shapes, so we define an `Image` class for images in general. The `Image` class is the parent of the `Car` class, and it contains both an instance of Java's built-in `Image` class and a `SmartRectangle` to draw the outline of the `Image`. Figure 9.9 shows the relationships among these classes.

```
1    /**
2     * Chapter 9: CarProxy.java
3     * Illustrates the Proxy Pattern.
4     */
5    public class CarProxy implements Mover, Accelerator {
6        private Car _car; // peer object
7
8        public CarProxy () {
9            super();
10           _car = null; // default
11       }
12       public void setCar (Car car) {
13           _car = car;
14       }
15
16       // methods for forwarding messages
17       public void move () {
18           if (null != _car)
19               _car.move();
20       }
21       public void setSpeed (int xSpeed, int ySpeed) {
22           if (null != _car)
23               _car.setSpeed(xSpeed, ySpeed);
24       }
25       public void setSelected (boolean aValue) {
26           if (null != _car)
27               _car.setSelected(aValue);
28       }
29       public int getMinBoundX() {
30           if (null != _car)
31               return _car.getMinBoundX();
32           else return 0;
33       }
34       public int getMaxBoundX() {
35           if (null != _car)
36               return _car.getMaxBoundX();
37           else return 0;
38       }
39       public int getMinBoundY() {
40           if (null != _car)
41               return _car.getMinBoundY();
```

Listing 9.5 ■ The CarProxy class (*continued on next page*)

```
42              else return 0;
43         }
44         public int getMaxBoundY() {
45              if (null != _car)
46                   return _car.getMaxBoundY();
47              else return 0;
48         }
49    }
```

Listing 9.5 ■ The `CarProxy` class

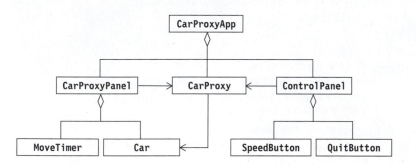

Figure 9.8 ■ Class diagram for `CarProxyApp`.

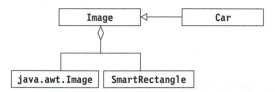

Figure 9.9 ■ Class diagram for the `Images` in `CarProxyApp`.

Start, as usual, by considering the class that contains the `main` method, here, the `CarProxyApp` (shown in Listing 9.6). As you can see, this method is almost identical to the `ColorHolderApp`, except that here the class instantiates a proxy instead of a holder object.

An overview of `CarProxyPanel` is shown in Listing 9.7. The constructor initializes the two objects we want to appear in the panel (two images of cars) and a proxy, and sends the proxy car a message that it's now "selected" (and therefore, should appear with a black box around it).

The `MoveTimer` sends its message to this panel, which (as shown in Listing 9.8) passes it on to the two cars. Each car moves at its own speed, however, which could be 0—if so, the car will stay in the same location.

```
1    /**
2     * Chapter 9: CarProxyApp.java
3     * A window that contains two panels,
4     * one with pictures of cars and one with buttons
5     * that control those cars (through a proxy).
6     */
7    public class CarProxyApp extends javax.swing.JFrame {
8        public CarProxyApp (String title) {
9            super(title);
10           this.setSize(600, 450);
11           CarProxy proxy = new CarProxy();
12           CarProxyPanel carProxyPanel = new CarProxyPanel(proxy);
13           ControlPanel controlPanel = new ControlPanel(proxy);
14
15           // layout, etc. omitted-see code on CD or website
16       }
17
18       public static void main(String[] args) {
19           CarProxyApp app = new CarProxyApp("Design Patterns II: Proxy");
20       }
21   }
```

Listing 9.6 ■ The `CarProxyApp` class

```
1    /**
2     * Chapter 9: CarProxyPanel.java
3     * Panel that contains images for the
4     * CarProxyApp
5     */
6    public class CarProxyPanel extends javax.swing.JPanel
7            implements Mover {
8        private final int INTERVAL = 100; // attribute
9        private Car _car1, _car2; // components
```

Listing 9.7 ■ The `CarProxyPanel` class (*continued on next page*)

```
10        private MoveTimer _timer;
11        private CarProxy _proxy; // peer object
12
13        public CarProxyPanel (CarProxy aProxy) {
14            super();
15            _car1 = new Car("redCar.jpg", this, 100, 10);
16            _car2 = new Car("car2.jpg", this, 10, 160);
17            _timer = new MoveTimer(INTERVAL, this);
18            _proxy = aProxy;
19            _car1.setSize(137, 50); // originally 1372 x 500
20            _car2.setSize(137, 50); // originally 1372 x 500
21            _proxy.setCar(_car1); //car1 is selected at first
22            _proxy.setSelected(true);
23            this.setBackground(java.awt.Color.WHITE);
24            this.addMouseListener (new MyMouseListener(this));
25        }
26
27        public void startTimer(){
28            _timer.start();
29        }
30        // move method
31        // paintComponent method
32        // code for mouse listener
33    }
```

Listing 9.7 ■ The `CarProxyPanel` class)

```
1    public void move() {
2        _car1.move();
3        _car2.move();
4        this.repaint();
5    }
```

Listing 9.8 ■ `CarProxyPanel`'s move method

The `paintComponent` method is familiar, except that instead of the `draw` and `fill` methods associated with graphical shapes, `Images` have a `paint` method. (See Listing 9.9.)

Finally, the mouse-handling code (shown in Listing 9.10) follows our standard event-handler recipe.

```
1    public void paintComponent (java.awt.Graphics aBrush) {
2        super.paintComponent(aBrush);
3        java.awt.Graphics2D betterBrush =(java.awt.Graphics2D) aBrush;
4        _car1.paint(betterBrush);
5        _car2.paint(betterBrush);
6    }
```

Listing 9.9 ■ CarProxyPanel's paintComponent method

What's new is what actually happens when the mouse is clicked. When the mouse is clicked, we unselect whatever was selected before, and check to see if the click was inside either of the images. If yes, we reset the proxy and call setSelected on the new current car. Finally, we repaint the CarProxyPanel.

```
1    private class MyMouseListener
2            extends javax.swing.event.MouseInputAdapter {
3        private CarProxyPanel _panel; // peer object
4
5        public MyMouseListener (CarProxyPanel aPanel) {
6            _panel = aPanel;
7        }
8        public void mouseClicked(java.awt.event.MouseEvent e){
9            _proxy.setSelected(false); // unselect old image
10           if ( _car1.contains(e.getPoint())) {
11               _proxy.setCar(_car1); // reset proxy
12               _proxy.setSelected(true); // select new image
13           }
14           else if (_car2.contains(e.getPoint())) {
15               _proxy.setCar(_car2); // reset proxy
16               _proxy.setSelected(true); // select new image
17           } else { // click outside both cars
18               _proxy.setCar(null); // reset proxy
19           }
20           _panel.repaint();
21       }
22   }
```

Listing 9.10 ■ CarProxyPanel's MyMouseListener class

The `ControlPanel` class (shown in Listing 9.11) is very similar to the `ControlPanel` class we've seen in earlier examples. It instantiates a row of three `SpeedButtons`, each associated with a different speed (forward, back, and stop) and a row that contains a `QuitButton`.

The `QuitButton` is exactly the same as the class we have used in earlier examples. The `SpeedButton` (shown in Listing 9.12) takes as parameters a name, an *x* speed, a *y* speed, and a responder object. Its class definition is new, but very similar to the `ColorButton` class. Both illustrate the event-handler recipe.

Each `SpeedButton` knows its own speed and has a peer object that's an `Accelerator`. Objects that implement the `Accelerator` interface have a `setSpeed` method. When clicked, the `SpeedButton` sends a message to its `Accelerator` to change its speed to the button's own speed, just as the `ColorButtons` each sent a message to a `Colorable`

```
 1   /**
 2    * Chapter 9: ControlPanel.java
 3    * Contains buttons for CarProxyApp.
 4    */
 5   public class ControlPanel extends javax.swing.JPanel {
 6       private final int REVERSE = -10; // attributes (both x-speeds)
 7       private final int FORWARD = 10; // (y-speeds are 0)
 8
 9       public ControlPanel (Accelerator anAccelerator) {
10           super(new java.awt.GridLayout(0, 1));
11
12           // speed buttons (all connected to CarProxy)
13           SpeedButton reverseButton = new
14               SpeedButton("Reverse", REVERSE, 0, anAccelerator);
15           SpeedButton stopButton = new
16               SpeedButton("Stop", 0, 0, anAccelerator);
17           SpeedButton forwardButton = new
18               SpeedButton("Forward", FORWARD, 0, anAccelerator);
19           stopButton.setBackground(java.awt.Color.RED);
20
21
22           // code for layout, quit button omitted—see CD or website
23       }
24   }
```

Listing 9.11 ■ The `ControlPanel` class

```
 1    /**
 2     * Chapter 9: SpeedButton.java
 3     * Controls the speed of some Accelerator object.
 4     * Illustrates the event-handler recipe.
 5     */
 6    public class SpeedButton extends javax.swing.JButton {
 7        private int _xSpeed, _ySpeed; // attributes
 8        private Accelerator _accelerator; // peer object
 9
10        public SpeedButton (String aLabel, int xSpeed,
11                                    int ySpeed,
12                                    Accelerator anAccelerator){
13            super(aLabel);
14            _xSpeed = xSpeed;
15            _ySpeed = ySpeed;
16            _accelerator = anAccelerator;
17            this.addActionListener(new SpeedListener());
18        }
19
20        private class SpeedListener
21                implements java.awt.event.ActionListener {
22            public void actionPerformed(java.awt.event.ActionEvent e){
24                _accelerator.setSpeed(_xSpeed, _ySpeed);
25            }
26        }
27    }
```

Listing 9.12 ■ The SpeedButton class

object to change its color to the button's color. Here, the Accelerator is in fact a CarProxy, but the buttons could be re-used with any object that satisfies the Accelerator interface.

The Image class is new and fairly detailed. First, consider the constructor (shown in Listing 9.13). The Image constructor takes as parameters a file—the file that contains the picture we want our program to display—a panel that will contain the picture, and the (x, y) location of the picture. Java.awt.Toolkit is a class that takes care of various low-level details having to do with the relationship between Java's GUI components on the one hand and the operating system your program is running on, on the other. Each AWT component has a related toolkit, but we can use the default toolkit, as we do

```
 1   /**
 2    * Chapter 9: Image.java
 3    * Lets us include images in a program.
 4    */
 5   public class Image {
 6       private boolean _selected; // attribute
 7       private java.awt.Image _image; // components
 8       private SmartRectangle _imageOutline;
 9       private javax.swing.JPanel _panel; // peer object (and container)
10
11       public Image(String aFile,javax.swing.JPanel aPanel,
12                     int x, int y){
13           super ();
14           _selected = false;
15           _image = java.awt.Toolkit.getDefaultToolkit().getImage(aFile);
16           _panel = aPanel;
17           java.awt.MediaTracker tracker =
18               new java.awt.MediaTracker(_panel);
19           tracker.addImage(_image, 0);
20           try {
21               tracker.waitForAll();
22           }
23           catch(InterruptedException e) { }
24           if (tracker.isErrorAny()) {
25               System.out.println("Image failed to load.");
26               return;
27           }
28           // setting up the outline for the image
29           _imageOutline =
30               new SmartRectangle(java.awt.Color.BLACK);
31           _imageOutline.setSize(_image.getWidth(_panel),
32                                 _image.getHeight(_panel));
33           this.setLocation(x, y);
34           _panel.repaint();
35       }
36       // accessors & mutators omitted—see code on CD & website
37       // setSelected & paint methods—see below
38   }
```

Listing 9.13 ■ The Image class

here, to take a jpg file and turn it into a set of pixels that can be displayed in a Java `JFrame`. The `MediaTracker` is an object that keeps track of the current status of Java `Images`. We create a `MediaTracker` and give it the current `Image` to keep track of. The second parameter, 0, to `addImage` means that the `Image` is the first one on the `MediaTracker`'s list (Java often starts counting with 0 rather than 1).

In particular, we want the `MediaTracker` to keep track of whether the `Image` has loaded successfully. If it hasn't, Java might halt our program and send an `InterruptedException`. What's an exception? It's an object that contains information about something that's gone wrong with your program. For example, if you've been programming in Java as you read this book, you've almost certainly seen `NullPointerExceptions`, which you get when you send a message to a variable that hasn't been initialized.

We'd like to know if the picture has loaded, but we don't necessarily want to halt the program if it hasn't. `Try` and `catch` are Java keywords that we put around a block of code that might cause an exception, and then after the `catch` we say what we want to happen if the exception does occur. So in short, what this code says is that the `MediaTracker` should wait for the image file to load. If anything goes wrong, don't do anything (the empty brackets after the `catch`). But if there was some error, print a message for the user and stop executing the `Image` constructor. For more details on `try` and `catch`, see Chapter 18.

The `setSelected` and `paint` methods make sure that an outline is displayed around `Images` when—and only when—they've been selected by the user (see Listing 9.14). If the `Image` loads successfully, we go ahead and create a black `SmartRectangle` the same size and location as the `Image` to be its outline, and call the panel's `repaint` method to display the `Image`.

The remaining methods of the `Image` class perform familiar tasks such as setting the size and location of the `Image`. These methods are straightforward and can be found on the CD or the book's website, so we do not include them here.

Finally, the `Car` class. Its constructor (shown in Listing 9.15) creates an `Image`, associates it with a `CarProxy`, and gives it an initial speed of 0. The `Car`'s `setSpeed` method is a simple mutator method for the `_changeX` and `_changeY` variables, and its `getMinBoundX`, `getMinBoundY`, `getMaxBoundX`, and `getMaxBoundY` methods are the same as in the `BouncingBall` class in Chapter 8.

The `move` method has been changed slightly, however. Unlike the `BouncingBall`, these cars don't bounce diagonally around the window; they simply move horizontally until they reach a wall (that is, one of the edges of the panel that contains them) and then stop. The code for this version of move is shown in Listing 9.16. Whenever the Car reaches one of the edges of the JPanel that contains it, the appropriate _change variable is set to 0.

```
1   public void setSelected (boolean aValue) {
2       _selected = aValue;
3   }
4   public void paint(java.awt.Graphics2D aBetterBrush) {
5       aBetterBrush.drawImage(_image,
6                               (int)_imageOutline.getX(),
7                               (int)_imageOutline.getY(),
8                               _panel);
9       if (_selected) aBetterBrush.draw(_imageOutline);
10  }
```

Listing 9.14 ■ Image's setSelected and paint methods

```
1   /**
2    * Chapter 9: Car.java
3    * A subclass of Image with the capability
4    * of moving right and left.
5    */
6   public class Car extends Image implements Mover {
7       private int _changeX, _changeY; // attributes
8       private javax.swing.JPanel _panel; // peer (and container)
9
10      public Car (String aFilePath, javax.swing.JPanel aPanel,
11                  int x, int y) {
12          super(aFilePath, aPanel, x, y);
13          _changeX = 0; _changeY = 0;
14          _panel = aPanel;
15      }
16      // move method (see below)
17      // accessors & mutators-see CD & website
18  }
```

Listing 9.15 ■ The Car class

```
1    // stops moving at edge of frame
2    public void move() {
3        int nextX = (int)this.getX() + _changeX;
4        int nextY = (int)this.getY() + _changeY;
5        if (nextX <= this.getMinBoundX()) {
6            _changeX = 0;
7            nextX = this.getMinBoundX();
8        }
9        else if (nextX >= this.getMaxBoundX()) {
10            _changeX = 0;
11            nextX = this.getMaxBoundX();
12        }
13        if (nextY <= this.getMinBoundY()) {
14            _changeY = 0;
15            nextY = this.getMinBoundY();
16        }
17        else if (nextY > this.getMaxBoundY()){
18            _changeY = 0;
19            nextY = this.getMaxBoundY();
20        }
21        this.setLocation(nextX, nextY);
22    }
```

Listing 9.16 ■ Car's move method

The Proxy Pattern: recap. Here's a summary of our second design pattern:

Name: Proxy Pattern

Problem solved: sometimes it's easier not to deal directly with an object, for example because it's too expensive to create yet or because it changes from time to time during program execution. It's necessary to tell the object to perform some action, not just to get the object.

Structure: an interface defining some desired behavior; a set of one or more objects (actors) that implement the interface; a proxy object that also implements the interface, but simply forwards all method calls to one of the actors; and one or more client objects.

Pros and cons: Using a proxy pattern makes the client objects simpler. Client objects (like our `SpeedButtons`) don't need to know which object they're really dealing with. On the other hand, the Proxy Pattern requires us to create an extra object (the proxy) and make an extra method call each time the proxy is used (the client calls the proxy, who calls the actor, rather than the client dealing with the actor directly).

How can we tell when to use the Holder Pattern and when to use the Proxy Pattern? Compare the way the current color is used in Section 9.4 with the way the current car is used here. Here, we need to know which car is the current car in order to tell it to move. In Section 9.4, we needed to know the current color, not to tell the color to do something, but to use the color for something else. When you need to store a changing value for future use by other objects—a color, for example, or the score of a game—consider using the Holder Pattern. When you need to store a changing value in order to send it messages to perform some action, consider using the Proxy Pattern.

■ 9.6 ■ Working Out with **the Composite Pattern**—the space alien

Objectives:
- ☑ Practice writing programs with GUI interfaces
- ☑ Use the Composite Pattern

To illustrate our third design pattern, we want to model a movable object that is made up of several parts. Here are the specifications for our next program:

> Design a frame with a space alien and a slider. The space alien bounces around the window from one edge to another. Moving the slider sets the speed at which the alien bounces. The space alien should be composed of three ellipses, as in Figure 9.10.

keyconcept

Use the Composite Pattern when the same message (such as setLocation) can be sent to both simple and composite objects.

Start by underlining the nouns in the specifications:

> Design a <u>frame</u> with a <u>space alien</u> and a <u>slider</u>. The <u>space alien</u> bounces around the <u>frame</u> from one <u>edge</u> to another. Moving the <u>slider</u> sets <u>the speed</u> at which the <u>alien</u> bounces. The <u>space alien</u> should be composed of three <u>ellipses</u>.

Based on this grammatical analysis, our candidate classes include a `JFrame`, a `SpaceAlien`, a `JSlider`, and a `SmartEllipse`. As usual, we also use two `JPanels`, one to model the region in which the `SpaceAlien` is moving and one to hold the `JSlider` and a `QuitButton`.

When we're done, the output of the program should look something like Figure 9.11. This example is almost identical to the `GUIBounceApp` in Chapter 8; the important difference is that all the parts of the `SpaceAlien` must move at the same time.

Figure 9.10 ■ A space alien.

It's very common to want to send a command to an entire object, as opposed to one of its parts. In fact, you may have done so before you ever wrote a program. Have you ever used a program such as the Drawing toolbar in Microsoft Word™? If so, you may have used the Group command to combine parts of a shape together. When you use that command, you create a composite shape, and then you can cut, paste, or drag the shape as a whole. You can also ungroup the shape, if you want to edit or delete one of the individual parts.

The Composite Pattern is a solution to this problem. To use it, we create a composite object, say, `SpaceAlien`. To make all the parts respond at the same time, we send a message to the composite object, and the composite object forwards, i.e., delegates, the message to *all* of its parts (here, the head and the eyes). To ensure that this all works properly, we make the composite object and its parts both implement the same interface (here, `Mover`).

To really understand a pattern, it helps to see it implemented in several different contexts. Although we didn't have a name for it, we have already seen several examples of Composite, including the `Hat` in Chapter 2, which forwarded its `setColor` and `setLocation` messages to its parts, and the `Fish` in Chapter 7, which also forwarded its `setLocation` messages to its parts. This is a very common pattern in graphics.

The structure of Composite is very similar to that of Proxy. The main difference is that the Proxy object forwards a message to the *current* object it contains; the Composite object forwards a message to a *group* of objects (i.e., its parts) all at once. Both Proxy and Composite make it possible for their client objects to ignore the details of what is going on. Proxy lets the clients send the same messages, regardless of the fact that the object executing them may change from time to time; Composite lets the client objects send the same messages, regardless of whether an object is atomic or made up of several parts.

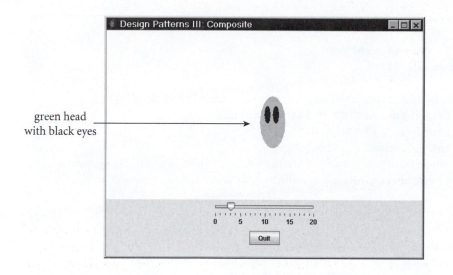

Figure 9.11 ■ Screenshot of `AlienApp`, a program that illustrates the Composite Pattern.

We present only the `SpaceAlien` class here, because the rest of the classes we need are very similar to code we have written before. Altogether, we need eight classes and two interfaces. `QuitButton`, `SpeedSlider`, `SmartEllipse`, `MoveTimer`, `Mover`, and `Accelerator` are the same as in earlier examples. The `AlienApp`, `AlienPanel`, and `ControlPanel` classes are the same, with minor changes (for example, to reflect the fact that we don't use any `ColorButtons` in this example). The full text of the code for this program can be found on the book's website and on the CD provided with the book.

Listing 9.17 gives the code for the `SpaceAlien` class. The `setLocation`, `setSize`, `fill`, and `draw` methods all simply delegate their tasks to the `SpaceAlien`'s component objects. The `move`, `setSpeed`, `getMinBoundX`, `getMinBoundY`, `getMaxBoundX`, and `GetMaxBoundY` methods are all identical to the corresponding methods for the `BouncingBall` class in Chapter 8, so they have been omitted. Finally, the `get` methods all refer to the `SpaceAlien`'s face: since the face contains the eyes, its location, height, width, and so forth are the same as those of the `SpaceAlien` itself.

The Proxy and Composite Patterns can be combined, for example in an implementation of the computer game Tetris. For those unfamiliar with the game, it involves shapes (made up of blocks) that fall one after another from the sky. The user presses keys to move the current object right, left, or down. Here, each key sends a message to a proxy, which forwards it to the current shape. The shape itself is a composite, however, so it in turn forwards the message to its components.

```
1   /**
2    * Chapter 9: SpaceAlien.java
3    * Models a space alien.
4    */
5   public class SpaceAlien implements Mover, Accelerator {
6       private final int HEIGHT = 96; // attributes
7       private final int WIDTH = 48;
8       private int _changeX, _changeY;
9       private SmartEllipse _face, _leftEye, _rightEye; // components
10      private javax.swing.JPanel _panel; // peer (and container)
11
12      public SpaceAlien (javax.swing.JPanel aPanel) {
13          super();
14          _changeX = 0; _changeY = 0;
15          _face = new SmartEllipse(java.awt.Color.green);
16          _leftEye = new SmartEllipse(java.awt.Color.black);
17          _rightEye = new SmartEllipse(java.awt.Color.black);
18          _panel = aPanel;
19          this.setSize(WIDTH, HEIGHT);
20      }
21      public void setLocation(int x, int y) {
22          _face.setLocation(x, y);
23          _leftEye.setLocation(x+8, y+18);
24          _rightEye.setLocation(x+24, y+18);
25      }
26      public int getX() {
27          return (int)_face.getX();
28      }
29      public int getY() {
30          return (int)_face.getY();
31      }
32      public double getMaxX() {
33          return _face.getMaxX();
34      }
35      public double getMaxY() {
36          return _face.getMaxY();
37      }
38      public void setSize (int width, int height) {
39          _face.setSize(width, height);
40          _leftEye.setSize(width/4, height/3);
41          _rightEye.setSize(width/4, height/3);
```

Listing 9.17 ■ The SpaceAlien class (*continued on next page*)

```
42          }
43          public double getWidth () {
44              return _face.getWidth();
45          }
46          public double getHeight() {
47              return _face.getHeight();
48          }
49          // move, setSize, and bounds methods omitted—see CD or website
50
51          public void fill(java.awt.Graphics2D aPaintBrush) {
52              _face.fill(aPaintBrush);
53              _leftEye.fill(aPaintBrush);
54              _rightEye.fill(aPaintBrush);
55          }
56          public void draw(java.awt.Graphics2D aPaintBrush) {
57              _face.draw(aPaintBrush);
58              _leftEye.draw(aPaintBrush);
59              _rightEye.draw(aPaintBrush);
60          }
61      }
```

Listing 9.17 ■ The `SpaceAlien` class

The Composite Pattern: recap. Here's a summary of our third design pattern:

Name: Composite Pattern

Problem solved: how a client object can send a message to a composite object and have the message passed on to all the object's parts at the same time.

Structure: A composite object, its parts (which are themselves objects), an interface that is implemented by both the composite object and the individual parts, and one or more client objects.

Pros and cons:

■ Pros:
   □ Simplifies the code in the client objects, because the client object doesn't need to worry about whether the object it's dealing with is a composite or an individual object.
   □ Extensible. It's easy to add new types of components, a `MovableRectangle`, for example.

      ☐ Flexible. A composite object could be made up of other composite objects, which in turn are made up of composite objects, etc. Messages would still be passed on until they reach the primitive objects that can execute them.

■ Cons: it may be a little too easy to add components. Here, for example, anything that's `Movable` would qualify as a component. There's nothing to prevent you from ending up with a system made up of an electron, a bicycle, and the planet Saturn.

■ Summary ■

In this chapter, we introduce the idea of design patterns and give three examples with an implementation of each. Design patterns are tested solutions to problems in object-oriented design.

The first pattern we introduce is the Holder Pattern. This pattern is useful whenever a program contains a value that is used by two or more other objects. The `Cursor` class in Chapter 5's `SketchApp` program is a holder. The `Graphics2D` paintbrush object is in part a holder—one of its functions is to hold the current color, rotation, etc. It doesn't quite fit the Holder Pattern, however, because it holds more than one value, and because it has so much additional functionality. The example given here for the Holder Pattern is the current color selected in a drawing program.

The second pattern covered here, the Proxy Pattern, is useful whenever one or more client objects need to address other objects indirectly. Here we use an example of a set of buttons that affect only the current shape (whichever shape the user has selected most recently). Without a proxy, all the buttons need to update their references each time the user clicks on a shape; with a proxy, the buttons don't need to change, only the proxy needs to update its reference.

The third pattern covered here, is the Composite Pattern, which is particularly useful in graphical applications. In fact, we've seen it already, both in the `Hat` example in Chapter 2 and in `FishApp` in Chapter 7. Here we give an example of a program where a set of buttons must move a picture of a space alien that is made up of three ellipses, one for the head and one for each of the eyes. In general, the Composite Pattern is useful whenever a command must be executed by all of the parts of a composite object; it is a form of delegation.

■ Self-Check Questions ■

(The answers to these questions can be found on the book's website, www.aw.com/sanders)

1. What is a design pattern?
2. List some patterns you used before reading this chapter and learning the term "design pattern."
3. What is the Holder Pattern? What problem does it solve, and what are its pros and cons?
4. What is the Proxy Pattern? What problem does it solve, and what are its pros and cons?
5. What is the Composite Pattern? What problem does it solve, and what are its pros and cons?

■ Exercises ■

Applying the Facts

1. List two additional problems where the Holder Pattern might be useful. Explain.
2. List two additional problems where the Proxy Pattern might be useful. Explain.
3. List two additional problems where the Composite Pattern might be useful. Explain.
4. Read in the *Design Patterns* book about a design pattern other than the ones described in this chapter. Find additional information about your pattern on the Web. Rewrite the description of the pattern in your own words. Identify the websites you looked at and discuss why they were (or were not) helpful in understanding this material.

■ Programming Projects ■

Modifying Programs

1. Modify `ColorHolderApp` so that all of the built-in colors (yellow, orange, magenta, and so forth) are included in the row of radio buttons.
2. Modify `ColorHolderApp` so that the shape is a `ColorRectangle` instead of a `ColorEllipse`.
3. Modify `ColorHolderApp` to add a `MovableRectangle` to the `MovingEllipsePanel`.

4. Modify `ColorHolderApp` so that there are several shapes that put together make a picture of a car and six different color buttons that can be used to change the color of each part of the car.

5. Modify `CarProxyApp` so that it uses pictures of balloons instead of cars, and make the balloons go up and down instead of sideways.

6. Modify `AlienApp` so that the picture shown is the snowman from Chapter 2 (including its hat). The slider should cause the entire snowman, including the hat, to move simultaneously.

7. Modify `AlienApp` so that the program displays the whole output of `SnowCartoon` from Chapter 2, including both the snowman and the sun. The user should be able to click on either the sun or the snowman, and the object selected should then be movable using the buttons.

Writing Programs

1. Revise the Tetris program from Chapter 8 (Question 3 in Writing Programs) so that it uses the Proxy Pattern.

chapter **10**

Advanced Arithmetic and Conditional Statements

OBJECTIVES

After reading this chapter, you should be able to:

☑ List and explain the types used to model real numbers in Java

☑ Read and write arithmetic expressions involving real numbers

☑ Read and write nested `if` statements

☑ Read and write `switch` statements

■ 10.1 ■ Introduction

In this chapter, we continue the discussion of arithmetic and conditional statements begun in Chapter 6. In Chapter 6, we showed how Java models integers and arithmetic expressions and how Java uses conditional statements to model choices.

For many applications, integers are not enough. For example, in our cookie factory, we might want to record the total profits for the year. These numbers are likely to have fractional parts: for example, $123,456,789.87 in profits (if we sell a lot of cookies!), not $123,456,789. Java, like other programming languages, gives us a way to model all real numbers, not just integers.

Java also provides a way to model more complex decisions than the ones in Chapter 6. In Chapter 6, we modeled immediate decisions, such as a car that changes direction at a fork in the road. Suppose we want to think several steps ahead—for example, if I turn right here then at the next corner I can turn left, right, or go straight, and if I turn left there, then ... . In this chapter, we discuss how to model this kind of decision.

■ 10.2 ■ **Concepts**

10.2.1 **Modeling real numbers**

As we have seen, Java has more than one built-in type for modeling integers. Which one we choose depends on how big the number is that we want to represent, and how much computer memory we have available for the representation.

Real numbers include both integers and numbers with fractional parts (also called **floating-point numbers**). To model floating-point numbers Java gives us more than one built-in type. Again, as for integers, we choose one of these types on the basis of the number we need to represent and the amount of computer memory available.

Determining which built-in type to use is an important modeling decision. A model of temperatures such as 98.6, or other data that is expressed in terms of numbers with fractional parts, should use floating-point numbers. On the other hand, for a model of something that can be counted, such as the number of cookies produced by the factory in a day or the number of space-alien pictures in a window, integers are a better choice.

10.2.2 **Operations on floating-point numbers**

Even though integers and real numbers are modeled by different datatypes in most programming languages, the same arithmetic operations can generally be performed on both. The rules of precedence are also the same for floating-point numbers as they are for integers.

Sometimes the operations have slightly different meanings. Division is one example: if we divide the integer 7 by the integer 2, the answer is 3; but if we divide the floating-point number 7.0 by the floating-point number 2.0, the answer is 3.5. And some operations apply to integers and not floating-point numbers, or vice versa. For example, the remainder operation only makes sense for integers.

10.2.3 **Casting and coercion**

keyconcept

Forcing a variable of one type to be considered as another is called coercion or casting.

What if we write an expression that includes both floating-point numbers and integers? For example, we might write 10.5 + 2 * 8.7342/17. When the expression is evaluated, the result must have one type only. Either the expression is invalid, or we need to choose what type the result will have.

Similarly, what if we assign a floating-point value to an integer variable, or vice versa? Should Java automatically convert the value so that it has the same type as the variable, or should it signal an error? If it converts the value, what should the value be converted to?

Java, like many languages, allows us to force an integer to be considered a floating-point number (or vice versa). This is another example of **coercion** or **casting**. We have already used explicit coercion to convert Java's Graphics objects into Graphics2D objects. **Implicit coercion** occurs when a language coerces one variable into another type without any code specifically telling it to do so. We see examples of implicit coercion in the next section.

keyconcept

Explicit coercion is the explicit statement that a variable of one type should be coerced into another. Implicit coercion occurs when a language coerces one variable into another type without any code specifically telling it to.

10.2.4 Modeling choices within choices

In Chapter 6, we showed how to model yes-no choices, choices with two alternatives, and choices with three or more alternatives. In this chapter, we consider more complex choices. Suppose, for example, that we're considering the following possibilities: the cookie factory is not producing enough cookies, it's producing enough cookies, and it's producing more cookies than we can sell. In each case, we have several possible responses. For example, if the factory is not producing enough cookies, we might get new cookie ovens or hire more employees; alternatively, if the factory is producing too many cookies, we might cut the least profitable line of cookies or spend more on advertising.

To model this kind of choice, we can use **nested conditionals**: conditional statements inside other conditional statements. We can say something like:

keyconcept

To model more complex decisions, we can use nested conditionals: conditional statements inside other conditional statements.

```
if the factory is not producing enough cookies then begin
    if ovens are old, buy new ovens
    else if not enough chefs, hire more chefs
    else buy more chocolate chips
end
else if factory is producing too many cookies then begin
    if no one likes peanut-butter cookies, stop making
        peanut-butter cookies
    else design new ad campaign
end
```

A flow chart for this decision is given in Figure 10.1. There are several things to note about this diagram.

- Although there are several paths through the diagram from Previous Statements to Next Statements, each time the program is executed, it must choose *exactly one* of those paths.

- It is possible to do nothing. For example, if the first two conditions are both `false` (that is, if the cookie factory is making the right amount of cookies), we continue to the next part of the program without taking any action.

- The nested conditional statements have the same form as a simple conditional statement.

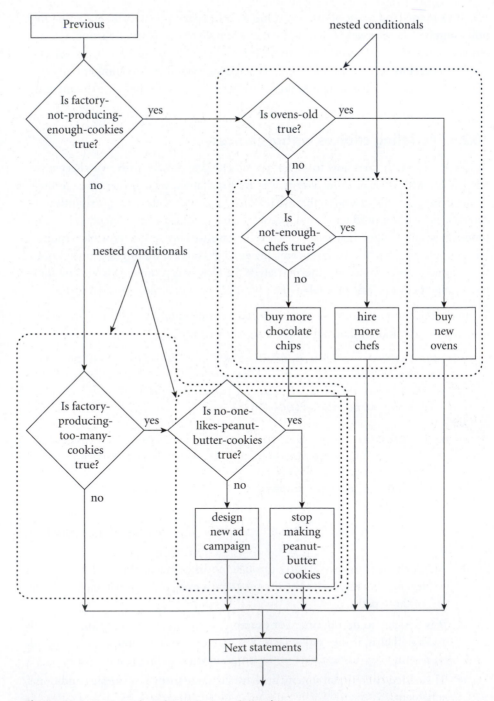

Figure 10.1 ■ Flow chart for nested conditional.

■ Wherever we see a block of code, another conditional statement can be substituted. We can have conditional statements nested inside conditional statements, nested inside more conditional statements, and on and on, in order to model more and more complex decisions. It is rare, however, to need more than one level of nesting.

■ 10.3 ■ **Mechanics**

In this chapter, we continue our cookie-factory example. In addition to keeping track of how many cookies the factory produces in a day, the factory manager now also wants to know approximately how many cookies we are producing per hour. Finally, for packaging reasons we need to know the area of the cookie. We're going to need to decide the best way to represent each of these results for a day-end report.

10.3.1 **Floating-point numbers in Java**

In Chapter 6, we noted that computers have different ways of storing numbers with different precision and that Java provides four different levels of precision for integers called `byte`, `short`, `int`, and `long` in order of increasing precision. The more precise the number, the more memory it uses.

Java provides only two built-in types for floating-point numbers, `float` and `double`. Because of the way these numbers are stored in the computer's memory, in both positive and negative numbers, a **float** ranges in magnitude from $0.14012985 * 10^{44}$ (at its closest to zero) up to $3.4028237 * 10^{38}$ (at its farthest from zero). A **double** has a much larger range, from $4.9 * 10^{324}$ up to $1.7976931348623157 * 10^{308}$. The greater the range, the more memory a number uses.

Table 10.1 summarizes the possible values of the numbers that can be represented by each of Java's built-in types, along with the amount of computer memory used by each (measured in the basic unit of computer memory, a **bit**).

> **keyconcept**
> Java gives us a way to model real numbers. The types used to model real numbers in Java are `float` and `double`.

Table 10.1 ■ Numeric datatypes with possible values for each.

Type	Minimum value	Maximum value	Computer memory used (bits)
`byte`	−128	127	8
`short`	−32768	32767	16
`int`	−2,147,483,648	2,147,483,647	32
`long`	−9,223,372,036,854,775,808	9,223,372,036,854,775,807	64
`float`	$−3.4028237 * 10^{38}$	$+3.4028237 * 10^{38}$	32
`double`	$−1.7976931348623157 * 10^{308}$	$+1.7976931348623157 * 10^{308}$	64

Using Java's floating-point numbers is quite straightforward. In fact, we have used them already. When we defined `ColorEllipse` in Chapter 7, we defined it as a subclass of `Ellipse2D.Double`. `Ellipse2D.Double` is a subclass of `Ellipse2D` whose height, width, location, and rotation are represented using `doubles`.

Consider our cookie factory. First we want to know how many cookies we produce. We probably won't produce more than two billion in a day, so we can use an `int` for this. The manager wants to know how many cookies we are producing per hour, and since averages usually involve fractions, let's use a floating-point number; a `float` should be precise enough. To represent the number of hours, a `byte` is sufficient because generally the number is reset whenever it reaches twenty-four. Next, suppose we want to compute the surface area of a cookie. The surface area will likely have a fractional part, but is a relatively small number, so a `float` should be sufficient. We'll also need to store the radius of the cookie to compute the area, and that should be a `float` as well.

Note that we are being more careful here than we usually need to be. To make things easy on yourself, simply use `int` for integers and `double` to model real numbers. We only need to be very careful if we're doing scientific computation where we want to preserve maximum precision or if we have a huge data set.

Let's take a look at what we have so far.

```
public class CookieFactory {
    private int _totalCookies;
    private byte _numHoursWorked;
    private float _cookiesPerHour, _cookieArea,
        _cookieRadius;

    public CookieFactory() {
        _totalCookies = 0; // always initialize, for
        _numHoursWorked = 0; // safety
        _cookiesPerHour = 0.0;
        _cookieArea = 0.0;
        _cookieRadius = 1.5;
    }
}
```

10.3.2 Arithmetic operations on floating-point numbers, casting, and coercions

Here's a method for computing cookies produced per hour.

```
public void computeCookiesPerHour() {
    _cookiesPerHour = _totalCookies/_numHoursWorked;
}
```

Both _totalCookies and _numHoursWorked are ints. Therefore, _totalCookies/ _numHoursWorked is computed using integer division. Then the result is implicitly coerced to a float, because _cookiesPerHour is a float. We call this **implicit coercion**, because Java does it automatically; we don't have to add any Java syntax to make it happen.

Does this computation give the result we want? Consider an example. If the factory produced 13,683 cookies in eight hours, the result is rounded down to 1710, and then when the value is stored in _cookiesPerHour, it becomes 1710.0. The answer should be 1710.375.

To get the answer we want, we need to use floating-point division, and to make Java use floating-point division, we need one of the numbers being divided to be a float. If either of the values is a float, the result of the division will be a float. But both of the variables are declared as ints.

To cause one of these variables to be a float, we use **explicit coercion**, like this:

```
public void computeCookiesPerHour() {
    //change _numHoursWorked to a float so we get a
    //float as the result of our division
    _cookiesPerHour = _totalCookies /
                        (float)_numHoursWorked;
}
```

Before _numHoursWorked we put the new base type (float) in parentheses to indicate that we want our variable to be converted to that type. This notation is Java's syntax for explicit coercion. (The conversion happens for this calculation only; the next time we use _numHoursWorked, it will be an int again.)

This method now includes both implicit and explicit coercion. _numHoursWorked is explicitly coerced from int to float. _totalCookies is then *implicitly* coerced to the same type as _numHoursWorked, so that Java can compute the quotient of the two.

Java does implicit coercion only in certain cases. It implicitly coerces a byte to an int or an int to a float, but not the other way around. For example, the code fragments:

```
float annualProfits;
    ...  // compute value for annualProfits
int result = annualProfits; // error
```

and

```
byte numHours = 600; // error
```

both generate errors.

Java is willing to perform implicit coercions as long as the result is at least as precise as the initial expression (that is, the result has a type that is at least as low down in Table 10.1). If we convert a `byte` to a `short` or an `int` to a `float`, no information is lost. If we go the other way, however (from a type lower in the table to one higher in the table), the value might have to be approximated. If there's any chance that information might be lost in a coercion from one numeric type to another, Java requires us to state explicitly that the coercion should be done.

When else can we assign a value of one type to a variable of another? Most notably, when we polymorphically assign an instance of a subclass (actual type) to a variable declared as a superclass (declared type). Here again, Java implicitly coerces something of one type (the subclass instance) to another type (the superclass's type). Once again, Java only makes implicit coercions in one direction: to assign an instance of a superclass to a variable declared as one of its subclasses, we must use explicit coercion.

10.3.3 Java's `Math` class: static variables and methods

Let's now write the factory's `CookieArea` method. The formula for the area of a cookie is πr^2 (we'll assume the cookie is completely flat). But how should we model π? It's not an integer, but it's used in many different applications. If each programmer chooses his or her own approximation, some might use 3.1, some 3.14, some 3.141, and so forth. Java has done us the favor of creating a class to help us out in situations like these—it's called the `Math` class (yup, it's a very original name).

keyconcept

Class variables (also called `static` variables) are shared by all instances of a class.

Java's `Math` class is composed of a number of **class methods** and **class variables** that we can use in any Java program. All the variables we have seen so far are specific to an instance of a class. That is, every time an instance is created, Java sets aside memory for that instance's copy of the instance variables, separate from any other instance's copy of those variables. **Class variables** belong to a class as a whole. The first time Java encounters a class, it sets aside memory for any class variables, and all members of the class share that same copy of the class variables. Class variables are created by using the Java keyword `static`, so they are also called **`static` variables**.

Static variables are useful for constant values that all instances of the class need to share, such as the value of π. It is dangerous to use `static` variables for values that may change, however. For a value that needs to be accessed by several different objects, it is safer to use the Holder Pattern: by putting the value in a Holder and providing accessor and mutator methods, we can control access to the value.

keyconcept

Class methods (also called `static` methods) are executed on behalf of the entire class.

Just as class variables are shared by all instances of a class, **class methods** are executed on behalf of the entire class and not on a specific instance of the class. Because class methods are the same for all instances of the class, they cannot refer to instance variables, whose values are different for each instance. Class methods are also called `static` methods. You have already seen the most common example of a `static` method—it's the `main` method. Another example is the `pow(int x,int y)` method in the `Math` class that raises *x* to the power *y*. Because class methods are the same for every instance of a class, we don't need to create an instance to use them. We can just say, for example, `Math.pow(2, 3)`, and Java computes the result (8) for us.

With these tools, we can now write our `computeCookieArea` method:

```
public void computeCookieArea() {
    _cookieArea = Math.PI * Math.pow(_cookieRadius, 2);
}
```

The `Math` class includes many other useful methods, including trigonometry functions (`sin`, `cos`, `tan`, etc.), `min`, and `max`.

10.3.4 **Random numbers**

Often in programs it's useful to generate a random number. One standard example is modeling the roll of a die. Another example might be if we wanted to give the fish in the simulated fish tank in Chapter 7 a different initial speed each time the program is run. There's a method in Java's `Math` class, called `random`, that almost does what we want. It returns a different number between 0.0 and 1.0 each time it is run. (The number may be equal to 0.0, but it is always less than 1.0.)

There are two problems with this method. First, it returns a `double`, and we usually want an integer (we're never going to roll a 2.5 on our die). Second, we often want a different range. For example, here we want one of the numbers from 1 to 6 for our die.

Here's a method that's more general than the one provided by Java:

```
public static int randomNumber(int low, int high) {
    return low + (int)(Math.random()*(high-low+1));
}
```

Let's hand-simulate an example to see how this works. Suppose we are using our method to simulate the roll of a die. We call our new method like this:

```
dieRoll = randomNumber(1, 6);
```

because 1 is the lowest value possible on our die and 6 is the highest. The expression `high — low + 1` evaluates to 6 − 1 + 1, or 6. The lowest value `Math.random()` could return is 0.0. In that case, `Math.random()*6` is 0.0, which is explicitly coerced to 0. Then we add the value of `low`, which is 1, and get a `dieRoll` of 1. So far so good—the lowest possible roll of our die should be a 1.

Now what's the highest possible roll? We get the highest roll when `Math.random()` returns the highest possible number. Whatever that number is, Java guarantees it is less than 1. For simplicity, say it's 0.99999. Multiply that by 6, and we have 5.99994. When we coerce this value to an `int`, however, Java drops the fractional part of our number, so it becomes 5. When we add 1 to that, we get 6, so our `randomNumber` returns a 6, and the highest possible `dieRoll` is 6.

We can use this method any time we want a random integer, as long as we know the lowest and highest possible values. To make it widely available, let's create a class called `Utilities` and put the method in that class, as shown in Listing 10.1. Later on, if we find other methods and constants of general use, we can add them to this class.

10.3.5 Constants: how, where, and when to define them

keyconcept

The Java syntax for declaring a constant is just like the syntax for declaring a variable, except for the keyword `final`. The keyword `final` means it's constant.

Often in programs there are numbers that are used over and over again and have a constant value throughout the life of the program. These numbers are called **constants**. One example of a constant might be π; another might be the speed of light.

In Java, the syntax for declaring a constant is just like the syntax for declaring a variable, except for the keyword `final`. The keyword `final` means that the value of this "variable" can never change; in other words, it's constant.

Where is the best place to declare a constant? Some constants affect only an individual class. In that case, declare the constant inside the class, like this:

```
private final int OATMEAL_COOKIE_RADIUS = 1.5;
```

```
 1    package chapter10;
 2
 3    /**
 4     * Chapter 10: Utilities.java
 5     * A file for methods we want to be able to use in many different
 6     * programs.
 7     */
 8    public class Utilities {
 9        public static int randomNumber (int low, int high) {
10            return low + (int) (Math.random()* (high-low+1));
11        }
12    }
```

Listing 10.1 ■ The `Utilities` class

Unlike variables, constants *must* be initialized when they are declared, because their value can never change afterward. It's now or never, if you want to give them a value. The value of the constant should be a number (such as 102 or 98.6), a `String` (such as "Hello, reader!") or another constant that has already been given a value.

What about constants that affect more than one class? Where should they be defined? In that case, we define a class and put our constants in the class, like this:

```java
public class CookieConstants {
    public static final float COOKIE_RADIUS = 1.5;
    public static final short TIME_IN_OVEN = 18;
    public static final short EXTRA_DOUGH = 10;
    public static final short BATCH_COUNT = 1200;
}
```

So that the constants will be generally accessible, we make them `public`, and so that they will be accessible without creating an instance of the class, we make them `static`.

Before Java 1.5, we could refer to the constants in the `CookieConstants` class using their qualified name, like this:

```java
CookieConstants.COOKIE_RADIUS
```

Java 1.5 allows us to refer to our constants simply by name, by importing them into another class. The syntax for importing constants is similar to the syntax for importing libraries such as `java.swing.*`. We can import all of the `CookieConstants` into the `CookieFactory` class like this:

```java
package cookieFactory;
/** We are showing only the methods that are affected
    by the use of constants.
**/
import static cookieFactory.CookieConstants.*;
public class CookieFactory {
    private int _totalCookies;
    private short _numHoursWorked;
    private float _cookiesPerHour, _cookieArea;

    public CookieFactory() {
        _totalCookies = 0;
        _numHoursWorked = 0;
        _cookiesPerHour = 0.0;
        _cookieArea = 0.0;
    }
```

```
    public void bakeBatch() {
        this.makeDough(BATCH_COUNT + EXTRA_DOUGH);
        this.putCookiesInOven(TIME_IN_OVEN);
        _totalCookies += BATCH_COUNT;
    }

    public void computeCookieArea() {
        _cookieArea = Math.PI *
                        Math.pow(COOKIE_RADIUS, 2);

    }
}
```

Alternatively, if we want to import an individual constant, rather than all the `static` definitions contained in `CookieConstants`, we can say:

```
import cookieFactory.CookieConstants.COOKIE_RADIUS;
```

without the wildcard.

Note the slight difference in syntax between import statements for constants and for libraries: for constants, we add the keyword `static`. With the wildcard *, as here, this statement imports anything from class `CookieConstants` that is declared `static`. In fact, if class variables or class methods were contained in `CookieConstants`, they would be imported as well. These import statements are also referred to as **static imports**.

To make static imports work, we have to make one additional change: the file being imported must be part of a named package. As explained in Chapter 2, `package` is a Java keyword for a group of related classes and interfaces. Up to now, we have used code from packages, such as `javax.swing` and `wheels.users`, but we have not defined packages of our own.

`Packages` are a way of organizing a program. We can use them to group related classes and interfaces together. For this reason, although we could technically make a program work by putting only the file we want to static-import into a package, we put all the files in the program into the same package.

To put a file in a package, we need to add just one line of code at the beginning of the file:

```
package <packageName>;
```

By convention, package names start with a lower-case letter. Thus, for example, our cookie constants, above, are in a `package` called `cookieFactory`. We add the same line

```
package cookieFactory;
```

to each of the class and interface files in the program.

The other steps needed to make Java packages work depend on the programming environment you are using. For this reason, and because our programs have been relatively small, we have avoided using packages up to now. When we do not explicitly put a class in a Java package, it is automatically placed in the default package. The default package works well enough for small programs. To make static imports work, however, we need a named package, so it's worth taking the time at this point to find out how packages work in your programming environment.

Now that you know how to define constants, we introduce two new style conventions and one warning. First, the conventions:

1. Constants should be named using all capital letters, with underscores separating one word from the next in multiword names.

2. Except for –1, 0, 1, and 2 (and –1.0, 0.0, 1.0, and 2.0), numbers should never appear in code. Always use a named constant. That way, readers of the code (including yourself) can easily tell what the number is there for. In addition, if you use a particular constant more than once, it's very helpful to be able to change it once in the constant definition, instead of searching through all the code files and asking yourself questions like "Is this 1.5 the radius of the cookie? Or is it part of the calculation of overtime pay?"

Now the warning: You may have been wondering if you could make an instance variable accessible the same way as a constant, like this:

```
public static int _totalCookies;
```

The answer is, technically, yes. You can. But it's strongly discouraged. Note that this variable isn't `final`. If you declare it `public static`, any other object in your program can modify it, and if it is changed in some way you don't like, you'll have a hard time tracking down how that happened. In effect, you are throwing away one of the main benefits of using objects in the first place. Don't do it! Instead, as discussed in earlier chapters, if a variable is closely associated with one class but used by others, define accessors and mutators for the variable. If a variable is equally useful to two or more classes, put it in a Holder.

10.3.6 **Modeling choices within choices: nested conditionals**

Suppose our cookie factory isn't producing enough cookies. Once we determine that there's a problem, the action we take depends on the cause, and there are several possible causes. To model this logic, we need a nested conditional statement.

To write a nested conditional in Java, we simply use an if-statement as one of the statements inside another if-statement (between the curly brackets). We can nest if-statements inside if-statements inside other if-statements to make progressively more precise decisions.

For example, we can write:

```
if (!this.isProducingEnoughCookies()) {
    if (this.isMachinesBroken())
        this.fixMachine();
}
```

Here we introduce a new coding convention:

> When writing nested if-statements, always put curly brackets around the block of statements to be executed.

By using brackets around the statements to be executed and indenting properly, it's much easier to see which statements go with which condition.

One exception to this convention: technically, the syntax we introduced in Chapter 6 for a series of three or more alternative actions could be considered a set of nested if statements in Java. Instead of

```
if (_weather.isSnowing()) {
    this.goSledding();
}
else if (_weather.isRaining()) {
    this.dance();
}
else if (_weather.isSunny()) {
    this.goToBeach();
}
else {
    this.studyJava();
}
```

we could write:

```
if (_weather.isSnowing()) this.goSledding();
else {
    if (_weather.isRaining()) this.dance();
    else {
        if (_weather.isSunny()) this.goToBeach();
        else {
            this.studyJava();
```

```
        }
      }
    }
```

The first style shows much more clearly, however, that we are talking about a set of alter-native actions, so when we have a series of alternative actions, we will continue to line up each else with the original if.

10.3.7 **Short-circuiting**

Consider the following code fragment. What is the value of n after it has executed?

```
int n = 1;
if(false && (2 == n++)) {
    System.out.println("Went into the if clause");
}
System.out.println(n);
```

You should avoid writing code like this, since conditional incrementing is very hard to read and understand! Nevertheless, it is useful to know how it works in case you encounter this kind of statement in someone else's code.

Since the left side of the boolean expression always evaluates to false, the right side is never evaluated. Hence n remains at its initial value, 1. This method of evaluating the conditional expression is called **short-circuiting**, because the second part of the expression is not evaluated.

Here's an example where short-circuiting might be useful. Suppose we want to call a method, but the instance variable we're calling the method on might be null. We can say:

```
if (_cookie != null && _cookie.getType() != OATMEAL)
```

If the _cookie variable is null, short-circuiting helps us out: the second half of the expression is not executed, and we do not get a null pointer exception.

A boolean expression in which the left side of an || ("or") evaluates to true is also short-circuited. For example, consider the code fragment for a robot cookie-chef:

```
if (cookieSales > 1000000 || _clock.getTime() >= 5) {
    this.goHome();
}
```

The cookie robot will go home if cookie sales top $1,000,000 or if it's 5 o'clock. Because the value of the whole boolean expression must be true, the robot won't bother to check the clock if sales go over the limit. If for some reason you want both parts of

keyconcept
Short-circuiting is omitting the evaluation of part of a conditional expression because the value of the whole expression is already known.

the expression to be evaluated, you can avoid short circuiting by using & and | as your *and* and *or* operators.

10.3.8 **Switch statement**

Normally, when we model a set of mutually exclusive alternatives in Java, we use `if-else-if` statements. But sometimes there is a special case when all of these choices depend on the value of a single integer variable. For example, let's assume that various parts of the cookie factory are making different kinds of cookies, and the manager sometimes wants to make random spot checks on these areas to make sure they are running smoothly. We need a method to determine which area should be checked.

```
public void checkRandomArea() {
    int areaNumber = randomNumber(1,4);
        //get random number between 1 and 4
        //inclusive
    if (areaNumber == 1)
        this.checkChocolateChipCookieArea();
    else if (areaNumber == 2)
        this.checkDoubleChocolateCookieArea();
    else if (areaNumber == 3)
        this.checkSugarCookieArea();
    else this.checkFactoryBookkeeping();
}
```

keyconcept

Java's `switch` statement is a special form of the `if-else-if` statement.

As an alternative, to make it easy to code this special case, Java provides the `switch` statement, which is really just a special form of the `if-else-if` statement.

The variable on which a `switch` statement bases its decision is called the **selector**. A selector cannot be any sort of complex data type, nor can it be a fractional number. It must be one of the integer primitive types (or a character, but we won't discuss that in these chapters). The value of this selector determines which action(s) should be taken.

Let's rewrite our `checkRandomArea` method using a `switch` statement. The first thing we need is a selector. Suppose we have an `int areaNumber`. Once we have the selector, we begin the `switch` statement with

```
switch(areaNumber) {
```

The body of the `switch` statement is composed of cases, and there is one case for each value of the selector. Each case begins with the keyword `case`.

Here's the revised method:

```
public void checkRandomArea() {
```

```
    int areaNumber = randomNumber(1,4);
        //get random number between 1 and 4
        //inclusive
    switch(areaNumber) {
            case 1 : this.checkChocolateChipCookieArea();
                    break;
            case 2 : this.checkOatmealRaisinCookieArea();
                    break;
            case 3 : this.checkDoubleChocolateCookieArea();
                    break;
            case 4 : this.checkSugarCookieArea();
                    break;
            default : this.checkFactoryBookkeeping();
    }
}
```

We can have as many statements involved in each `case` as we want, and we don't need braces to mark the beginning and end. In order to keep the `switch` statements readable, however, it is a good idea to write separate methods that we can call from each `case` for which we have more than a few lines.

Note the keyword `default`. The `default` is executed if `areaNumber` doesn't match any of the values given in the other `cases`. Java doesn't require us to have a `default`, but it is always a good idea to include one.

A `break` statement is inserted at the end of each case to say that "the `switch` statement is done, we can go on." If no `break` is inserted, the next case is executed (even if the selector does not match the case) and so on until a `break` (or something else that changes the flow of control) is reached. For example, if there is a `return`, the `break` is not necessary, since we are already leaving the method containing the `switch` statement, and nothing else is executed. A flow-chart for `switch` statements is given in Figure 10.2.

Now suppose that our oatmeal raisin cookie is the most popular cookie and we therefore want to check that area a little more often than the others. If we delete the `break` statement before that `case`, the random check is weighted to hit the Oatmeal Raisin cookie area more often, as follows:

```
public void checkRandomArea() {
    int areaNumber = randomNumber(1,4);
        //get random number between 1 and 4
        //inclusive
    switch(areaNumber) {
            case 1 : this.checkChocolateChipCookieArea();
            case 2 : this.checkOatmealRaisinCookieArea();
```

```
                    break;
        case 3 : this.checkDoubleChocolateCookieArea();
                    break;
        case 4 : this.checkSugarCookieArea();
                    break;
        default : this.checkFactoryBookkeeping();
    }
}
```

Every time `areaNumber` is 2, the `RaisinCookieArea` is checked; every time it is 1, both the `ChocolateChipArea` and the `RaisinCookieArea` are checked. It's not clear from this code, however, that the `break` was omitted on purpose; this is a very easy mistake to make.

To make it clearer that we want the oatmeal cookies to be checked more often, it's better to dedicate more possible selector values to that area, as follows:

```
public void checkRandomArea() {
    int areaNumber = randomNumber(1,5);
        //get random number between 1 and 5
        //inclusive
    switch(areaNumber) {
```

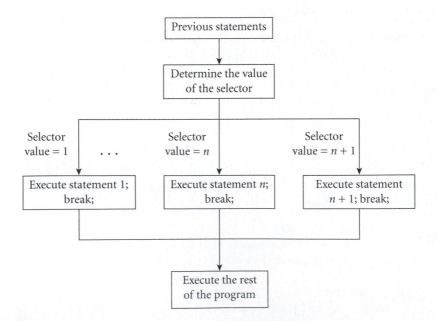

Figure 10.2 ■ Flow of control in a switch statement.

```
        case 1 : this.checkChocolateChipCookieArea();
                 break;
        case 2,5 : this.checkOatmealRaisinCookieArea();
                   break;
        case 3 : this.checkDoubleChocolateCookieArea();
                 break;
        case 4 : this.checkSugarCookieArea();
                 break;
        default : this.checkFactoryBookkeeping();
    }
}
```

 ■ **10.4** ■ Working Out with

floating-point numbers, nested conditionals, and random numbers—ColorBounceApp

Objectives:
☑ Practice using arithmetic
☑ Use nested conditionals
☑ Use random number function to control program output

In this section, we develop a version of GUIBounceApp from Chapter 8 modified to change colors randomly as it bounces. Here are the specifications:

> The ball should bounce continuously from one side of the window to another, changing direction each time it hits an edge. When it changes direction, it should also change color. Two possible colors are associated with each edge. The program should randomly choose between the two colors.

For this program, we need ten files: Colorable, Accelerator, Mover, MoveTimer, SmartEllipse, Utilities, ColorBounceApp, BouncePanel, BouncingBall, and BounceConstants. The first five—Colorable, Accelerator, Mover, MoveTimer, and SmartEllipse—are the same as in Chapters 7 and 8. The only change we need to make is to add the statement

```
    package chapter10;
```

at the beginning of each file. The Utilities file is given in Listing 10.1. So we can reuse most of the code we need, and we only have to define four new classes for this program: ColorBounceApp, BouncePanel, BouncingBall, and BounceConstants. As usual, we start with the subclass of JFrame (here, ColorBounceApp, shown in Listing

10.2). This code is very familiar. We create a `JFrame`, give it a title and a size, make the program exit when we close the frame, and create the contents of the `JFrame`, a `BouncePanel`. The only really new thing here is line 9, where we import a class that contains our constant definitions. This import statement lets us use the constants `FRAME_WIDTH` and `FRAME_HEIGHT` in line 14. Recall that by convention, constants' names are in upper-case letters.

Next, consider the `BouncePanel` class (shown in Listing 10.3). `BouncePanel` is a subclass of `JPanel`. The class has two methods, a constructor and a version of `paintComponent`. The constructor sets the `JPanel`'s color to white, creates an instance of class `Ball`, and then sets the location and size of the `Ball`. Finally, following our event-handler recipe, it creates a timer with itself as a listener and starts the timer.

This code is also very familiar, again with the exception of the imported constants class.

```
1    package chapter10;
2    /**
3     * Chapter 10: ColorBounceApp.java
4     * Displays a window that contains a single panel that in turn
5     * contains a ball that bounces from one side
6     * to another, changing color and direction each time it hits an edge.
7     */
8    import javax.swing.*;
9    import static chapter10.BounceConstants.*;
10
11   public class ColorBounceApp extends JFrame {
12       public ColorBounceApp (String title) {
13           super(title);
14           this.setSize(FRAME_WIDTH, FRAME_HEIGHT);
15           this.setDefaultCloseOperation(JFrame.EXIT_ON_CLOSE);
16           this.add(new BouncePanel());
17           this.setVisible(true);
18       }
19
20       public static void main (String [ ] args) {
21           ColorBounceApp app = new
22               ColorBounceApp ("Chapter 10: ColorBounceApp");
23       }
24   }
```

Listing 10.2 ■ The `ColorBounceApp` class

Notice how easy it is to find the constants, with names in capital letters. The `BouncingBall` class (shown in Listing 10.4) is the same as the `BouncingBall` class in Chapter 8, except for two things. First, we have made the changes necessary to use

```
1    package chapter10;
2
3    /**
4     * Chapter 10: BouncePanel.java
5     * Contains a colorful bouncing ball.
6     */
7    import java.awt.*;
8    import javax.swing.*;
9    import static chapter10.BounceConstants.*;
10
11   public class BouncePanel extends JPanel implements Mover {
12       private BouncingBall _ball; // components
13       private MoveTimer _timer;
14
15       public BouncePanel () {
16           super();
17           _ball = new BouncingBall (Color.red, this);
18           _timer = new MoveTimer(INTERVAL, this);
19           _ball.setLocation(BALL_X, BALL_Y);
20           _ball.setSize(BALL_WIDTH, BALL_WIDTH);
21           this.setBackground(Color.white);
22           _timer.start();
23       }
24
25       public void move() {
26           _ball.move();
27           this.repaint();
28       }
29
30       public void paintComponent (Graphics aBrush) {
31           super.paintComponent(aBrush);
32           Graphics2D betterBrush = (Graphics2D) aBrush;
33           _ball.fill(betterBrush);
34       }
35   }
```

Listing 10.3 ■ The `BouncePanel` class

the `BounceConstants`. Second, we have modified the `move` method so that the `BouncingBall` will change color.

The revised `move` method contains the code to move the `BouncingBall` around the `JPanel` and make it change color. At each move, we need to determine whether the ball has hit one of the edges of the `JFrame`. If it has, we need to choose a new color. The choice of new colors depends on the edge we have hit. As a result, we need to use a nested conditional statement.

The outer conditional has one branch for each of the edges we can hit: top, bottom, left, and right. Each branch tests for a particular edge, and if that edge is hit, determines how to change the direction. Note that we test for the right side and bottom side using the width and height of the `JPanel`, not the `JFrame`—the size of the `JFrame` includes the border containing its title, maximize and minimize buttons, and so forth.

Inside each branch, we have another conditional. If the `randomNumber` method returns a 0, we choose one color; if not, we choose the other.

```
 1    package chapter10;
 2
 3    /**
 4     * Chapter 10: BouncingBall.java
 5     * The same as the BouncingBall from Chapter 8, with two changes: (1)
 6     * the code is contained in a package and static imports a file of
 7     * constants and (2) the move method is modified so that
 8     * the bouncing ball changes color randomly when
 9     * changing direction.
10     */
11    import java.awt.*;
12    import javax.swing.*;
13    import static chapter10.BounceConstants.*;
14
15    public class BouncingBall extends chapter10.SmartEllipse
16        implements Mover, Accelerator, Colorable {
17        private int _changeX, _changeY; // attributes
18        private JPanel _panel; // peer object (and container)
19
20        public BouncingBall(Color aColor, JPanel aPanel){
21            super(aColor);
22            _changeX = INIT_X_SPEED;
```

Listing 10.4 ■ The `BouncingBall` class (*continued on next page*)

```
23            _changeY = INIT_Y_SPEED;
24            _panel = aPanel;
25        }
26        public void move() {
27            double nextX = this.getX()+_changeX;
28            double nextY = this.getY()+_changeY;
29            if (nextX < this.getMinBoundX()) {
30                if (Utilities.randomNumber(0,1)==0){
31                    this.setColor(Color.blue);
32                }
33                else {
34                    this.setColor(Color.red);
35                }
36                _changeX *= -1;
37                nextX = this.getMinBoundX();
38            }
39            if (nextX > this.getMaxBoundX()) {
40                if (Utilities.randomNumber(0,1)==0){
41                    this.setColor(Color.green);
42                }
43                else {
44                    this.setColor(Color.orange);
45                }
46                _changeX *= -1;
47                nextX = this.getMaxBoundX();
48            }
49            if (nextY < this.getMinBoundY()) {
50                if (Utilities.randomNumber(0,1)==0){
51                    this.setColor(Color.magenta);
52                }
53                else {
54                    this.setColor(Color.yellow);
55                }
56                _changeY *= -1;
57                nextY = this.getMinBoundY();
58            }
59            if (nextY > this.getMaxBoundY()) {
60                if (Utilities.randomNumber(0,1)==0){
61                    this.setColor(Color.cyan);
62                }
63                else {
```

Listing 10.4 ■ The BouncingBall class (*continued on next page*)

```
64                    this.setColor(Color.black);
65                }
66                _changeY *= -1;
67                nextY = this.getMaxBoundY();
68            }
69            this.setLocation(nextX, nextY);
70        }
71        // insert rest of methods from Chapter 8's BouncingBall
72    }
```

Listing 10.4 ■ The `BouncingBall` class

Finally, let's examine the `BounceConstants` class (shown in Listing 10.5). This class is a simple list of constant declarations. By putting them in the same place, we can ensure that the same values are used throughout the program. In addition, we can change them easily. For example, to experiment with different speeds for the ball, we need only change the values of `INIT_X_SPEED` and `INIT_Y_SPEED` in this file.

```
1    package chapter10;
2
3    /**
4     * Chapter 10: BounceConstants.java
5     * The constants used by all the classes in ColorBounceApp, collected
6     * in one place.
7     */
8    public class BounceConstants {
9        public static final int FRAME_WIDTH = 600; // attributes
10       public static final int FRAME_HEIGHT = 450;
11       public static final int BALL_WIDTH = 80;
13       public static final double BALL_X = 75.0;
14       public static final double BALL_Y = 75.0;
15       public static final int INIT_X_SPEED = 6;
16       public static final int INIT_Y_SPEED = 4;
17       public static final int INTERVAL = 100;
18   }
```

Listing 10.5 ■ The `BounceConstants` class

■ Summary ■

In this chapter, we have seen how to model real numbers using the floating-point base types `float` and `double`. We've seen how to write a method that generates random numbers. And we've seen how to model complex decisions using nested conditionals. Finally, we've seen a special syntax for writing mutually exclusive conditional statements where the choices depend on the value of a single integer variable, the `switch` statement.

■ Self-Check Questions ■

(The answers to these questions can be found on the course website www.aw.com/sanders)

1. What are the two datatypes Java provides for modeling real numbers?
2. When should we use one of the datatypes Java provides for modeling integers, and when should we use one of its datatypes for modeling real numbers?
3. What is the difference between integer division and division where the arguments are real numbers?
4. What is coercion?
5. What is implicit coercion?
6. What is explicit coercion?
7. When does Java perform implicit coercions?
8. What is the Java syntax for an implicit coercion?
9. What is a nested conditional?
10. What is a class method (static method)?
11. What is a class variable (static variable)?
12. Check the online documentation for Java's `Math` class (at http://java.sun.com) and list three mathematical constants contained in the class.
13. Check the online documentation for Java's `Math` class (at http://java.sun.com) and list three methods contained in the class.
14. Do we need to instantiate the `Math` class in order to use one of its methods? Why or why not?
15. What is the syntax for defining a constant in Java? Explain each keyword that you use.
16. What is the convention for naming constants?
17. What is the syntax for a nested if-statement in Java?

18. Compare and contrast Java's built-in `random` method with the `randomNumber` method given in this chapter.

19. What is a `static` import statement? When is it used?

20. What is short-circuiting?

21. What is a `switch` statement?

22. Compare and contrast `switch` statements and `if-else` statements.

■ Exercises ■

Applying the Facts

1. For each of the following, indicate which of Java's numeric datatypes you would use to model it, and explain why. If more than one datatype applies, choose the one that uses the least memory.

    a. The number of days in a week
    b. The number of days in a year
    c. The number of minutes in a year
    d. The current population of the United States
    e. The current population of the world
    f. The height of a human being in meters
    g. The distance from the Earth to the moon
    h. The distance from the Earth to the sun
    i. The mileage on a car

2. Suppose we have a variable named `hoursWorked` that should contain a real number. Write two Java statements declaring this variable, each giving it a different datatype.

3. What is the result of the following arithmetic computations in Java:

    a. 2/3
    b. 2.0/3.0
    c. 2 + 3.5
    d. 2.5 + 3
    e. 2/3 + 2.5

4. Using only the basic arithmetic operations, write a method that returns the ceiling of a number. The ceiling of a number is the smallest integer larger than that number. For example, 4.0 is the ceiling of 3.5. 10.0 is the ceiling of 9.1. –4.0 is the ceiling of –4.5.

5. Declare a constant to hold the number of trees in the city or town where you live.

6. Declare a constant to hold the height in meters of the tallest tree in the city or town where you live.

7. Recall that we can create our own custom colors in Java by creating a new instance of the `Color` class

   ```
   new Color(red, green, blue)
   ```

   where `red`, `green`, and `blue` are `int` variables that each have some value from 0 to 255.

   a. What type would the Java designers have used for these variables if they wanted to save as much memory as possible?

   b. Write a `randomColor` method, using the `randomNumber` method from this chapter, that returns a new random color each time it is called.

8. Suppose we have declared a class called `MyConstants` to hold the constants in a program. Write a Java statement that, when included in another class A, make it possible to use those constants in class A.

9. What is the value of `n` after each of the following groups of statements is executed? Explain your answers.

   a. `n = 19;`
      `(6 > 7) && n++;`

   b. `n = 6;`
      `(6 > 7) || n++;`

   c. `n = 2;`
      `(6 < 7) && n++;`

   d. `n = 83;`
      `(6 < 7) || n++;`

10. Write a method containing a nested `if-then-else` statement that takes a number from 1 to 365 and (assuming it's not leap year) returns a `String` containing the month corresponding to that number.

11. Run `ColorBounceApp` and consider it as a test of our `randomNumber` method.

    a. Count how often each color appears, until the ball has hit each wall 20 times. How many times does each color appear?

    b. How would you modify the program so that this count is performed automatically?

■ Programming Projects ■

Modifying Programs

1. Modify `ColorBounceApp` so that the number of times each color appears is counted, and totals for each color are displayed in a `JLabel` after every 100 bounces. How often does each color appear:

   a. After 100 bounces?
   b. After 500 bounces?
   c. After 1000 bounces?

   What do you conclude about the randomness of the `randomNumber` method?

2. Modify `ColorBounceApp` so that instead of a bouncing ball, the space alien from Chapter 9 is bouncing around the frame (the space alien should not change color). Make sure to use the composite pattern in this program.

3. Modify `ColorBounceApp` so that instead of changing color when it hits a wall, the ball speeds up or slows down. It should speed up by ten pixels at a time until it reaches a maximum speed of 50, then slow down until it reaches 0, then speed up again.

Writing Programs

1. Write a program to display a clock on the screen. The clock should have a black circular face and two hands, one red and one cyan. There should be no numbers. The hands should both rotate, and the minute hand should be twelve times as fast as the hour hand.

2. Write a program that repeatedly picks a random location at the top of the frame and then causes a "raindrop" (i.e., a small ellipse) to fall from that location. Each raindrop should fall from the top of the frame all the way to the bottom and then disappear.

3. Modify the program from question 2 so that the raindrops are each a different, randomly chosen color.

4. Modify the program from question 2 so that the raindrops appear in groups of two or three, all at random locations.

■ New Coding Conventions ■

- When writing nested if-statements, always put curly brackets around the block of statements to be executed.

- One exception: for a series of three or more alternatives (if/else if/.../else), continue to line up each `else` with the original `if`.

- Constants should be named using all capital letters.

- Except for −1, 0, 1, and 2 (and −1.0, 0.0, 1.0, and 2.0), numbers should never appear in code. Always use a named constant instead.

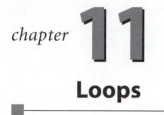

chapter **11**

Loops

OBJECTIVES

After reading this chapter, you should be able to:

- ☑ Explain how a computer program models repeated actions
- ☑ Explain the difference between definite and indefinite loops
- ☑ Give examples of situations when you would use a `for` loop, a `while` loop, and a `do-while` loop
- ☑ Read and write `for` loops
- ☑ Read and write `while` loops
- ☑ Read and write `do-while` loops
- ☑ Explain the sentinel, best-value, and accumulator recipes and use them in programs
- ☑ Use hand-simulation to find bugs in loops

■ 11.1 ■ Introduction

Suppose we want to program a cookie robot to make a thousand cookies. Or suppose we want to program the robot to keep filling bags of cookies every day for a year, or to calculate and record the cookie factory's profits every day. In each case, we need to tell it to repeat the same basic steps—the steps needed to make one cookie, fill one bag, or perform one calculation—over and over again.

So far, if we wanted to make the computer execute the same step over and over, we had to write the same line of code over and over. That's okay if we want to execute a step two or three times, but a thousand? We could cut and paste the code, but.... Appropriate laziness tells us there should be a better way. Moreover, what if we don't know how many times we want the steps to be repeated? What if, for example, we want to program the robot to add cookies to the bag until it is full? Cut and paste won't solve this problem, because we don't know how many cut and pastes to do.

With loops, we can write a block of statements once and tell the computer to repeat it.

The answer is loops. With **loops**, we can write a block of statements once, and tell the computer to repeat it, either a fixed number of times, or until a given condition has been met. In this chapter, we discuss loops, Java's loop syntax, and how to avoid the most common errors involving loops.

■ 11.2 ■ Concepts

There are two broad categories of loops. The first, **definite loops**, repeat a set of statements a predetermined number of times. The second, **indefinite loops**, repeat a set of statements an unknown number of times, stopping when a specified condition is met. Another term for repeating a block of statements is **iteration.**

Definite loops repeat a set of statements a predetermined number of times.

Both kinds of loops have simple syntax, but they are a common source of bugs. Consider the following loop, which used to be common in the instructions on shampoo bottles:

Lather.

Rinse.

Repeat.

Indefinite loops repeat a set of statements an unknown number of times, stopping when a specified condition is met.

What would happen if we gave these instructions to a literal-minded robot? It would stay in the shower until it rusted and fell apart, lathering and rinsing over and over again. A loop like this that never halts is called an **infinite loop**. You will almost undoubtedly write an infinite loop at some point. Other problems with loops include loops that never start and loops that execute the wrong number of times.

Loops are particularly useful when dealing with a collection of objects. We briefly introduce a Java class called a `Vector` that models a list and show how to process the objects in the `Vector` using a loop, for example displaying all the shapes stored in a `Vector`. `Vectors` are considered in more detail in Chapter 13. We also introduce a design pattern called Iterator that is useful in connection with collections of objects, such as `Vectors`.

■ 11.3 ■ Mechanics

11.3.1 `Vectors`

Caution: This discussion holds for Java 1.5 only. `Vectors` have been changed in Java 1.5 with the introduction of generics.

It would often be useful to be able to model a group of objects. For example, up to now, when we wanted to have ten `Ellipses` in a panel, we've had to give each of them a name—say, `_ellipse1`, `_ellipse2`, `_ellipse3`, … `_ellipse10`. Each time we want to repaint the panel, we have to repaint each `Ellipse` separately.

```
_ellipse1.fill(aBetterBrush);
_ellipse2.fill(aBetterBrush);
_ellipse3.fill(aBetterBrush);
...
_ellipse10.fill(aBetterBrush);
```

As usual, when we find ourselves writing the same code over and over, it's time to be appropriately lazy. It's time to ask, "Isn't there an easier way?"

It would be convenient to define a class that modeled a list of `Ellipses`, say, `EllipseList`, and store all our `Ellipses` in an instance of that list. That way, we could simply say:

```
_ellipseList.paint();
```

and all ten (or 100, or 1000) `Ellipses` in the panel would be repainted.

Most of the remaining chapters, in fact, deal with different ways to define groups of objects (also known as data structures). A **data structure** is a collection of objects that could have been stored in individual variables but have instead been organized in some way and given a single name and set of operations. The operations vary depending on the data structure, but they all include some way of accessing the individual pieces of data. All higher-level programming languages provide one or more built-in data structures.

keyconcept

A data structure is a group of objects connected in some way and given a single name.

One of the simplest data structures in Java, the `java.util.Vector`, is a built-in class that models a list. All of the items in the list (called **elements**) belong to the same class, or some subset of that class. When we declare a `Vector`, we give the class its elements belong to in angle brackets, like this:

```
java.util.Vector <SomeClassName> vectorName;
```

Note that here the angle brackets *are a required part of the syntax.* So for example, if we want to declare a list of `SmartEllipses`, we can write:

```
java.util.Vector <SmartEllipse> _ellipseList;
```

keyconcept

The Java Vector class is a data structure that models a list.

This `_ellipseList` can hold as many `SmartEllipses` as we like. To refer to a particular `SmartEllipse` in `_ellipseList`, we can use `Vector`'s `elementAt` method and give the position in the list of the `SmartEllipse` we're interested in, like this:

```
_bigEllipse = _ellipseList.elementAt(6);
```

If we declare a `Vector` of `SmartEllipses`, everything in the `Vector` must be a

SmartEllipse. We can also add an instance of a subclass of `SmartEllipse`, like `BouncingBall`, but not objects that are instances of some other class. Thus, for example, we can say

```
_ellipseList.add(new SmartEllipse());
```

or

```
_bouncingBall = new BouncingBall();
_ellipseList.add(_bouncingBall);
```

but not

```
_ellipseList.add(new SmartRectangle());
```

To remove the first object from `_ellipseList`, we write:

```
SmartEllipse ellipse = _ellipseList.remove(0);
```

Note that this line of code is removing the zeroth element of the `Vector`. Alternatively, we say that this line of code is removing the element whose **index** is 0. Vectors start counting at 0, so the index of the first element of the `Vector` is 0, the index of the next element is 1, the index of the third element is 2, and so forth. (See Figure 11.1).

To remove a particular element, say `_currentEllipse`, from our `Vector`, we can write:

```
_ellipseList.remove(_currentEllipse);
```

Since we already have a reference to the element we're deleting, Java doesn't return it; instead, the return type of `remove` is a `boolean`: `true` if the deletion succeeded, `false` if it didn't.

Java provides many built-in methods for `Vector`s; some of the most useful are summarized in Table 11.1.

```
To Do

  0 — Get up.
  1 — Eat breakfast.
  2 — Log in.
  3 — Read mail.
     .
     .
     .
     .
```

Figure 11.1 ■ A `Vector` models a list in which the first item is always #0.

Table 11.1 ■ A few of the methods of the `java.util.Vector` class.

Method	Description
`Vector <ClassName>()`	Constructs an empty `Vector` to hold elements of type `ClassName`. The angle brackets are required.
`boolean add(ClassName element)`	Adds the specified element of type `ClassName` to the `Vector`.
`ClassName elementAt(int index)`	Returns the object of type `ClassName` at the given location in the `Vector`.
`boolean isEmpty()`	Returns `false` if the `Vector` contains any elements, otherwise `true`.
`boolean remove(ClassName element)`	Removes the first occurrence of the given instance of class `ClassName` from a `Vector`.
`ClassName remove(int index)`	Removes the `Object` at the given position from a `Vector`.
`ClassName set(int index, ClassName element)`	Changes the value of the object of type `ClassName` at the given location in a `Vector` to the given object.
`int size()`	Returns the number of elements in the `Vector`.

Finally, suppose we want a list of `SmartEllipses` that has some additional methods of its own, besides the methods shared by all `Vectors`. For example, suppose we want to find the largest, find the smallest, or compute the sum of the areas of all the ellipses in the list. We can define a subclass of `java.util.Vector<SmartEllipse>`, like this:

```
public class EllipseList extends Vector<SmartEllipse>{
    ...
    public java.awt.Color largest() {
        ... // to be defined below
    }

    public double smallest() {
        ... // to be defined below
    }

    public double totalArea() {
        ... // to be defined below
    }
}
```

11.3.2 **Indefinite loops:** `while` **loops**

Often when programming we want some action to be executed several times. For example, suppose we want to program our cookie factory to fill a bag with cookies. If the bags are small and hold only three cookies each, we can write our code like this:

```
private Vector<Cookie> _cookieBag;
    ...
_cookieBag.add(new Cookie());
_cookieBag.add(new Cookie());
_cookieBag.add(new Cookie());
```

That's not particularly elegant, but it's easy. We just have to type it once and then cut and paste. It's not so easy, however, for a package that holds several dozen cookies. And if we want to specify a condition—say we want to say "keep adding cookies until the package weighs at least a pound"—this cut and paste solution won't work at all.

keyconcept

Java's indefinite loops are the while and do-while loops. The do-while loop is guaranteed to run at least once; the while loop may not run at all.

All programming languages provide a solution: loops. If we want an action to be repeated but we don't know in advance how many times, we use an **indefinite loop**. Java provides two indefinite loops, the **while** and **do-while** loops. They are very similar; the only difference between them is that the `do-while` loop is guaranteed to run at least once while the `while` loop may not run at all.

We'll start with the `while` loop. Let's write a method for our cookie factory to fill a bag of cookies. Since the number of cookies may differ per bag, we don't know exactly how many cookies we'll need to add. We want to say something like, "While the bag is not yet full (that is, while it still weighs less than a pound), add another cookie." Therefore an indefinite loop is appropriate here.

While loops are very easy to write. They start with the keyword `while` followed by a `boolean` expression in parentheses, like this:

```
while (<boolean condition>) {
    <statements to be executed>
}
```

keyconcept

The loop condition is a boolean expression that must be `true` for the loop to continue.

The syntax is exactly the same as for a simple `if`-statement: a keyword followed by a condition plus a block of statements. The only difference is that the keyword is `while` instead of `if`. As with `if`-statements, the `boolean` condition can be as complicated as necessary (though of course, the more complicated it is, the more difficult it may be to debug).

A `while` statement not only looks like a simple `if`-statement, it works almost the same. Java evaluates the condition and then, if it's `true`, executes the block of statements. Here the condition is known as the **loop condition** and the block of statements is known as the loop body. The **loop body** is the group of statements to be executed each time the loop is repeated. Like the body of a method or if-statement, the loop body can include either one or multiple statements (and these statements can themselves be loops). If the loop body includes more than one statement, we must indicate the beginning and end of the loop body using curly brackets; if there's only one statement, the curly brackets are optional.

There's only one difference between a simple if-statement and a while loop, but it's a major one: when Java is done executing the statements in the body of a while loop, instead of continuing with whatever comes afterward, as it does for if-statements, Java goes back and evaluates the loop condition again. If the loop condition is still true, Java executes the statements in the loop body again. It continues to evaluate the loop condition and execute the loop body over and over again until the loop condition is false. Figure 11.2 shows a flow chart for Java's while statement.

Suppose we define a subclass of Vector<Cookie> called CookieBag with additional methods such as getWeight, and a class CookieConstants with appropriate constant definitions. Using a while statement, our method for filling a cookie bag might look like this:

```java
public void fillCookieBag(CookieBag aCookieBag) {
    while (aCookieBag.getWeight() <
            CookieConstants.FULL_WEIGHT)
        aCookieBag.add(new Cookie());
}
```

> **keyconcept**
> The loop body is the block of statements to be executed each time the loop is repeated. Any executable statement, including another loop, can be in the loop body.

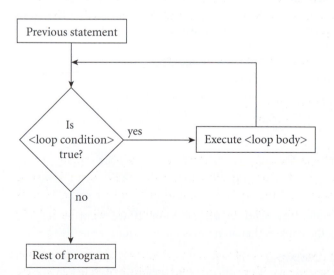

Figure 11.2 ■ Flow of control of while loop.

In other words, check to see if the cookie bag is full; if not, add another cookie; and repeat until the bag is full. Note that if the bag is full to begin with, no cookies are added to the bag. While loops, like if-statements, are never executed at all if the condition is false from the start.

Just like if-statements, while loops can have loop bodies that include more than one statement. To have more than one statement in a loop body, we enclose the statements in curly braces. For example, if our factory robot picks each cookie up off the assembly line before putting it in a bag, then we could write:

```java
public class CookieRobot {
    ...
    public void fillCookieBag(CookieBag aCookieBag) {
        while (aCookieBag.getWeight() <
                CookieConstants.FULL_WEIGHT){
            Cookie cookie = this.pickupCookie();
            aCookieBag.add(cookie);
        }
    }
}
```

We can nest loops inside loops. Suppose instead of filling cookie bags, we want to tell the robot how to fill a whole box full of bags of cookies, ready to be shipped. Using similar pickupBag and pickupCookie methods, we could write:

```java
public class CookieRobot {
    ...
    public void fillBox(ShippingBox aBox) {
        while (!aBox.isFull()) {
            CookieBag bag = this.pickupCookieBag();
            while (bag.getWeight() <
                    CookieConstants.FULL_WEIGHT){
                Cookie cookie = this.pickupCookie();
                bag.add(cookie);
            }
        }
    }
}
```

We can also nest an if statement inside a while loop. If we want to tell the CookieRobot to pack only the cookies that aren't broken, we could write:

```java
public class CookieRobot {
    ...
    public void fillCookieBag(CookieBag aCookieBag) {
```

```
    while (aCookieBag.getWeight() <
            CookieConstants.FULL_WEIGHT){
        Cookie cookie = this.pickupCookie();
        if (!cookie.isBroken())
            aCookieBag.add(cookie);
    }
  }
}
```

keyconcept

The Iterator Pattern provides a way for clients to access a data structure's contents without knowing all the inner details of how the data structure is set up.

11.3.3 Iterators

When we have a list in a program, we often want to go through the whole list and do something to each element: display each element on the screen, count the elements, double the size of each element, etc. This is such a common task that there's a design pattern for it, called Iterator.

The Iterator Pattern is one of the patterns in the original *Design Patterns* book. When we have a variable like a `Vector` that holds more than one value, Iterator provides a way for clients to access the variable's contents without knowing all the inner details of how the `Vector` is set up. Iterator supplies methods to find the beginning of the list, to tell whether we're at the end of the list, and to retrieve the next element of the list.

keyconcept

The Java class `Iterator` implements the Iterator Pattern.

Java provides an implementation of the Iterator design pattern called, as you might expect, `Iterator`. Some useful methods of Java's `Iterator` class are summarized in Table 11.2.

Table 11.2 ■ Java's `Iterator` class.

Method	Description
`boolean hasNext()`	Returns `true` if the Iterator has more elements left to visit.
`ClassName next()`	Returns the next element in the Iterator's collection.
`void remove()`	Removes from the underlying collection the last element returned by the iterator.

Here's how a Java `Iterator` works with a `Vector`. Suppose we have a list called `ellipseList`, and we want to display each of the ellipses.

```
//first create an Iterator associated with this Vector
java.util.Iterator<SmartEllipse> iterator =
    ellipseList.iterator();
// then let it retrieve the elements of the Vector for us
```

```
while (iterator.hasNext()) {
    SmartEllipse ellipse = iterator.next();
    aPaintBrush.draw(ellipse);
}
```

First, we create an `Iterator` for our particular list. The `Iterator` must be associated with the list from the beginning, because it needs to know how to find information in this list. Java `Iterators`, like `Vectors,` are associated with a particular type in angle brackets when they are declared.

Then we use a `while` loop to traverse the list. An indefinite loop works here, because we can tell when we reach the end of the list by using the `Iterator`'s `hasNext` method. As long as the `Iterator` says there's another element, we get that element, put it in the variable `ellipse`, and `draw` it.

11.3.4 Indefinite loops: `do-while`

If we know that a bag is empty to begin with and want to make sure we add at least one cookie to the bag, we can use a `do-while` loop. This loop is the same as the `while` loop except the loop condition is at the end of the statements in the body instead of the beginning. (Compare Figures 11.2 and 11.3). As a result, the loop body is executed once before the condition is tested. We begin the loop with the keyword `do`, follow with the body statement(s), and finish with the keyword `while` and the loop condition in parentheses (followed by a semicolon).

Rewriting our `fillCookieBag` method with a `do-while` loop yields:

```
public void fillCookieBag(CookieBag aCookieBag) {
    int numCookies = 0;
    do {
        aCookieBag.add(new Cookie());
        numCookies++;
    }
    while (aCookieBag.getWeight() <
            CookieConstants.FULL_WEIGHT);
}
```

As usual, the loop body is enclosed in curly braces, which are optional if there is only one statement in the loop body.

keyconcept

Java's definite loop is the for loop.

11.3.5 Definite loops: the `for` loop

Java's definite loop is the **for loop**. The `for` loop lets us specify the number of times we would like a certain block of code to be repeated. For example, if our cookie factory

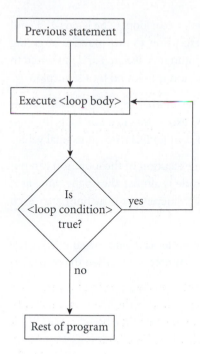

Figure 11.3 ■ Flow of control of do-while loop.

ships individual bags of cookies in large boxes and each box contains 50 bags, we might program a `for` loop to tell an industrial robot to add a bag to the box 50 times. Here's the code for that loop:

```
for (int i = 0; i < 50; i++)
    this.addCookiePackageToBox();
```

This is a very standard `for` loop. The syntax of the loop body is exactly the same as in `while` loops: there can be either one statement or more than one, and if there are more than one, they must be surrounded by curly brackets.

The loop declaration, the code in parentheses after the keyword `for`, is the new part of `for` loops, so let's consider it carefully:

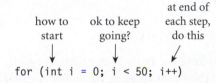

The loop counter, i, is declared as a local variable to the for loop. (The letters i, j, and k are traditionally used for loop counters, a rare exception to our practice of giving variables longer, more mnemonic names). First, the counter is declared and initialized to 0, a common practice in programming. This initialization is followed by a semicolon.

Next the loop condition, i < 50, is given, followed by another semicolon. Loop conditions in for loops are similar to those in while loops, except that in a for loop, the loop condition usually involves checking to see if the loop counter has reached its final value.

Finally, the code says what should be done after each execution of the loop. You can put any statements you want here, but in practice, the code is almost always the same as it is here: add one to the value of the loop counter (i.e., increment it by one) after each time through the loop.

This loop executes exactly 50 times: once when the counter is 0, once when it is 1, once when it is 2, and so on, up to the last time, when the counter is 49. When the counter is 50, the loop will halt.

Figure 11.4 contains a flow chart for Java's for loop.

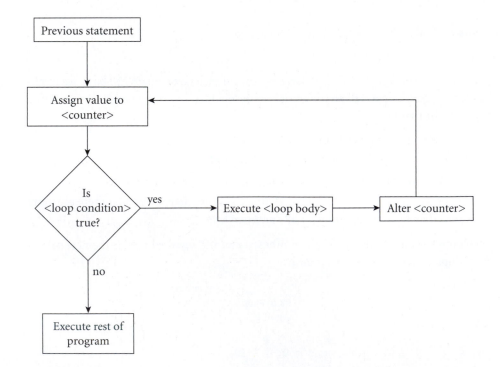

Figure 11.4 ■ Flow of control of for loop.

There are many ways to make a `for` loop do what you want. Take some time to experiment with initializing your loop counter and determining the best loop condition. Many problems can arise if these are not chosen carefully. Also keep in mind that you can alter your loop counter in any way you like. So if you prefer to start with a high number and count down using the `--` operator, that is perfectly acceptable (and more appropriate for some situations). In this case the loop continues until the counter reaches the lower limit.

11.3.6 `Break` and `continue` in loops

There are times when we don't want to execute an entire loop. Java allows us to stop a loop early with `break` and `continue` statements.

The `break` statement causes an immediate exit from a loop. `Break` is also used, as we saw in Chapter 10, to skip the remainder of a `switch` statement.

Suppose we're modeling a household robot that should take 20 cookies out of the cookie jar and put them on a plate to serve to guests. The robot will look pretty silly if there are only twelve cookies in the jar and it reaches in eight more times anyway. We can tell it to stop when the cookie jar becomes empty using a `break` statement, like this:

```java
for (int i = 0; i < 20; i++) {
    if (_cookieJar.empty()) {
        break;
        // only take a cookie if there is one!
    }
    _plate.add(_cookieJar.remove(i));
}
this.serveCookies(_plate);
```

When the `break` statement is executed, Java stops executing the loop and continues on to whatever statements come afterward (in this case, serving however many cookies there were in the jar).

You should know how to read `break` statements, but avoid writing them. If you find yourself using a `break` statement in a loop, think twice: chances are good that you don't need it. For example, we could easily rewrite this loop without a `break` statement. Think for a moment about what we want to happen. We want the character to take cookies out of the jar until 20 cookies have been taken—or there are no more cookies. In other words, the real loop condition is "while i is less than 20 *and there are cookies in the jar.*"

With the new condition, we can rewrite the code like this:

```
for (int i = 0; i < 20 && !_cookieJar.empty(); i++) {
    _plate = _cookieJar.remove(i);
}
this.serveCookies(_plate);
```

The revised version of the code is shorter, and the logic is simpler, easier to read, and easier to debug.

If we use a `continue` statement, Java doesn't halt the loop entirely; it just skips to the end of the current iteration of the loop and (as the name of the statement indicates) continues with the next iteration. In a `while` or `do while` structure, execution continues by evaluating the loop-continuation condition. In a `for` structure, execution continues by incrementing the counter and then evaluating the loop condition.

A `continue` statement can be useful if you are looping over a list of data and you want to skip processing of data that is somehow illegal. For example, suppose you're trying on shirts on a rack, one hanger at a time, but you want to skip the hangers that don't have a shirt:

```
// we'd like to try on shirts that hang on a rack
for (int i = 0; i < 20; i++) {
    if (!rack.isShirtOnHanger(i)) {
        // if there's no shirt on the current hanger, skip
        // to the next iteration
        continue;
    }
    // only do this if there's a shirt on current hanger
    shirtToTry = rack.shirtOnHanger(i);
    this.tryOnShirt(shirtToTry);
}
// more code here
```

11.3.7 Choosing between loops

We could get by with only one of these three loops. For example, `while` loops can be rewritten as `for` loops. Instead of

```
while (<condition>) {
    // do something
}
```

just write:

```
for ( ; <condition>; ) {
```

```
        // same statements in loop body as in while loop
    }
```

Similarly, `for` loops can be written as `while` loops, either of them can be translated into `do-while` loops, and `do-while` loops can be translated into either of the other two.

To make your code as readable as possible, however, we strongly recommend that you use each loop in the type of situation for which it was intended:

1. Use `for` loops when you know exactly how often you want a block of code to be executed. (Put 50 cookie bags in the box.)

2. Use `while` loops when you want a block of code to be executed an indefinite number of times until some condition is met. (While the cookie jar is not empty, keep removing cookies.)

3. Use `do-while` loops when you want a block of code to be executed at least once and an indefinite number of times after that. (Ask a guest how many cookies he or she wants; while the answer is greater than the number of cookies left, ask again.)

11.3.8 Recipes for writing loops

There are several common recipes for writing loops and working with `Vectors`, depending on the task we want to perform. We describe three here.

1. Using a sentinel.

2. Finding the best value in a `Vector` (using whatever definition of "best" is appropriate to the particular problem).

3. Computing an aggregate value based on all the elements of the `Vector`.

These recipes can be used with either definite or indefinite loops.

The sentinel recipe. A sentinel is an arbitrary value used to signal that we have reached the end of a sequence of values. For example, suppose the `CookieRobot` keeps packing cookies into bags until it sees a broken cookie, at which point it must stop the assembly line. Then we could write:

```
public class CookieRobot {
    ...
    public void fillBox(ShippingBox aBox) {
        while(!aBox.isFull() && !assemblyLine.isHalted()){
            CookieBag bag = this.pickupCookieBag();
            Cookie cookie = this.pickupCookie();
            while (bag.getWeight() <
```

```
                        CookieConstants.FULL_WEIGHT &&
                        !cookie.isBroken()){
                    bag.add(cookie);
                    Cookie cookie = this.pickupCookie();
                }
                if (cookie.isBroken())
                    assemblyLine.halt();
            }
        }
    }
```

The basic idea is that some particular value—here, a broken cookie—indicates that a series of items has ended. The sentinel recipe is often useful when a program is getting input from a user. Have you been asked by a computer game when the game is over, "Do you want to play again?" In that case, the program is probably looping, playing the game over and over until the user clicks on (or types) "No."

Finding the best value in a collection. (also called the **high or low water-mark** recipe) Suppose we want to give the `CookieBag` class a method to compute the largest number of chocolate chips in any of its cookies:

```
public class CookieBag extends Vector<Cookie> {
    ...
    public int getMaxNumChips() {
        int maxNumChips = 0;
        for (int i = 0; i < this.size(); i++){
            Cookie cookie = this.elementAt(i);
            if (cookie.getNumChips() > maxNumChips)
                maxNumChips = cookie.getNumChips();
        }
        return maxNumChips;
    }
}
```

Here's how the recipe works.

1. Declare a "most-wanted" variable that holds the worst possible value of the variable. (Here, this is 0, since the smallest number of chips a cookie could have is 0.)

2. Consider each element of the `Vector` one by one. Compare the value associated with each element with the current best value. When we find a better value, that becomes the new best. (Here, for example, suppose the first cookie has five chips. That's more than 0, so the `maxNumChips` becomes 5. Then suppose the second cookie contains four chips. Four is less than 5, so

`maxNumChips` stays unchanged. Then if the third cookie contains six chips, 6 will become the new value of `maxNumChips`, and so on.)

3. After all the elements of the `Vector` have been considered (after the end of the loop body), the value we're looking for (here, the largest number of chips) will be stored in the most-wanted variable (here, `maxNumChips`).

Incidentally, this code shows how we can use a `for` loop to process the elements of a `Vector` if we use the `Vector`'s `size()` method to get the number of elements in the loop. Compare this with using an `Iterator`, as discussed earlier.

Computing an aggregate value based on all the elements. (also called the **accumulator recipe**) Suppose instead of the maximum number of chips in a single cookie, we want to know the total number of chips contained in all the cookies in the bag. In that case, we could write:

```
public class CookieBag extends Vector<Cookie> {
    ...
    public int getTotalNumChips() {
        int totalNumChips = 0;
        while (!this.isEmpty()) {
            Cookie cookie =
                this.remove(this.size()-1);
            totalNumChips += cookie.getNumChips();
        }
        return totalNumChips;
    }
}
```

Again, we initialize a variable before the loop, modify it inside the loop body, and use its final value after the end of the loop body. The difference is that here, we're not just storing a single best value in the variable; instead, we're accumulating an aggregate value.

11.3.9 Debugging loops

Loops are one of the most frequent causes of bugs in programs. Therefore it is important to think your loops out carefully in advance and hand-simulate them to make sure they will do what you want. By **hand-simulation**, we mean writing down on paper what happens after each statement is executed. Use a column for the loop counter (if the loop is a `for` loop), the loop test, and any other variables that may be affected by the execution of the loop. Each row represents one time through the loop.

For example, consider the following loop. Suppose we want to add two cookies to a cookie bag. (We wouldn't normally use a loop to add just two things, but to keep the simulation short, we'll make the example small.)

keyconcept
Loops are one of the largest sources of bugs in programs. Hand-simulate loops carefully.

```
CookieBag bag = new CookieBag(); // initially empty
for (int j=0; j<3; j++) { // This code has a bug—what?
   Cookie cookie = this.pickupCookie();
   bag.add(cookie);
}
```

Table 11.3 shows how we might simulate this loop. Aha! We actually have three cookies in the bag, when we wanted two. By hand-simulating the loop, we can see that it executes one too many times. To fix it, we need to modify either the initial value of the loop counter or the loop condition.

Table 11.3 ■ Hand-simulating a loop.

Loop counter (j)	Loop test	bag
(before loop starts)	- - -	Bag is empty.
0	true	Go into loop, add one cookie, bag now contains one cookie.
1	true	Go into loop, add one cookie, bag now contains two cookies.
2	true	Go into loop, add one cookie, bag now contains three cookies.
3	false	Loop halts. Final total: three cookies in bag.

You're probably thinking, "No way would I do this if there were ten iterations of the loop, let alone 100!" There must be a better way; that's why we wanted the computer to execute the loop instead of us in the first place! And yet, some hand-simulation is essential if we're going to catch all the bugs in our programs. In addition students who hand-simulate code on exams are far more likely to get the answers right.

Here's a strategy. Instead of trying all the iterations through the loop, try the first one or two, then perhaps one in the middle, and then the last two. Here's another example. Suppose we want to compute the sum of the numbers from 1 to 120 with the following loop. What will happen?

```
public int sum() { // This code doesn't work—why?
   int runningTotal = 0;
   for (int i = 1; i > 120; i++) {
      runningTotal += i;
   }
   return runningTotal;
}
```

Table 11.4 shows a hand-simulation of this loop. Here, it's the loop test that is wrong, because < was used where > was intended. It is `false` before the loop ever starts, so the numbers are never added up. The value returned is 0, rather than the desired sum. And luckily, we could discover the error after simulating only the first two iterations of the loop.

Table 11.4 ■ Hand-simulation of another loop.

Loop counter (`i`)	Loop test	`runningTotal`
(before loop starts)	- -	0
1	false	Loop body never executed

Here's a third example. This time we want the product of the numbers from 1 to *n* (i.e., *n* factorial):

```java
public int factorial(int n) { // doesn't work—why?
    int tempProduct = 0;
    for (int i = 1; i <= n; i++)
        tempProduct *= i;
    return tempProduct;
}
```

We can hand-simulate this loop as in Table 11.5.

Table 11.5 ■ Hand-simulation of a third loop.

Loop counter (`i`)	Loop test	`tempProduct`
(before loop starts)	- - -	0
1	true	0 * 1 = 0
2	true	0 * 2 = 0
...	. . .	...
10	true	0 * 10 = 0
11	false	No change

Here the initial and final values of the loop counter and the loop test are all correct. The problem is the variable `tempProduct`. It starts out at 0, so every time you multiply it by one of the other numbers, the result is still 0. Again, we could identify the bug after evaluating only the first and last iterations of the loop.

In sum, many different things can go wrong with loops. Some common symptoms include:

1. Some statements aren't being executed that should be, or are being executed when they shouldn't.

   a. Check to see if the curly brackets around the loop body are in the right place. (Using an editor that indents your code automatically makes it much easier to spot this problem.)

2. The program never seems to halt. Very probably you have an infinite loop; in other words, the loop condition never becomes `false`.

   a. Does the program have a way to change the loop condition? There should either be something in the code itself, or some external condition such as a value the user types in, that makes it change during processing.

   b. Is the initial condition set correctly?

   c. Do you change the condition in an `if` statement whose body is never executed?

3. The loop executes one too many or one too few times ("off-by-one" errors).

   a. Check how you used relational operators in your loop condition. Did you say <= when you meant <, or vice versa?

   b. Did you have the loop start at 0 when you meant 1, or 1 when you meant 0?

   c. Did you change the value of a `for`-loop counter inside the body of the loop? A loop counter is meant to keep track of how many times the loop has been executed. Changing the value of the loop counter within a loop body can throw off the count and force the loop to either end at the wrong time or continue too long. If you ever want to change the value of the loop counter, copy its value to another variable so that the loop counter itself remains intact.

Hand-simulation is the best way to catch such errors. In an interesting program, the loop probably executes too many times to write down a row for each execution. In that case, try the first one or two, last one or two, and a typical time through the loop.

11.3.10 Flow of control

Flow of control is the order in which the steps of a computer program are executed. We've now seen all of the common flow-of-control mechanisms:

- Method invocation
- Conditional statements
- Loops

The simplest flow of control in a Java program is in a program with a single object and only one method, the `main` method and no conditions or loops. In that case, each step in the `main` method is executed one after another, in order, and then the program halts. Control flows from the first statement of the `main` method to the last, one statement at a time, in order.

Any interesting Java program involves more than one object, however, and, as we have seen, the objects in a program interact with each other through method invocations. Method invocations make flow of control a little more complicated, but not much. We still follow the program execution starting with the first line of the `main` method. When one method invokes another, control is transferred to the first step of the second method; when the second method is done executing, control is transferred back to the next point in the first method (see Figure 11.5). Although this flow of control jumps from one location in the program to another, there is still only one path through the program; there are no choices.

Conditional statements mean that there are alternative paths through a program. Some

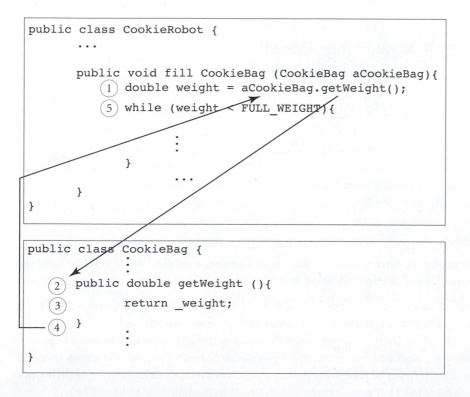

Figure 11.5 ■ Flow of control with method calls.

statements may never be executed at all. And loops mean that some statements may be executed more than once. Still, no matter how complex the processing inside one of these constructs, we can be guaranteed that control flows from a single entry point to a single exit, as shown by the flowcharts, so that the overall flow is still linear.

Outside events such as mouse clicks or button pushes may cause the flow of control of a program to jump to a new location (the event handler) at unexpected moments. Because we don't know exactly when these events will occur, we need to consider various possibilities when hand-simulating our programs. Still, we do know that program execution is still relentlessly linear. At any given point, only one statement is being executed at a time, and if we know which external events have occurred, we can still predict what the flow of control should be.

Note: We can make Java appear to do more than one thing at a time by using threads. Threads are outside the scope of this book; they are basically separate sequences of statements that appear to be executed in parallel because the computer goes back and forth among them so quickly. At any given time, however, the computer is still doing exactly one thing.

■ 11.4 ■ Working Out with Loops—`ButterflyApp`

Objectives:
- ☑ Use loops
- ☑ Use `Vectors`
- ☑ Display a large number of objects (here, lines) in a window

In this section, we illustrate loops with a program that uses a `Vector` to store the lines that make up a complicated shape, far more complicated than the ellipse, fish, and snowmen we have seen so far. A screenshot of the program we're going to write is shown in Figure 11.6.

We need only three classes: a subclass of `JFrame`, a subclass of `JPanel` to hold the shapes, and a `Butterfly` class. `ButterflyApp`, the subclass of `JFrame`, is shown in Listing 11.1. There's nothing new about this class.

`ButterflyPanel`, the subclass of `JPanel` that we use (shown in Listing 11.2), is also very familiar. There's a constructor that creates three instances of `Butterfly`, with different colors and locations, and a `paintComponent` method that draws them on the screen. As in the composite pattern, these two methods delegate a lot of their work to the `ButterflyPanel`'s components (the three instances of `Butterfly`).

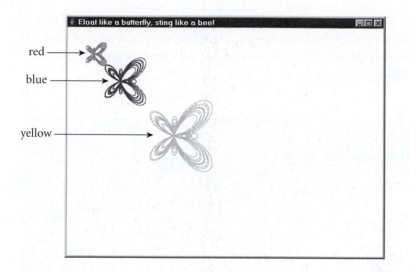

Figure 11.6 ■ Screenshot of `ButterflyApp`.

```
1    /**
2     * Chapter 11: ButterflyApp.java
3     * A window that contains a panel
4     * that displays butterflies.
5     * Similar to the SnowCartoon in Chapter 2, except that
6     * the butterfly pictures are made up of thousands of parts.
7     */
8    public class ButterflyApp extends javax.swing.JFrame {
9       public ButterflyApp (String title) {
10          super(title);
11          this.setSize(600, 450);
12          this.add(new ButterflyPanel());
13          this.setDefaultCloseOperation(javax.swing.JFrame.EXIT_ON_CLOSE);
14          this.setVisible(true);
15       }
16
17       public static void main (String [ ] args) {
18          ButterflyApp app = new ButterflyApp(
19             "Float like a butterfly, sting like a bee!");
20       }
21    }
```

Listing 11.1 ■ The `ButterflyApp` class

The complexity comes in the `Butterfly` class. This butterfly is an implementation of an algorithm found in C. A. Pickover, *Computers and the Imagination* (1991), a fascinating book about mathematical patterns, aesthetics, and computer graphics. The code for this class is shown in Listing 11.3.

```
1    /**
2     * Chapter 11: ButterflyPanel.java
3     * Instantiates and draws three instances
4     * of Butterfly.
5     */
6    public class ButterflyPanel extends javax.swing.JPanel {
7        private Butterfly _butterfly, _butterfly2, // components
8            _butterfly3;
9
10       public ButterflyPanel () {
11           super();
12           _butterfly = new Butterfly(50, 50, 6,
13                                       java.awt.Color.red,
14                                       this);
15           _butterfly2 = new Butterfly(100,100, 12,
16                                       java.awt.Color.blue,
17                                       this);
18           _butterfly3 = new Butterfly(200,200, 18,
19                                       java.awt.Color.yellow,
20                                       this);
21           this.setBackground(java.awt.Color.white);
22       }
23
24       public void paintComponent(java.awt.Graphics aBrush){
25           super.paintComponent(aBrush);
26           java.awt.Graphics2D aBetterBrush =
27               (java.awt.Graphics2D) aBrush;
28           _butterfly.draw(aBetterBrush);
29           _butterfly2.draw(aBetterBrush);
30           _butterfly3.draw(aBetterBrush);
31       }
32   }
```

Listing 11.2 ■ The `ButterflyPanel` class

```
 1   /**
 2   * Chapter 11: Butterfly.java
 3   * Uses loop to create thousands of small lines that together make up
 4   * a picture of a butterfly. Stores them in a Vector.
 5   */
 6   import java.awt.*;
 7   import java.awt.geom.*;
 8   import javax.swing.*;
 9
10   public class Butterfly {
11       private Color _color; // attributes
12       private int _xOffset, _yOffset, _scaleFactor;
13       private java.util.Vector <Line2D.Double> _outline; // component
14       private JPanel _panel; // peer object (and container)
15
16       public Butterfly (int anXOffset, int aYOffset, int aScaleFactor,
17                 Color aColor, JPanel aPanel){
18           super();
19           _color = aColor;
20           _xOffset = anXOffset;
21           _yOffset = aYOffset;
22           _scaleFactor = aScaleFactor;
23           _outline = new java.util.Vector<Line2D.Double>();
24           _panel = aPanel;
25
26           // now add the lines that make up the butterfly to _outline
27           double rho, x, y, prevX, prevY, scaledX, scaledY;
28           prevX = 0; prevY = 0;
29           for (double theta = 0; theta <= 100*Math.PI; theta += 0.010) {
30               rho = Math.exp(Math.cos(theta)) - 2*Math.cos(4*theta)
31                   + Math.pow(Math.sin(theta/12.0), 5);
32               x = rho * Math.cos(theta); // convert to x-y coordinates
33               y = rho * Math.sin(theta);
34               // make butterfly larger
35               scaledX = (x*_scaleFactor) + _xOffset;
36               scaledY = (y*_scaleFactor) + _yOffset;
37               if (theta != 0) {
38                   _outline.add(new Line2D.Double(
39                       prevX, prevY, scaledX, scaledY));
40               } // end if
```

Listing 11.3 ■ The `Butterfly` class (*continued on next page*)

```
41                    prevX = scaledX;
42                    prevY = scaledY;
43              } // end for
44         } // end constructor
45
46         public void draw (Graphics2D aPaintBrush) {
47              Color oldColor = aPaintBrush.getColor();
48              aPaintBrush.setColor(_color);
49              java.util.Iterator<Line2D.Double> iterator
50                   = _outline.iterator();
51              while (iterator.hasNext()) {
52                   Line2D.Double line =
53                   (Line2D.Double) iterator.next();
54                   aPaintBrush.draw(line);
55              }
56              aPaintBrush.setColor(oldColor);
57         }
58    }
```

Listing 11.3 ■ The Butterfly class

Start by considering the mathematical equation for this butterfly:

$$\rho = e^{\cos(\theta)} - 2\cos(4\theta) + \sin^5\left(\frac{\theta}{12}\right)$$

Instead of the familiar x and y coordinates, here we're using the polar coordinates ρ and θ. Recall that ρ is the distance of the point from the origin and, if we draw a line from the origin to the right (at 3 o'clock) and a second line from the origin to our point, θ is the angle between those two lines (see Figure 11.7). So this equation says that in our Butterfly the distance of a point from the origin depends, in a complicated way, on the angle.

We can translate this equation into Java easily, since the Math class provides the exponential and trigonometry functions we need:

```
double rho, theta;
rho = Math.exp(Math.cos(theta)) - 2*Math.cos(4*theta)
            + Math.pow(Math.sin(theta/12.0), 5);
```

But in order to draw a point in a window, we need x and y values, not ρ and θ. We can convert from polar coordinates to Cartesian x and y coordinates using the following formulas:

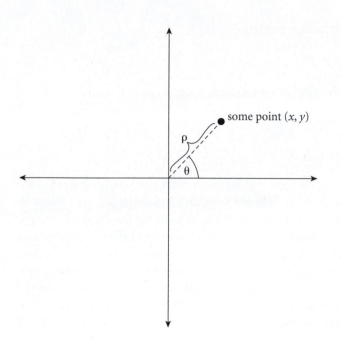

Figure 11.7 ■ Polar coordinates ρ and θ.

$$x = \rho \cos (\theta)$$
$$y = \rho \sin (\theta)$$

When we translate this into Java, we have:

```
x = rho * Math.cos(theta);
y = rho * Math.sin(theta);
```

So if we have θ, the angle, we can compute ρ, the distance from the origin of one of the points in our butterfly; and if we have ρ and θ, we can compute x and y.

But all that just gives us the location of one point. To get enough points to draw the butterfly, we need to consider many angles and get the x and y value for the point at each angle. Since we can't draw a continuous line, we can use a `for` loop to compute many points, create many small lines, one from each point to the next, and store the small lines in a `Vector`:

```
prevX = 0; prevY = 0;
for (double theta=0; theta<=100*Math.PI; theta+=0.010) {
    rho = Math.exp(Math.cos(theta)) - 2*Math.cos(4*theta)
          + Math.pow(Math.sin(theta/12.0), 5);
    x = rho * Math.cos(theta); // convert to x-y coords.
```

```
        y = rho * Math.sin(theta);
        ...
        if (theta != 0) {
          _outline.add(
              new java.awt.geom.Line2D.Double(prevX,prevY,x,y));
        }
        prevX = x;
        prevY = y;
    }
```

This is close, but we're not quite there yet. We don't want just one `Butterfly`, we want three. And we want them to be different sizes, and located in different places in the window. To change the size of the `Butterfly`, we multiply the (x, y) values by a `_scaleFactor`. To move the `Butterfly` to a different point in the window, we add constants (`_xOffset` and `_yOffset`) to the x and y values. These variables—`_scaleFactor`, `_xOffset`, and `_yOffset`—are parameters to the `Butterfly`'s constructor, so we can supply different values each time we instantiate a `Butterfly`. The color is also a parameter, so we can draw `Butterflies` of different colors. The code that creates all the lines and adds them to a `Vector` is shown in lines 26–43 of Listing 11.3.

Finally, in the `Butterfly`'s `draw` method (lines 46–57 of Listing 11.3), we use an `Iterator` to go through the `Vector` and draw each of the lines in the `Butterfly` one after another.

Compile the program and run it. Modify the code to change the color and location of the butterflies. Add a loop to `ButterflyPanel` to instantiate twenty small butterflies in different locations around the window. Vary the program until you are comfortable with how it works.

■ Summary ■

In this chapter, we introduced a new kind of control statement called a loop. With loops, we can write a block of statements once and tell the computer to repeat it, either a fixed number of times or until a given condition has been met. Java provides three loops: the `for` loop, the `do-while` loop, and the `while` loop. `For` loops are most suitable for situations where we know in advance that we want a given block of statements to be executed a certain number of times. `While` loops are suitable for situations where we want a block of statements to be executed until a certain condition becomes `false`; `do-while` statements are suitable for situations where we want a block of statements to be executed once and then repeated as necessary until a certain condition becomes `false`.

We also introduced a Java class called `Vector` that models a list of objects. `Vectors` are an example of a data structure, that is, a collection of related objects that are connected in some way and given a single name. In later chapters, we examine several more data structures, including arrays, lists, stacks, queues, and trees.

If we want client objects to be able to access a data structure's contents without knowing all the inner details of how the data structure is set up, we can use the Iterator Pattern, which supplies methods to find the beginning of the structure, to tell whether we're at the end of the structure, and to retrieve the next element of the structure. The Java class `Iterator` implements the Iterator Pattern.

Both conditional branching and looping must be done very carefully since errors in syntax (mismatched braces, missing semicolons, and the like) and semantic errors (mistakes in the condition) can lead to code that compiles but produces results that are unexpected and difficult to debug. Careful hand-simulation, while tedious, will save you time.

■ Self-Check Questions ■

(The answers to these questions can be found on the course website, www.aw.com/sanders)

1. How do computer programs model repeated actions?
2. What is the difference between a definite and an indefinite loop?
3. Give examples of situations when you would use a `for` loop, a `while` loop, and a `do-while` loop.
4. What is the function of a `break` statement in a loop?
5. What is the function of a `continue` statement in a loop?
6. What is a `Vector`?
7. Describe two common sources of bugs in programs with loops.

■ Exercises ■

Applying the Facts

1. Write code to declare a `Vector`.
2. Write a line of code to add a `ColorRectangle` in the third position of a `Vector`.
3. Write a `for` loop to add 50 cookies to a `Vector`.
4. Write a line of code to remove the element in the fifth position in a `Vector` and assign it to a variable of type `ColorArc`.

5. Write a `for` loop to remove 50 cookies from a `Vector`. Be sure to check before removing each cookie to see if the `Vector` is empty.

6. Write a `while` loop to remove cookies from a `Vector` one at a time until the `Vector` is empty.

7. Which of Java's loops would be most appropriate for a robot that is going to perform each of the following tasks:

   a. Wrap a present for each of the ten people in your family.
   b. Polish the car until it shines.
   c. Give the user of an ATM the opportunity to perform a transaction. Ask whether he or she wants to perform another transaction. Repeat until he or she says no.
   d. Have fun, fun, fun 'til Daddy takes the T-Bird away.

8. Suppose we have the following code to draw nine circles in a grid pattern:
```
for (int i = 0; i < 3; i++) {
    for (int j = 0; j < 3; j++) {
        this.drawCircle(i*30, j*30, 10);
        //parameters are xPos, yPos, and radius
    }
}
```
This code calls the `drawCircle` method (which takes the x and y coordinates of the circle as parameters) nine times.

   a. What are the coordinates of the circles?
   b. Draw the result of this nested `for` loop (numbering each circle to show the order in which they were drawn).

9. Compare and contrast the use of `Iterators` and `for` loops to process `Vectors`. What are their pros and cons? Which do you prefer? Why?

Debugging Programs

1. `for (int i = 0, i < 50, i++ ) {...}`

2. `for (int i = 0; i < 50; i--) {...}`

3.
```
int i = 0;
    do while (i < 10) {
        this.eatCookie();
        i++;
    }
```

4.
```
public void fillShoppingCart(ShoppingCart shoppingCart) {
    while (!shoppingCart.isEmpty()) {
        this.addItemToCart();
    }
}
```

```
5. // we'd like to taste all 32 ice cream flavors
       for (int i = 0; i < 32; i++) {
           if (iceCreamFlavor.isEmpty(i) ) {
               break;
           }
           this.tasteIceCream(i);
       }
6. // still trying to taste the 32 ice cream flavors
           private Vector _flavors;
               ...
           for (int i = 1; i <= 32; i++) {
               this.tasteIceCream(_flavors.elementAt(i));
           }
7. private JLabel _label;
           ...

           _label.setText("Before loop.");
           int numLoops = 0;
           while (numLoops < 5) {
               if (numLoops == 3) continue;
               _label.setText("In loop number: " + i);
               numLoops++;
           }
           _label.setText("Loop is now done.");
```

■ Programming Projects ■

Modifying Programs

1. Modify the SnowCartoon from Chapter 2 so that it contains a house, a snowman, a sun, and a tree. Use a Vector to store all four objects, and use a loop in the paintComponent method to display them.

2. Modify the BouncingBallApp program from Chapter 8 so that three balls of different sizes and colors are bouncing around the window. Use a Vector to store the three bouncing balls, and use a loop in the paintComponent method to display them.

3. Modify the FishApp from Chapter 7 so that three or more fish are swimming in the fish tank. Use a Vector to store all the fish, and use a loop in the paintComponent method to display all the fish.

4. Modify the `ColorHolderApp` from Chapter 9 so that there are ten shapes of various sizes in the window, some ellipses and some rectangles. Use a `Vector` to store all of the shapes, and use a loop in the `paintComponent` method to display all the shapes.

5. Modify the `ButterflyApp` so that the butterflies are green, magenta, and pink.

6. Modify the `ButterflyApp` so that the butterflies are in order by decreasing rather than increasing size.

7. Modify the `ButterflyApp` by changing the constants used in the original equation. What differences can you make in the shape of the butterflies?

8. Modify the `ButterflyApp` so that a new `Butterfly` is created wherever the user clicks in the window. It should always be red and the same size as the small `Butterfly` in the original program.

9. Modify the program from question 8 so that the user can select a color using color buttons, and then click to create a new butterfly of that color. Make sure to use the Holder Pattern from Chapter 9.

Writing Programs

1. Use a `for` loop to write a program that draws a bull's-eye on the screen. The bull's-eye should consist of seven concentric circles that alternate in color.

2. Write a program that displays a fish tank. Use a `while` loop to keep adding fish to the tank until a fish of each color has been added to the tank. The color of each fish added to the tank should be chosen at random from the list of built-in Java colors.

12

Recursion

OBJECTIVES

At the end of this chapter, you should be able to:

☑ Define recursion

☑ Recognize and give examples of recursion

☑ Use recursion appropriately to solve problems

☑ Explain the tradeoffs involved in using recursion vs. iteration

■ 12.1 ■ Introduction

"A journey of a thousand miles begins with a single step," according to the familiar proverb. This doesn't give us a plan for the whole trip, but it gives us a plan to get from the thousand-mile journey to a shorter one: take a step. Suppose your step is, say, two feet long. Then after you take it, you have a journey of 999 miles, 5278 feet left.

A journey of 999 miles, 5278 feet, however, also begins with a single step. If we apply the same plan—start with one step—to this new journey, we have a journey of 999 miles, 5276 feet left. And this shorter journey also begins with a single step. By applying the same plan to smaller and smaller trips, we eventually complete our whole trip.

We could write our plan like this:

```
public class Traveler {
    public int _stepLength;
    ...
    public void takeJourney (int aNumMiles) {
        if (aNumMiles == 0) return;
        this.takeStep(_stepLength);
        this.takeJourney (aNumMiles-_stepLength);
    }
}
```

Notice that the `takeJourney` method calls itself. At first, this might seem like an error—like saying "To take a journey, just take a journey." But that's not quite right. Literally, the code says, take a journey by taking one step and then taking a *shorter* journey. As long as each journey is shorter than the one before, we will eventually get to a journey of 0 miles, and then we'll be done.

This technique—having a method call itself—is called **recursion**. If used properly, it is an elegant example of divide and conquer by delegation. In this chapter, we discuss how, and when, to use recursion to solve programming problems.

keyconcept

Recursion is a technique for solving problems that are self-similar, that is, problems that contain one or more pieces that are the same kind of problem as themselves, but easier to solve.

■ 12.2 ■ Concepts

Recursion is a flow-of-control mechanism, like iteration. Some languages, like FOR-TRAN for much of its history, only support iteration, and others, like early versions of Lisp, only support recursion. Java provides both.

Recursion is a particularly natural technique for solving problems that are self-similar. A **self-similar problem** is a problem that contains one or more pieces that are the same kind of problem as the original problem, but easier to solve. When we use recursion to solve a self-similar problem, we break a problem down into easier subproblems, solve them (by breaking them down in turn into easier problems), and finally combine the solutions to the subproblems to build up larger and larger solutions, until we have a solution to the original problem. Thus, recursion is a form of the general divide-and-conquer strategy that we have seen in this text many times.

keyconcept

To use recursion, we need a self-similar problem, a base case, and a method of making the problem closer to the base case.

To use recursion, we need:

1. a problem that contains one or more subproblems that are similar to itself
2. a version of the problem that is simple enough to be solved by itself, without recursion (known as the **base case**)
3. a way of making the problem simpler so that it is closer to (and ultimately becomes the same as) the base case

In our journey problem, how does this work?

1. the journey itself contains shorter journeys
2. the base case that we can solve by itself is the journey of 0 miles (just stop walking)
3. the method of making the problem simpler is to take a step

keyconcept

The base case is a version of the problem being solved that is simple enough to solve directly, without a recursive call.

If we accidentally leave out the base case, or if somehow the subproblems are never reduced to the base case, we have the equivalent of an infinite loop.

■ 12.3 ■ Mechanics

The Java syntax for recursion is very simple: we just write a method that calls itself. In this section, we'll consider two different ways of using recursion: one where a problem is reduced to one subproblem, and a second where a problem is broken down into more than one subproblem. Then we'll look at some common bugs in recursive programs, and finally, we'll consider how to choose between iteration and recursion for a particular program.

keyconcept
In Java, recursion is modeled by a method that calls itself.

12.3.1 An example with one recursive call: factorial

Consider the following problem:

> Three students, Gillian, Juan, and Kawai, all like cookies. There are three cookies, one chocolate chip, one oatmeal, and one peanut butter cookie. How many ways can they distribute the cookies among themselves?

Suppose Gillian chooses first. She has three choices. Suppose she picks the oatmeal cookie. Then Juan goes next. He has two choices. He picks the chocolate chip. Finally, Kawai has only one choice, and he takes the peanut butter. Whatever Gillian picks, two cookies are left and Juan has two choices. Whatever Juan picks, Kawai has to take whatever is left. So the total number of ways the cookies can be divided up is 3 * 2 * 1, or six ways.

Now suppose we want to solve this problem for four, or five, or 30 students. If there are four students and four cookies, the first student has a choice of four cookies, the second student has a choice of the three that are left, the third student has a choice of two, and the last student has a choice of one. The total number of choices is 4 * 3 * 2 * 1, or 24. If there are five students, similarly, the number of ways they can divide up the cookies is 5 * 4 * 3 * 2 * 1, or 120. When we get up to 30, though, just writing the product down becomes inconvenient.

Let's model the problem mathematically. As a shorthand, mathematicians write the product of the numbers from 1 to n as "n factorial," or even more briefly, "$n!$" For example:

$1! = 1$
$2! = 2 * 1 = 2$
$3! = 3 * 2 * 1 = 6$
$4! = 4 * 3 * 2 * 1 = 24$
$5! = 5 * 4 * 3 * 2 * 1 = 120$

Our problem is to compute the product of the first n numbers, or `factorial(n)`.

Let's consider the requirements for recursion, one by one. We need:

1. A problem that contains one or more subproblems that are similar to itself. `Factorial(n)` contains a simpler problem, which is computing the product of the first n-1 numbers, or `factorial(n-1)`.

2. A base case of the problem that is simple enough to be solved by itself, without recursion. Mathematicians say `factorial(1)` is 1 by definition, so we'll take that as the base case.

3. A way of making the problem simpler so that it is closer to (and ultimately becomes the same as) the base case. How can we get from `factorial(n)` to `factorial(n-1)`? Easily—factor out the n. `factorial(n)` is the same as `n*factorial(n-1)`.

In Java, we can write this solution to the `factorial` problem as follows:

```
public class RecursiveMath {
    // code elided

    public static long factorial (int n) {
        if (n == 1)
            return 1;
        else
            return
                n * this.factorial(n-1);
    }
}
```

This code is very straightforward; you could probably have understood it without reading this chapter. The only new feature of the code is that the factorial method calls itself. We are used to a method invoking *other* methods, but this method invokes itself.

Consider `factorial(5)`, for example. `factorial(5)` calls `factorial(4)`, which calls `factorial(3)`, which calls `factorial(2)`, which calls `factorial(1)`. The reason this works is that the parameter gets smaller and smaller until we reach the base case, `factorial(1)`. We know how to answer `factorial(1)` without calling factorial again—it's 1—so the recursion stops there.

keyconcept

The record of information related to a method invocation, such as the values of its parameters and local variables, is called an activation record.

When a method calls itself, the mechanics are basically the same as when calling another method. As with separate methods, each invocation (message send) has its own copy of the parameters and local variables and shares access to instance variables. The record of information related to a method invocation, such as the values of its parameters and local variables is called an **activation record**. (Here the term activation is a synonym for invocation.)

The number of times a method is called is the **depth of recursion**. For example, if *n* is 1, factorial is only called once, so the depth of recursion is 1. If *n* is 10, factorial is called 10 times, so the depth of recursion is 10, and so on.

With recursion, many activations of a single method may exist at once. At the base case, as many activations exist as the depth of recursion. As illustrated in Figure 12.1, each activation has its own activation record, which is is stored on the **activation stack**. (For more about stacks, see Chapter 14.)

Incidentally, note that the `factorial` method assumes $n >= 1$. Such assumptions are called **preconditions** and should be documented and checked.

keyconcept

The number of times a recursive method calls itself is the depth of recursion.

keyconcept

With recursion, many activations of a single method may exist at once. Each has its own activation record.

12.3.2 **An example with more than one recursive call: Towers of Hanoi**

The Towers of Hanoi is a one-person game invented by French mathematician Edouard Lucas in the nineteenth century. To start, the player has three pegs and a set of *n* disks, each of a different size, placed on the leftmost peg with the largest on the bottom, then the next largest, and so on, as shown in Figure 12.2.

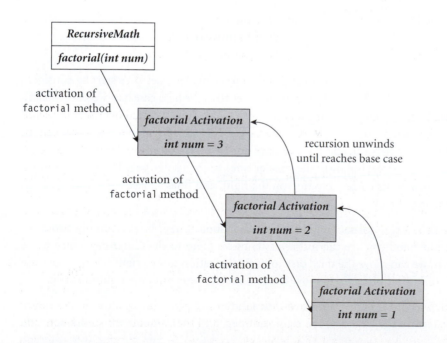

Figure 12.1 ■ Multiple method activations illustrated for three factorial.

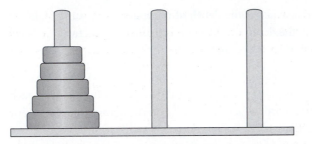

Figure 12.2 ■ Starting position for the Towers of Hanoi game.

The rules of the game are:

1. Move one disk at a time.
2. No disk can be placed on top of a smaller disk.
3. All disks must end up on the right-hand peg.

Does this problem contain subproblems that are simpler than the original? Yes—the problem of moving a smaller number of disks.

What is the base case in this problem? The simplest version of the problem is when we just have one disk: then all we have to do is to move one disk from the leftmost peg to the rightmost peg, and we're done. So let's call that the base case.

Is there a way to move from a larger problem to a smaller one? Let's start by considering a small example. The smallest example other than the base case has two disks, so let's start with that. We can't move them both at the same time. And we can't move the small one to the rightmost peg first, because the larger one can't go on top of it. What can we do? Take the top disk off, and then we have our base case, a pile with only one disk. So suppose we move the top disk (the smaller one) to the center peg. Then we can move the larger disk to its correct position on the right, and finally place the smaller disk on top of the larger disk.

Now we have a plan for moving two disks, what about three? If we can move two disks to the right-hand peg, we can just as easily move them to the center peg. Once we've done that, we can move the third disk to its final location on the right. Then we can use the two-disk solution again to move the two smaller pegs onto the rightmost peg.

To move *four* disks, we use our three-disk solution to move the top three to the center peg, then move the largest to the rightmost peg, and then use the three-disk solution again.

Even if we had a very large pile, say 100 disks, we could use a similar plan: move 99 disks to the center peg, then move the bottom disk to the rightmost peg, then move 99 disks from the center peg to the rightmost peg. Moving 99 disks to the center peg would involve moving 98 disks to the right-hand peg, then moving the 99th disk to the center peg, and then moving the 98 disks from the right-hand peg to the center peg. And similarly for moving 98 pegs, 97 pegs, and so on down to 1.

Our general plan for n disks, then, can be summarized like this (assuming we have a function `otherPole` that takes two poles and returns the third one). To move n disks from pole A to pole B:

1. move $n - 1$ disks from A to otherPole(A, B).

2. move the nth disk to B.

3. move $n - 1$ disks from otherPole(A, B) to B.

The original problem of moving n disks contains two simpler problems of moving $n - 1$ disks, plus the base case. How do we move from the simpler problem to the more difficult one? By agreeing to move the bottom disk once the top $n - 1$ are out of the way. And what is our base case? The case we know we can do for sure, moving one single disk.

Here's some pseudocode for this example:

```
// n is number of disks, aSource is starting pole,
// aDestination is finishing pole
public void hanoi (int n, Pole aSource, Pole aDestination) {
    if (n == 1)
        this.move(aSource, aDestination);
    else {
        Pole otherPole = this.otherPole(aSource,
                                    aDestination);
        this.hanoi(n-1, aSource, otherPole);
        this.move(aSource, aDestination);
        this.hanoi(n-1, otherPole, aDestination);
    }
}
```

`otherPole` is a method that takes two poles and returns the third, and `move` moves a disk from one `Pole` to another. Both are simple methods, so altogether the program is very short. But try hand-simulating this for n > 4—that is, writing down each disk move, one by one. Compared to writing out all the steps, the recursive solution is compact and elegant. A way of thinking about a recursive problem decomposition is to say: "If I assume for the moment that I know how to solve the problem for a simpler version (typically for $n - 1$), then how can I reframe my problem to take advantage of that solution?"

12.3.3 **Debugging tips**

The two main problems we need to watch out for when using recursion are:

1. No base case is given.

2. The subproblems never get to the base case.

What would happen if we didn't have a base case? Suppose our `takeJourney` method looked like this:

```
public class Traveler { // buggy recursive code
    public int _stepLength;
    ...
    public void takeJourney (int aNumMiles) {
        this.takeStep(_stepLength);
        this.takeJourney (aNumMiles-_stepLength);
    }
}
```

We'd just keep taking one step after another.

What would happen if the problem never got closer to the base case? Suppose our algorithm looked like this, for example:

```
public class Traveler { // buggy recursive code
    public int _stepLength;
    ...
    public void takeJourney (int aNumMiles) {
        if (aNumMiles == 0) return;
        this.takeStep(_stepLength);
        this.takeJourney (aNumMiles +_stepLength);
    }
}
```

> **keyconcept**
>
> Tail recursion is a simple form of recursion in which a method calls itself only once, and the recursive call is the last statement. It is particularly easy to convert to iteration.

The more we walk, the longer the trip gets! So, again, our trip would never end. If you are having problems with a recursive program, check for the base case, and use hand-simulation to make sure that in each recursive call the program is getting closer to it.

12.3.4 **Choosing between iteration and recursion**

For many problems, including the factorial problem, we can use either a recursive or an iterative solution. Problems like `factorial` are particularly easy to convert to an iterative solution, because they use a simple form of recursion called tail recursion. With **tail recursion,** a method only calls itself once, and the recursive call is the last statement in the method.

For example, here's an iterative version of `factorial`:

```
public class IterativeMath {
    // code elided

    public static long factorial (int n) {
        long result = 1;
        for (int i = 2; i <= n; i++) {
            result *= n;
        }
        return result;
    }
}
```

This loop follows the basic accumulator recipe introduced in Chapter 11: Initialize a variable; use the variable inside the loop to hold an answer that is improved each time through the loop; after the loop is done, find the final answer in the variable, ready for us to use (or return).

The conversion from tail recursion to iterative code is so straightforward that optimizing compilers can make it automatically. Other types of recursion can also be converted into iteration, but the process of conversion and the resulting code are generally more complex.

Going in the opposite direction, iterative code, on the other hand, can always be converted to recursive code. For example, consider the following definite loop that the `CookieRobot` from Chapter 11 could use to fill a cookie box with the maximum number of packages:

keyconcept
Iterative code can always be converted into recursive code.

```
public class CookieRobot { // iterative solution
    ...
    public void fillBox() {
        for (int i = 0;i < CookieConstants.NUM_PACKAGES; i++)
            this.addCookiePackageToBox();
    }
}
```

This code can be written recursively as follows:

```
public class CookieRobot {
    ...
    public void fillBox() { // recursive solution
        this.addCookiePackages(0);
    }
}
```

```java
public void addCookiePackages(int numPackagesAdded) {
    // base case: all done
    if (numPackagesAdded == CookieConstants.NUM_PACKAGES)
        return;

    // general case
    this.addCookiePackageToBox();
    this.addCookiePackages (numPackagesAdded++);
    }
}
```

The basic idea is to make the loop variable into a parameter, and use the negation of the loop condition as the base case.

A similar technique works for indefinite loops. Consider the following code for an indefinite loop, also a `CookieRobot` method:

```java
public class CookieRobot {
    ...
    public void fillCookieBag(CookieBag aBag) {
        while(!aBag.isFull())
            aBag.addCookie();
    }
}
```

This can be converted to recursive code as follows:

```java
public class CookieRobot {
    ...
    public void fillCookieBag(CookieBag aBag) {
        // base case: bag is full
        if (aBag.isFull()) return;

        // general case: add one cookie and then continue
        this.addCookie();
        this.fillCookieBag(aBag);
    }
}
```

Again, the exit condition becomes the base case.

If it's always possible to use either recursion or iteration, how can we choose between them? It's a question of *design*. In order to make this design choice, we need to consider two questions:

1. whether recursion or iteration is best suited to the problem

2. if recursion is better suited, whether the benefits of recursion are worth the possible cost in efficiency

keyconcept

Recursion (except for tail recursion) is less efficient than iteration, because time and space are needed to handle the extra parameters, local variables, and return values.

Let's consider these questions in order. How can we tell if recursion or iteration is best suited to the problem? Recursion works best for tasks that are naturally self-similar, like the Towers of Hanoi. With experience, you will gain a sense for which technique is a better fit.

Second, we also need to consider the tradeoffs involved. Tail recursion, as mentioned earlier, can be automatically translated into iteration by many compilers, but other forms of recursion are generally slower than the iterative solution. Recursion is slower because multiple method calls are activated at the same time. It takes time for the system to handle the parameters, local variables, and return values involved in method calls. On the other hand, a solution that matches the problem is generally easier to write and to read. As a result, it's also easier to debug and to maintain.

keyconcept

If recursion matches the problem, it is generally easier to write, read, debug, and maintain.

In the end, you will have to make a judgment call. For some applications, speed is critical. For some, being able to write a program quickly and easily is key. And for applications that are used for many years and maintained by many different programmers, ease of maintenance is a priority.

■ 12.4 ■ Working Out with Recursion—`SpiralApp`

Objectives:
☑ Write a simple recursive program

In this section, we look at a program that uses recursion to display a spiral. A screenshot of our program is given in Figure 12.3.

Suppose we draw this shape with a pencil, starting at the outside and working in. If we do that, the spiral is made up of the first line we draw, plus another smaller spiral. The smaller spiral starts at the end of the first line and is drawn at a slightly different angle. This observation gives us most of what we need to create a recursive program to draw the spiral:

1. a smaller subproblem: the smaller spiral
2. how to get from a larger problem to a smaller one: draw the first line and turn

The only other thing we need is a base case. Each line is slightly smaller than the one before, so we can say that the base case is one where the line is too small. (We'll define "too small" more precisely soon.)

We'll use three classes: `SpiralApp`, `SpiralPanel`, and `Spiral`. `SpiralApp`, shown in Listing 12.1, is identical to the `ButterflyApp` class from Chapter 11, except for minor changes.

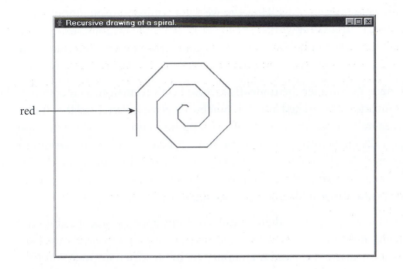

red

Figure 12.3 ■ Screenshot of `SpiralApp`.

```
1    /**
2     * Chapter 12: SpiralApp.java
3     * The usual subclass of JFrame.
4     */
5    public class SpiralApp extends javax.swing.JFrame {
6       public SpiralApp (String title) {
7          super(title);
8          this.setSize(600, 450);
9          this.add(new SpiralPanel());
10         this.setDefaultCloseOperation(
11             javax.swing.JFrame.EXIT_ON_CLOSE);
12         this.setVisible(true);
13      }
14
15      public static void main (String [ ] args) {
16         SpiralApp app =
17             new SpiralApp("Recursive drawing of a spiral.");
18      }
19   }
```

Listing 12.1 ■ The `SpiralApp` class

`SpiralPanel` (shown in Listing 12.2) is very similar to `ButterflyPanel`.

The new and interesting code, and in particular, the use of recursion, is all in the `Spiral` class. An overview of the code for the `Spiral` class is shown in Listing 12.3. The instance variables include, most importantly, `_firstLine` (for the first line we draw) and `_rest`, for the other, smaller `Spiral` within our `Spiral`. The other variables include the length of the first line and the color of the whole `Spiral`. To make the `Spiral` easier to see, we draw a wider line; the thickness of the line is given in a constant, `STROKE_WIDTH`.

The constructor includes the first example of recursion in the `Spiral` class. The idea is this:

1. instantiate the first line of the `Spiral`
2. if that line's too small, we're done (the base case)
3. otherwise (the general case), instantiate another `Spiral` that starts with a smaller line

In order to instantiate the `Spiral`'s first line, we need both endpoints. We only have the starting point, but we do have the length of the line and the angle at which it should

```
1    /**
2     * Chapter 12: SpiralPanel.java
3     * Instantiates and displays a Spiral.
4     */
5    public class SpiralPanel extends javax.swing.JPanel {
6        private Spiral _spiral; // component
7
8        public SpiralPanel () {
9            super();
10           _spiral = new Spiral (150, 200, 80, 4,
11                                 Math.PI/2, Math.PI/4,
12                                 java.awt.Color.red);
13           this.setBackground(java.awt.Color.white);
14       }
15       public void paintComponent (java.awt.Graphics aBrush){
16           super.paintComponent(aBrush);
17           java.awt.Graphics2D aBetterBrush =
18               (java.awt.Graphics2D) aBrush;
19           _spiral.draw(aBetterBrush);
20       }
21   }
```

Listing 12.2 ■ The `SpiralPanel` class

```
1    /**
2     * Chapter 12: Spiral.java
3     * Uses recursion to create and then display a picture of a spiral.
4     */
5    public class Spiral {
6        private java.awt.Color _color; // attributes
7        private double _length;
8        private final int STROKE_WIDTH = 2;
9        private java.awt.geom.Line2D.Double _firstLine; // components
10       private Spiral _rest;
11
12       public Spiral (double x, double y,
13                      double length, double lengthChange,
14                      double angle, double angleChange,
15                      java.awt.Color aColor){
16           super();
17           _color = aColor;
18           _length = length;
19           double endX = computeEndX(x, angle, length);
20           double endY = computeEndY(y, angle, length);
21           _firstLine = new java.awt.geom.Line2D.Double (x, y,
22                                                          endX, endY);
23           if (_length <=3) { // base case: line is short enough
24               _rest = null; // (just makes default explicit)
25           }
26           else { // general case: not done yet
27               _rest = new Spiral(endX, endY,
28                                  _length - lengthChange, lengthChange,
29                                  angle - angleChange, angleChange,
30                                  aColor);
31           }
32       }
33       public double computeEndX (double x, double angle, double length) {
34           return x + length * Math.cos(angle);
35       }
36       public double computeEndY (double y, double angle, double length) {
37           return y - length * Math.sin(angle);
38       }
39
40       public void draw (java.awt.Graphics2D aPaintBrush) {
```

Listing 12.3 ■ The Spiral class (*continued on next page*)

```
41              java.awt.Color savedColor = aPaintBrush.getColor();
42              aPaintBrush.setColor(_color);
43              java.awt.Stroke savedStroke = aPaintBrush.getStroke();
44              aPaintBrush.setStroke(new java.awt.BasicStroke(STROKE_WIDTH));
45              aPaintBrush.draw(_firstLine);
46              aPaintBrush.setStroke(savedStroke);
47              aPaintBrush.setColor(savedColor);
48              if (_length <= 3) // base case: draw shortest line
49                  return;
50              else // general case: not done yet
51                  _rest.draw(aPaintBrush);
52          }
53  }
```

Listing 12.3 ■ The `Spiral` class

be drawn. With a little bit of trigonometry, we can use that information to write methods that compute the *x* and *y* values of the end point (see Figure 12.4).

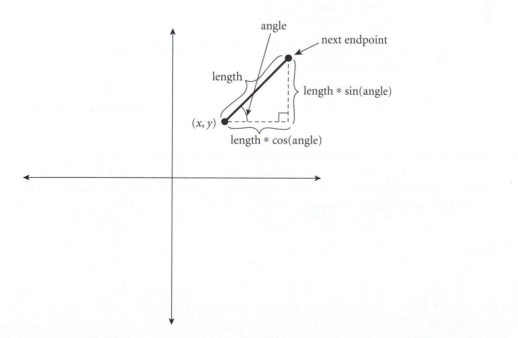

Figure 12.4 ■ Computing the second endpoint of the next line to be added to the `Spiral`.

Given the x and y values of the endpoint, we can instantiate the line.

```
_firstLine = new java.awt.geom.Line2D.Double (x, y,
                                    endX, endY);
```

Once we've instantiated the first line, we check to see if it's too small. Fairly arbitrarily, we decide that the smallest line we want to draw is three pixels. If the length of the current line is less than or equal to three pixels, that's the end of the `Spiral`; we simply set the `_rest` instance variable to `null`. (This is the default, but it's helpful to say so explicitly, just so it's clear you didn't forget to initialize the variable.)

If we haven't reached the base case yet, then our `Spiral` contains another smaller `Spiral`, and so we call the `Spiral` constructor to initialize it, as shown in Listing 12.3. When we create the next `Spiral`, we give it a smaller length (`_length – _lengthChange`). That way, each time we call the constructor, we're getting closer and closer to the base case.

Just as we use recursion to create the `Spiral`, we use recursion to draw it. After drawing the `_first` line in the usual way, the `draw` method includes the following code:

```
if (_length <= 3) // base case
    return;
else // general case: not done yet
    _rest.draw(aPaintBrush);
```

In other words, if we just drew the base-case line (three pixels or shorter), we're done; otherwise, draw the rest of the `Spiral`.

Notice how both of these methods, the constructor and the `draw` method, simply follow the structure of the `Spiral` itself: first they process the first line of the `Spiral`; then they process the rest of it.

That's it! That's all you need for your first recursive program. Compile, test, and run this program. Then modify it as suggested in the exercises until you're comfortable that you understand how it works. In particular, try converting the recursive code to an iterative solution. Which do you prefer? Why?

■ 12.5 ■ Working Out with Recursion—`TreeApp`

Objectives:
☑   Write a program in which a method calls itself twice

In this section, we show you a program that requires two recursive calls, rather than just one, to do its job. Instead of a spiral, this program draws the tree in Figure 12.5.

To draw a spiral, at each step, we changed direction and drew one new line; to draw this tree, at each step, we need to choose two new angles and draw two new lines. To put it another way, each spiral was made up of one line, plus another smaller spiral; each tree is made up of one line plus *two* smaller trees.

This program, like the last one, is made up of three classes: a subclass of `JFrame` (`TreeApp`), a subclass of `JPanel` (`TreePanel`), and a class modeling the shape itself (`Tree`). The `TreeApp` class (shown in Listing 12.4) is the same as `SpiralApp`, with only minor changes.

The `TreePanel` class (shown in Listing 12.5) is very similar to the corresponding `SpiralPanel` class. The only significant differences are the initial location and angle given to the `Tree`.

The differences between the `Tree` and the `Spiral` are found in the `Tree` class shown in Listing 12.6. Both `Tree` and `Spiral` contain constructors, methods for computing

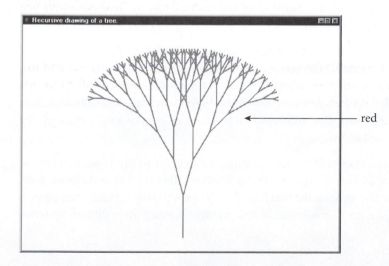

Figure 12.5 ■ A drawing of a tree created by a doubly recursive program.

```
1    /**
2     * Chapter 12: TreeApp.java
3     * The usual subclass of JFrame.
4     */
5    public class TreeApp extends javax.swing.JFrame {
6        public TreeApp (String title) {
7            super(title);
8            this.setSize(600, 450);
9            this.add(new TreePanel());
10           this.setDefaultCloseOperation(
11               javax.swing.JFrame.EXIT_ON_CLOSE);
12           this.setVisible(true);
13       }
14
15       public static void main (String [] args) {
16           TreeApp app =
17               new TreeApp("Recursive drawing of a tree.");
18       }
19   }
```

Listing 12.4 ■ The `TreeApp` class

the endpoints of the first line, and `draw` methods. Both have the same instance variables, and use the same code to compute and instantiate the endpoint of the first line. But the recursive code in `Tree`—in the constructor and in the `draw` method—requires two recursive calls, instead of just one.

After instantiating the first line, the `Tree`'s constructor initializes the two subtrees. If we've reached the base case, both subtrees are `null`; otherwise, we create two subtrees each starting with a shorter line (whose length is `_length-lengthChange`). Can you spot the other difference between the two subtrees? Right—it's the angle at which their first line should be drawn. One subtree's line is drawn at `angle-angleChange`; the other, at `angle+angleChange`.

The `draw` method works similarly: After drawing the first line of the `Tree`, it draws the two subtrees. Again, as with the `Spiral`, the code follows the structure of the `Tree` itself. It's very natural to say, "process the first line; then process the left subtree; then process the right subtree." An iterative solution to this problem is much more difficult to write.

```
1    /**
2     * Chapter 12: TreePanel.java
3     * The usual subclass of JPanel
4     */
5    public class TreePanel extends javax.swing.JPanel {
6        private Tree _tree; // component
7
8        public TreePanel () {
9            super();
10           _tree = new Tree (300, 400, 80, 10,
11                             Math.PI/2, Math.PI/12,
12                             java.awt.Color.red);
13           this.setBackground(java.awt.Color.white);
14       }
15       public void paintComponent (java.awt.Graphics aBrush){
16           super.paintComponent(aBrush);
17           java.awt.Graphics2D betterBrush =
18               (java.awt.Graphics2D) aBrush;
19           _tree.draw(betterBrush);
20       }
21   }
```

Listing 12.5 ■ The TreePanel class

```
1    /**
2     * Chapter 12: Tree.java
3     * Uses recursion to create and display a picture of a tree.
4     */
5    import java.awt.*;
6    import java.awt.geom.*;
7
8    public class Tree {
9        private Color _color; // attributes
10       private double _length;
11       private final int STROKE_WIDTH = 2;
12       private Line2D.Double _firstLine; // components
13       private Tree _leftSubTree, _rightSubTree;
14
15       public Tree (double x, double y,
16                    double length, double lengthChange,
```

Listing 12.6 ■ The Tree class (*continued on next page*)

```
17                      double angle, double angleChange,
18                      Color aColor){
19          super();
20          _color = aColor;
21          _length = length;
22          double endX = computeEndX(x, angle, length);
23          double endY = computeEndY(y, angle, length);
24          _firstLine = new Line2D.Double (x, y,endX, endY);
25          if (_length <=3) { // base case: line is short enough
26              _leftSubTree = null;
27              _rightSubTree = null;
28          }
29          else { // general case: not done yet
30              _leftSubTree = new Tree (endX, endY,
31                                       _length-lengthChange,
32                                       lengthChange,
33                                       angle - angleChange, angleChange,
34                                       aColor);
35              _rightSubTree = new Tree (endX, endY,
36                                        _length-lengthChange,lengthChange,
37                                        angle + angleChange, angleChange,
38                                        aColor);
39          }
40      }
41      public double computeEndX (double x, double angle, double length){
42          return x + length * Math.cos(angle);
43      }
44      public double computeEndY (double y, double angle, double length){
45          return y - length * Math.sin(angle);
46      }
47
48      public void draw (Graphics2D aPaintBrush) {
49          Color savedColor = aPaintBrush.getColor();
50          aPaintBrush.setColor(_color);
51          Stroke savedStroke = aPaintBrush.getStroke();
52          aPaintBrush.setStroke(new BasicStroke(STROKE_WIDTH));
53          aPaintBrush.draw(_firstLine);
54          aPaintBrush.setStroke(savedStroke);
55          aPaintBrush.setColor(savedColor);
56          if (_length <= 3) base case: drew shortest line
57              return;
```

Listing 12.6 ■ The Tree class (*continued on next page*)

```
58              else { // general case: not done yet
59                  _leftSubTree.draw(aPaintBrush);
60                  _rightSubTree.draw(aPaintBrush);
61              }
62          }
63      }
```

Listing 12.6 ■ The `Tree` class

There are other types of recursion we have not discussed in this chapter. **Indirect recursion** occurs when two or more methods work together to act recursively. For example, it would be indirect recursion if one method, method A, called another method, Method B, which in turn called method A. Indirect recursion can be particularly difficult to debug, because it's necessary to track through several method calls even to find out that it's happening. For example, if you mistakenly write in Java a `paintComponent` method that calls `repaint`, you set up a chain of indirect recursive calls: `repaint` always calls `paintComponent`, which in turn calls `repaint`, which calls `paintComponent`, and so forth. This creates an infinite sequence of recursive calls that can be very difficult to track down. **Polymorphic recursion** occurs when a method in instance A invokes itself on another instance B that may not even belong to the same class. In polymorphic recursion, one of the instances must ultimately act as the base case.

■ Summary ■

Recursion is a technique for solving problems that contain subproblems that are similar to, but simpler than, the original problem. To use recursion, we must:

1. identify a subproblem that is of the same type as the original problem
2. define a way of breaking the problem down into the simpler problem
3. find a base case, or simpler problem that can be solved directly without recursion

For some problems, a recursive solution is easier to write than an iterative solution; the resulting code is sometimes (not always) less efficient. Choosing between iteration and recursion is a judgment call, based on the requirements of the problem being solved.

■ Self-Check Questions ■

(The answers to these questions can be found on the book's website, www.aw.com/sanders)

1. Define recursion and give an example.
2. What is a self-similar problem? Give an example other than the ones in the text.
3. Define tail recursion.
4. What is an activation record, and where are activation records stored?
5. What are the tradeoffs involved in using recursion vs. iteration?

■ Exercises ■

Applying the Facts

1. Explain how a `for` loop can be converted to recursive code, with a code example.
2. Explain how a `while` loop can be converted to recursive code, with a code example.
3. If one move is necessary to move one disk in the Towers of Hanoi problem, three moves are necessary to move two disks, and seven moves are necessary for three disks, how many would you conjecture are necessary for four disks? for n disks? Explain.
4. Prove your answer to question 2. (*Hint*: try proof by induction.)

5. Hand-simulate the iterative solution to the Towers of Hanoi for $n = 4$. That is, given three poles, A, B, and C, and four disks, D1, D2, D3, and D4 (where D4 is the largest), list in order each disk that must be moved, with its start location and destination, if all disks start on pole A and must end on pole C.

Debugging Programs

Identify the bugs (if any) in each of the following code fragments. Explain your answers.

1.
```
public void doHomework (int numProblems) {
    this.doProblem();
    this.doHomework(numProblems);
}
```

2.
```
public void eatDinner (int dinnerSize) {
    this.takeBite();
    this.eatDinner(dinnerSize - this.getBiteSize());
}
```

3.
```
public void weedGarden (int numWeeds) {
    this.weedGarden(numWeeds);
}
```

■ Programming Projects ■

Modifying Programs

1. Modify `SpiralApp` so that the spiral is blue instead of red.

2. Modify `SpiralApp` so that the spiral is upside down.

3. Modify `SpiralApp` so that the spiral turns clockwise instead of counter-clockwise.

4. Modify `SpiralApp` so that the program displays two identical spirals at different locations.

5. Modify `SpiralApp` so that the program displays three spirals of three different colors.

6. Modify `SpiralApp` so that the program displays three spirals of three different sizes and three different colors.

7. Modify `SpiralApp` so that the program displays a new spiral at any location where the user clicks in the window. Each spiral should be a red spiral of the same size given in the original program. All the `Spirals` should be stored in a `Vector`.

8. Modify `TreeApp` so that the tree is upside down, like a real computer-science tree.

9. Modify `TreeApp` so that the tree is a different color.

10. Modify `TreeApp` so that the tree's branches branch off at a greater angle (and overlap less).

Writing Programs

1. Use recursion to write a program that displays concentric circles. It should start with a circle of a given size and recursively draw smaller and smaller circles inside the original circle until the circles are too small to display clearly.

2. Use recursion to divide a window into smaller and smaller parts. Start by drawing vertical and horizontal lines that divide the window into four smaller rectangles, then draw lines that divide the four smaller rectangles into even smaller rectangles, and so on. Stop when one of the lines being drawn is ten pixels long or less.

3. Use recursion to write a program that displays a smiley face (that is, a circle containing two round eyes and a smile). Each eye of the smiley face should also be a smiley face, and each eye of those smiley faces should be a smiley face, and so on, until the smiley faces are too small to display clearly. (Thanks to Robert Duvall for this idea.)

13

Arrays, Vectors, and ArrayLists

OBJECTIVES

After reading this chapter, you should be able to:

☑ Read and write Java programs using arrays, `Vectors`, and `ArrayLists`

☑ Compare and contrast arrays, `Vectors`, and `ArrayLists`

■ 13.1 ■ Introduction

Suppose we want to adapt the fish tank from Chapter 7 so that 20 fish are displayed in the fish tank. We could define a `FishTankPanel` with 20 instance variables (`_fish1`, `_fish2`, `_fish3`, etc.), one for each fish, and have `paintComponent` send a message to each one of them every time the `FishTankPanel` is repainted. This solution works, but it's far from ideal. Defining 20 instance variables in a single class is possible, but it's pretty ugly—not to mention inconvenient.

In Chapter 11 we saw how to solve this kind of problem using a `Vector`. In this chapter, we introduce two alternatives to `Vectors` called arrays and `ArrayLists` and compare and contrast the different solutions.

■ 13.2 ■ Concepts

To model a fish tank with 20 fish we can simply declare one variable, called, say, `fishList`, as an array of fish. With an array, we don't need a name for every fish. The fish are identified by their position in the array, just as they would be in a `Vector`. The same is true for an `ArrayList`, a Java built-in class like `Vector` that also holds a collection of items.

The larger the problem, the greater the benefit we get from using one of these data structures. Suppose we're modeling an airline's route map, including the hundreds of different cities where the airline goes. To solve this problem without a data structure, we'd have to declare hundreds of instance variables, one for each city; to solve it with arrays,

Vectors, or ArrayLists, we only need to declare a single instance variable and give the type of elements it holds.

The main differences between Vectors, ArrayLists, and arrays include:

1. Vectors and ArrayLists are extremely similar. This is not a coincidence: they have the same superclass (AbstractList), and they implement the same six interfaces.

2. Vectors and ArrayLists are more flexible than arrays. We need to declare in advance how many elements an array holds, but Vectors and ArrayLists can grow and shrink as needed.

3. Vectors and ArrayLists have the familiar Java class syntax; arrays have a different syntax, borrowed from older languages such as C.

4. Arrays are more efficient.

5. Arrays are not instances of a Java class nor are they a primitive type, like ints (although, as seen below, they are more like a primitive type than an object).

If we know in advance exactly how many objects we need to store, and efficiency is important, an array is better. If the amount of data is going to grow and shrink unpredictably, or if readability is more important than efficiency, a Vector or ArrayList is better.

■ 13.3 ■ Mechanics

Java provides a special syntax to access array elements. Arrays don't have any methods, and we cannot subclass them. ArrayList, on the other hand, is a built-in Java class, like Vector, with all the regular Java class syntax.

13.3.1 Declaring and initializing arrays, ArrayLists, and Vectors

keyconcept

The position of an element in an array is its index. The first index of a Java array, like a Vector, is always 0, and the last is length −1 (where length is the number of elements in the array).

In Java, every array element is an object reference, a primitive type, or (as we will see below) another array: fish, cities, the squares on a chessboard, the IDs of students in a class. All three data structures store these objects in numbered slots in a single block of memory, like reserved seats in a theater. If we have a 64-integer array, for example, we can look up the 22nd element in the array, or store a new int in the 46th place.

The position of an element is also called its **index**. The first index of a Java array, like the first position of a Vector or an ArrayList, is always 0. So in an array with 10 elements, the first one is in position 0 and the last one is in position 9. In an array with

986 elements, the first one is in position 0, and the last one is in position 985. This numbering is illustrated in Figure 13.1.

All the elements of an array must belong to the same type, called the array's **base type**. The base type must be given when the array is declared.

To declare an array in Java, the syntax is:

```
<type>[ ] <array-name>;
```

For <type>, put the type each slot in the array is to hold. It can be a primitive type, a class, an interface, or, as we shall soon see, another array. (`Vector` is a class, so arrays can even contain `Vectors`.) The square brackets and the semicolon are required, and the array name can be any legal Java variable name. The angle brackets are *not* part of the syntax, although they are part of the syntax for generic `Vectors` and `ArrayLists`.

Recall that to declare a `Vector` of graphical shapes, we could write:

```
Vector <Shape> myShapes;
```

To declare an `ArrayList`, we write essentially the same thing:

```
ArrayList <Shape> myShapes;
```

To declare an array, we write instead:

```
Shape [ ] myShapes;
```

This syntax tells the compiler that there will be a variable called `myShapes` in the program, that it will be an array (because of the [ ]), and that the elements of the array will be references to objects that either are `Shapes` or are instances of its subclasses. The syntax for all three declarations is exactly the same, regardless of whether the base type is an interface or a class.

To initialize an array, we must specify its size:

```
<array-name> = new <type>[<size>];
```

For example,

```
myShapes = new Shape[1000];
```

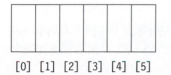

[0] [1] [2] [3] [4] [5]

Figure 13.1 ■ How Java arrays are numbered.

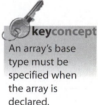
keyconcept
All the elements of an array must belong to the same class or a subclass of that class or implement the same interface. This class or interface is the array's base type.

keyconcept
An array's base type must be specified when the array is declared.

keyconcept
In Java, the length of an array must be given when the array is initialized.

This statement tells the compiler that our array will contain a thousand elements. It also causes the compiler to set aside space in memory for 1000 `Shapes`. Note, however, that no values are stored in the array yet. The array is initialized, but its elements are not. It's as if we've built a theater and put numbers on all the seats, but haven't let anyone sit in the seats yet. Java's way of indicating that the seats are empty is to set them to `null`. All array elements are `null` when the array is first initialized.

Since `Vectors` and `ArrayLists` grow and shrink depending on the number of elements they contain, we do not specify their size when we initialize them . If `myShapes` were a `Vector` of `Shapes`, instead of an array, we would initialize it like a class:

```
myShapes = new Vector <Shape>();
```

If it were an `ArrayList`, we could write:

```
myShapes = new ArrayList <Shape>();
```

In sum, all three initializations use the Java reserved word `new`. `Vectors` and `ArrayLists` use the standard syntax for Java classes; arrays have their own idiosyncratic syntax. Arrays specify their size; `Vectors` and `ArrayLists` do not.

13.3.2 Accessing and using elements

Now suppose we want to access, say, the tenth element of an array. If it's a `Vector`, we'd simply call the appropriate method, like this:

```
Shape currentShape = myShapes.elementAt(9);
```

`ArrayLists` do not have the `elementAt` method (one of the few methods they don't share with `Vectors`), but both `Vectors` and `ArrayLists` have a `get` method, so we could say:

```
Shape currentShape = myShapes.get(9);
```

regardless of whether `myShapes` is a `Vector` or an `ArrayList`. If `myShapes` is an array, the syntax for accessing the tenth element is:

```
int currentNum = scores[9];
```

The expression `scores[9]` is often pronounced "scores sub 9." All three data structures start counting at 0.

A reference to an array element can take the place of something of the same type in any Java expression. For example, to compute the total area of two shapes in an array `myShapes`, we could say:

```
double totalArea = myShapes[8].getArea() +
                   myShapes[9].getArea();
```

To perform the same computation if `myShapes` is a `Vector` or an `ArrayList`, we can write:

```
double totalArea = myShapes.get(8).getArea() +
                   myShapes.get(9).getArea();
```

To store a value in the seventh position of an array, we can write:

```
myShapes[6] = new SmartEllipse(java.awt.Color.red);
```

To store a shape in the seventh position of a `Vector` or an `ArrayList`, we write:

```
myShapes.add(6, new SmartEllipse(java.awt.Color.red));
```

13.3.3 Passing as parameters

We can declare an array as a parameter simply by adding brackets to the type of the formal parameter. For example,

```
public int sum (int [] numbers) {
    // code to compute sum of numbers in array
}
```

But the method code will need to know the length of the array (i.e., how many elements it contains). How can we handle this? We could pass the length as a second parameter (a traditional solution in languages such as C). In Java, there's a better solution. All arrays know their own length. Length can be accessed using the following syntax:

```
int arrayLength = <arrayName>.length;
```

The syntax for accessing the length of an array is the same as if arrays were a class and `length` were a `public` instance variable of that class.

Passing a `Vector` or an `ArrayList` as a parameter is no different from passing any other object as a parameter. Both classes provide a `size` method that returns their length.

13.3.4 Multidimensional structures

Arrays work nicely for modeling similar objects all in a line. But what if they're in a square? For example, suppose we want to model a chessboard. The squares aren't all lined up in a row; they're more like a grid. Sometimes it's important to identify the rows and columns that contain a particular piece—a rook, for example, can threaten other pieces in the same row or column of the chessboard. If all the squares are stored in a single long list, identifying rows, columns, or diagonals would be difficult.

keyconcept
An array in Java can have one, two, or more dimensions.

The natural way to model a chessboard is with a two-dimensional array. We can declare an array to be two (or more) dimensions in Java, just by adding more brackets. The declaration for a two-dimensional array is similar to that for a one-dimensional array:

```
Square [][] gameBoard = new Square [8][8];
```

And accessing elements of a two-dimensional array is similar to accessing elements of a one-dimensional array:

```
currentSquare = gameBoard]i][j];
```

In fact, we can think of a two-dimensional array as just a one-dimensional array of one-dimensional arrays. GameBoard[0] refers to one of the one-dimensional arrays; so does gameBoard[2]; GameBoard[0][5] refers to element 5 in array 0 of gameBoard. Vectors can also contain other Vectors, and ArrayLists can contain ArrayLists. But for a fixed-size object like a chessboard, a two-dimensional array is the best choice.

Arrays with three or more dimensions work similarly to two-dimensional arrays. In general, we just need one pair of brackets per dimension. For example, if we want a three-dimensional game board, we can declare it like this:

```
int [][][] gameBoard3d = new int [x][y][z];
```

Consider gameBoard[0] for a moment. That's one of the arrays contained in the two-dimensional gameBoard. But is it a row or a column? For reasons having to do with the way Java (and most other programming languages) store arrays in memory, many computer scientists think of gameBoard[0] as a row, and gameBoard[0][4] as the element in column 4 of that row. (The technical name for this is **row-major ordering**, because it seems to make rows more important than columns.)

With row-major ordering, here are the array indices we would use for each cell of an array with three rows and five columns.

(0,0)	(0,1)	(0,2)	(0,3)	(0,4)
(1,0)	(1,1)	(1,2)	(1,3)	(1,4)
(2,0)	(2,1)	(2,2)	(2,3)	(2,4)

The rows come first, so grid[1][2] is the element in row 1, column 2. The next element, grid[1][3], is the element in row 1, column 3.

Now that you've been working with graphics for a while, this ordering should look strange to you. What's wrong with it? Recall that when we want to indicate a pixel location, we give the *x* value (i.e., the column) first, and then the row (or *y* value). With "pixel" ordering, therefore, we would use the following indices for each cell of the same array:

(0,0)	(1,0)	(2,0)	(3,0)	(4,0)
(0,1)	(1,1)	(2,1)	(3,1)	(4,1)
(0,2)	(1,2)	(2,2)	(3,2)	(4,2)

Because the columns come first, this ordering is known as **column major**.

We strongly recommend that for graphics programs you use column-major order in declaring and accessing your arrays. The first number you give when you declare an array should be the number of columns, and the second number, the number of rows, like this:

```
Square gameBoard [numColumns][numRows];
```

Then when you want to access row 7, square 3, you can access it like this:

```
currentSquare = gameBoard[3][7];
```

In this way, the locations you use for arrays will be the same as the locations you must use for pixels, and as a result, your code will be much easier to write and debug. The locations we use have no effect on how Java stores the array data—it is still stored in row-major order. But the underlying implementation doesn't matter; as long as we store and access the data consistently in column-major order, the code will work fine regardless of how Java accesses the individual memory elements.

keyconcept
We strongly recommend that you use column-major ordering for two-dimensional arrays, because it is consistent with the coordinate system used for locations in a window.

13.3.5 Debugging tips: common array errors

The most common error in working with arrays is using an out-of-bounds index. *Remember that the array goes from 0 to n − 1.* If the index is less than zero or greater than $n - 1$, Java will throw something called an `ArrayIndexOutOfBounds` exception. If this happens and you haven't written code to handle the exception, your program will crash. (See Chapter 18 for a discussion of exception handling.) Contrast this behavior with `Vectors` and `ArrayLists`, which simply grow as necessary to hold the number of items added to them.

One very common recipe for checking array indices is to use a `for` loop:

```
for (int i = 0; i < <arrayName>.length; i++){
    ... <arrayName> [i] ...

}
```

As long as the loop conditions are written correctly, the array access inside the loop will cause no problems.

Just as with one-dimensional arrays, we need to be careful to avoid out-of-bounds indices with two-dimensional arrays. Like one-dimensional arrays, two-dimensional arrays start at 0. The only difference is that now we need to know the number of both rows and columns.

Just like one-dimensional arrays, two-dimensional arrays are smart enough to know their own dimensions. How does this work? Recall that we can think of a two-dimensional array as an array of one-dimensional arrays. Since we're using column-major order, we actually have an array of *columns*. So if we have an array named gameBoard, gameBoard.length gives us the number of columns. We could say, for example:

```
numColumns = gameBoard.length;
```

How can we find the number of rows? Well, the number of rows is the same as the number of elements in each column. So if we pick one column and find out its length, we'll know the number of rows. All the columns are the same, so suppose we pick column 0. Then we can find out the number of rows like this:

```
numRows = gameBoard[0].length;
```

If we wanted to use a row-major array, we would simply reverse these. Similar issues apply to higher-dimensional arrays, but these are much less common in practice than one- and two-dimensional arrays.

Some additional errors to watch out for include:

■ Assigning a scalar value to an array

```
int [ ] numList = 5; // ERROR
```

This will fail as a type mismatch because numList is an array and 5 is an int.

■ Assigning an array to a scalar

```
int[ ] numList = new int [5000];
int firstItem = numList; // ERROR
```

Again, there's a type mismatch. This will fail, because firstItem (on the left of the assignment statement) is an int and numList, on the right, is an array.

■ Assigning arrays of different dimension to each other

```
int [ ] numList = new int [5000]
int [ ] [ ] matrix = new int [500][10];
numList = matrix; // ERROR
```

This error causes an error message that looks like this:

Incompatible type for =. Can't convert int[ ] to int [ ][ ]

There's a similar message when one array contains, say, Squares and the other contains ints.

13.3.6 **Comparing and contrasting arrays, `Vectors`, and `ArrayLists`**

Table 13.1 summarizes the major differences among `Vectors`, `ArrayLists`, and arrays. Arrays are clearly quite different from the other two, but even after examining the table, you may be wondering what the difference is between `Vectors` and `ArrayLists`. They're not just similar on the surface; they are both implemented using arrays, which are resized automatically when necessary. If you dig deeper and look at the online Java documentation, you will discover that `Vectors` and `ArrayLists` are basically equivalent, except that `Vectors` are synchronized and `ArrayLists` are not. For purposes of the code we write in this book, whether or not a data structure is synchronized does not matter, so for our purposes, they are equivalent.

keyconcept

`ArrayLists` and `Vectors` are almost identical; they have the same superclass, implement the same interfaces, and are both implemented using resizable arrays. The difference between them is that `Vectors` are synchronized and `ArrayLists` are not.

13.3.7 **The mainline revealed**

Now we've looked at arrays, we can finally explain what the mainline is doing. Consider the line included in every program:

```
public static void main (String [] args) {
```

Table 13.1 ■ Array, `Vector`, and `ArrayList`.

Array	Vector and ArrayList
Ordered	Ordered
Needs to be initialized with size	Doesn't need to be initialized with size
Size is fixed when initialized	Grows as new elements are added

Declaration looks like:
`Shape []myShapes;`
	Declaration looks like:
	`java.util.Vector <Shape> myShapes;`
	`java.util.ArrayList <Shape> myShapes;`

Initialization looks like:
`myShapes = new Shape[1000];`
	Initialization looks like:
	`myShapes = new java.util.Vector<Shape>();`
	`myShapes = new java.util.ArrayList<Shape>();`

Accessing an element looks like: `myShapes[6]`	Accessing an element looks like: `myShapes.get(6)` (if `Vector`, can also say `myShapes.elementAt(6)`)
Must check to see if array location is in bounds before adding element	Need not check to see if location is in bounds
Not a class	Java class, with usual syntax for declarations and initializations
Almost universal part of programming languages	Relatively new idea (though not unique to Java)
More efficient	Less efficient, but more flexible

The reserved words `public` and `void` are both familiar. `Static` means that the method can be called without actually instantiating the class containing the method. This is necessary because nothing can be instantiated until the mainline is called. From this chapter, we now know that the formal parameter `args` to `main` is an array of `Strings`. What this means is that if we run a program from a shell such as DOS, Unix, or the Terminal program in Apple's OSX, we can give it arguments like this:

```
MyProgram arg1 arg2 arg3 ...
```

Then those arguments will be given to `main` and the array `args` will store them. So `args[0]` is arg1, `args[1]` is arg2, etc.

We could use these arguments, for example, to write a program that repeats whatever the user types in:

```
public class Echo {
    public Echo ( ) {
    }

    public static void main (String [ ] args) {
        for (int j = 0; j < args.length; j++) {
            System.out.println(args[j]);
        }
    }
}
```

If we compile this class definition and then enter the following in a shell:

```
Echo hello from me
```

We'd get the output:

```
hello
from
me
```

Since we're not writing command-line programs, we won't need to use arguments to `main` for this book, but we wanted to tell you what the magic was all about.

■ 13.4 ■ Working Out with Arrays—`ClickApp`

In this section, we create a program that displays a grid of squares. Squares are initially white; when the user clicks on a square, it changes color to red, and then alternates between white and red each time it is clicked. Figure 13.2 contains a screenshot of the program running, after a few squares have been clicked:

Our implementation of this program includes three classes, `ClickApp`, `ClickPanel`, and `ClickSquare`. A class diagram for these classes is given in Figure 13.3.

`ClickApp` is the starting point, since it contains the `main` method. It's the same as usual, except for minor changes (see Listing 13.1).

The `ClickPanel` contains one large rectangle, the background, and a two-dimensional array of small squares (see Listing 13.2). Its constructor (shown in Listing 13.3) initializes a rectangle large enough to hold all the desired rows and columns of small squares, with some room in between. Then it initializes a two-dimensional array of smaller squares (`ClickSquares`). When the small squares are drawn on top of the background, the background showing between the small squares will look like lines.

The `paintComponent` method draws the background in blue and then sends a `fill` message to each of the squares, as shown in Listing 13.4.

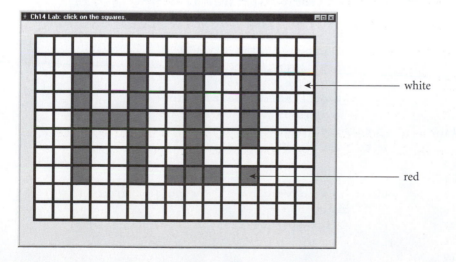

Figure 13.2 ■ Screenshot for `ClickApp`.

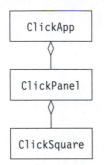

Figure 13.3 ■ Class diagram for the `ClickApp` program.

Finally, `MyMouseListener` follows our usual pattern: the `JPanel` contains an inner class with a `mouseClicked` method. When the mouse is clicked, `MyMouseListener` checks all the relevant shapes displayed in the panel until it finds the one that was clicked (if any), and forwards the `mouseClicked` message to that square.

There are two recipes to notice here. First, we use a nested `for` loop to search a two-dimensional array. `For` loops are very well suited, and very commonly used, for array

```
1   /**
2    * Chapter 13: ClickApp.java
3    * The window for our program illustrating arrays.
4    */
5   public class ClickApp extends javax.swing.JFrame {
6       public ClickApp(String title){
7           super(title);
8           this.setSize(600, 450);
9           this.setDefaultCloseOperation(
10              javax.swing.JFrame.EXIT_ON_CLOSE);
11          this.add(new ClickPanel());
12          this.setVisible(true);
13      }
14
15      public static void main (String [ ] args) {
16          ClickApp app = new
17              ClickApp("Ch13 Lab: click on the squares.");
18      }
19  }
```

Listing 13.1 ■ The `ClickApp` class

```
1    /**
2     * Chapter 13: ClickPanel.java
3     * The panel for our program illustrating arrays.
4     * Holds a two-dimensional array of clickable squares.
5     */
6    import java.awt.geom.*;
7    public class ClickPanel extends javax.swing.JPanel {
8        private final static int OFFSET = 25; // attributes
9        private final static int LINE_WIDTH = 5;
10       private final static int CELL_WIDTH = 30;
11       private static int NUM_COLS = 15;
12       private static int NUM_ROWS = 10;
13       // components
14       private Rectangle2D.Double _background;
15       private ClickSquare[][] _squares;
16
17       // constructor, paintComponent go here
18       // and then MyMouseListener inner class
19   }
```

Listing 13.2 ■ The `ClickPanel` class

```
1    public ClickPanel() {
2        // _background is behind squares, looks like
3        // lines between squares
4        _background = new
5          Rectangle2D.Double(OFFSET,OFFSET,
6                          LINE_WIDTH + NUM_COLS*(CELL_WIDTH+LINE_WIDTH),
7                          LINE_WIDTH + NUM_ROWS*(CELL_WIDTH+LINE_WIDTH));
8        _squares = new ClickSquare[NUM_COLS][NUM_ROWS];
9        for (int col=0;col<NUM_COLS;col++)//fill _squares
10         for (int row=0;row<NUM_ROWS;row++)
11           _squares[col][row] = new ClickSquare(
12               OFFSET + LINE_WIDTH +
13                 col * (CELL_WIDTH + LINE_WIDTH), // x
14               OFFSET + LINE_WIDTH +
15                 row * (CELL_WIDTH + LINE_WIDTH), // y
16               CELL_WIDTH, this);
17       this.addMouseListener(new MyMouseListener());
18   }
```

Listing 13.3 ■ The `ClickPanel`'s constructor

```
1    public void paintComponent(java.awt.Graphics aPaintBrush) {
3        super.paintComponent(aPaintBrush);
4        java.awt.Graphics2D pen = (java.awt.Graphics2D) aPaintBrush;
5
6        // first, draw the background
7        java.awt.Color savedColor = pen.getColor();
8        pen.setColor(java.awt.Color.blue);
9        pen.fill(_background);
10
11       // then the squares
12       for (int col = 0; col < NUM_COLS; col++)
13           for (int row = 0; row < NUM_ROWS; row++)
14               _squares[col][row].fill(pen);
15       pen.setColor(savedColor);
16   }
```

Listing 13.4 ■ The ClickPanel's paintComponent method

searching and processing. Second, we set a boolean variable foundSquare to false before we begin our search. By setting it to true when we find what we're looking for (if ever), we can stop the for loops at that point and avoid searching the whole array, as shown in Listing 13.5.

```
1    private class MyMouseListener
2            extends java.awt.event.MouseAdapter {
3        public void mouseClicked(java.awt.event.MouseEvent e){
4            boolean foundSquare = false;
5            for (int col = 0; col < NUM_COLS && !foundSquare; col++){
6                for (int row = 0; row < NUM_ROWS && !foundSquare; row++) {
7                    if (_squares[col][row].contains(e.getPoint())){
8                        foundSquare = true;
9                        _squares[col][row].mouseClicked(e);
10                   }
11               }
12           }
13       }
14   }
```

Listing 13.5 ■ The ClickPanel's inner class MyMouseListener

The third of our three classes, `ClickSquare`, is basically a `SmartRectangle`. It knows its own color, and it knows how to alternate colors between red and white when it's clicked on (see Listing 13.6.)

```java
1   /**
2    * Chapter 13: ClickSquare.java
3    * A smarter rectangle: in addition to knowing its
4    * color and knowing how to draw itself, it knows how
5    * to change color when it's clicked on.
6    */
7   public class ClickSquare
8           extends java.awt.geom.Rectangle2D.Double {
9       private ClickPanel _panel;
10      private java.awt.Color _myColor,_clickColor;
11
12      public ClickSquare(int x, int y,
13                         int aWidth,ClickPanel aPanel){
14          super(x,y,aWidth,aWidth);
15          _panel = aPanel;
16          _myColor = java.awt.Color.white;
17          _clickColor = java.awt.Color.red;
18      }
19      public void setColor(java.awt.Color aColor) {
20          _myColor = aColor;
21      }
22      public void fill(java.awt.Graphics2D aPaintBrush){
23          java.awt.Color savedColor = aPaintBrush.getColor();
24          aPaintBrush.setColor(_myColor);
25          aPaintBrush.fill(this);
26          aPaintBrush.setColor(savedColor);
27      }
28      public void mouseClicked(java.awt.event.MouseEvent e){
29          if ( _myColor.equals(java.awt.Color.white))
30              this.setColor(_clickColor);
31          else
32              this.setColor(java.awt.Color.white);
33          _panel.repaint();
34      }
35  }
```

Listing 13.6 ■ The `ClickSquare` class

Compile, test, and run this program. When you have it working, try modifying it as indicated in the exercises.

■ Summary ■

Arrays, Vectors, and ArrayLists are linear data structures that allow us to store a collection of items using a single variable. Vectors and ArrayLists are nearly identical: they have the same superclass and implement the same interfaces. Arrays do not use the standard Java class syntax; instead, they use a syntax inherited from older languages. All the objects in one of these data structures must belong to the same class or implement the same interface. The programmer must specify in advance how many objects an array will contain, but Vectors and ArrayLists vary in size as necessary when elements are inserted and deleted. For loops are commonly used for processing all the elements of an array.

■ Self-Check Questions ■

Mastering the Facts

1. What is an array?
2. What is an array element?
3. What is the index of an array element (in general)?
4. What is the index of the first element of an array?
5. What is the index of the last element of an array?
6. How many dimensions can a Java array have?
7. List four common errors to watch for when using arrays.
8. What is row-major ordering?
9. What is column-major ordering?
10. Why is row-major ordering generally preferred?
11. Why is column-major ordering easier for graphical programs?
12. Explain the syntax of the first line of the main method, word by word.

■ Exercises ■

Applying the Facts

1. Write a Java statement declaring an array of 70 integers, to hold all the final grades for a class.

2. Write a Java statement declaring a two-dimensional array that holds ten columns of 70 integers, to hold all the class grades for an entire semester.

3. Write a Java method that takes a one-dimensional array of `ints` as a parameter and returns the sum of all the elements in the array.

4. Write a Java method that takes a one-dimensional array of `ints` as a parameter and returns the average of all the elements in the array.

5. Write a Java method that takes a one-dimensional array of `Shapes` as a parameter and returns `true` if the shapes are sorted from left to right (i.e., if the *x* value of the location of each `Shape` is less than or equal to the *x* value of the location of the next `Shape`).

6. Write a Java method that takes a one-dimensional array of `Shapes` as a parameter and returns `true` if all the `Shapes` in the array are blue.

7. Write a Java method that takes a two-dimensional array of `Squares` as a parameter and returns `true` if there's a row in which all the `Squares` are green.

8. Write a Java method that takes a two-dimensional array of `Squares` as a parameter and returns `true` if there's a column in which all the `Squares` are green.

9. Write a Java method that takes a two-dimensional array of `Squares` as a parameter and returns `true` if there's a diagonal in which all the `Squares` are green.

10. Write a Java method that takes a two-dimensional array of `Squares` as a parameter and returns `true` if there's a row, column, or diagonal in which all the `Squares` are yellow.

11. Write a Java method that takes a two-dimensional array of `ints` in which there are the same number of rows and columns, and returns `true` if all of the rows, columns, and diagonals add up to the same number. For example, in the array

    $$
    \begin{array}{ccc}
    8 & 1 & 6 \\
    3 & 5 & 7 \\
    4 & 9 & 2
    \end{array}
    $$

    each of the rows, columns, and diagonals adds up to 15. (Such an array is called a "magic square.")

Debugging Programs

Identify the errors, if any, in each of the following code fragments. Explain your answers.

1. To compute the product of all the numbers in an array `numList`:

    a. ```
        int total = 1;
        for (int j = 1; j < numList.length; j++)
            total = total*j;
        return total;
        ```

    b.  ```
        int total = 1;
        for (int j = 0; j < numList.length-1; j++)
            total = total*j;
        return total;
        ```

    c. ```
        int total = 0;
        for (int j = 0; j < numList.length-1; j++)
            total = total*j;
        return total;
        ```

2.  To find a number *n* in the array `numList`:

    a.  ```
        boolean found = false;
        for (int j = 1; j < array.length; j++) {
            if (equal(results[j], desiredNumber))
                found = true;
        return found;
        ```

    b. ```
        boolean found = true;
        for (int j = 0; j < array.length-1; j++) {
                if (equal(results[j], desiredNumber))
                    found = false;
        return found;
        ```

## ■ Programming Projects ■

### Modifying Programs

1.  Modify `ClickApp` to add a control panel with buttons that let the user choose the color the squares will have when they're clicked on. (*Hint*: use a Holder to contain the current color.)

2.  Modify the program developed in question 1 so that there is a grid of tiny circles to be clicked on, instead of squares (similar to the toy LiteBrite™).

3.  Modify `ClickApp` so that instead of changing color, the squares display an image of an X or an O.

4.  Modify the program from question 3 to create a TicTacToe program.
        ```

Writing Programs

1. Fair and loaded dice. (Thanks to Ed McDowell for this idea.)

    a. Write a program that displays a picture of a die in a window, like this:

    b. Underneath the die there should be a button labeled "Roll." Each time the "Roll" button is pushed, a random-number generator should determine which face of the die is displayed next.

    c. As the die is rolled, keep a running total in an array of how often each face of the die comes up: so many 1s, so many 2s, etc. Display these totals in the window next to the die.

    d. If the die is fair and the user rolls it often enough, the totals for each face should be approximately the same. Are they? How many times do you think you should roll the die before you reach a conclusion?

2. Modify the program from question 1 so that every time the button is pushed, the die is rolled a thousand times, not just one, and the totals are posted only at the end of each thousand rolls. Compile, test, and run your program. Now do you think the die is fair? Why or why not?

chapter **14**

Introduction to Data Structures

OBJECTIVES

After reading this chapter, you should be able to:

- ☑ Define the term "abstract datatype" (ADT)
- ☑ List the operations associated with the ADT's stack, queue, list, and dictionary
- ☑ Implement a stack, a queue, a list, and a dictionary in Java
- ☑ Use implementations of stack, queue, list, and dictionary appropriately to solve simple programming problems

■ 14.1 ■ Introduction

Suppose you're rushing to class one morning. You go out to get in your car and realize that it has been parked in. You and your roommates have a long driveway. Since you got home first last night, you were the first one in the driveway, and there are cars parked behind you. You now need to wake up your roommates and ask them to move their cars. Moreover, they have to move their cars in a specific order: the last one to get home last night must back out of the driveway first.

We can model this situation using a structure known as a **stack**. When items are added to a stack, just as when cars are parked in the driveway, they are added in the order in which they arrive, and the last one added is the first one removed. Stacks are useful for modeling many things: the pile of papers on your desk, the pile of cards you draw from in a card game, the trays in the dining hall, and the order in which employees are laid off when a strict seniority rule is followed.

You have used software implementations of stacks already. The "back" button on your Web browser takes you back to the place you visited most recently. The "undo" option in your word processor undoes the most recent change. Both of these maintain a list of items (sites visited, changes made) and need to see the last item added to the list first, so they are naturally implemented using a stack.

Stacks can be—and have been—implemented in many different ways, but we don't need to know anything about the implementation to say that modeling a particular situation calls for a stack or that a piece of software is implemented using a stack. All we need to know is that there's a list of objects that we can add to or remove from, and when we remove an item from the list, we can only remove the one that was added most recently.

keyconcept

An abstract datatype (ADT) is a language-independent specification of a collection of data and operations on that collection to store, retrieve and manipulate the data.

In computer science, an abstract, language-independent specification of a collection of data and operations on that collection to store, retrieve, and manipulate the data is known as an **abstract datatype (ADT)**. The notion of an ADT transcends particular programming languages or even language types, and ADTs can be implemented in both object-oriented and procedural programming languages. ADTs such as stacks, queues, dictionaries, and trees are important throughout computer science—they are covered in detail in data structures courses and you will encounter them in most of the other courses you take, including (for example) programming language design, operating systems, and database systems.

What we provide in this book is just a brief introduction to this important topic. Here we introduce four of the most common ADTs, stack, queue, list, and dictionary, and show how to define and implement them in Java.

Note: Many languages provide built-in implementations of some ADTs. Java, for example, provides implementations of Stacks, among others, and provides a set of interfaces and classes, called the **Java Collections Framework**, to make it easier for you to implement additional ADTs for yourself. Once you understand how ADTs work, you'll find it relatively easy to learn to use Java's (or another language's) implementations.

■ 14.2 ■ **Concepts**

Since ADTs consist of a name and a list of operations, which ADT we choose depends on the operations we need. Consider the following problems:

1. (The example given above) We want to model a driveway where cars are parked, one behind the next.

2. We want to model a line of cars waiting at a tollbooth. Cars join the line at one end (the back) and leave from the other (the front).

3. We want to model one of the lanes of traffic in a four-lane highway. Cars can enter or leave the lane at any point by shifting to an adjacent lane.

4. We want to model the Registry of Motor Vehicles, which maintains a collection of information about drivers' licenses and regularly checks each license to see if it needs to be renewed.

5. We want to model a garage that has a collection of information about the cars on which it has worked. When you take your car in for repairs, the garage needs to locate information about your car.

ADTs are implemented in a programming language by concrete data structures. A **data structure** is a collection of elements organized in some way, like an array, a `Vector`, or an `ArrayList`. The elements can belong to any arbitrary class, such as `Car` or `Spiral`.

14.2.1 Stacks

For the first problem, we need to be able to add and delete elements (since cars come and go in the driveway), and for our model to be accurate, we need to make sure that the last car to arrive is the first one to leave. The ADT stack provides just the operations we need: insert an element and delete the element that was most recently added. These operations are traditionally known as `push` and `pop`, respectively. Stacks also provide an operation `isEmpty` that lets us determine whether there are any elements, and some stacks provide an operation `peek` that lets us look at the top element without removing it.

Stacks are useful for modeling situations like the one in the first problem, where the last element to be added is the first one to be removed. This problem is illustrated in Figure 14.1. For this reason, implementations of the ADT stack are also known as **last-in-first-out (LIFO) data structures**.

One of the most common applications of a stack is the execution stack. When a program is executed, Java creates an **activation record** for each method each time it is called. This record contains important information about the method, including the values of its local variables and parameters. Programming languages use an implementation of a

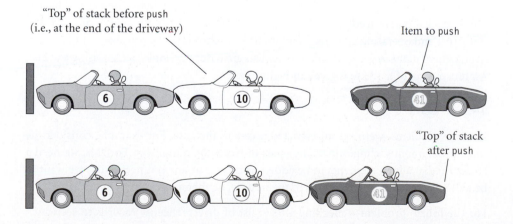

Figure 14.1 ■ Car being pushed onto a stack in the driveway.

stack called the **execution stack** to track the activation records. When a method calls another method, Java adds the activation record of the new method to the stack. When the new method is finished, its activation record is removed from the stack and the program continues with the previous method. This explains why the values of local variables and parameters are lost when a method is done executing: the activation record containing those values has been popped off the execution stack.

14.2.2 Queues

The other four examples illustrate common types of problems for which stacks are a bad solution. Take the second problem: to model cars waiting in line at a tollbooth, we need to be able to add cars at the end of the line, remove cars from the front of the line, and prevent them from being added or deleted anywhere else. If we use a stack to solve this problem, new cars will always join the line at the front instead of the back! We need some structure that models an orderly line, where elements are added only at the end.

> **keyconcept**
>
> A queue is a first-in-first-out ADT: elements are added at the end of the list and the first one added is deleted first. Operations include enqueue, de queue, and isEmpty.

The ADT that provides exactly the operations we need for the second problem is called a **queue**. The queue operations are traditionally called `enqueue`, `dequeue`, and `isEmpty`. `Enqueue` adds an element at the end of the line; `dequeue` removes an element from the front of the line; and `isEmpty`, like the stack operation, tests to determine whether the queue has any elements.

Queues are useful for modeling many things: the line of customers waiting to be checked out in a store, the line of cars at a drive-through bank, and the list of movies requested from an online service. In each case, the first item in is the first one out. For this reason, implementations of the ADT queue are also known as **first-in-first-out (FIFO) data structures**.

You have used software queues already. Java uses a queue to manage the events (such as mouse clicks) that it needs to handle. Operating systems maintain queues of processes. Both Java and operating systems maintain lists of items (events, processes) and need to handle them in the order received, so these lists are naturally implemented using a queue. An illustration of a queue is given in Figure 14.2.

14.2.3 Lists

In some problems, we need unrestricted access to the data. For example, consider the third problem: modeling one of the lanes of traffic on a highway. For this, we need a structure that allows elements to be added or deleted at any point. Because we want to be able to add and delete elements in the middle, neither a stack nor a queue will work.

For the fourth problem—checking a fixed list of drivers' license records to see which licenses need to be renewed—stacks and queues are again too limited. To solve this

Figure 14.2 ■ Cars joining a queue (i.e., being enqueued).

problem, we don't need to be able to insert or delete anything, but we do need to be able to access all of the elements, one after another. (And if we want our model to be useful for very long, we'll have to be able to insert and delete elements as well.)

We can solve both of these problems using an ADT called a **list**. Lists are more general than stacks or queues. Lists, stacks, and queues are all linear, but lists allow us to add, delete, or access elements at any point. We can think of stacks and queues as special cases of lists that limit us to inserting, deleting, and accessing elements in a particular place. The place where an element is located is called its **position** in the list. Each element in a list has a position. To insert an element, we simply give the position that it should go in. (Inserting or deleting an element naturally affects the positions of all the elements that follow it in the list.)

The third and fourth problems illustrate two general types of problem for which the ADT list is useful:

keyconcept
A list is an ADT that supports unrestricted inserts, deletes, and access to elements at any location in the collection.

1. simple list-processing problems, where we need to be able to go through a fixed sequence of items one by one and perform some task using values from each element of the list

2. random-access problems, where we need to be able to access, insert, or delete individual elements at any location within a sequence

Other examples of simple list-processing problems include: going through a list of student records and computing each student's average; going through a list of rectangles and displaying each rectangle in a window; and going through a list of library books and making a list of all the books that are overdue. Lists can be implemented using arrays, `Vectors`, and `ArrayLists`.

Simple list-processing and random-access problems can be solved with stacks or queues, but the solutions are quite awkward. The key fact about stacks and queues is that they restrict access to their contents. When we want unrestricted access, that is, when we want to be able to work with any—or all—of the items, the ADT list is a better choice.

14.2.4 **Dictionaries**

To solve our fifth problem, searching for information about a particular car that needs to be repaired, we need to find a particular element that may be anywhere in the collection. At first glance, this problem seems like a candidate for the ADT list. A list would work, but it would be slow: there is no guarantee that the information in a list is in any particular order, so we just have to check each element until we find the right one. Imagine trying to look up a name in the phone book if the names were in a completely random order!

The ADT dictionary is designed for this type of problem. In dictionaries, unlike stacks, queues, and lists, each element has a value called a **key** that is used to identify that element. For example, when you look someone up in your address book, you probably look him or her up by name. The key value in the address book is the person's name; the element is the entire entry, including name, address, phone number, etc. The key value doesn't have to be something that's actually stored in the element, however; it can be computed when needed. For example, if we want to store graphical shapes sorted by their area, it suffices for each graphical shape to have a `computeArea` method.

> **keyconcept**
>
> A dictionary is an ADT in which the elements are sorted according to a particular key value they contain. Operations include insert, delete, and search.

Unlike the elements of a list, the elements of a dictionary are in order, sorted according to the value of their keys: largest to smallest, coldest to warmest, most boring to most fun, anything as long as we can tell where each element belongs (see, e.g., Figure 14.3). When each new element is added, the location where it is placed depends on its key. Because the elements of a dictionary are sorted, it is much easier to find them, just as the phone book's alphabetical order makes it easier to look up names.

Don't be misled by the name "dictionary": the information associated with the key doesn't have to be a definition. In fact, it can be anything. In our car-repair example, the key could be the make and model of a car, and the information might be anything related to that type of car. Another typical example of a dictionary is an online address book: when you look up someone's name, you find his or her address, telephone number, and perhaps email address.

14.2.5 **Implementing ADTs with linked lists**

To implement an ADT, we need a concrete data structure. You have probably noticed the similarity between the list ADT and the arrays, `Vectors`, and `ArrayLists` discussed in the previous chapter. The list ADT—and the other ADTs discussed in this chapter—can all be implemented with `Vectors`, `ArrayLists`, or (with a bit more effort) arrays.

Another popular solution is to create a node for each element and link them together into a longer sequence, like a daisy chain. Each node contains one element and a reference to the next node. These sequences of linked nodes are known as **linked lists**. We use linked lists for each of the implementations in this chapter. For details of implementations using arrays, `ArrayLists`, or `Vectors`, see a data structures text.

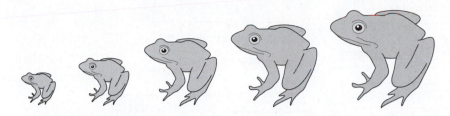

Figure 14.3 ■ A sorted list.

14.2.6 **Instance diagrams**

There is a piece of the UML language that is particularly useful in describing data structures: the instance diagram. By now, you're familiar with class diagrams and how they show the relationships among classes. **Instance diagrams**, also called **object diagrams**, show the important properties of specific instances and how the instances relate to one another. These diagrams let you take a snapshot of the object instances in your program at a particular moment during its execution. In other words, they show the state of the program at that moment.

Instance diagrams look exactly like class diagrams except:

- The top third of the box, instead of the <className>, has <instance name: class Name>. The instance name is optional. If the instance name is missing, the notation is <:className>.

- The second third of the box, instead of <variable name>: <type name>, has <variable name> = <value>.

- The bottom third of the box, for methods, is omitted (since all instances have the same methods).

Instances have values for each of the properties of their class, and the main distinction between a class diagram and an instance diagram is that these property values are shown. In addition, methods are omitted from instance diagrams, since they are the same for all instances of a class. The same rectangles are used for the boxes in instance diagrams and in class diagrams, and the same arrows are used to connect an instance with its parts, its superclass, and its associated peer instances.

Consider the instance diagram given in Figure 14.4. It shows two cars, one red with a four-cylinder engine and one blue with a six-cylinder engine. Both cars are located in the same city, Providence.

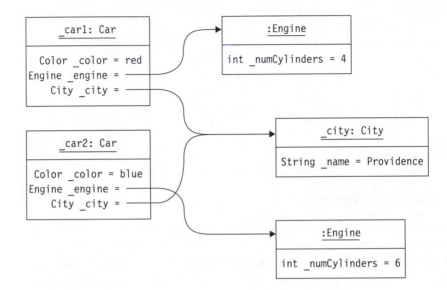

Figure 14.4 ■ An instance diagram for a red car and a blue car.

Note that the values of attributes are included in the instance box for a particular instance, while the values of components and peer objects are given their own instance boxes. Two instances of the same class, such as the two instances of `Car` shown here, have the same instance variables (in this case, `_color`, `_engine`, and `_city`). They may or may not have the same values for these properties. Here, the two instances of `Car` have two different values for `_color`. Naturally, each `Car` has its own `Engine`. On the other hand, they are located in the same `City`.

Contrast this instance diagram shown in Figure 14.4 with the class diagram for the same classes given in Figure 14.5. The class diagram has one box for `Engine` instead of two, and one box for `Car`. It does not include the values of the instance variables, but it includes the signatures of the methods associated with each class. Class diagrams are good for showing the overall structure of a program; instance diagrams show the state of a program at a particular moment in time during the program's execution.

■ 14.3 ■ **Mechanics**

In this section, we give straightforward, traditional implementations of stacks, queues, and dictionaries using linked lists.

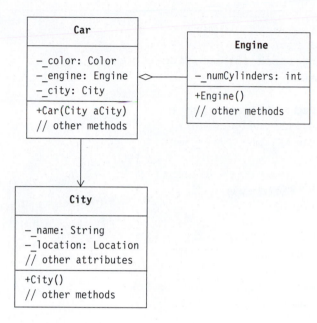

Figure 14.5 ■ A class diagram for the class Car.

14.3.1 **The Node class**

All the data-structure implementations in this chapter use the same simple definition of a Node (shown in Listing 14.1).

This Node class is basically a holder for two instance variables: a reference to an element and a reference to the next node in the sequence. The elements in the data structure can belong to any class. An element may model a car, or a graphical shape, or an entry in an address book, for example. The Node has accessors for both instance variables and a mutator for the _next variable. No mutator is provided for the _element variable, because the contents of a Node never change after the Node is created.

The only new feature in this syntax is the angle brackets, which are similar to the syntax for Vectors. That's because both this Node class and Java's built-in Vector class

are examples of Java's **generics**, new in Java 1.5. By using generics, we can say, "This is how a Node works—these are its properties and capabilities, whatever it holds. You tell me what type of element you want to put in it." Later on, when some client code uses our Node implementation, it can say what goes in the Node the same way we did for Vectors. For example, if it wants a Node that contains a Spiral, it could say,

```
private Node<Spiral> _node;
```

```
1    /**
2     * Chapter 14: Node.java
3     * The building block for our Stacks, Queues, and
4     * Dictionaries.
5     */
6    public class Node <ElementType> {
7        private ElementType _element;
8        private Node <ElementType>_next;
9
10       public Node(ElementType element) {
11           _element = element;
12           _next = null;
13       }
14       public ElementType getElement() {
15           return _element;
16       }
17       public Node <ElementType>getNext (){
18           return _next;
19       }
20       public void setNext (Node <ElementType>aNode){
21           _next = aNode;
22       }
23   }
```

Listing 14.1 ■ The Node class

What this definition says is that if the user declares, say, a Node<Spiral>:

■ This Node will contain a Spiral

■ The next Node is a Node<Spiral> like this one

■ The constructor must be given a Spiral as a parameter

■ The getElement method returns a Spiral

■ The getNext method returns a Node<Spiral> like this one

■ The setNext method takes a Node<Spiral> like this one as a parameter

In other words, when you declare a Node<Spiral>, "Spiral" is substituted for "ElementType" throughout the definition. We could declare a Node<Snowman>, or a Node<SpaceAlien>, or any other kind of Node using this same definition. In fact, Java's generics give us the opportunity to be appropriately lazy in a new way. One single class definition works for many different types of object.

In earlier versions of Java, we would have had to either write a separate implementation of `Node`s for each type of object we wanted to store, or write a version of `Node` that holds an `Object`. Neither of these solutions is satisfactory. A `Node` that holds `Object`s is easy to add to—it can hold anything—but the compiler can't check whether the right things are being put in it, or whether the contents of the `Node` are being used correctly. We would have to add code to make these checks, or simply trust that the client code would use the `Node` correctly (not a good idea). If we wrote a separate implementation of `Node` for each type of object, the compiler would be able to do these checks for us, but we would have to write a lot more code, much of it redundant. Generics make possible a much more elegant solution.

14.3.2 A `StackADT` interface

To define our ADTs precisely, we use an interface to specify the necessary operations. For example, the interface for stacks is shown in listing 14.2.

This says exactly what we want, that any implementation of the ADT stack must provide these three operations.

14.3.3 The `Stack` class

The `Node` class is simple, because all the work of implementing the required `Stack` methods is done in the `Stack` class. Nevertheless, even `Stack` is not very long, as shown in Listing 14.3.

When a new `Stack` is created, the `_top` is `null`. When the first element is `pushed`, a `Node` is created to hold it and the `_top` is assigned that new `Node`. When the next element of the `Stack` is `pushed`, again a new `Node` is created to hold it and to become the top of the stack. This newest `Node` must now point to the `Node` that was pushed before it, and `_top` is reset to point to the new `Node`.

```
1    /**
2     * Chapter 14: StackADT.java
3     * The interface for our implementation of Stacks.
4     */
5    public interface StackADT <ElementType>{
6        public void push (ElementType aType);
7        public ElementType pop();
8        public boolean isEmpty();
9    }
```

Listing 14.2 ■ The `StackADT` interface

```
1    /**
2     * Chapter 14: Stack.java
3     * A linked-list implementation of a Stack.
4     */
5    public class Stack <ElementType>
6        implements StackADT <ElementType>{
7            private Node <ElementType> _top;
8
9            public Stack () {
10               _top = null;
11           }
12           public void push (ElementType element) {
13               Node <ElementType> nodeToAdd =
14                   new Node <ElementType>(element);
15               nodeToAdd.setNext(_top);
16               _top = nodeToAdd;
17           }
18           public ElementType pop () {
19               if (this.isEmpty())
20                   return null;
21               else {
22                   ElementType topElement = _top.getElement();
23                   _top = _top.getNext();
24                   return topElement;
25               }
26           }
27           public boolean isEmpty() {
28               return (_top == null);
29           }
30    }
```

Listing 14.3 ■ The Stack class

The diagram in Figure 14.6 shows a sequence of Stacks (reading from left to right): first, an empty Stack, then a Stack after the first element has been pushed, and then a Stack after two elements have been pushed. Note that each new Node is added on top of the older ones in the Stack.

When an element is popped off the Stack the whole process is reversed: the top Node is removed, _top is changed so that the second Node becomes the _top, and then the element from the former _top Node is returned. The test for whether a Stack is empty

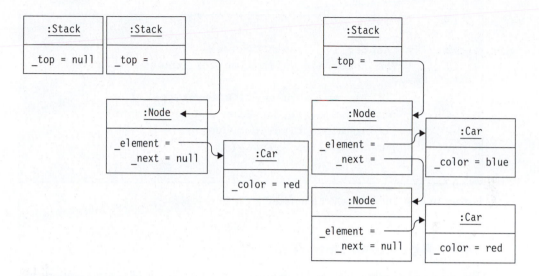

Figure 14.6 ■ Pushing `Nodes` onto a `Stack` (or, reading from right to left, popping them off).

is simply whether `_top` is `null`. `Pop` is the opposite of `push`, so you can see this process simply by reading Figure 14.6 in the opposite direction, from right to left.

When we create a `Stack`, we fill in the type of element we want it to hold. For example, we can declare a `Stack` of `SmartEllipses` like this:

```
Stack<SmartEllipse> _ellipseStack;
```

Java substitutes `SmartEllipse` for `ElementType` everywhere in the `Stack` definition. The instance variable `_top`, for example, becomes a `Node<SmartEllipse>`, and `SmartEllipse` is then substituted for `ElementType` in the `Node` definition as well. Anything that is pushed on `_ellipseStack` has to be a `SmartEllipse`; when something is popped off the `_ellipseStack`, that too has to be a `SmartEllipse`. All these things are checked by the Java compiler.

The `isEmpty` method raises a design question: what should happen if client code tries to `pop` a `Node` from an empty stack? Here, the `isEmpty` method simply returns `null`. Alternatively, we could return an error message. Our solution leaves the client code free to handle the situation in its own way; returning an error message ensures that the client code cannot inadvertently ignore the situation. Both solutions have their advantages. In Chapter 18, we will see a third solution, using exceptions.

```
1    /**
2     * Chapter 14: QueueADT.java
3     * The interface definition for Queues.
4     */
5    public interface QueueADT<ElementType> {
6        public void enqueue(ElementType element);
7        public ElementType dequeue ();
8        public boolean isEmpty();
9    }
```

Listing 14.4 ■ The QueueADT interface

14.3.4 A QueueADT interface

For queues, like stacks, all we need is an interface that specifies the required operations and a single class implementing the interface. The QueueADT interface is shown in Listing 14.4.

14.3.5 The Queue class

Like the Stack class, the Queue class (shown in Listing 14.5) is quite simple.

The Queue has two instance variables, one referring to the _head of the Queue (so we know where to remove Nodes) and one referring to the _tail (so we know where to add them). When a new Queue is created, its _head and _tail are null. This is true for all empty Queues; in fact, all we need to do is to check to see if the _head Node is empty, and that's what the isEmpty method does.

When the first Node is enqueued, a Node is created to hold it and the _head and _tail of the Queue are both set to point to it. Later, when a new element is added to a non-empty Queue, a new Node is created to hold it. The _tail Node is modified so that its _next variable points to the new Node, and the Queue's _tail variable is modified to refer to the new Node that has been added at the end of the Queue. Figure 14.7 is an instance diagram illustrating Nodes being added to a Queue.

When an attempt is made to remove a Node from an empty Queue, dequeue returns null. Otherwise the data of the first Node in the Queue is returned, and the _head variable is reset to point to the second Node. Figure 14.8 illustrates Nodes being removed from a Queue. The Node that is removed is always the Node at the head of the Queue (unlike Stacks).

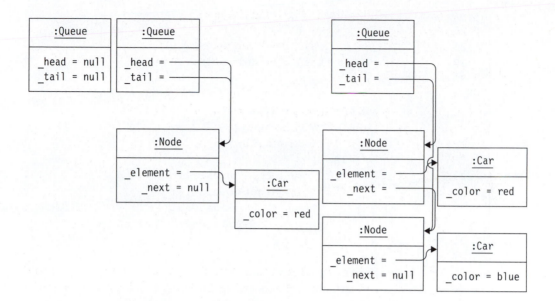

Figure 14.7 ■ From left to right: an empty `Queue` and the same `Queue` after enqueuing first one `Node` and then a second `Node`.

```
1    /**
2     * Chapter 14: Queue.java
3     * A linked-list implementation of Queues.
4     */
5    public class Queue<ElementType>
6        implements QueueADT<ElementType>{
7            private Node <ElementType> _head;
8            private Node <ElementType> _tail;
9
10           public Queue () {
11               _head = null;
12               _tail = null;
13           }
14           public void enqueue (ElementType element) {
15               Node<ElementType> nodeToAdd =
16                   new Node<ElementType> (element);
17               if (this.isEmpty()) {
18                   _head = nodeToAdd;
19                   _tail = nodeToAdd;
```

Listing 14.5 ■ The Queue class (*continued on next page*)

```
20              } else {
21                  _tail.setNext(nodeToAdd);
22                  _tail = nodeToAdd;
23              }
24          }
25          public ElementType dequeue () {
26              if (this.isEmpty())
27                  return null;
28              else {
29                  ElementType nodeToReturn =
30                      _head.getElement();
31                  _head = _head.getNext();
32                  return nodeToReturn;
33              }
34          }
35          public boolean isEmpty() {
36              return (_head == null);
37          }
38      }
```

Listing 14.5 ■ The Queue class

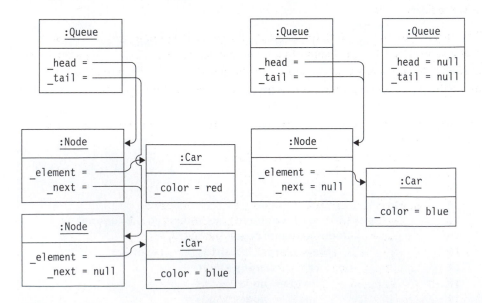

Figure 14.8 ■ From left to right: a Queue with two Nodes, then the same Queue with the head Node removed, and finally, the Queue with both Nodes removed (an empty Queue).

14.3.6 A `ListADT` interface

The operations we need in order to implement the list ADT include:

- Insert an element at a given position
- Delete an element (from anywhere in the list)
- Return the first element of the list
- Given an element, return the next element of the list
- Determine whether the list is empty

Listing 14.6 shows an interface specifying these operations.

14.3.7 Implementing `List` and the Iterator design pattern

All the operations we need are built into Java's `Vector` and `ArrayList` classes, except for the two methods for traversing the list. `Vector` has a `firstElement` method but not a next method; `ArrayList` has neither.

We could extend `Vector` and `ArrayList` and add the methods we need, but Java provides a better solution. Writing these two methods requires us to know something about the internal structure of a data structure and its other methods, which isn't ideal. We'd prefer a solution that lets us examine the elements of a list in order, independent of how the list is implemented.

The problem of examining all the elements of a collection of objects comes up so often that a solution to it is encoded in the design pattern Iterator: create a separate object called an Iterator that knows how to access the elements of a collection in order. Think of the Iterator as a tour guide: it shows us all the elements of the collection in order, but

```
 1    /**
 2     * Chapter 14: ListADT.java
 3     * An interface for Lists.
 4     */
 5    public interface ListADT<ElementType>{
 6        void add (int index, ElementType element);
 7        boolean remove (ElementType element);
 8        boolean isEmpty();
 9        ElementType firstElement();
10        ElementType next ();
11    }
```

Listing 14.6 ■ The ListADT interface

we don't need to worry about where to start, what order to visit the elements in, or how to get from one element to the next.

Java's `Vectors` and `ArrayLists` have a method `iterator` that returns an implementation of the Iterator design pattern:

```
Iterator<ElementType>iterator=
                    _vector.iterator();
```

The `iterator` method returns an `Iterator` that is specifically associated with this instance of `Vector`. Similarly, if we want an iterator for an `ArrayList`, we can say:

```
Iterator<ElementType>iterator=
                    _arrayList.iterator();
```

An `Iterator` object has two required methods: `hasNext`, which returns true if the list has another element; and `next`, which returns the next element in the list, an object of type `ElementType` (that is, whatever type we have stored in the `Vector`). Thus, to get the next element of `_vector`, we can now say

```
if (iterator.hasNext())
    return iterator.next();
else
    return null;
```

For the list implementation in this chapter, for simplicity, we write the `firstElement` and `next` methods specified in the interface. As you read through the discussion, consider how you might define an `iterator` method for our lists.

14.3.8 A `DictionaryADT` interface

As we did for stacks and queues, we now define an interface `DictionaryADT` specifying the required operations. We make it a generic interface, as we did for stacks and queues, so that each `Dictionary` contains a particular `ElementType`.

A first draft of the `DictionaryADT` interface is shown in Listing 14.7.

Just giving a parameter type for the `Elements` isn't enough; now we also need to specify a type for the keys somehow. Luckily, Java lets us list additional parameters between the angle brackets, separated by commas, just as we can have more than one ordinary parameter in a method's parameter list. Version 2 of the interface, shown in Listing 14.8, adds a type parameter for the keys.

This change doesn't quite solve all our problems, however. First, we need to say somehow that each element has to have a key—this interface says nothing about the relationship between elements and keys. And second, we need to say that it must be possible to compare the keys to one another.

```
1    /**
2     * Chapter 14: DictionaryADT.java
3     * Version 1, based on the ListADT interface
4     */
5    public interface DictionaryADT<ElementType> {
6       public void insert (ElementType element);
7       public void delete (_____ aKey);
8          //search returns null if element not found
9       public ElementType search (_____ aKey);
10      public boolean isEmpty();
11   }
```

Listing 14.7 ■ The `DictionaryADT` interface (version 1 of 5)

```
1    /**
2     * Chapter 14: DictionaryADT.java
3     * Version 2, adding a type for the keys
4     */
5    public interface DictionaryADT
6          <KeyType, ElementType>{
7       public void insert (ElementType element);
8       public void delete (KeyType aKey);
9          //search returns null if element not found
10      public ElementType search (KeyType aKey);
11      public boolean isEmpty();
12   }
```

Listing 14.8 ■ The `DictionaryADT` interface (version 2 of 5)

Consider what we want from the elements. We don't care if the key is stored in the element or if the element has some way of computing it. Basically, we want the element to have a `getKey` method. As long as there's an accessor method that returns the key, we don't care how.

Since we're implementing the `Dictionary` in Java, requiring that the element have certain capabilities means we need an interface. Since we only need one method, the interface (shown in Listing 14.9) is very simple.

All `KeyProviders` have to do is to implement an accessor method that returns keys of a particular type.

```
1    /**
2     * Chapter 14: KeyProvider.java
3     * The interface for elements of a Dictionary.
4     */
5    public interface KeyProvider<KeyType> {
6        public KeyType getKey();
7    }
```

Listing 14.9 ■ The KeyProvider interface

Let's revise the DictionaryADT again to incorporate this new restriction on the elements. The third version of our interface is shown in Listing 14.10.

The syntax

    E extends KeyProvider<K>

is Java's way of saying that whatever class we substitute for E when we create a dictionary must also implement the KeyProvider<K> interface. (Why the Java designers used extends here instead of implements is unclear, but they did.)

Because this code is getting quite long, we have chosen to use the short variable names K and E instead of KeyType and ElementType, adding a brief comment to explain what the variable names refer to. For the same reason, it is usually recommended that you use short variable names with generics. If you find the longer ones helpful, however, you may want to continue using them for now.

We also need to be able to place a restriction on the keys. Given two keys, we need to be able to say whether they're equal, or if not, which one is greater than the other. Fortunately, Java has a built-in Comparable interface that requires just that.

Using Java's Comparable interface, we can revise our DictionaryADT interface as shown in Listing 14.11.

What this revised interface now gives us is a guarantee that it will be possible to say whether any two keys are equal, and if not, which one is "greater" than the other—as long as they define "greater" the same way.

What if two keys define "greater" differently? What will happen if we have two elements of a Dictionary whose keys are Comparable, but one thinks "greater" means "flies higher" and the other thinks "greater" means "swims better" (see Figure 14.9)? Then whichever object we ask, it will say that it's greater than the other one:

    _frog.isGreaterThan(_stork);

```
1    /**
2     * Chapter 14: DictionaryADT (version 3)
3     * Adds requirement that elements have keys.
4     */
5
6    public interface DictionaryADT
7       <K, E extends KeyProvider<K>> {
8       // K is class for keys, E is class for elements
9       public void insert (E element);
10      public void delete (K aKey);
11      //search returns null if element not found
12      public E search (K aKey);
13      public boolean isEmpty();
14   }
```

Listing 14.10 ■ The `DictionaryADT` interface (version 3 of 5)

```
1    /**
2     * Chapter 14: DictionaryADT (version 4)
3     * Adds requirement that keys be comparable.
4     */
5
6    public interface DictionaryADT
7          <K extends Comparable,
8           E extends KeyProvider<K>> {
9       // K is class for keys, E is class for elements
10      public void insert (E element);
11      public void delete (K aKey);
12      //search returns null if element not found
13      public E search (K aKey);
14      public boolean isEmpty();
15   }
```

Listing 14.11 ■ `DictionaryADT` interface (version 4 of 5)

and

     `_stork.isGreaterThan(_frog);`

will both return true.

Figure 14.9 ■ Comparing apples and oranges.

That can't be right. Our interface doesn't quite work yet. Somehow we want to be able to say that each key can be compared—not with objects in general, but with other objects of the same type. In terms of generics, we want our keys to be `Comparable<K>`, not just `Comparable`. We need the interface itself to be generic. Fortunately, in Java 1.5, the `Comparable` interface now is generic, so we revise our `DictionaryADT` interface one last time, as shown in Listing 14.12.

This interface now says that a `DictionaryADT` is a class with `insert`, `delete`, `search`, and `isEmpty` methods, where each element has a key of a given type, and the keys can be compared with each other.

14.3.9 **The `Dictionary` class**

Besides the ADT interface, as usual, we define a class that implements the interface. We start by writing a basic framework for this class using the `DictionaryADT` interface, as shown in Listing 14.13.

We have provided an instance variable, `_first`, for the first `Node` in the list, and filled in the details for the two simplest methods. The constructor creates an empty `Dictionary` with `_first` equal to `null`. The `isEmpty` method simply checks to see if `_first is null`.

The `insert`, `delete`, and `search` methods are very similar to one another. Each method starts by calling a related method that keeps track of which `Node` it's considering. For example, consider the `search` method, shown in Listing 14.14.

```
1    /**
2     * Chapter 14: DictionaryADT.java
3     * Adds requirement that keys be comparable to each
4     * other.
5     */
6
7    public interface DictionaryADT
8            <K extends Comparable<K>,
9             E extends KeyProvider<K>> {
10        // K is class for keys, E is class for elements
11        public void insert (E element);
12        public void delete (K aKey);
13        //search returns null if element not found
14        public E search (K aKey);
15        public boolean isEmpty();
16    }
```

Listing 14.12 ■ DictionaryADT interface (version 5 of 5)

This method says, "If you want to find a key value in a list, start looking for it in the first Node of the list. If you find a Node that contains an element with the right key value, extract the element and return it."

The insert, delete, and search methods each have a helper method. The helper methods, searchAux, insertAux, and deleteAux, each start with the _first Node and consider the rest of the Nodes in the Dictionary one by one until they reach the right place—the place to add a new Node, or the Node to be deleted, or the Node being searched for. Each of these methods calls itself. This is a very natural use of recursion: if you can't find something in one Node, try again in the next one. (See Figure 14.10).

First consider the searchAux method, shown in Listing 14.15.

To understand how this works, it is necessary to understand the compareTo method, which is the method required by Java's Comparable interface. Each type of key will define compareTo in its own way, but the basic signature is the same for all of them, and it's not exactly what we might want. Instead of something like this:

```
public interface Comparable <T> {
    public boolean equals (T item);
    public boolean isGreaterThan (T item);
    public boolean isLessThan (T item);
}
```

```
1    /**
2     * Chapter 14: the Dictionary class
3     * A linked-list implementation of dictionaries.
4     */
5    public class Dictionary
6        <K extends Comparable<K>, E extends KeyProvider<K>>
7        implements DictionaryADT<K,E> {
8        // K is class for keys, E is class for elements
9        private Node<E> _first;
10
11       public Dictionary () {
12           _first = null;
13       }
14
15       public void insert (E element) {
16           // discussed below
17       }
18
19       public E search (K key) {
20           // discussed below
21       }
22
23       public void delete (K key) {
24           // discussed below
25       }
26
27       public boolean isEmpty() {
28           return (_first == null);
29       }
30   }
```

Listing 14.13 ■ The Dictionary class

```
1    public E search (K key) {
2        Node<E> resultNode = this.searchAux(key, _first);
3        if (resultNode == null)
4            return null;
5        else
6            return resultNode.getElement();
7    }
```

Listing 14.14 ■ The Dictionary class's search method

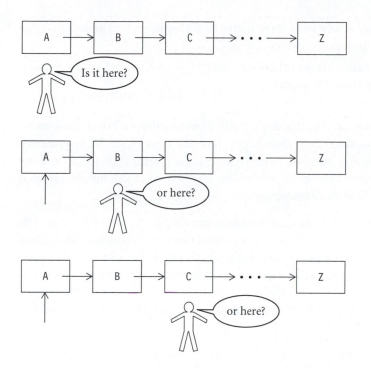

Figure 14.10 ■ Checking each node, one at a time.

```
1    private Node<E> searchAux (K keyToFind,
2                               Node<E> currNode) {
3       if (currNode == null) return null;
4       else {
5          K currKey = currNode.getElement().getKey();
6          int comparison = keyToFind.compareTo(currKey);
7          if (comparison > 0) // keyToFind > currKey
8             return null;
9          else if (comparison == 0) // the keys are equal
10            return currNode;
11         else // keep looking
12            return this.searchAux(keyToFind,
13                                  currNode.getNext());
14      }
15   }
```

Listing 14.15 ■ The `Dictionary` class's `searchAux` method

where the methods say clearly what we're testing and give us back an answer of `true` or `false`, Java gives us this:

```
public interface Comparable <T> {
    int compareTo (T item);
}
```

According to the documentation, this single method can take the place of all three methods in the previous version of the interface: to indicate `lessThan`, the `compareTo` method returns a negative number; to indicate `equals`, it returns 0; and to indicate `greaterThan`, it returns a positive number. This is very economical, but the previous solution would have been more readable.

`Why do we use the Comparable` interface, you might ask, if it makes our code harder to read? Because some of the data types we most often use as keys, such as `String`, already implement Java's `Comparable` interface. If we defined our own interface, we would also have to define classes to implement that interface, for example, by extending the `String` class. It's appropriately lazy to use the `Comparable` interface and the classes that already implement it. We compensate for the lack of readability by adding comments to our code, as shown.

`Delete` follows the same pattern. First, call a second method that takes two parameters, the element we want to delete and the `_first Node`, the beginning of the list (see Listing 14.16).

The second method, called `deleteAux` and shown in Listing 14.17, again considers four possibilities:

1. Is the current node `null`? If so, we're done.

2. If not, is its value greater than the one we're looking for? If so, the element we need to delete isn't there, and we're done.

3. If not, is its value equal to the value we're looking for? If so, we've found it, and we're done.

4. Otherwise, keep looking.

If the current `Node` is `null`, or if the element stored in the current `Node` is greater than the one we're looking for, then we didn't find what we were looking for and we're done.

```
1    public void delete (K key) {
2        _first = this.deleteAux(key, _first);
3    }
```

Listing 14.16 ■ The `Dictionary`'s `delete` method

```
1    private Node<E> deleteAux (K keyToDelete, Node<E> currNode) {
2        if (currNode == null) {
3            return null;
4        }
5        else {
6            K currKey = currNode.getElement().getKey();
7            int comparison = keyToDelete.compareTo(currKey);
8            if (comparison > 0) // keyToDelete > currKey,
9                return currNode;//should have been found already
10           else if (comparison == 0) // the keys are equal
11               return currNode.getNext();
12           else { // current element too small, not there yet
13               currNode.setNext(this.deleteAux (keyToDelete,
14                                           currNode.getNext()));
15               return currNode;
16           }
17       }
18   }
```

Listing 14.17 ■ The Dictionary's deleteAux method

If the value of the current Node is equal to the value we're looking for, we found it, and we make the changes needed to remove the Node from the list. And finally, if we haven't found it, we keep going. (See Figure 14.11.)

The code for the two delete methods is very similar to the code for search and searchAux—after all, we have to search for the right Node to delete. But there's one difference. The client code calling search wants to retrieve an element, so we return an element. The client code calling delete doesn't need any value returned, but the internal structure of the list may be modified if a Node is deleted. Because we're modifying the structure of the list, each Node needs to know if it should still be connected to the one that follows it, so deleteAux returns a Node.

```
1    public void insert (E element) {
2        _first = this.insertAux(new Node<E>(element),
3                                _first);
4    }
```

Listing 14.18 ■ The Dictionary's insert method

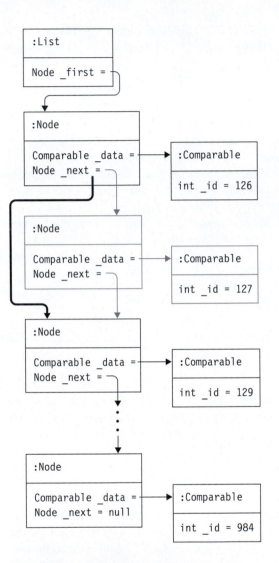

Figure 14.11 ■ Deleting a Node from a List.

The insert method is similar to delete and search, except that it takes an element and creates a new Node to hold it (see Listing 14.18).

The method says, "If you want to insert a new element, create a node to contain it, and then look at the first Node to see if that's the right place to insert it."

If this were a `Stack` or an unsorted list, we could simply put the new Node in the front of the list. Instead, `insertAux` looks at each `Node` until it finds the right place to put the new one (see Listing 14.19).

Here's the basic idea: we want to put the new `Node` right before the first `Node` we find whose value is *greater* than the new `Node`'s value. (See Figure 14.12.) There are four possibilities:

1. The current `Node` is `null`. This means we have reached the end of the dictionary without finding any `Nodes` whose key values are greater than the key value of the current `Node`—so the new `Node` belongs at the end of the dictionary.

2. The key value of the element contained in the new `Node` is greater than the key value of the current `Node`'s element. In this case, we keep on looking.

3. The key value of the element contained in the new `Node` is equal to the key value of the current `Node`'s element. In this case, we do nothing—we don't want to have elements with duplicate keys stored in the list.

```
 1   private Node<E> insertAux(Node<E> nodeToAdd,Node<E> currNode){
 2       if (currNode == null) {
 3           return nodeToAdd;
 4       }
 5       else {
 6           K currKey = currNode.getElement().getKey();
 7           K keyToAdd = nodeToAdd.getElement().getKey();
 8           int comparison = keyToAdd.compareTo(currKey);
 9           if (comparison > 0) { // found the spot, add it in
10               nodeToAdd.setNext(currNode);
11               return nodeToAdd;
12           }
13           else if (comparison == 0) { // keys are equal
14               return currNode;
15           } // just quit, don't insert duplicate
16           else { // currKey is less, so keep looking
17               currNode.setNext(this.insertAux(nodeToAdd,
18                                                currNode.getNext()));
19               return currNode;
20           }
21       }
22   }
```

Listing 14.19 ■ The `Dictionary`'s `insertAux` method

4. The only other possibility is that the key value of the element contained in the new Node is less than the key value of the current Node's element. This means we've found the right location, and we make the changes needed to insert the new Node immediately before the current Node.

Again, as with searching and inserting values into the list, recursion is the natural solution: if you can't find the right element at this Node, just look at the next one.

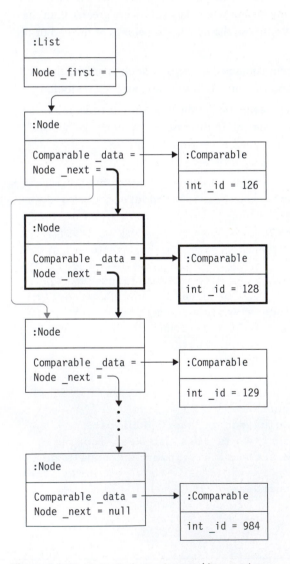

Figure 14.12 ■ Node being inserted into a List.

■ 14.4 ■ Working Out with **Data Structures**—Driver Programs

When we implement a key data structure, it's important to test it thoroughly before using it. Suppose we want a program to test our stack class, for example. We have several requirements for this program:

- It should call all the required methods
- It should allow us to push and pop arbitrary numbers of elements
- It should provide some visual feedback on what is happening
- It should be easy to plug in different stack implementations for testing

A program that is written just to test another program is called a **driver**. A driver program doesn't have to do anything interesting in itself—we can use our stacks for interesting tasks later. First, we need to see if they work.

A screenshot of a sample driver program is given in Figure 14.13. (Full code for this program is given on the CD and the book's website.) It displays a panel and two buttons, labeled "Push" and "Pop." When the user clicks on "Push," a small square is pushed onto the stack, and the modified stack is displayed. When the user clicks on "Pop," the top square is popped from the stack and disappears from the display as well. Because this program uses graphics, it is a bit more elaborate than a simple driver that would deal merely with manipulating primitive types such as integers or text strings; the advantage is that you can easily see the code is working, as the stack grows and shrinks.

> **keyconcept**
> A driver program is a program whose only purpose is to test another program.

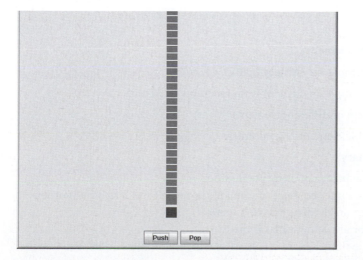

Figure 14.13 ■ Screenshot for StackApp.

We have similar requirements for a program to test our `Queue` class:

- It should call all three of the required methods
- It should allow us to `enqueue` and `dequeue` arbitrary numbers of elements
- It should provide some visual feedback on what is happening
- It should be easy to plug in different stack implementations for testing

A screenshot of a driver program for the `Queue` class is given in Figure 14.14. (Again, full code is given on the website.) It displays a panel and two buttons, labeled "Enqueue" and "Dequeue." When the user clicks on "Enqueue," a small square is added to the end of the queue, and the modified queue is displayed. When the user clicks on "Dequeue," the top square is removed from the queue and disappears from the display as well.

The queue starts at the bottom right-hand side of the window and grows to the left; when it reaches the left-hand side of the window, it moves up and all the way to the right, then continues back to the left, and so on. Here, the blue square in the bottom row on the right is in the front of the line; the five earlier squares have already been `dequeued`. The green square on the left is the last square in the bottom row; it is followed by the yellow square at the right-hand end of the second row.

Suppose we have similar driver programs for each of our data structures; the next question is: What kind of tests do we want to run? What evidence will satisfy us that our code actually works? The problem is that, as for any really interesting program, we can't try every single possibility. We could create and manipulate an extremely large number of structures, even with this simple interface. So we need to choose our tests carefully. Here are some ideas to get you started:

1. Add some elements.
2. Remove some elements.
3. Attempt to remove an element that isn't there.
4. Attempt to remove an element from an empty structure.
5. Insert a variety of different elements.
6. Insert the same element several times.
7. For a dictionary:
   a. Insert a sequence of elements in order.
   b. Insert the same sequence of elements in reverse (or scrambled) order.
   c. Search for an element that isn't there.
   d. Search for an element that is there.
   e. Delete the first element, the last element, one in the middle, and one that isn't there.

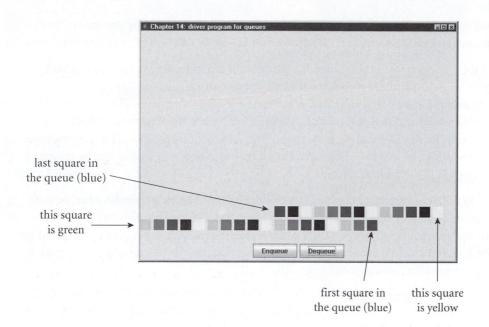

last square in
the queue (blue)

this square
is green

Enqueue   Dequeue

first square in   this square
the queue (blue)   is yellow

Figure 14.14 ■ Screenshot for `QueueApp`.

Do enough tests to convince yourself (and your instructor) that the code for your data
structure is really working.

■ Summary ■

In this chapter, we have introduced the idea of an abstract datatype (ADT) with four
examples: stack, queue, list, and dictionary. An abstract datatype (ADT) is an abstract,
language-independent specification of a collection of data and operations on that collection to store, retrieve, and manipulate the data. The notion of an ADT transcends particular programming languages or even language types, and ADTs can be implemented
in both object-oriented and procedural programming languages. The idea is closely
related to and in Java is best expressed by Java's interfaces.

Software implementations of stacks that we use frequently include the back button on
a web browser, the undo operation in a word processor, and the stack of activation records
used during program execution. In each case, the last item in is the first one out. For
this reason, implementations of the stack ADT are also known as last-in-first-out (LIFO)
data structures.

Queues model lines: the line of customers waiting to be checked out in a store, the line
of cars in the drive-through at a bank, or the list of movies you have requested from an

online service. In each case, the first item in is the first one out. For this reason, implementations of the queue ADT are also known as first-in-first-out (FIFO) data structures.

A list is a sequence of things in order. We can add things to the list or delete them at any point, not just at the beginning or the end. We can also look at anything in the list. Lists are useful for modeling situations like a lane of traffic, where new elements are added and removed at different locations, and situations where we need to store and process a group of items. For example, if we have a program that displays several different shapes in a window, we can store them in a list, so that each shape in the list can be repainted whenever the window is repainted.

A dictionary is useful in situations where we want to look up particular items in a collection of information based on some value (called a **key**). The elements of the collection are sorted based on the key, in order to make searching easier, and inserts need to be handled carefully in order to keep the collection sorted. We can use a dictionary to model an online address book.

We showed how to use instance diagrams to illustrate the state of a data structure at different points. Instance diagrams are another piece of the UML language; they are particularly useful for illustrating operations on data structures.

Finally, we discussed how to use driver programs, programs that are written to test another piece of code, and how, given a driver program, to choose appropriate tests for our data structures.

■ Self-Check Questions ■

Mastering the Facts

1. What is an abstract datatype and why are they useful? Explain.
2. Explain in your own words what a Stack is, and give three examples of possible applications of a Stack.
3. What are the three main operations associated with a Stack? Give their names and explain briefly what they do.
4. What is an instance diagram, and how does it differ from a class diagram? Explain and give an example.
5. What is an activation record?
6. What is the execution stack?
7. How does the use of an execution stack explain why local variables become undefined after a method has finished executing?
8. What should happen when client code attempts to pop from an empty stack? Discuss at least two possible solutions, choose one, and defend your choice.

9. Explain in your own words what is meant by a Queue in computer science, and give three examples of possible applications of a Queue.

10. Give an example of a situation that cannot be modeled by a queue (other than examples given earlier in the chapter). Explain your answer.

11. What are the three main operations associated with a Queue? Give their names and explain briefly what they do.

12. What is FIFO, and why is a Queue a FIFO datatype?

13. Give an example of a situation that can be modeled by a List, that cannot be modeled by either a Stack or a Queue. Explain.

14. What is the list ADT? Explain, and give three examples of possible applications.

15. What is the dictionary ADT? Explain, and give three examples of possible applications.

■ Exercises ■

Applying the Facts

1. Write code to declare and initialize a Stack that holds SmartShapes.

2. Write code to declare and initialize a Stack that holds StudentRecords.

3. Draw instance diagrams:
   a. Showing the state of an empty Stack of SmartRectangles
   b. Showing the state of a Stack after the insertion of two SmartRectangles
   c. Showing the state of the Stack after the deletion of one of the SmartRectangles

4. Write code to declare and initialize a Queue that holds LicenseRecords.

5. Draw instance diagrams
   a. Showing the state of the Queue after the enqueuing of the first, second, third, and fourth LicenseRecords.
   b. Then showing the state of the Queue after the dequeuing of the first, second, third, and fourth LicenseRecords.

6. When we test a queue implementation, we can't try all possible combinations of enqueues and dequeues: there's an infinite number of them. That's usually the case for any interesting piece of software.
   a. How can we choose which tests are most important?
   b. What tests would convince you that the Queues work? Explain.

b. What tests would convince you that the `Queues` work? Explain.

c. What do you think would convince another user? Explain.

7. Online movie services allow the user to keep a queue of movies, and send the first movie in the queue whenever an old movie is returned. But they also let the user reorder the queue. Explain how you might go about implementing the operation "take the 31st movie in my queue and move it to the head of the queue." How will you find the movie? How will you put the queue back together after you remove it?

8. (Continuing the previous example) Explain how you might implement the operation "Take the 31st movie in the list and move it to position 99." How will you find the movie? How will you put the queue together after you remove it? What should happen if there are only 73 elements currently in the queue?

9. Write a code fragment to declare and initialize a list of `SpaceAliens`.

10. Write a code fragment to declare and initialize a dictionary that contains `StudentRecords`.

11. Repeat exercises 7 and 8 using a list. Which ADT do you prefer for this task? Why?

Debugging Programs

Identify the error(s), if any, in each of the following program fragments. Explain your answer.

1.
```
private Stack<CafeteriaTray> _stack;
        . . .
_stack = new Stack<CafeteriaTray>();
_stack.pop();
```

2.
```
private Queue<OnlineCustomer> _customers;
        . . .
_queue = new Queue<OnlineCustomer>();
_queue.dequeue();
```

3.
```
private Dictionary<Addresses> _addressBook;
        . . .
_addressBook = new Dictionary<Addresses>();
_addressBook.find("Dorothy");
```

Programming Projects

Writing Programs

1. Write a program that reads in a string of characters (letters, symbols, and/or numbers) and outputs the same string in reverse order. (Refer to Chapter 18 for more information about Java's `String` class if necessary.)

2. A palindrome is a sentence that reads the same forwards and backwards. One famous example is the sentence "Able was I ere I saw Elba," as Napoleon might have commented after his exile to that island. One of the shortest is the exclamation "O." Using a stack, write a program that reads in a `String` supplied by the user and determines whether it is a palindrome.

3. A web page includes pairs of what are called "tags": <html>, </html>, <title>, </title>, <head>, </head>, and so forth. Tags are surrounded by pointed brackets (<, >) and tags that occur in pairs have a forward slash just inside the left bracket of the closing tag. The last tag started must be the first one closed. Using a stack, write a program that takes html input and determines whether the html tags are properly matched.

4. Write a program that maintains a list of movies that you want to see. The program should allow you to add to the end of the list, remove items from the beginning of the list, and determine whether the list is empty. It should provide a nice visual interface and should display the complete list upon request. Optional: allow the user to select an item and specify a new position (e.g., 4) for it in the list, reorder the list, and display the reordered list.

5. Voicemail or answering-machine messages are stored in a queue: the first message left is the first one you hear. Write a program that displays two "telephones" in a window (i.e., textboxes). In one textbox, the user should be able to enter messages; in the other textbox should appear a queue of headers for the pending messages, each with a time and date.

6. Queues are particularly useful for simulations. Suppose you are having trouble with your computer; you call the number for the helpdesk and are placed on hold.

   a. Suppose a customer calls this number every two minutes, there are five customer-service agents, and each phone call, on average, takes ten minutes. On paper, work out how long you will spend on hold.

   b. Write a program that simulates this situation using a queue for all the customers who are currently on hold. It should give a timestamp to each user based on the time he or she called, `enqueue` and `dequeue` 100 customers, and then display the number of customers served, the minimum, maximum, and average amounts of time the customers spend on hold, and the minimum and maximum lengths of the queue. Statistics should be displayed for each agent as well: number of customers served and amount of time (if any) spent idle.

c. Modify the program in (b) so that each customer has associated with it a randomly chosen number n between 0 and 60, where n is the number of minutes a customer-service agent spends on the line with that customer. (0 indicates that the customer hung up while on hold.) Your program should display the same statistics as in (b), plus the minimum, average, and maximum time spent with each customer.

d. Modify the program so that a customer's n-value (from (c)) is reset to 0 whenever that customer has waited 15 minutes or more on hold. Now print the same statistics as in (c).

e. Add sliders that let the user vary
    i.   the number of customer-service agents on duty
    ii. The frequency with which customers arrive

    How many agents does it take to minimize the wait time without any agent ever being idle (after the start of the simulation)?

7. Design and implement a version of Queues using arrays.

8. Design and implement a version of Queues using Vectors.

9. Write a program that maintains a list of movies that you want to see, in order of how soon you want to see them. The program should include the title of each movie and its release date (*Wizard of Oz,* 1939). The program should allow you to add or remove movies from anywhere in the list, and determine whether the list is empty. It should provide a nice visual interface and should display the complete list upon request.

10. Reimplement your program from question 9 so that the movies are sorted in order by the date when they were released. If you have written your program well, you should need to modify only the isEqualTo, isGreaterThan, and isLessThan methods.

11. Design, write, and test an implementation of the ADT list using Vectors.

12. Design, implement, and test an implementation of the ADT list using arrays.

13. Design, implement, and test an implementation of the ADT dictionary using Vectors.

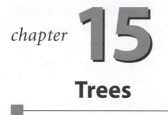

chapter **15**

Trees

OBJECTIVES

After reading this chapter, you should be able to:

☑ List three things that can be modeled with a tree but not with a linear data structure

☑ Implement a binary search tree in Java

☑ Compare and contrast binary search trees and linked lists as strategies for implementing the ADT dictionary

☑ Use a binary search tree appropriately to solve simple programming problems

■ 15.1 ■ Introduction

So far, all our data structures have been linear: that is, they put all their elements in a line, one after another. Sometimes this line is sorted:

And sometimes it isn't:

But the elements of the structure are always organized into a line.

Not everything we want to model is a line. What if we want to model someone's family tree? Or an organizational chart? For tasks like this, we need a data structure called a **tree**. Trees are used to model data that is organized into a hierarchy.

■ 15.2 ■ Concepts

15.2.1 Modeling with trees

A picture of a computer-science "tree" is shown in Figure 15.1. Like our linked-list implementations of stack, queue, and list, the tree in Figure 15.1 is a collection of nodes. The arrows point from a node to the nodes that follow it (the nodes we called "next" in talking about linked lists, except that these nodes can have more than one "next" node). This tree is drawn upside down (with its root at the top), like all computer-science trees.

A tree has a precise mathematical definition. It is a finite set T of one or more nodes such that:

<key concept>
A tree is a data structure that lets us model many things we could not model with linear data structures.
</key concept>

1. Exactly one of T's nodes has no predecessor. This is called T's **root node**.
2. The remaining nodes can be partitioned into disjoint sets $T_1, T_2, ..., T_m$.
3. Each one of those sets T_i is also a tree. These sets T_i are called **subtrees** of T (Figure 15.2).

We've already seen a lot of hierarchies like this. Inheritance hierarchies are trees. All Java classes are part of a single tree, with `Object` at the root. The classes in `Wheels` are part of the larger Java class inheritance hierarchy. For example, see Figure 15.3.

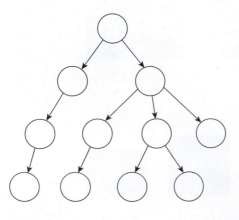

Figure 15.1 ■ Diagram of a tree.

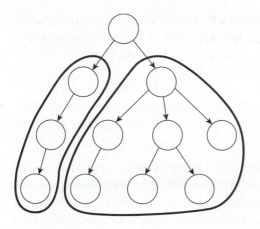

Figure 15.2 ■ The same tree with the root node's subtrees circled.

In this hierarchy, if one thing is higher than another, it's more *general*. So in this hierarchy, Shape is the most general, RectangularShape is more general than Ellipse or RoundedRectangle, and Shape is more general than ConversationBubble. Note that we can't compare all the pairs of classes. Consider Ellipse and Rectangle, for example: neither one of them is more general than the other. Because we can put these classes partly in order—some things are in order relative to one another, but not all—mathematicians call this a **partial order**. Because we can't put all of the elements of the group in order, none of the linear ADTs would work to model this set of relationships.

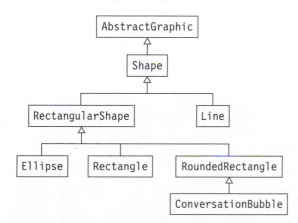

Figure 15.3 ■ A class-hierarchy example of a tree.

Containment hierarchies can also be modelled with a tree. For example, we might have a `JFrame` that contains a `JPanel` that contains both a `DrawingPanel` and a `ButtonPanel`, where the `ButtonPanel` contains three `RadioButtons`. A containment-hierarchy tree is shown in Figure 15.4. Here, the higher levels *contain* more components. The lower levels, on the other hand, are contained by whatever is above them. So the `JFrame` contains everything else. The `ButtonPanel` contains only the three `JRadioButtons`. The `JRadioButtons` are contained by the `ButtonPanel`, the `JPanel`, and the `JFrame`.

As shown in these diagrams, trees represent both a group of nodes and a kind of relationship among them. You could draw two diagrams for the same exact classes for a program you're writing, one showing the inheritance hierarchy and the other showing the containment hierarchy. If you wanted to, you could draw a third hierarchy showing the level of difficulty of each of the classes. Even though exactly the same nodes appear in two diagrams, the relationships among them can be different.

Before we continue, let's introduce some terminology to help us talk about trees. We've already mentioned the **root node**, the single node in the tree that has no predecessors. That's the node labeled A in Figure 15.5. The new terms we'll use to talk about trees include:

- **Edge.** The line (or link) connecting one node directly to another. These are represented by arrows in the tree in Figure 15.5. For example, there's an edge from C to F, but no edge from F to G.
- **Parent node** and **child node.** Child nodes are what we called "next" nodes in stacks, queues, and lists. A parent node is the "previous" node. Thus, C is the

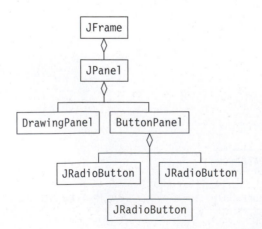

Figure 15.4 ■ A containment-hierarchy example of a tree.

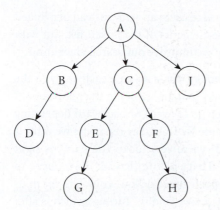

Figure 15.5 ■ Another computer-science tree, with labeled nodes.

parent node of E and F; F is a child node of C. On the diagram, arrows go from a parent node to each of its children.

- **Leaf node.** A leaf node is a node with no children. These are also called **external nodes**. Nodes with children are called **internal nodes**.

- **Depth (or level) of a node.** The depth of a node is the number of edges you have to follow from that node to get to the root. For example, the depth of D is two and the depth of G is three.

- **Height of a tree.** The height of a tree is the depth of the deepest node (i.e., the maximum number of edges it takes to get from the root to a node). The height of the tree in Figure 15.5 is three.

- **Degree of a node.** The degree of a node is the number of children it has. For example, the degree of node A is three, and the degree of node C is two. (What is the degree of a leaf node?)

15.2.2 Implementing dictionary operations efficiently with trees

Trees can help us implement certain collections of objects and their relationships more efficiently, as well as letting us model relationships we couldn't model with a linear data structure. Consider search, for example. Recall how we implemented search in the `Dictionary` class in Chapter 14: the `Dictionary` asked the first node and, if necessary, the second node, and so on. Imagine how that would work if the list had one node for each name in the phone book. If we were searching for someone whose name begins with "Z," we might have to look through the entire list to get to the end. If we were searching for "Ada," we might find it on the first try. On average, we'd always have to look at every name in the first half of the book.

Suppose we implement the `DictionaryADT` interface using an array instead of a linked list. The elements of the array are sorted, like the elements of the linked list, but with an array we can access any element we want. Can we improve our search algorithm?

A sorted array of names is a lot like the phone book (if you assume each entry in the phone book is a single element). How do we usually look up names in the phone book? We open the book somewhere in the middle, then go forward or backward depending on where the name we see is in relation to the name we want. Say the name we want is "Pascal." We open up the book in the middle. If we're very lucky, the name is right there. If not, say the name we see is "Mauchly." That's before "Pascal," so we need to look later in the book. We've ruled out half of the book already! Now we look in the middle of the *second* half of the book. Suppose the name we find is "Turing," which is after "Pascal." Now we've ruled out another quarter of the book. Next, we open the section of the book between "Mauchly" and "Turing" and we find "Nygaard." And so forth. Every time we look at a name, we either find what we want or, at worst, we cut in half the amount of the list we have left to search.

Let's quantify the difference in search time. For a linked-list implementation of List, the worst-case scenario for search is that we have to look at every single item in the List. If there are n things in the dictionary, then the search time is proportional to n. With

SOME GREAT NAMES IN COMPUTER SCIENCE

Ada, Countess of Lovelace (1815–1852). British mathematician and assistant to Charles Babbage, she is often considered the first computer programmer. The Ada programming language is named after her.

Babbage, Charles (1791–1871). British inventor of the all-mechanical Difference Engine and Analytical Engine (both designed for automatic numerical computation). Although the Analytical Engine implementation was never completed, it is generally considered the first computer.

Mauchly, John (1907–1980). American computer scientist who, with Presper Eckert, designed the ENIAC (one of the first digital computers) and the UNIVAC (one of the first commercial computers).

Nygaard, Kristen (1926–2002). Norwegian computer scientist who, with Ole-Johan Dahl, designed the programming language Simula, which introduced important concepts of object-oriented programming, including classes, objects, and inheritance.

Pascal, Blaise (1623–1662). French mathematician and philosopher, after whom the programming language Pascal is named. Constructed an early mechanical calculator.

Turing, Alan (1912–1954). British mathematician and cryptographer. Made major contributions to theoretical computer science and artificial intelligence. The Turing Test, Turing Machine, and Turing Award are all named after him.

the phone-book method, at worst, we have to look at $\log_2 n$ items. The difference between these two values is illustrated in Table 15.1.

Consider the difference:

Table 15.1 ■ Comparison of n and $\log_2 n$

n (number of items in list)	$\log_2 n$
1	0
2	1
4	2
16	4
256	8
1024	10
1048576	20

When n is over a million, $\log_2 n$ is still only 20. This is clearly what we want!

There's one problem with using an array, however: inserts and deletes. Every time we add an element to the middle of an array, we need to shift other elements over to make room. Every time we remove an element from the middle of an array, we need to shift other elements over to fill in the gap. And unless we make the array much too large (and waste space), we run the risk of running out of room.

In sum, the linked-list implementation of `Dictionary` gives us inefficient search but allows us to allocate memory as needed; the array-based implementation gives us efficient search but we must allocate a fixed amount of memory up front and choose between wasting memory and the risk of running out of room.

Can we get the best of both worlds? Yes. If we implement the `DictionaryADT` interface using a **binary tree**—that is, a tree in which each internal node has no more than two children—it turns out that we can get just what we want.

In particular, what we want is a **binary search tree**. In a binary search tree, not only does each internal node have degree 1 or 2 but, in addition, for each node, the data in its left subtree is smaller than its own data and the data in its right subtree is larger.

Figure 15.6 shows an example. In every case, the nodes in the left subtree contain data that is earlier in the alphabet. For example, to the left of the root C are nodes that contain A and B. To the left of G are nodes that contain D, E, and F. Similarly, the nodes in the right subtree of a node always contain data that is later in the alphabet. For example, H is later than G, and D, E, F, G, and H are all later than C.

keyconcept
A binary tree is a tree whose nodes all have degree 0, 1, or 2.

keyconcept
A binary search tree is a binary tree in which, for each node, the data in its left subtree is smaller than its own data and the data in its right subtree is larger.

The tree in Figure 15.6 is a fairly well-balanced tree. **Balanced tree** is a technical term, but roughly speaking it means that no one branch of the tree is much longer (or shorter) than any other. A **full binary tree**—a tree where all nodes of depth less than the height of the tree have two children and the rest have 0—is perfectly balanced.

Figure 15.7 shows an unbalanced tree. Note that this is also a binary search tree. Each internal node has one child, and the value in the left subtree of each node is less than the value in that node. But the tree is linear in shape. If we started at the root looking for "A," we'd have to look just as far as if the tree were a linked list.

There are sophisticated algorithms for making sure that binary trees are balanced and stay balanced as nodes are added and deleted. In this chapter, we'll present some simpler algorithms to get you started working with trees. For now, just remember that search can be just as inefficient in an unbalanced tree as in a linked list.

15.2.3 **In-order, pre-order, post-order**

Suppose you want to search through the data values from a data structure in some systematic order. With an array, you can look at them in any order you want, since arrays have random access. With a linked list, you don't have much choice: you just go in order, starting with the first node and going to the second, the third, etc. With a tree there are several possibilities. We will illustrate three of the best-known orders using the tree in Figure 15.8.

When visiting the nodes of a tree, we always start with the root, and for the three orders discussed here, we always visit the nodes in the same order (See Figure 15.9): go left until you can't go any farther, then back up until you find a node with a right child, go right to that child, then go left as far as you can, and so forth until you've visited all the nodes in the tree.

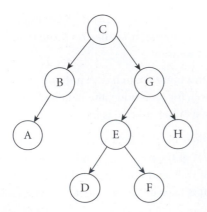

Figure 15.6 ■ A binary search tree.

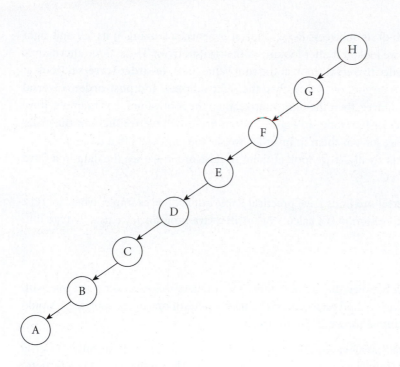

Figure 15.7 ■ An unbalanced tree.

The question is when we look at the *value* in a node. We have an opportunity to look at the value of the root node right at the beginning, and we have the opportunity to examine the value of any node each time we visit it.

As you can see from the arrows in Figure 15.9, we often have more than one opportunity to look at the value in a node. Do we look at it right away (on the first visit) and

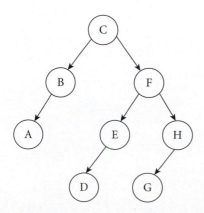

Figure 15.8 ■ Another example of a binary search tree.

then look at each of its subtrees? Do we look at it between looking at its left and right subtrees? Or do we look at it after looking at the two subtrees? These three alternatives are called **pre-order traversal** (look at the root value first), **in-order traversal** (look at the left subtree, then the root value, then the right subtree), and **post-order traversal** (look at the left subtree, then the right subtree, then the root value). For example, if we look at the values of the nodes in Figure 15.9 in pre-order, we see them in the order CBAFEDHG. If we look at them in in-order, we see the same data in a different order: ABCDEFGH. And finally, if we look at them in post-order, we see the data in a third order: ABDEGHFC.

These tree-traversal methods have practical applications. For example, when we type an arithmetic expression into a calculator (or in a Java program), we usually type it in this form:

    2 * 3

with the operator between the two operands. If we think of this expression as a tree, with the operator at the root and each operand being the value of one of the subtrees, it would look like this example shown in Figure 15.10.

To get the normal (infix) version of this expression, 2 * 3, we do an in-order traversal of the tree. What if we do a pre-order traversal of the tree? Then we get * 2 3 (prefix notation). And if we do a post-order traversal of the tree, we get 2 3 * (postfix notation).

The infix notation for arithmetic expressions, the most familiar one, is used by most calculators, but there are some calculators that use postfix. Calculators that use postfix

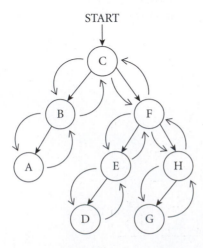

START

Figure 15.9 ■ Binary search tree: Arrows show the order in which the nodes are visited.

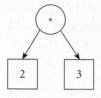

Figure 15.10 ■ An expression tree.

notation are called **RPN calculators**, for "reverse Polish notation," after the Polish logician Lukasiewicz, who showed the advantages of pre-order notation over in-order notation—no parentheses are necessary.

The RPN notation looks a little unusual, but it doesn't make much difference for a simple expression like this one. Consider a really complicated arithmetic expression, though, like

    ((5 * 2)+(3 / 4)) - (5 * (7 + 8))

The expression tree corresponding to this expression is shown in Figure 15.11. Now do a post-order traversal of the tree to translate this into postfix notation:

    5 2 * 3 4 * + 5 6 - 7 8 / + -

Postfix notation doesn't need any parentheses and can be evaluated in a single scan from left to right: each time you come to an operator, its operands are immediately to its left. Thus we can group this as ((5,2, *),(3, 4, *)),+), etc., without actually needing those parentheses! This notation takes some getting used to, but many people come to like it.

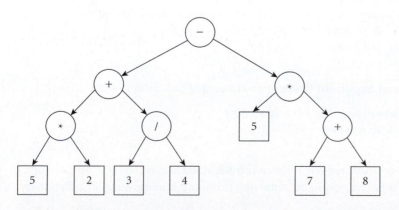

Figure 15.11 ■ A more complicated expression tree.

How can we mechanically evaluate a post-order expression in a single left-to-right pass? Whenever we see a number, we push it on a stack; when we see an operator, we pop the two most recent numbers off the stack, perform the calculation indicated by the operator, and push the intermediate result back on the stack. With the usual notation (corresponding to an in-order traversal), we must look for expressions in parentheses, which may be on the far right of the expression, and evaluate them first, so we may need to read through the expression several times.

The programming language Lisp (used in artificial intelligence applications) has a prefix notation for arithmetic expressions that corresponds to a pre-order traversal of the tree. The above expression, for example, would be written:

```
(- (+ (* 5 2) (/ 3 4))  (* 5 (+ 7 8)))
```

This notation also has its advantages. There are lots of parentheses (it has been said that "Lisp" stands for "lots of irrelevant and silly parentheses"), but using prefix notation means that arithmetic operators have the same syntax as all other functions: the name of the function (or operator) comes first, then the parameters.

■ 15.3 ■ **Mechanics: Binary Search Trees**

We want our binary search tree to implement the `DictionaryADT` interface defined in Chapter 14:

```
public interface DictionaryADT
        <K extends Comparable<K>,
          E extends KeyProvider<K>> {
    // K is class for keys, E is class for elements
    public void insert (E element);
    public void delete (K aKey);
        //search returns null if element not found
    public E search (K aKey);
    public boolean isEmpty();
}
```

Each element must implement the `KeyProvider` interface from Chapter 14:

```
public interface KeyProvider<K>{
    public K getKey ();
}
```

Although trees are structured very differently from linked lists, we will use them to implement the same behavior: adding to, removing from, and finding things in a dictionary.

15.3.1 **Declaring the `BinarySearchTree` class**

Our `BinarySearchTree`, like our `Stacks` and `Queues`, is made up of a collection of linked nodes. The first node in the collection is called the "root," however, and instead of having one "next" node, internal nodes in binary search trees have two, a "left child" and a "right child."

Each `Node` contains data: a reference to some `Element` (for example, an entry in an address book with the name, address, and phone number of some person). As required by the `KeyProvider` interface, each `Element` has a `getKey` method that returns a key. The keys of the `Elements` in the `Dictionary` belong to some class that implements Java's `Comparable` interface.

The `BinarySearchTree` class includes a reference to the first `Node` in the `List` and provides the four methods required by our `List` interface: `insert`, `delete`, `isEmpty`, and `search`. A class diagram for our `BinarySearchTree` implementation is given in Figure 15.12.

The `BinaryTree` is a collection of `Nodes`. Each `Node` has a left and right child (either or both of which may be `null`) and contains an `Element`. The `Node`'s children may change during the execution of the program, but its element does not; thus the children have both accessors and mutators, but the element has only an accessor.

A `Node`'s element can contain any amount of information, but it must have a method `getKey` that returns some key value. E is the class the element will belong to; K is the class of the key value. We don't know yet what E and K will stand for. E might be an entry in an address book, and K might be a `String` that holds a person's name. Alternatively, E might be a graphical shape, and the `getKey` method might compute and return the shape's area.

Using this class diagram, we can easily create a skeleton definition of the `BinarySearchTree` class (shown in Listing 15.1). We're on our way!

For the `Node` class, we fill in all the code right away. It's easy, since we use almost the same `Node` class as in Chapter 14. (See Listing 15.2.)

The primary difference between this `Node` class and the one in Chapter 14 is that this one has references to its two child `Nodes`, `_left` and `_right`, instead of a single reference to a `_next` `Node`. In this tree, a `Node` is a leaf node if it has no children, that is, if its `_left` and `_right` references are equal to `null`.

The instance diagram for a newly constructed, empty `BinarySearchTree` is given in Figure 15.13. As each `Node` is added, it is `inserted` into the tree in order according to the key value of the element it contains (for example, the name of a person.) Figure 15.14

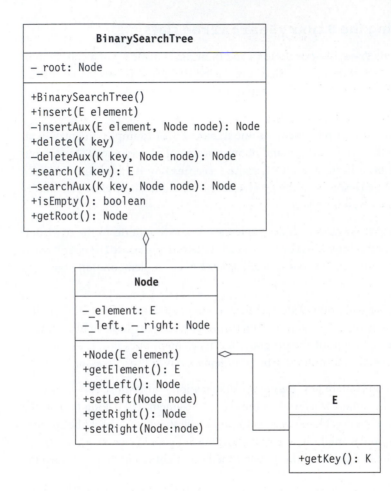

Figure 15.12 ■ Class diagram for Binary Search Tree.

shows an instance diagram of a `BinarySearchTree` that contains three `Nodes`. This `BinarySearchTree` is part of the implementation of an address book. The elements of the dictionary are address-book entries. Recall that the elements can be any type of object that implements the `KeyProvider` interface. Each element must have a `getKey`

```
1    /**
2     * Chapter 15: BinarySearchTree.java
3     * A second implementation of DictionaryADT.
4     */
5    public class BinarySearchTree
```

Listing15.1 ■ The `BinarySearchTree` class (*continued on next page*)

```
 6          <K extends Comparable<K>, E extends KeyProvider<K>>
 7          implements DictionaryADT<K,E> {
 8          // K is class for keys, E is class for elements
 9          private Node<E> _root;
10
11          public BinarySearchTree() {
12              _root = null; // tree empty so far
13          }
14
15          public void insert (E element) {
16              // to be described below
17          }
18          private Node<E> insertAux (Node<E> nodeToAdd,
19                                     Node<E> currNode) {
20              // to be described below
21          }
22
23          public E search (K keyToFind) {
24              // to be described below
25          }
26          private Node<E> searchAux(K keyToFind,
27                                    Node<E> currNode) {
28              // to be described below
29          }
30
31          public void delete (K key) {
32              // to be described below
33          }
34          private Node<E> deleteAux (K keyToDelete,
35                                     Node<E> currNode) {
36              // to be described below
37          }
38
39          public boolean isEmpty() {
40              if (_root == null)
41                  return true;
42              else return false;
43          }
44          public Node<E> getRoot() {
45              return _root;
46          }
47      }
```

Listing 15.1 ■ The `BinarySearchTree` class

method that returns some kind of key. Here, the key is the person's name, so the `getKey` method simply returns the value stored in the `_name` field.

Now let's fill in the blanks in the `BinarySearchTree` class, starting with `insert`. The `insert` method is easier to write if it has two parameters, the `Node` we're inserting and the `Node` we're currently looking at as the start of our search for the right place to insert the new `Node`. A common recipe when we want an additional parameter to carry along information is to define a second helper method that has an extra parameter, as we did for the dictionary implementation in Chapter 14. See the definition in Listing 15.3.

```java
1    /**
2     * Chapter 15: The BinaryTree's Node class
3     * Similar to the Node class for Stacks, but with two
4     * child nodes.
5     */
6    public class Node<E> {
7        private E _element;
8        private Node<E> _left, _right;
9
10       public Node(E element) {
11           _element = element;
12           _left = null;
13           _right = null;
14       }
15       public E getElement() {
16           return _element;
17       }
18       public Node<E> getLeft() {
19           return _left;
20       }
21       public void setLeft (Node<E> aNode) {
22           _left = aNode;
23       }
24       public Node<E> getRight() {
25           return _right;
26       }
27       public void setRight (Node<E> aNode) {
28           _right = aNode;
29       }
30   }
```

Listing 15.2 ■ The `BinaryTree`'s Node class

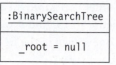

Figure 15.13 ■ Instance diagram for empty `BinarySearchTree`.

The new value of the `_root` will be whatever the `insertAux` method returns. When the first `Node` is inserted, that `Node` will become the `_root`. Otherwise, the new `Node` will be inserted somewhere below the root, so that this call to `insertAux` will just return the old reference to `_root`.

All the interesting work happens inside `insertAux` (shown in Listing 15.4). If the `_root` is null, we simple make the new `Node` into the `_root`. Otherwise, we compare the key value of the element being added with the key value of the element in the current `Node`. If the new key value is less (if the `compareTo` method returns a negative number), then call `insertAux` recursively on the left subtree; if the new key value is greater (if the `compareTo` method returns a positive number), then call `insertAux` on the right subtree. Otherwise, if the new key value is equal to the one in the element stored at the current `Node`, just do nothing—this implementation of dictionary doesn't allow duplicates.

Note that with this algorithm, inserting data in different orders can give you different trees. As remarked above, inserts and deletes can lead to very unbalanced trees. For example, if we insert data in the order A B C, we get a tree that looks like the one shown in

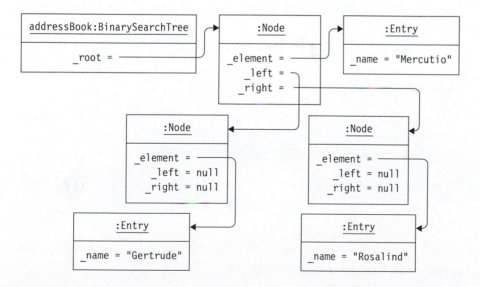

Figure 15.14 ■ Instance diagram for `BinarySearchTree` with three `Nodes`.

the figure on the left in Figure 15.15. But if we insert data in the order C B A, we get a tree that looks like the one shown in the figure in the middle in Figure 15.15. And if we insert data in the order B A C, we get a nice balanced tree like the one shown in the figure on the right in Figure 15.15.

```
1    public void insert (E element) {
2        _root = this.insertAux(new Node<E> (element), root);
3    }
```

Listing 15.3 ■ The BinarySearchTree's insert method

```
1    private Node<E> insertAux (Node<E> nodeToAdd, Node<E> currNode) {
2        if (currNode == null) {
3            return nodeToAdd;
4        } else {
5            K currKey = currNode.getElement().getKey();
6            K keyToAdd = nodeToAdd.getElement().getKey();
7            int comparison = keyToAdd.compareTo(currKey);
8            if (comparison < 0) {// new key is less, go left
9                Node<E> leftChild = currNode.getLeft();
10               if (leftChild == null)
11                   currNode.setLeft(nodeToAdd);
12               else
13                   this.insertAux(nodeToAdd, leftChild);
14           }
15           else if (comparison > 0) {//new key greater, go right
16               Node<E> rightChild = currNode.getRight();
17               if (rightChild == null)
18                   currNode.setRight(nodeToAdd);
19               else
20                   this.insertAux(nodeToAdd, rightChild);
21           }
22           // else new key already there, do nothing
23           return currNode;
24       }
25   }
```

Listing 15.4 ■ The BinarySearchTree's insertAux method

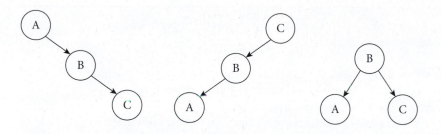

Figure 15.15 ■ `BinarySearchTrees` created by inserting the same data in different orders.

The `search` method works similarly to `insert`. It first calls a helper method with an additional parameter (as shown in Listing 15.5.) If the auxiliary method returns a `Node`, extract the element it contains and return it; otherwise, return `null`. Note that the client code for this method doesn't even have to know that there are `Nodes` in our representation; it gives us a key and gets back an element containing the key and (probably) additional information as well.

Once again, all the interesting work is done in the helper method (as shown in Listing 15.6.) If the key we're looking for is less than the key value of the current `Node`, look in the left subtree of the current `Node`; if it's greater, look in the right subtree; and if it's equal, return this `Node` itself.

Finally, the last of the required methods, `delete`, starts out in the same way as `insert` and `search` by calling a helper method with an additional parameter (as shown in Listing 15.7). Once again, the `_root` becomes whatever value is returned by the helper method; it changes only if the element with the key to be deleted is actually stored at the root. And once again, all the interesting work is done by the helper method.

The helper method faces a new problem, however: what if we have to remove a `Node` from the tree that has two children? We start off by searching for the `Node` to be deleted,

```
1   public E search (K keyToFind) {
2       Node<E> resultNode = this.searchAux(keyToFind, _root);
3       if (resultNode == null)
4               return null;
5       else
6               return resultNode.getElement();
7   }
```

Listing 15.5 ■ The `BinarySearchTree`'s search method

```
1    private Node<E> searchAux(K keyToFind, Node<E> currNode) {
2        if (currNode == null) return null;
3        else {
4            K currKey = currNode.getElement().getKey();
5            int comparison = keyToFind.compareTo(currKey);
6            if (comparison < 0) // go left
7                return this.searchAux(keyToFind, currNode.getLeft());
8            else if (comparison > 0) // go right
9                return this.searchAux(keyToFind,
10                                      currNode.getRight());
11           else // found it!
12               return currNode;
13       }
14   }
```

Listing 15.6 ■ The `BinarySearchTree`'s `searchAux` method

```
1    public void delete (K key) {
2        _root = this.deleteAux(key, _root);
3    }
```

Listing 15.7 ■ The `BinarySearchTree`'s `delete` method

and if we don't find it, no problem—we're done. If we do find it, but it doesn't have any children, we just remove it. (See Figure 15.16.) If it has just one child, we remove the `Node` and put its child in its place. (See Figure 15.17.) But what if there are two children?

Consider the code for `deleteAux` (shown in Listing 15.8.) The first part of this code is very similar to `search` and `insert`. As usual, we compare the key value we're interested

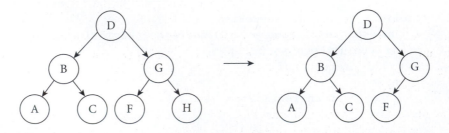

Figure 15.16 ■ Deleting a `Node` (H) with no children.

```
1    private Node<E> deleteAux (K keyToDelete,
2                        Node<E> currNode) {
3      if (currNode == null) {
4          return null; // nothing to delete here and no children
5      }
6      else {
7          K currKey = currNode.getElement().getKey();
8          int comparison = keyToDelete.compareTo(currKey);
9          if (comparison > 0) { // go right
10             currNode.setRight(deleteAux(keyToDelete,
11                                     currNode.getRight()));
12             return currNode;
13         }
14         else if (comparison < 0) { // go left
15             currNode.setLeft(deleteAux(keyToDelete,
16                                     currNode.getLeft()));
17             return currNode;
18         }
19         else { // found it!
20             Node<E> left = currNode.getLeft();
21             Node<E> right = currNode.getRight();
22             if (left == null)
23                 return right;
24             else if (right == null)
25                 return left;
26             else // node being deleted has two non-null children
27                 return this.insertAux (right, left);
28         }
29     }
30   }
```

Listing 15.8 ■ The `BinarySearchTree`'s `deleteAux` method

in with the key value at the current `Node`. If the key we're trying to delete is less than the key value at the current `Node`, we go left and look in the left child; if the key we're trying to delete is greater than the key value at the current `Node`, we go right and look in the right subtree.

When we find a match it gets more interesting. If the current `Node` is the one we need to delete, then we first check its child `Node`s. If one of them is `null`, the other one takes the place of the current `Node`. (If they're both `null`, we arbitrarily pick the right `Node`.) So far, so good.

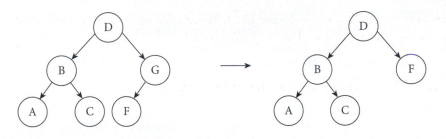

Figure 15.17 ■ Deleting a Node (G) with one child.

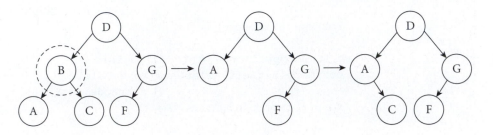

Figure 15.18 ■ Deleting a Node (B) with two children.

If the Node being deleted has two children, though, what happens? We start by substituting the left child for the current Node. But we still have the right child, along with any children it may have, to worry about. Here's the trick: we take that right child and insert it all over again into the tree. Specifically, we insert it into the subtree whose root is the former left child. The right child's children, if any, will continue to be its children, so when the right child is inserted, they're fine. (See Figure 15.18.)

■ 15.4 ■ Working Out with Trees—Driver Program

Just as with the data structures in Chapter 14, we need to test the binary search tree code before we can use it; and to test it, we need a simple driver program. If you wrote a driver program to test the dictionary ADT in Chapter 14, you could use the same one here, since both the linear implementation from Chapter 14 and the binary search tree code shown here implement the dictionary ADT.

A driver program in which the data structure is displayed in tree form is more challenging, since laying out the tree in a window can be difficult. A screenshot illustrating one possible solution is shown in Figure 15.19. Readers are encouraged to implement this driver; the code can be found on the book's website.

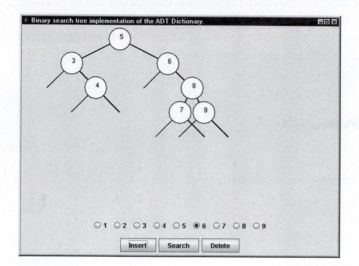

Figure 15.19 ■ A screenshot showing a driver program testing our `BinarySearchTree` classes.

■ Summary ■

This chapter introduced a data structure called a tree. Trees can be used to model any-thing with a hierarchical structure, such as an organization chart, Java's class inheritance, or a family tree. We introduced a particular type of tree, the `BinarySearchTree`, and gave an implementation of the `DictionaryADT` using a `BinarySearchTree`. Binary search trees provide a more efficient implementation of `search` than the linked-list implementation in Chapter 14.

■ Self-Check Questions ■

Mastering the Facts

1. What is the definition of a tree in computer science?
2. Define the following terms:
    a. Root node
    b. Edge
    c. Parent node
    d. Child node
    e. Leaf node
    f. Internal node
    g. Depth (or level) of a node
    h. Height of a tree
    i. Degree of a node
    j. Binary tree
    k. Binary search tree
    l. Balanced tree
    m. In-order traversal
    n. Pre-order traversal
    o. Post-order traversal
    p. RPN calculator

■ Exercises ■

Applying the Facts

1. Give three examples of things that can be modeled better with a tree than with a linear data structure.
2. Compare and contrast binary search trees and linked lists as strategies for implementing the ADT `Dictionary`.

■ **Programming Projects** ■

Modifying Programs

1. Modify the code given in the chapter so that the `BinarySearchTree` keeps its data sorted in reverse order (from largest to smallest).

2. Modify the code given in the chapter so that the `BinarySearchTree` allows nodes with duplicate keys.

Writing Programs

1. Implement the binary search tree code given in the chapter to create an address book for the pizza places near campus. Include the name and phone number of each place.

2. Write a driver program with a GUI interface that allows the user to insert data into and remove data from a `Dictionary` and display the contents of the `Dictionary`. Implement the back end of your program first using a linked list, then using a binary search tree. The user interface should be attractive and easy to use, and should not change when the back-end implementation changes.

16

Sorting and Searching

OBJECTIVES

After reading this chapter, you should be able to:

☑ Define and explain the importance of algorithm analysis

☑ Define and give examples of recurrence relations

☑ Define worst-case performance, constant-time algorithms, linear algorithms, quadratic algorithms, and exponential algorithms

☑ Define linear and binary search

☑ Give the algorithm and worst-case run time for bubble sort, insertion sort, selection sort, and merge sort

☑ Compare and contrast bubble sort, insertion sort, selection sort, and merge sort

☑ Define hash table

☑ Compare and contrast the efficiency of searching in unsorted arrays, sorted arrays, linked lists, trees, and hash tables

■ 16.1 ■ Introduction

Think back to Chapter 1, where we presented a list of criteria for evaluating models:

- how well it satisfies its purpose
- appearance
- reliability
- usability
- flexibility
- maintainability
- efficiency

In this chapter, we look at **algorithm analysis**: ways to analyze the efficiency of a model. By **efficiency**, we mean the extent to which a model makes effective use of resources.

For example, in Chapters 14 and 15, we saw that dictionary search can be implemented in two different ways, using linked lists and binary trees, and that one of them generally runs much more quickly than the other.

All things being equal, everyone would like programs to run faster. Everyone would like programs to take up less memory and hard disk space on their computers. Everyone would like programs to use as little network bandwidth as possible, if only because waiting for the network can really slow a program down. We can't usually achieve all of these goals at once, however, so it's also important to understand the tradeoffs between one problem solution and another.

Algorithm analysis is such an important topic that nearly every undergraduate computer-science major takes at least a full course in it. This course presents a toolbox of useful designs that have been developed over the years to solve various problems, as well as techniques for analyzing and comparing those designs. Naturally, we can't present all of this material in one chapter. Our objective is just to give you a taste and pique your interest—and also to show you the advantages of being concerned about performance. The difference between an inefficient solution to a problem and an efficient one can be tremendous.

Accordingly, we focus on two extremely common tasks that we have explored already in previous chapters: sorting (putting a collection of items in alphabetic or numeric order) and searching (looking for a particular item in a collection). Searching and sorting are part of many different programs, from the software the registrar at your college uses to look up your transcript to Web search engines. Indeed, they are estimated to be the most common tasks executed by computers. Because these tasks are so common, they have also been much studied, and a lot is known about different algorithms for solving them. To simplify the discussion, we look only at the computing-time various algorithms for these tasks might take.

■ 16.2 ■ Concepts

Before we talk about how to make a program run faster, we need to be able to measure how fast it runs. And before we can measure how fast a program runs, we need to know what we mean by "fast."

One obvious way of telling how fast a program runs is to run it on a particular machine at a particular time and time it. Unfortunately, the results depend on the type of machine, the operating system, the other software installed on the machine, the particular programming language the program is written in, the quality of the compiler for that language, and many other details specific to a given hardware/software configuration. This

<key concept>
keyconcept

The analysis of algorithms is a subfield of computer science that considers how efficiently an algorithm uses resources such as time, space, and network bandwidth.
</key concept>

method is very useful if you want to see how the particular software you plan to use will work on the specific computer that you're planning to use, but we'd like something more general.

To get a more general measure, we turn to one of the principal themes of this book: abstraction. What do all searching and sorting tasks have in common? Any time we're searching, we're searching through a collection of items, such as integers or character strings. Any time we're sorting, we're also sorting a collection of items. In both cases, that collection can be counted. Let N be the number of items in the collection. Instead of measuring the time of an algorithm in seconds or in computer cycles, we measure how many steps it takes in relation to N. If we can say that algorithm A always (or even on average) sorts a collection of N things in fewer steps than algorithm B, we have a really useful fact that is independent of the details of a particular machine, operating system, or programming language.

Another detail we need to worry about is the actual input to the algorithm. For example, recall from Chapter 15 that the speed of searching in a binary tree depends on the shape of the tree (i.e., the average depth of the nodes and how much the depth varies) and that the shape of binary trees depends on the order in which data is inserted into the tree. There are several approaches to abstracting away from this detail, but the one we consider here is **worst-case time complexity,** $T(N)$: the maximum running time T (measured in number of steps, not clock time) of an algorithm over all possible inputs of size N.

keyconcept

Worst-case time complexity ($T(N)$) is the maximum running time T (measured in number of steps) of an algorithm over all possible inputs of size N.

The last detail we abstract away is numerical. Suppose $T(N)$ for one algorithm is $2N^2$, another is $6N^2$, and another is $18N^2 + N + 17$. We put these all in the same category, based on the fastest-growing term, N^2. An algorithm with any of these runtimes is said to be $O(N^2)$. This stands for "on the order of N squared," and is pronounced "big oh of N squared," or "oh of N squared."

Table 16.1 ■ Examples of big-oh notation.

Expression	Big-oh notation
6	$O(1)$
$17N$	$O(N)$
$2N + 3$	$O(N)$
$\log_2 N$	$O(\log_2 N)$
$83N + \log_2 N + 16$	$O(N)$
$16N^2 + 79N + 2$	$O(N^2)$
$2^N + 76N^2 - 17$	$O(2^N)$

keyconcept
To figure out the big-oh notation for a function take the largest N term in its $T(N)$ and remove its constants.

There's a precise mathematical definition of big-oh notation, but intuitively, to figure out the **big-oh notation** for a function, we take the largest N term and remove its constants. Table 16.1 shows some examples of functions and their value in big-oh notation.

To give you a feeling for the difference among $O(1)$, $O(N)$, $O(N^2)$, and $O(2^N)$, Table 16.2 shows values for 1, N, N^2, and 2^N, for different values of N. 1 is constant (of course). N increases linearly. N^2 increases quadratically, more quickly than N, and 2^N starts out slowly but then accelerates exponentially and thus increases more quickly than N raised to any positive exponent.

Table 16.2 ■ Various rates of growth.

1	N	N^2	2^N
1	1	1	2
1	10	100	1024
1	20	400	1,048,576
1	30	900	1,073,741,824
1	40	1600	1,099,511,627,776

keyconcept
Algorithms are divided into groups based on their worst-case running time: constant-time, linear, quadratic, exponential, etc.

It may seem strange to consider 1,000,000N and N both as $O(N)$, but mathematically we think of N as being, very, very large so that the effect of the constant is not noticeable. This is called "asymptotic behavior." It is useful to characterize and compare algorithms according to their asymptotic behavior. Nevertheless, bear in mind that this analysis works best for programs that deal with really huge numbers of data items.

16.2.1 Sorting: overview

Now that we've got a couple of analytical tools in place, let's look at some real algorithms. First, sorting. Sorting involves taking a collection of N items (which we may get one at a time or all at once) and making sure they are in order. Imagine you have several shelves of CDs, you can't ever find the one you want anymore, and you've decided to put them in some kind of order. Your first choice—talk your roommate into organizing them—has failed, so you need a quick and easy way to do it yourself.

We'll consider four simple, classical solutions to this problem: bubble sort, insertion sort, selection sort, and merge sort. They work just fine for collections ranging from hundreds to thousands of items, and only when we have to process orders-of-magnitude larger collections do we need more refined sorting methods. A nice animation of these and other sorting algorithms can be found at http://www.cs.ubc.ca/spider/harrison/Java/sorting-demo.html.

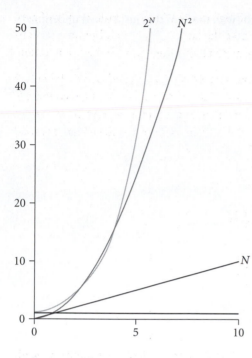

Figure 16.1 ■ Various rates of growth.

16.2.2 **Bubble sort**

With bubble sort, we look at two things at a time. Say we start with the first two CDs on the left end of the first shelf. The CDs are supposed to be in alphabetical order left-to-right by composer or performer (according to which one you're most likely to be looking for). We look at each pair of neighboring CDs, switch them if they're not in order, and move on to the next pair.

Here's our row of CDs to begin with:

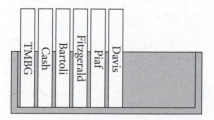

And here's what it looks like after each switch (with the item that just moved underlined):

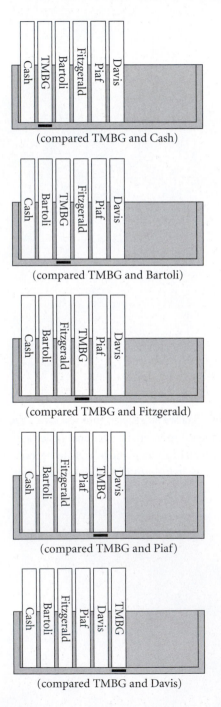

(compared TMBG and Cash)

(compared TMBG and Bartoli)

(compared TMBG and Fitzgerald)

(compared TMBG and Piaf)

(compared TMBG and Davis)

Notice how the alphabetically "largest" item, the TMBG (The Might Be Giants) CD, has "bubbled" its way to the end, one move at a time. This behavior is what gives the sort its name.

There's one problem, though: we've made it all the way to the end, and the CDs still aren't in order. What to do? Well, do it again, starting from the left, but this time, we don't need to go all the way to the right end, because we know that the CD on the right is in the right place.

Here's what happens the second time through:

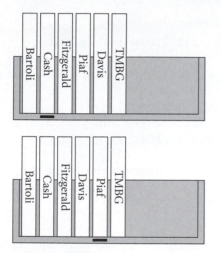

We're still not done, so we do it again. Now we know that the *two* CDs on the right are in the right place, so we can stop just before we get to them.

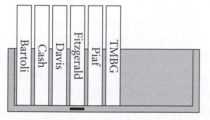

Now all the CDs are in order, so we should be done—but we're not. Why not? Remember that the algorithm only looks at two CDs at a time. If we stand back and look at the whole list, yes, we can see that they're all in order, but all we know from looking at two at a time is that we did some switches the first time through, and then we did some switches again the second and third times. For all we know, there may be more (and, in fact, it may take more than three iterations).

We won't know we're done until we go all the way through the list without making any switches. So we go through one more time. "Bartoli, Cash"—yes. "Cash, Davis"—yes. "Davis, Fitzgerald"—yes. "Fitzgerald, Piaf"—yes. "Piaf, They Might Be Giants"—yes. In sum, we go through the list over and over, switching CDs every time we find two neighbors that are not in order, until we can go all the way through once without making any switches. In each iteration we can avoid checking one fewer item than in the previous iteration.

This might seem like a lot of work, but is it? Let's try to measure the amount more precisely, starting with some pseudocode for bubble sort:

```
lastPositionToCheck = N;
    //to the right of this counter all items are sorted
    sorted = false
    while ( (lastPositionToCheck >1) and (!sorted)) {
       sorted = true // hope for the best
       for (int j = 2; j<=lastPositionToCheck; j++){
             compare the CDs in position j-1 and position j
             if they are in the wrong order {
                 a. swap them
                 b. sorted = false // remember the swap
       }
       lastPositionToCheck --
    }
```

The most important steps to count are the data comparisons and the data swaps. Ignoring the other steps simplifies the analysis and has little effect on the results, since they occur no more often than the comparisons.

How many data comparisons and swaps does bubble sort require? There's one data comparison and at most one swap inside the `for` loop, which in turn is inside a `while` loop. In the worst case, the `while` loop is executed $N - 1$ times. It stops being executed as soon as either (1) `lastPositionToCheck` is less than or equal to 1 or (2) the CDs become sorted. If it is possible for the CDs to remain unsorted until the N-1st time through the loop, then the loop will be executed $N - 1$ times—and it is in fact possible. (See if you can figure out under what conditions that would happen.)

The first time through the `while` loop, the `for` loop is executed $N - 1$ times, the second time through the loop it is executed $N - 2$ times, then $N - 3$ times, all the way down to 1. There's a formula for the sum of the numbers from 1 to $N - 1$: the total is $\frac{N(N - 1)}{2}$, or $\frac{1}{2}N^2 - \frac{1}{2}N$. Thus, every time the `for` loop is executed, we have $\frac{N(N - 1)}{2}$ data comparisons and up to $\frac{N(N - 1)}{2}$ swaps (or $\frac{1}{2}N^2 - \frac{1}{2}N$ of each, or $N^2 - N$ combined steps).

Note: The quick way to verify this useful sum is to pair the smallest and largest number, i.e., $1 + (N-1)$, then the next smallest and largest, $2 + (N-2)$, and so on, with each sum being N and there being $\frac{(N-1)}{2}$ such pairs.

From this analysis, we can say that bubble sort is $O(N^2)$. In other words, in order to sort your CDs using bubble sort, in the worst case, the number of steps is roughly proportional to the square of the number of CDs you have. If you have 100 CDs, that's 10,000 steps, which would take quite a while! Appropriate laziness motivates us to see if we can find a more efficient solution.

16.2.3 Insertion sort

Insertion sort works like this. Imagine that your CDs have all fallen off the shelves into a big pile on the floor:

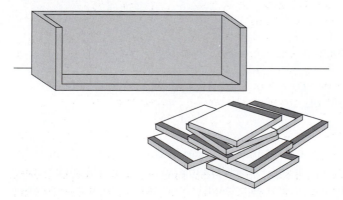

1. Pick any CD up off the floor and put it on the leftmost end of the top shelf. Now you have a sequence of CDs that's in order, even if it only includes one CD.

2. Pick up another CD and put it in order within the sequence of CDs that is already in place (i.e., either before or after the only one you have so far). Now you have a sequence of two.

3. Repeat until all the CDs are in place on the shelf.

This method would work just as well if the CDs were all on the shelf: make a space on the left-hand side of the top shelf for the ordered sequence, and take CDs one by one from the out-of-order part of the shelf (over on the right). Insertion sort is probably already familiar to you if you play cards: it is the way many people sort the cards in their hand.

Here's an example. Choose a CD—say, the TMBG CD—and put it on the left side of the shelf.

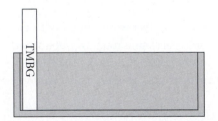

Then choose another, say the CD by Edith Piaf. "Piaf" comes before "They," so move TMBG over and put Piaf on the left.

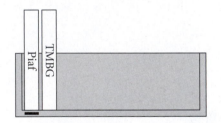

Next is a CD of piano music by Clara Schumann. Start by comparing it with the rightmost CD, They Might Be Giants. It goes to the left of that, so move They Might Be Giants over, and compare Schumann with Piaf. Schumann belongs to the right of Piaf, so we've found the right place, in the middle:

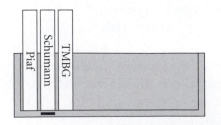

Next, a CD by Ella Fitzgerald. Now we have to compare with all three of the CDs that are there in turn, starting with TMBG, and move all three of them to put the new one in place:

On the upside, we always have a subsequence of CDs that is completely in order. On the downside, we have to keep moving CDs over to make room for the newly inserted one.

This doesn't seem quite so bad as bubble sort. But appearances might be deceptive. We do have to keep moving CDs over to make room for the newly inserted one. Let's make the comparison between insertion sort and bubble sort precise, starting with some pseudocode:

```
Put the first CD into the ordered sequence.
for (CDnum = 2; CDnum <= N; CDnum++) {
int shelfPosition;
    for (shelfPosition = CDnum-1; shelfPosition > 0
              and new CD belongs to the left of
                 the CD at shelfPosition;
              shelfPosition--) {
          move the CD at shelfPosition over;
    }
    Put the new CD in place.
```

The outer loop runs $N - 1$ times. Each time through the outer loop, for CD number j, at worst, the inner loop runs $j - 1$ times. In other words, if you happen to pick up the CDs in exactly backward order, every time you put one on the shelf, you have to move all the CDs that are already there over to make room. Thus, the inner loop could run a total of $1 + 2 + ... + (N - 2)$, or $\frac{(N - 1)(N - 2)}{2}$, times.

For each iteration of the inner loop, assuming we go through the loop the maximum number of times, there is one data comparison (inside the loop condition) and one data move. The final line (actually putting the CD on the shelf) is executed once each time through the outer loop, or $N - 1$ times. If we count putting the CD on the shelf as a move (as we should), we have a total of $\frac{(N - 1)(N - 2)}{2}$ data comparisons and $\frac{(N - 1)(N - 2)}{2} + (N-1)$, or $\frac{N(N - 1)}{2}$ data moves. Combining the two, we have a total of $(N - 1)^2$ operations. This is the same number of moves as the swaps we counted for bubble sort, and moves take less time. In addition, insertion sort has slightly fewer comparisons than bubble sort. Still, both algorithms are $O(N^2)$. Let's try to do better.

16.2.4 Selection sort

Selection sort works like this:

1. Look through all your CDs, find the one that goes first, and put it in place on the shelf.

2. Look through all the rest of the CDs ($N - 1$ of them), find the one that goes second, and put it to the right of the first one on the shelf.

3. Look through all the rest of the ($N - 2$) CDs, find the one that goes third, and put it to the right of the second one on the shelf.

4. Repeat until you have put all the CDs on the shelf.

By now, you should have an idea what's coming. Before we put CD number i on the shelf, we have to look through $N - i + 1$ elements to find it. So first we search through a pile of N CDs, then $N - 1$ CDs, then $N - 2$ CDs, etc., and we do N such searches. Yes, you're right—selection sort too is $O(N^2)$, although with different constants.

In addition to the worst-case analysis we have done here, we can also do a best-case analysis (what is the *minimum* amount of time this algorithm takes to sort N items) and an average-case analysis (generally, how much compute time an algorithm takes, averaged over all possible sequences of inputs). The average-case analysis, even though it is more difficult to compute, may well be the most important in practice.

Table 16.3 summarizes the relative performance of bubble sort, insertion sort, and selection sort, based on all three types of analysis.

As you can see, even though all three algorithms are $O(N^2)$, there are still differences among them. In the worst case, they are all about the same, but in the average case, insertion sort is better than the other two, and in the best case, both bubble sort and insertion sort are better than selection sort ever is. For small values of N, however, all of these algorithms work fine; your best strategy is probably to pick the one you feel most comfortable coding.

Table 16.3 ■ Comparison of bubble sort, insertion sort, and selection sort.

	Bubble	Insertion	Selection
Best-case	N	N	$\frac{N^2}{2}$
Average-case	$\frac{N^2}{2}$	$\frac{N^2}{4}$	$\frac{N^2}{2}$
Worst-case	$\frac{N^2}{2}$	$\frac{N^2}{2}$	$\frac{N^2}{2}$

16.2.5 **Merge sort**

We've now seen three very different ways of getting the CDs in order on the shelf, and they're all depressingly slow (unless you have only a very few CDs). Can we do any better?

Yes: merge sort, using the magic of recursion, can do much better. Here's the starting point. Suppose somehow we had all the CDs divided into two groups, and each group was already in order:

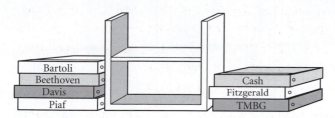

All we'd have to do is:

1. compare the items at the beginning of the two lists
2. pick the first one (Bartoli, in this case)
3. put it on the shelf to the right of what's already there
4. repeat until all the CDs are on the shelf

And best of all, in order to get an item to put on the shelf, we only need to make one comparison (between the two first items) and one move (from a pile to the shelf)! The time we need to do this is proportional to the number of CDs, or N.

The only catch, of course, is that our CDs are *not* in two neatly sorted piles. So here's what we do:

1. arbitrarily divide them into two roughly equal piles (Don't spend any time on it, just make sure the piles are about the same size.)
2. sort each of the smaller piles
3. merge the two sorted piles together

How can we sort the smaller piles? By dividing each of *them* into two smaller piles, sorting those piles, and merging them together. Basically, we just keep dividing up the piles until there are only two elements in each pile, and sort those two (which we can do trivially). Then we have a lot of sorted pairs. Combine them into sorted groups of four, then combine them into sorted groups of eight, and so on, until we have the whole pile sorted.

This process of sorting pairs, then combining the pairs, and so forth is shown in Figure 16.2. This should remind you of a tree! And if we think of it as a tree, the analysis becomes clear. The number of levels at which we have to merge is the height of the tree, which is $\log_2 N$. At each level, we have to deal with all N CDs, but we just have to do one move and at most one compare per CD, on average. So the total is $N * \log_2 N$, and merge sort is $O(N \log_2 N)$, which grows considerably more slowly than N^2.

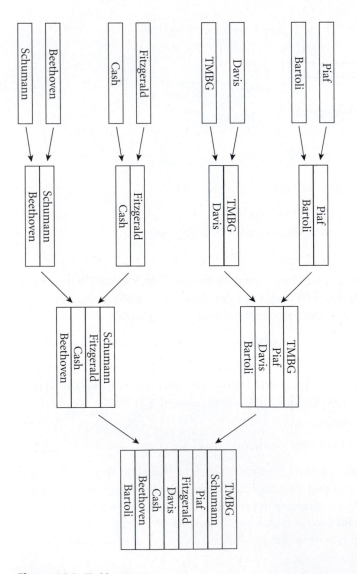

Figure 16.2 ■ Merge sort.

Because we only look at the first element of each list at each stage, merge sort is particularly useful for sorting linked lists, and also for sorting sequences of data that are so large they can't be read into memory all at once. And by starting with pairs of elements in the first place, then combining sorted pairs into sorted quadruples, and so on to do a nonrecursive "bottom-up" merge-sort, we can even avoid the overhead of recursion.

16.2.6 Recurrence relations

A **recurrence relation** (also called **recurrence**) is a recursive definition of a function. In other words, the function's value at one point is given in terms of its value at another point. For example, we might say:

$T(N) = 2^* \, T(N-1)$

The recurrence relation by itself is not enough to define a function. We also need to know its value at at least one point, which serves as the base case. For example, the definition above might include a value for $T(1)$:

$T(1) = 6$

Otherwise, we could define $T(N)$ in terms of $T(N-1)$, $T(N-1)$ in terms of $T(N-2)$, and on and on, but the definition would never stop. We would never be able to compute an actual value.

Often recurrences are very natural ways to express the time complexity of an algorithm. For example, with merge sort, the time it takes to sort N items is two times the time it takes to sort $\frac{N}{2}$ items plus the N steps it takes to merge the two sublists:

$$T(N) = 2^*T\left(\frac{N}{2}\right) + N$$

We'd like to translate this recurrence into a closed form. The definition of a function is in **closed form** if it is written in terms of a fixed number of basic operations. To get a closed form for a recurrence, we need to rewrite the function definition without recursion.

To get an idea of how to do that, let's unwind the definition by successive substitution of the original relation:

$$T(N) = \qquad\qquad\qquad 2^*T\left(\frac{N}{2}\right) + n$$

$$T(N) = 2^* \left[2^*T\left(\frac{N}{4}\right) + \left(\frac{N}{2}\right)\right] + N = 4^*T\left(\frac{N}{2}\right) + 2N$$

$$T(N) = 4^* \left[4^*T\left(\frac{N}{8}\right) + \left(\frac{N}{4}\right)\right] + 2N = 8^*T\left(\frac{N}{8}\right) + 3N$$

keyconcept

Four classic algorithms for sorting the elements of a collection are bubble sort, insertion sort, selection sort, and merge sort. The first three are all $O(N^2)$. Merge sort is much faster at $O(N \log_2 N)$.

keyconcept

Recurrences (recursive definitions of functions) are often very natural ways to express the time complexity of an algorithm.

When does this stop? Well, how long does it take us to sort one item? Just the one step it takes to "merge" the pile. So we'll say that

$$T(1) = 1$$

Then we just keep dividing $\frac{N}{2}, \frac{N}{4}, \frac{N}{8}, \ldots$ until the result is 1.

If you take a course in analysis of algorithms, you'll learn some tricks for solving these recurrences. But for now, just see if you can find any patterns. There are several patterns in this recurrence:

- At each step, we're multiplying T by powers of two: $2^1 = 2, 2^2 = 4, 2^3 = 8$, etc.
- At each step, we're dividing N by the same power of two
- When we multiply T by the ith power of 2, 2^i, we also add $i * N$

So we can rewrite the recurrence like this:

$$T(N) = 2^i * T\left(\frac{N}{2^i}\right) + i * N$$

We know that $T(1) = 1$, so when $\frac{N}{2^i} = 1$ we can substitute 1 for $T\left(\frac{N}{2^i}\right)$. Let's solve for i to find out when $\frac{N}{2^i} = 1$:

$$\frac{N}{2^i} = 1$$
$$N = 2^i$$
$$i = \log_2 N$$

Now if we substitute $\log_2 N$ for i and 1 for $T\left(\frac{N}{2^i}\right)$, we get:

$$T(N) = 2^{\log_2 N} * 1 + (\log_2 N) * N$$
$$= N + N \log_2 N$$

So $T(N) = N + N \log_2 N = O(N \log_2 N)$. And for mergesort, we have a worst-case run-time of $O(N \log_2 N)$.

For another example of a recurrence relation, consider the Towers of Hanoi problem from Chapter 12. Recall that we have three pegs (A, B, and C) and N disks, all of different sizes, as shown in Figure 16.3. To begin with, the disks are all on peg A, with the largest disk on the bottom. Each disk in the pile is a little smaller than the one below it.

The goal is to transfer all N disks from peg A to peg C. The rules are:

1. Move one disk at a time.
2. Never put a larger disk above a smaller one.

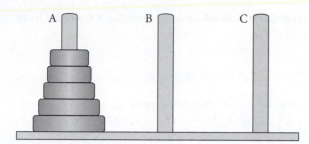

Figure 16.3 ■ Towers of Hanoi.

As we saw in Chapter 12, the recursive solution to this problem is:

1. Temporarily move $N - 1$ disks from peg A to peg B.
2. Move the largest disk (the only one left) from A to C, where it belongs.
3. Move $N - 1$ disks from B to C.

Using a recurrence relation, we can easily write down the number of moves this solution will take:

$$T(N) = 2 * T(N - 1) + 1$$

To move N disks, move $N - 1$ disks twice (steps 1 and 3) and move one disk once (step 2).

We need to know when to stop. How much work would we have to do to move one disk? Just one move. So

$$T(1) = 1$$

By unwinding the recurrence, we get:

$$T(N) = 2 * [2 * T(N - 2) + 1] + 1 = 4 * T(N - 2) + (2 + 1)$$
$$= 4 * [2 * T(N - 3) + 1] + (2 + 1) = 8 * T(N - 3) + (4 + 2 + 1)$$
$$= 8 * [2 * T(N - 4) + 1] + (4 + 2 + 1) = 16 * T(N - 4) + (8 + 4 + 2 + 1)$$

Where we go from here depends on noticing patterns. Notice that when we have $T(N - i)$ on the right, we always multiply it by 2^i: $2^2 * T(N - 2)$, $2^3 * T(N - 3)$, etc. And when we multiply by 2^i, we're always adding on all the smaller powers of i: 2^{i-1}, 2^{i-2}, ..., down to 1.

Let's rewrite the equation in terms of these powers of two:

$$T(N) = 2^i * T(N - i) + 2^{i-1} + 2^{i-2} + ... + 1$$

We can get rid of $T(N - i)$ when $T(N - i) = 1$. What value of i will set $N - i$ equal to 1?

$$N - i = 1$$
$$N = 1 + i$$
$$N - 1 = i$$

Now we can substitute $N - 1$ for i and 1 for $T(N - i)$, and we get:

$$T(N) = 2^{N-1} * 1 + 2^{N-2} + 2^{N-3} + \dots + 1$$

In other words, $T(N)$ is the sum of the first $N - 1$ powers of 2. This is called a **geometric sum,** and it turns out there's a formula for it:

$$T(N) = 2^N - 1$$

So we say that the recursive algorithm for solving the Towers of Hanoi is $O(2^N)$. An algorithm that is $O(2^N)$ is also called an **exponential algorithm**, because its worst-case runtime is an exponential function of the number of elements in the input. Exponential algorithms are typically not viable for problems with large N; we must look for faster algorithms or ones that don't give optimal solutions or only approximate answers. Sometimes, even a nonrecursive algorithm runs exponentially, and it is the province of analysis-of-algorithms and computational-complexity research to characterize the intrinsic difficulty of problems.

16.2.7 **Searching: overview**

Searching is one of the most fundamental computer tasks. We often need to search for data, such as a book in the library catalog or a particular topic on the Web. In addition, as we have seen with stacks, queues, lists, and trees, we may need to search as part of an insert or delete operation, in order to find the correct place for data to be added or removed. Searching is so important that we sort our data in order to make searching faster.

As with sorting, we analyze four different search methods. The efficiency of the searches we discuss depends at least as much on the data structure we are searching in as it does on the process we use. So we'll be talking about searching in arrays, linked lists, binary trees, and a new data structure called a "hash table."

16.2.8 **Searching: arrays**

keyconcept

Linear search is $O(N)$.

How we search in an array depends on whether it's ordered or not. If it's not ordered, the best we can do is start at the beginning of the array and check each item until we find the one we want (or reach the end of the array without finding it). This technique is called **linear search**.

At worst, with linear search, we have to check every single item in the list. And the worst case includes every time the item we're looking for is not in the list, any time we need to make sure we find duplicates, as well as the times when the item we want is actually at the very end of the list. Linear search takes $O(N)$ time. (We also say that the algorithm runs in "linear time," meaning that the time is a linear function of the number of elements.) While that may seem good compared to our sorting algorithms, we can do better.

keyconcept
Binary search is $O(\log_2 N)$.

If our array is sorted, we can use binary search. **Binary search** in an array is similar to searching in a binary search tree:

1. If the array has N elements, we start by checking element $\frac{N}{2}$.

2. If that's the item we want, we're done.

3. If the item we're looking for is earlier in the list than element $\frac{N}{2}$, we now consider elements 1 to $\left(\frac{N}{2}\right) - 1$.

4. If the item we're looking for is later in the list than element $\frac{N}{2}$, we now consider elements $\left(\frac{N}{2}\right) + 1$ to N.

5. Either way, we pick the element in the middle of our new subarray, and compare it with the one we're looking for.

6. Repeat this whole process until we've either found the element we're looking for or reduced the size of the array to 1, and the only element left is not the one we want.

At each step, we perform one operation (comparing the data we find with the data we're looking for), and we cut the size of the array we have left to search in half. How many times can we go on cutting something in half before we get it down to 1? $\log_2 N$. Just like merge sort, binary search is $O(\log_2 N)$. If an algorithm's runtime is proportional to the logarithm of the number of elements in the input, as these are, we say that it is a **logarithmic-time** algorithm.

Search is extremely fast in a sorted array, but, insert might not be. If we're inserting a new element at the beginning of an array, we have to move all the other $N - 1$ elements of the array over to make room for it. If the array is full and we need to copy it over into a new larger array to make room for the new item, we'll have to copy all $N - 1$ items. Any time we delete an item in the middle of the array, we need to move items over to fill in the empty space. As a result, our worst-case time for insert and delete in an array is $O(N)$. This time applies to Java's `Vectors` and `ArrayLists` as well as to arrays, since the `Vector` and `ArrayList` classes are implemented using arrays. Consequently we use arrays only if the volume of inserts and deletes is relatively low, especially compared to the volume of searches.

16.2.9 **Searching: linked lists**

Instead of an array, suppose our data is stored in a linked list like the one we implemented in Chapter 14. Whether or not the list is sorted, we have to start with the first node and look at one node at a time. If

- The data we're looking for is in the last node in the list
- The data we're looking for isn't in the list at all
- We need to check for duplicates

then we need to look at every single item in the list. In effect, it's the same situation as searching an unsorted array: the worst-case runtime for searching in a linked list is $O(N)$.

Since search is part of insert and delete (because you have to search for the right place to insert or delete), insert and delete also have a worst-case time of $O(N)$. Inserts and deletes are simpler to implement in linked lists than they are in arrays, since we don't need to worry about moving or copying data. Unfortunately, their runtime isn't any faster.

16.2.10 **Searching: binary trees**

Binary trees offer some of the advantages of both arrays and linked lists. As long as the tree is approximately balanced, we can effectively do a binary search, so that search time and insert time are both logarithmic. There are three disadvantages, compared to linked lists:

1. We may need to do some work to keep the tree balanced, especially if there are frequent inserts and deletes.
2. There's an extra reference in each node, taking up some additional space.
3. And, as we saw in Chapter 15, deletes are somewhat more complicated.

Because of this overhead, it makes sense to use a tree for searching only if large amounts of data are being stored. Industrial-strength databases, which may store millions of items, typically use a form of balanced trees. For a small problem, a linked-list solution is efficient enough, and it is quicker and easier to code.

16.2.11 **Searching: n-ary and hybrid trees**

What if, instead of a binary tree, we use a tree in which each node has three children? Or 10? Or 100? An **n-ary** tree is a general term for a tree in which each node has n children. The larger n is, that is, the more children each node has, the shallower the tree will be. For example, if two trees both have 20 internal nodes, and one is a binary tree and the other is a 10-ary tree (a tree where each node has ten children), then the 10-ary tree will be shallower as shown in Figure 16.4.

If the tree is shallower, then we won't have to search as far. To be precise, a binary tree has $O(\log_2 N)$ search time, a tree where each node has three children has $O(\log_3 N)$ search time, a tree where each child has 100 children has $O(\log_{100} N)$ search time, and so on. The difference between $\log_2 N$ and $\log_{100} N$ isn't that great, however. Some sample values are given in Table 16.4.

In other words, a search with a binary tree might take six or seven times as long as it would with a tree that has 100 branches. Compared to an N of a million, however, this

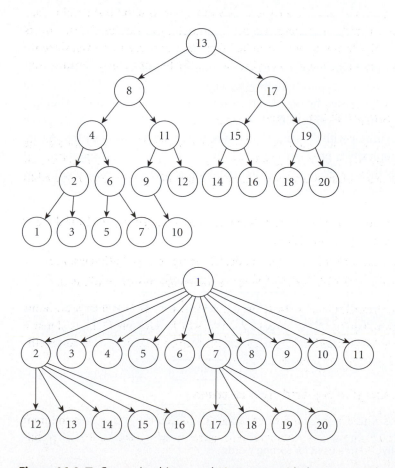

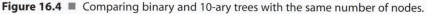

Figure 16.4 ■ Comparing binary and 10-ary trees with the same number of nodes.

isn't a big difference. Moreover, the more children each node has, the more space the links take up and the more complicated the node processing is. In general, binary trees are therefore far more prevalent for searching and sorting than n-ary trees.

Table 16.4 ■ Comparison of approximate search times for trees with 2, 10, and 100 branches per Node.

N	$\log_2 N$ (approx.)	$\log_{10} N$	$\log_{100} N$
1	0	0	0
10	3.3	1	0.5
100	6.6	2	1
1000	10.0	3	1.5
10,000	13.3	4	2
1,000,000	19.9	6	3

Another possibility is a **hybrid tree**, a tree in which the root has a large number of children but other internal nodes only have two (see Figure 16.5). One possible application for a hybrid tree, as suggested by the picture, is for sorting words or names. They can be inserted into the tree according to the first letter of each word: within that tree, each group of words beginning with the same letter can be organized into a binary tree. Again, the additional complexity is probably not worth the small gain in searching speed, but it is suggestive—is there perhaps another technique for significantly reducing the size of the subarrays to be searched in an initial step?

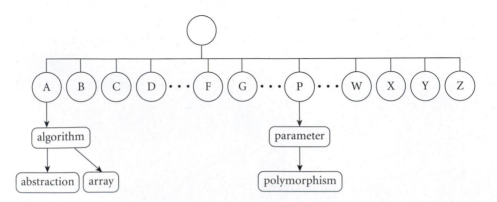

Figure 16.5 ■ A hybrid tree used for sorting words.

16.2.12 **Searching: hash tables**

Suppose we have a single-level tree in which each element is one of the children of the root. Then we could use each key as an index and go from the root to its child immediately. Insert, delete, and search each take one step (i.e., they're $O(1)$). An algorithm that is $O(1)$ is said to be a **constant-time** algorithm.

Even better than using a tree, we can use an array. If each piece of data has a unique key from 1 to N and we use an array of size N, we can simply use the key to index into the array without going through the root (see Figure 16.6.)

> **keyconcept**
>
> A hash table is a combination of an array and a hash function. In practice, searching is nearly 0(1) with a hash table.

Sounds perfect, right? But consider how it might work in practice. A local theater identifies its subscribers by their phone number. It has approximately 500 subscribers. United States phone numbers are ten digits, long, however:

```
(123) 456-7890
```

If a programmer sets up an array for the theater that uses phone numbers as an index, the array will need to have a size of a billion. `Insert`, `delete`, and `search` could all be done in constant time, but .9999995% of the space in the array would be wasted. An array like this in which most of the elements are empty is called a **sparse array**.

Another issue is choosing the right key. Do we want to use phone numbers or another number that's already associated with our data, such as (in the United States) social security numbers? Or assign an arbitrary number to each subscriber? What if our data doesn't have an obvious number associated with it (like the variable names in a program)?

A **hash table** is a combination of an array and a function (called a **hash function**) that takes any of the pieces of data we want to store and returns a number that we can use as an index into the array. In the theater example, the hash function was phoneNumberOf(subscriber). (We assume here that each subscriber reports exactly one phone number to the theater). As long as each piece of data is stored in a separate location in the array, `insert`, `delete`, and `search` each have exactly two steps:

1.   Use the hash function to find the right location for the data.

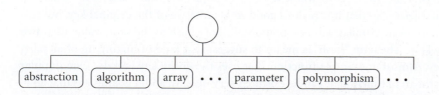

Figure 16.6 ■ The ideal tree for searching, with every leaf node at depth 1.

2. Perform the desired operation (i.e., insert the data into the array, `delete` it, or report whether it was found).

If each piece of data is stored in a separate location in the array, then `insert`, `delete`, and `search` all have constant time. But the trick clearly is to use a hash function that doesn't create a sparse array—we need something like a 3- or 5- digit identifier for our movie subscribers to get a smaller array that will be much denser. Typically we use the hash function to calculate integers based on names (or other strings) identifying a record. For example, the theater might use a hash function that assigns a number to each letter of the alphabet—1 for A, 2 for B, and so forth—and adds up the numbers assigned to each subscriber's name.

What if the hash function returns the same value for two different pieces of data? What if, for example, two different subscribers (say, two college roommates) have the same phone number? What if, instead of phone numbers, they decided to use birthdays (since there are only 365 of them)? Even if we calculate a number based on the key, the hash function may return the same result for two different inputs. For example, with the hash function described in the last paragraph, "Bob" and "Dan" both hash to 19. Each location in the hash table is known as a **bucket**—what if two pieces of data end up in the same bucket?

When the hash function returns the same value for two different pieces of data so that they end up in the same bucket, we have what is called a **collision**. The bigger the hash table, the less likely it is that a collision will occur; the smaller the hash table, the more likely. Note that while the hash function must yield the same answer each time, it doesn't have an inverse—we can't tell from any generated identifier what the original item was.

There are a number of solutions to the problem of collisions in hash tables. First, we need a good hash function. A good hash function distributes the data almost evenly across the buckets, so as to minimize collisions. As an example of a bad hash function, suppose we use only 26 buckets and store the theater subscribers in buckets according to the first letter of their last name. Not only will there be a lot of collisions (which we could have predicted, since there are 500 subscribers and only 26 buckets), but the data will be very unevenly distributed: many subscribers will end up in the "M" bucket and few if any in the "Z" bucket.

A good hash function uses the whole key (for example, the whole last name instead of just its first letter) so that it is really a good representative of the original key, but two keys that are nearly similar will not be more likely to hash to the same value than two arbitrary keys. The term "hash" is meant to suggest that kind of mixing up of all parts of the key. Almost any simple function that uses the entire key will do. One popular choice is the mod function. It can be executed very quickly, and it guarantees that all of the hash values are legal array indexes into the hash table. For best results, use a prime as the size of the hash table.

Using mod as the basis for the hash function works like this:

1. Take the number that is being used as the key (or a number based on the computer representation of the key, assuming it is alphanumeric). Suppose that the number is k and the size of the hash table is s.

2. Compute k mod s.

If the key is 512, for example, and the size of our table is 101, the hash value will be 7. Even with a good hash function, there are some collisions. It's simply not practical, except for very small problems, to have an array that's large enough to hold every possible key value separately. When we have a collision, we need a fallback strategy: an alternative location for the data. One solution is to associate a linked list with each bucket. Instead of finding data in the array itself, the algorithm looks in the first node of the linked list, then if necessary the second, and so on (see Figure 16.7). Alternatively, we could associate a binary tree with each bucket and store data in the nodes of the binary tree.

The worst-case time for searching in hash tables would arise if every single element hashed to the same bucket. In that case, the time would be that of a linear search over N items, i.e., $O(N)$. In practice, however, collisions are rare enough that hash tables very often give us near constant-time performance, something that can't be matched by any of the alternatives we've discussed. Putting even a collection of a million items in 511 buckets, assuming a good hash that produces few empty slots and a near-uniform number of collisions, gives us an approximate bucket size of only 2000 items, which can be binary-searched very quickly.

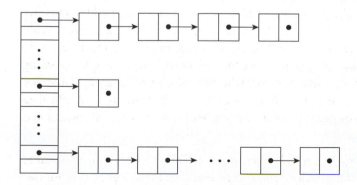

Figure 16.7 ■ Hash table with linked lists for collisions.

■ Summary ■

In this chapter, we have attempted to give you some of the flavor of algorithm analysis, one of the most fascinating and important topics in computer science. We have looked at four sorting algorithms, bubble sort, insertion sort, selection sort, and merge sort, and considered searching in the context of four data structures, arrays, linked lists, trees, and hash tables.

We can only give you an overview of this material. There's a vast literature on algorithm analysis, and if you continue with computer science, you will probably take a full-length course in this material. But it is important to understand even now that there are often different ways to solve the same problem, and that both the data structure we choose to organize our data and the process we design for working on that data can strongly affect the efficiency of our programs.

In addition, we have seen that the comparison of two different solutions is not just a matter of opinion. The analysis of different solutions can be very precise, and we have had a glimpse of some of the powerful mathematical techniques for that analysis.

■ Self-Check Questions ■

1. Define the following terms:
    a. Algorithm analysis
    b. Big-oh notation
    c. Constant-time algorithm
    d. Logarithmic-time algorithm
    e. Linear algorithm
    f. Quadratic algorithm
    g. Constant-time algorithm
    h. Exponential algorithm
    i. Recurrence
    j. Recurrence relation
    k. Closed form
    l. Linear search
    m. Binary search
    n. Hybrid tree
    o. *N*-ary tree
    p. Hash table
    q. Hash function
    r. Bucket
    s. Collision

2. List the steps involved in bubble sort and give its worst-case runtime.

3. List the steps involved in insertion sort and give its worst-case runtime.

4. List the steps involved in selection sort and give its worst-case runtime.

5. List the steps involved in merge sort and give its worst-case runtime.

6. Which of the sort algorithms has (have) the best worst-case performance?

7. Which of the sort algorithms is (are) quadratic?

8. What is fastest: linear time, logarithmic time, constant time, quadratic time, or exponential time? Explain, with examples.

9. What is the worst-case performance for searching in:

   a. An unsorted array
   b. A sorted array
   c. A linked list
   d. A binary tree
   e. An n-ary tree
   f. A hash table
   g. A sorted Java `Vector`
   h. A sorted Java `ArrayList`

10. What should a good hash function do?

■ Exercises ■

Applying the Facts

1. Hash tables are very good for insert, delete, and search, but they're not at all good for sorting data. Explain why not.

2. Suppose you are assigned to write a program that stores data about each student in your class (name, contact information, grades on exams, etc.) in a hash table. What hash function would you choose and why? Discuss.

3. Compare and contrast arrays, linked lists, binary trees, and hash tables for sorting data. When would you use each one and why?

4. Suppose you have a very dynamic problem where inserts and deletes happen much more frequently than searches. Which data structure would you choose and why?

5. Analyze the worst-case runtime of the implementations we gave for the dictionary ADT in Chapters 14 and 15.

■ **Programming Projects** ■

Writing Programs

1. The searching and sorting algorithms in this chapter can be used to implement the dictionary ADT. Write an implemention of the dictionary ADT that stores 100 numbers in a sorted array and performs binary search on the array.

2. Rewrite the program from question 1 so that it uses a linked list rather than an array. Which do you prefer, and why? Are there circumstances under which you would prefer the other solution? What are those circumstances?

3. Rewrite the program from question 1 so that it uses a binary tree. Which of the three versions of the program do you prefer, and why?

4. Write an implementation of the dictionary ADT that stores data about each student in a class (name, contact information, grades on exams, etc.) in a hash table.

chapter **17**

Strings and Text I/O

OBJECTIVES

After reading this chapter, you should be able to:

☑ Declare, define, and use `String` variables

☑ Use the built-in `String` functions

☑ Display text in a `JFrame` using a `JLabel` or `TextArea`

☑ Read in text input using a `TextArea` or `TextBox`

■ 17.1 ■ Introduction

Suppose you start a company, My Cool Company. It has a website, www.myCoolCompany.com. Now you want to write a standard webpage that will generate webpages automatically, to be hosted at that website. Alternatively, suppose you want to encrypt a webpage. Suppose you want to write a program to search through a webpage for a particular phrase. Or suppose you're writing a program—almost any kind of program—and you want to let the user type in commands, instead of just using the mouse or pressing a button.

To solve these problems, we need to write programs that represent and manipulate words: read them in, store them inside the program, modify them, and display the results. In this chapter, we discuss some of the ways in which text is stored and manipulated inside a Java program, and also some of the ways in which text can be read in from and output to the user using a graphical user interface (GUI).

■ 17.2 ■ Concepts

Most programming languages have a way of representing text. Basically, **text** is anything a user can type in from the keyboard, such as "Hello," or "Put a circle on the screen at (25, 150)," or a list of names and addresses, or "http://www.myCoolCompany.com."

There are a few basic things we'd like to be able to do with text. We'd like to be able to combine two pieces of text. For example, if the user types in "www.myCoolCompany.com" and we know the default beginning of a URL is "http://," we would like our program to automatically create the string "http://www.myCoolCompany.com." We'd like to be able to search a piece of text. For example, suppose we want to count how many times the word "cool" occurs on our webpage. We'd like to be able to compare one piece of text to another, to see if they're equal or maybe put them in order. For example, we might like to sort a list of names and addresses. We might like to be able to replace one piece of text with another. For example, we might want to take a standard webpage and fill in the blanks with appropriate values.

Here we look at some of the operations Java provides for manipulating text; we also look at some of the mechanisms Java provides for reading in and outputting text using GUIs.

■ 17.3 ■ Mechanics: `Strings`

In order to illustrate various ways to manipulate text, we use interfaces like the one in Figure 17.1. This picture was taken immediately after the text in the left-hand box was entered and the button "Reverse string" was clicked. A string such as "able was I ere I saw elba" that is the same when reversed is called a **palindrome**. In Section 17.4, we'll show how to create this interface, add different buttons, and vary the textboxes, depending on the operations we want to perform.

First, though, let's see what goes on behind the scenes. One of Java's built-in classes is the **`String` class**, designed to hold text. It is part of `java.lang`, so we can use it with-

Figure 17.1 ■ Screenshot from `String` Demo with multiple buttons.

out any `import` statements. `String` is a **final class** in Java, so it cannot have any subclasses. Declaring a `String` variable is just like declaring any other variable:

```
String url;
```

Any text inside double quotation marks is a **`String` literal**, that is, an instance of the `String` class that we can use in our programs. We have seen examples of this already in debugging statements, for example,

```
System.out.println("Inside method foo of class bar.");
```

We can also use `String` literals to initialize `String` variables:

```
String url = "http://www.myCoolCompany.com";
```

Since `String`s are a class, we can initialize `String` variables using a constructor, the same way we generally initialize objects:

```
String url = new String("http://www.myCoolCompany.com");
```

The first way is shorter and easier to type. Not only that, it turns out that it's more effi-cient as well, so we use it from here on (see the `String` section of the Java Tutorial at http://java.sun.com/docs/books/tutorial/java/data/strings/html for details).

17.3.1 Combining `Strings`

Java provides the special operator + for combining `Strings`. For example, if we say,

```
String url = "http://" + "www.myCoolCompany.com";
```

then the value of `url` is "`http://www.myCoolCompany.com`." Combining `Strings` is also called **concatenation.**

We can use the + operator to concatenate `String` variables as well as `String` literals. For example, suppose we have a `String` variable `defaultURLstart` whose value is "`http//:`". We can combine this prefix with the rest of the URL like this:

```
String homePage = defaultURLstart +
        "www.myCoolCompany.com"
```

The value of `homePage` is then "`http://www.myCoolCompany.com`."

Finally, suppose we want to generate the URLs for webpages for all the employees of myCoolCompany. If the names of the employees are stored in an array `employeeNames`, we can say:

```
String [ ] employeeURLs = new
            String[employeeNames.length];
```

```
for (int i = 0; i <employeeNames.length; i++){
    employeeURLS[i] = homePage + "/" + employeeNames[i];
```

17.3.2 **Extracting parts of Strings**

keyconcept
String has a substring method that returns part of the String.

Java provides the method `substring` to return a new `String` that is a substring of the given `String`. The first parameter is the location of the first character of the substring in the original `String`, and the second parameter is one *more* than the location of the last character of the substring. As with arrays, the first location in a `String` is position 0.

Thus, for example, if we say

```
String homePage = "http://www.myCoolCompany.com";
```

then the value of

```
homePage.substring(0, 1)
```

is the `String` "h". The value of

```
homePage.substring(0, 7)
```

is the `String` "http://".

17.3.3 **Comparing Strings**

keyconcept
Java provides three methods to test Strings for equality. In three different ways: the == operator, equal, and equalsIgnore Case.

Java provides three ways to test `Strings` for equality that depend on how strict we want to be. The "==" operator returns true only if two `String` variables refer to the same location in memory. For example, if we have:

```
String defaultPrefix = "http://";
s1 = defaultPrefix;
```

then the expression

```
s1==defaultPrefix
```

returns `true`.

The `equals` method returns `true` if two `Strings` contain the same characters in the same order. For example, suppose we want to test whether a particular URL is the one we're looking for. If we have

```
String companyURL = "www.myCoolCompany.com";
```

and

```
String desiredURL = "www.myCoolCompany.com";
```

then the expression

```
companyURL == desiredURL
```

is `false` because the two identical strings are stored in two different places in memory. On the other hand, the method call

```
companyURL.equals(desiredURL);
```

returns `true`.

Finally, suppose we have a URL but we're not sure it is capitalized the same way as the website does. Suppose we have, for example,

```
String companyURL = "www.myCoolCompany.com";
```

and

```
String desiredURL = "www.myCOOLcompany.com";
```

The method call

```
companyURL.equals(desiredURL);
```

now returns `false`.

Java provides a built-in method `equalsIgnoreCase` that returns `true` when two `Strings` contain the same letters in the same order, even if some upper-case letters in one `String` are lower-case in another. The method call

```
companyURL.equalsIgnoreCase(desiredURL);
```

returns `true`.

Figure 17.2 is a screenshot of a program that lets the user test these three definitions of equality. The user enters two `Strings` on the left and clicks a button to indicate which equality test is to be used. The result of testing the two input `Strings` then appears on the right. This screenshot was taken just after the user clicked the "Equals" button. Note that we have reused most of the interface from our previous example; a second input box has been added and the buttons (and the related operations) are new, but the general layout and use of buttons is the same.

17.3.4 **Reversing Strings**

Suppose we want to write a method that takes a `String` and returns its reverse. For example, if the input is "Java", the output should be "avaJ".

Here's the skeleton of our method, with a local variable `reverse` to hold the result as we build it, step by step.

```
public String reverse (String text) {
    String reverse = "";
    // to be added
}
```

The variable `reverse` is initialized with the empty `String`. The **empty `String`** is a `String` that has a length of 0 and is written `""`. If you combine it with any other `String`, you get that `String` (just as when you add 0 to a number, you get back the original number). For example,

```
"hello" + ""
```

is the `String "hello"`. We will be adding the letters from `myString` to `reverseString`, starting with the last letter and working backward.

Whatever `String` we have, we can use the `length` method to find out how long it is, so we know how many letters we have to copy. Since we know how many there are, a `for` loop is a good choice. We can use the `substring` method to pull out one character at a time. To get character `i-1` from a `String`, we write:

```
text.substring(i-1,i)
```

And finally, to add each character to the `reverse String`, we can say:

```
reverse += text.substring(i-1,i);
```

Note the += operator. This operator can be expanded in the same way as for integers: thus

```
string1 += string2;
```

is shorthand for

```
string1 = string1 + string2;
```

Now we can put all the pieces together:

```
public String reverse (String text) {
        int len = text.length();
        String reverse = "";
        for (int i = len; i > 0; i--) {
            reverse += text.substring(i-1, i);
        }
        return reverse;
    }
```

We use this method in the `StringDemo` program.

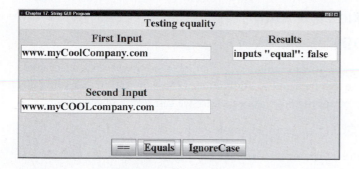

Figure 17.2 ■ Screenshot from `EqualTestApp` program.

17.3.5 Summarizing the `String` class

The `String` class methods and operators we have discussed so far, plus a few others, are summarized in Table 17.1. For the complete list, go to http://java.sun.com/reference/api/index.html, select the online Java documentation for the version of Java you are running, and look at the documentation for the `String` class.

Table 17.1 ■ Summary of the `String` class.

String operator or method	Brief description
`+`	Creates a new `String` made up of copies of its two operands
`String substring (int start, int end)`	Returns a `String` that is a copy of the substring of this `String` that starts at `start` and ends at position `end-1`
`==`	Returns true if two `Strings` contain the same characters in the same order, in the same case, stored in the same location in memory
`boolean equals (String otherString)`	Returns true if this `String` and `otherString` contain the same characters in the same order, in the same case
`boolean equalsIgnoreCase (String otherString)`	Returns true if this `String` and `otherString` contain the same characters in the same order, regardless of case
`boolean endsWith (String suffix)`	Returns true if this `String` ends in `suffix`
`boolean startsWith (String prefix)`	Returns true if this `String` starts with `prefix`
`int length()`	Returns the length of this `String`. (Contrast arrays: for an array A, the syntax would be `A.length`.)
`String toLowerCase()`	Returns a copy of this `String` with all upper-case letters converted to lower-case
`String toUpperCase()`	Returns a copy of this `String` with all lower-case letters converted to upper-case

■ 17.4 ■ Working Out with **Strings**—GUI Text I/O

In this section, we first show how to build a GUI that lets users input text, select operations to be performed on that text, and see the results of those operations. Creating this GUI is another example of appropriate laziness, since we can re-use it several times.

We then customize the GUI to create three simple applications:

1. `EchoApp`. Echoes whatever the user types in.
2. `StringMethodsApp`. Tests miscellaneous `String` methods.
3. `EqualTestApp`. Takes two `Strings` and compares the three different ways of testing them for equality.

These examples can be adapted to create a variety of simple text I/O programs.

17.4.1 A boilerplate GUI for simple text I/O programs

In this GUI, we need to read in text input by the user and display text for the user. Three of the classes Java provides for these purposes are `JLabel`, `JTextField`, and `JTextArea`.

1. `JLabel` lets us display a small amount of text that cannot be edited by the user.
2. `JTextField` lets us read in or display a single line of text. Text displayed may or may not be editable.
3. `JTextArea` lets us read in or display more than one line of text. Text may or may not be editable.

Our implementation includes two classes, `StringGUI` and `LabeledTextBox`. `StringGUI` is an `abstract` class that defines the general layout of components in the window. Each window contains a `JLabel` and two or more `LabeledTextBoxes`. The `JLabel` indicates what the program is about (for example, "Testing Equality" in Figure 17.2). The `LabeledTextBoxes` are a combination of a `JTextField` (for inputting or outputting text) and a `JLabel` that serves as a caption for the `JTextField`. With minor modifications, `JTextAreas` can be substituted for the `JTextFields`; this increases the number of lines available for input and output.

The code for `StringGUI` is given in Listing 17.1. `StringGUI` is a `JFrame`. It implements `ActionListener` because it's going to listen for `JButton` input. It includes two `LabeledTextBoxes`, one for the input and one for the output. It has a separate `JPanel` to hold the `JButtons`. The `JFrame`, `JPanel`, and `JButtons` are all familiar from Chapter 8.

```
 1    /**
 2     * Chapter 17: StringGUI.java
 3     * A basic framework for String I/O programs.
 4     */
 5    import java.awt.event.*;
 6    import java.awt.*;
 7    import javax.swing.*;
 8
 9    public abstract class StringGUI extends JFrame
10                           implements ActionListener {
11       private JPanel _buttonPanel;
12       protected LabeledTextBox _inputBox; //use in subclass
13       protected LabeledTextBox _resultBox;//use in subclass
14       protected Font _defaultFont; // use in subclass
15
16       public StringGUI(String title){
17          super("Chapter 17: String GUI program");
18          this.setDefaultCloseOperation(JFrame.EXIT_ON_CLOSE);
19          _defaultFont = new
20             Font("Times New Roman",Font.BOLD,30);
21
22          // create and put title for particular app in NORTH
23          JLabel label = new
24             JLabel(title,SwingConstants.CENTER);
25          label.setFont(_defaultFont);
26          label.setBackground(Color.yellow);
27          label.setOpaque(true);
28          this.add(label, BorderLayout.NORTH);
29
30          // create and place input and result areas
31          _inputBox = new
32             LabeledTextBox("Input",12,true,_defaultFont);
33          this.add(_inputBox, BorderLayout.WEST);
34          _resultBox = new
35             LabeledTextBox("Results",12,false,_defaultFont);
36          this.add(_resultBox, BorderLayout.EAST);
37
38          // put some space in CENTER
39          JPanel middleSpace = new JPanel();
40          middleSpace.setPreferredSize(new Dimension(50,300));
41          this.add(middleSpace,BorderLayout.CENTER);
```

Listing 17.1 ■ The StringGUI class (*continued on next page*)

```
42
43          // create and add a place for buttons in SOUTH
44          _buttonPanel = new JPanel();
45          _buttonPanel.setLayout(new FlowLayout());
46          this.add(_buttonPanel, BorderLayout.SOUTH);
47       }
48    public abstract void actionPerformed(ActionEvent e);
49
50    public void addMethodButton(String label,
51                                ActionListener listener) {
52       JButton button = new JButton(label);
53       button.setFont(_defaultFont);
54       button.addActionListener(listener);
55       _buttonPanel.add(button);
56       }
57    }
```

Listing 17.1 ■ The `StringGUI` class

Line 14 introduces a new Java built-in class, `Font`. This class contains information about font type and size to use in displaying text in a Java GUI. In lines 19 and 20, the `StringGUI` constructor initializes the `_defaultFont` variable with a new instance of the `Font` class. The actual values of the parameters to the `Font` constructor should be familiar: the font we choose here is 30-point Times New Roman boldface.

Working from the top of the `JFrame` down, the first thing we want to create is a title. It should appear centered at the top of the `JFrame`, with a yellow background, and it should not be editable by the user. The part of the code that makes this happen is lines 22 through 28. Here we create a `JLabel`, center it, give it the default font, set its color to be yellow, make it opaque, and then add it to the top of the `JFrame`.

Starting on line 30, we create the `LabeledTextBoxes`. The first parameter to the `LabeledTextBox` constructor is the desired label (a `String`), the second is the width of the `TextBox`. The fourth is the desired font. Note that the third parameter is different in the two `LabeledTextBoxes`. This parameter determines whether the text in the `LabeledTextBox` is editable by the user. Accordingly, it's `true` for the `_inputBox`, and `false` for the `_resultBox`.

Next, we add some space in the middle. Trial and error indicates that this amount of space looks attractive; you can vary it according to your own preference.

Next, we create a space for `JButtons` and add it to the bottom of the `JFrame`. No `JButtons` are added yet. Similarly, in line 49, we leave the `actionPerformed` method `abstract`. The details of what `JButton` or `JButtons` to add, and what the program's response should be when they are pressed, are given in the specific applications that extend the `StringGUI` class. Finally, in lines 51–56, we provide a method for subclasses to use when defining the `JButtons` to be added to the `StringGUI`.

Now consider the second piece of our interface, the `LabeledTextBox` class (shown in Listing 17.2). Lines 16 and 17 initialize the `LabeledTextBox`'s two components, the `JLabel` and the `JTextField`. The text of the `JLabel` and the width of the `JTextField` are both variables, supplied as parameters when the `JTextField` is created. We set the background of the `JTextField` to white to give it the customary appearance. Note that, unlike the `JLabel` in the `StringGUI` class, this one does not have its background color set; instead, we use the default background, which is the same color as the `JFrame`. The fonts for the `JLabel` and the `JTextField` are the same; like the text of the `JLabel` and the width of the `JTextField`, they are supplied as parameters to the `JTextField` constructor. In addition, the `editable` parameter determines whether the user can edit the `JTextField`.

In sum, this is a very general `JTextField` with an associated label. The label, the width, the font, and whether the text in the `JTextField` is editable are all determined when the individual instances of `LabeledTextField` are created.

To make `JLabeledTextBox` work with `JTextAreas` instead of `JTextFields`, three changes are necessary. First, declare an instance of `JTextArea`:

```
public JTextArea _textArea;
```

Then initialize it with two parameters, rather than one. For a `JTextArea`, we need to give both the width and the number of lines:

```
public _textArea = new JTextArea(numLines, charWidth);
```

(Unlike other Java classes, this one puts height first and width second.)

Finally, make the text wrap from one line to the next:

```
_textArea.setLineWrap(true);
```

A version of the `EchoApp` program that works with `JTextAreas`, `LongEchoApp`, is included in the code provided with this book.

```java
1   /**
2    * Chapter 17: LabeledTextBox.java
3    * The basic building block of our program, a text label over a white
4    * text field. Used for either input or output.
5    */
6   import java.awt.event.*;
7   import java.awt.*;
8   import javax.swing.*;
9
10  public class LabeledTextBox extends JPanel {
11      private JTextField _textBox;
12      private JLabel _label;
13
14      public LabeledTextBox(String label, int charWidth,
15                            boolean editable, Font font) {
16          _label = new JLabel(label,SwingConstants.CENTER);
17          _textBox = new JTextField(charWidth);
18          _textBox.setBackground(Color.white);
19          _label.setFont(font);
20          _textBox.setFont(font);
21          _textBox.setEditable(editable);
22
23          // innerPanel used so _label and _textBox stay same
24          // size even if the LabeledTextBox is later resized
25          // (by its container changing)
26          JPanel innerPanel = new JPanel();
27          innerPanel.setLayout(new GridLayout(2,1));
28          innerPanel.add(_label);
29          innerPanel.add(_textBox);
30          innerPanel.setMaximumSize(innerPanel.getPreferredSize());
31          this.setLayout(new FlowLayout());
32          this.add(innerPanel);
33      }
34      public String getText() {
35          return _textBox.getText();
36      }
37      public void setText(String string) {
38          _textBox.setText(string);
39      }
40  }
```

Listing 17.2 ■ The LabeledTextBox class

17.4.2 **A simple program: EchoApp**

We start with a very simple application, one that just echoes the text input by the user. We extend the `StringGUI` class to create the interface shown in Figure 17.4. The code for `EchoApp` is given in Listing 17.3.

This code is very simple; most of the work has been done in the first two classes. All we do here is add a `JButton` (the "echo!" button), define the `actionPerformed` method to provide the response when the `JButton` is pushed, and write a main method that instantiates this class. The `actionPerformed` method simply gets the text input by the user from the `_inputBox` and copies it into the `_resultBox`. The `getText` method returns a `String`, which is then passed as a parameter to the `setText` method of the `_resultBox`.

```
1    /**
2     * Chapter 17: EchoApp.java
3     * Extends StringGUI to create an application that echoes
4     * text input by the user.
5     */
6    import java.awt.event.*;
7    import java.awt.*;
8    import javax.swing.*;
9
10   public class EchoApp extends StringGUI {
11       public EchoApp(String title) {
12           super(title);
13           this.addMethodButton("echo!",this);
14           this.pack();
15           this.setVisible(true);
16       }
17
18       public void actionPerformed(ActionEvent e) {
19           _resultBox.setText(_inputBox.getText());
20       }
21
22       public static void main(String [] args) {
23           EchoApp app = new EchoApp("String Demo:echoing input");
24       }
25   }
```

Listing 17.3 ■ The EchoApp class

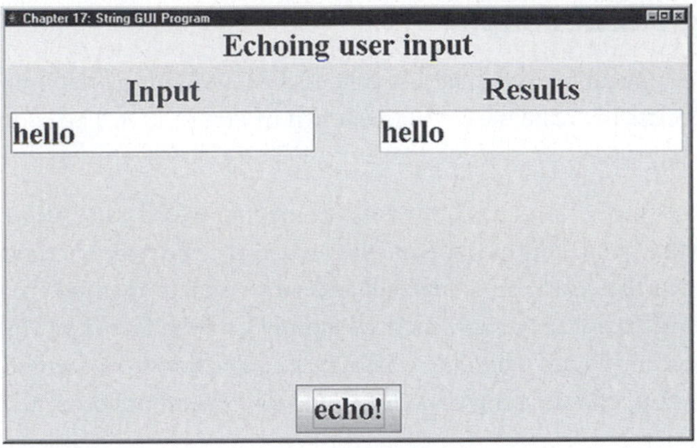

Figure 17.4 ■ Screenshot of EchoApp

17.4.3 **A second application: StringMethodsApp**

Listing 17.4 gives the code for the program whose interface we showed in Figure 17.1. This program gives the user two additional options besides echoing the input: computing its length and reversing it.

Here we add three JButtons to the interface. The actionPerformed method chooses which action to perform based on the label of the JButton that is pressed. In each case, we use the getText method to get the String entered by the user from the _inputBox. If the "echo string" is pressed, we then copy that String into the _resultBox, as in Listing 17.3. If the "show length" button is pressed, we call String's length method on the input String. Finally, if the "reverse string" button is pressed, we call the reverse method on that String.

17.4.4 **A third application: EqualTestApp**

The third and final example in this section is EqualTestApp, whose interface is shown in Figure 17.2. For this program, as you can see, we need two input boxes. StringGUI only provides one input box, so we extend StringGUI to create a new class with two. The code for this class, TwoInputStringGUI, is given in Listing 17.5.

To get the new layout, we first declare a second input box. Then we create a JPanel called inputSpace to hold the two input boxes and give it a GridLayout, so the two input boxes will appear in a column. Then we add the two input boxes to the inputSpace, and add the inputSpace to the left-hand side of the JFrame.

```
1   /**
2    * Chapter 17: StringMethodsApp.java
3    * Extends the StringGUI class to create a program that tests
4    * several String methods.
5    */
6   import java.awt.event.*;
7   import java.awt.*;
8   import javax.swing.*;
9
10  public class StringMethodsApp extends StringGUI {
11      public StringMethodsApp(String title) {
12          super(title);
13          this.addMethodButton("Echo string",this);
14          this.addMethodButton("Show length",this);
15          this.addMethodButton("Reverse string", this);
16          this.pack();
17          this.setVisible(true);
18      }
19      public void actionPerformed(ActionEvent e) {
20          String buttonLabel = e.getActionCommand();
21          if (buttonLabel.equals("Echo string")) {
22              _resultBox.setText(_inputBox.getText());
23          }
24          else if (buttonLabel.equals("Show length")) {
25              _resultBox.setText("Input length: " +
26                                  _inputBox.getText().length());
27          }
28          else if (buttonLabel.equals("Reverse string")) {
29          _resultBox.setText(this.reverse(
30                          _inputBox.getText()));
31          }
32          else {
33              System.out.println(
34                  "Problem with StringMethodsApp's actionPerformed.");
35          }
36      }
37      public String reverse (String text) {
38          int len = text.length();
39          String reverse = "";
40          for (int i = len; i > 0; i--) {
41              reverse += text.substring(i-1, i);
```

Listing 17.4 ■ The StringMethodsApp class (*continued on next page*)

```
42              }
43          return reverse;
44      }
45      public static void main(String [] args) {
46          StringMethodsApp app = new StringMethodsApp(
47              "Testing String methods");
48      }
49  }
```

Listing 17.4 ■ The StringMethodsApp class

```
1   /**
2    * Chapter 17: TwoInputStringUI.java
3    * Framework for programs with two input Strings.
4    */
5   import java.awt.event.*;
6   import java.awt.*;
7   import javax.swing.*;
8
9   public abstract class TwoInputStringGUI
10         extends StringGUI {
11      protected LabeledTextBox _inputBox2;
12
13      public TwoInputStringGUI(String title){
14          super(title);
15
16          // create and place input and result areas
17          JPanel inputSpace = new JPanel();
18          inputSpace.setLayout(new GridLayout(0, 1));
19          _inputBox = new
20             LabeledTextBox("First Input",22,true,_defaultFont);
21          _inputBox2 = new
22             LabeledTextBox("Second Input",22,true,_defaultFont);
23          inputSpace.add(_inputBox);
24          inputSpace.add(_inputBox2);
25          this.add(inputSpace, BorderLayout.WEST);
26      }
27  }
```

Listing 17.5 ■ TwoInputStringGUI

```
1    /**
2     * Chapter 17: EqualTestApp.java
3     * Extends TwoInputStringGUI to create a program that
4     * lets user to experiment with the different tests for equality.
5     */
6    import java.awt.event.*;
7    import java.awt.*;
8    import javax.swing.*;
9
10   public class EqualTestApp extends TwoInputStringGUI {
11       public EqualTestApp(String title) {
12           super(title);
13           this.addMethodButton("==", this);
14           this.addMethodButton("Equals",this);
15           this.addMethodButton("IgnoreCase",this);
16           this.pack();
17           this.setVisible(true);
18       }
19   public void actionPerformed(ActionEvent e) {
20       String buttonLabel = e.getActionCommand();
21       if (buttonLabel.equals("Equals")) {
22           String result = Boolean.toString(
23               _inputBox.getText().equals(
24               _inputBox2.getText()));
25           _resultBox.setText(
26           "inputs \"equal\": " + result);
27       }
28       else if (buttonLabel.equals("==")) {
29           String result = Boolean.toString(
30               _inputBox.getText() == _inputBox2.getText());
31           _resultBox.setText("inputs \"==\": " + result);
32       }
33       else if (buttonLabel.equals("IgnoreCase")) {
34           boolean result =
35               _inputBox2.getText().equalsIgnoreCase( _inputBox.getText());
36
37           if (result)
38                   _resultBox.setText("ignoring case: equal");
39           else
40                   _resultBox.setText("ignoring case: not equal");
```

Listing 17.6 ■ The `EqualTestApp` class (*continued on next page*)

```
42                }
43                else {
44                    System.out.println(
45                    "Problem with EqualTestApp's actionPerformed.");
46                }
47            }
48        public static void main(String [] args) {
49            EqualTestApp app = new EqualTestApp("Testing equality");
50        }
51    }
```

Listing 17.6 ■ The EqualTestApp class

Listing 17.6 gives the code for the EqualTestApp class. It extends TwoInputStringGUI to create the interface and functionality shown in Figure 17.2. Just as in the previous program, we add three JButtons. The difference lies in the response to those buttons, specified in the actionPerformed method. Again, we use the JButton's labels to determine which action to take, and the getText method to get the user's input. The difference is that we're now getting input from two input boxes, rather than one. Also creating the text to be displayed in the result box requires a little extra work. The equals method and the == operator return boolean values, rather than Strings, so we use the toString method of the Boolean class to convert these values to Strings before adding them to the result.

■ Summary ■

In this chapter, we have shown how to declare, initialize, and use variables of Java's `String` class to represent and manipulate text in a Java program. Text is basically the numbers, letters, and punctuation you can type in from the keyboard. Instances of the class `String` hold text; operations on `Strings` include concatenation, comparing two `Strings`, extracting parts of a `String`, and reversing a `String`.

In addition, we have presented two variations on a boilerplate GUI that can be used for a variety of different programs involving text input and output. Finally, we showed how to customize the boilerplate GUIs to produce three concrete applications: one to echo the user's input, the second to test various operations on the user's input, and the third to let the user experiment with different definitions of equality for `Strings`. This GUI can easily be adapted to create similar text I/O programs.

■ Self-Check Questions ■

1. Go to http://java.sun.com and find the documentation on `JLabel`. Skim the documentation and write a brief (1–2 paragraph) summary. Don't worry if it doesn't all make sense; some of it will, and the more practice you have navigating this online documentation, the easier it gets.

2. Follow the link from the documentation to the tutorial on `JLabels`. Read the tutorial and try out the examples.

3. Similarly, go to http://java.sun.com and find the documentation on `JTextField`. Skim the documentation and write a brief (1–2 paragraph) summary.

4. Go to http://java.sun.com and find the documentation on `String`. Skim the documentation and write a brief (1–2 paragraph) summary.

■ Exercises ■

Applying the Facts

1. Given the statement

   ```
   String s = "Able was I ere I saw Elba";
   ```

   a. What is the value returned by `s.length()`?
   b. What is the value returned by `s.charAt(3)`?
   c. What happens if the method call is `s.charAt(40)`?
   d. What `String` is returned by the method call `s.substring(1, 5)`?

2. Suppose you have two `String` variables, `msg` and `name`, that hold the message you want to print out and the name of the current user, respectively. Write a statement that creates a new `String` variable, `output`, and initializes it by concatenating `msg` and `name`.

3. Look up the dates for the signs of the zodiac and write a conditional statement that takes a birth month and date as input (as integers) and returns the corresponding zodiac sign.

Debugging Programs

1. Find the bug(s) in the following code:

```
public String reverse (String text) {
    int len = text.length();
    String reverse = "";
    for (int i = len; i >= 0; i--) {
        reverse += text.substring(i-1, i);
    }
    return reverse;
}
```

■ Programming Projects ■

Modifying Programs

1. Modify the `Echo` program to change the default font (check the online Java documentation to find out what fonts are available).

Writing Programs

1. Write a program that reads in text and outputs the same text, but
   a. entirely in lower-case.
   b. entirely in upper-case.

2. Write a program that reads in text and outputs the length of the longest word in the input.

3. Suppose you have been hired to censor the school newspaper, and you want to automate the task. Write a program that reads in text and substitutes "CENSORED" for every word in the input that is four characters long.

4. To decode messages, it is useful to know the frequency of the different letters in the English language. To obtain results from some small samples, write a program that reads in text and outputs the number of a's, b's, c's, etc., in the input. For example, if the input is "The cat sat on the mat," the output should be:

a 3   c 1   e 2   h 2   m 1   n 1   o 1   s 1   t 5

(In Chapter 18, we will see how to perform this task on a text file.)

5. Write a program that reads in text in a `TextArea` and outputs the number of lines, words, and characters.

6. Write a program that reads in a `String` and outputs all the substrings of that `String`. If the input is "cat," for example, the output should be "c ca cat a at t."

7. Write a program that acts as a "Scrabble® Assistant." It should read in text in a `TextBox` consisting of 2–7 letters A–Z, and output all the combinations that can be made with the input letters. If the input is "cat," for example, the output should be "cat cta act atc tac tca ca ac ct tc at ta c a t." (For now, we leave it to the user to determine which of these are actual words.)

8. Write a program that prompts the user for his or her birthday and outputs the zodiac sign for that birthday (a listing of which birthdays fall in which sign can be found in your local newspaper or on the Web).

9. Write a program that prompts the user for his or her name, reads it in using a `TextBox`, and prints out the first verse of "Happy Birthday" with the person's name inserted.

10. Here is the HTML for a very simple webpage:

    ```
    <HTML>
    <TITLE>Jane's Excellent Webpage</TITLE>
    <BODY>This webpage belongs to Jane Doe. It's going to be GREAT!
    </BODY>
    </TITLE>
    ```

    Write a program that prompts the user for his or her first and last name using `TextFields` and displays the HTML for the above webpage with their name inserted in the appropriate locations.

11. Many newspapers carry word problems known as "scrambles" or "anagrams." These puzzles involve taking a word, or a group of letters that looks like a word, and unscrambling it to find the real word. For example, "cat" is an anagram of "act." Write a program that prompts the user for two strings and determines whether one is a scrambled version of the other.

12. Write a program that prompts the user for his or her full name and generates a logname consisting of the user's first initial and last name. For example, if the input is "Florence Nightingale," the output should be "fnightingale." If the input is "Martin Luther King, Jr.," the output should be "mking." If the input is "Thurston Howell IV," the output should be "thowell."

13. Write a program that prompts the user for two integers, reads them in, and outputs

    a. their sum
    b. their difference
    c. their product
    d. their quotient

14. Write a program that reads in an integer and outputs all of its factors.

15. Write a program that reads in a positive integer and outputs a message indicating whether the input is a prime number, a composite number, or an error (that is, not a positive integer).

16. Write a program that

    a. reads in the temperature in Fahrenheit and outputs the temperature in Celsius.

    b. reads in the temperature in Celsius and outputs the temperature in Fahrenheit.

17. Write a program that

    a. reads in a distance in miles and outputs the distance in kilometers.

    b. reads in a distance in kilometers and outputs the distance in miles.

18. Write a program that reads in the length of a trip in miles and the number of gallons used and outputs the number of miles per gallon.

19. Write a program that prompts the user for the radius and x and y positions of a circle and outputs a picture of the circle.

20. Write a program that prompts the user for the height, width, x, and y positions of a rectangle, and outputs a picture of the rectangle.

21. Write a program that prompts the user for a dollar amount and returns the amount written out in full, as on a check. For example, if the input is $123.47, the output should be "one hundred twenty-three and forty-seven hundredths dollars."

22. Write a program that takes a positive integer in base 10 notation and returns the `String` corresponding to the number's unary notation. Unary notation for a number n is a sequence of n 1's in a row. For example, if the input is 5, the output should be "11111."

chapter 18

Console I/O, File I/O, and Exceptions

OBJECTIVES

After reading this chapter, you should be able to:

☑ Write programs that:
- ✓ read from the keyboard
- ✓ write to a console window
- ✓ read text from a file
- ✓ write text to a file
- ✓ read objects from a file
- ✓ write objects to a file

☑ Define the term "exception" and explain how exceptions are implemented in Java

☑ Write code to propagate or handle exceptions

☑ Explain the difference between checked and unchecked exceptions in Java

■ 18.1 ■ Introduction

Whatever we do on a computer, whether we're editing a paper, creating a picture, writing a Java program, working with a spreadsheet, or playing a game, there's almost always a way to save what we're doing and come back to it later. Often programs save other information as well, such as our preferences or our high scores in a game. When we save that information, it's put in a **file**: a collection of data with a name that is stored in the computer's long-term memory. In this chapter, we'll see how to make a program read input from or send output to a file. We'll also see how to make a program read input that the user types at the keyboard or output it to the computer screen.

When we're working with input and output, things can go wrong that are out of the programmer's control: the user may enter the wrong type of data, for example, or the file we're trying to open may not exist, or the user may not have the necessary permissions to open it or write to the desired location. In Java, these problems cause the system to create an **exception**: an object that records information about an error or unusual situation that occurs while a program is running. You have probably seen examples of exceptions such as the `NullPointerException` when running your programs. Just as we wrote event handlers to take care of events such as mouse clicks, in this chapter we'll see how to write **exception handlers**, code for handling exceptions.

■ 18.2 ■ Concepts

18.2.1 Console I/O

Before graphical user interfaces were developed, most computer users communicated with a computer through a **console**. There was an empty screen with room for maybe 30 lines of text and a **prompt** to the left of a line of text near the top, some phrase or character indicating that the computer was waiting for the user to type something. Indeed, your computer probably still lets you start up a **console window** that looks and works like an old computer console. There's a picture of a console window on a Macintosh in Figure 18.1.

Console windows on other operating systems look slightly different, but the basic idea is the same: a window with lines of text, such as we might type on a typewriter. On the left-hand side of the top line in this window is the prompt "[k-sanderss-Computer:~]" to tell us what folder we're in, followed by "ks%." Many operating systems allow users to customize this prompt, so we could make it say something like "Hello!" or "Quack!" if we wanted to.

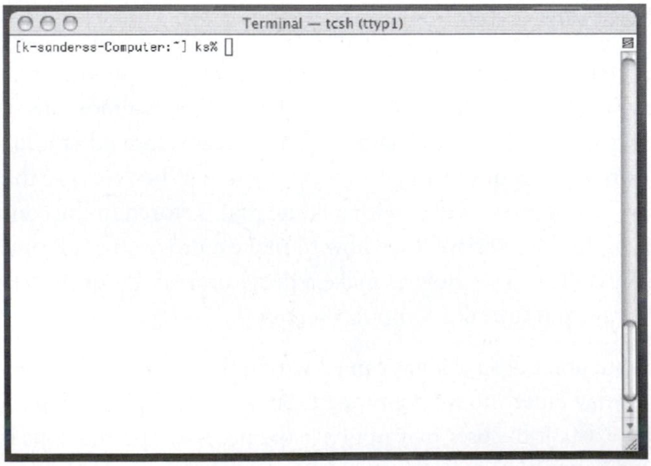

Figure 18.1 ■ Screenshot of a Macintosh console window.

In a console window, instead of clicking on an icon or selecting a program's name from a menu, as we would with a GUI interface, we simply type the program's name along with any parameters it needs (see Figure 18.2).

Here we invoke the Java compiler (javac), give it the name of a file to compile (Hello.java), and hit "enter." The compiler executes without any comment, so the compile was successful. The prompt is back, so it's our turn again.

Besides running programs, we can also enter data for a program to use by way of the console. Data that we type into a console window for a program to use is called **keyboard input** or **console input**. Data displayed by the program in the console window is called **console output**. Together, console input and output are referred to as **console I/O**.

Figure 18.3 shows what happens when we run the program we just compiled, which is a simple console I/O program. After compiling, we tell Java to run our program (java Hello). The program asks for a name, we type one in, and the program reads in the name, makes it part of a message by string concatenation, and prints the message out. When we run the program again using a different name, we get a different message.

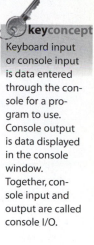

keyconcept
Keyboard input or console input is data entered through the console for a program to use. Console output is data displayed in the console window. Together, console input and output are called console I/O.

18.2.2 File I/O

Console I/O is rare nowadays, however, compared to file I/O. **File I/O**, getting data from or saving it to a file, is part of all the programs we use most often, from email to web browsers to word processors. From an object-oriented programmer's point of

keyconcept
File I/O is the process of a program's getting data from a file or saving it to a file.

```
○ ○ ○              Terminal — tcsh (ttyp1)
[k-sanderss-Computer:~] ks% javac Hello.java
[k-sanderss-Computer:~] ks% []
```

Figure 18.2 ■ Running a program at a console window.

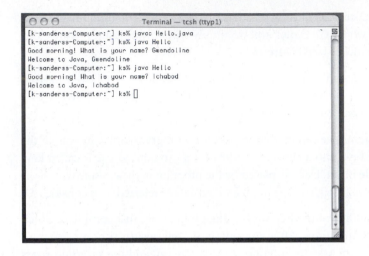

Figure 18.3 ■ Running a console I/O program.

view, files are objects with properties and methods. The properties of a file include, among other things, its name and its location in the computer's long-term memory. The location of a file is given by its **path**, a string that indicates how to find the file. The exact form of the path depends on the operating system. In Unix, a path might look like:

/home/sanders/book/ch8-examples/Fish.java

In Windows on a PC, the same file might have the path:

C:\Windows\Desktop\book\ch8-examples\Fish.java

Both of these paths give the location of a file named "Fish.java" contained in a folder named "ch8-examples," which in turn is contained in a folder named "book." In this Unix path, the "book" folder is contained in a folder named "sanders"; in the Windows path, it's contained in a folder named "Desktop."

In addition to properties, files have operations. There are accessor methods to return the name of the file and its path. There are also operations to **open** and **close** a file. It's necessary to open a file before reading from it or writing to it; it's a good idea to close it when we're done. The sequence of bytes flowing to or from an open file is called a **stream**.

The operations to read from or write to a file depend on what kind of a file it is. **Text files** are files containing characters that you can type on a keyboard: words, numbers, words in other alphabets such as Greek, and so forth. The source files for your Java programs are text files, for example, and so are the html source files for webpages. Your computer probably has both a text editor and a word processor; the text editor creates text files and the word processor normally does not (though it probably does have a "save as text" option). **Binary files** are files that may include text but also include some symbols that cannot be represented as text. Word processors generally work with binary files, for example and the .class file created by the Java compiler is a binary file. Image files, such as those ending in .gif or .jpg, are binary files.

18.2.3 Saving objects to files and reading them back in

Our Java programs are made up of objects, so we often want to save object instances. What distinguishes one instance of an object from another? Its state. If we don't care about remembering the values of the instance variables for a particular instance, a new one may suffice, but if we do, we must be able to store and retrieve a particular instance. Suppose we have a `Student` class, for example, that has instance variables for the student's name and ID number. `Student` "Miranda" with ID #1 is different from `Student` "Ferdinand" with ID #2. In order to start again where we left off, we need to remember that we were working on the record for `Student` "Miranda" and not `Student` "Ferdinand."

There are two problems with saving object instances. First, objects usually have more than one instance variable, so there's more than one thing to save. Second, what if, instead of primitive types like integers or `Strings`, the instance variable of an object contains a reference to another object? What if the `Student` has an `_address` instance variable that refers to an object of type `Address`? Or what if, on a `GameBoard` for a checkers game that is made up of an array of `Squares`, some of the `Squares`, the ones that have pieces on them, contain references to `Piece` objects? There could be references to references to references to references. Ideally, we'd like our programming language to provide a way to save all this information—all the instance variables and all the contents of any objects that are referred to by instance variables—at once. As we will see, Java does just that.

18.2.4 Exceptions

Suppose you're sitting at home studying, and you're interrupted. If you're interrupted by your telephone, you can either answer it or just ignore it. If you're interrupted by a fire alarm, you will probably stop and take action immediately. And some interruptions you can anticipate and prevent—for example, you can turn your telephone off so that it won't ring while you're studying.

As you have probably seen, Java can interrupt your program. At certain points during the execution of a program, Java instantiates an object called an exception. An **exception** is an object that records information about a problem, or perhaps just something unusual, that happened during program execution. After instantiating the exception, Java looks for some

keyconcept

Text files are made up of the characters that you can type on a keyboard. Binary files may include text but also include some symbols that cannot be represented as text.

keyconcept

An exception is an object that contains information about a problem or something unusual that occurred during program execution.

code to handle it. This process is called **throwing an exception**. Java's most familiar exception is probably the `NullPointerException`, but there are many others.

In a program, throwing an exception interrupts whatever else the program is doing and transfers control to the system. The system then looks for some code to deal with the problem. If an object provides this code itself, we say that it **handles** the exception. Code written to handle an exception is called an **exception handler** (just as an "event handler" deals with events such as mouse clicks). Alternatively, if an object delegates the problem to another object (as you might ask your roommate to answer the phone), we say that it **propagates** the exception. In that case, the second object also has the choice of handling the exception or propagating it. In certain cases, ignoring the exception is also a reasonable strategy.

The best design often depends on what type of interruption it is. Is the interruption one that:

1. should have been avoided?
2. is too rare to worry about in advance, but can be dealt with when it happens?
3. can't be either avoided or solved by our program?

Sometimes, especially during the implementation and testing phases of programming, there are problems that could have been avoided but were not. For example, suppose we forget to initialize a variable. We could plan ahead to supply some default value if this happens and attempt to continue the program's normal execution, but it's better for the program to notify us so we can fix the problem. Here ignoring the exception and letting the program crash is the best solution.

Some problems are so serious that they can't be avoided; not only that, if they do happen, we can't cope with them at all: if the power to the computer is interrupted, for example, or there's a problem with the Java Virtual Machine. Returning to the program's normal operation is not an option. In this case, we have no choice but to let the program crash.

More interesting design questions are raised by the problems that can and should be solved. There are many such problems. For example, suppose our code lets the user open a file, but he or she inputs the name of a nonexistent file. Or suppose the user attempts to divide by zero. Or suppose we write a stack implementation and the client code attempts to pop an empty stack. All these events are outside of the programmer's control, but we can predict that (even if rarely) they all will happen.

Later in this chapter, we see how to write code that throws an exception when a problem occurs. But in order to write code to throw an exception, we need to anticipate that a problem might happen. And we already know another technique for dealing with predictable problems: use a conditional statement to test whether the problem has occurred. For example, application programmers can use the `isEmpty()` method before attempting to pop a stack.

How can we choose between conditional tests and exceptions? It depends how often the event we're checking for occurs. Conditionals are evaluated every time the code is run. If we're checking for something that happens rarely, exceptions are more efficient. We don't have to think about exceptions until they are thrown. To put this decision in real-life terms, if we're looking for clutter to be picked up around the house, it makes sense to check continuously to see if some clean-up is needed. On the other hand, it doesn't make sense to keep picking up the phone to see if someone's on the line. Instead, we wait for it to interrupt us.

Consider a programming example: implementing a stack. In the stack implementation in Chapter 14, the stack code itself uses a conditional statement to handle the problem of popping elements from an empty stack; this is the equivalent of checking continuously to see if there's a problem. When the client code calls `pop`, the stack is rarely empty. This situation is more like the phone ringing than like picking up clutter. Exceptions might be a better solution.

If we decide that we're dealing with a phone call rather than just clutter, the next question is who's going to answer the phone: in programming terms, which part of the code should handle the situation. Should the stack code itself deal with popping an empty stack, or should that issue be left to the programmers who write client code that uses the stack?

Different solutions are appropriate for different applications. If the application is an RPN calculator, for example, the stack is popped when the user enters an operator. Suppose that instead of typing "2 3 +," the user types "2 +." The calculator sees the "+," pops the "2" off the stack, and then discovers that the stack is empty. The calculator could simply crash at this point, but a more user-friendly design would push the "2" back on the stack and give the user an error message and a chance to enter the second argument. Alternatively, suppose the application is a "Back" button for a web browser. If the user clicks on the back button too many times, the browser should probably just ignore the clicks and do nothing. Thus, there's a good argument for delegating the handling of the empty-stack problem to the application programmers. If we delegate the task, however, we should make it clear that we're leaving the problem up to them. By throwing an exception, we can give the application programmers the freedom to solve the problem in different ways, but still remind them that the problem must be solved.

■ 18.3 ■ **Mechanics**

18.3.1 **Console I/O**

Outputting information to the console window is easy in Java. It is a highly platform-dependent process, but Java hides the details from us. Java has an object that represents the console window called `System.out`. `System.out` is an instance variable in the `System` class and by default, it refers to the console window. It's always open and ready for output, and because it's so frequently used, it's a public instance variable. `System.out` is an instance of the `PrintStream` class (because it sends a stream of information to the console window). It's particularly easy to use because instances of `PrintStream` never throw exceptions; they just do what we tell them to.

Suppose we want to print the message, "Work! Work! Work!" in the console window. There are two methods we can use. We can say:

```
System.out.print("Work! Work! Work!");
```

In that case, the message will appear on the screen with the prompt to the right of it, like this:

```
Work! Work! Work!ks%
```

Or we can say:

```
System.out.println("Work! Work! Work!");
```

Unlike `System.out.print`, `System.out.println` automatically adds a newline at the end of a message, so in this case, the message will appear on the screen and the cursor will be at the beginning of the next line, like this:

```
Work! Work! Work!
ks%
```

To put newlines in the middle of a message, we use the character code '\n.' For example, we can say:

```
System.out.print("Work!\nWork!\nWork!\n");
```

Now each word of our message will appear on a separate line, like this:

```
Work!
Work!
Work!
ks%
```

By adding `'\n'` at the end of the message, we can make `print` have the same output as `println`. Thus, the following two statements have the same output:

```
System.out.println("Work! Work! Work!");
System.out.print("Work! Work! Work!\n");
```

Both statements cause the message "Work! Work! Work!" to appear in the console window on a single line, followed by a new line.

So far, all our examples have involved giving a `String` argument to `print` or `println`. Conveniently, these methods can also take `boolean`, `int`, `double`, or `Object` arguments. We use either constant values or variables in which a value has been stored. Listing 18.1 shows a program that tests all of these capabilities.

The output of this program is:

```
Testing console output:
First an integer: 12
Next two booleans:
true
false
Now a double:
The value of PI is: 3.141592653589793
Finally, an object:
java.awt.geom.Ellipse2D$Double@e53108
```

The output when we ask `System.out` to print an object isn't very useful, so we probably want to define a new method for printing objects. But printing primitive types works fine.

We can combine different types of output in a single `print` or `println` statement using the + operator to concatenate `Strings` together. For example, we could shorten the program in Listing 18.1 by combining some of the lines, as shown in Listing 18.2. The output of this version of the program is exactly the same as that of the previous one.

Finally, in addition to constants or variables, we can use method calls as arguments to `print` or `println`, as long as they return one of the kinds of value that `print` and `println` can handle. For example, suppose we want to print the height and width of an `Ellipse2D.Double`. We can add the following line of code:

```
System.out.println("The height of the ellipse is "
                   + ellipse.getHeight()
                   + " and its width is "
                   + ellipse.getWidth()
                   + ".");
```

```
1    /**
2     * Chapter 18: ConsoleOutput.java
3     * Run this program in a console window to test Java's
4     * console I/O.
5     */
6    import java.awt.geom.*;
7
8    public class ConsoleOutput {
9        public ConsoleOutput() {
10           System.out.println("Testing console output:");
11           System.out.print("First an integer: ");
12           System.out.println(12);
13           System.out.println("Next two booleans: ");
14           System.out.println(true);
15           System.out.println(false);
16           System.out.println("Now a double: ");
17           System.out.print("The value of PI is: ");
18           System.out.println(Math.PI);
19           Ellipse2D.Double ellipse = new Ellipse2D.Double();
20           ellipse.setFrame(30, 40, 50, 60);
21           System.out.println("Finally, an object: ");
22           System.out.println(ellipse);
23       }
24
25       public static void main(String [] args) {
26           ConsoleOutput app = new ConsoleOutput();
27       }
28   }
```

Listing 18.1 ■ The ConsoleOutput class

That line of code adds the following output to our program:

```
The height of the ellipse is 60.0 and its width is 50.0.
```

Statements like this are an old-fashioned but simple (and useful) way of debugging your program. If you want to find out which methods are being called or what the value of a particular variable is at a particular point, you can just insert one of these statements and print out the information you need to the console.

Now suppose instead of just writing to the console, we also want our program to get input from the user. Console input used to be tricky in Java, but Java 1.5 has made it

```
1     /**
2      * Chapter 18: ConsoleOutput.java
3      * Listing 18.1 modified to use concatenation.
4      */
5     import java.awt.geom.*;
6
7     public class ConsoleOutput {
8         public ConsoleOutput () {
9             System.out.println("Testing console output:");
10            System.out.println("First an integer: " + 12);
11            System.out.println("Next two booleans: "
12                               + "\n" + true
13                               + "\n" + false);
14            System.out.println("Now a double:");
15            System.out.println("The value of PI is: " + Math.PI);
16            Ellipse2D.Double ellipse = new Ellipse2D.Double();
17            ellipse.setFrame(30, 40, 50, 60);
18            System.out.println("Finally, an object: "
19                               + "\n" + ellipse);
20        }
21
22        public static void main(String [] args) {
23                ConsoleOutput app = new ConsoleOutput();
24        }
25    }
```

Listing 18.2 ■ The `ConsoleOutput` class with concatenation

much easier. Java has an object called `System.in` that by default corresponds to the keyboard. Just like `System.out`, it is a public instance variable in the `System` class and is always ready for use.

Instead of reading information directly from `System.in`, however, we create a `Scanner` object to do it for us, like this:

```
Scanner scanner = new Scanner(System.in);
```

Notice that we have to tell the `Scanner` that we want it to look at `System.in`; as we will see soon, `Scanner`s can also read information from files.

What does the `Scanner` do for us? Well, remember that `System.in` sends us a stream of data. Putting your head in a stream—or even a water fountain—and trying to drink can be overwhelming. What the `Scanner` does is break down the stream of data and give it to us in smaller, more manageable units—like bottled water. The units of input provided by the `Scanner` are called **tokens**.

It's time for an example. Suppose we've just asked the user for his or her name:

```
System.out.print("What's your name? ");
```

To read in the name when the user types it, we write the following code:

```
Scanner scanner = new Scanner(System.in);
String response = scanner.nextLine();
```

This code grabs everything the user types until he or she hits "Enter" and puts it in the `String` variable `response`. In other words, it uses "bottles" that are the size of a line of input and labeled `String`. To make sure the code works, we can have the program echo back what the user input. Suppose we ask for the user's name and then have the program greet him or her by name.

```
System.out.println("Hello: " + response);
```

Please see Listing 18.3 for the full program. Note that we have to import `java.util`, the package that contains the `Scanner`.

```
1    /**
2     * Chapter 18: ScannerApp.java
3     * Uses Java 1.5's new Scanners to read in console input.
4     */
5    import java.util.*;
6
7    public class ScannerApp {
8        public ScannerApp() {
9            System.out.print("What's your name? ");
10           Scanner scanner = new Scanner(System.in);
11           String response = scanner.nextLine();
12           System.out.println("Hello, " + response);
13       }
14       public static void main (String [] args) {
15           ScannerApp app = new ScannerApp();
16       }
17   }
```

Listing 18.3 ■ The ScannerApp class

Here's the output of that program (omitting the system prompts for brevity, with user input in boldface type):

```
java ScannerApp
What's your name? Ada
Hello, Ada
```

The `Scanner`'s `nextLine` method works well for some problems. For example, we could write a program that echoes everything the user inputs, a console version of the GUI `EchoApp` in Chapter 17. (See Listing 18.4.)

This program scans in everything the user types, line by line, and repeats it until the user enter a 'q.' A sample dialog looks like this:

```
Start of echo program:
Hello
Hello
How are you?
How are you?
```

```
1    /**
2     * Chapter 18: Echo.java
3     * A console version of the GUI EchoApp in Chapter 17.
4     */
5    import java.util.*;
6
7    public class Echo {
8        public Echo() {
9            System.out.println("Start of echo program: ");
10           Scanner scanner = new Scanner(System.in);
11           String currentLine = "";
12           while (!currentLine.equals("q")) {
13               currentLine = scanner.nextLine();
14               System.out.println(currentLine);
15           }
16           scanner.close();
17       }
18       public static void main (String [] args) {
19           Echo echo = new Echo();
20       }
21   }
```

Listing 18.4 ■ The Echo class

q

q

Sometimes, however, it's useful to get input in bottles of a different size or type. Fortunately, the `Scanner` class provides lots of different sizes and shapes of bottles. For example, we can ask it to give us the next `double`, or the next `int`, or the next `boolean`, or the next `String`.

Suppose we ask the user to enter an integer, for example:

```
System.out.print("Enter an integer, any integer: ");
Scanner scanner = new Scanner(System.in);
```

To read in the integer, we can say:

```
int number = scanner.nextInt();
```

As usual, we can check to see if it worked by echoing back what the user entered:

```
System.out.println("Your number is: " + number);
```

Please see Listing 18.5 for the full program.

```
1    /**
2     * Chapter 18: EchoInteger.java
3     * A program that echoes integers, rather than general
4     * text.
5     */
6    import java.util.*;
7
8    public class EchoInteger {
9        public EchoInteger() {
10           System.out.print("Enter an integer, any integer: ");
11           Scanner scanner = new Scanner(System.in);
12           int number = scanner.nextInt();
13           System.out.println("Your number is: " + number);
14       }
15       public static void main (String [] args) {
16           EchoInteger app = new EchoInteger();
17       }
18   }
```

Listing 18.5 ■ The `EchoInteger` class

Sample output for this code is:

```
Enter an integer, any integer: 26
Your number is: 26
```

Similarly, we could ask the user to enter a `boolean` and use the `nextBoolean` method to read it into a `boolean` variable, or ask for a `double` and use the `nextDouble` method to read it into a `double` variable, and so forth. If the user enters the wrong type of input, an `InputMismatchException` is thrown (more about these below).

Some of the methods of the `Scanner` class are summarized in Table 18.1. (For a full description, see the `Scanner` documentation online at http://java.sun.com/j2se/1.5.0/docs/api/allclasses-noframe.html.))

Table 18.1 ■ Scanner methods.

To read in a value of type:	Use Scanner method:	
boolean	boolean	nextBoolean()
double	double	nextDouble()
float	float	nextFloat()
int	int	nextInt()
long	long	nextLong()
short	short	nextShort()
String (whatever input appears in the next line, up to the next newline)	String	nextLine()
String (whatever input appears up to the next space, tab, or newline)	String	next()

18.3.2 Exceptions

What if we write a program using one of these methods, and the user enters the wrong thing? Anything the user types can be interpreted as a `String`, so we're not likely to run into problems with `nextLine`. But what if we ask for an integer (using `nextInt()`) and get a `String`? Let's try and see:

```
Enter an integer, any integer: two
```

We get an error message like this:

```
    Exception in thread "main"
java.util.InputMismatchException
        at java.util.Scanner.throwFor(Scanner.java:818)
```

```
     at java.util.Scanner.next(Scanner.java:1420)
     at java.util.Scanner.nextInt(Scanner.java:2029)
     at java.util.Scanner.nextInt(Scanner.java:1989)
     at EchoInteger.main(EchoInteger.java:8)
```

We get a similar result if we enter a `boolean`, or a `double`, or a number that's too big for an `int` (so it should have been declared a `long`). The `nextInt` method throws an exception.

There are two useful things about this error message. First, Java identifies what kind of exception is being thrown. The `nextInt` method has created an `InputMismatchException`, a subclass of `Exception` designed for, well, situations just like this: when the type of the input does not match the type of the variable into which it is being read. You've probably seen similar messages already, about `NullPointerExceptions` or `ArrayOutOf BoundsExceptions`. The second useful thing about this message is the stack trace. Associated with each `Exception` object in Java is this detailed information about which method threw the `Exception` and which methods were on the call stack at the time. Here you are told that the error in your program was at line 8 of `EchoInteger`, which called several built-in `Scanner` methods.

The `Exception` class has over forty built-in subclasses. `InputMismatchException`, `NullPointerException`, and `ArrayOutOfBoundsExceptions` are just three of many `Exception` classes in Java. Figure 18.4 shows the basic framework and the exceptions that

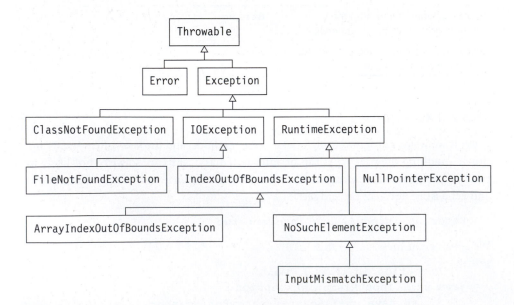

Figure 18.4 ■ Part of Java's `Exception` hierarchy.

you are most likely to see. Let's start at the top. `Throwable` sounds like an interface name, but it is actually a class, the superclass for all of Java's `Error` and `Exception` objects.

`Throwable` has three important subtrees.

1. `Error` and its subclasses correspond to the problems we can't avoid and can't solve. One of its subclasses, for example, is `VirtualMachineError`.

2. `RuntimeException` and its subclasses are the exceptions that the compiler does not force us to address. Some of these are problems we should have fixed but didn't. There's no need to write an exception handler for a `NullPointerException`, for example: instead, we should track down the pointer in question and initialize it. `RuntimeExceptions` also include some problems that we can and probably should solve, `InputMismatchExceptions`, for example. If we want to ignore them, however, we can do so.

3. Finally, the subtree that includes `Exception` and all its other subclasses (not including `RunTimeException`) consists of problems that not only can and should but must be addressed. They must be addressed because they are **checked exceptions**: that is, the Java compiler checks any method that might throw one of these exceptions and requires it to either provide an exception handler or explicitly propagate the exception. We will see an example of a checked exception below under File I/O when we discuss the `FileNotFoundException`. The only unchecked exceptions in Java are `RuntimeException` and its subclasses.

Now let's return to our `InputMismatchException`. Since this is an unchecked exception, we don't have to deal with it at all. In fact, that's why our original version of the code compiled and ran. We can just assume that the user will enter a value of the right type, and most of the time the user probably will.

On the other hand though, it's pretty ugly to have the code just crash when the user enters the wrong kind of value. Can we use a conditional to check the input? In fact, the `Scanner` class has a number of helpful methods in case we want to make this test. We can use `hasNextInt()`, for example, if we want to know whether the next token is an `int`. Similarly, there are `hasNextDouble()`, `hasNextBoolean()`, and so forth. These methods are summarized in Table 18.2.

Suppose we use `hasNextInt` to check whether the next token in the input is an `int`. Our program now looks like Listing 18.6.

Table 18.2 ■ More Scanner methods.

To check input for a value of type:	Use Scanner method:
boolean	boolean hasNextBoolean()
double	boolean hasNextDouble()
float	boolean hasNextFloat()
int	boolean hasNextInt()
long	boolean hasNextLong()
short	boolean hasNextShort()
A particular String value	boolean hasNext(String)
Any additional input (up to the next whitespace)	boolean hasNext()
An additional line of input	boolean hasNextLine()

```
1   /**
2    * Chapter 18: EchoInteger2.java
3    * Uses conditional statements to test for invalid input.
4    */
5   import java.util.*;
6
7   public class EchoInteger2 {
8      public EchoInteger2() {
9         System.out.print("Enter an integer, any integer: ");
10        Scanner scanner = new Scanner(System.in);
11        if (scanner.hasNextInt()) {
12           int number = scanner.nextInt();
13           System.out.println("Your number is: " + number);
14        }
15        else
16           System.out.println("Not a number. Try again.");
17     }
18     public static void main (String [] args) {
19        EchoInteger2 app = new EchoInteger2();
20     }
21  }
```

Listing 18.6 ■ The EchoInteger2 class

If we run this revised program with the same input as above, we don't get an exception any more:

```
Enter an integer, any integer: two
Not a number. Try again.
```

The downside of this design is, though, that every time this code is run, the program checks to see if the input really is an integer, even if we know that 999 times out of a thousand, it will be.

Our third option, if we don't want to (or can't) ignore a possible exception and don't want to check for one every time, is to write an exception handler. There are three parts to an exception handler: the `try` block, the `catch` block, and the `finally` block.

First, we identify the lines of code that might throw an exception and surround them with a try block:

```
try {
    // one or more Java statements
}
```

We have a choice about where to put the `try` block. At a minimum, it needs to be around the statement that can throw an exception, which in our case is

```
int number = scanner.nextInt();
```

We don't want to print the number out if it hasn't been read in, however, so we include the statement that prints the number in the `try` block as well.

Now that we've announced that the code might throw an exception, we provide an exception handler. The `catch` blocks are the exception handlers. Here's an example:

```
catch (InputMismatchException e) {
    System.out.println("Not a number. Try again.");
}
```

This is a very simple handler that just prints out an error message.

If we take out the conditional statements that we added earlier and substitute these `try` and `catch` blocks, we get the code shown in Listing 18.7.

When we run this code, two things can happen:

1. The user enters an integer.
2. The user enters some other type of data.

In the first case, the program works as usual: the `try` and `catch` blocks make no difference to the normal operation of the program. In the second case, however, the new

```
1    /**
2     * Chapter 18: EchoInteger3.java
3     * Uses try and catch to test for invalid input.
4     */
5    import java.util.*;
6
7    public class EchoInteger3 {
8        public EchoInteger3() {
9            Scanner scanner = new Scanner(System.in);
10           System.out.print("Pick an integer, any integer: ");
11           try {
12               int number = scanner.nextInt();
13               System.out.println("You said " + number);
14           } catch (InputMismatchException e) {
15               System.out.println("Not an integer, try again.");
16           }
17           scanner.close();
18       }
19       public static void main (String args[]) {
20           EchoInteger3 app = new EchoInteger3();
21       }
22   }
```

Listing 18.7 ■ The `EchoInteger3` class

code does make a difference: `nextInt` still throws an exception, but now the program doesn't crash. Because we have enclosed the code in a `try` block and provided a `catch` block, the message "Not an integer. Try again" is printed.

The `try` and `catch` blocks together look like this:

```
try {
    // Java statements that might throw exception
} catch (...) {
    // first handler
} catch (...) {
    // second handler
}
```

We have some choice about where to place the `try` block, but there's no choice about the `catch` blocks: they have to come immediately after the `try` block.

If there are two or more `catch` blocks, Java picks the first one that matches. For example, if we have

```
try {
    // code that might throw exception
} catch (InputMismatchException ime) {
    ...
} catch (FileNotFoundException fe) {
    ...
}
```

and the code throws a `FileNotFoundException`, the second `catch` block will be matched. If there is no matching `catch` block, Java looks at the calling method (if any) and on back up the call stack.

What if there are two catch blocks that match? Java picks the first one of the two. For example, if we have:

```
try {
    // code that might throw exceptions
} catch (FileNotFoundException fe) {
    ...
} catch (InputMismatchException ime) {
    ...
} catch (Exception e) {
    ...
}
```

and the code inside the `try` block throws a `FileNotFoundException`, the first `catch` block will be executed, not the third, even though both of them match.

If there are `catch` blocks for two related exceptions, it is important to put the more general one last (as in the above example). Otherwise, the specific one will never be matched. Here, for example, the `catch` block for `Exception` is first:

```
try { // DON'T DO THIS
    // code that might throw exceptions
} catch (Exception e) {
    ...
} catch (InputMismatchException ime) {
    ...
} catch (FileNotFoundException fe) {
    ...
}
```

If there's a `FileNotFoundException`, it will always match the first `catch` block in this code, so the third one is never executed.

18.3.3 **File I/O**

Now suppose we want our program to read data in from a file. The process is nearly the same as for console input. For example, suppose we want to revise the `Echo` program (Listing 18.4) so it reads data from a file and then prints it to the console. For convenience, here's that program:

```
import java.util.*;


public class Echo {
    public Echo() {
        System.out.println("Start of echo program: ");
        Scanner scanner = new Scanner(System.in);
        String currentLine = "";
        while (!currentLine.equals("q")) {
            currentLine = scanner.nextLine();
            System.out.println(currentLine);
        }
        scanner.close();
    }
    public static void main (String [] args) {
        Echo echo = new Echo();
    }
}
```

We need to make four small changes. First, we need to add the statement:

```
import java.io.*;
```

since both the `File` and `FileNotFoundException` classes are contained in that library.

Second, we need to create a `File` object corresponding to the file we want to read from. Just as Java has a `System.in` object corresponding to the keyboard, it has a `File` class, whose instances correspond to a file. Don't be confused by the name `File`: when we create a new instance of `File`, we're not creating the file itself, we're creating an object that connects our program to a file. The file must already be there. (If you haven't created it already, now would be a good time.)

The `File` class has several methods, but for now, all we need to do is to call its constructor. The name of the file (or the full path, if it's not in the current folder) is the parameter to the `File` constructor. For example, if the name of the input file is "testData.dat," the code for creating the `Scanner` looks like this:

```
Scanner scanner = new Scanner(new File("testData.dat"));
```

The third change we need to make is to deal with an exception. The `File` constructor can throw a `FileNotFoundException`. Since that's a checked exception, the compiler won't compile our program until we either provide an exception handler or explicitly propagate the exception (i.e., delegate handling it to another part of the code).

Suppose we want to propagate the exception. All we have to do is to state in the method header that it throws that particular type of exception. For example, here we'd say

```
public Echo() throws FileNotFoundException {
```

Fourth, if another method calls `Echo()`, because `Echo` is delegating the problem of dealing with this exception, the second method must also either provide a handler or state

```
 1    /**
 2     * Chapter 18: FileToConsole.java
 3     * Reads input from a file and outputs to the console.
 4     */
 5    import java.util.*;
 6    import java.io.*;
 7
 8        public class FileToConsole {
 9            public FileToConsole() throws FileNotFoundException {
10                Scanner scanner = new Scanner(new File("testData.dat"));
11                String currentLine = "";
12                while (!currentLine.equals("q")) {
13                    currentLine = scanner.nextLine();
14                    System.out.println(currentLine);
15                }
16                scanner.close();
17            }
18            public static void main (String [] args)
19                    throws FileNotFoundException {
20                FileToConsole app = new FileToConsole();
21            }
21        }
```

Listing 18.8 ■ The `FileToConsole` program

```
1     import java.io.*;
2     import java.util.*;
3
4     public class ConsoleToFile {
5         public ConsoleToFile() throws IOException {
6             System.out.println("Enter data for file, q to quit: ");
7             Scanner scanner = new Scanner(System.in);
8             PrintWriter writer = new PrintWriter("outputData.dat");
9             String currentLine = "";
10            while (!currentLine.equals("q")) {
11                currentLine = scanner.nextLine();
12                writer.println(currentLine);
13            }
14            writer.close();
15            scanner.close();
16        }
17        public static void main (String [] args)
18                throws IOException {
19            ConsoleToFile consoleToFile = new ConsoleToFile();
20        }
21    }
```

Listing 18.9 ■ The `ConsoleToFile` class

that it too is handing off the problem (using another `throw` statement):

```
public static void main(String [ ] args)
                throws FileNotFoundException {
```

With those four small changes (plus a change in the program's name), we have our program. It is given in Listing 18.8, with major modifications to Listing 18.4 shown in bold.

This program opens the file "testData.dat" (assuming it exists in the same folder as the program) and prints its contents in the console window.

Now suppose we want to go the other way. Suppose we want to save data in a file. For example, suppose we want to read in everything the user enters at the keyboard and save it in a file to be edited later.

How can we modify this code so that it prints to a file instead? A solution is shown in Listing 18.9 (with significant modifications to Listing 18.4 in boldface type). This solution uses a `PrintWriter`, an output stream that can write text to a file.

■ 18.3 ■ Working Out with File I/O—Saving and restoring objects

Now suppose we want to save objects. Without special language support, this would be quite difficult. We would need to save each instance variable of each object, each instance variable of the objects it refers to, and so forth and so on. Fortunately, Java lets us save everything at once.

Suppose the class `Character` records information about various fictional characters, including their name, ID, and home, as shown in Listing 18.10.

To save instances of `Character`, we have to declare it `Serializable`. ("Serializable" means something that can be arranged in a series; in computer science, it refers particularly to transmitting data, one byte after another.) `Serializable` is an unusual interface. It doesn't contain any methods; it just signals to the compiler that this is a class

```
 1    /**
 2     * Chapter 18: Character.java
 3     * A record of information about a fictional character.
 4     */
 5    import java.io.*;
 6
 7    public class Character implements Serializable {
 8        private String _name;
 9        private int _ID;
10        private String _home;
11
12        public Character(String name,int id,String home){
13            _name = name;
14            _ID = id;
15            _home = home;
16        }
17
18        public void printCharacter () {
19            System.out.println("Character: " + _ID);
20            System.out.println("Name: " + _name);
21            System.out.println("Home: " +
22                               _home +"\n");
23        }
24    }
```

Listing 18.10 ■ The `Character` class

whose instances might be saved to a file. So all we need to do is put it in the class header, as shown above. We don't need to define any methods. If the instance variables of this object refer to other objects, they have to be `Serializable` too. If any piece of the object is not `Serializable`, then the whole process fails.

Suppose we have a program that creates instances of four `Characters`:

```
_char1 =
    new Character("Rosalind", 1, "Forest of Arden");
_char2 =
    new Character("Caliban", 2, "cave");
_char3 =
    new Character("Antipholus", 3, "Syracuse");
_char4 =
    new Character("Cressida", 4, "Troy");
```

To save all this information to a file, we need a new kind of stream:

```
ObjectOutputStream ostream = new ObjectOutputStream(
            new FileOutputStream("savedObjects.dat");
```

The `ObjectOutputStream` connects to a `FileOutputStream`, which (as before) connects directly to a file.

Once we have all the streams connected together, we can save our `Characters` like this:

```
ostream.writeObject(_char1);
ostream.writeObject(_char2);
ostream.writeObject(_char3);
ostream.writeObject(_char4);
ostream.close();
```

> **keyconcept**
> The shape classes defined in `java.awt.geom` do not implement `Serializable`, so that saving any object containing instances of these shapes to a file, involves defining subclasses of the shapes that implement `Serializable`. These classes must also define their own `readObject` and `writeObject` methods.

To read the objects back in, we need to connect together the input streams for objects. This is just the opposite of creating the output stream.

```
ObjectInputStream istream = new ObjectInputStream(
            new FileInputStream("savedObjects.dat");

Character charFromFile1 =
    (Character) istream.readObject();
```

`ReadObject` returns a value of type `Object`, so we cast it to match the `Character` type that we need.

Listing 18.11 shows `CharApp`, a class that saves and reads in information about `Character` objects.

```
1    /**
2     * Chapter 18: CharApp.java
3     * Stores and reads in information about objects.
4     */
5    import java.io.*;
6    public class CharApp {
7        private Character _char1, _char2, _char3, _char4;
8
9        public CharApp() {
10           _char1 = new Character("Ulysses", 5, "Ithaca");
11           _char2 = new Character("Isabella", 6, "Vienna");
12           _char3 = new Character("Hal", 7, "London");
13           _char4 = new Character("Portia", 8, "Belmont");
14
15           System.out.println("The created characters:");
16           _char1.printCharacter();
17           _char2.printCharacter();
18           _char3.printCharacter();
19           _char4.printCharacter();
20       }
21       public void  saveCharacters(String fileName) {
22           try {
23               ObjectOutputStream ostream =
24                   new ObjectOutputStream(
25                       new FileOutputStream(fileName));
26               ostream.writeObject(_char1);
27               ostream.writeObject(_char2);
28               ostream.writeObject(_char3);
29               ostream.writeObject(_char4);
30               ostream.close();
31           }
32           catch(Exception e) {
33               System.out.println("Read failed.");
34           }
35       }
36       public void readCharacters(String fileName) {
37           Character charFromFile1= null;
38           Character charFromFile2= null;
39           Character charFromFile3= null;
40           Character charFromFile4 = null;
```

Listing 18.11 ■ The CharApp class (*continued on next page*)

```
41          try {
42              ObjectInputStream istream =
43                  new ObjectInputStream(
44                      new FileInputStream(fileName));
45              charFromFile1 =
46                  (Character) istream.readObject();
47              charFromFile2 =
48                  (Character) istream.readObject();
49              charFromFile3 =
50                  (Character) istream.readObject();
51              charFromFile4  =
52                  (Character) istream.readObject();
53          }
54          catch (Exception e) {
55              System.out.println("Read failed.");
56          }
57
58          System.out.println("The read-in characters:");
59          charFromFile1.printCharacter();
60          charFromFile2.printCharacter();
61          charFromFile3.printCharacter();
62          charFromFile4.printCharacter();
63      }
64
65      public static void main(String[] args){
66          CharApp app = new CharApp();
67          app.saveCharacters("CharacterFile.dat");
68          app.readCharacters("CharacterFile.dat");
69      }
70  }
```

Listing 18.11 ■ The CharApp class

Try out this program, modify it to add different instance variables, and test it until you are comfortable with reading and writing simple objects.

One caveat is necessary here. As noted above, if we want to serialize an object, not only that object but all of its parts must implement the Serializable interface. Unfortunately, the shape classes contained in java.awt.geom, which were used in Wheels and most of the programs in this book, do not implement Serializable. In order to save any objects containing these shapes, say a gameboard or a picture, we must do some extra work. First, we must define subclasses of those shapes that implement `Serializable`. Those subclasses must also define their own `readObject` and `writeObject` methods. For further information, see the online Java documentation related to the `Serializable` interface.

■ Summary ■

In this chapter, we have shown how to write programs that read input from the keyboard, write to the console window, read from or write to text files, and save and read files of object instances. Most programs need to save data to a file or read data from a file at some point, so the file I/O routines, and especially the object I/O routines, are very important.

There is a lot of detail involved in both I/O and exceptions. Much of this detail is outside the scope of this book, but you now have a framework and the basic tools you need to get started using both.

■ Self-Check Questions ■

1. Define the following terms:
    a. Exception
    b. Handle an exception
    c. Propagate an exception
    d. Exception handler
    e. Checked exception
    f. Unchecked exception
    g. Console window
    h. Prompt
    i. Console I/O
    j. File I/O
    k. File
    l. Text file
    m. Binary file
    n. Opening a file
    o. Closing a file
    p. Stream

2. What kind of blocks must follow a `try` block in Java? Where must they go? Give an example.

■ Exercises ■

Applying the Facts

1. In the Echo program in Listing 18.3, the loop condition looks like this:

    ```
    while (!currentLine.equals("q")) {
    ```

    What would happen if the code read

    ```
    while (currentLine != "q") {
    ```

    instead? Why?

2. Explain how exception handlers are implemented in Java.

■ Programming Projects ■

Modifying Programs

1. Modify the Echo program in Listing 18.3 so that it asks the user for a filename, opens that file, and displays the contents of the file in the console window.

2. Modify the Echo program in Listing 18.3 so that it asks the user for two filenames, opens both files, and copies the contents of the first file into the second.

3. Modify the Echo program in Listing 18.3 so that it handles the exception by printing a message to the user, instead of propagating it.

Writing Programs

1. Write, implement, and test a program that gets a list of names and phone numbers from the user, inserts them in some implementation of the Dictionary ADT, and lets the user save the whole address book to a file and read it back in later. For simplicity, use a console interface.

2. Reimplement the program in question 1 with a graphical user interface.

3. Revise the `SketchApp` program from Chapter 5 so that the user can save a picture to a file and work on it again later. For simplicity, always save the picture to the same file (overriding old pictures as necessary).

4. Modify the program in question 3 so that the user can select the name of the file in which to save his or her picture and the name of the file to open when editing an old picture.

Index

2D (two-dimension) graphical shapes   211–258

&& (ampersand ampersand)   196

<> (angle brackets)   31, 367, 449

* (asterisk)   **39, 73**

{ } (curly braces)   27, 199, 348

. (dot)   44, 74

= (equals)   33, 194–195

== (equals equals)   197, 536

! (exclamation mark)   196, 399

!= (exclamation mark equals)   **197**

< (left angle bracket)   197

<= (left angle bracket equals)   197

– (minus)   37, 105, 194

–– (minus minus)   196

\n (backslash n)   562

(( )) (parentheses)   32, 59

% (percent)   194

+ (plus)   37, 105, 194, 535

+= (plus equals)   538

++ (plus plus)   195

 # (pound sign)   105

> (right angle bracket)   197

>= (right angle bracket equals)   197

; (semicolon)   30

_ (underscore)   30

|| (vertical bar vertical bar)   196

A

absolute positioning   77, 217–218, 266
   See also GUI

abstract,
   See also inheritance
   categories   108
   classes   107–108, 128, 130, 134–135, 248
   datatypes, *See* ADTs (abstract datatypes)
   keyword   107
   methods   107–108, 129

abstraction,
   See also complexity
   as complexity management tool   55, 90
   polymorphism as example of   158
   search and sorting commonalties   507

access(ing),
   array elements   424–425
   instance variables   229–230
   type desired, as ADT choice criteria   442
   unrestricted   444–445
   variable and methods, by classes   111

accessor(s),
   See also mutators
   methods   68
   recipe   151–152

accumulator recipe   381, 405

activation(s),
   record   400, 443
   recursion   401
   stack   401

actual parameters,
   See parameters

actual type,
   See type(s)

addition arithmetic operator   194
   See also arithmetic; mathematics; operators

address,
   object   29

ADTs (abstract datatypes) 441–478
See also data structure(s); dictionary(s); generics;
list(s); queue(s); stack(s); type(s)
Alexander, Christopher 302
algorithm(s),
See also big-oh notation; design; design patterns;
recipes
analysis 505–532
classification 508
complexity 518–522
constant-time 508, 527, 529
evaluation 507–508
exponential-time 508, 522
logarithmic-time 518, 520, 523
quadradic-time 508
sorting 508–522
term description 3
alias(es),
actual vs. formal parameters 61
AlienApp (example application) 327–332
analysis,
See also design; evaluation; testing
algorithms 505–532
average-case 516
best-case 516
example applications, *See* example applications
interfaces 137
loop termination conditions 377
model creation role 20
recursive problem decomposition 403
roles 135
waterfall model component 9
worst-case 507–516
ancestor class 100
animations,
See also move; rotation
bouncing ball 230–235
creating 225
events and 225–235
fish tank 234
annotations of UML diagrams 38–39
appropriate laziness,
See abstraction; design patterns; generic; inheritance;
recipes; reuse, code
arcs,

modeling 244–246
arguments (command line) 430
See also main method; running programs
arithmetic,
See also mathematics; primitive, types
operators 184–185, 194–195, 340–342
statements 183–210, 335–364
arranging components,
See layout(s)
array(s),
See also data structure(s)
ClickApp example application 431–436
declaration 422–424
elements 422, 423
GridLayout content arrangement 269
index 422
initialization 422–424
length 425
linked lists vs. 484–485
multidimensional 425–427
searching 523–524
sparse 527
Vector, ArrayList, and 421–439, 422, 429
ArrayLists 421–439
arrows UML notation 38, 100
assembly language 4
assignment,
objects vs. primitive types 193
operator 33
arithmetic operator use with 194–195
statements 33–34, 196
type matching rules for 158–161
association (peer object) 37
See also attributes; components; properties; in Holder
pattern 305
asymptotic behavior 508
attribute(s),
See also association (peer object); capabilities; prop-
erty(s); role(s)
Graphics object as collection of 222
initialization semantics 148
term description 20
average-case analysis 516
AWT (Abstract Windowing Toolkit) 211–258, 322

B

backslash n ( )   562

balanced trees   486

`BallApp` (example application)   213–224, 230

bandwidth,
  program use   506

base,
  case   398, 402, 407, 414
  class   100
  type   423

behavior,
  See also interface(s); role(s)
  asymptotic   508
  modeling   134, 156

benchmarks,
  See driver(s)

best-case analysis   516

big-oh notation,
  See also algorithms; analysis; testing
  introduction to   506–508
  searching   523–526, 529
  sorting   512–513, 515–518

binary,
  code   7
  digit (bit)   3, 339
  files   559
  trees   485–490, 523–527

binding (dynamic)   174

bit (binary digit)   3, 339

`BlobApp` (example application)   113–121

body delimiters   27

boolean,
  logic   185–188
  operators   196–197
  primitive type   196

bottom-up design   103
  See also design

bouncing ball animation   230–235

`BouncingBall` (example application)   225–235

bounding boxes   77, 243, 246
  See also drawing; shapes

bounds/boundary,
  cases   171–172

moving car specification   314
  range   39

break statement   351, 377–378
  See also debugging; flow of control

bubble sort   509–513, 517
  See also big-oh notation; searching; sorting

bucket   528
  See also hash

bugs   6, 12–13
  See also debugging

`ButterflyApp` (example application)   386–392

button(s),
  See also event(s); GUI; widgets
  classes   307–308
  color   287–289
  cursor interaction with   168
  mouse click interaction   166
  push   264, 270–271
  radio   264, 271–272
  toggle   264

byte,
  code   8
  term description   2

`byte` keyword   192, 339
  See also integers; primitive type(s)

C

C programming language   422

capabilities   56, 108, 247
  See also methods; properties; role(s)
  class commonalties   128
  generic types relationship to   449
  modeling   31–37, 137
  term description   20

`CarProxyApp` (example application)   311–327

Cartesian coordinates,
  converting polar coordinates to   390–392

case,
  base   400, 402, 404, 409
  keyword   350
  text   537

casting   222, 336–339
  See also coercion; type(s)

catch keyword   324, 573–576
    See also exceptions

categorization/categories,
    abstract   108
    as complexity-handling tool   99
    modeling<   100
    modeling   134

central processing unit (CPU)   2
    See also hardware

checked exceptions   571

child,
    class   100
    node   482

choices,
    See also conditional; flow of control; performance
    ADT criteria   442
    complex   337, 338, 347–349
    flow charts   190, 191

class(es),
    See also inheritance; interface(s); type(s)
    abstract   107–108, 128, 130, 134–135, 248
    ancestor   100
    base   100
    child   100
    constants   345
    declaration   26–29
    definition   26–29, 148–150
    derived   100
    descendent   100
    hierarchy   481
    inner   220, 229
    interface   36
    methods   342–343
    modeling things and categories with   134
    names   27
    parent   100
    term description   21
    UML diagrams   37
    variables   342–343
    writing   137–138

class-definition recipe   148–150

classification,
    algorithm   508

ClickApp (example application)   431–436

closed form   519
    See also function(s)

code,
    binary   7
    byte   8
    object(s)   7
    reuse   41, 81, 100, 128
    source   7
    support   8

coding conventions   348

coercion   336–339
    See also casting; polymorphism; type(s)
    explicit   222, 341
    implicit   337, 341

coherency,
    design importance for both classes and interfaces   136

collection,
    See also data structure(s); set(s)
    LIFO (last in first out)   441
    loops as control structure for   366

collision   528

color(s),
    See also GUI
    built-in   75
    buttons   287–289
    change   247
    methods   249
    modeling   305–306
    paintbrush   223
    user control   282
    in user interfaces   272

ColorBounceApp (example application)   353–358

ColorHolderApp (example application)   303–311

column-major ordering   427

combining,
    See addition; concatenation

command line arguments   430
    See also main method; running programs

comments,
    See also design
    commenting out code   28, 83
    documentation   27
    inline   27
    standard   28
    term description   27

commutative operators   195

See also operators

comparison,
  See also conditionals; equality; relation; relational
     operators
  `Comparable` use for 460
  of keys 458–462
  program execution speed 506–508
  strings 536

compilation,
  See also JVM (Java Virtual Machine); syntax
  compile term description 7
  compiler term description 5
  process characteristics 8–9

complexity,
  algorithm 518–522
  management, *See also* abstraction; design; divide and
     conquer; encapsulation; hierarchy; inheritance;
     modeling; polymorphism; type(s)
  management, b 22–23, 99, 158, 313, 388
  worst-case time 507

component(s),
  See also association (peer object); peers; widgets (GUI
     components)
  hierarchy 22
  relationship 38, 116

Composite design pattern 327–332
  See also design patterns
  `FishApp` use 241
  as Gang of Four design pattern 303

composite objects 80–90, 144
  Composite pattern use 327–332
  events and 236–246
  interface use 142–147

computer,
  background 1–15
  graphics 40
  hardware 1–3
  program 4
  software 3–4

"Computers and the Imagination",
  by Pickover, Clifford A. 388

concatenation 535, 565
  See also string(s)

conditional(s),
  See also comparison; equality; exceptions; flow of

     control; loops; relational operators
  advanced operations 335–364
  arithmetic and 183–210
  event handling use 233
  exceptions vs. 561
  introduction 185–188
  polymorphism vs. 191–192
  statements 385

Conner, Brook 303

console I/O **555–586**
  See also I/O

constant(s) 218
  See also string(s); variable(s)
  boolean 185
  definition of 344–347
  importing 345
  Java built-in colors 75
  naming conventions 347
  static variables use for 342

constant-time algorithm,
  See also algorithm(s)
  big-oh notation representation of 508, 527
  hash table searching 529

constructors,
  See also method(s); object(s)
  modeling capabilities with 31–33
  not used in interfaces 129
  with parameters 61–63
  superclass 109

containers/containment,
  See also inheritance; peer(s)
  hierarchy 482
  objects that know their 144, 152–153
  as peer objects 142
  in Proxy pattern classes 315
  relationship 116

continue keyword 377–378

control flow,
  See flow of control

conventions,
  See also design
  coding 348
  constructor 34
  instance variable 34
  naming, *See* name(s)/naming, conventions

ordering   53
spacing   52–53
style   52–53, 347
UML class diagrams   37

coordinates,
converting polar coordinates to Cartesian   390–392

counting,
measuring vs.   336
in searching and sorting algorithm evaluation   507

coupling (class),
complexity increase due to   313

CPU (central processing unit)   2
See also hardware

creating,
See constructors; instantiation; new keyword

cursor,
See also GUI; widgets (GUI components)
buttons interaction with   168

curves,
See also graphics
modeling   244–246

D

DaisyApp (example application)   200–205

data structure(s),
See also ADTs; array(s); ArrayList; collection(s);
    dictionary(s); FIFO; LIFO; list(s); node(s);
    queue(s); stack(s); streams(s); tree(s); Vectors
hierarchical   480
introduction to   441–478
multidimensional   425–427
term description   367

datatypes,
See ADTs; type(s)

debugging   6, 12–13
See also design; errors; exceptions
arrays   427–428
console output use for   564
ease   407
infinite loops   384
loops   381–384
method calls   63
off-by-one   384

recursion   404
save and restore use to avoid   223
superclass method calls importance   222

declaration,
See also defining/definition; initialization; variable(s)
ArrayList   422–424
of arrays   422–424
class   26
instance variable   30, 148
strings   535
vectors   367, 422–424

declared type,
See type(s)

decomposition,
See also recursion
recursive problem   403

decrement operators   195–196
See also operators

deep property equality   189

default keyword   351

default values   150–151
recipe   150

defining/definition,
See also declaration; initialization
class   26, 148
constants   344–347
constructor   63
GUIs   266
interfaces   129–130
method   148

definite loops   366
conversion to recursive code   405
for use   374–377

degree of node   483

delegation recipe   36

deleting   466–468
See also inserting
nodes   468, 497–500

depth,
of node   483
of recursion   401

derived class   100

descendent class   100

design,
  See also analysis; complexity management;
      model(ing); representation
  algorithm efficiency analysis   505–532
  array, `Vector`, and `ArrayList`   421–439
  bottom-up   103
  class coupling   313
  color vs. text   272
  component vs. inheritance   249
  composite object interaction   144
  conditionals vs. exceptions   561
  conditionals vs. polymorphism   191–192
  criteria   107–108, 505
  draw methods   251
  equality semantics   189
  event-handling code   226–230
  examples, See, example applications
  fill methods   251
  global variables   305
  hash functions   528
  instance variable visibility precautions   113
  interfaces   131, 134–136, 261
  loops   377–379
  models   505
  polymorphism   160–161
  principles   128
  recursion vs. iteration   404–407
  search data structure choices   523–524
  serialization   582
  skills   102
  testing   171, 471–473
  toolkit building   246–252
  top-down   103
  user interfaces   259–266
  user-centered   263
  as waterfall model component   10
  Wheels library replacement   246–252
design patterns   301–334
"Design Patterns",
  by Erich Gamma, RIchard Helm, Ralph Johnson, and
      John Vlissides   302
design patterns,
  See also appropriate laziness; Composite design pat-
      tern; Holder design pattern; Iterator design pat-
      tern; Proxy design pattern; recipes; reuse, code
  recipes relationship to   147

devices,
  See hardware
diagrams,
  class   447–448
  instance   447–448, 495
dictionary(s)   446, 490
  See also ADTs; data structures(s)
  implementation   448–470, 449, 458–470
  searching   464–465, 483–486
disk   2, 506
  See also hardware
divide and conquer   22
  See also complexity, management; design
division arithmetic operator   194
do keyword   370
do-while indefinite loop   374, 379
  See also flow of control; loops
documentation comment   27
double keyword   339
  See also arithmetic; float keyword; primitive type(s);
      real numbers
drawing,
  See also GUI; window(s)
  animations   243
  curves   244
  GUI widgets   168–171
  on a sketchpad   166
  programs   303–313
  recursion use   411
  shapes   221–224
  smart   250–251
drivers   471–473, 471, 500–501
  See also testing
Duvall, Robert   303
dynamic   182
  binding   174

E

EchoApp (example application)   545
edge   482
  See also tree(s)
  detection   232
efficiency,

See also big-oh notation; design
array advantage   422
inner class advantage   220
model   505
term description   24

elements,
See also ADTs; data structure(s)
array   422–423
list   373, 457–458
term description   367
vector   368

ellipses,
arcs based on   244–246
placing in a JPanel   218

else keyword   189, 199

empty,
stack   453
string   538

encapsulation   22, 37
See also inheritance; object-oriented, programming;
        polymorphism
accessor support of   152
inner class value for   220
mutator support of   152
violation   113

enqueing operation   456

equality,
See also comparison; conditionals; relational
        operators
deep property   189
identity   189
object   188–198
operator   197
strings   536–537

EqualTestApp (example application)   546

errors,
See also debugging; exceptions
syntax   6

evaluation,
See also big-oh notation
algorithm   508
of conditional expressions   349
of models   23, 505

event(s)   225
See also ActionEvent; exceptions; flow of control

animation and   225–235
composite shape handling and   236–246
designing event-handling code   226–230
flow of control use   386
handling   259–300, 276–282, 276, 277, 444
Java event model   225–230
mouse   277–281
user input response   264

example applications,
AlienApp   327–332
BallApp   213–224, 230
BlobApp   113–121
BouncingBall   225–235
ButterflyApp   386–392
CarProxyApp   311–327
ClickApp   431–436
ColorBounceApp   353–358
ColorHolderApp   303–313
DaisyApp   200–205
EchoApp   545
EqualTestApp   546
FirstApp   42–45
FishApp   236–246
GUIBounceApp   282–294
MovableHatApp   142–147
MovableSunApp   136–141
QueueApp   472–472
SketchApp   166–173
SnowCartoon   80–90
SpiralApp   407–412
StackApp   471
StringDemo   538
StringMethodsApp   546–548
SunCartoon   70–78
TreeApp   413–417

exception handling   324, 559–561, 569–577
See also debugging; errors

execution,
examples   44–45
program   6
speed   506–508
stack   443–444, 444

exiting a loop   377, 405

explicit coercion   222, 337, 341
See also casting; coercion; type(s)

exponential,

See also algorithm(s); function(s)
functions   390
time algorithm   508, 522
expression(s)   489
arithmetic   185
boolean   186
conditional   349
trees   185
extending interfaces   42, 100, 133
See also class(es); inheritance
extends keyword   103, 460
external node   483
extreme programming   11–12

F

factorial,
iteration version   405
recursion version   399–401
factoring commonalties,
See also complexity
inheritance as tool for   101
similar vs. dissimilar objects   135
false (Java-defined primitive value)   196
fast,
See speed
FIFO (first-in-first-out) data structures   444
See also ADTs; data structure(s)
file(s),
See also hardware; I/O
binary   559
close   558
I/O   555–586
open   558
reading objects from   559
saving objects to   559
serialization   579–583
text   558
final keyword   218, 344, 534
finally keyword   573–576
See also exceptions
FirstApp (example application)   42–45
FishApp (example application)   236–246
flexibility   24

See also design
benefit   101, 157
as model evaluation criterion   505
float keyword   339
floating-point numbers   336–342, 353–358
See also arithmetic; double keyword; float keyword; integers; primitive type(s); real numbers
Florida 2000 presidential ballot,
as bad user interface design example   260
flow of control   384–386
See also break statement; conditional, statements;
do-while statement; event(s), handling; flow
chart(s); for statement; if statement; if-
else statement; if-else-if statement;
loops; method(s), invocation; recursion;
switch statement; while statement
for keyword   374–377, 379, 427
See also flow of control; loop(s)
formal parameters,
See parameters
full binary trees   486
fully qualified names   75
function(s),
See also mathematics; recursion
exponential   390
hash   527–529, 529
mathematical   57
method   57
mod   529
recurrence relations   518–522
trigonometry   343

G

Gamma, Erich   302
Gang of Four   302
generic,
See also ADTs; polymorphism; type(s)
interfaces   451, 454, 457, 458–462
programming   158
types   449–451
geometric,
shapes   246
sum   522

global variables   305

glossary,
   See term descriptions and key concepts

grammar   5
   See also semantics; syntax

graphics/graphical,
   See also bounding boxes; buttons; GUI; menus;
         mouse; WIMP; windows
   computer   40
   shapes   40–42, 211–258

greater than operator   197
   See also operators

greater than or equal to operator   197
   See also operators

grouping objects   327–332

growth rate   508–509
   See also big-oh notation

GUI (Graphical User Interface),
   components, *See* widgets (GUI components)
   event-handling   259–300
   text I/O   540–550

GUIBounceApp (example application)   282–294, 327

H

handling,
   See also events; exceptions; flow of control
   event   259–300
   exception   324, 560
   mouse input   277–281

hard disk   2

hardware   1–3

hash,
   See also ADTs; data structure(s)
   functions and tables   527–529

height of a tree   483

Helm, Richard   302

hierarchy   480–483
   See also data structure(s); inheritance; tree(s)
   component   22
   containment   482
   inheritance   23
   parts   22

high or low watermark recipe   380–381

high-level programming language   5

Holder design pattern   303–313
   Proxy design pattern use compared with   314, 327
   as static variable alternative   342, 347

I

I/O,
   See also exceptions
   console   555–586
   file   555–586
   text   533–554

icons   264
   See also GUI

IDE (integrated development environment)   7

identifier(s)   27

identity equality   189

if keyword   189, 198

if statement   189, 198, 348, 370–373, 372
   See also flow of control

if-else statement   189, 199
   See also flow of control

if-else-if statement   350
   See also flow of control

immutable   194
   See also constants

implementation,
   interface   129–130, 134, 159–160
   as waterfall model component   10

implements keyword   129

implicit coercion   337, 341
   See also casting; type(s)

import   73
   constants   345
   keyword   73
   packages   73–75
   static   346

in-order traversal of binary trees   486–490

increment operators   195–196
   See also operators

incremental development   70, 108

indefinite loops   366

See also flow of control; loops
conversion to recursive code   405
`do-while` use   374
`while` statement   370
indentation conventions   52
index (array)   422
infinite loop   366, 384
infix notation   488–490
inheritance   99–126, 100
   See also class(es); encapsulation; interface(s); object-oriented, programming; peers; polymorphism; role(s)
   hierarchy   23, 480
   method   104–106, 111
   multiple   101
   polymorphism   159, 161–163
   properties   108–111
   simple   102–104
   single   101
initialization   32
   See also declaration; definition
   arrays   422–424
   constants   345
   instance variables   148
   peer objects   148
   strings   535
   vectors   422–424
inline comment   27
inner class   220, 229–230
input(s),
   See also output(s); stream(s)
   devices, *See* hardware
   event handling   276–282
   mouse   277–281
   number of   507
   program   171
inserting,
   insertion sort   513–516, 517
   nodes into a list   468–470
   order of   495–496
   unrestricted   444–445
insertion sort   513–516
   See also big-oh notation; searching; sorting
instance(s),
   See also class(es); inheritance; object(s)

diagrams   447–448, 495
term description   21
variables   29–31, 30, 64–67, 112–113, 129, 148
   See also, properties   21
instantiation   31
`int` keyword   192, 339
   See also integers; primitive type(s)
integers   192, 192–194, 339
   See also arithmetic; `byte` keyword; `int` keyword; `long` keyword; numbers; primitive type(s); `short` keyword
interface(s)   127–156
   See also class(es); inheritance; type(s)
   class   36
   defining for `ColorShape` capabilities   248
   generic   451, 454, 457, 458–462
   polymorphism   163–164, 307
   user   259–300
      See also GUI
internal node   483
internationalization,   133
interpreter   8
invocation,
   constructor   63
   method   36, 385
   recursion, *See* activation
is-a relationship   100
iteration   366
   See also flow of control; loops; recursion
   recursion vs.   404–407
Iterator design pattern   373–374
   List implementation use   457–458

J

Java Collections Framework   442
   See also ADTs; data structures
Java programming language   4–6
Java virtual machine (JVM)   8
   See also compilation
Java2D   212, 246–247, 247
`javadoc` program,
   documentation comment handling   28

Johnson, Ralph,
    as Gang of Four member   302
JVM (Java virtual machine)   8

K

key concepts,
    See term descriptions
keyboard input   557
keys   446
    See also dictionary(s); hash, tables
    of comparing   458–462
    modeling   458–462
keywords   7, 26
    Java, *See*, `abstract`; `break`; `byte`; `case`; `catch`;
        `default`; `double`; `else`; `extends`; `float`;
        `if`; `implements`; `import`; `int`; `long`; `new`;
        `package`; `private`; `protected`; `public`;
        `random`; `short`; `static`; `super`; `this`; `try`;
        `void`

L

labels   275, 540, 543, 544
language(s),
    computer   3, 4, 5, 264, 422, 490
    natural   4
last-in-first-out (LIFO) data structures,
    See LIFO (last-in-first-out) data structures
law of least astonishment   263
layouts (window)   217, 264, 266–270
    See also GUI
leaf node   483
length of array   425
less than operator   197
    See also operators
less than or equal to operator   197
    See also operators
level of node   483
library(s)   73
    Wheels   40–42, 70–72, 113–114, 246–252
lifetime   66, 67
    See also scope
LIFO (last-in-first-out) data structures   441, 443–444

    See also ADTs; data structure(s)
line(s)   41
linear,
    search   523
    time algorithm   508
linked lists,
    See list(s), linked
Lisp programming language   490
list(s)   444–445
    See also ADTs
    deleting nodes from   468
    implementation as ADT   457–458
    inserting nodes into   468–470
    linked   446, 484–485, 490, 524
    manipulating each element   373, 457–458
    modeling   367
    position   445
    searching   465
listener(s)   225
    event-handling role   226
    mouse events   277
literals (string)   535
local variables   64–67
location,
    See also layout(s); positioning
    methods   250
    screen   55
    specification   77–78, 86
logarithmic-time algorithm   523
    See also algorithm(s)
    binary tree searching   525–526
    sorting   518, 520
logic/logical,
    boolean   185–188, 185
    operators   186–187
`long` keyword   192, 339
    See also integers; primitive type(s)
look and feel   24
loop(s)   365–396, 405, 407, 427
    See also flow of control; iteration; recursion

M

machine language   3

main method   44, 429–430

mainline   44

maintenance/maintainability   10, 24, 407, 505

Math (Java-defined class)   234, 342–343, 390

mathematics,
  See also arithmetic; exponential functions; factorial; Math (Java-defined class); numbers; trigonometry
  PI constant   234
  radians angle measurement   234
  tree definition   480

measuring,
  See also algorithms; testing
  counting vs.   336
  speed   506–508

megabyte (MB)   3

memory   2, 506
  See also hardware

menus   264
  See also GUI

merge sort   517–518, 519, 520
  See also big-oh notation; searching; sorting

message(s),
  See method(s), invocation

method(s)   55–98
  See also capabilities; constructors; generic; inheritance; local variables; parameters; return value
  abstract   107–108
  accessor   151–152
  activation records   443
  bodies   129
  boolean   187
  class   342–343
  definition   148
  invocation   385
  main   44
  modeling capabilities with   34–37
  mouse   113–114
  multiple interface definitions   133
  mutator   151–152
  overloading   68–69, 162–163
  overriding   104–106
  resolution   111–113, 160, 164–165
  signatures   128
  term description   31

mod arithmetic operator   194
  See also operators

mod function,
  hash function use   529

model(ing)   18–19
  See also design; representation
  attributes vs. components vs. peer objects   148
  capabilities   31–33, 34–37, 56
  categories   100, 134
  common capabilities   128
  complex choices   337, 347–349
  counting vs. measuring   336
  current color   305–306
  curves   244–246
  equality semantics   189
  evaluation   505
  extreme programming   11–12
  FIFO data structures   444
  hierarchies   480–483
  integers   192–194
  LIFO data structures   441, 443–444
  lists   367
  mathematical points   169
  numbers   184, 192–194, 336, 339–342
  polymorphism vs. conditionals   191–192
  properties   29–31
  recursion   399
  roles   127, 134
  software   9–12, 23
  spiral   11
  techniques   102
  things(s), See, class(es)
  time   225–235
  unrestricted insertion and deletion   444–445
  waterfall   9–11

mouse,
  See also GUI
  clicks   166
    See also event(s)
  input   277–281
  methods   113–114, 169
  move operations   144

MovableHatApp (example application)   142–147

MovableSunApp (example application)   136–141

multidimensional data structures   425–427

multiple,
    inheritance   101
    interfaces   130
multiplication arithmetic operator   194
mutator(s)   68
    methods   62
    recipe   151–152

N

N,
    in worst-case time complexity and big-oh notation
            507
n-ary trees   525–527
name(s)/naming,
    classes   27
    conventions   27, 52, 129, 151, 346
    fully qualified   75
    instance variables   30, 64
    interfaces   129
    naming   30, 34, 64, 75
    objects   73–75
    packages   346
natural language   4
negation arithmetic operator   194
nested,
    classes, *See* inner classes
    conditionals   337, 338, 347–349, 353–358
    `if` statements   199
    panels   267–269
    while loops   372
new keyword   33, 44, 130
    See also instantiation
newlines   562
node(s)   480, 482, 483
    See also data structure(s)
not equal to (!=) operator   197
    See also operators
notation,
    See big-oh notation; conventions; infix notation;
            postfix notation; prefix notation; reverse Polish
            notation (RPN)
notification   225
null (Java-defined type)   33

numbers,
    See also arithmetic; mathematics; primitive, types
    modeling   184, 192–194, 336, 339–342
    naming conventions   347
    primitive types, (table)   339
    random   343–344
    real   336
    relational operators   197–198
    value range and size   339

O

O,
    in big-oh notation   507
object(s)   17–50
    See also object-oriented programming
    address   29
    assignment   193
    code   7
    composite   80–90, 142–147, 236–246, 327–332
    diagrams, See, instance, diagrams
    equality   188–198
    names   73–75
    peer   34, 148
    reading   559
    saving   559, 579–583
object-oriented programming,
    See class(es); encapsulation; inheritance; interface(s);
            object(s); polymorphism
off-by-one bug   384
operators,
    addition   194
    arithmetic   184–185, 194–195, 194
    assignment   33
    boolean   196–197
    commutative   195
    decrement   195–196
    division   194
    equality   197
    greater than   197
    greater than or equal to   197
    increment   195–196
    less than   197
    less than or equal to   197
    logical   186–187
    multiplication   194

negation   194
not equal to   197
precedence   198
relational   188, 197–198
remainder   194
string   535
subtraction   194

order(ing),
ADT choice criteria   442
column-major   427
conventions   52
dictionaries as example of   446
in-order traversal of binary trees   486–490
insertion   495–496
of instance variable initialization   148
LIFO (last-in-first-out)   441
parameters   63–64
partial   481
post-order traversal of binary trees   486–490
pre-order traversal of binary trees   486–490
with relational operators   188
row-major   426
sorting as strategy for   508–522

output devices,
See hardware

overloading   68–69, 162–163
See also inheritance; method(s); overriding

overriding   101, 104–106, 119
See also inheritance; method(s); overloading

P

package keyword   346
package(s)   73–75, 346–347
paintbrush   222–223
palindrome   534
panel(s),
nested   267–269, 269–220
parameters   56–58
See also generic; method(s)
actual   57, 59–60, 193–194
constructors with   61–63
formal   57, 59–60, 193–194
method calls   63
passing   193, 425

polymorphism vs.   158
superclass property access with   110
syntax, definition, and invocation   59–63
type matching rules for   158–161
variables vs.   64–67

PARC (Palo Alto Research Center)   264
parent,
class   100
node   482
partial,
ordering   481
overriding   101, 106, 119
parts hierarchy   22
path   558
peer(s),
See also inheritance
performance,
See also algorithm(s); big-oh notation; searching;
sorting
linked lists vs. array searching   484–485
program algorithms   505–532
recursion vs. iteration   407
Pickover, Clifford A.,
"Computers and the Imagination"   388
pixels   40
point (mathematical)   169
pointer   29
polar coordinates   390–392
policies,
setting   108
polymorphism   157–182, 191–192, 222, 307, 342, 417
See also coercion; encapsulation; generic; inheritance;
object-oriented, programming
portability   266
position(ing),
absolute   77, 217–218, 266
array elements   422–423
change   247
list   445
relative   77, 86
post-order traversal of binary trees   486–490
postfix notation   488–490
pre-order traversal of binary trees   486–490

precedence   185, 198

precision   192, 342

predicates   197

prefix notation   488–490

primitive type(s)   62, 184
See also type(s)
numeric,
See `byte` keyword; `double` keyword; `float` keyword; `int` keyword; integers; `long` keyword; real numbers; `short` keyword
objects vs., assignment   193

`private` keyword   109, 110, 113, 229

procedure   57

process management   444

program(s)   18
computer   4
executing   6
running   6
speed   506–508
testing   12–13, 471–473

programming,
ease   407
extreme   11–12
language   4–6
tools for   6–8

prompt   556

propagation,
exception   560

property(s),
See also association (peer object); attributes; capabilities; components; instance, variables
access management   151–152
class   37
deep   189
equality   189
generic types relationship to   449
inheriting   108–111
instance variable declaration representation of   30
modeling   29–31
term description   20

`protected` keyword   110, 111

Proxy design pattern   303, 311–327

pseudo-inheritance   108–111, 109

`public` keyword   26, 113, 345

push,
buttons   264, 270–271
See also, widgets
stack operation   453

quadradic-time algorithm   508
See also algorithm(s)

queue(s)   444, 448–470
See also ADTs; data structures

Q

`QueueApp` (example application)   472–473

R

radio buttons   264, 271–272
See also widgets

RAM (random-access memory)   2

random,
access   2, 444–445
keyword   343
numbers   343–344, 353–358

rate of growth   508–509
See also big-oh notation

reading objects   559

real numbers   336, 339–342
See also arithmetic; `double` keyword; `float` keyword; numbers

recipe(s),
See also appropriate laziness; design patterns; reuse, code
accessor   151–152
accumulator   405
class-definition   148–150
creating a panel to fit inside a window   216
default-value   150
delegation   36
design pattern relationship to   147
event handling   277
loops   379–381
mutator   151–152
nested panels   268
objects that know their container   152–153
save-and-restore   223
term description   3

record activation   400, 443

recurrence relations   518–522
  See also function(s); recursion

recursion   397–420, 463, 470, 517–522
  See also flow of control; iteration

reference   29

relational operators   188, 197–198
  See also comparison; conditionals; equality; operators

relations,
  recurrence, *See* recurrence relations

relationships,
  class   38, 100
  component   116
  containment   116
  is-a   100

relative positioning   77, 86

remainder,
  arithmetic operator   194

representation   19, 30, 184
  See also design; model(ing)

reserved words   7, 26

resolution (method)   111–113, 160, 164–165
  See also method(s)

responder   226, 228
  See also event(s), handling

return,
  See also functions; type(s); value(s)
  statements   68
  types   57, 58, 67–68
  value   57, 58

reuse,
  See also complexity, management; design; design
      patterns
  code   41, 81, 100, 101, 128

reverse Polish notation (RPN)   489

reversing strings   537–539

role(s)   127, 128, 134, 135, 291
  See also capabilities; inheritance; interface(s)

root node   480

rotation   234, 247, 249
  See also animation; move

row-major ordering   426

RPN (reverse Polish notation)   489

running programs,
  See also exceptions
  command line arguments   430
  console I/O   558
  term description   6

S

safe types   194
  See also type(s)

save-and-restore recipe   223

saving objects   559, 579–583

scope   65, 66, 67
  See also generic; lifetime; type(s); variables

screen,
  See window(s)

search(ing)   464–465, 467–468, 483–486, 488, 491–500,
      505–532
  See also big-oh notation; sorting

selection sort   516–517
  See also big-oh notation; searching; sorting

selector   350

self-similar problem   398, 407

semantics   6, 148, 189
  See also syntax

sending messages,
  See method(s), invocation

sentinel recipe   379–380

serialization   579–583

shapes (graphical)   40–42, 211–258
  See also GUI

short keyword   192, 339
  See also integers; primitive type(s)

short-circuiting   349–350, 349

signatures   68–69, 128, 133
  See also methods

simple,
  inheritance   102–104

single inheritance   101

size,
  array   423
  change   247
  methods   250

specification 424
window 214
SketchApp (example application) 166–173
sliders 264, 272–275
    See also GUI
    adding to ControlPanel 289
    ControlPanel with 292–293
Smalltalk language 264
SnowCartoon (example application) 80–90
software 3–12, 23
solution domain 19
sorting 505–532
    See also big-oh notation; searching
source,
    code 7
    event-handling role 226
space for program,
    storage and running 506
spacing conventions 52
    See also conventions
speed,
    See also algorithm(s); analysis; big-oh notation
    measuring 506–508
    user control 282
spiral model 11
SpiralApp (example application) 407–412
stack(s) 401, 441, 443–444, 448–470
    See also ADTs; data structures
standard comment 27
state 21, 448
    See also instance variable(s)
statement(s),
    arithmetic 183–210, 335–364
    assignment 33–34, 196
    conditional 183–210, 335–364, 385
    if 189, 198
    if-else 189, 199
    return 68
    switch 350–353
    termination 30
    while 370
static 182
    See also constant(s)

class 342, 343
    constant class definition use 345
    imports 346
stream(s) 558, 565–569, 578
    See also data structure(s) I/O
string(s) 197–198, 276, 429–430, 533–554
    See also constant(s); text
StringDemo (example application) 538
StringMethodsApp (example application) 546–548
structure,
    data, *See* data structure(s)
    node 482
    program 448
stub(s) 108, 283, 285
    See also abstract, methods interfaces
style,
    See conventions
subclass(ing) 101, 369, 534
    See also class(es)
subpanel,
    See panel(s), nested
substrings 536
subtraction arithmetic operator 194
subtrees 480
subtypes 159
    See also type(s)
SunCartoon (example application) 70–78
super keyword 106, 109
superclass 100, 101, 109, 222
    See also class(es); inheritance
support code 8
Swing 211–258, 265–266
    See also AWT
switch keyword 350
switch statement 350–353
    See also flow of control
syntax,
    See also semantics
    ArrayList 423, 424–425
    arrays 422, 423, 424–425, 425
    assignment with arithmetic operators 195
    class name vs. class constructor call 33
    class-definition recipe 149–150

constant definition   344
constructor   32, 63
curly braces ()   27, 199
do-while loop   374
errors   6
for loop   375
generics   449
importing constants   345–347
inner classes   229
instance variable declaration   30, 31
interface   129
method   34, 36, 60, 106
nested if statements   199
public instance variables   113, 138
recursion   399
subclass definition   103
Vector   367, 423, 424–425
while statement   370

T

T(N) (worst-case time complexity),
   as algorithm evaluation measure   507
tail recursion   406
term descriptions and key concepts,
   absolute positioning   77, 217
   abstract,
      classes   107, 108
      datatypes   442
      keyword   108
      methods   107, 129
   accessor, methods   68
   activation,
      record, methods   443
      record, recursion   400
      stack   401
   actual,
      parameters   57
      type   159, 182
   address, object   29
   ADTs (abstract datatypes)   442
   algorithm(s)   3
      analysis   505, 506
      constant-time   527
      exponential-time   522
      logarithmic-time   523

ancestor class   100
and (Java-defined primitive boolean operator)   196
animations, creating   225
application   40
appropriate laziness   41
arithmetic, expression   185
array(s),
   index   422
   sparse   527
assembly, language   4
asymptotic behavior   508
attribute(s)   20
average-case analysis   516
balanced tree   486
base,
   case   398
   class   100
   type   423
behavior,
   asymptotic   508
   interface modeling of   134
best-case analysis   516
big-oh notation   507
binary,
   code   7
   digit (bit)   3
   files   559
   search   523
   tree   485, 525
bit (binary digit)   3, 339
body delimiters   27
boolean,
   boolean   186
   constants   185
   (Java-defined primitive type)   196
   logic   185
   methods   187
   variables   185
bottom-up design   103
bounding boxes   77
bucket   528
bugs   6, 12
buttons,
   push   264
   radio   264
   toggle   264
byte   2

code(s)   8
  keyword   192
capabilities   20
casting   222, 337
central processing unit (CPU)   2
checked exceptions   571
child,
  class   100
  node   482
class(es)   21
  abstract   107, 108
  ancestor   100
  base   100
  child   100
  declaration   26
  definition   26
  derived   100
  descendent   100
  inner   220
  interface   36
  methods   342
  modeling things and categories with   134
  parent   100
  variables   342
closed form   519
code,
  binary   7
  byte   8
  object(s)   7
  source   7
  support   8
coercion   337
collision   528
column-major ordering   427
command line arguments   430
commenting out   28, 83
comments   27
compilation   7
compile   7
compiler   5
complexity management   22
computer,
  graphics   40
  program   4
concatenation   535
conditional(s)   185
console   556

I/O   557
  window   556
constant   218, 344
  boolean   185
  time algorithm   527
constructor   31
  superclass   109
conventions   27
coupling   313
CPU (central processing unit)   2
data structures   367, 443
debugging   6, 12
declaration   26, 30
declared type   159, 182
deep property equality   189
defining/definition, class   26
definite loops   366
degree of a node   483
depth,
  node   483
  recursion   401
derived class   100
descendent class   100
design,
  bottom-up   103
  interfaces   261
  patterns   302
  top-down   103
  user interfaces   261
  user-centered   261
devices,
  input   2
  output   2
diagrams, instance   447
dictionary(s)   446
disk, hard   2
divide and conquer   22
documentation comment   27
double keyword   339
drivers   471
dynamic   182
edge   482
efficiency   24, 505
elements   367
empty string   538
encapsulation   2, 22
equality,

deep property   189
    identity   189
    operator   197
    strings   536
evaluation, models   23
event(s)   225
    handler   276
exception   324, 555, 559
    checked   571
    handler   556, 560
    propagation   560
    throwing   560
execution, stack   444
explicit coercion   222, 341
exponential-time algorithm   522
expression   185
    arithmetic   185
    boolean   186
extending   42, 100
    interfaces   133
external node   483
extreme programming   11
`false` (Java-defined primitive value)   196
FIFO (first-in-first-out) data structures   444
file   555
    binary   559
    close   558
    I/O   557
    open   558
    text   558
flexibility   24
floating-point numbers   336
flow chart(s)   189
`for` loop   374
formal parameter   57
full binary tree   486
fully qualified names   75
functionality   24
functions,
    hash   527
    method   57
generic, types   449
geometric sum   522
grammar   5
greater than operator   197
greater than or equal to operator   197
hand-simulation   381

handle   276
hard disk   2
hardware   1
hash,
    function   527
    table(s)   527
height of a tree   483
hierarchy,
    component   22
    inheritance   23
    parts   22
high-level programming language   5
icons   264
IDE (integrated development environment)   7
identifier(s)   27
identity, equality   189
`if` statement   189, 198
`if-else` statement   189, 199
immutable   194
implementation, interface   134
implicit coercion   337
import   73, 346
in-order traversal   488
incremental development   70
indefinite loops   366
index, array   422
indirect recursion   417
infinite loop   366
inheritance   23, 100
    hierarchy   23
    method resolution   111
    multiple   101
    polymorphism   159
    single   101
initialization   32
inline comment   27
inner class   220, 229
input, devices   2
instance   21
    diagrams   447
    variable, declaration   30
    variables   29
instantiation   31
`int` keyword   192
integrated development environment (IDE)   7
interface   127, 128, 259
internal node   483

interpreter 8
invocation, method 36
is-a relationship 100
iteration 366
Java, byte code 8
Java Collections Framework 442
JVM (Java virtual machine) 8
key 446
keyboard input 557
keywords 7, 26
law of least astonishment 263
leaf node 483
less than operator 197
less than or equal to operator 197
level of a node 483
library 41, 73
lifetime 66
line 41
linear search 523
linked lists 446
list 445
listener 225
literals, string 535
local, variables 64
logarithmic-time algorithm 523
logic, boolean 185
long keyword 192
look and feel 24
loop 366
   body 371
   condition 370
machine language 3
main method 44
mainline 44
maintainability 24
MB (megabyte) 3
memory 2
menus 264
method 31
   resolution 111
modeling 18
multiple inheritance 101
mutator 62, 68
N in worst-case time complexity and big-oh notation
   507
n-ary trees 525
names,

fully qualified 75
   interfaces 129
natural language 4
not equal to operator 197
not (Java-defined primitive boolean operator) 196
notification 225
O (big-oh notation) 507
object 18
   address 29
   code 7
object-oriented,
   program 18
   programming 18
operators, relational 188
or (Java-defined primitive boolean operator) 196
output, devices 2
overloading 69
   method 69
overriding 101
   partially 101
package 73
   keyword 346
palindrome 534
parameters 56
parent,
   class 100
   node 482
partial order 481
partially override 101
parts hierarchy 2, 22
path 558
peer objects, objects 20
pixels 40
pointer 29
polymorphic recursion 417
polymorphism 157, 182
position, list 445
positioning,
   absolute 77
   relative 77, 86
post-order traversal 488
pre-order traversal 488
precedence 185
preconditions of recursion 401
predicates 197
primitive types 62, 184
private keyword 109

procedure   57
program   18
programming,
   language   4
   language, high-level   5
prompt   556
propagation, exception   560
property   20
   deep, equality   189
   equality   189
protected keyword   110, 111
pseudo-inheritance   109
public keyword   26
push buttons   264
queues   444
radio buttons   264
RAM (random-access memory)   2
random-access memory (RAM)   2
recipes, See, recipes
recurrence relations   518
recursion   398
reference   29
relational operators   188
relations, recurrence   518
relationships, is-a   100
relative positioning   77, 86
reliability   24
reserved words   7, 26
resolution, method   111
return,
   statements   68
   types   57, 58
   value   57, 58
reverse Polish notation calculator   489
robust   24
roles   128
root node   480, 482
row-major ordering   426
RPN calculator   489
running, programs   6
safe types   194
scope   65, 66
selector   350
self-similar problem   398
semantics   6
serialization   579
set, methods   62

short keyword   192
short-circuiting   349
signature   68
single inheritance   101
sliders   264
solution domain   19
source, code   7
sparse array   527
specialize   100
specification   9
spiral, model   11
stack   441, 443
   activation   401
   execution   444
standard comment   27
state   21
static   342
   imports   346
   keyword   182
stream   558
string, literals   535
stub   108, 283
subclass   100, 101
substrings   536
subtrees   480
subtypes   159
super keyword   106
superclass   100, 101
   constructor   109
support, code   8
syntax   6
   errors   6
T(N) (worst-case time complexity)   507
tail recursion   404
testing, exhaustive   171
text   264, 533
   editor   7
   files   558
this keyword   153
throwing an exception   560
toggle buttons   264
tokens   566
top-down design   103
trace   45
transparent, interface   263
tree   480
   height   483

`true` (Java-defined primitive value)   196
truth tables   186
types   21
usability   24
user interface   260
   design   261
user-centered design   261
views, interface use for restricting   128
visibility   26
walkthrough   45
widgets   264
WIMP (windows, icons, menus, and pointer)   264
worst-case,
   analysis   507
   time complexity (T(N))   507
testing   10, 12–13, 171, 471–473
   See also big-oh notation; debugging; drivers
   example applications, *See* example applications
Tetris computer game   329
text   264
   See also GUI; string(s)
   editor   7
   files   558
   I/O   533–554
   user interface use   272
"The Timeless Way of Building",
   by Christopher Alexander   302
themes,
   See abstraction; appropriate laziness; complexity,
      management
things (modeling),
   See class(es)
`this` keyword   150, 153
thread(s)   386
   See also flow of control
throwing exceptions   560
   See also exceptions
time   225–235
   See also big-oh notation
   complexity of an algorithm   518–522
   constant-time algorithm   508, 527
   event handling   225
   exponential-time algorithm   508, 522
   lifetime   66
   linear-time   508

logarithmic-time algorithm   518, 520, 523
quadradic-time algorithm   508
worst-case time complexity   507
title (window)   214
   See also GUI
toggle buttons   264
   See also widgets
tokens   565–569
   See also streams   text
tools (software)   6–8
top-down design   103
   See also design
Towers of Hanoi game   401–403, 521–522
trace   45
tradeoffs,
   commonality vs. uniqueness   128
   recursion vs. iteration   406
transparent interface   263
traversal,
   See also trees
   binary trees   486–490
tree(s)   100, 413–417, 479–503, 480–501, 524–527
   See also data structure(s)
`TreeApp` (example application)   413–417
trigonometry   390, 411
   See also arithmetic; mathematics; real numbers
   functions   343
`true` (Java-defined primitive value)   196
truth tables   186, 186–187
`try` keyword   324, 573–576
   See also exceptions
two-dimension (2D) graphical shapes   211–258
type(s),
   See also ADTs; casting; class(es); coercion; generic;
      interface(es)
   actual   159, 164, 173–173, 182
   assignment   158–161, 193
   base   423
   declared   159, 173–173, 182
   generic   449–451
   numeric, See,
      `byte` keyword
      `double` keyword

`float` keyword
`int` keyword
integers
`long` keyword
real numbers
`short` keyword
parameter   59–60, 158–161
primitive   62, 184, 193, 339
return   57–58, 67–68
safe   194
strict matching   162
term description   21
variable   30, 157

U

UML (Unified Modeling Language)   37–39, 100, 130, 447–448
user interface design   260, 261, 272
    See also GUI
user-centered design   261
    See also design

V

value(s)   20, 57–58, 68, 150, 336
    See also variable(s)
variables,
    See also constant(s)   value(s)
    boolean   185
    class   342–343
    criteria for choice   66
    global   305
    instance   29–31, 64–67, 112–113, 148
    lifetime   66–67
    local   64–67
    method use   64–67
    objects vs. primitive types   193
    parameters   64–67
    scope   65–66, 67
    string   535
    types   157
Vectors   366–369, 373, 386–392, 421–439
    See also array(s); ArrayList
visibility   26, 30, 32

See also encapsulation; scope
Vlissides, John   302
void keyword   35

W

walkthrough   45
waterfall model   9–11
    See also modeling; spiral model
Wheels library   40–42, 70–72, 113, 246–252
while loop   370–373, 379
    See also flow of control   loop(s)
widgets (GUI components)   264
    See also buttons; GUI; icons; menus; mouse; sliders; text; windows
wild cards   73
WIMP (windows, icons, menus, and pointer)   264
window(s)   55, 211–258, 264–270
    See also GUI
worst-case,
    analysis   507–516
    time complexity (T(N))   507
writing,
    classes   137–138
    files   578
    interfaces   137

X

Xerox PARC (Palo Alto Research Center)   264

Z

Zeno's paradox,
    See recursion